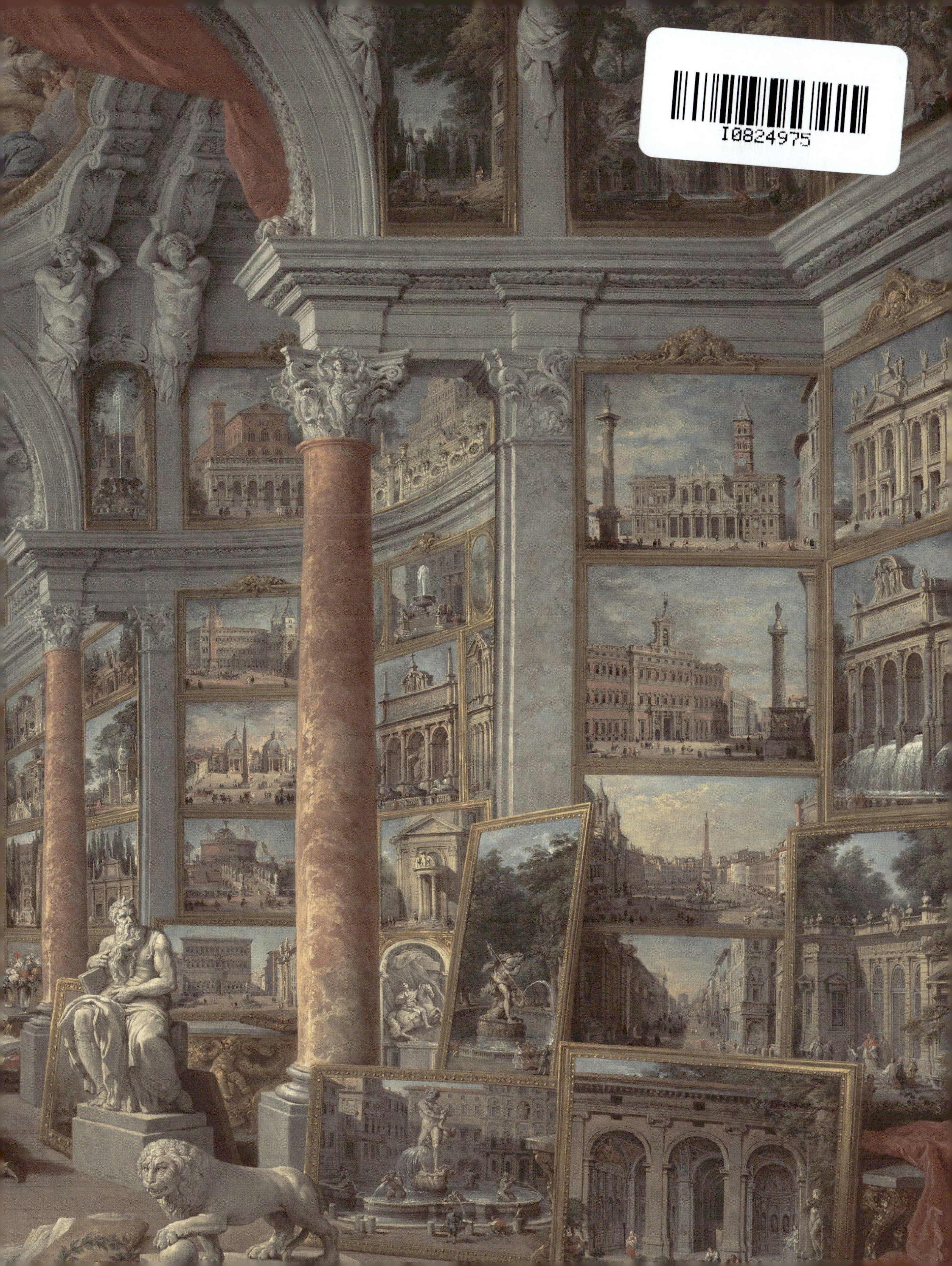

THE MADMAN'S GALLERY

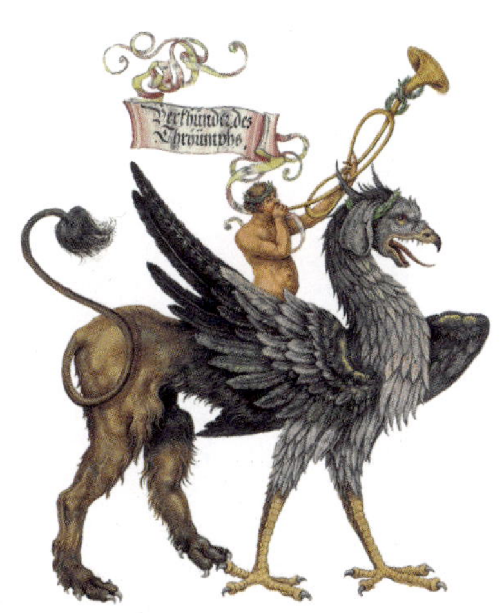

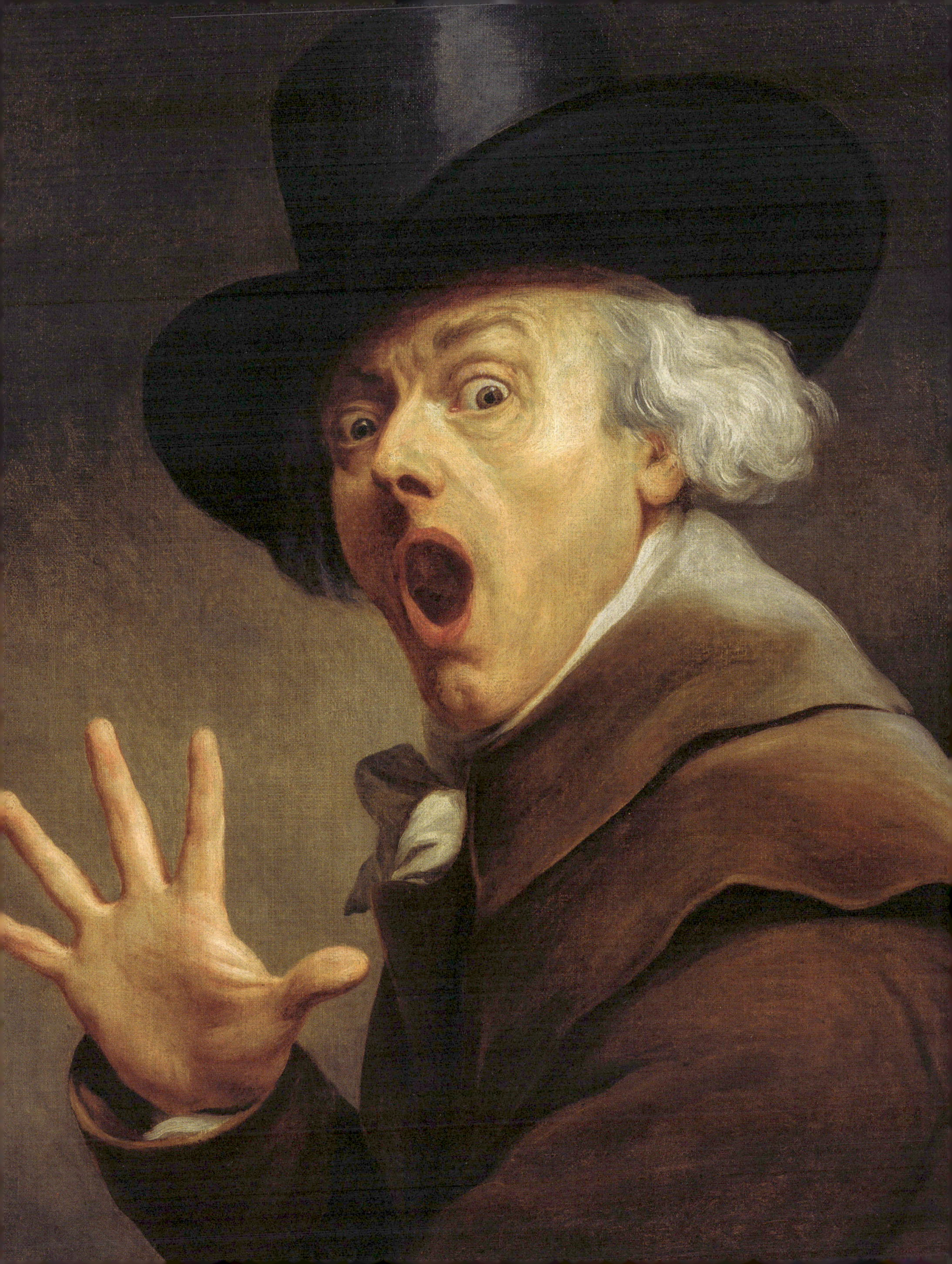

The MADMAN'S GALLERY

The Strangest Paintings, Sculptures and Other Curiosities from the History of Art

EDWARD BROOKE-HITCHING

CHRONICLE BOOKS
SAN FRANCISCO

MMXXIII

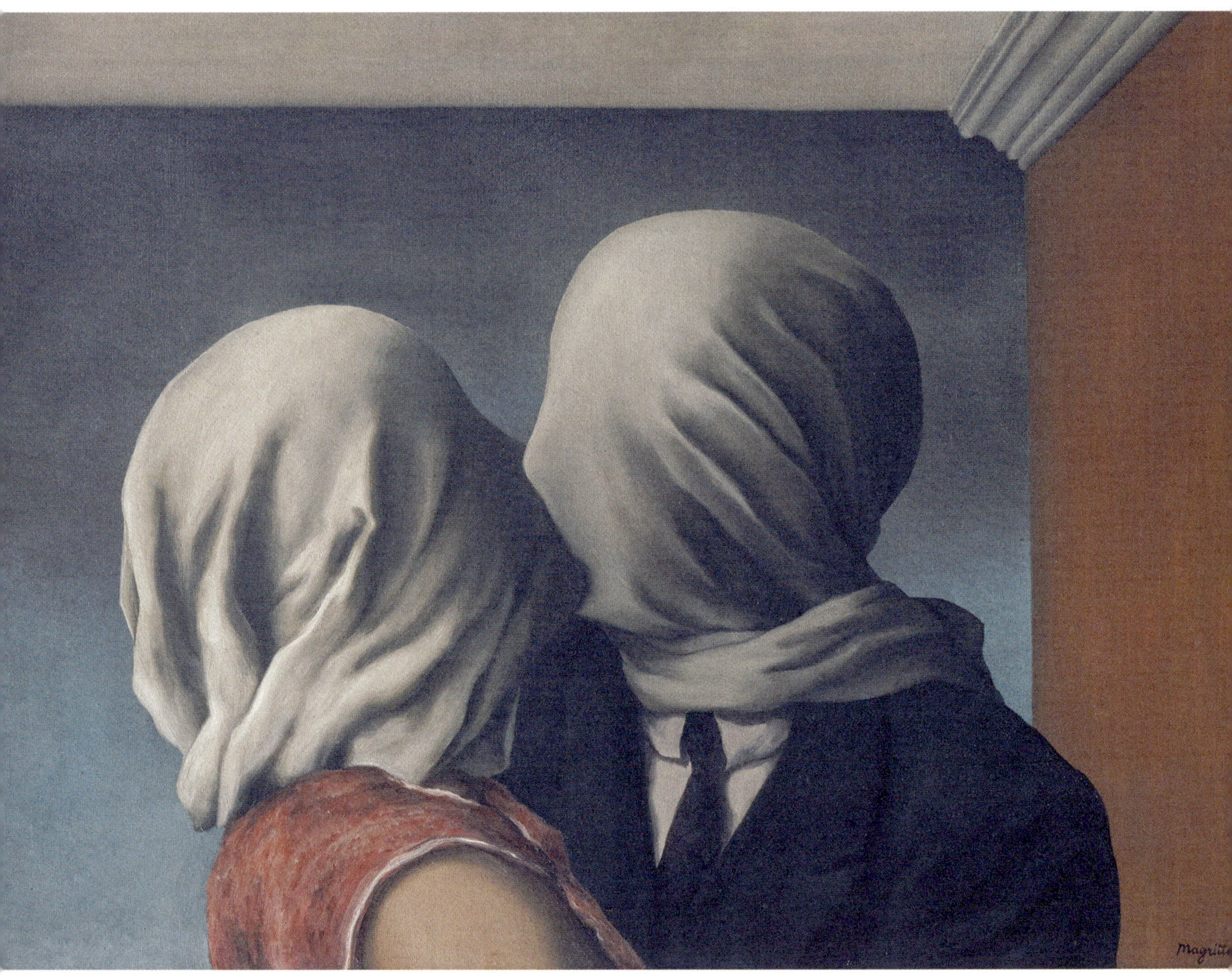

ABOVE: *René Magritte's* The Lovers, *1928.*

PREVIOUS PAGE: The Surprise *(1790s), Joseph Ducreux.*

For D.

CONTENTS

Introduction **8**

Venus of Hohle Fels (38,000-33,000BC) and Other Fertility Art **16**

Nebra Sky Disc (*c.*1600BC) **22**

Colossal Heads of the Olmec (*c.*900BC) **26**

Tomb of the Diver (*c.*480BC) and Other Art Made to Be Buried **30**

Statue of Glycon, the False Snake Deity (late second century) **36**

Doom Paintings (twelfth-thirteenth centuries) **38**

Portrait of the Devil, *Codex Gigas* (early thirteenth century) **42**

Japanese *Kusozu* (thirteenth-nineteenth centuries) and the Art of Death **44**

Ripley Scroll (fourteenth century) **48**

Wound Man (fifteenth-seventeenth centuries) **52**

Arnolfini Portrait (1434), Jan van Eyck **56**

Crucifixion Diptych (*c.*1460) and the Tricky Art of Restoration **60**

Portrait of Federico da Montefeltro (*c.*1473-5), Piero della Francesca **64**

The Garden of Earthly Delights (1490-1500), Hieronymus Bosch **68**

Unicorn Tapestries (1495-1505) **72**

Mona Vanna, the Nude Mona Lisa (*c.*1510), Gian Giacomo Caprotti da Oreno **78**

Triumphal Procession of Emperor Maximilian I (1512-26), Hans Burgkmair the Elder and Others **82**

The Ugly Duchess (*c.*1513), Quentin Matsys **88**

St Christopher Dog-head (sixteenth-eighteenth centuries) **92**

Fool's Cap Map of the World (*c.*1580-90) **96**

The Composite Art of Arcimboldo (1563-*c.*1590) **98**

Gabrielle d'Estrées and One of Her Sisters (*c.*1594) **102**

The Legend of the Baker of Eeklo (*c.*1550-1650), after Cornelis van Dalem **104**

Man Consumed by Flames (1600-10), Isaac Oliver **106**

Artemisia Gentileschi's *Judith Slaying Holofernes* (1612-13) and the Art of Revenge **110**

Christ in the Storm on the Sea of Galilee (1633) and the Art of Theft **112**

Tapuya Woman (1641) and the Art of Cannibalism **115**

Portrait of Barbara Van Beck (*c.*1650) **118**

The Temptation of St Anthony (*c.*1650), Joos van Craesbeeck **124**

Ángeles Arcabuceros – The Art of the Angel Musketeer (seventeenth century) **128**

Central African *Minkisi* Power Figures (seventeenth-twentieth centuries) **132**

Competition on the Ponte dei Pugni in Venice (1673), Joseph Heintz the Younger **134**

Typus Religionis (*c.*1700) and the Art of Blasphemy **138**

Lucifer's New Row-Barge (*c.*1722) and the Art of Satire **142**

Joseph of Cupertino Takes Flight… (eighteenth century), Ludovico Mazzanti **144**

The Imaginary Prisons of Giovanni Battista Piranesi (1750) **148**

The Ghost Heads of Franz Xaver Messerschmidt (1770-83) **154**

Henry Fuseli's *The Nightmare* (1781) and the Art of Dreaming **158**

Mr Barker's Monster Panoramas (1789) **161**

Interior of a Kitchen (1815), Martin Drölling **164**

Francisco Goya's *Black Paintings* (1819-23) **168**

Hikeshi-banten (nineteenth century) and the Art of Fighting Fire **172**

The Coronation of Inês de Castro in 1361 (*c.*1849), Pierre Charles Comte **176**

The Fairy Feller's Master-Stroke (1855-64), Richard Dadd **178**

Portrait of Madame X (1884), John Singer Sargent **180**

Reply of the Zaporozhian Cossacks to Sultan Mehmed IV (1880-91), Ilya Repin **184**

The Roses of Heliogabalus (1888), Sir Lawrence Alma-Tadema **187**

Bream in 25 Feet of Water Off the West Coast of Scotland (1910), Zarh Pritchard **189**

Fate of the Animals (1913), Franz Marc **192**

Raoul Hausmann's *The Art Critic* (1919-20) and the Art of Dada **194**

Georgiana Houghton and Spiritualist Art (nineteenth-twentieth centuries) **198**

The Persistence of Memory (1931), Salvador Dalí and Surrealist Art **204**

The Wounded Deer (1946), Frida Kahlo **210**

The *Eternity* of Arthur Stace (1932-67) **212**

James Hampton's *The Throne of the Third Heaven*… (*c.*1950-64) and Other Outsider Art **214**

Merda d'Artista (1961), Piero Manzoni **220**

Mondo Cane Shroud (1961), Yves Klein **224**

The Art of Pierre Brassau (1964) **228**

The *Getty Kouros* (twentieth century) and Other Fakes and Forgeries **232**

Marina Abramović and Performance Art **236**

Portrait of Edmond de Belamy (2018) and Other Art by Artificial Intelligence **240**

Select Bibliography **244**

Index **246**

Picture Credits **254**

Acknowledgements **255**

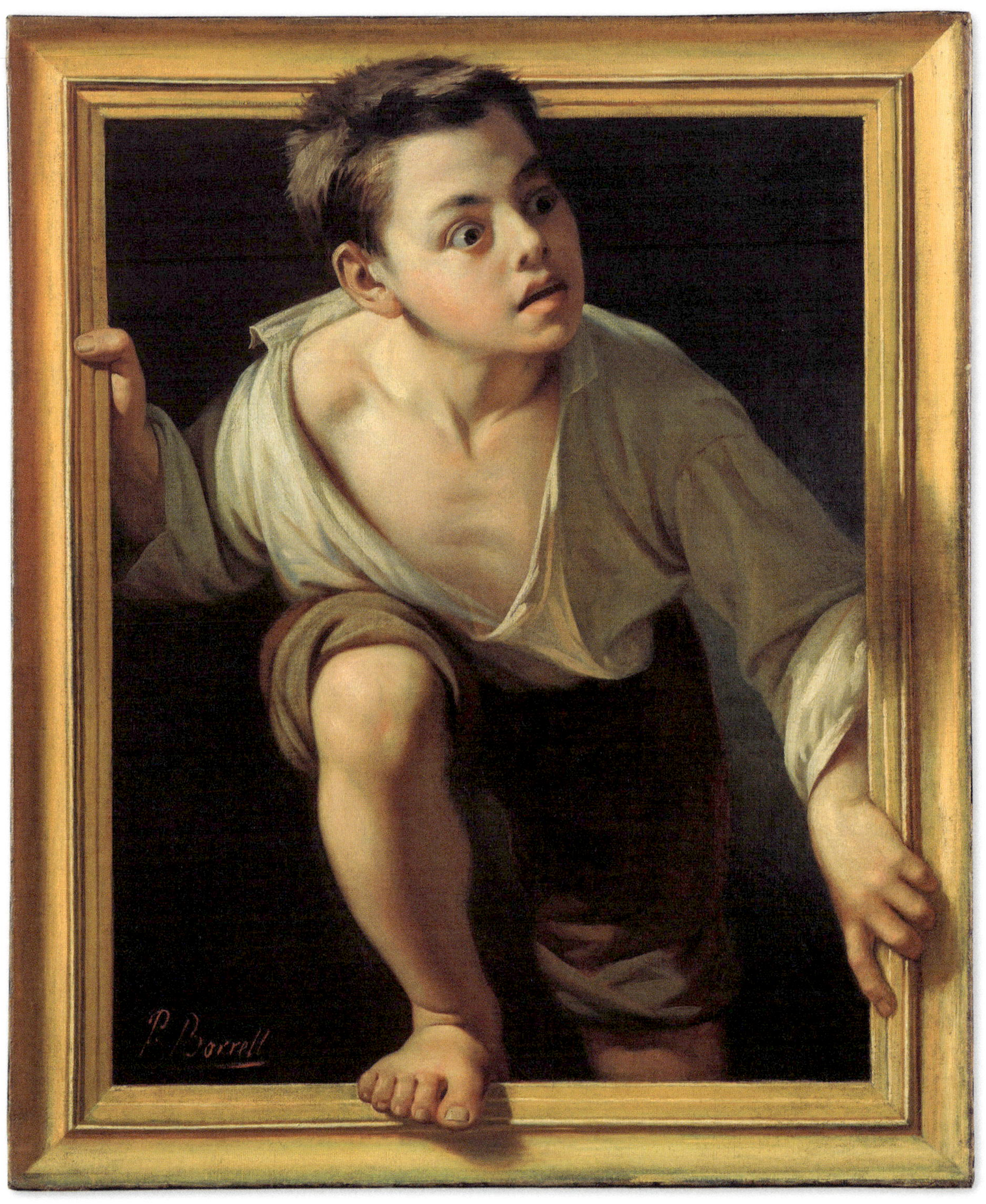

The line between the real and the fictitious is blurred as the young subject emerges wide-eyed into the world, in Spanish painter Pere Borrell del Caso's Escaping Criticism *(1874), one of the greatest works of* trompe l'oeil *(trick the eye) art ever created.*

INTRODUCTION

'Art evokes the mystery without which the world would not exist.'

René Magritte

On 1 July 1936 the great surrealist artist Salvador Dalí stood before a crowd at London's New Burlington Galleries, as part of the first International Surrealism Exhibition. Dressed in a diving suit and clutching two dogs on leads in one hand and a billiard cue in the other, he launched into a passionate lecture on surrealist art. Very little of this was picked up by the audience, though, for Dalí was also wearing a sealed copper-and-brass diving helmet. This sort of thing was to be expected at an exhibition that had opened with a lecture given by the surrealism co-founder André Breton dressed entirely in green, smoking from a green pipe, while the poet Dylan Thomas went around offering guests teacups filled with boiled string ('Do you like it weak or strong?'). Dalí continued with his muffled address, gesturing wildly as people strained to listen, until his colleagues realised that his frantic movements were actually appeals for help: he was suffocating inside the helmet. The poet David Gascoyne leapt forward and managed to jimmy open the helmet with the billiard cue, as the audience applauded, thinking it was all part of the show.

It was from reflecting on this curious episode and other similarly strange stories from the history of art that the idea for this book came about in 2015, a particularly strong year of comparable artistic oddness. Banksy had just opened his *Dismaland Bemusement Park* exhibition in North Somerset, England, converting an entire derelict seaside tourist venue into a dark and twisted parody of Disneyland, drawing over 150,000 visitors from around the world. Elsewhere, performance artist Stelarc was growing a human ear and attaching it to his own arm, with the idea of adding a microphone to eavesdrop on conversations. (Ears were a particular trend – in the same year, the artist Diemut Strebe exhibited *Sugababe*, a living bioengineered replica of Vincent van Gogh's severed ear using genetic samples taken from the van Gogh family.)[1] Meanwhile, the town of Borja in northern

---

1 'If a *scientist* were to cut his ear off,' once grumbled the biologist Sir Peter Medawar (1915-87), 'no one would take it as evidence of a heightened sensibility.'

Spain was reporting a record year for tourism, with visitors keen to see the disastrous art 'restoration' conducted by Cecilia Giménez in 2012, an octogenarian untrained amateur, of the local fresco known as *Ecce Homo*, which had hit headlines around the world (see page 61 for this and other such episodes).

While Stelarc was growing his ear and Señora Giménez was enduring another year of ridicule, I was putting together material for an illustrated book called *The Madman's Library* (2020), which collected the strangest books and manuscripts – literary 'curiosities' – as a way of examining the more obscure and intriguing pockets of literary history. The antiquarian book world, with its looming walls of dark leather bindings and obscure jargon, can seem like a closed private club to the uninitiated. But from growing up in a rare antiquities shop as the son of a dealer, the lesson one learns is that a historical curiosity with a captivating story can make even the most complex area of specialist study instantly accessible. The art world can possess that same intimidating complexity of scholarship and critical theory; but just as with literature, there is, of course, a riotous, humorous history of genius, eccentricity and imaginative experimentation to explore, as stories like these few examples go to show.[2]

While the bulk of art history books focus on the revolutionary and traditionally revered works, *The Madman's Gallery* is intended to offer an alternative guided tour of art history, focusing instead on the oddities, the forgotten, the freakish, all with stories that offer glimpses of the lives of their creators and their eras. There are, of course, a number of infamous works included in these ranks, but it is not for their masterpiece status that they were selected to be hung in this hypothetical gallery of curiosities; rather they were chosen for a strangeness salient in both their time and today. The inclusion of these notorious works is counterbalanced by pieces that will hopefully make for new discoveries to those reading these pages. For example, for every Hieronymus Bosch triptych (see page 68) and its dark universe of nightmarish creatures, there is the extraordinary *Lucifer's New Row-Barge* (see page 142) or the work of Zarh H. Pritchard, the first

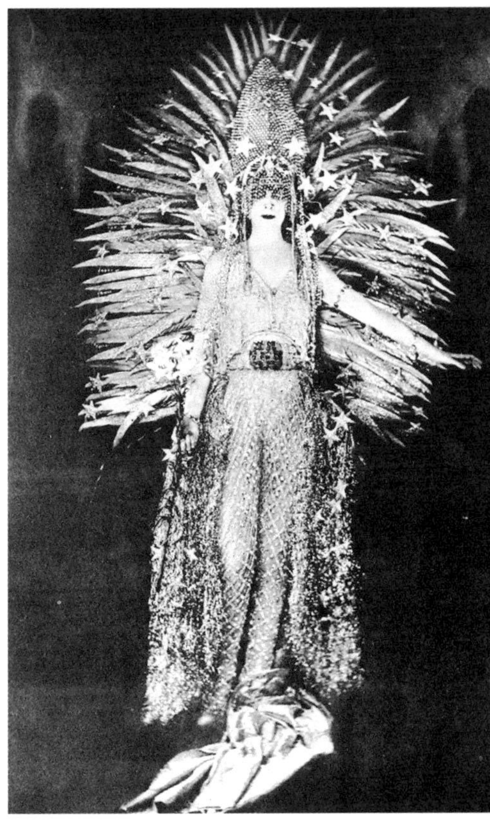

Marchesa Luisa Casati in 1922. A figure of the Belle Époque and muse of surrealist and Futurist artists including Man Ray, Casati endeavoured to be a 'living work of art', and collected wax likenesses of herself in wigs of her own hair. Her dress, commissioned from the costume designer of the Ballets Russes, featured tiny electric bulbs that once short-circuited and gave her such a great electric shock that the blast caused her to somersault backwards.

2 Here's another one. In February 1976 a group of performance artists calling itself Ddart spent a week walking 240km (150 miles) in a giant circle around the Norfolk countryside, wearing hats resembling ice-cream cones with a 3m (10ft) pole balanced on top. When questioned, the men were unable to explain the meaning behind the piece.

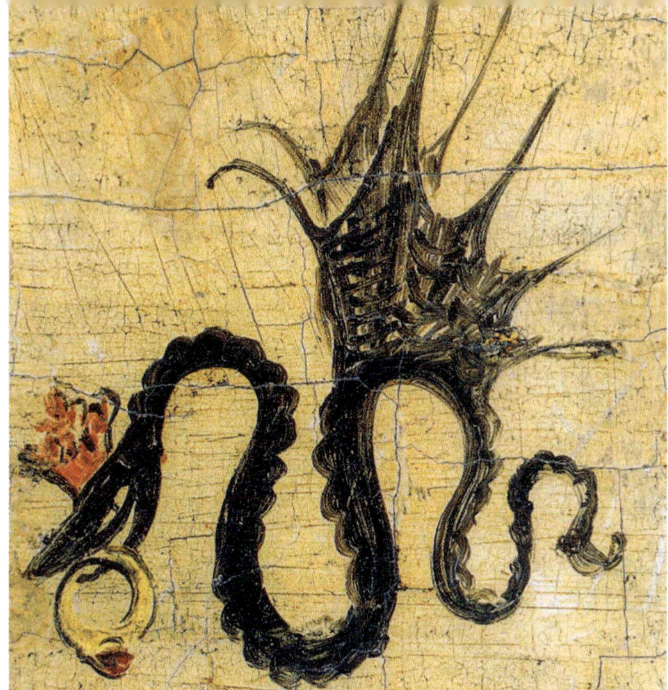

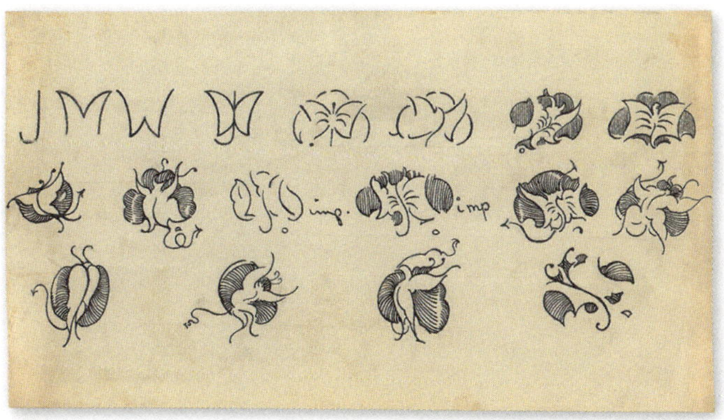

Why sign a work with one's name? In 1508, the German painter Lucas Cranach the Elder (c.1472-1553) was granted his own coat of arms – a winged serpent – which he thereafter used as his signature, like this example of 1514 (left). By the 1870s James McNeill Whistler (1834-1903) was signing his paintings and prints with his butterfly design, which he even used for letters, notes and invitation cards. His butterfly symbol (below left) was so popular that customers who had bought his paintings before he began using it would bring back their purchase for him to add the butterfly.

person to paint under water (see page 189). While there will be those already familiar with the *Imaginary Prisons* of Giovanni Battista Piranesi, perhaps more novel will be the seventeenth-century Peruvian *Ángeles arcabuceros* tradition of depicting finely dressed gun-slinging angels (see page 128) or the nude versions of the Mona Lisa produced at the same time as da Vinci's masterpiece (see page 78) and thought to be based on a lost original by the virtuoso himself.

What was also important when choosing the artworks to feature here was to make a global sweep for curiosities, to show the delightful, drunken variety of creative imaginations across vastly different traditions, geographies and eras. In Japan, for example, we find the starkly beautiful *kusozu* (decomposition watercolours) of the thirteenth to nineteenth centuries, akin to the European *memento mori* as reminders of our mortal frailty (see page 44); while from the nineteenth century we examine the beautiful *hikeshi-banten* (see page 172), works of art worn by those fighting fire. In Chinese history, too, the eccentric artist lives as large as it does in Europe. When we think of paint-hurling artists we tend to consider twentieth-century figures like Jackson Pollock (1912-56); when we should also add Wang Hsia (*fl.* 785-805), whose work sadly has not survived. Known as 'Ink-flinger Wang', the *Register of Notable Painters of the T'ang Dynasty* of 840 recounts how Wang loved to get drunk and work by throwing ink on silk at random, smearing it with his hands, his feet and his backside, and then produce shapes of mountains and rivers out of the chaos. 'When he was drunk, he would spatter ink on it, laughing and singing all the while. He would kick it, smear it with his hands, sweep his brush about or scrub with it.' (The writer Chang Yen-yuan (*fl.* 847) mentions Ink-flinger Wang also enjoyed drunkenly dipping the topknot of his hair in the ink, and then head-butting the fabric.)

Each artwork here is also chosen to represent not just its particular art movement, but a wider theme, too. So, for example, by entering the ethereal Tomb of the Diver (see

This self-portrait – one of the most unusual items in the collection of the Metropolitan Museum of Art, New York – was painted by the American miniaturist Sarah Goodridge (1788-1853). Beauty Revealed *measures just 6.7 × 8cm (2⅝ × 3⅛ in), and was presented by the artist as a token of affection to her close friend and occasional sitter, the statesman Daniel Webster (1782-1852).*

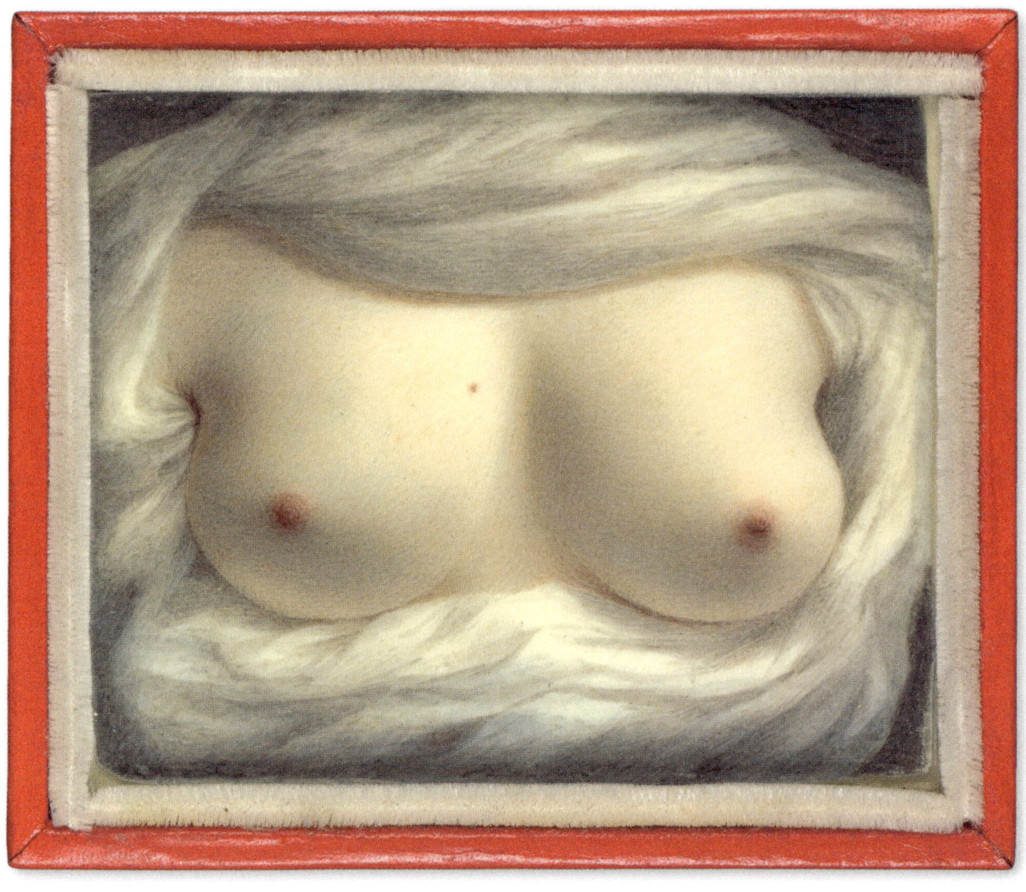

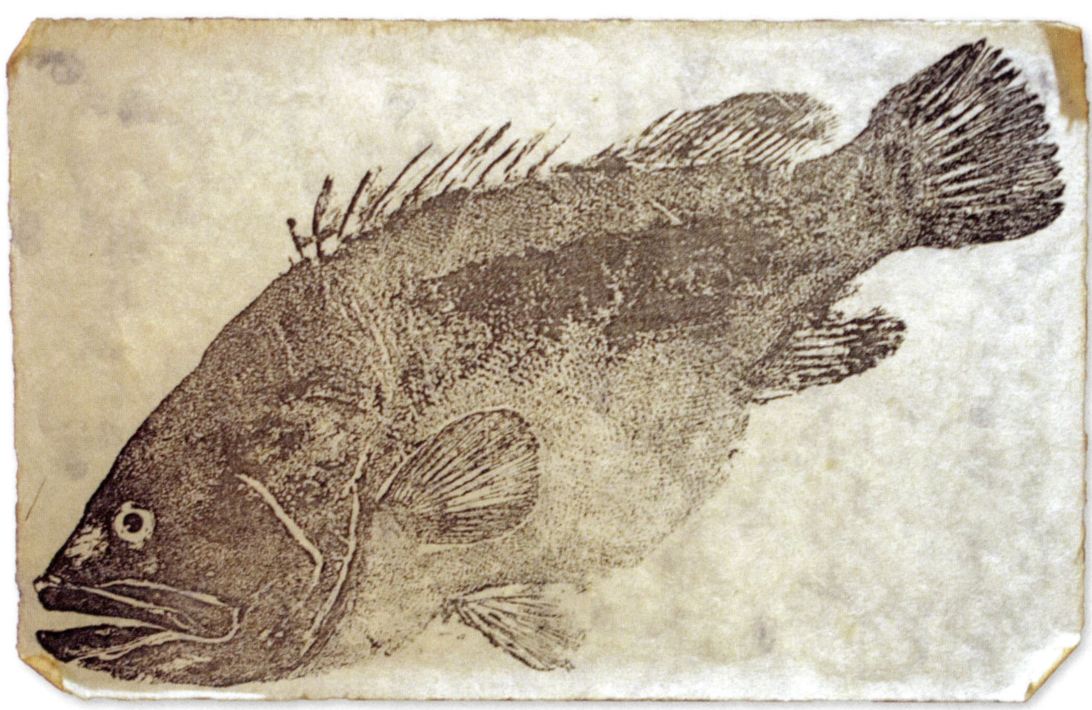

Gyotaku *is a traditional Japanese technique for printing with fish, which originated with fishermen recording their catches in the mid-nineteenth century. The fish or other sea creature is smeared with sumi ink and pressed onto* washi *(rice paper).*

page 30) we explore art that was made to be buried; when examining Henry Fuseli's *The Nightmare* (see page 158) and the apocalyptic visions of Albrecht Dürer (see page 159), we wander through the subconscious landscapes of the art of dreaming. The work of the mysterious Pierre Brassau (see page 228) takes us into the area of the artistic hoax, while with the devastating story of Artemisia Gentileschi (see page 110) we explore the idea of art as revenge, and so on.[3] In this gallery hangs stolen art, Outsider art, art made to be destroyed and art made from people, scandalous and satirical art, art of the heart and the art of men in flames. Here is the art of ghosts, the art of madness, imaginary art, art of dog-headed people, the first portrait of a cannibal, and a painting of the Italian monk who levitated so often he's recognised as the patron saint of aeroplane passengers.

---

3 The practice of taking revenge through art is alive and well. In 2015 Daphne Todd, the first female president of the Royal Society of Portrait Painters, admitted that she had decided to take revenge on 'an obnoxious young gentleman' whose portrait she had been commissioned to paint. She added devil horns to the picture, which would become visible only after 50-100 years as the top layer of paint fades. 'I don't think I did anything wrong on this particular portrait of this young gentleman,' she told *The Independent*, 'as it didn't affect the final painting. What they have hanging on their wall is a perfectly sensible painting.'

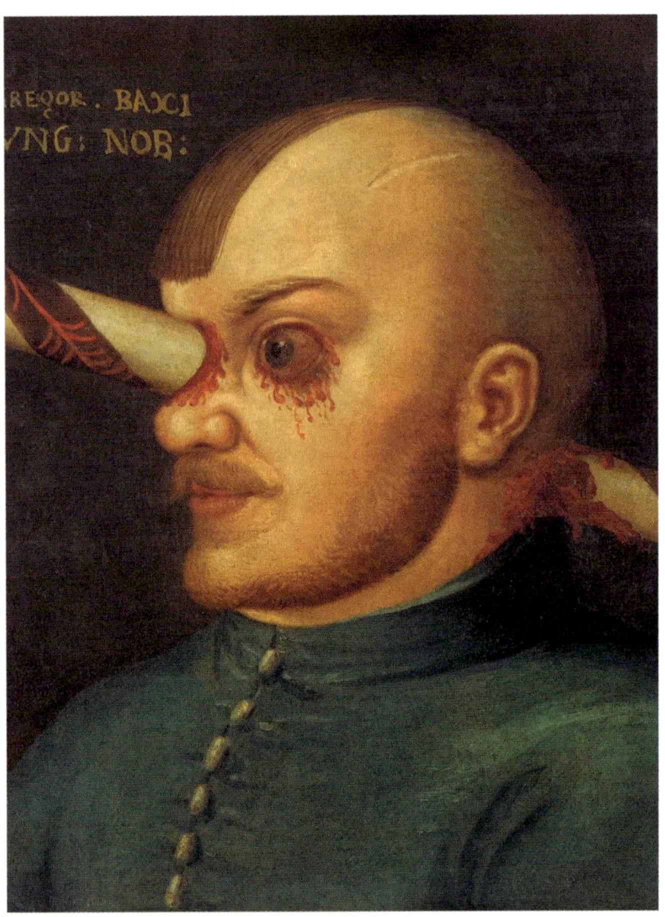

Opposite: *Giuseppe Arcimboldo's* Four Seasons in One Head *(c.1590), thought to be a self-portrait by the artist in the 'winter' of his life, and forming a summary of his career. (For more, see The Composite Art of Arcimboldo,* page 98*).*

Left: *A startling painting in the curiosity collection of Archduke Ferdinand II at Ambras Castle in Innsbruck. The sixteenth-century portrait is thought to be of the Hungarian nobleman Gregor Baci, whose head was impaled with a lance during a jousting tournament. He lived for another year with the sawn-off piece of lance in his head. The lance's white paint was likely made of zinc oxide, preventing infection.*

Below: The Floating Church of the Redeemer of Philadelphia, *the only remaining image of an aquatic church, conceived in 1847 by the Churchmen's Missionary Association for Seamen, which had it built on two 27m (90ft), 100-tonne barges. It sailed around the Delaware river to attend to the needs of mariners in its various ports.*

From prehistoric art to pieces created by artificial intelligence, these objects work to show how artistic imagination has developed to aid our understanding of ourselves, our world and the meaning of our existence. The personalities of the artists are palpable in their works, undimmed by the centuries that have passed. These are works with symbolism and meaning still to interpret, stories to unpick and messages to decipher. In one sense an artwork is an impossible thing, a small, portable anomaly of space-time in which the volume and weight of its story and meaning are many times that of the physical dimensions of its container. These works are the densest of these dark stars of meaning, illustrating how art has been the common language of our species from before language itself existed. 'If I could say it in words,' explained the twentieth-century American artist Edward Hopper, 'there would be no reason to paint.' So, let's begin the conversation.

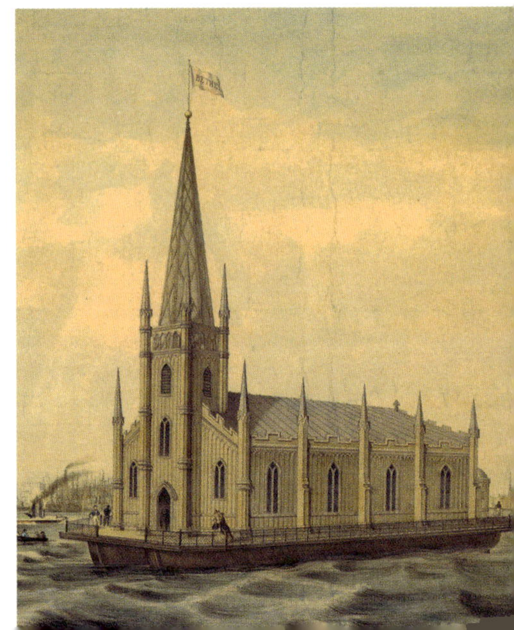

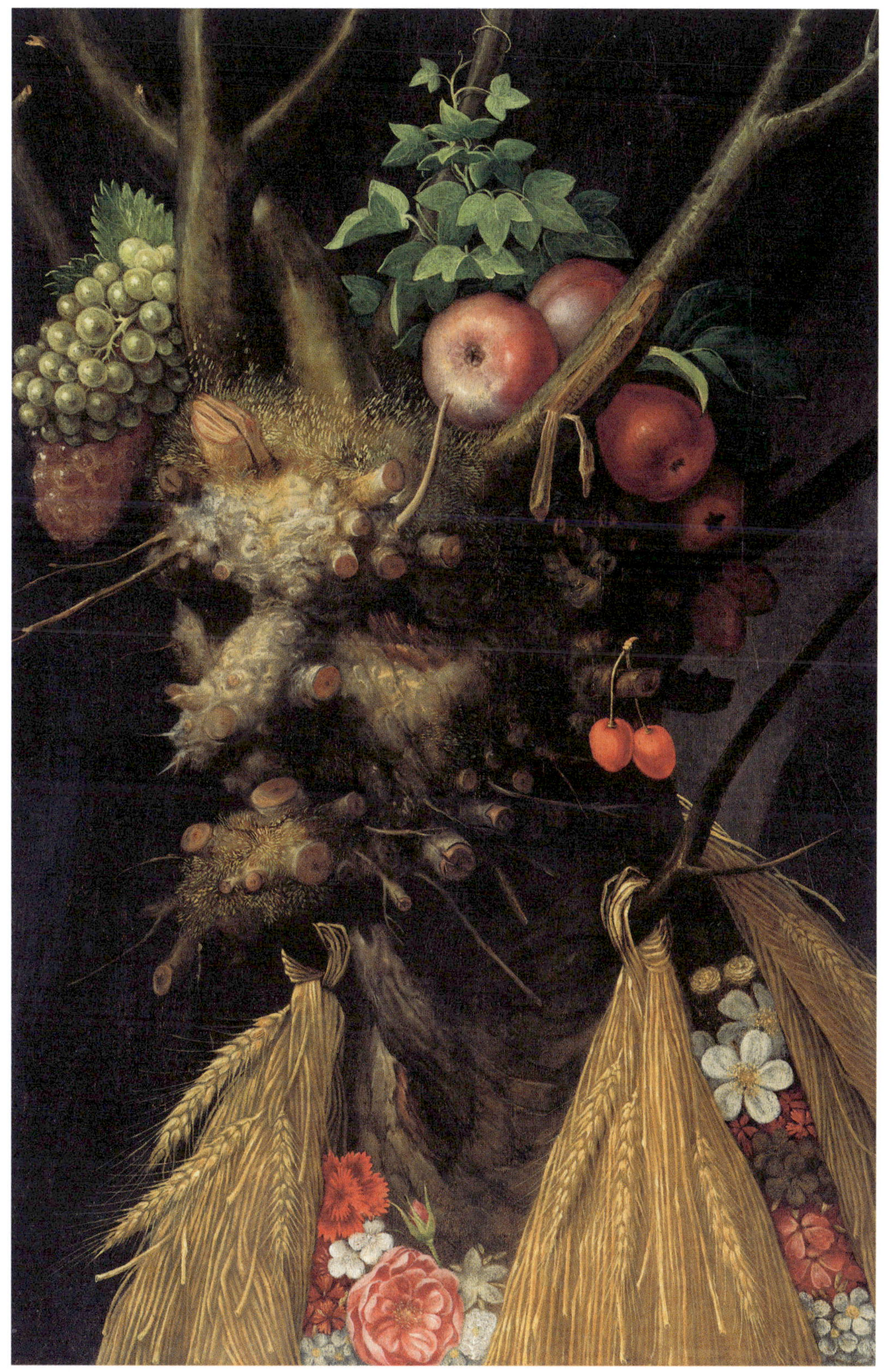

VENUS OF HOHLE FELS (38,000-33,000 BC) AND OTHER FERTILITY ART

Where and when did art begin? Despite centuries of investigation and debate, the origins remain disputed. Yet what can be said is that over 35,000 years ago, in the Hohle Fels (German for 'hollow rock') cave in the Swabian Jura of southwestern Germany, a prehistoric artist picked up a tusk of a woolly mammoth and carved the earliest known depiction of a human being.

As it happens, that artist also set a precedent for the type of curiosity collected in this book, for the *Venus of Hohle Fels* is a deeply strange and mysterious object. It is also not something to be found in art histories prior to 2008, as that is the year it was discovered by an archaeological team led by Nicholas J. Conard of the University of Tübingen. The curious figure was found apart in six fragments in a layer of clay silt about 3m (10ft) below ground level in the hall of the Hohle Fels cave, a remarkable site that has proved to be a kind of Palaeolithic cabinet of curiosities yielding many similarly exciting discoveries. (Elsewhere in the cave, for example, was discovered a flute carved from a vulture bone, dated to 42,000 years and so the oldest known musical instrument.) At just 6cm (2½in) in height, the fragile *Venus of Hohle Fels* could disappear in a closed fist, and yet somehow it survived the violence of millennia to rewrite established assumptions about prehistoric carving and revise the dating of such art by a staggering 7000 years earlier than previously thought.

But what exactly are we looking at? The figurine is headless; instead there is a carved ring protruding between the shoulders, suggesting that the sculpture was probably worn around the neck as a pendant. The Venus bears exaggerated buttocks and genitals; while below her bulging breasts are placed her delicately carved hands and fingers, at the end of two short arms. Her torso is scratched with deep horizontal lines, perhaps representing clothing, while her legs are as stumpy as the arms, suggesting that it is her sexual features that are the focus.

Though she is far older, this places her within the ranks of other Palaeolithic Venus figures that have been uncovered around Europe, like the *Venus of Willendorf* (Austria), the *Venus*

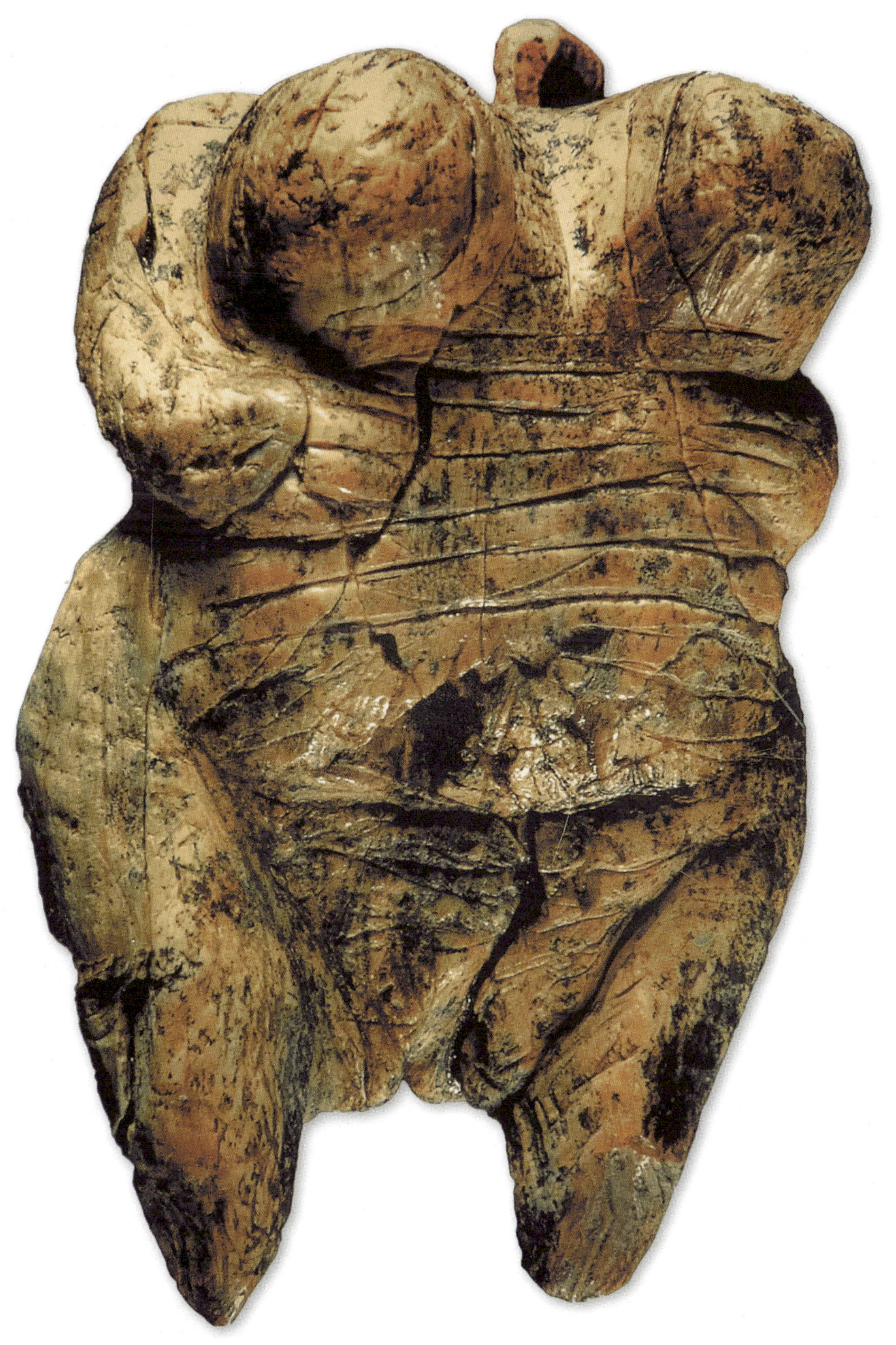

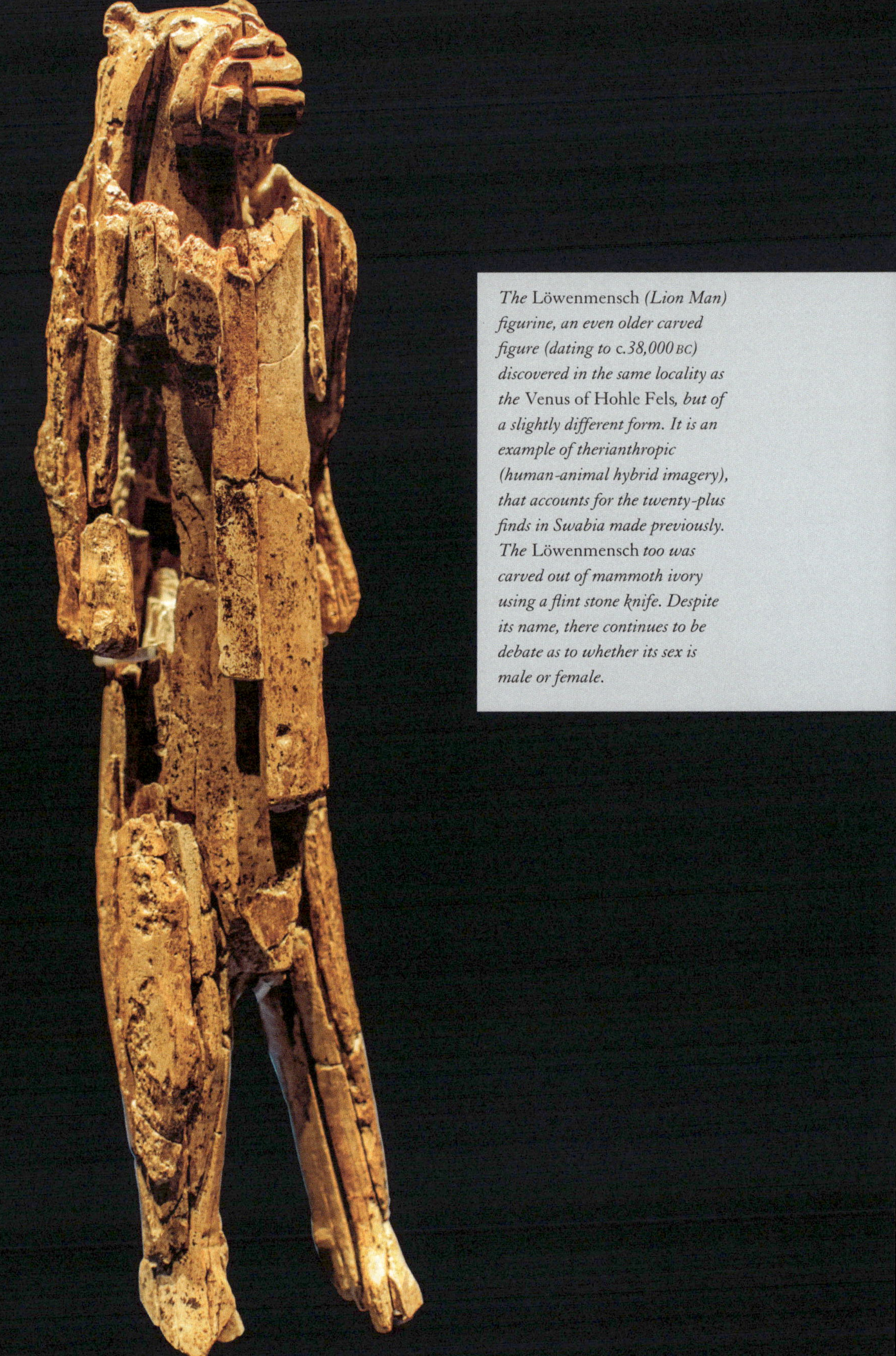

The Löwenmensch *(Lion Man) figurine, an even older carved figure (dating to* c.*38,000* BC*) discovered in the same locality as the* Venus of Hohle Fels, *but of a slightly different form. It is an example of therianthropic (human-animal hybrid imagery), that accounts for the twenty-plus finds in Swabia made previously. The* Löwenmensch *too was carved out of mammoth ivory using a flint stone knife. Despite its name, there continues to be debate as to whether its sex is male or female.*

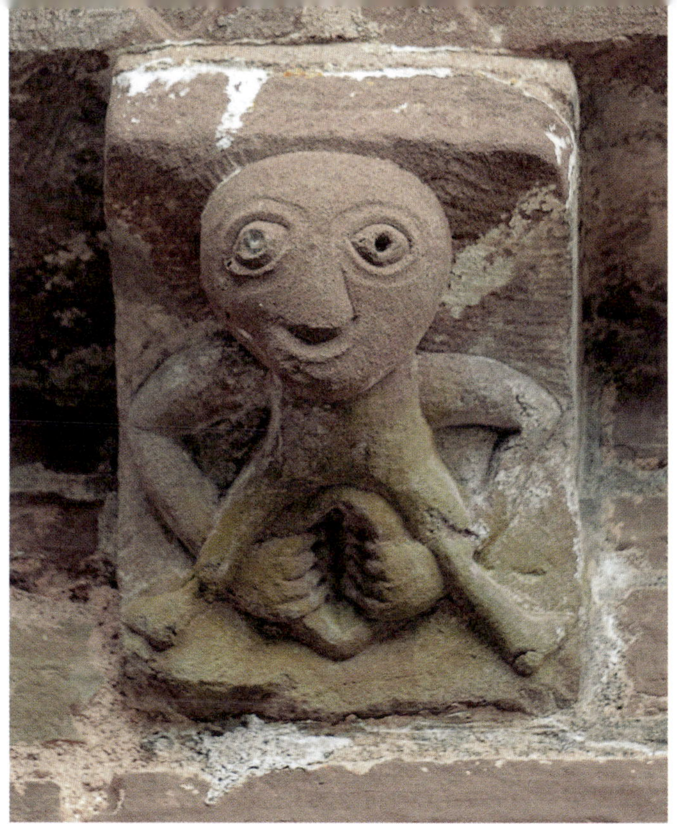

LEFT: *Fast-forward to twelfth-century Europe and we find the Sheela na gig grotesque carvings on churches such as this at the Church of St Mary and St David, built c.1140 at Kilpeck, Herefordshire, England. One theory as to their origin and the reason behind their exaggerated vulva is that they represent a pagan fertility goddess; another is that they were used to ward off death, evil and misfortune.*

RIGHT: *Thousands of these metal badges survive in Europe from the Middle Ages, and were worn by Christians on pilgrimage. They commonly feature animated vulvas and penises performing actions like climbing ladders, wearing hats and riding horses. The example shown here is known in the scholarship as* Pussy Goes a Hunting. *Very little contemporary literature mentions these early souvenirs and so their meaning is mysterious. Probably symbolising fertility, it has also been suggested that – like the Sheela na gig – they were used to ward off evil, or perhaps to signify availability for sexual encounters.*

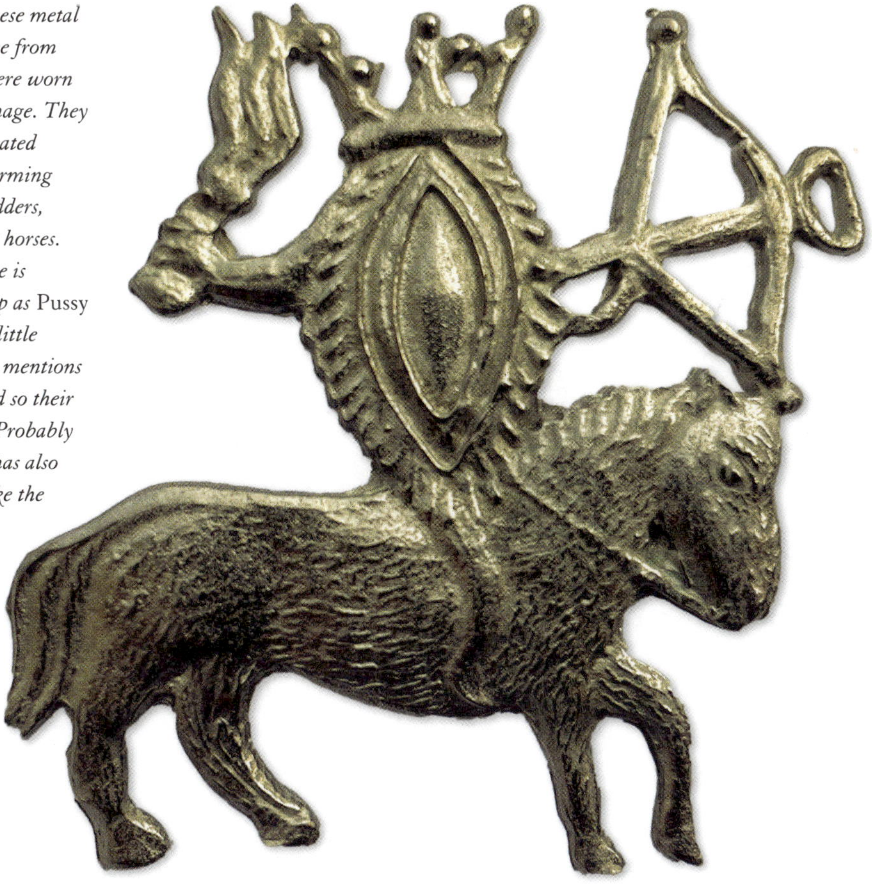

of Monpazier (France), the *Venus of Dolní Věstonice* (Czech Republic) and the *Venus of Savignano* (Italy). The meaning of these figures has long been the subject of debate, but they are commonly thought to be fertility symbols, perhaps even of fertility deities, of enough significance to justify the immensely time-consuming process of carving them using primitive tools.

Today our popular impression of Upper Palaeolithic Europe abounds with the images of male Ice Age hunters chasing around woolly mammoths and other megafauna; how exciting then that this ancient artwork of female iconography offers clues to a whole other side of early Stone Age life, while also marking a seismic milestone in mankind's creative development.

The extraordinary Italian fresco known as the Albero della Fecondità *(Fertility Tree), known locally as the 'penis tree'. Created in 1265, it was discovered in 1999 in the street-level loggia (balcony) of a thirteenth-century, former wheat store close to Piazza Garibaldi, Naples. During preservation work following its discovery, restorers were accused of prudishly erasing several sets of testicles – this they denied, attributing the change to the necessary removal of salt and calcium deposits.*

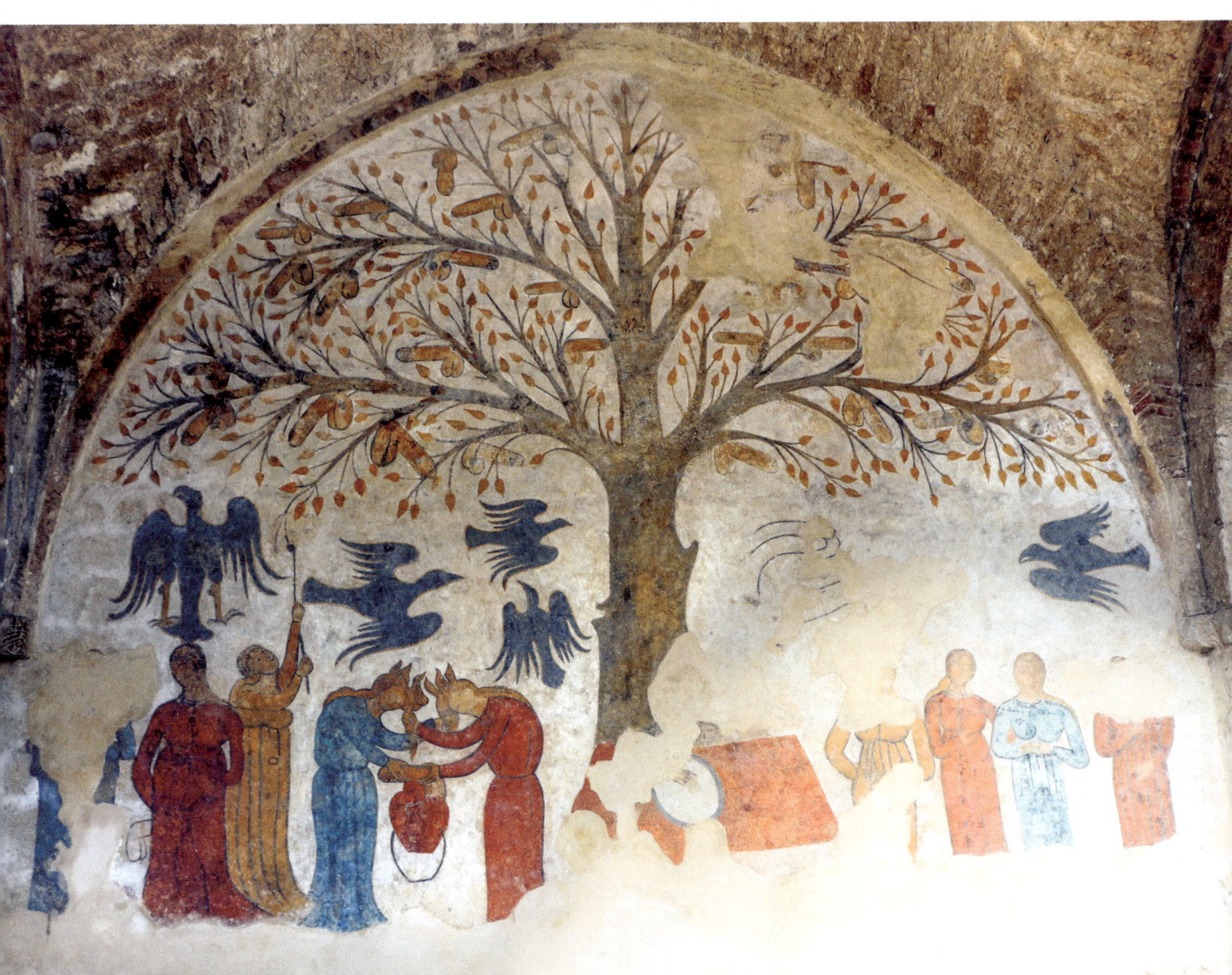

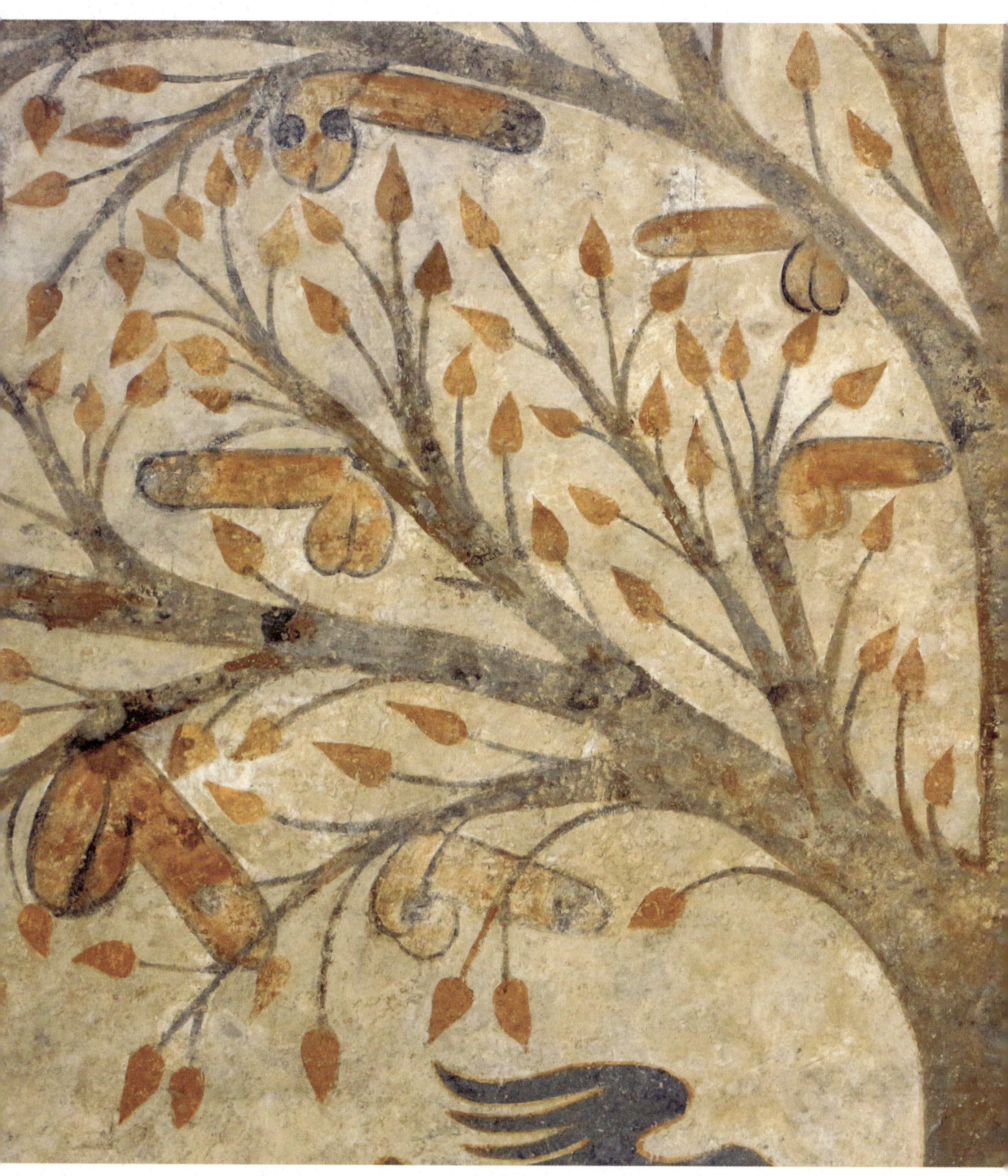

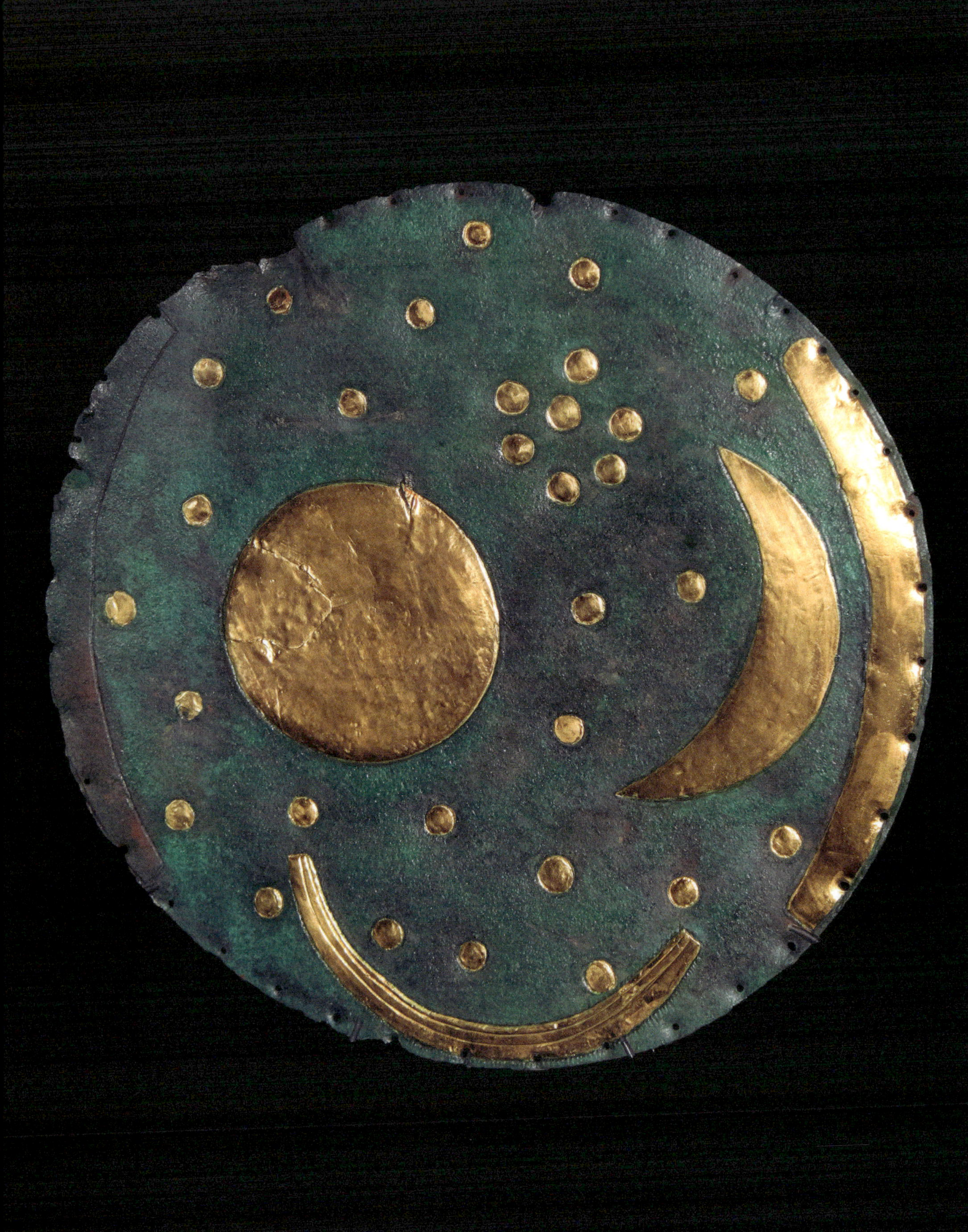

NEBRA SKY DISC (*c.*1600 BC)

A remarkable artistic find was made in 1999 when two amateur archaeologists of the more criminal persuasion – otherwise known as grave-robbers – uncovered a Bronze Age treasure trove at a site near Nebra, Saxony-Anhalt, in Germany. Among the small pile of two bronze swords, two hatchets, a chisel and pieces of spiral bracelets, they found this stunning bronze disc, 12in (30cm) in diameter, oxidised to a glowing blue-green patina and inlaid with symbols of gold. There is no other object remotely like it in the history of European archaeology.

The looters (who were later prosecuted and, on appealing for leniency, had their sentences increased) sold the stash to an underground antiquities dealer in Cologne, and for two years the disc and its burial companions changed hands on the black market. It wasn't until 2002, when the disc was recovered by authorities after a sting operation led by Dr Harald Meller of the State Museum of Prehistory in Halle, Germany, that the true significance of the Nebra sky disc began to be realised.

Through radiocarbon analysis of the axes and swords with which it was buried, the disc has been associatively dated to *c.*1600 BC and the Bronze Age Unetice culture. This means that the Nebra sky disc is verified as the oldest confirmed depiction of the cosmos in existence – an astounding discovery that questions the traditional thinking of Bronze Age Europe as a place of intellectual darkness in the shadow of the enlightened cultures of ancient Egypt and Greece. The disc has a surprising sophistication: its inlaid symbols clearly include the sun and moon, and, while these are surrounded by an apparently random sprinkle of stars, the prominent stellar grouping just north of the centre is recognisable as the Pleiades cluster, just as they would have shone in the Bronze Age sky over northern Europe.

Even more intriguing are the interpretations of the two curved golden bands (one of which is missing) along its edges. These span 82 degrees, which matches the angle the sun is seen to travel along the horizon between the high midsummer sunset and the low midwinter sunset. In other words, the disc might well have been a functional device to mark the solstices precisely as they would have occurred in Nebra, which would have been of significant use for agriculture. The third

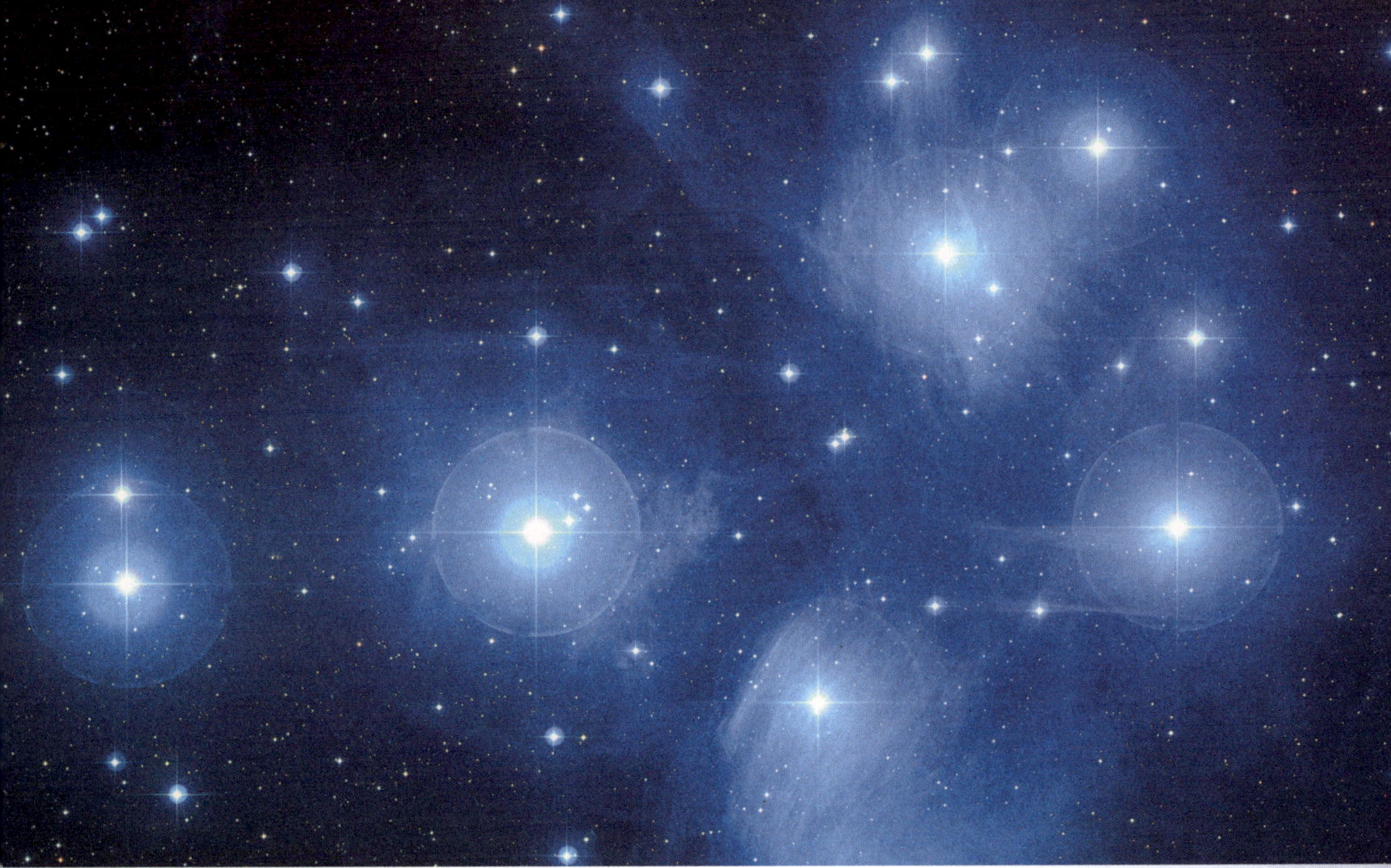

golden arc, distinctive in that it curves upwards away from the edges, has been variously interpreted as the Milky Way, or perhaps a rainbow. The leading theory, however, has thrilling implications. Might the golden curve represent a 'solar barge' or 'sun boat', the vessel that transported the sun-god Ra during the night according to Egyptian mythological tradition? Could the sphere of ancient Egyptian cultural influence have spread this far at this time?

The idea of such international involvement is not as far-fetched as it seems. A geochemical survey conducted in 2011 found that, while the copper elements of the disc could be traced to local mines, its gold and tin content were identified as originating from Cornwall, southwest England, a distance of more than 1100km (700 miles) as the crow flies. The disc reveals not just an overlooked sophistication of its authorial culture, but also the existence of a substantial metal trade from the British Isles towards central Germany, and perhaps even Egyptian mythological inspiration if it is indeed a solar vessel depicted. Little wonder, then, that in 2013 the Nebra sky disc was designated by the United Nations Educational, Scientific and Cultural Organization (UNESCO) as 'one of the most important archaeological finds of the twentieth century'.

A composite image of the Pleiades star cluster, captured between 1986 and 1996 at the Palomar Observatory, California.

OPPOSITE: *The unique Berlin Gold Hat, a ceremonial hat of embossed gold dating to the Late Bronze Age, c.1000-800* BC, *discovered in southern Germany or Switzerland. A Bronze Age operator would have used it as a solar and lunar calendar, predicting eclipses and other celestial events.*

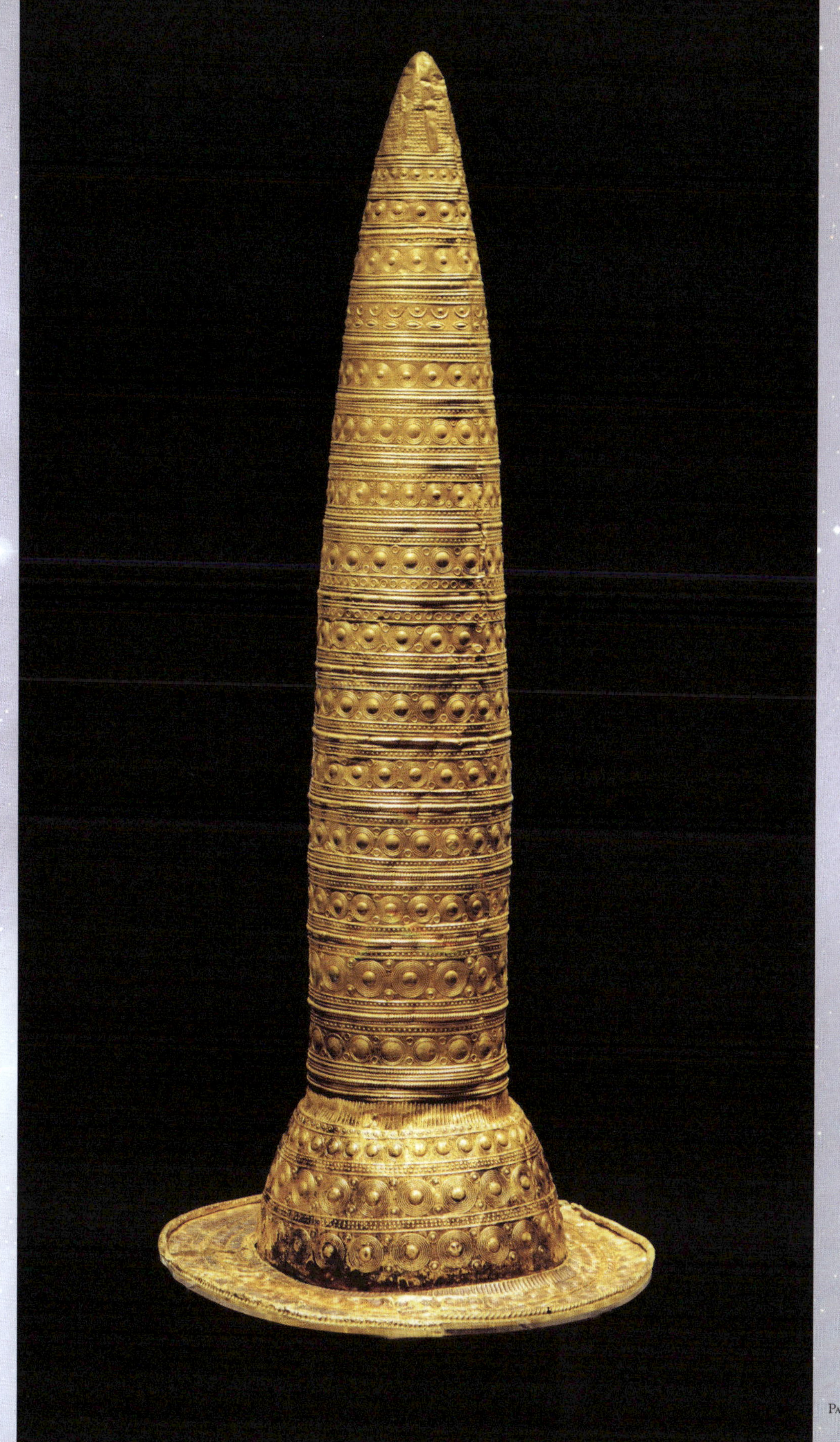

COLOSSAL HEADS OF THE OLMEC (*c.*900 BC)

In Mesoamerica, long before the Aztec and their intricate goldwork,[1] before the Maya and their hieroglyphic writing, before even the Zapotec and their dazzling geometric textiles, there were the Olmec and their giant heads. San Lorenzo, the oldest discovered centre of this first great Mesoamerican civilisation (which is often referred to as the 'mother culture' of the region), is dated to *c.*1150-900 BC, and yet the skill of Olmec sculptors arguably eclipses that of all later civilisations of the region. When the site was first excavated, the artistry exhibited in the tiny jade figures, architectural adornments and other materials was so advanced, despite being made around a thousand years before the advent of Maya civilisation, that a number of archaeologists refused to believe their antiquity.

---

1 'I have never seen in all my days that which so rejoiced my heart, as these things,' wrote the great German Renaissance artist Albrecht Dürer (1471-1528) when he first glimpsed Aztec artworks of gold and silver brought back from the New World. 'For I saw among them amazing artistic objects, and I marvelled over the subtle ingenuity of the men in these distant lands.' Sadly very few of these gold and silver artworks survive, as most were melted down to make currency.

An Olmec head, now the collection of the National Museum of Anthropology, Mexico.

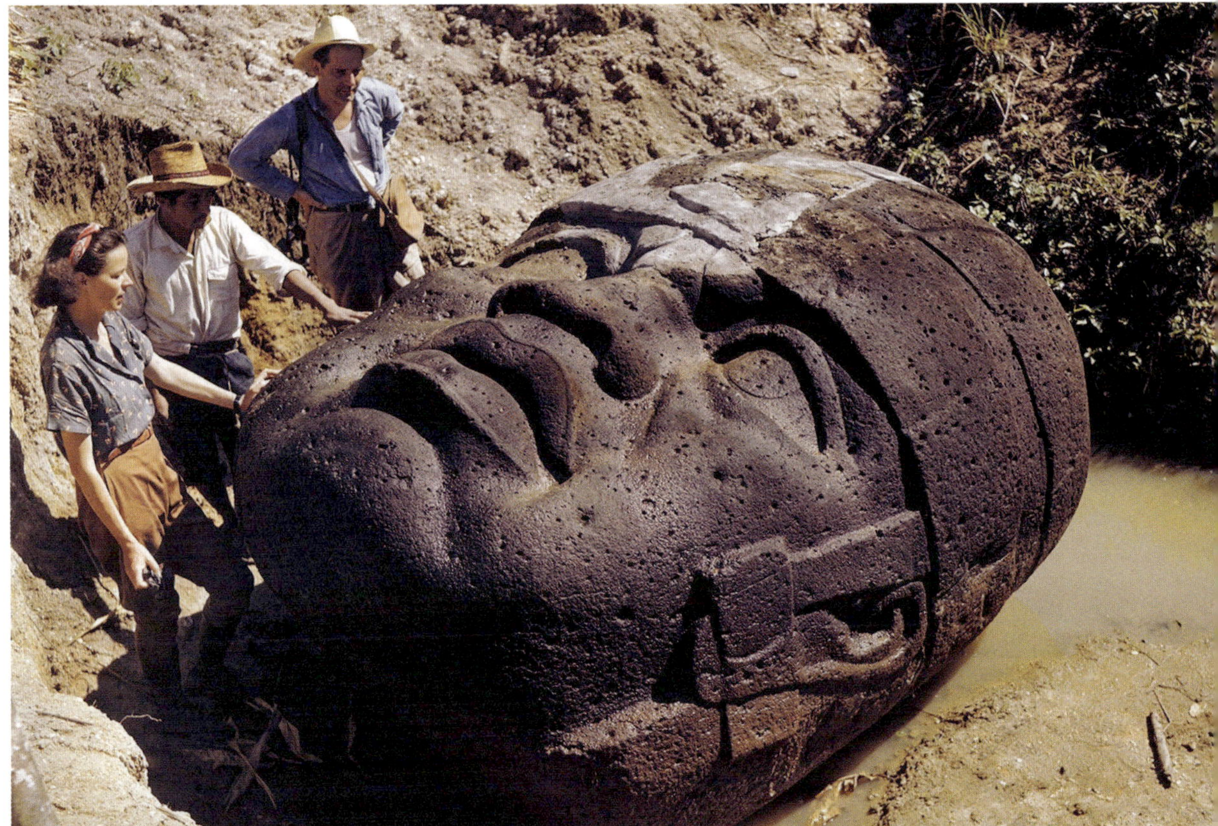

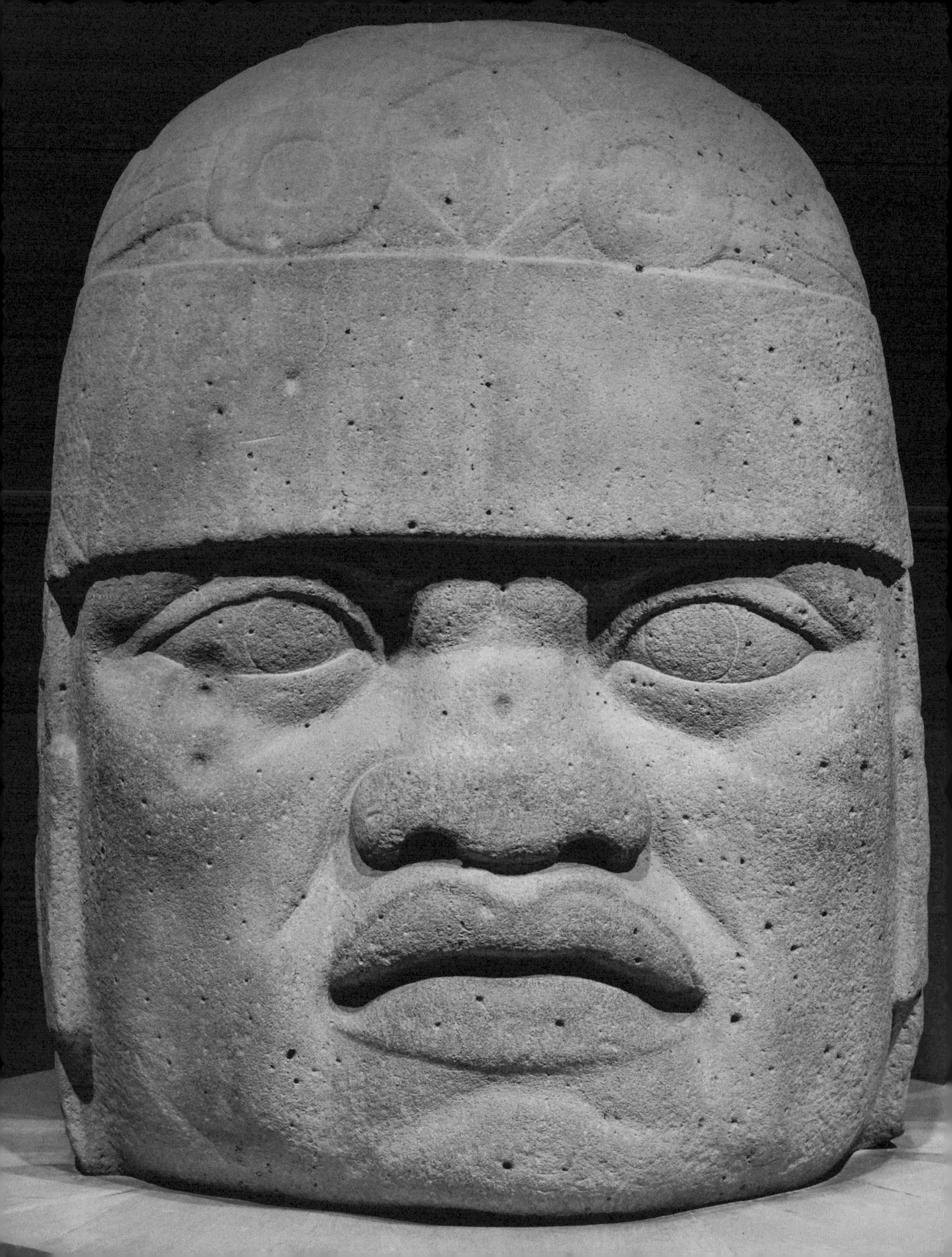

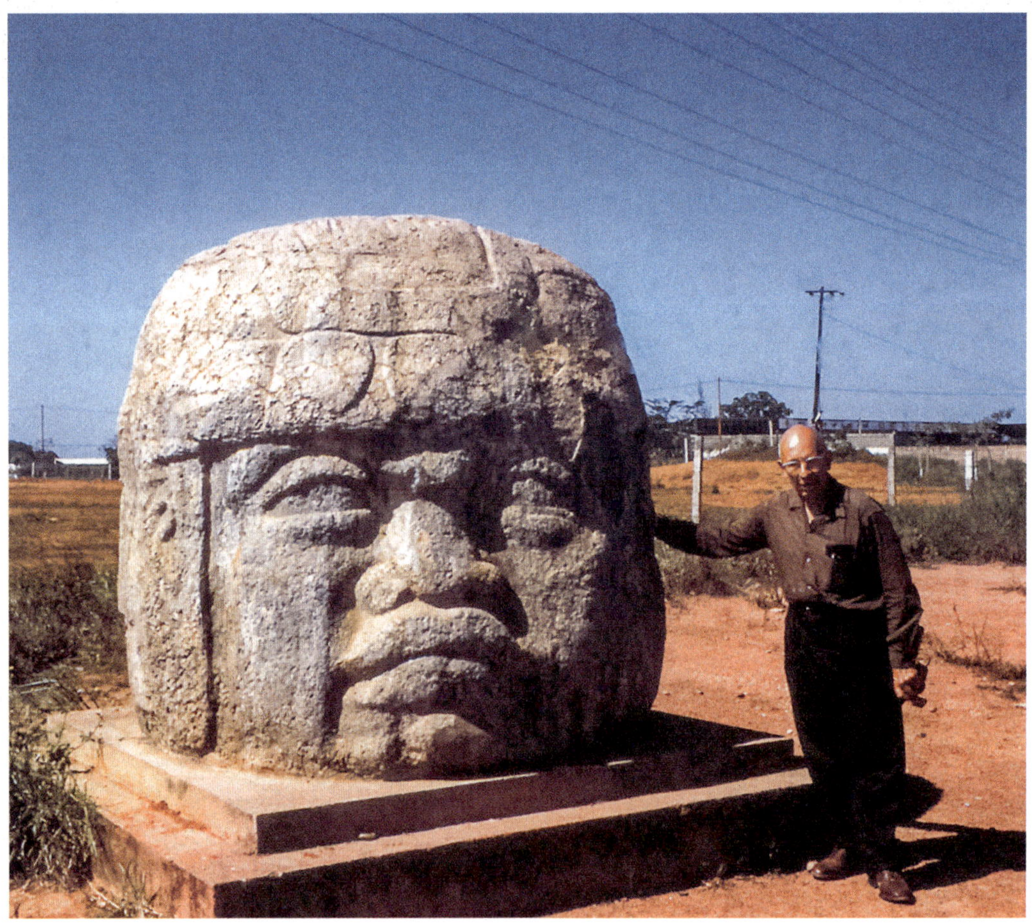

An Olmec head, Mexico, in a photo taken c.1960 by Dr C.N. Caldwell.

Among the wealth of extraordinary stone monuments discovered at San Lorenzo, the most startling are the 'colossal heads', which can stand as tall as 3.4m (11.2ft), carved from solid basalt boulders. Seventeen of the heads have been discovered so far, each with wide staring eyes, a flat nose and thick lips, and weighing up to 25 tonnes. The last detail makes remarkable the fact that some have been found some 95km (60 miles) from the nearest basalt quarry. It's thought they were carved from basalt in the Tuxtla Mountains to the northwest, then dragged down to the nearest navigable waterway and carried on rafts up the Coatzacoalcos river to San Lorenzo. An astonishing amount of labour would have been involved in their relocation.

The heads' sizes are matched only by their scale of mystery. Why they were made, and who they portray, remains a matter of debate, as does the enigma of why they appear to have been ceremoniously mutilated. The leading theory, based on the fact that they were discovered arranged in a line and buried after the damage was inflicted, suggests that each head represents a ruler whose likeness was destroyed as part of a funerary ritual, or perhaps to mark the transfer of power to their successor. However, each head also appears to be wearing a piece of headgear reminiscent of a protective helmet, which has led to the suggestion that the heads are of players of a rubber-ball game that we know, from other figurines, was played at San Lorenzo. It's this tantalising riddle as to the purpose of the monuments that helps render the scale and expressive power of the Olmec artworks as fascinating to the modern viewer as it surely must have been for those who first saw the gargantuan heads.

Over 3000 years since the Olmec carved their giant heads presumed to be of their leaders, the tradition is alive and well in Williamsburg, Virginia, USA. There one can find a set of 6m (20ft) statues of the American presidents created by the artist David Adickes, which have languished in a field since 2010, quietly disintegrating as they await a site suitable for their display to the public.

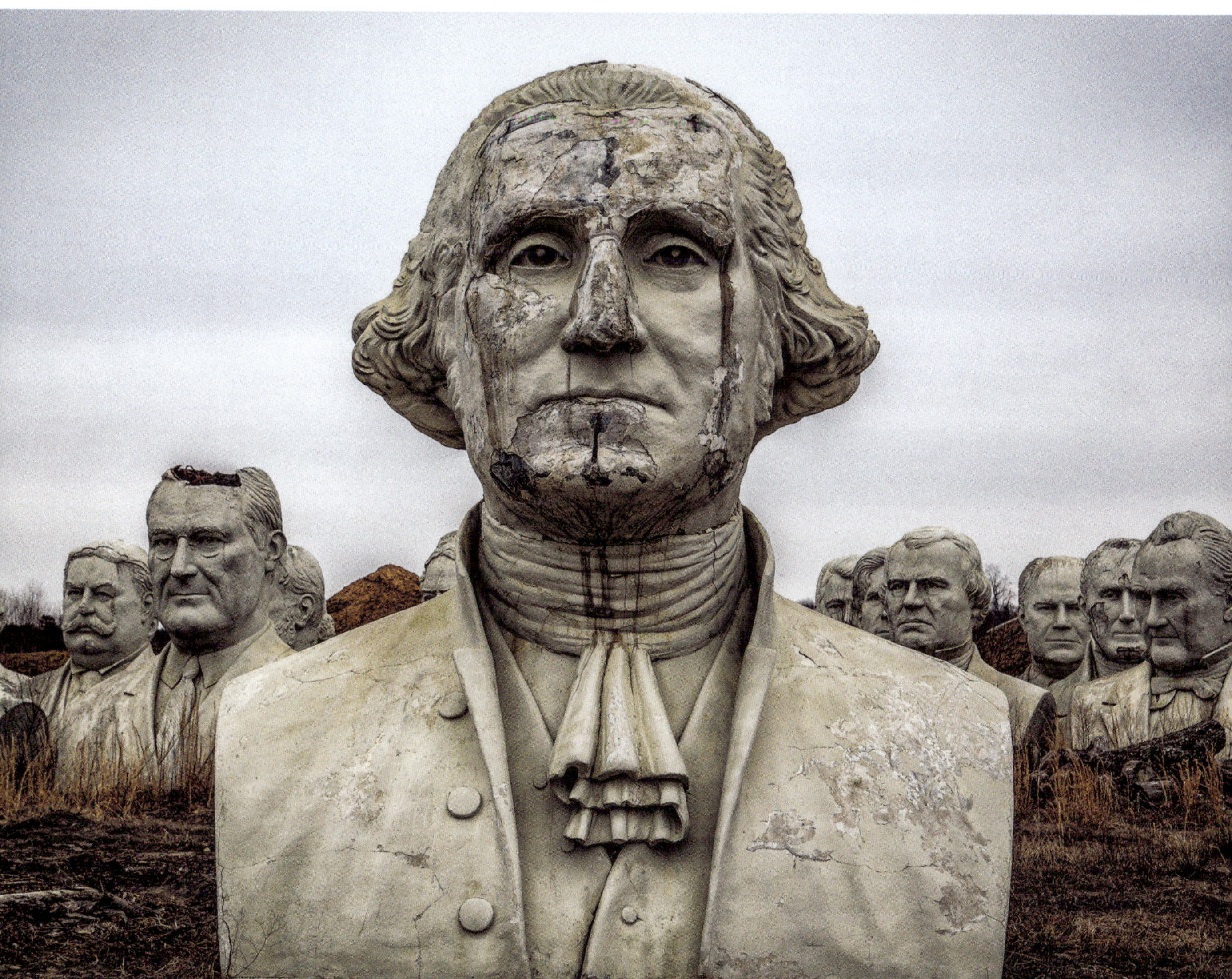

TOMB OF THE DIVER (*c.*480 BC)
AND OTHER ART MADE TO BE BURIED

Some works of art were never meant to be seen – at least, not by the eyes of the living. Funerary art, designed to be entombed or buried with the deceased, is a custom of cultures around the world. While popular awareness is dominated by famous examples like Tutankhamun's tomb and China's Terracotta Army,[1] buried with Emperor Qin Shi Huang in 210-209 BC to protect him in the afterlife, there are also a few more curious examples that help illustrate just how art can illuminate eras and personalities otherwise swallowed up by the dust of time.

These continue to be found today – a recent example is the discovery of the true nature of a treasure found in King Tutankhamun's tomb. Though the tomb was unearthed in 1922 by Howard Carter (1874-1939), it was only in 2016 that researchers from the Polytechnic University of Milan concluded that the beautifully crafted, gold-hilted dagger found within the wrappings of the mummified pharaoh was of a startling composition of iron, nickel and cobalt, which 'strongly suggests an extraterrestrial origin'. The composition of the dagger's blade is identical to that of a meteor found in the city of Mersa Matruh. In other words, King Tut possessed a true weapon of the heavens.

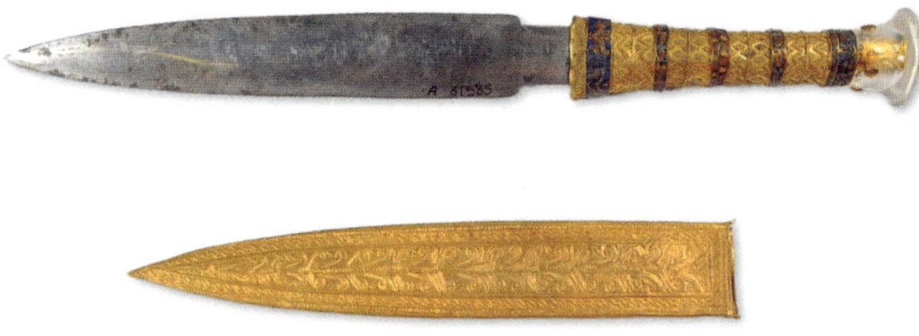

Tutankhamun's meteorite dagger – one of two knives discovered in 1925 hidden among the wrappings of Tutankhamun's mummified corpse. The blade is made of iron, which was rarer and more valuable than gold at the time.

1 An extraordinary fact about the estimated 8,000 soldiers, 130 chariots with 520 horses, and 150 cavalry of the Terracotta Army is that no two faces are alike. The heads were moulded, but the Qin artisans were under imperial orders to craft the faces by hand, furnishing each figure with unique features and expressions to represent a unique personality. A cunning warrior has graceful eyebrow and eyes, while the eyes of a brave soldier are wide and staring. A large head with a wide face, bushy eyebrows and big eyes denotes a simple and honest soldier.

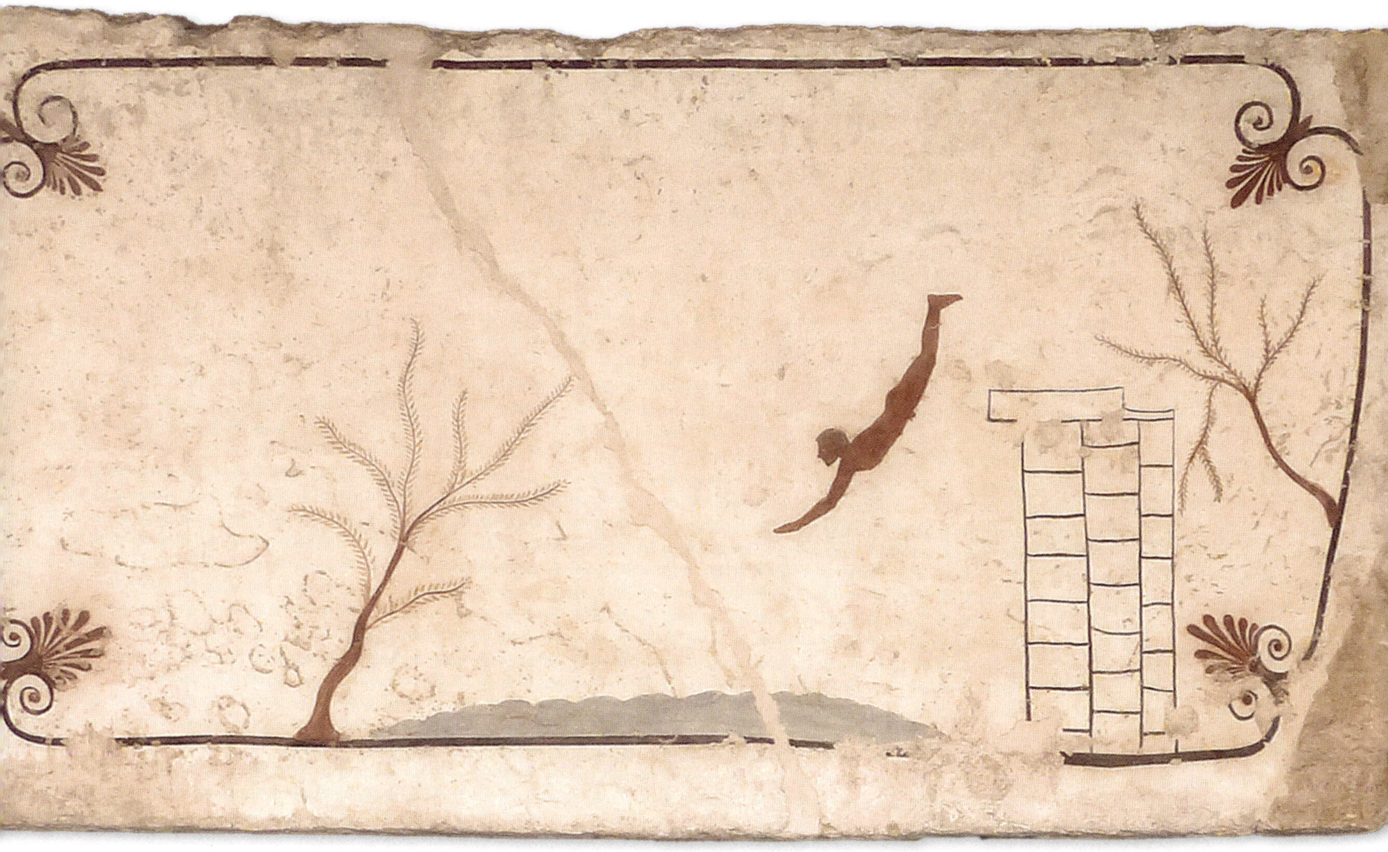

The painted ceiling slab of the Tomb of the Diver, showing a young man plunging into the eternity of the afterlife.

Other excavations have turned up equally extraordinary treasures. Noblemen of the Maya, for example, have been found buried with drinking jars in the shape of an animal head, designed to allow their spirits to enjoy the luxury of sipping cocoa in the afterlife. Elsewhere, burial sites of the Moche civilisation of northern Peru, which flourished AD *c.*100-800, have contained strange carved figures of male 'zombie' figures with genitals of enormous proportions. These sexually active, living cadavers were thought to exist in the underworld, and possess the ability to masturbate and produce great quantities of semen to fertilise the living earth.

The most remarkable survival featured here is known as the painted Tomb of the Diver. The ancient Greek writers describe a tradition of monumental wall paintings, but virtually no examples exist, and it was almost entirely from studying ceramic vessels that we formed our knowledge of Greek painting. Until 1968, that is, when the Italian archaeologist Mario Napoli discovered an extraordinary monument during his excavation of a necropolis just south of the ancient Greek city of Poseidonia (later renamed Paestum by the Romans) in southern Italy.

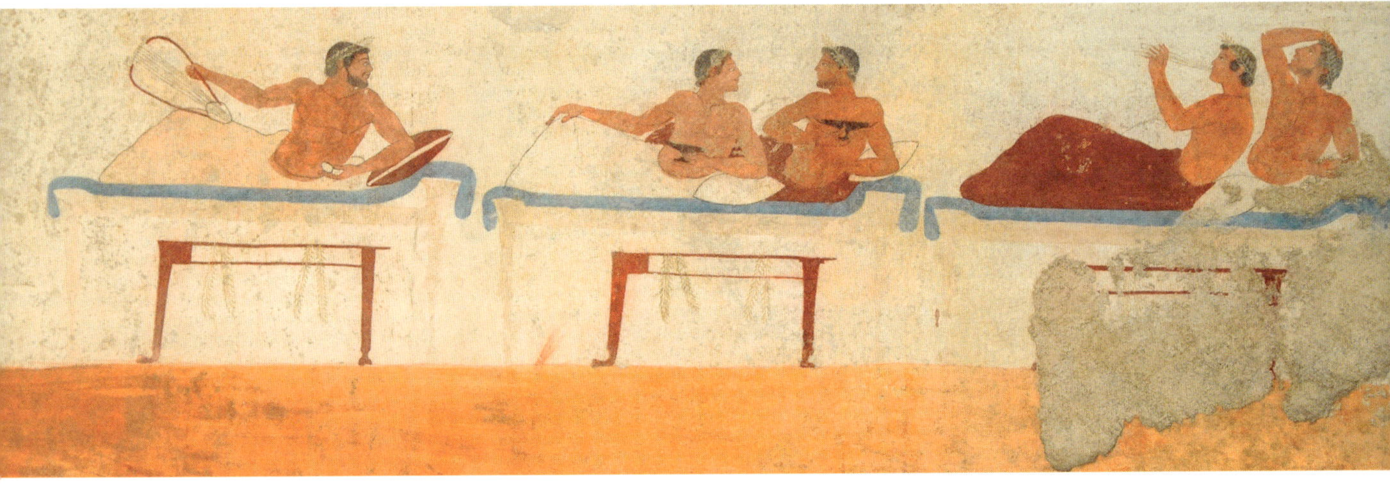

Created *c.*470 BC, the tomb comprises five travertine slabs (forming four walls and a ceiling) set into bedrock, each painted with a fresco. On the walls of the tomb are scenes of reclining young men assembled for a symposium, the ancient Greek equivalent of a boozy knees-up – a commemorative montage, it appears, of the young man enjoying his life to the full in better days. Of particular note is the figure brandishing his *kylix* (a wide shallow drinking cup) above his head. This was a popular ancient Greek party game known as *kottabos*, in which the reclining drinkers would deftly sling the last dregs of their wine through the air in one unbroken liquid missile at a target in the middle of the room. The best players had the aim of a spitting cobra and were held in a similar level of regard as those who threw the javelin. The game was heavily gambled upon and, because of the element of luck involved, the performance of each *kottabos* contestant was viewed as an omen of their future successes, especially in affairs of the heart.

The symposium scenes are thought to have been painted by a minor artist – the ceiling slab, on the other hand, by a master. The painting shows a young man (assumed to be the deceased resident of the tomb) diving from a high platform into calm blue water. This is interpreted as a metaphorical scene – the young man, in the prime of life, plunges from the world of the living into death's great eternal sea. The rarity of this cannot be overstated, not just in its depiction of the afterlife but also because – of the thousands of Greek tombs of this time that have been excavated – the Tomb of the Diver is the only one to feature frescoes of a human subject.

ABOVE: *The symposium scene on the north wall of the Tomb of the Diver.*

OPPOSITE: *This Moche ceremonial vessel represents a sexually active, living cadaver of the underworld. His exaggerated proportions emphasise his ability to masturbate and produce semen to fertilise the living earth.*

BELOW: *This jaguar-head jar, AD 300-600 (Early Classic), was a luxury item made to be buried with a Maya nobleman or noblewoman in their tomb, to provide them with drinking chocolate in the afterlife.*

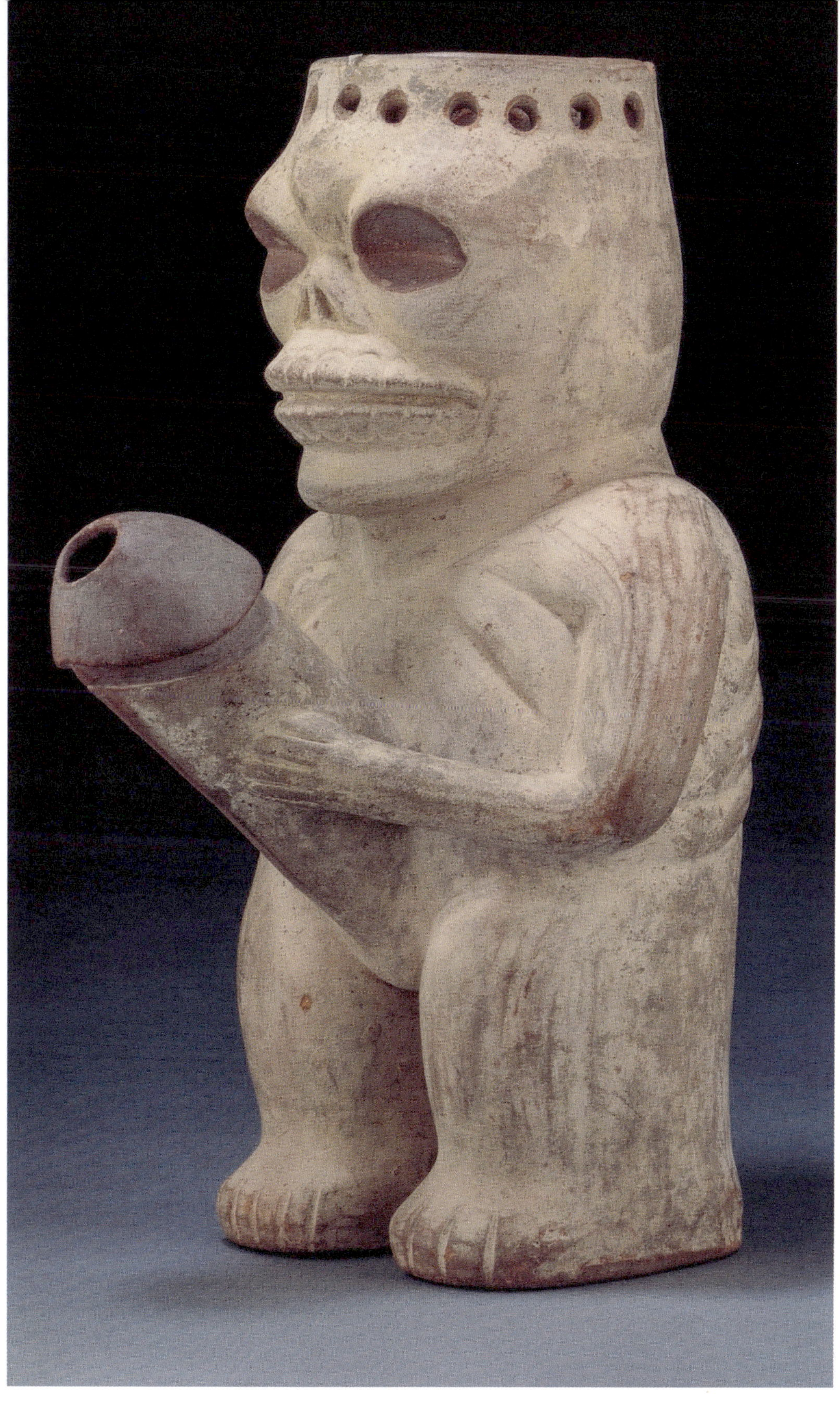

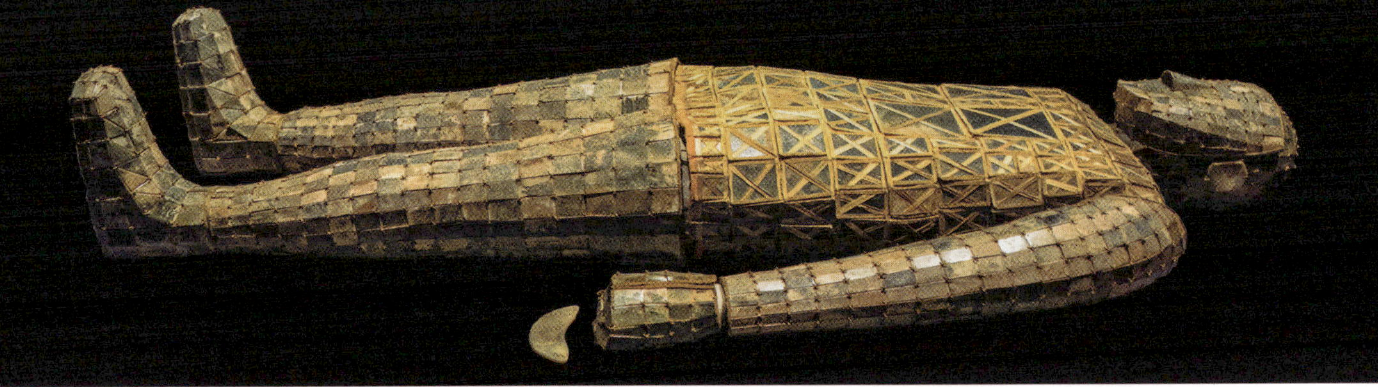

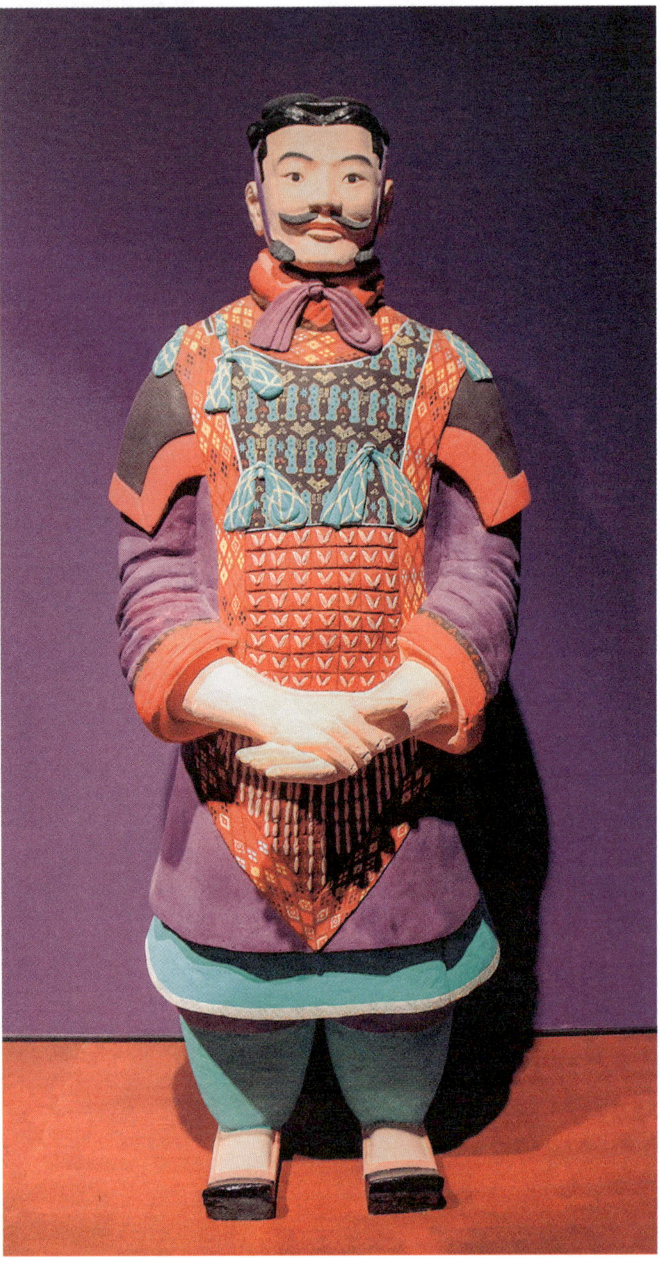

Above: *In 1968, the same year that the Tomb of the Diver was uncovered, across the world in China an archaeological discovery of equal importance was made. The jade burial suit of Princess Dou Wan (d. c.118-104* BC*) was found in her tomb in Hebei Province and was swiftly declared a national treasure. Such suits of precious stones, stitched with gold and silver, were designed to protect their wearer in the afterlife.*

Left: *A recreation of how the figures of the famous Terracotta Army would have originally looked at the time of their creation. When they were uncovered in 1974 by farmers of Lintong County, China, their colourful lacquers reacted with the air and rapidly dissolved to leave only the plain terracotta beneath.*

Opposite: *A representation of the sarcophagus lid of K'inich Janaab' Pakal, seventh-century* ajaw *(ruler of Palenque), found in the Temple of the Inscriptions, the largest Mesoamerican stepped pyramid structure ever discovered. This astonishingly beautiful afterworld depiction shows Pakal caught between two worlds, perpetually tumbling down into the gaping jaws of the underworld while above him is the heavenly* muan *bird, perched atop the Cosmic Tree.*

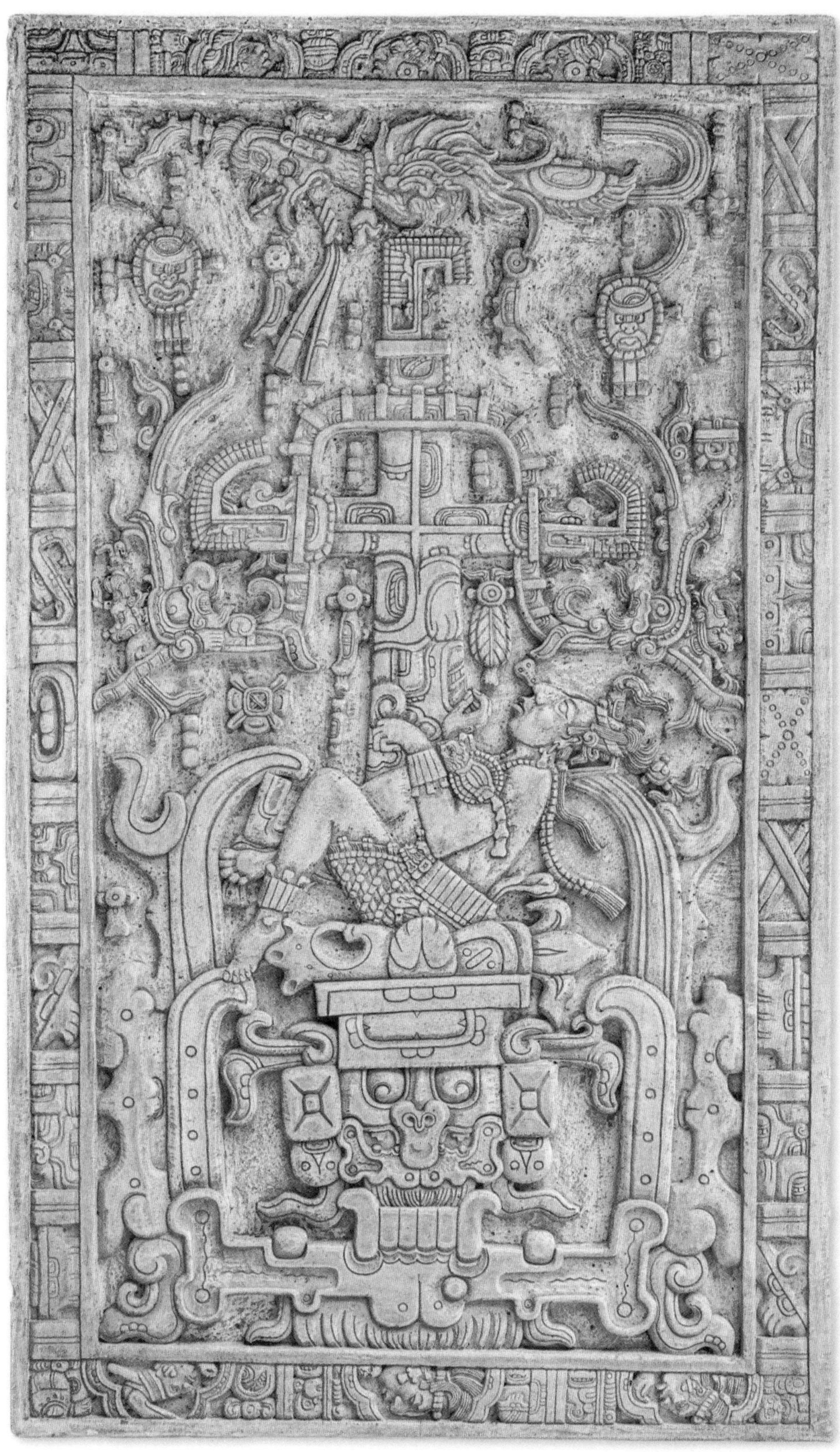

STATUE OF GLYCON, THE FALSE SNAKE DEITY (LATE SECOND CENTURY)

Perhaps it's the distinctly human ears on the snake of this second-century marble statue that first strike you as odd, or maybe the thick mop of human hair running elegantly down to where shoulders would be. Even stranger is the story behind this curious and confusing carving, which involves a con artist, a snake deity and a hand puppet.

The statue was discovered deep beneath the former Pallas railway station in Constanța, Romania, during excavation work in 1995, but we need to go back over 1800 years earlier to find Alexander of Abonoteichos (AD *c*.105-*c*.170), the principal character of the story as related by the Syrian writer Lucian of Samosata (AD *c*.125-after 180). Little is known of Alexander, a Greek mystic who used fake tablets and a hand puppet to found his prophetic snake cult. We do know he was the classical equivalent of a quack, grifting the gullible with touring medical shows around Greece and pretending to be a prophet of the goddess Soi. He struck gold, though, with his invention of Glycon.

Lucian tells us how Alexander created and buried in the temple of the healing god Asclepius a set of forged tablets that prophesied the appearance of Asclepius in Alexander's hometown, Abonoteichos. When the 'relics' were stumbled upon, every mystic and follower in the region travelled to the town to erect a new temple to Asclepius and await his arrival. Cue Alexander: dressed in prophet's robes, he cut open a goose egg to reveal inside a live snake (a tame one that he had set in place earlier). Pointing at the serpent, he announced that Asclepius had returned in serpent form, and henceforth wished to be known as Glycon.

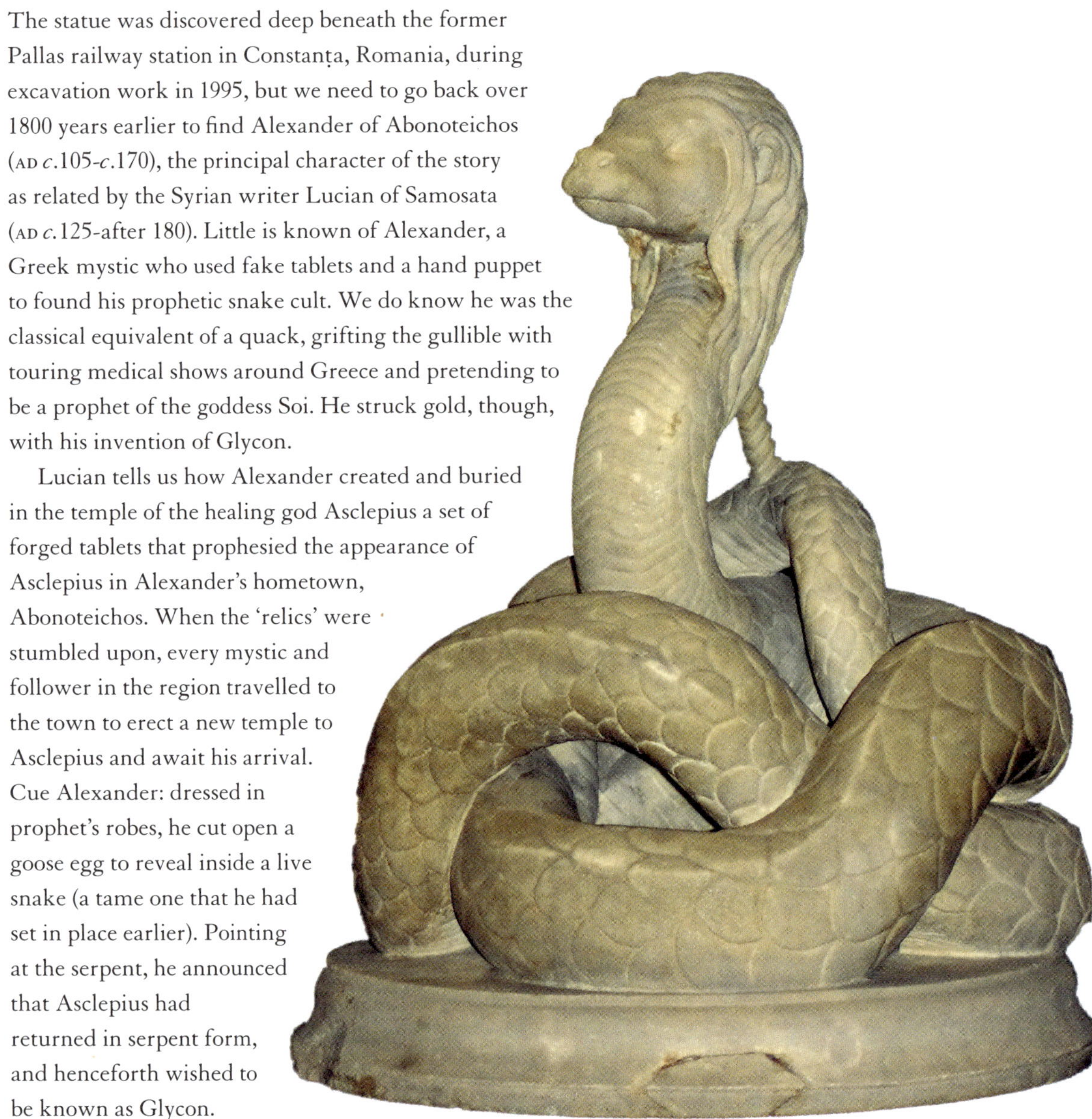

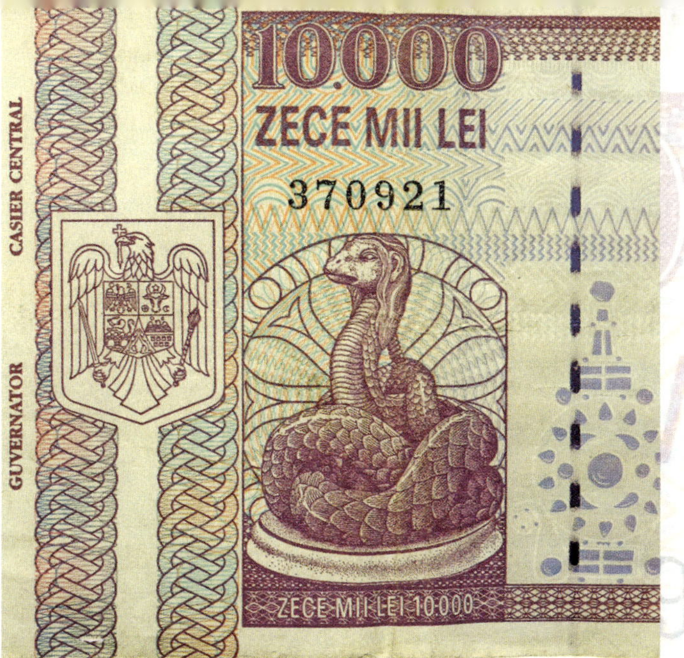

The Romanians celebrated the discovery of the Glycon statue by depicting Glycon on a banknote of 10,000 lei in 1994.

Alexander was his communicatory vessel. Eager believers bought into it without question, and Alexander's snake cult grew swiftly in popularity. Divine aid with fertility was a common focus of Macedonian cults, and Alexander's was no different. Barren women brought Glycon offerings in the hope of falling pregnant, and if these failed, writes Lucian, Alexander would humbly offer his intimate services as a solution.

Alexander's success was largely down to two things. He was able to reply with uncanny accuracy to his followers' questions, having secretly read their sealed messages to Glycon ahead of time. And there was also the fact that Glycon (in the form we see here) would appear in his hand, as a live snake with human features and long blond hair. Well, sort of. According to Lucian, this incarnation was a hand puppet made from linen that 'would open and close its mouth by means of horsehairs; and a forked black tongue also controlled by horsehairs, would dart out'.

This didn't seem to interfere with the cult's popularity spreading beyond the Aegean region. There are records of the Roman senator Publius Mummius Sisenna Rutilianus announcing himself as protector of Glycon's oracle, and of Marcus Aurelius consulting the prophesies of Alexander and Glycon. From archaeological evidence, it appears Alexander's snake cult lived on for over 100 years after his death *c.* AD 170. Even today, his legacy has not entirely faded – in 1993 the English writer and occultist Alan Moore declared himself a follower of Glycon, choosing the fake deity over all others 'because I'm not likely to start believing that a glove puppet created the universe or anything dangerous like that'.

DOOM PAINTINGS
(TWELFTH-THIRTEENTH CENTURIES)

In 1869 Rev. Henry Shepherd, rector of the church of St Peter and St Paul in Chaldon, Surrey, was watching decorators prepare the walls for limewashing when he noticed a flare of red pigment burst through the old pale coating. Work was immediately halted, and the old wash gradually stripped from the walls, to reveal the breathtaking sight of the enormous, 5.3 × 3.5m (17¼ × 11¼ft), two-tone mural in dark red and yellow ochre shown here. Such Doom paintings, sometimes simply referred to as 'Dooms', served as gigantic billboard warnings to reform sinful ways or face the graphic consequences. Usually they were painted on the western wall of a church, so they were the last thing worshippers saw while filing out after a service.

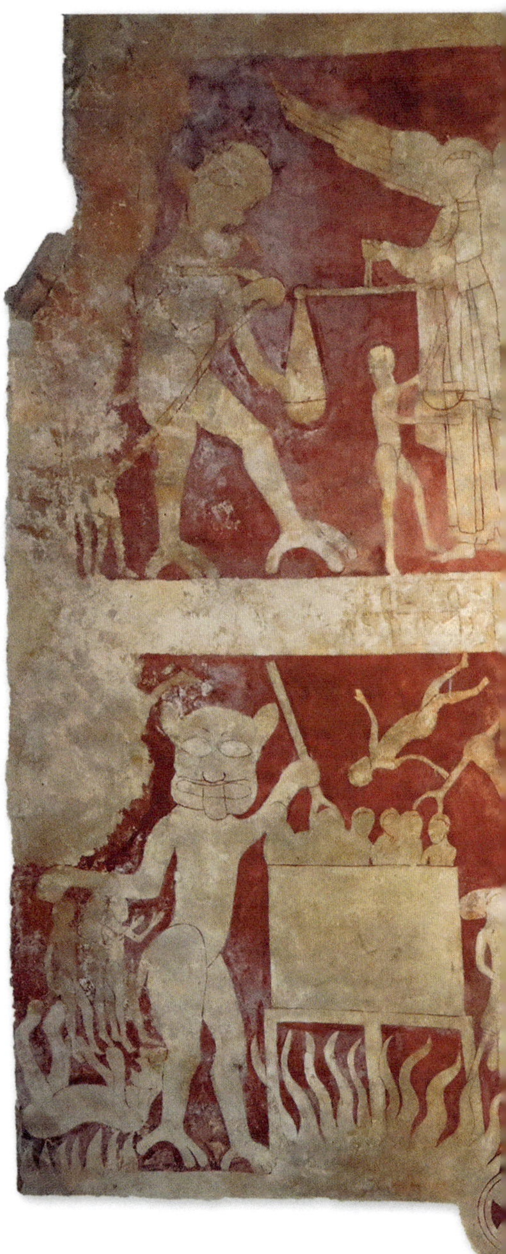

In the enormous Chaldon example, which is thought to have been painted *c.*1140 by a travelling artist-monk well versed in Greek ecclesiastical art, there is a lot to take in. The dead have their sins and virtues weighed by giant angels in the top left corner; an archangel marshals a demon back into the jaws of hell with his flagged standard in the top right; and, in the centre, sinners attempt to ascend the Ladder of Salvation to heaven but tumble back down to hell, where multiple spike and fire-based tortures are in full swing. These are the spiritual machinations that will follow the Last Judgement, when every deceased person in history will be bodily resurrected to face the judgement of Christ, who will weigh the virtues of both 'the quick and the dead' (2 Timothy 4:1). The virtuous will pass to heaven, the sinful to hell (Matthew 25:30: 'And cast ye the unprofitable servant into outer darkness: there shall be weeping and gnashing of teeth').

Doom murals are the great hidden jewels of Christian churches around the world, though mainly concentrated in Europe. In the UK, there are about sixty known surviving examples besides the Chaldon mural, all in wildly varying

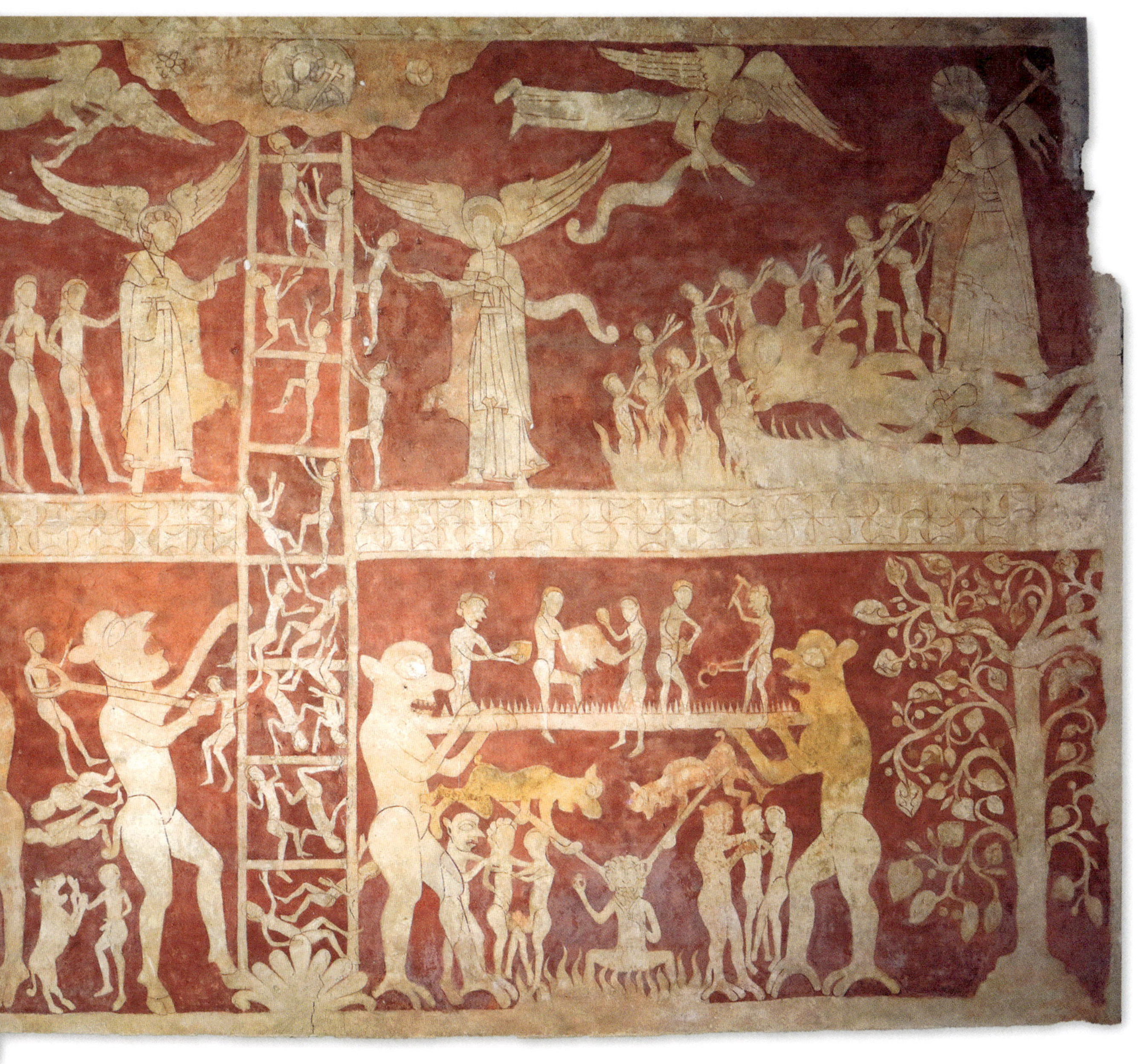

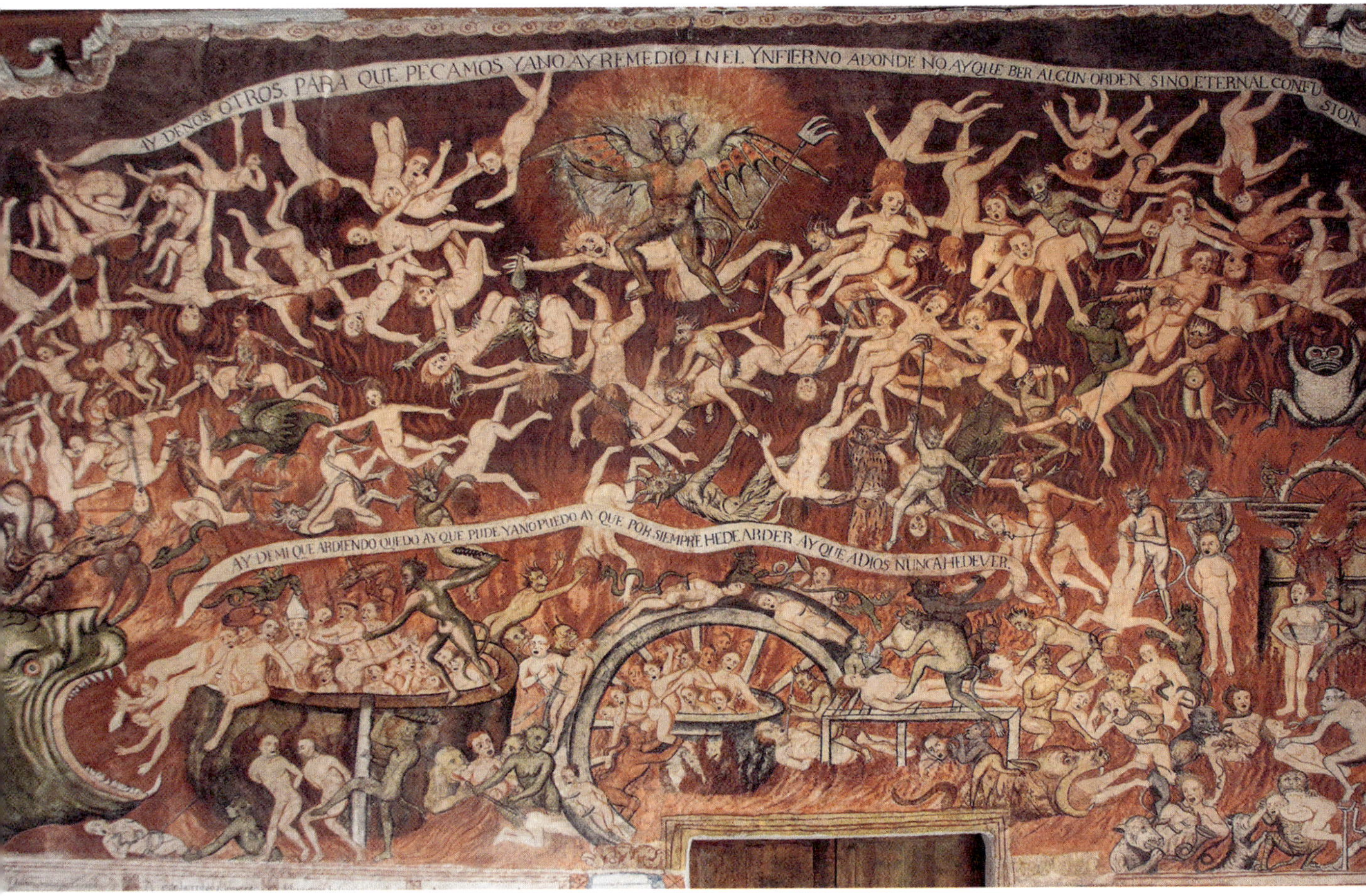

states of preservation, but most freely open to public visitation. Most date from the twelfth or thirteenth centuries until the Counter-Reformation, which began with the Council of Trent (1545-63). Sadly most Dooms, in English churches at least, were destroyed by government authority during the English Reformation. Others were painted over, like the Chaldon mural, or have simply disintegrated over time. The Doom in the church of South Newington, Oxfordshire, for example, exists in just a few remaining scraps on the wall above the chancel, offering starkly beautiful artistic remnants of painted faces of the 'saved'. There are traces too of the resurrected dead cheerfully emerging from their coffins to joyously join the living in anticipation of passage to heaven. Doom, it seems, is not all doom and gloom.

Above: *A Peruvian Doom mural depicting hell, painted by Tadeo Escalante (fl. 1802-40) in 1802 at San Juan Bautista in Huaro.*

Opposite: *The mouth of hell from* The Hours of Catherine of Cleves *(c.1440), the greatest surviving Dutch illuminated manuscript. The 'hell-mouth' is a traditional medieval motif, originating from the Anglo-Saxon period, of a terrifying doorway to Satan's subterranean kingdom in the form of a giant animal's maw, from which tortured souls and demons reach out in agony: a graphic warning of the consequences of leading an un-Christian life.*

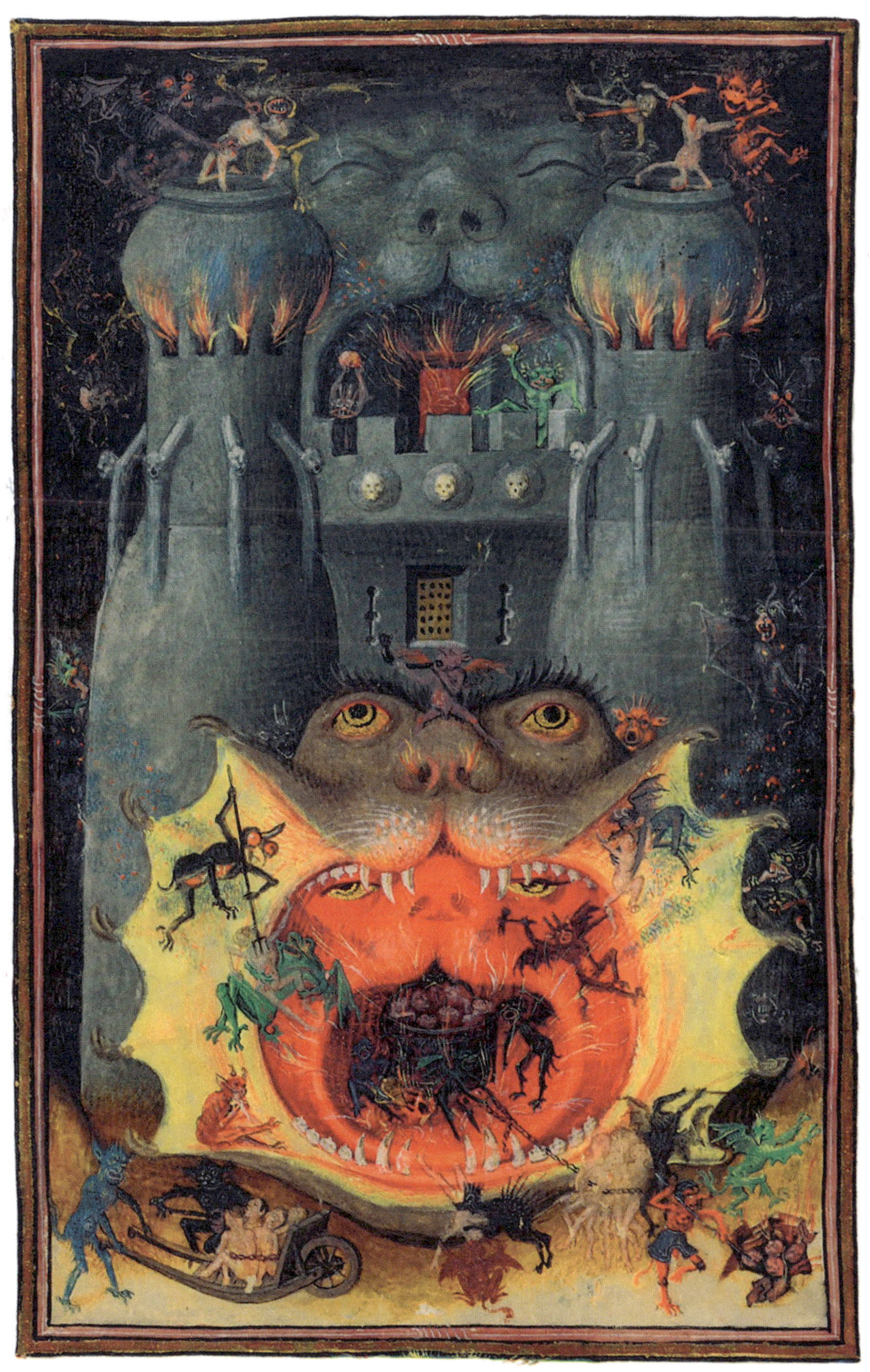

PORTRAIT OF THE DEVIL, CODEX GIGAS (EARLY THIRTEENTH CENTURY)

On the evening of 7 May 1697 a fire broke out at Stockholm's royal castle, and as it spread to the library a panicked curator grabbed the world's largest existing illuminated medieval manuscript – weighing 75kg (165lb) – and hurled it out of a high window. According to the theologian Johann Erichsons (1700-79), the massive book landed heavily and squarely on a passerby. Not that it would have been much comfort to the person who involuntarily broke its fall, but the book was worth saving at all cost because of its extraordinary beauty and origin story, particularly for the unusual painting it held on the recto of the 290th folio – a portrait of the Devil, drawn from life.

The *Codex Gigas*, literally 'giant book' (with a length of 92cm/36in), otherwise known as the 'Devil's Bible', carries with it the legend that it was written and illustrated in one night, with the assistance of Lucifer. The story goes that in the early thirteenth century, in the Benedictine monastery of Podlažice in Bohemia, a scribe known as Herman the Recluse was condemned by his abbot to be immured (walled up alive) for breaking his vows. After pleading for his life, Herman was told he would be spared the sentence, on the rather unfair condition that he write down all of humanity's knowledge in twelve hours. Herman wrote frantically, but at midnight he admitted defeat and, with no response to his prayers for help, in desperation he prayed to the Devil. These prayers were answered. By morning, Lucifer had completed the beautifully illuminated work and, in thanks, Herman painted in the book a full-page portrait of his infernal ghostwriter. In it, the Devil poses in a primal crouch or squat, his taloned hands raised and bursting out of the page to claw at the soul of the reader, while two separate long red tongues snake their way from between his teeth.

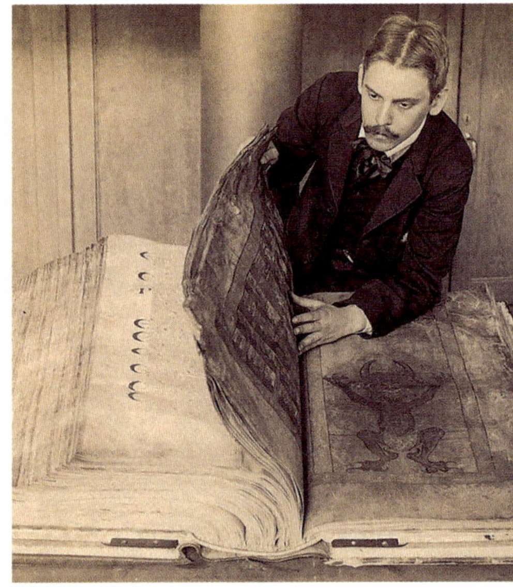

A cautious reader examines the portrait of the Devil in the Codex Gigas *in 1906.*

The author of the *Codex Gigas* certainly packed a lot into the volume, which required 100 donkey hides to make the 309 parchment sheets for its 1m- (1yd-) high pages. Even among the tradition of Romanesque monasteries producing large books, it is extraordinary. Its modern curators estimate that the hulking work is likely to be the product of between twenty and thirty years' labour. This would be the time needed to copy out an entire Vulgate Bible (the principal Latin version), as well as other popular works including Isidore of Seville's entire

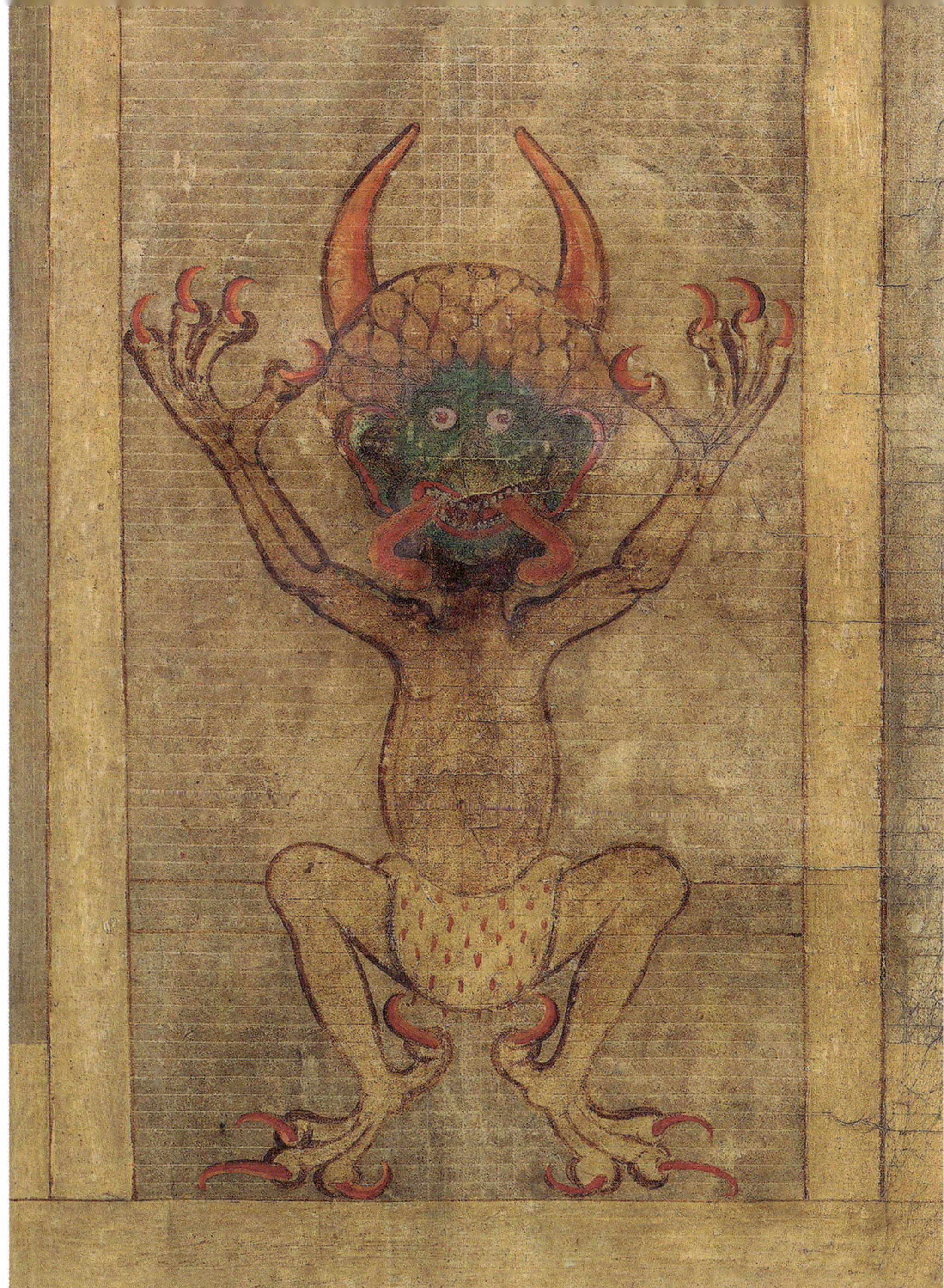

encyclopaedia, *Etymologiae*, assorted medical compilations and two books by Constantine the African.

The *Codex Gigas* currently resides in the National Library of Sweden at Stockholm, having been moved there after the fire at Stockholm castle. It is rarely out on public display, however, as its vellum pages darken when exposed to ultraviolet light – or perhaps because it's thought that the Devil is best kept safely trapped between its closed bindings.

Portrait of the Devil, Codex Gigas *(early thirteenth century)*

JAPANESE *KUSOZU* (THIRTEENTH-NINETEENTH CENTURIES) AND THE ART OF DEATH

Decorating walls with scenes of decomposition may not fit with the modern taste, but this particular art of dying was an important theme in Japanese Buddhist imagery for hundreds of years between the thirteenth and nineteenth centuries. *Kusozu* (pictures of the nine aspects) is a style of painting that depicts in nine vignettes the process of decomposition of a cadaver left out among the flora and fauna of nature. This is a process that was not particularly feared but approached pragmatically – many Buddhist cultures practise 'sky burials', for example, where human corpses are left exposed on mountain tops and in forests to be devoured by the birds and wild animals.

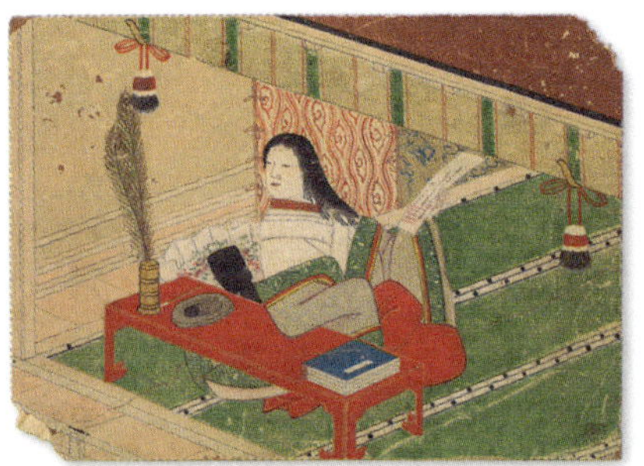
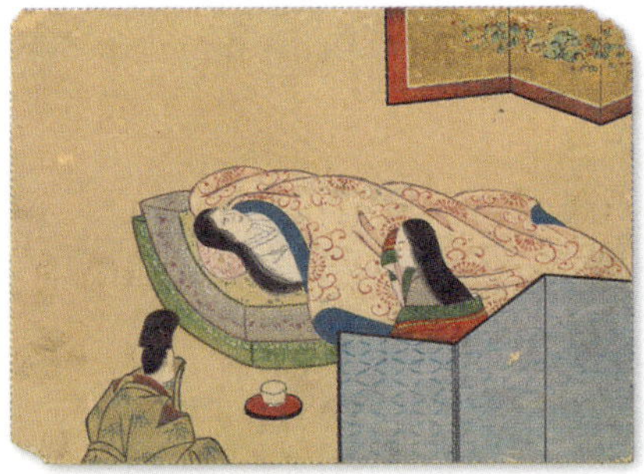
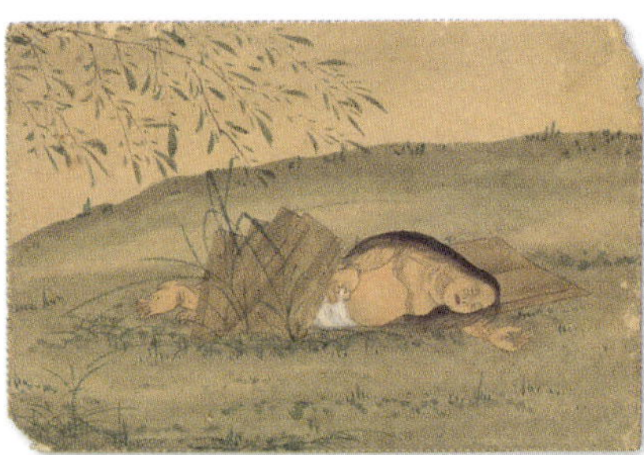
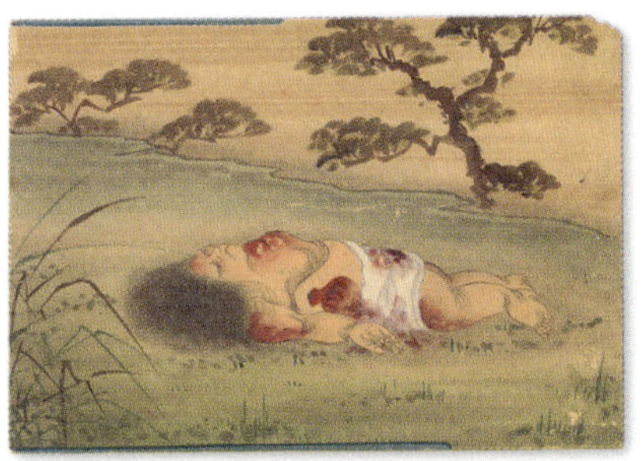
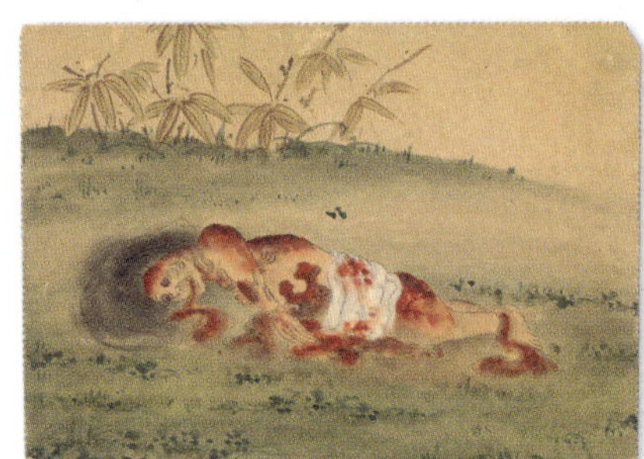
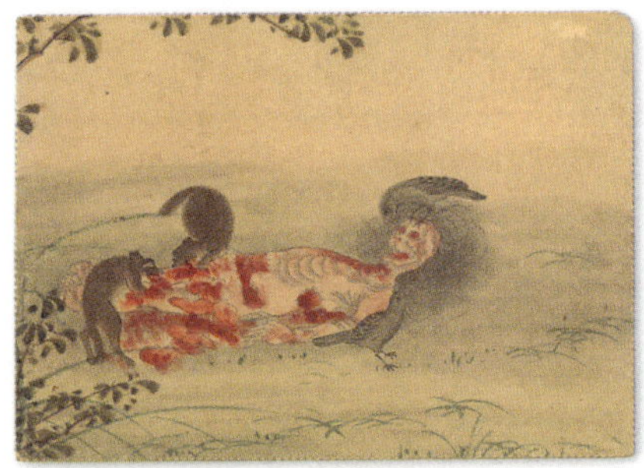
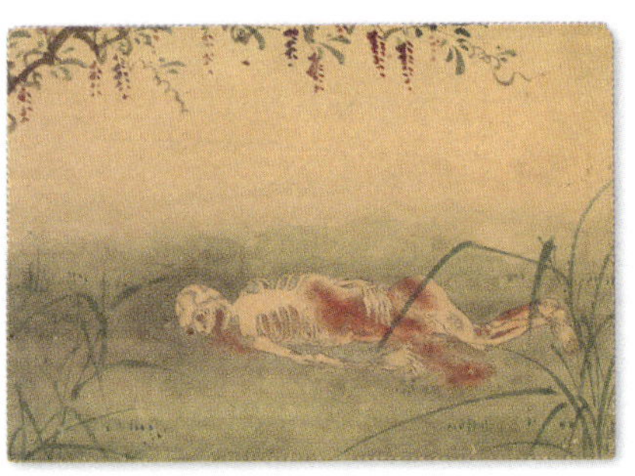
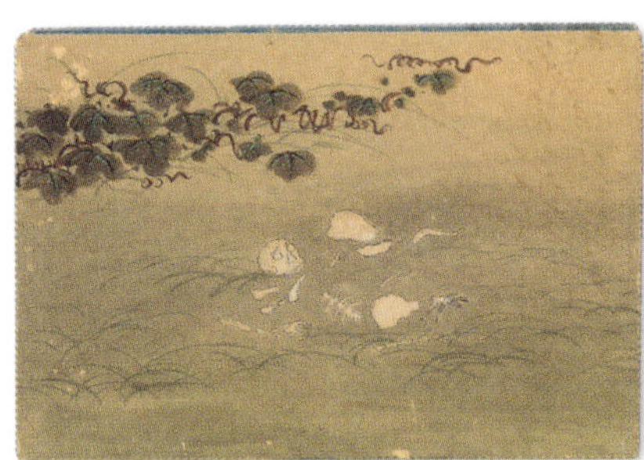
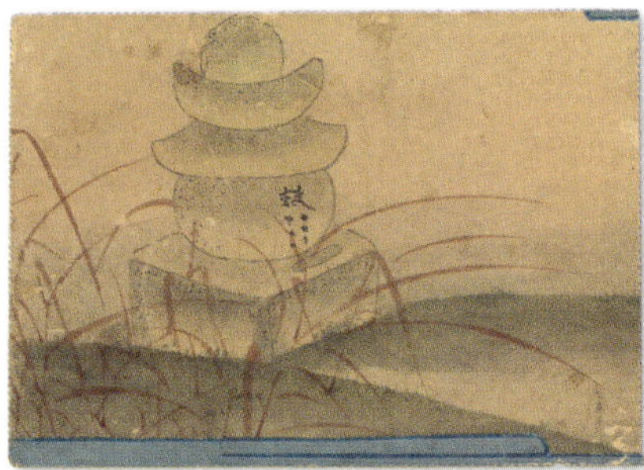

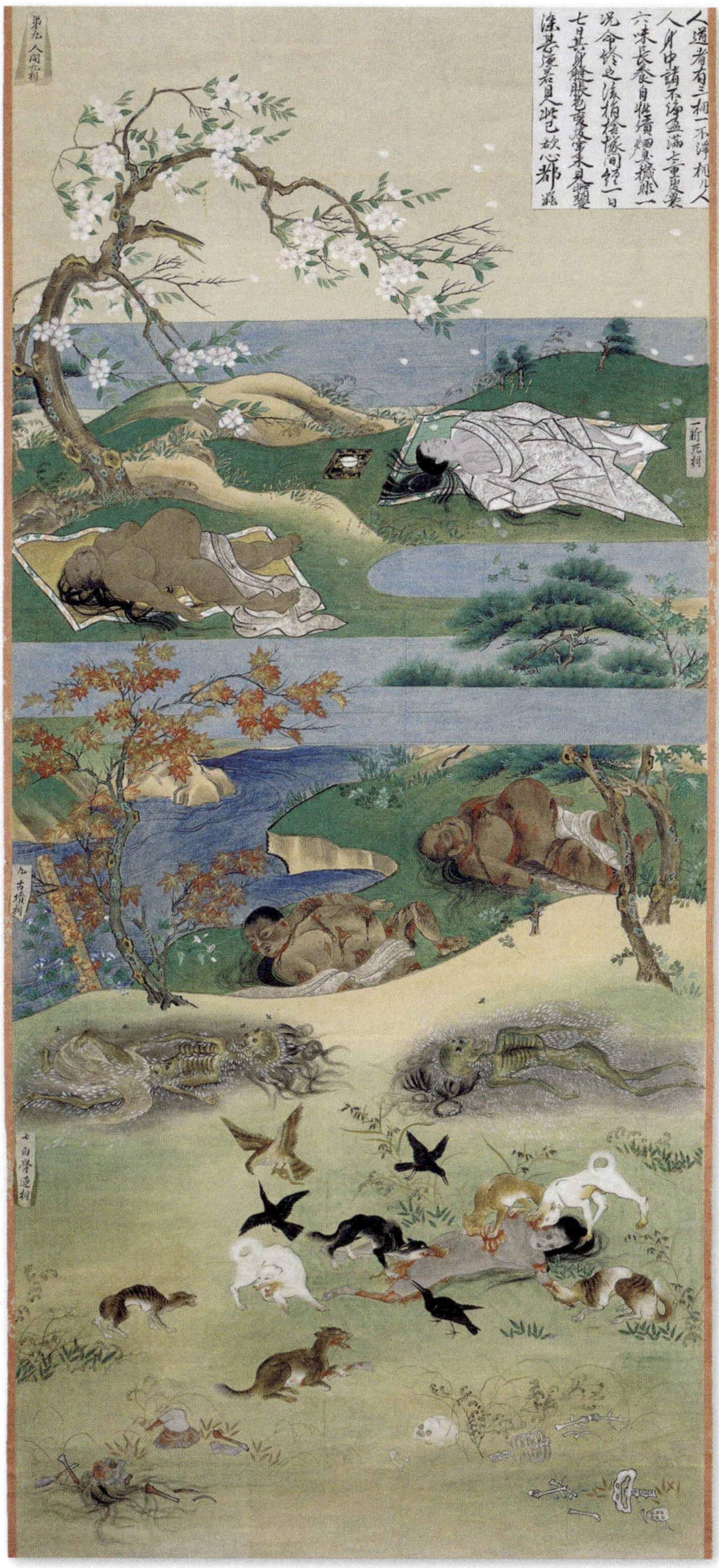

Left: A nineteenth-century copy of a thirteenth-century original kusozu*, showing the nine stages of human decomposition*

Opposite: *An eighteenth-century set of Kusozu paintings.*

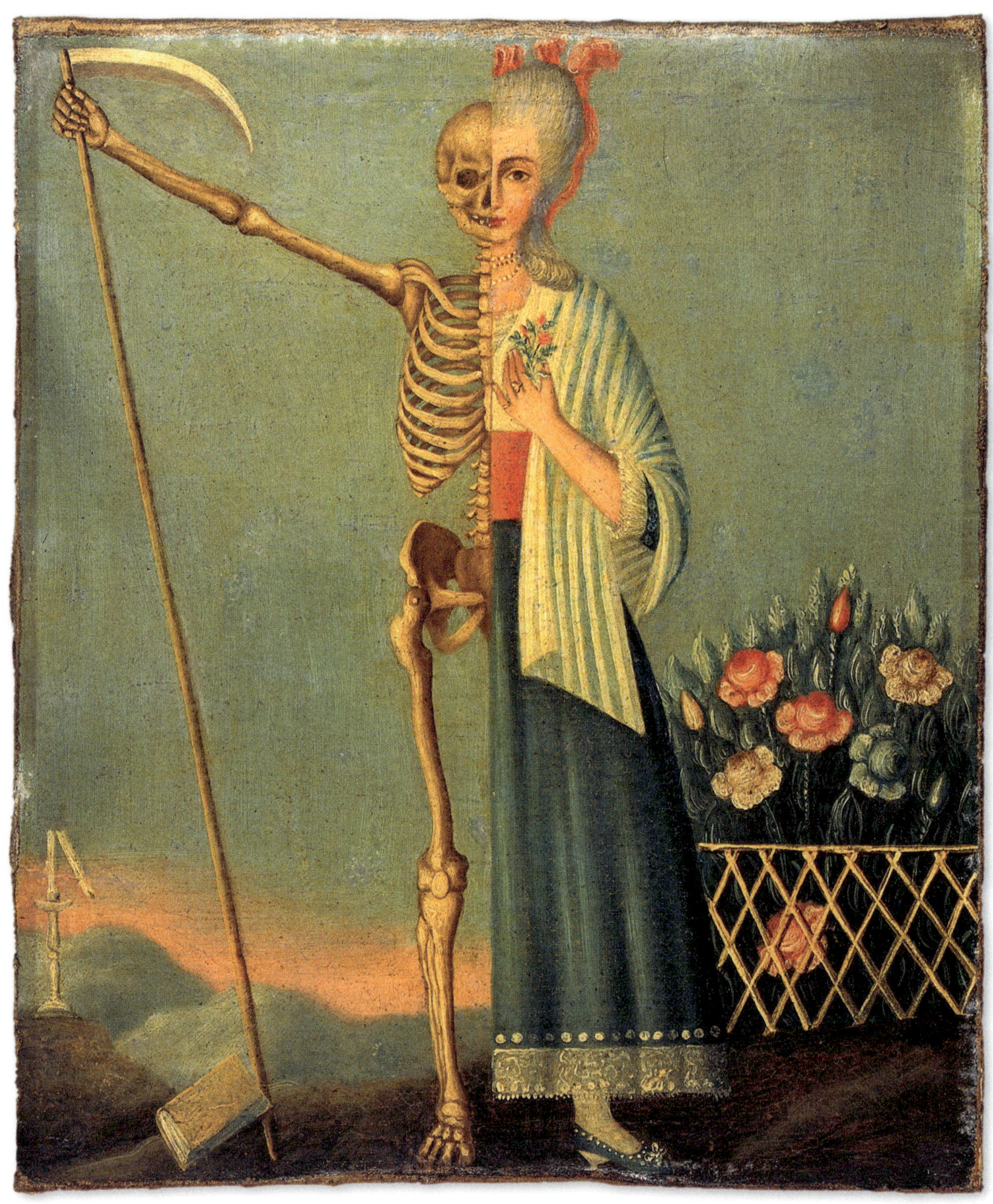

Life and Death, *a* memento mori *oil painting from the eighteenth century. The female figure represents both the pleasures of life on the right side, and the ultimate pointlessness of these pursuits through the inevitability of death, on the left.*

Kusozu depictions are commonly found in poetry, narrative literature, woodblock books, prints and paintings, and a huge number of hanging scrolls and hand-scroll paintings found in temples across Japan, still serving their religious function. As unsettling as they are to modern Western eyes, the art serves as a vital teaching instrument and meditation aid in Buddhist philosophy. Similar to the *memento mori* in European history, in which death-themed objects and paintings were kept as humbling reminders of mortality, *kusozu* were used to highlight the impermanence and foul nature of the mortal body. In every known surviving example of *kusozu*, incidentally, the body in question is always that of a woman – perhaps because the female form was thought of as more vulnerable, but also because depicting the gruesome sight of a rotting female form would instil a revulsion and so negate temptations of the flesh in monks and devotees.

The rotting corpse is the consequence of the journey of the soul through the great cycle of life, death and rebirth known as samsara; that is, until one is liberated from the great wheel by achieving nirvana (extinguishment), reached only when one has managed to put out the 'three fires' or 'three poisons' of *raga* (greed), *dvesha* (aversion) and *moha* (ignorance). The corpse was one of three things that inspired Siddhartha Gautama (*c*.563-*c*.483 BC) to find the path of enlightenment and become the historical Buddha, and so as a symbol it is of utmost importance. Death is 'the greatest of all teachers,' said the Buddha. In Buddhist temples *kusozu* were used for *kan* (contemplation) and were displayed during Obon (Festival of the Dead) on the fifteenth day of the seventh lunar month, when Buddhists reflect on their destinies on the wheel of transmigration.

The paintings shown on page 44 are a set believed to have been painted in the eighteenth century, and are typical in format: the first image of the woman, who in this example is identified with the ninth-century poet Ono no Komachi (*c*.825-*c*.900), is shown indoors at a table writing a farewell poem, her face pale and preoccupied. In the second image she is dead, laid out on the floor and covered with a blanket surrounded by mourners. In the third her body is outdoors surrounded by the nature that will consume her. In the remaining and quite graphic imagery the corpse putrefies and disintegrates until she is just bones pecked apart by birds. The final painting shows only a burial stupa, the symbol of the Buddha – all earthly pride and vanity has vanished, all advantages and barriers of birth and other human divisions are irrelevant; and the cycle of reincarnation begins anew.

RIPLEY SCROLL
(FOURTEENTH CENTURY)

'Oh, ye seekers after perpetual motion, how many vain chimeras have you pursued? Go and take your place with the alchemists!' scoffs Leonardo da Vinci (1452-1519) in his diaries, somewhat undermining claims that he too was a dabbler in alchemy. While da Vinci, that stickler, preferred observation- and evidence-based science, the alchemists pursued more elusive goals in their ancient branch of natural philosophy. Their main three aims were to discover the method of *chrysopoeia* (the transmutation of base metals into noble metals like gold and silver); to concoct an elixir that would bestow its drinker with immortal life; and to create a panacea that could cure any illness. ('And many have made a trade of delusions and false miracles,' grumbles da Vinci, 'deceiving the stupid multitude.')

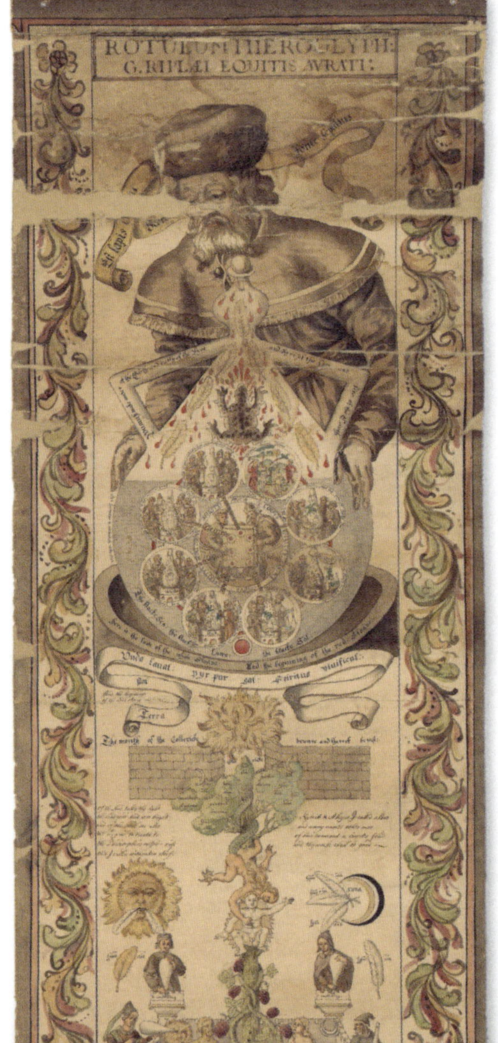

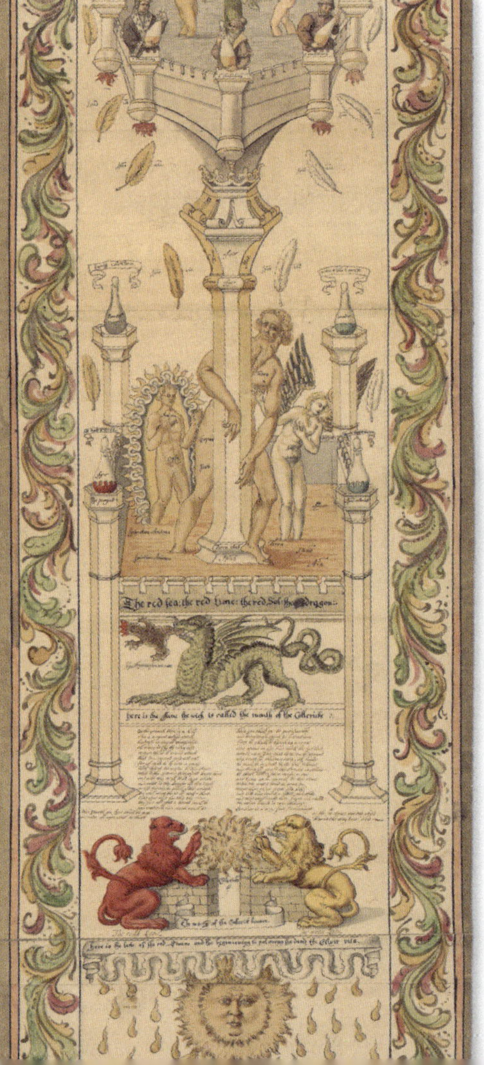

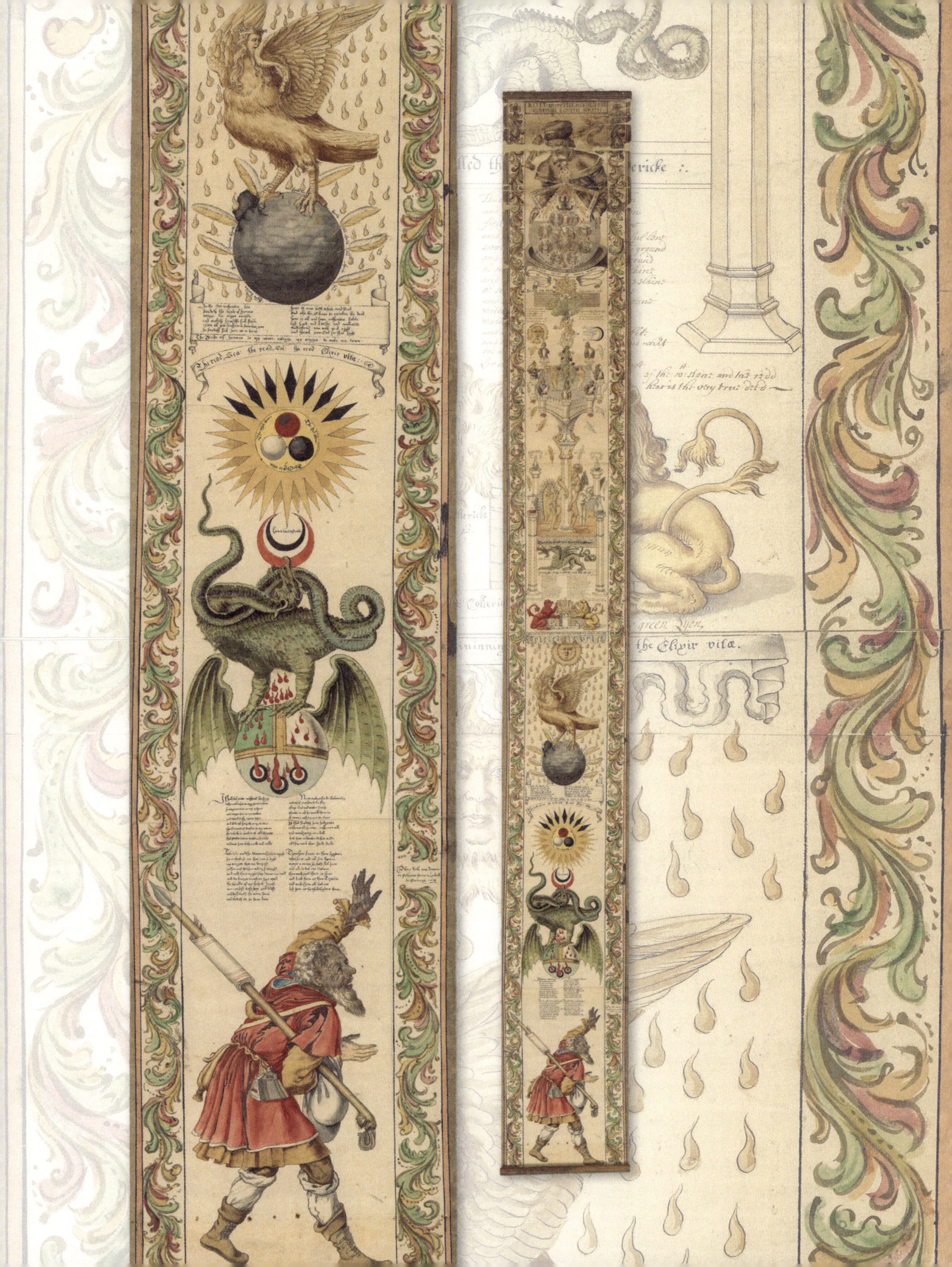

the Elixir vitæ

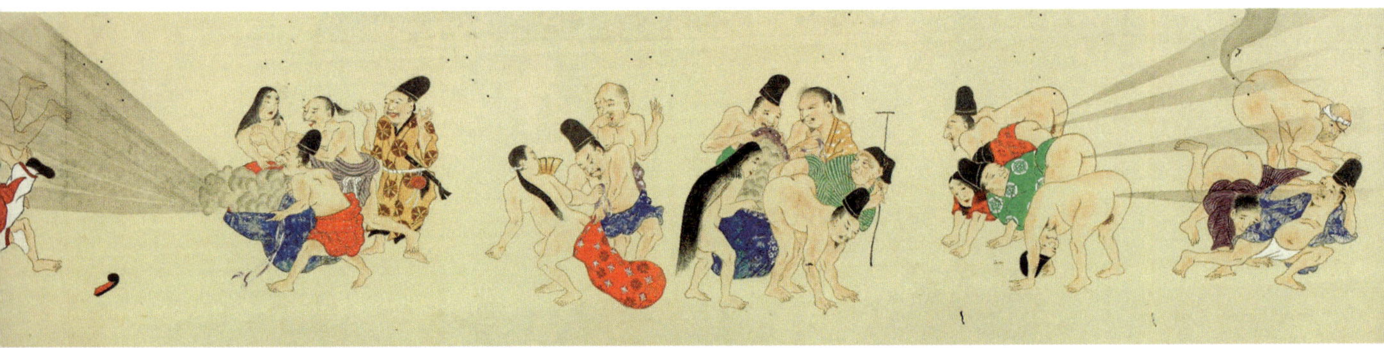

A scroll of equal, yet very different, strangeness – He-Gassen *('Fart competitions') is a Japanese scroll of the Edo period (1603-1868) by an unknown artist, depicting characters exercising flatulence against each other, likely as satire.*

As with practitioners of any secretive art, no self-respecting alchemist would be seen without an extensive library of manuscripts and scrolls of ancient knowledge. Many of the surviving illustrated examples of these are exquisitely beautiful, painted by artists working with a visual language of symbols and motifs unique to the tradition – but the Ripley Scroll is surely the most striking. Twenty-three copies are known to exist, all based on a lost original, the longest of which runs to around 6m (20ft) in length. The cryptic document sets out coded instructions to perform the manufacture of the Philosopher's Stone, an object that would allow the alchemist to achieve successful *chrysopoeia* and convert base metals to gold.

The scroll takes its name from George Ripley (*c*.1450-*c*.90), an Augustinian canon at Bridlington in Yorkshire and author of the *Compound of Alchymy*…, a poem written in Middle English in 1471, but published in 1591. By 1700 Ripley had taken on a near-mythical status and a large number of alchemical works had been credited to him, most of which – including the Ripley Scroll – are considered to be false accreditations and more likely composite works of various creators.

The artwork of the Ripley Scroll lays out the transmutation process with a parade of mystical symbolism, a number of which have never been decrypted. In the top section the legendary Greek-Egyptian figure Hermes Trismegistus (a combination of the Greek god Hermes and the Egyptian god Thoth), whose teachings formed the basis of the philosophy Hermeticism, grasps an alchemical flask over a furnace. Inside are eight roundels revealing the stages in creating the white Philosopher's Stone, revolving around the central roundel showing Hermes bestowing a book of his alchemical secrets to George Ripley. Below this is a pool representing a chemical bath, with snakes coiling around the tree, the symbol of wisdom and knowledge. Adam – sulphur – and Eve – mercury

– come together in the solution (or, in another interpretation, these two are having their souls of silver and gold extracted). Beneath this scene is a dragon eating a toad – the white stone is now a black stone, and next, when mixed again with sulphur (the red lion) and the ore from which is taken (the yellow lion), the black stone is heated over fire, and becomes the all-powerful red stone.

The resulting restorative vapours of the successful creation process is represented in the next illustration, the golden Bird of Hermes, which symbolises regeneration. Below it are the three coloured forms of the Philosopher's Stone, which together form the Elixir of Life. Here too are its promised fruits – the radiating sun signifies gold, the crescent moon silver. These are held aloft by a dragon known as the Serpent of Arabia, the blood of which was said to be *aqua fortis* (nitric acid), which bleeds from its belly onto the Philosopher's Stone at its feet. And finally, the figure at the end of the scroll is perhaps George Ripley (or the true illustrator of the scroll), dressed in the humble guise of a pilgrim and holding a strange staff, which at one end is a quill wrapped in a scroll, and at the base is a shod hoof.

The scroll has had undimmed admiration through the centuries. For all his renown in scientific investigation, Isaac Newton was also a keen alchemist apparently influenced by a copy of the Ripley Scroll – in his notes has been found a diagram he drew of the alchemist's flask in the opening section. This admiration continues today – of the twenty-three copies, the only Ripley Scroll in private hands sold in 2017 for £584,750. A bargain at the price, one could say, if it turns out the scroll does indeed hold the alchemical secrets of which it boasts.

A mysterious painting of a group of nude bathers, from the cryptic work known as the Voynich Manuscript. *Found in Italy in 1912 by a Polish rare-book dealer named Wilfrid Voynich, the 246 pages of illustrations of strange plant life, bathers and writing in an impenetrable alien language have never been deciphered.*

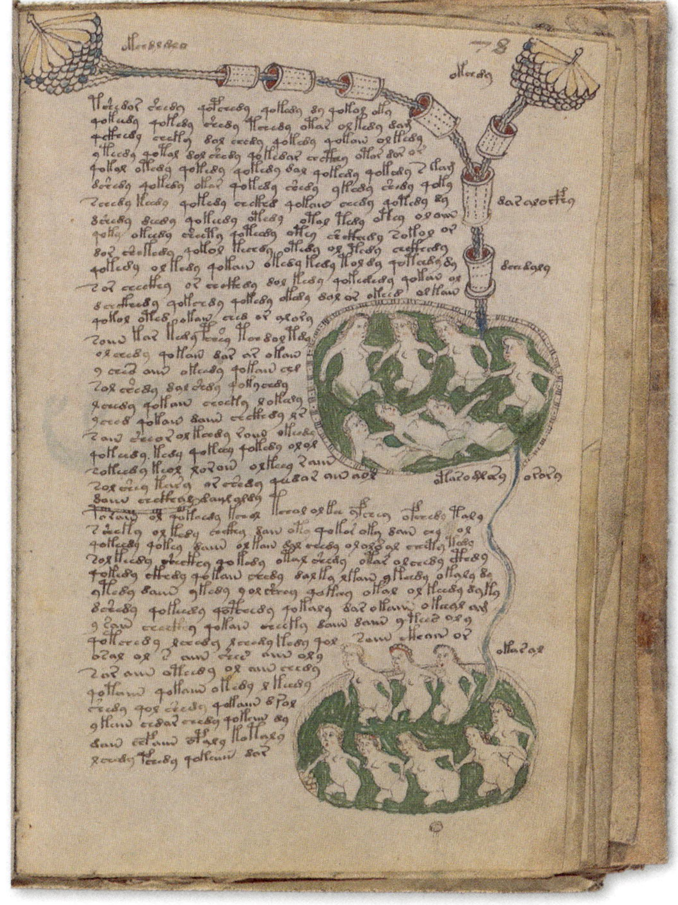

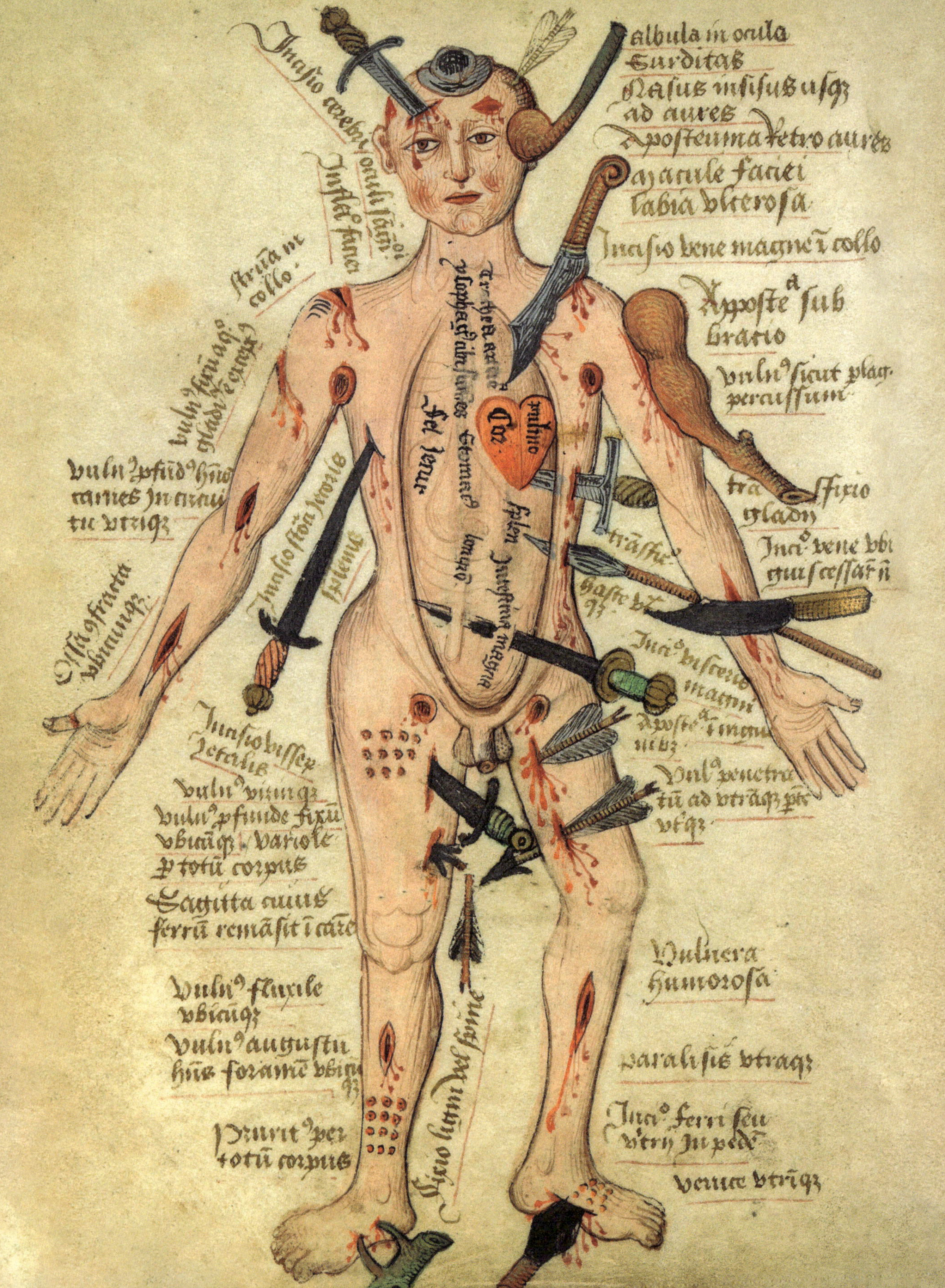
albula in oculo
Surditas
Nasus incisus usqz ad aures
Apostema retro aures
Macule faciei
labia ulcerosa
Incisio vene magne i collo
Fel
Cor
Splen
Vulnera humorosa
paralisis utraqz
Pruritus per totū corpus
Sagitta cuius ferrū remāsit i carne
Variole p totū corpus

WOUND MAN (FIFTEENTH-SEVENTEENTH CENTURIES)

Pity the poor *Wound Man*, for he suffers just about every conceivable violent injury, and all at once, although he does seem to be taking it rather well. All over his body are bleeding cuts – to the brow, the shoulders, the wrists and shins – as well as arrows fired into his head and thighs. His arteries have been sliced open and his body has been pierced with an array of knives and swords, including one thrust into his side that is revealed to have pierced his heart; another has entered his digestive system. A club is embedded in his arm. Thorns and spears puncture his feet. His right thumb looks a little sore, too. But there is hope for the *Wound Man*. His penetrated heart still beats, he can be saved and the recommended treatments for each unfortunate affliction are written beside the injury.

The *Wound Man* illustration first began to appear in German manuscripts in the fourteenth century, most notably in the works of the Bavarian surgeon Ortolf von Baierland, who offered the figure as an easy reference guide to quickly finding the correct cure for a patient's particular ailment. That is not to say that the advice in the accompanying captions of various *Wound Man* iterations was purely scientific, in the sense that we understand today, at least. Magic was also employed. Charms and chants calling on Christ, the Virgin Mary or the Three Kings were just as much an ingredient in the therapy as poultices, balms and practical advice on how to remove the offending objects without incurring massive haemorrhage.

For over 200 years the *Wound Man* appeared in medical treatises, appearing in print as late as 1678, in the London surgeon John Browne's *Compleat Discourse of Wounds* in rather dashing neoclassical form, with updated weaponry, as shown on p.55.

Incidentally the *Wound Man* was not a lone figure in these medieval surgical texts offering illustrated instructions – see also his companion, the Zodiac Man. For most of history the constellations were believed to be inextricably linked with the health of the human body. Medical astrology saw a desperate surge in popularity during the fourteenth century in Europe with the devastation wreaked by the Black Death, and the Zodiac Man took his place in texts with equal importance as the *Wound Man* who bore buboes as part of his traumatic collection of body art. We can see the 'science' of this approach

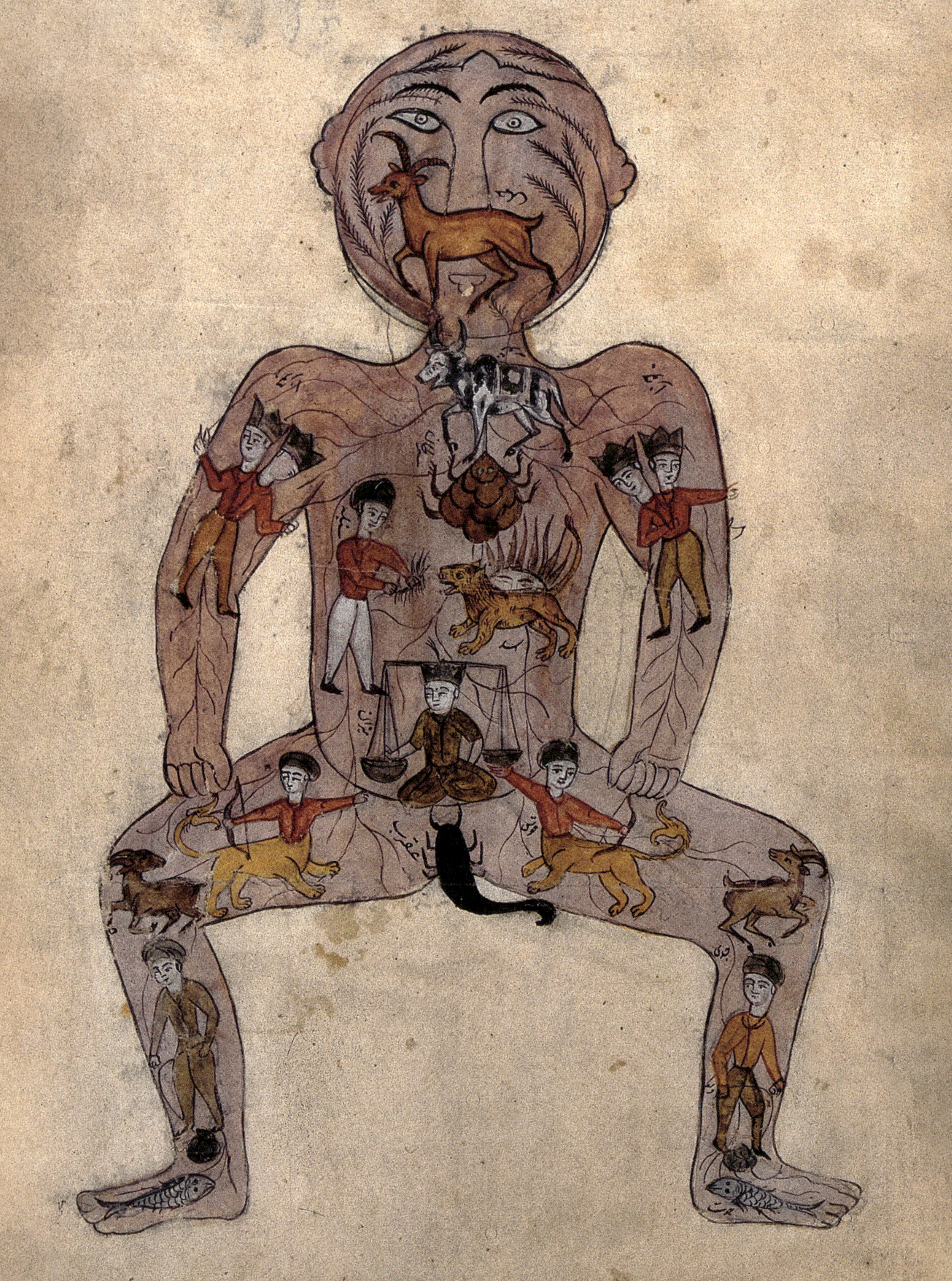

in the nineteenth-century Persian zodiac-linked anatomical painting (opposite). In the picture, each sign of the zodiac is shown to correspond with a body part. Pisces are linked to the feet; Aries, with the ram's sacred associations, marks the head. In European versions, Latin inscriptions in the four corners expand on the medicinal properties of the zodiac signs. Physicians incorporated astrology into their diagnoses, and current star positioning and the patient's own star chart had to be factored into the technique and timing of the surgery.

Opposite: The Zodiac Man. *Nineteenth-century watercolour painting by a Persian artist.*

Below: *An updated* Wound Man, *from the London surgeon John Browne's* Compleat Discourse of Wounds *(1678).*

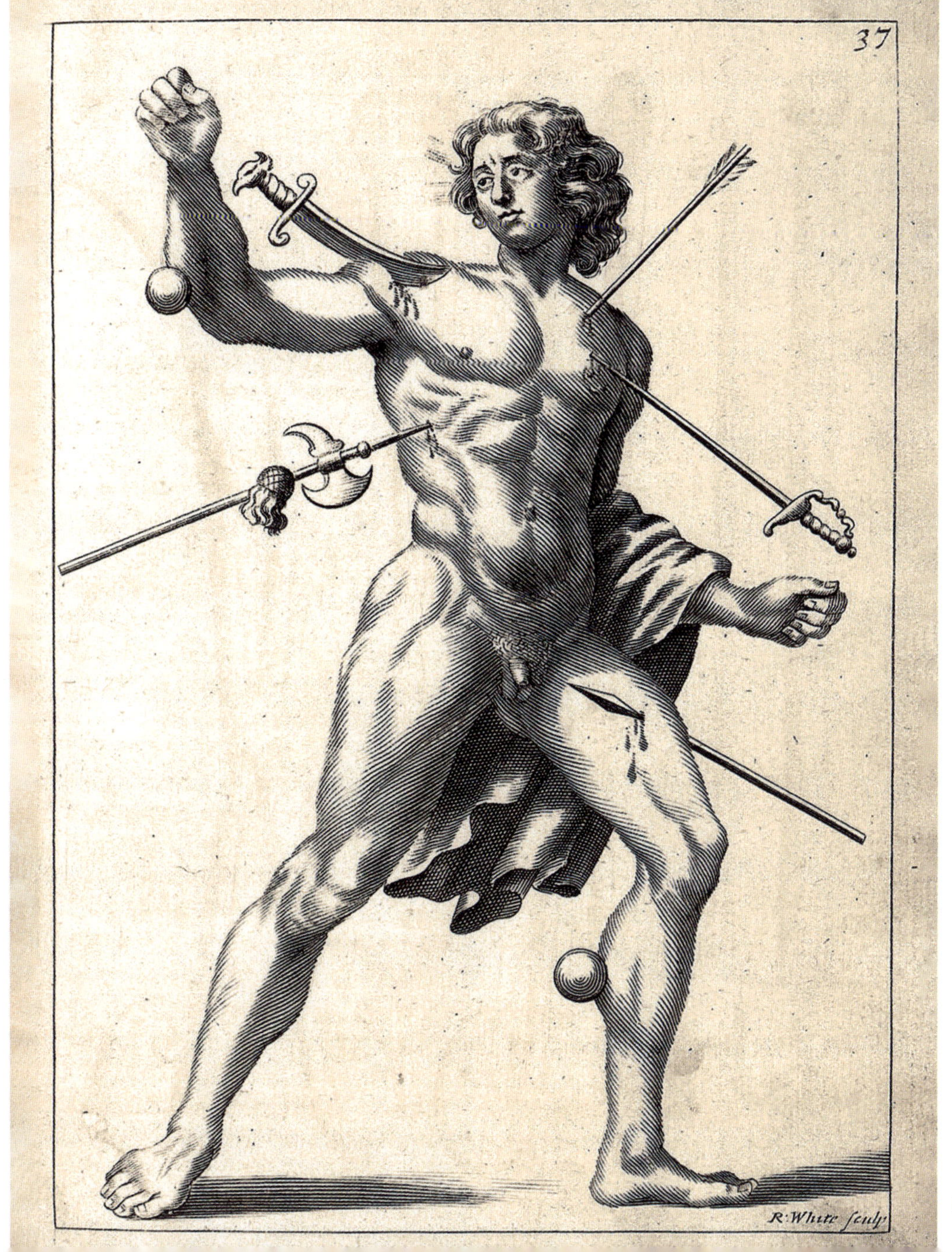

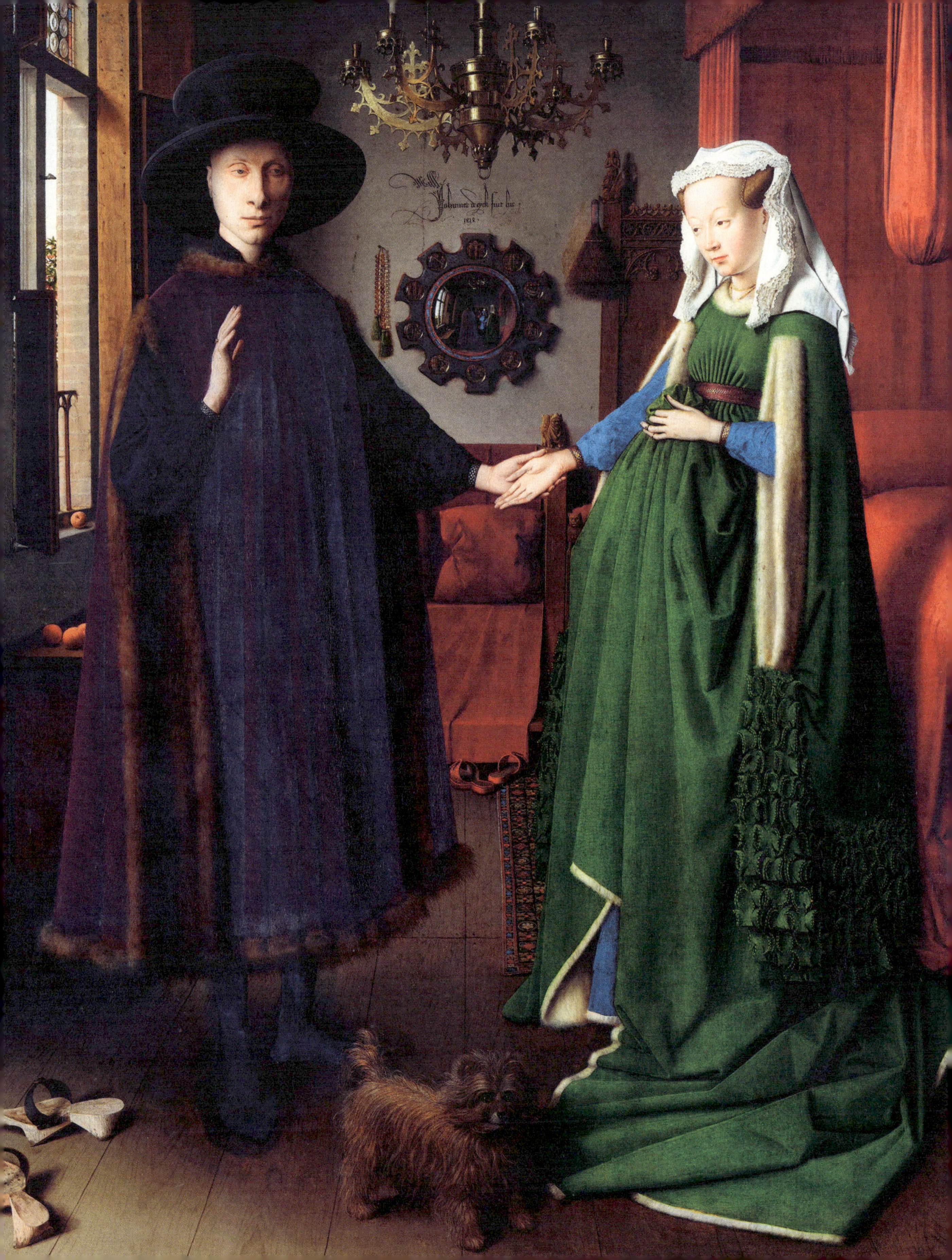
Johannes de eyck fuit hic
1434

ARNOLFINI PORTRAIT (1434), JAN VAN EYCK

Few paintings have been subjected to the same kind of obsessive scrutiny as the *Arnolfini Portrait* of 1434 by Jan van Eyck (*c.*1390-1441). It is a painting of deceptive strangeness that slowly builds as one takes in the symbols and other clues scattered around the composition. Every single feature of this private room is a carefully selected component seemingly geared for the broadcast of one message: the wealth of the subject. The intricate metalwork of the gleaming chandelier, the infamous convex mirror, the stained-glass window, the hint at a garden outside with a cherry tree. Fruit, a luxury item, is scattered casually on the sill and nearby chest, and light spills into a room rich in expensive fabrics draped over the luxurious carved furniture in a soft crimson that contrasts with the colours of the opulent furs, silks, velvets and wools clothing the couple. An oriental carpet lies on the floor.

But then we look closer, and more curious details, and questions, emerge. Religious symbols abound: the convex mirror is decorated with ten roundels containing scenes from the Passion of the Christ. The man's patten shoes in the lower left (and those of his companion behind them) are apparently a reference to a passage in the Book of Exodus 3:5: 'Put off thy shoes from thy feet, for the place whereon thou standest is holy ground.' An indication of a sacred event taking place? The chandelier has only one lit candle, the seeing eye of God. The mirror is unblemished, a traditional symbol of the purity of Mary, Mother of God. Rosary beads hang beside it. The oranges represent fertility, the cherry tree love. (While at first glance it appears that the woman is pregnant, she is, in fact, clutching the raised bulk of her dress in the manner of the period.)

So who are the figures seen here? We do not know for certain. In the earliest inventory record, the pallid man was identified as 'Hernoul le Fin', or 'Arnoult Fin' – this is probably the Bruges-based Italian merchant Giovanni di Nicolao di Arnolfini, who would have been the right age at the time this painting was made. The woman is thought to be his undocumented second wife, whom he married after his first wife, Costanza Trenta, died in 1433. Recently the theory has been put forward that this is a posthumous portrait, begun when Costanza was alive, and finished a year after her death.

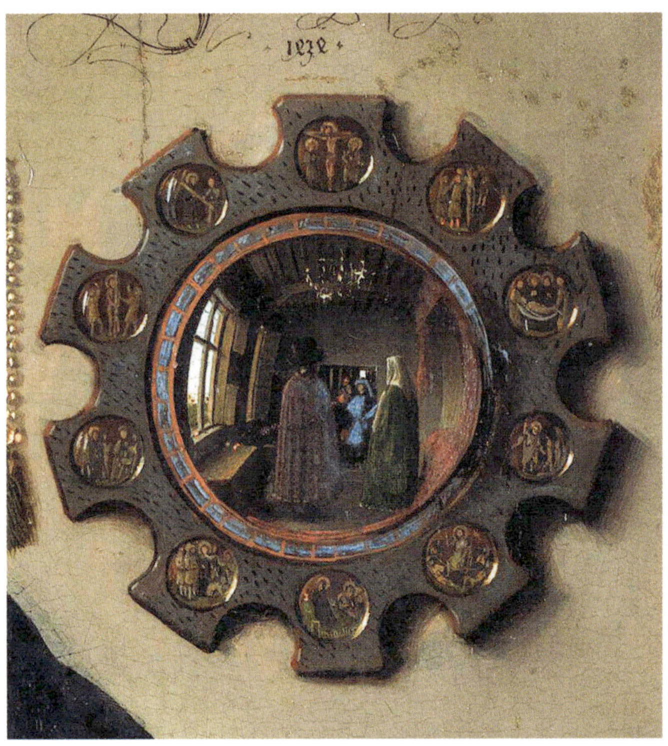

Left: *The convex mirror detail of the portrait, showing two figures standing opposite the couple, thought to be a self-portrait by van Eyck.*

Below and Right: *A detail from Rembrandt's famous* The Night Watch *(see page 63), thought to be a self-portrait snuck into the painting by the artist.*

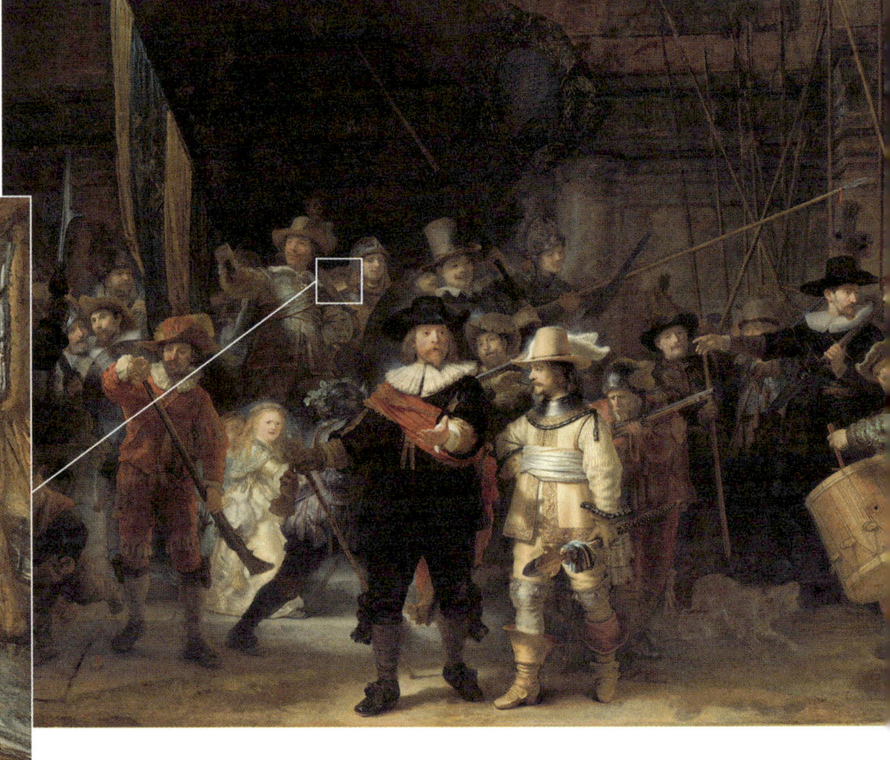

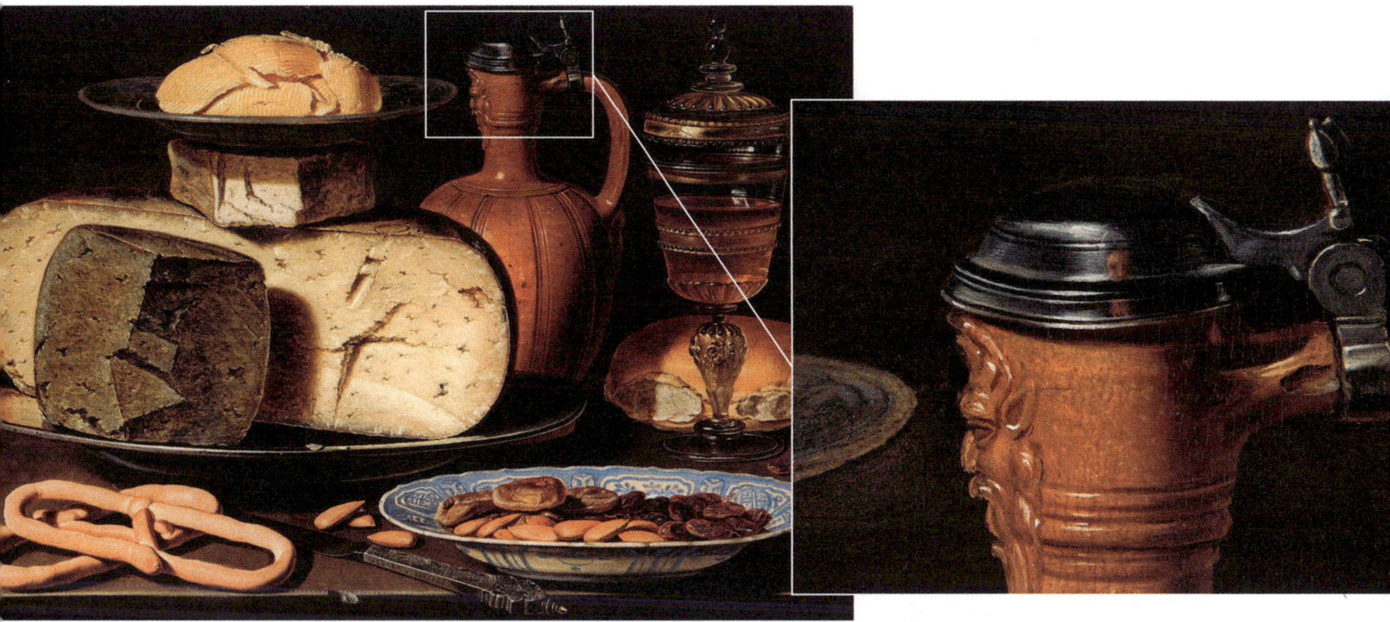

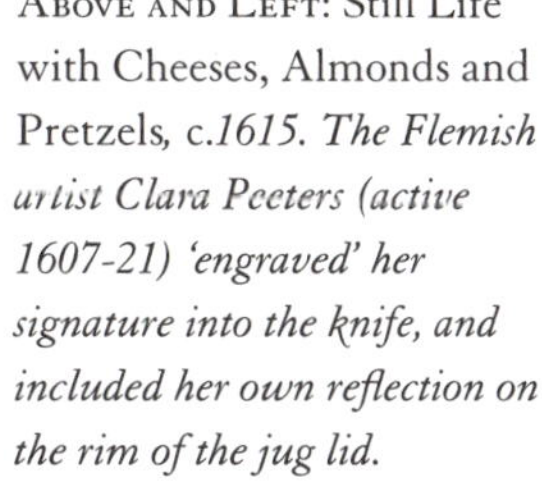

In 1934 the art historian Erwin Panofsky proposed the now-disputed idea that the painting served as a legal document of a marriage ceremony – the pose of the couple's hands appears reminiscent of taking vows in a marriage ceremony, and above the mirror we can see van Eyk's signature, more in the style of an official document than a painting: *Johannes de Eyck fuit hic. 1434* ('Jan van Eyck was here. 1434').

The most curious feature of all, though, is the convex mirror on the rear wall. It's a magnificent display of van Eyck's mastery of detail: the room is warped in perfect proportion in the reflection of the mirror, which also reveals two figures standing opposite the couple, outside the frame of the painting, from our point of view. Could this be a slyly inserted self-portrait of van Eyck himself, arriving with his assistant through the doorway?

Above and Left: Still Life with Cheeses, Almonds and Pretzels, c.*1615. The Flemish artist Clara Peeters (active 1607-21) 'engraved' her signature into the knife, and included her own reflection on the rim of the jug lid.*

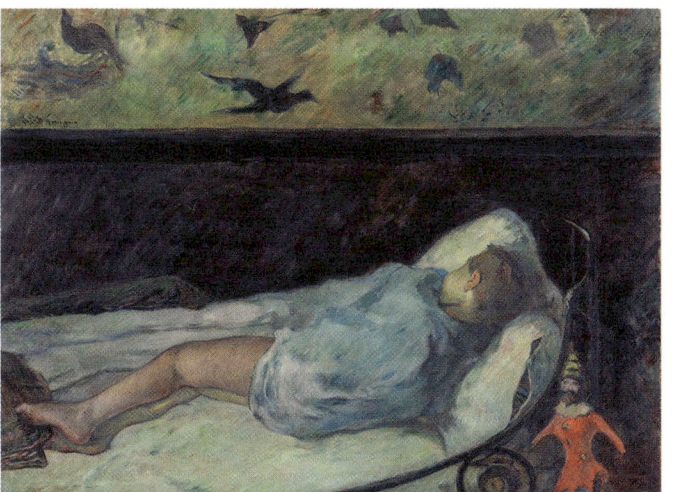

In The Little One Is Dreaming *(1881) Paul Gauguin (1848-1903) inserted himself as the toy jester in the lower-right corner of the scene.*

CRUCIFIXION DIPTYCH (*c*.1460) AND THE TRICKY ART OF RESTORATION

Artworks burn in the fire of time like everything else, with a susceptibility to any number of detriments (usually human-related) that can render restoration essential. Michelangelo's (1475-1564) Sistine Chapel frescoes, for example, were first restored as early as the sixteenth century after suffering water damage. In 2015, repair work was conducted at a Taiwanese gallery on a $1.5-million late-Baroque oil painting by Paolo Porpora (1617-73), entitled *Flowers* (*c*.1660), after a twelve-year-old visitor holding a drink accidentally tripped and punched a hole straight through it.

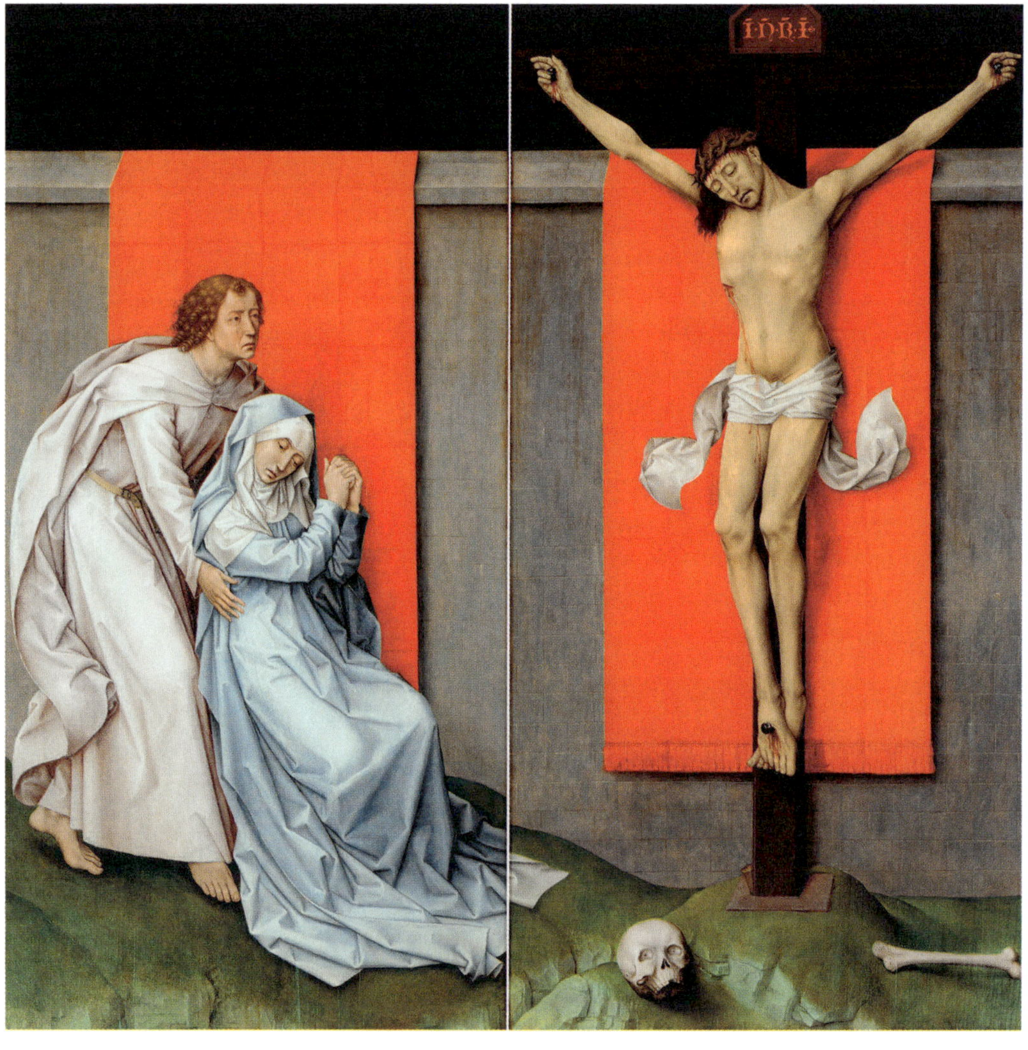

Leonardo da Vinci's *The Last Supper* is in a terrible state – in fact, it always has been. Its deterioration was noted soon after its completion. By using paints of an ephemeral nature on a thin exterior wall, humidity swiftly ravaged the masterpiece. 'The painting is all but ruined,' lamented Gian Paulo Lomazzo in the second half of the sixteenth century. Major, and often compromising, restorations have been conducted since 1726, and the result is that today, like a sinking ship of Theseus, just 42.5 per cent of *The Last Supper* is Leonardo's work; 17.5 per cent is lost. The remaining 40 per cent is the work of restorers.[1]

If the road to hell is paved with good intentions, as the proverb tells us, then it is a highway choked with the traffic fumes of the well-meaning amateur – and sometimes the not-so-forgivably-amateur art restorer. In 2012, when the authorities of Borja, Spain, were alerted to the radically altered condition of a fresco portrait of Jesus known as *Ecce Homo* (Behold the Man) in the Sanctuary of Mercy church, they at first assumed it to be the criminal act of a malicious vandal. But then it was learnt that it was an attempted 'restoration' by an untrained parishioner in her eighties named Cecilia Giménez, who had become so upset by the deterioration of the work made by Elías García Martínez in 1930 that she decided to take a crack at it herself. A BBC correspondent likened the resulting Giménez fresco to a 'crayon sketch of a very hairy monkey in an ill-fitting tunic', and the nickname *Ecce Mono* (Behold the Monkey) stuck.[2]

Even world-renowned experts have been guilty of destruction. Early nineteenth-century attempts to restore Old Master paintings were common but techniques were crude. Manuals recommended caking paintings in wood ash, then

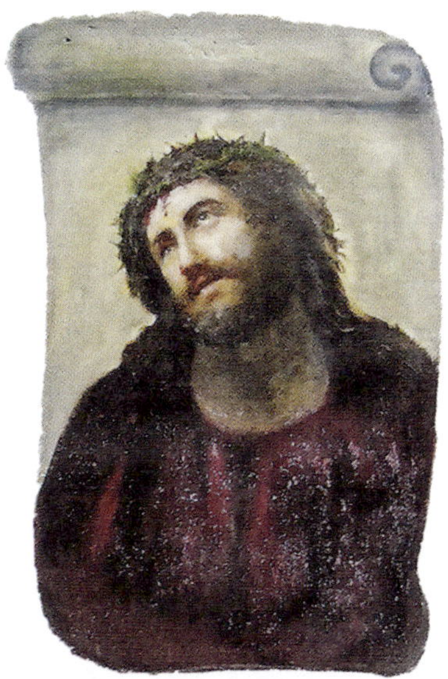

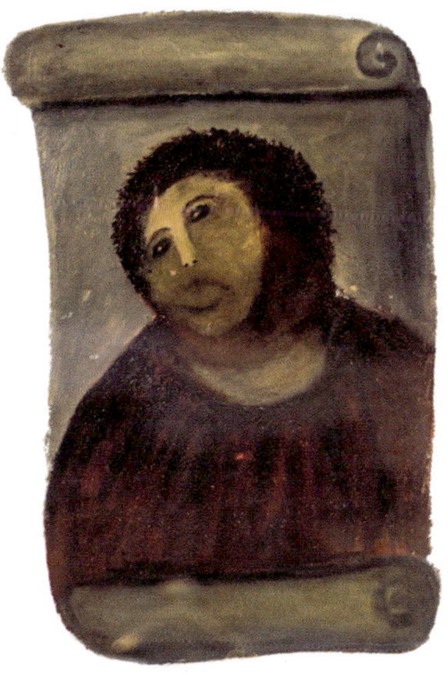

Above (Top and Bottom): Ecce Homo, *a fresco portrait of Jesus, before its 'restoration' and after.*

Opposite: *The* Crucifixion Diptych *of Rogier van der Weyden, completed* c.*1460.*

1 Frankly it's astonishing that any original detail remains at all, when one takes into consideration the workmen of 1652 who installed a doorway in the wall holding *The Last Supper* and cut into the lower-centre of the mural, slicing off Christ's feet. And then there was the occupation of Napoleon's army, during which they kept their horses in the same room as the painting and reportedly threw bricks at the apostles' heads. A bomb nearly destroyed it on 16 August 1943, and the acidic air pollution of post-war Milan and the effects of crowds of tourists have been detrimental ever since.

2 Ms Giménez's efforts did bring an unexpected boon to the town of Borja, however. The notoriety of her work spread so far around the world that by 2016 tourism increased to the town from an average of 6000 visitors to 200,000, raising tens of thousands of euros for local charities. It also led to the establishment of an 'interpretation centre' for her artwork.

wiping them clean with water, but this created a bitingly alkaline substance much more injurious to paintings than time and weather. By the early twentieth century a more scientific approach was being advised, but results still relied on the judgement of the restorer. Titian's *Bacchus and Ariadne* (*c.*1520) was controversially submitted by London's National Gallery for restoration by the painter Arthur Lucas between 1967 and 1969. Lucas would later boast that there was 'more of me than Titian in that sky'. What wasn't revealed to the public, nor the gallery's trustees, was that his 'cutting-edge' restoration rather horrifyingly included ironing the canvas painting directly onto a double-laminate 'Sundeala' board of compressed paper. (These boards have since become unstable.)

The stunning artwork featured on page 60 also possesses something of a rollercoaster ride of a restoration history. The *Crucifixion Diptych* of Rogier van der Weyden was completed *c.*1460, and eventually donated to the Philadelphia Museum of Art in 1933. The Virgin Mary collapses into the arms of St John the Baptist as she witnesses Christ elevated to the cross. The scene is carefully constructed – the tall, grime-covered walls push the figures towards us, as do the backings of rich red fabric. The midnight sky running across the top is just a thin strip, almost squeezed out of frame to keep the focus on the dramatic scene.

In 1941 the art restorer David Rosen was hired by the museum to return the painting to its original glory. He decided to strip it of its layers of discolouring varnish and the overpainting of the dark midnight of the sky, both of which he assessed as having been added by later artists. The grime was cleaned off the walls and the fabrics, the sky replaced with gold leaf. Only in 1990 was it realised that these had, in fact, been added by van der Weyden himself: the 'grime' was deliberate painting of lichen and water stains, to emphasise the purity and colours of the central figures; the darkening of the red cloth was to tonally alter bright vermillion to a rich crimson. These were not then restored as van der Weyden had intended (the painting had been put through enough, it was thought), but the midnight sky was returned, applied in such a way that later generations could revert to the gold leaf if desired.

A recent recipient of cutting-edge, transformative restoration techniques is Rembrandt's famed *The Night Watch*. But first a popular misconception should be cleared up: there is no night, nor night watch, in *The Night Watch*. The painting is actually a daytime scene, with the official title *Militia Company*

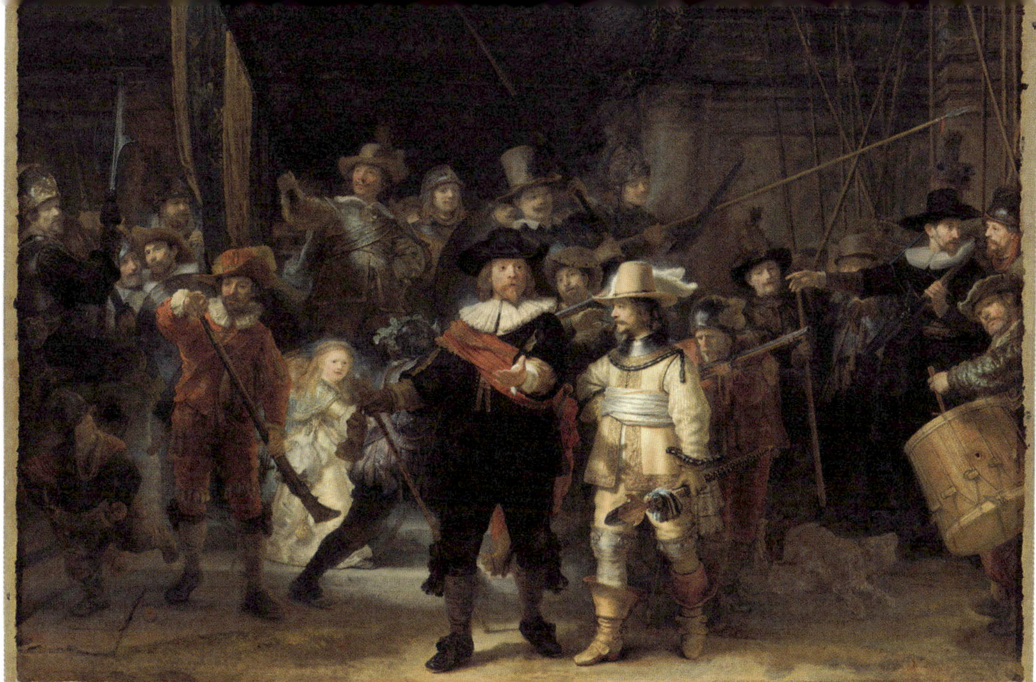

of District II under the Command of Captain Frans Banninck Cocq. Completed in 1642, the canvas is a group portrait of a platoon of Amsterdam's city guard, the Kloveniers militia. The men amble into formation as their captain orders his lieutenant to start the company marching out, in a groundbreakingly mobile depiction. The painting earned its nickname for the many layers of varnish originally applied by Rembrandt, which darkened over time to such an extent that the scene was plunged into apparent nocturnal gloom.

Rembrandt van Rijn's Militia Company of District II under the Command of Captain Frans Banninck Cocq *(1642), more commonly known as* The Night Watch.

Over the years it has been attacked three times: by knife-wielding perpetrators in 1911 (the varnish was so thick at this time that it actually deflected the blade) and again in 1975, while in 1990 a visitor sprayed it with acid. The most significant damage, however, was inflicted in 1715, when the painting was moved from the headquarters of the civic guard to the Amsterdam Town Hall. To fit Rembrandt's work between two columns, significant strips of the canvas on all four sides were sliced off – a common practice before the nineteenth century, but which today is akin to solving the problem of low ceilings by removing one's feet. This alteration resulted in the loss of two figures on the left side of the painting, the top of the arch, the balustrade and the edge of the step. The missing portions have never been found, but since July 2019 restorers at Amsterdam's Rijksmuseum have been studying the painting with stereomicroscopy and using artificial intelligence technology to piece together the details those lost borders contained.

PORTRAIT OF FEDERICO DA MONTEFELTRO (*c*.1473-5), PIERO DELLA FRANCESCA

Federico da Montefeltro (1422-82) was one of the most powerful *condottieri* (mercenary captains) of the Italian Renaissance. He and his freelance soldiers were engaged by Italian city-states to aid their bloody disputes, but after serving Florence for six years Federico and his knights were then employed by the Duke of Milan. During this time he suffered a terrible injury during a tournament, which resulted in the loss of an eye and a large scar that covered the right side of his face. It is for this reason that Federico takes a profile pose in this striking portrait of his likeness by Piero della Francesca (*c*.1415-92), who is believed to have worked on it between 1465 and *c*.1473-75. The painting of the Duke, with the Montefeltro hills rolling in the background, is considered one of the finest of the Italian Renaissance, and is actually part of a diptych, its companion being a portrait of Battista Sforza, Federico's wife, positioned in reverse to face her husband.

Less well known is the story behind the distinctive feature on display here, the Duke's nose, which was the victim of a separate tournament accident when it was broken badly and left crooked. Whether or not it was due to losing his half-brother Oddantonio da Montefeltro, Duke of Urbino, to an assassination conspiracy in 1444 (though there were murmurings that Federico was involved), Federico became paranoid that plans were afoot for his own assassination. For this reason, he commanded a surgeon to cut away a section of his nasal bridge, leaving the distinctive notch on view here. This greatly improved his field of view, reducing the risk of a sneak attack and facilitating a successful career as a field commander in battle.

Speaking purely of his martial accomplishments paints an incomplete picture of the man, however – nicknamed the 'Light of Italy', Federico is remembered as a significant contributory figure in the Italian Renaissance, commissioning the creation of the largest library outside that of the Vatican, which included its own scriptorium (writing room). The Light finally went out in 1482, when he was struck by fever, having never recovered from the loss of his wife Battista, who he referred to as 'the delight of my public and private hours'.

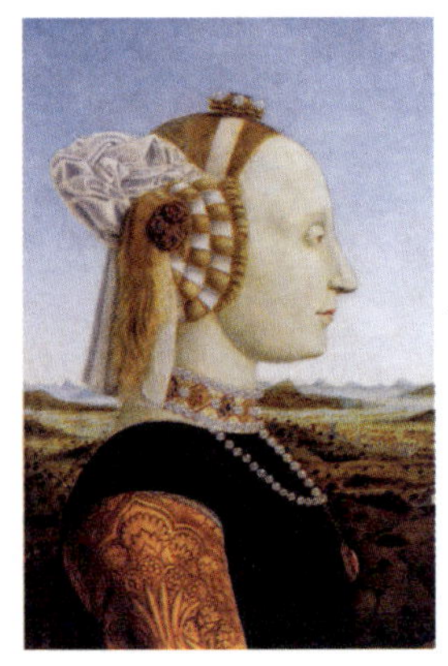
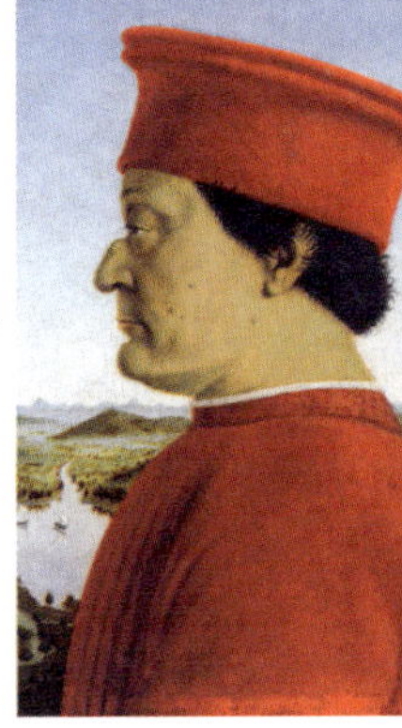

Above and Following Page: *The left-hand portrait of the* Diptych of Federico da Montefeltro and Battista Sforza.

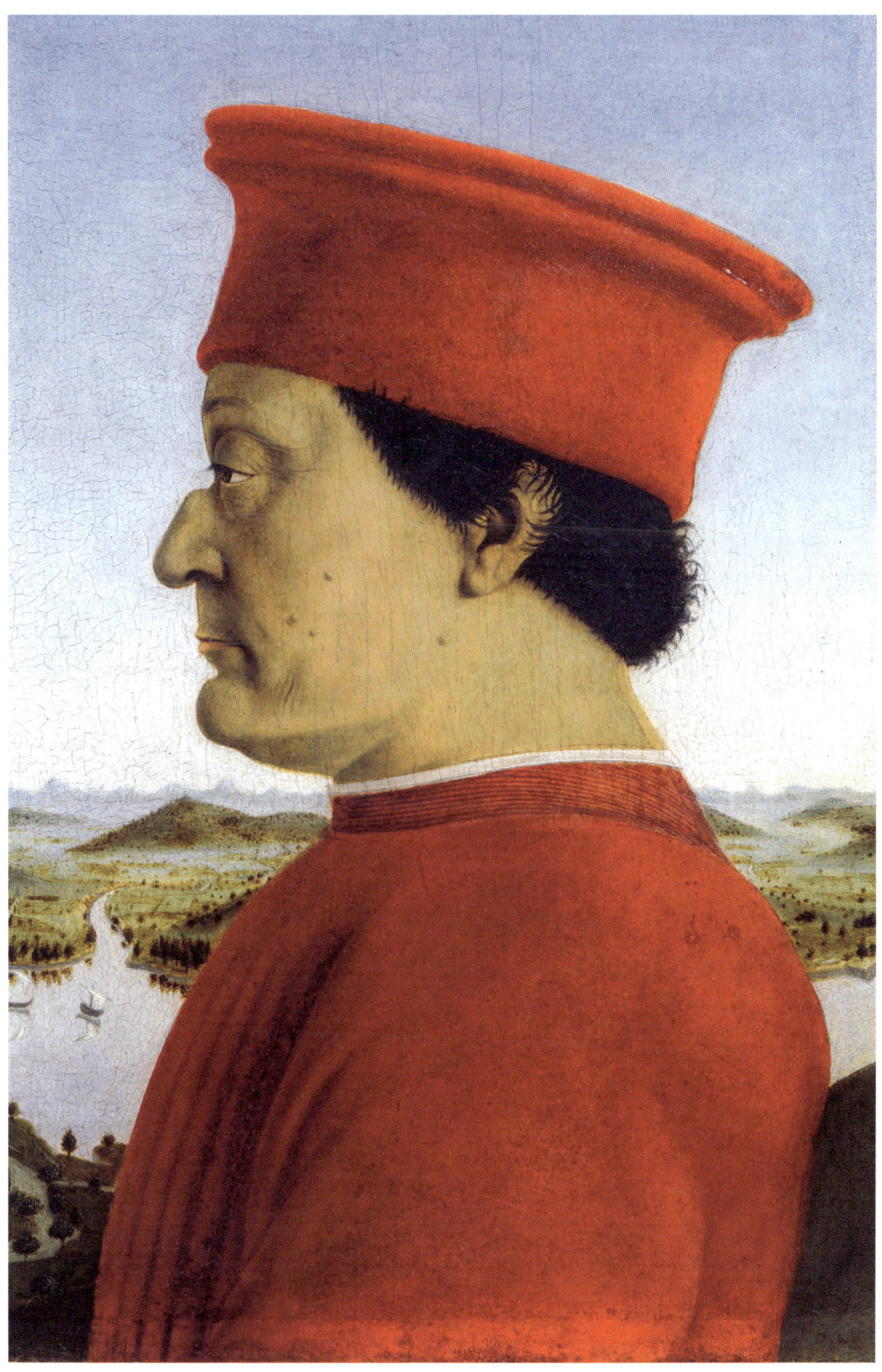

Portrait of Federico da Montefeltro *(c.1473-5), Piero della Francesca*

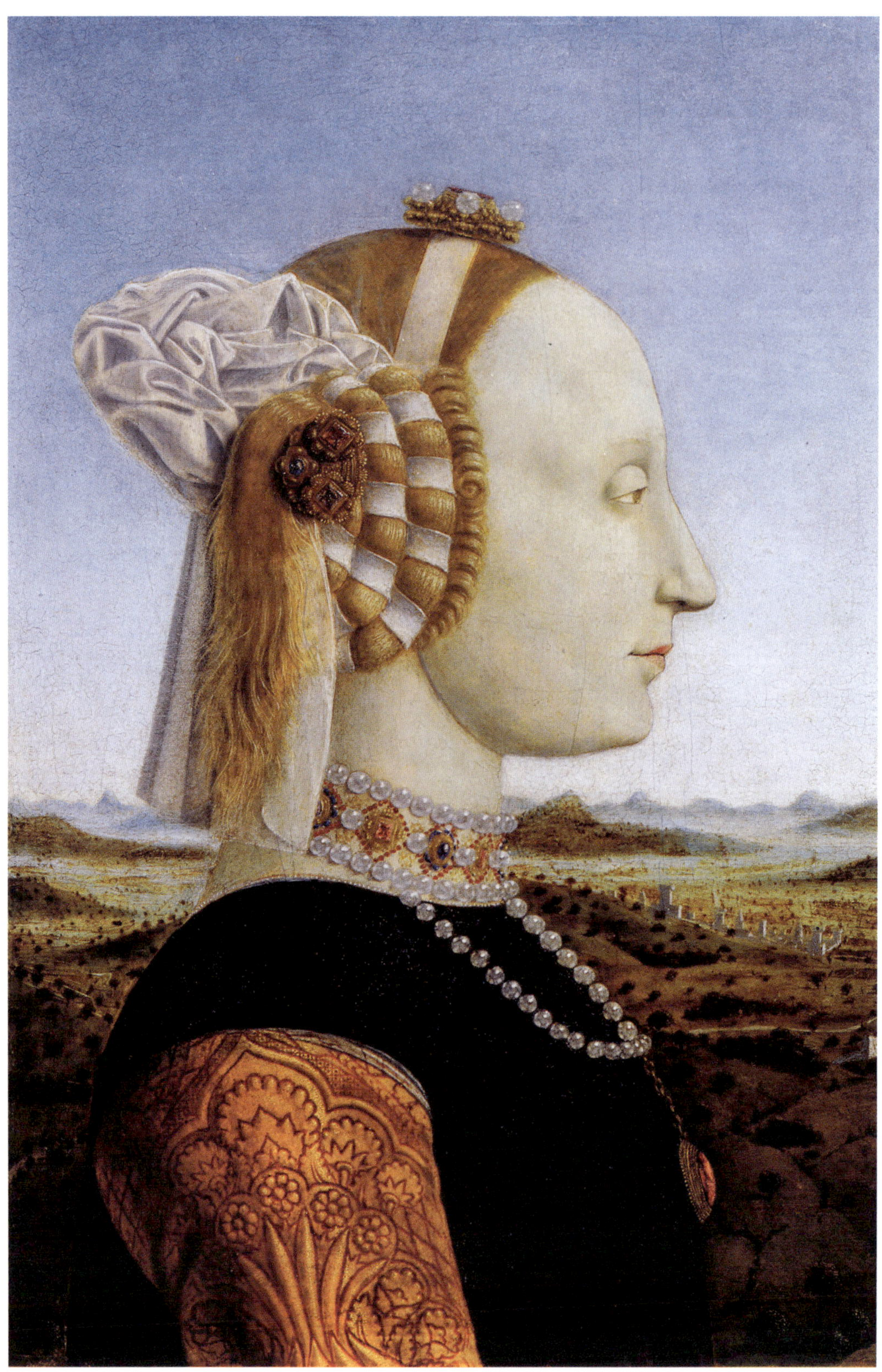

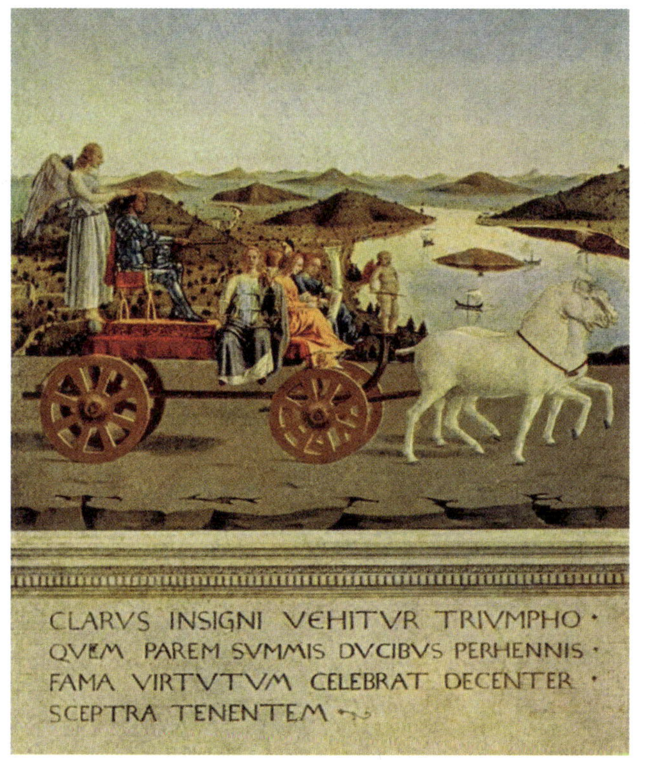

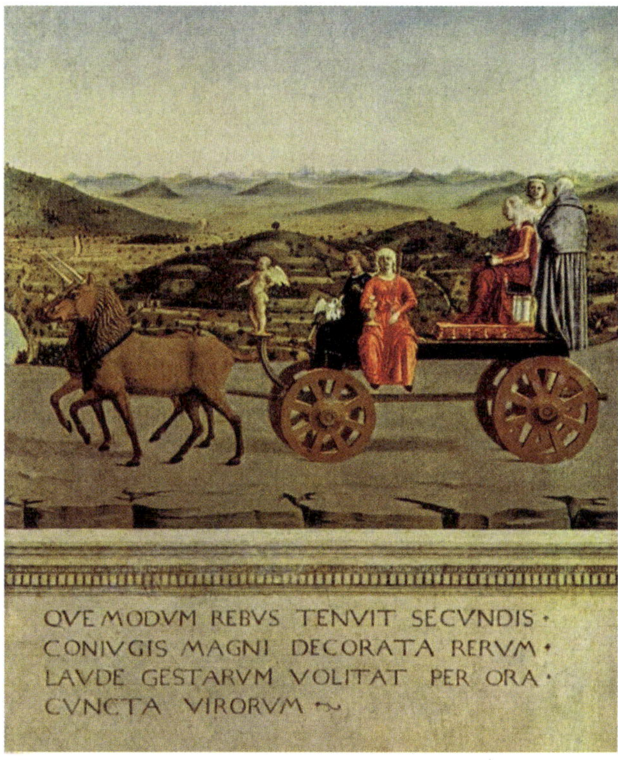

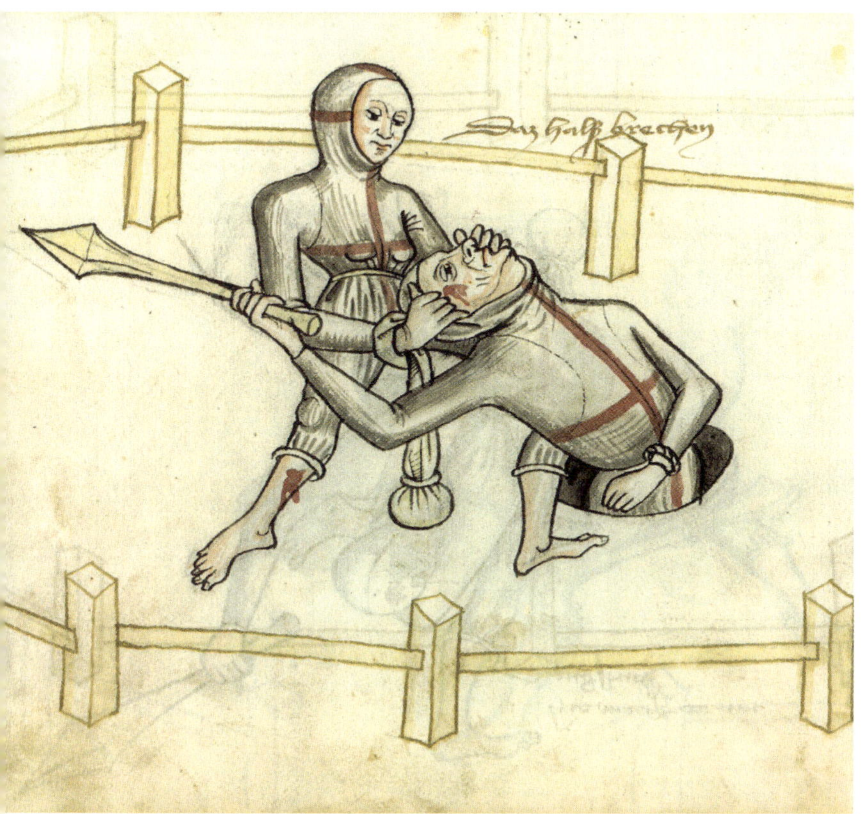

ABOVE: *The illustrations on the reverse of the two paintings – allegories of triumph, with an angel riding the carriage on the left, and unicorns pulling the car on the right.*

LEFT: *Mercenaries like Federico da Montefeltro often produced their own illustrated fighting manuals – a contemporary of Federico, German fencing expert Hans Talhoffer, produced perhaps the most curious. His* Fechtbuch *(Fight book, or Fencing book) created in 1459 features a series of nine illustrations of a man and a woman clashing in a bloody judicial trial by combat. The male physical advantage is countered with a hole cut into the floor of the ring, in which he stands, the ring rising up to his waist. The caption of the final image, in which both contestants lie bleeding on the floor, translates as 'Here they make an end of each other.'*

THE GARDEN OF EARTHLY DELIGHTS (1490-1500), HIERONYMUS BOSCH

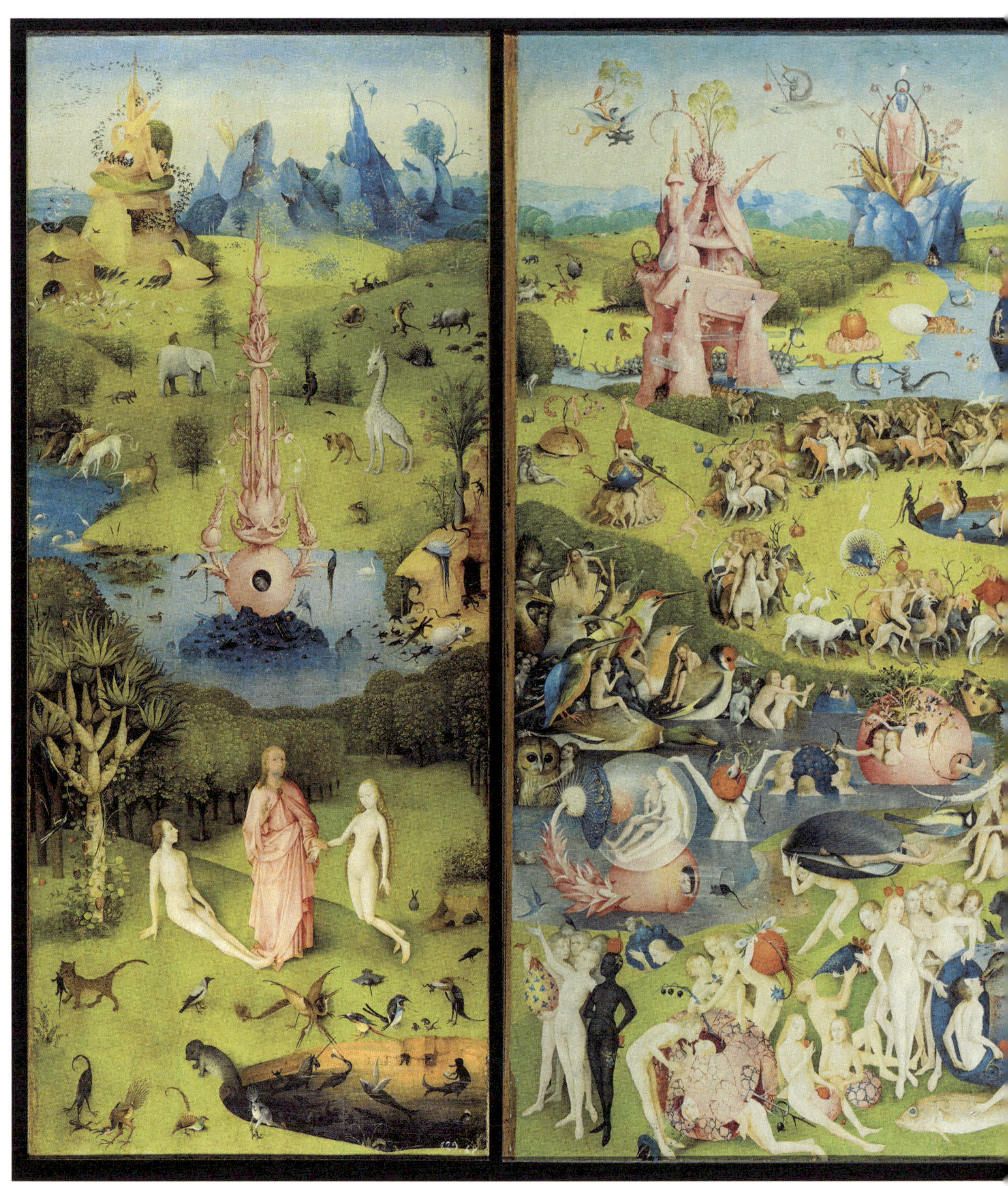

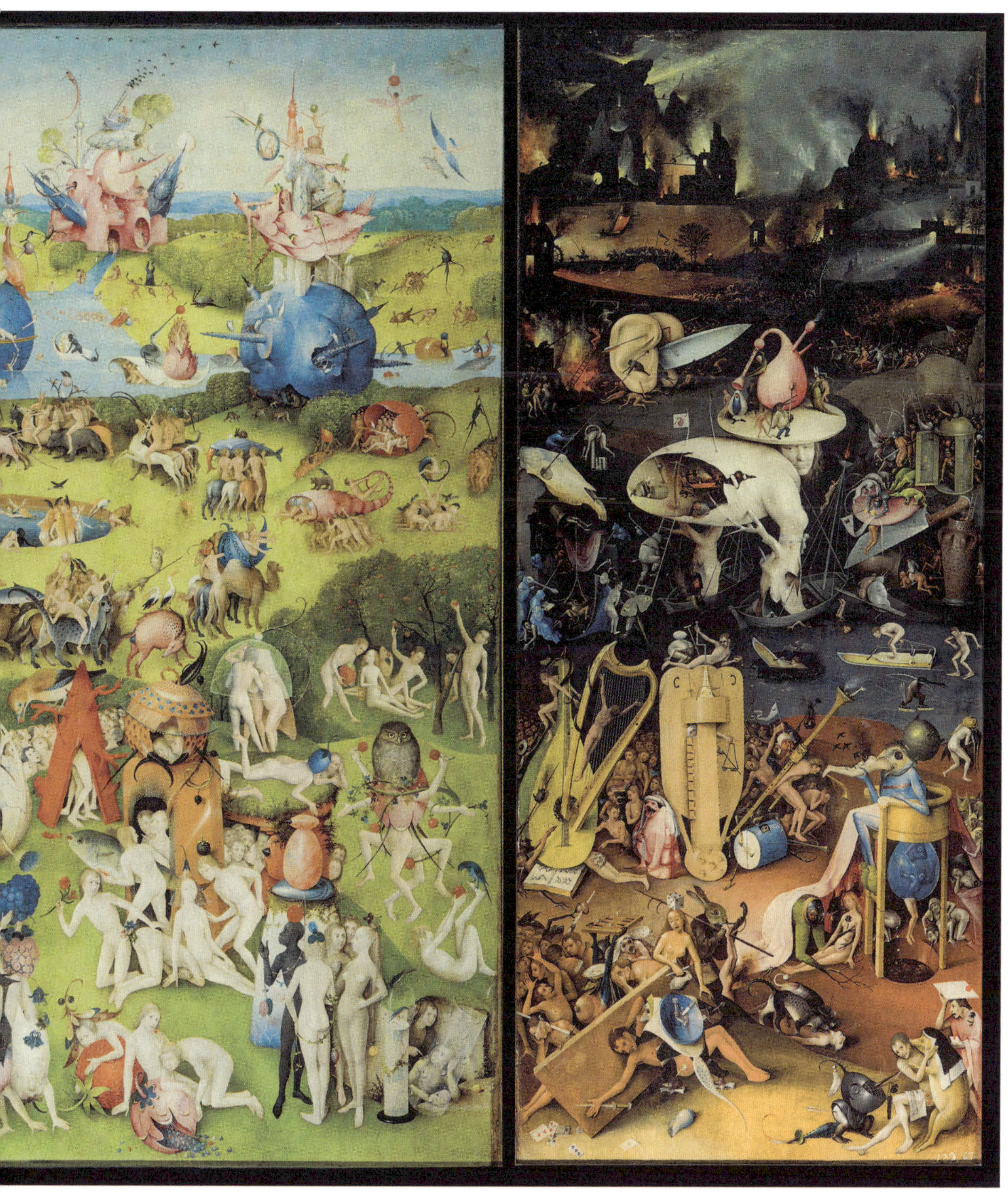

The Garden of Earthly Delights *(1490-1500), Hieronymus Bosch*

With the majority of strange and cryptic artworks one can feel a compulsion to expand one's understanding of the symbolism and other hidden meanings. But then there are the paintings of Hieronymus Bosch (*c.*1450-1516), whose infamous works of curiosity appear so alien and utterly unique that one almost *doesn't* want the veil to be drawn back, to allow one's own imagination to float forever like a lost cosmonaut through his otherworldly, fantastical atmospheres. Fortunately, for those wishing to maintain this mystery – at least about the man himself – there is little to ruin it. Almost nothing is known about the man with one of the most famous names in the history of art – and even that name was a later adoption. Born Jeroen van Aken in 's-Hertogenbosch, Netherlands, into a family of artists, he later changed his Christian name to the Latinised form, and his surname to represent his city. He was skilled in just about every medium – designing stained-glass windows, embroidery, brass work – but it was with oils that his imagination found its rocket fuel.

On first examination, *The Garden of Earthly Delights* is simply overwhelming in detail and scale. The three panels have a combined height of some 2m (6½ft) and width of 3.85m (12½ft) and are teeming with figures, flora and strange architecture – where does one start? Tryptychs are, by and large, designed to be read sequentially, and so moving from left to right we can begin to feel the structure of the painting's narrative. On the left is the Garden of Eden, with God bringing Adam and Eve together below a strange, towering bio-structure surrounded by water. It is an idyllic place and time before the arrival of the rest of the human race.

In the centre panel, mankind is in full utopian party mode, nakedly indulging in every pleasure and vice, all of which inevitably brings our species to the consequences of such wild, erotic abandon in the form of the hell of the right-hand panel. Musicians are tortured with their instruments; hunters are attacked by their prey; and the architecture is no longer biological but jagged and man-made. In the upper centre, strangest of all, we find a giant figure with the body of a hollow egg propped up on tree stumps with a human face that is believed to be a self-portrait by the artist. This is thought to be a counter to the Tree of Life in Paradise, just one example of how Bosch uses inversion in his overall moralising message about the fate of humanity.

The Garden of Earthly Delights is a painting that roars with the noise of its crowd, a chaotic ensemble that Bosch has, in fact, composed with rather traditional perspective and structure. The panels share the same horizon and distances of foreground, midground and background, and the elements of each are composed with balance, and comparative similarities – see the bodies of water in each panel, for example, like the renewing baptismal waters, and the architecture that shifts from the natural to the cold, dark industrial aesthetic of the hellscape.

Much of Bosch's extraterrestrial elements can be brought down to Earth with the context of his contemporary surroundings, and how they influenced his art and this painting in particular. The aforementioned giant tower in the first panel, for example, bears a striking resemblance to the elegant baptismal font of St John's Cathedral in Bosch's home city of 's-Hertogenbosch. As a member of the Illustrious Brotherhood of Our Blessed Lady, a religious confraternity, he would have been free to roam the cathedral and explore its manuscript archives.

Even the wild medley of monstrous and mythical creatures is rooted in real-world influence – the cathedral is decorated with ninety-five different grotesques and gargoyles, as well as carved figures in the wooden choir stalls, of snickering devils, anthropomorphised animals and men riding griffins, just as we find in the centre panel. There is clear influence, too, of the drolleries found in the margins of manuscripts. These small illustrations, doodled by bored and rebelliously satirical scribes, are often comical and lascivious: the figure in Bosch's hell panel, to the right of the hurdy-gurdy, bent over with a woodwind instrument protruding from his bottom, is – believe it or not – a common drollery motif.

We are still discovering wonders in the details of *The Garden of Earthly Delights*. In 2014 it was noticed that Bosch had painted musical notation on the bare backside of a figure in the hell panel (to the left of the figure with the inserted woodwind instrument). This was transcribed into modern notation for piano and a recording shared to YouTube, under the title *Hieronymus Bosch's Butt Song*. While it's unlikely that the plodding 49-note piece will set fire to the charts, it is extraordinary to hear 500-year-old music emanate from a painting already rich in marvels. One can't help but feel that Bosch would be nothing but delighted with the amount of serious attention given by modern scholars to his bum notes.

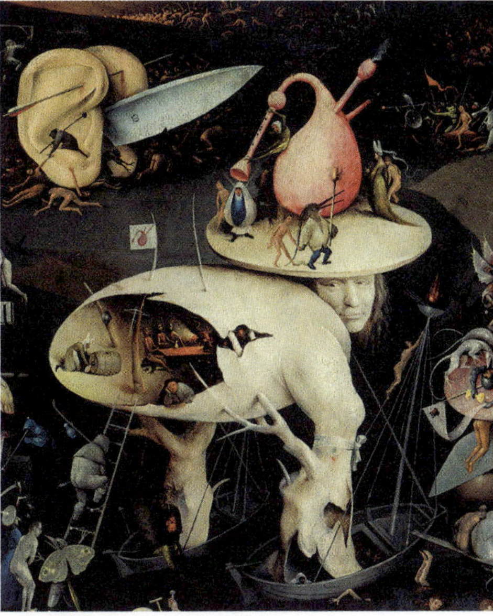

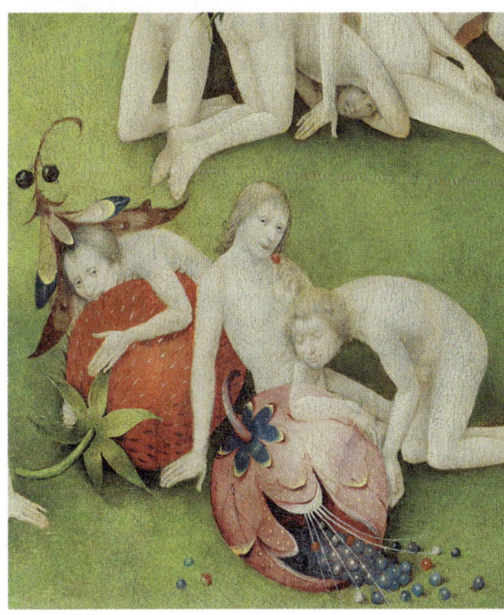

Above Top: *This detail of a humanoid tree in the right panel is thought to be an infernal mirroring of the Tree of Life in Paradise. The face is thought to be a self-portrait by Bosch.*

Above Bottom: *Lovers eat fruit in a metaphor for sex, while the peelings represent worthlessness.*

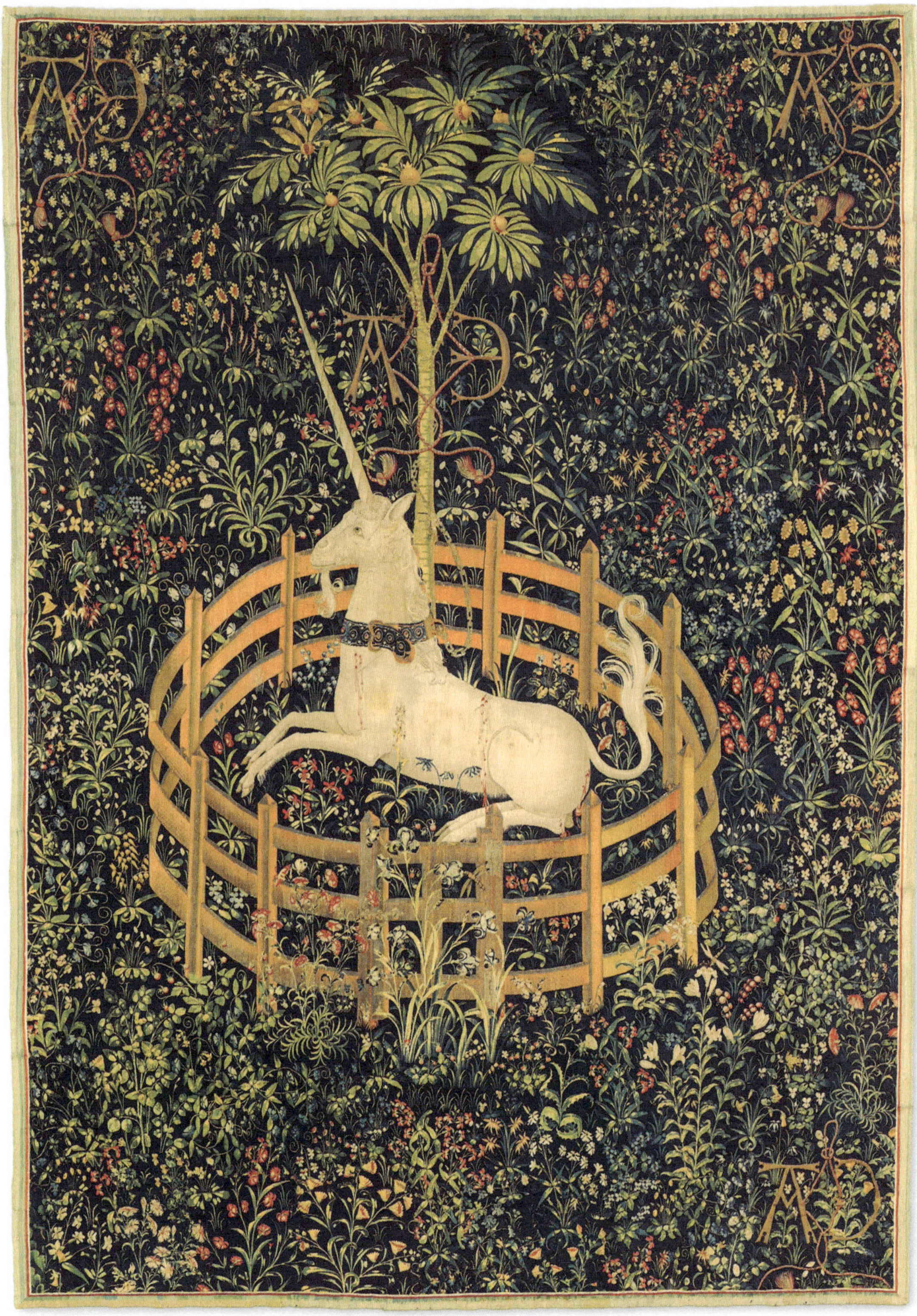

The Unicorn in Captivity.

UNICORN TAPESTRIES (1495-1505)

The elusive mythical unicorn can be tracked through history around the world, via its capture in art. Depictions of single-horned horses, goats and even wolves decorate statues, mosaics, pottery and tapestries from India to Africa and Europe. In ancient China the creature was known as the *qilin*, believed to have appeared at the birth of Confucius and other wise men. In the fifth century BC, the Greek historian Ctesias – likely repeating earlier Persian stories – documented its tricolour appearance and its single horn. Pliny the Elder describes the unicorn (in this case likely a rhinoceros) in his *Natural History* (AD 77-79): 'But the most fell and furious beast of all other, is the Licorne or Monoceros… one blacke horn he hath in the mids of his forehead… by report, this wild beast cannot possibly be caught alive.' Nearly 1600 years later the myth was still galloping through popular imagination, though scepticism was beginning to tighten its snare. 'Some conceive there is no such Animal extant,' Sir Thomas Browne writes cautiously in his wonderful *Pseudodoxia Epidemica* in 1646, a wonder-filled book designed to puncture the many popular misconceptions of his time.

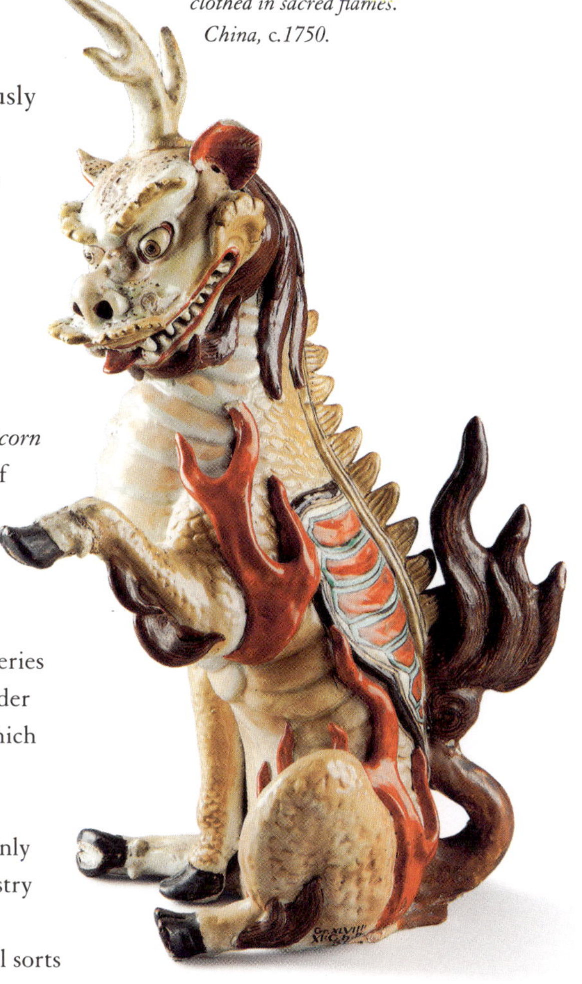

The fabled unicorn-like qilin, *clothed in sacred flames. China,* c.*1750.*

By then, the unicorn had come to symbolise everything from purity and divinity to fertility, seduction, healing and sacrifice. So perhaps it is of some surprise that, when it comes to the magnificent set of seven giant weavings of fine wool, silver and gold known as the *Unicorn Tapestries*, or *The Hunt of the Unicorn*, in the collection of the Metropolitan Museum of Art in New York, there is still no consensus as to what the unicorn and the scenes represent, why they were made or or who commissioned them. We also have no clue as to the identity of the artist of this most beautiful of mysteries inherited from the Middle Ages, with their dyes of madder (red), woad (blue) and weld (yellow) still vibrant, nor which order they should be presented in.

Are the tapestries encoded ceremonial marriage documents? An allegory of Christ's Passion? There certainly seem to be symbols of the latter (if not both). In the tapestry known as *The Hunters Enter the Woods*, the setting is a *millefleurs* background of a lush green field filled with all sorts of flowers and blossoming trees, including a cherry tree. (Some 101 species of plants are represented in the seven tapestries, of which eighty-five have been identified.)

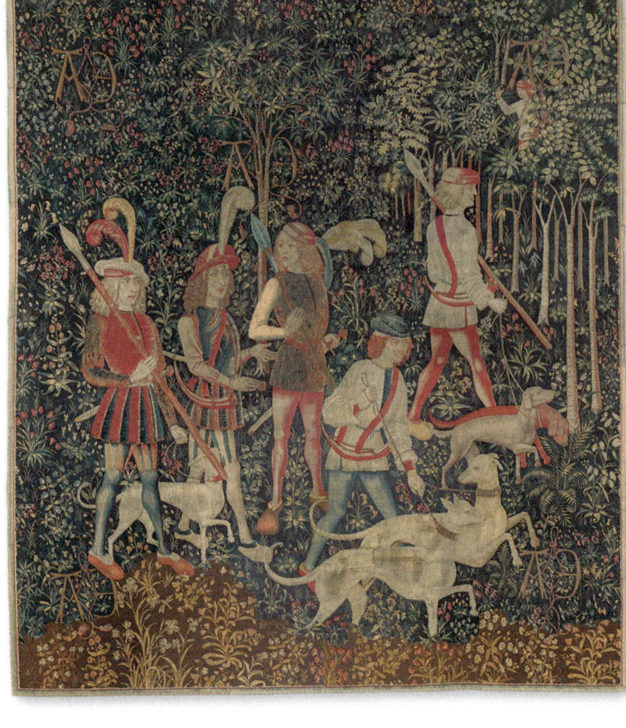

The Hunters Enter the Woods.

As our eyes adjust we notice the cipher 'A & E' woven into the trunk of the cherry tree, and then again in another four different parts of the scene – these letters, it is assumed, allude to the original owners of the tapestries, but their identities remain a mystery. The spotter in the tree waves excitedly to the hunters – the unicorn has been sighted. In *The Unicorn Is Found,* the beast is discovered before a fountain decorated with goldfinches and pheasants, dipping its horn into a stream to perhaps purify the water that pours from the fountain. Encircling this is a group of twelve hunters, the same number as Christ's disciples. Plants once used as medieval herbal antidotes to poisoning – sage, pot marigolds, orange – are dotted beside the stream.

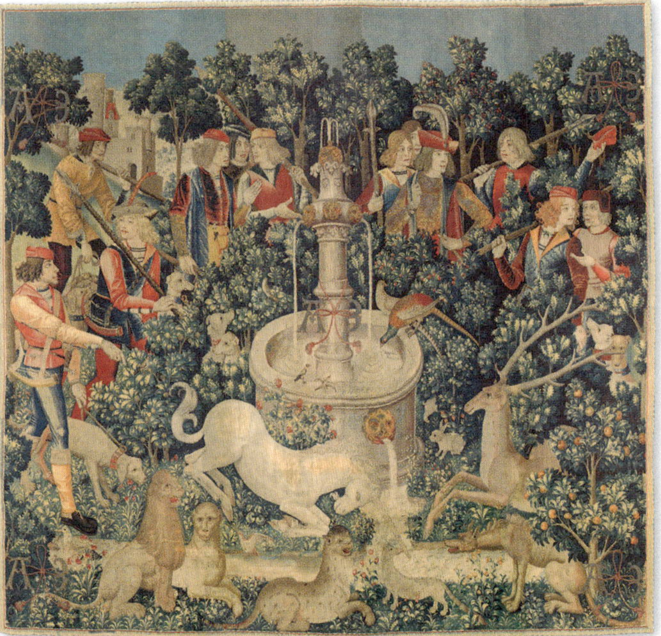

The Unicorn Is Found.

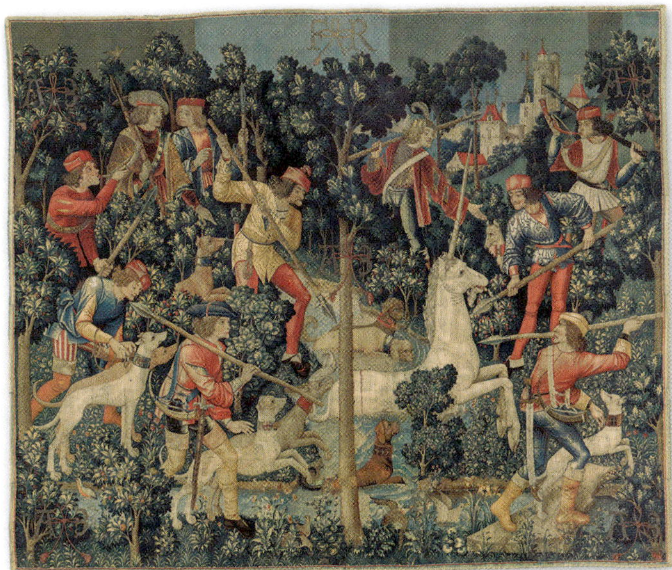

The Unicorn Is Attacked.

In *The Unicorn Is Attacked*, the scene is suddenly one of chaotic battle – horns are blown as the hunters attempt to plunge their lances into the animal's flesh as it leaps across the stream to escape. (Again the cipher 'A & E' can be found in the four corners and on the oak tree in the centre.) The injured creature fights back in *The Unicorn Defends Itself*, furiously kicking at a hunter while lacerating a greyhound nearly in two with its horn. The hunter blowing a horn in the lower-left corner carries a scabbard with the dangling inscription AVE REGINA C[OELI] (Hail, Queen of the Heavens).

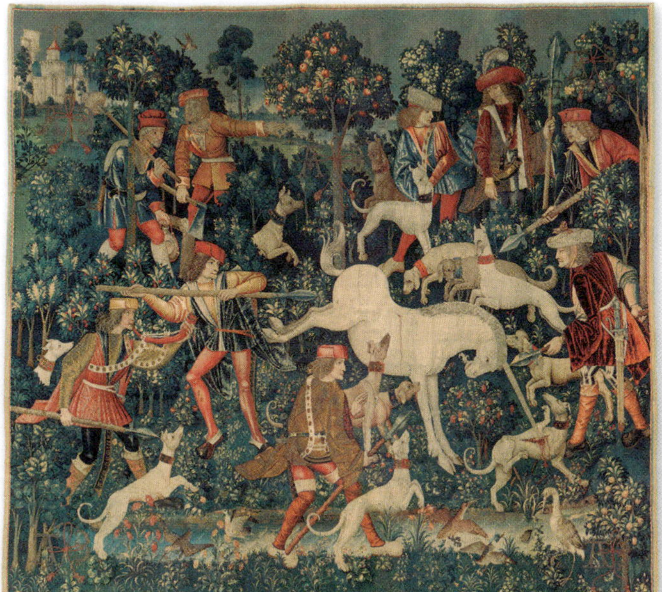

The Unicorn Defends Itself.

The Unicorn Captured by the Virgin exists in two small fragments, appearing to show the unicorn trapped in a fenced garden and submitting to a maiden, who signals to a hunter to sound the horn. *The Unicorn Is Killed and Brought to the Castle* contains two panels of story, and the clearest allegory to Christ's Passion. On the left we find the hunters stab the unicorn to death with their blades, with one of their number using a horn to catch the falling blood, reminiscent of depictions of the Crucifixion in which angels scoop Christ's blood in chalices. In the centre the unicorn is now slung across the back of a horse, its neck ringed with a crown of thorns like Christ, as it is presented to a group of royals.

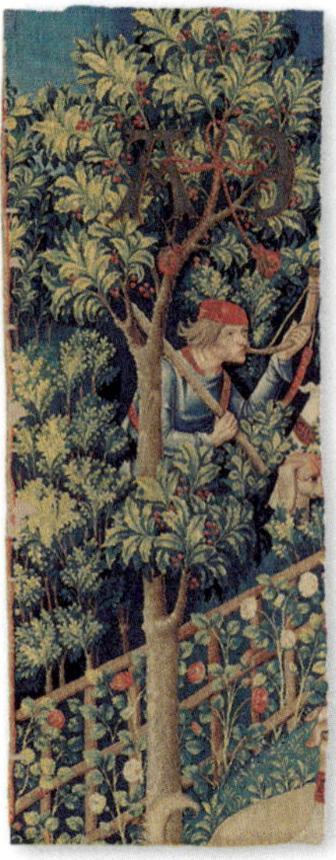

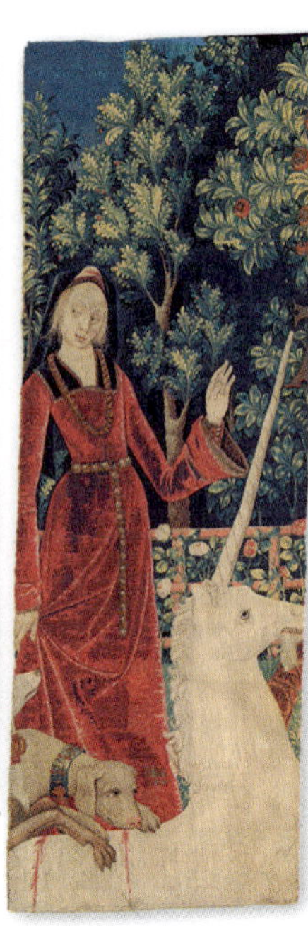

The Unicorn Surrenders to a Maiden.

And finally there is the most beloved of the tapestries, the main image shown at the beginning of this chapter, *The Unicorn in Captivity*, which might well have been created as a single piece and not as part of the series. The unicorn appears content in his captivity, loosely tied to a tree behind a fence he could easily leap over if he so wished. The tree bears ripe pomegranates, a medieval symbol of fertility and marriage, which has led to the hypothesis that this particular piece was made to be hung by the bed of a noble couple on their wedding night.

Solutions to the enigma of the tapestries have been confidently offered in the past. 'This puzzling quest is almost at its end,' wrote the first curator of the Met Cloisters (where they are displayed to this day), James Rorimer, in 1942, who had been handed the daunting task of their interpretation. The museum was donated the works in 1937 by the American financier John D. Rockefeller Jr (1874-1960), who had acquired them from the La Rochefoucauld family in 1922. The French nobles had owned them since at least 1680, although the tapestries had briefly left their possession in the 1790s, when they were looted during the French Revolution. They were later found with tattered edges and holes, having been used to wrap fruit trees over winter. Rorimer claimed to have found symbols in the weavings – including a knotted cord, a pair of striped tights and a squirrel – that he said revealed Anne of Brittany to have been their original owner, in celebration of her marriage to Louis XII in 1499.

In 1976 an assistant curator named Margaret Freeman published a book that overturned Rorimer's theories. While possible that they were made as part of a marriage celebration, the interpretation of the symbols didn't hold up. 'The squirrel of the tapestry may be intended to be symbolic,' she wrote, 'or

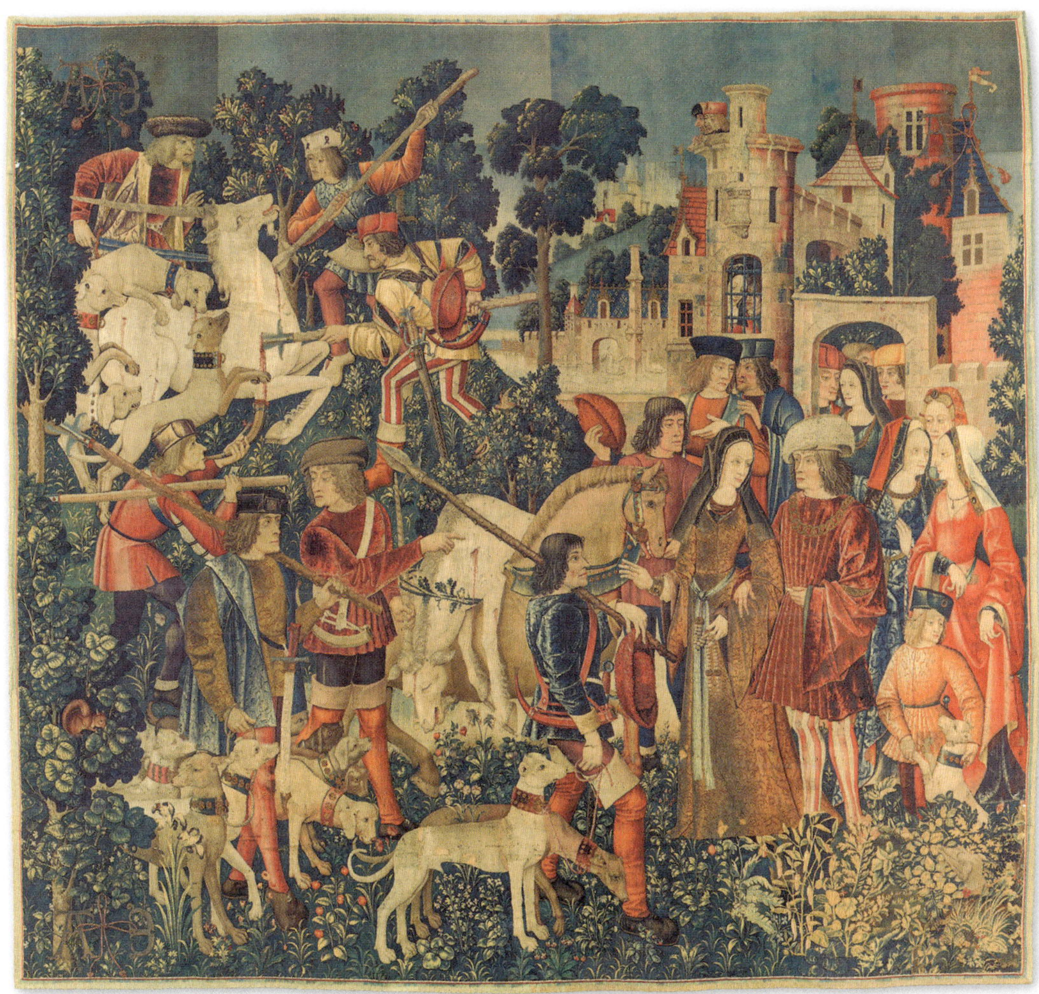

The Unicorn Is Killed and Brought to the Castle.

it may be present merely to call attention to the tree in which it sits.' As Rorimer's theories were gradually edited out of the museum's official guides, the information agreed as fact by consensus shrank to the extent that, as the former Met Cloisters lecturer Danielle Oteri has pointed out, today the wall labels that hang beside one of the world's most famous and intriguing set of artworks consist of about only one sentence each. 'It is among the greatest visual poems that I know. It is alluring and elusive like the unicorn itself,' Thomas P. Campbell, former director and CEO of the Metropolitan Museum of Art, told the *Paris Review* in 2020. 'I have no doubt that people will be spinning stories and interpretation for generations to come.'

MONA VANNA, THE NUDE MONA LISA (*c.*1510), GIAN GIACOMO CAPROTTI DA ORENO

Of the more than one million artworks in the collection of the Louvre, only one has ever been given its own postbox to cope with the amount of love letters it receives. The portrait of a woman thought to be the Italian noblewoman Lisa Gherardini by Leonardo da Vinci (1452-1519), known as *Mona Lisa*, or *La Gioconda* or *La Joconde*, is the most visited painting in the world and has had its fair share of notable admirers. Napoleon Bonaparte (1769-1821) had it hung on his bedroom wall at the Tuileries Palace for years and, when it was first exhibited in the Louvre in 1815, ardent visitors brought it gifts of flowers, poems and love notes.

On the morning of 21 August 1911 one admirer went a little too far and 'eloped' with the painting. Paris police scoured the city for suspects, at one point interrogating a 29-year-old Picasso (1881-1973), who four years earlier had innocently (he claimed) purchased two statues that had been stolen from the Louvre. Eventually, in December 1913, the painting was discovered in the closet of Vincenzo Peruggia, an ex-Louvre employee who had simply walked out with it hidden under his white worker's smock. The theft was a media sensation, telegraphed across the world and amplifying the painting's fame many times over.

Over the years *Mona Lisa* has endured rocks, acid and a coffee cup thrown at her, and today beams her famous enigmatic grin from behind bulletproof glass. The smile has captured curious minds around the world – some more than others. In 1852 a young artist named Luc Maspero leapt to his death from the fourth floor of a Paris hotel, leaving behind a note in which he'd written: 'For years I have grappled desperately with her smile. I prefer to die.' In 1910, another obsessed fan visited the painting and, overcome, shot himself before her.[1]

---

1 An attempt to conclusively analyse just what her smile betrayed was made in 2005 when researchers at the University of Amsterdam processed the image with 'emotion recognition' computer software, and announced that the smile was 83 per cent happy, 9 per cent disgusted, 6 per cent fearful and 2 per cent angry. Which I'm not sure gets us anywhere.

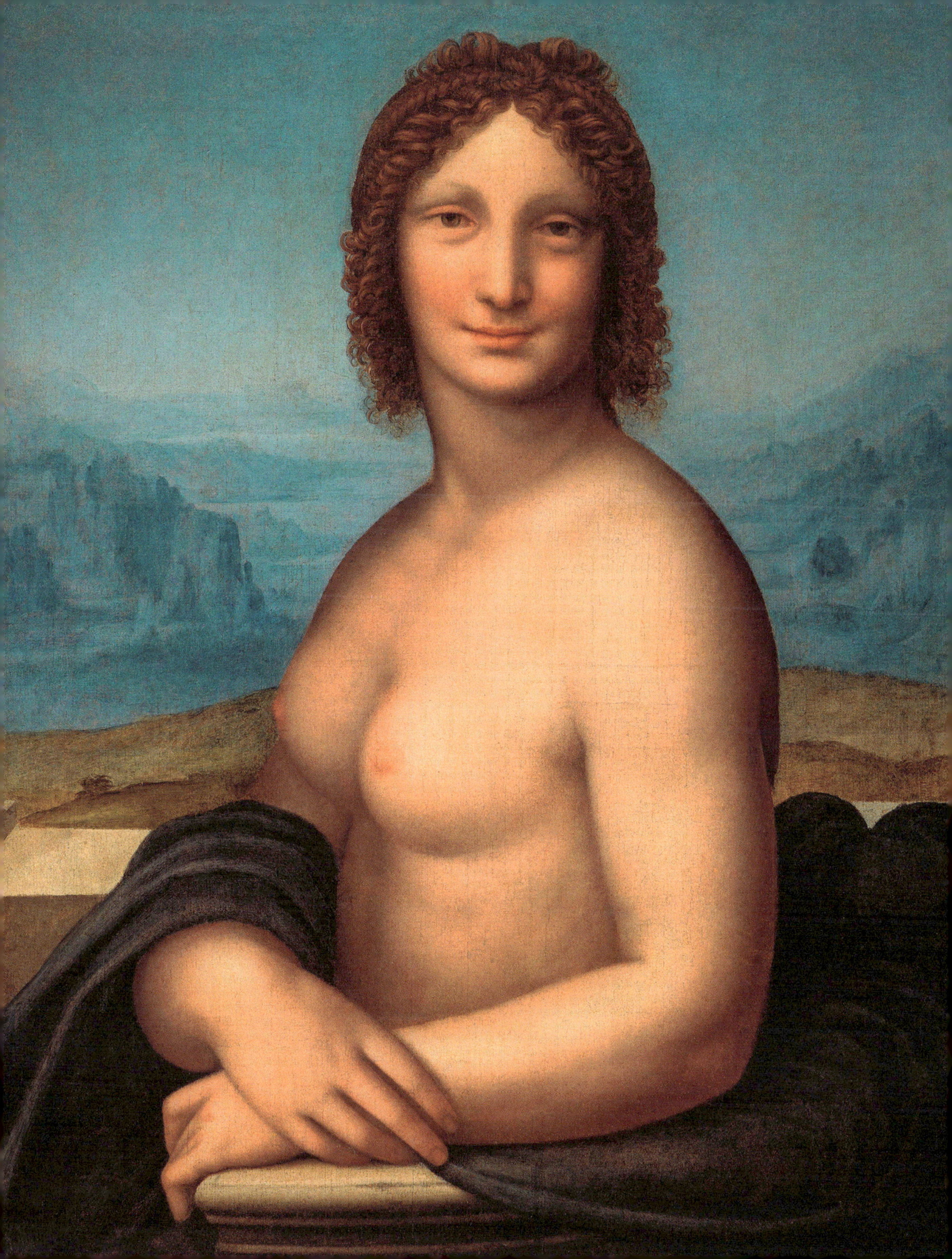

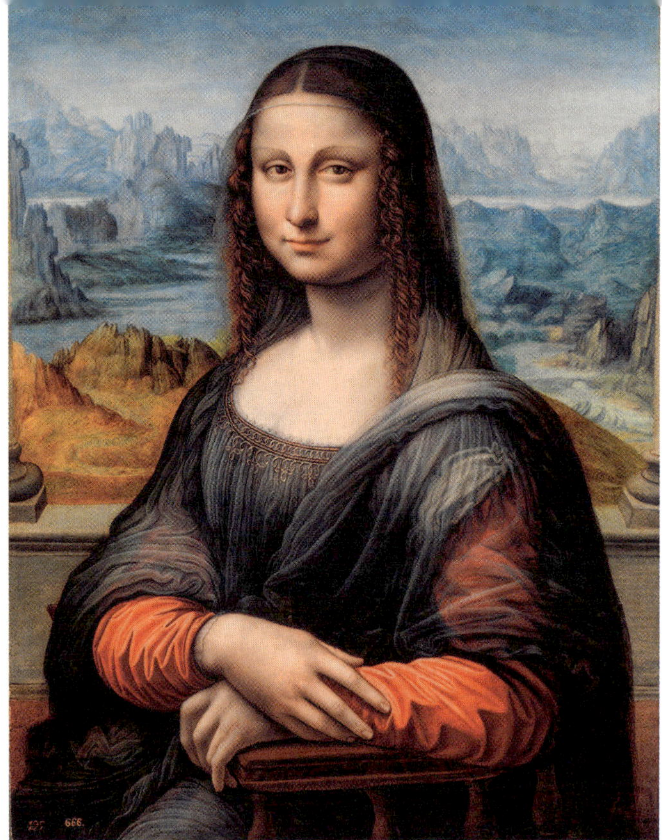

Left: *The* Mona Lisa *in Madrid's Prado Museum, painted from a slightly different perspective to the more famous work in the Louvre.*

Below: *The charcoal sketch known as* La Joconde Nue, *of disputed authorship but recently reappraised as the work of Leonardo himself, at least in part.*

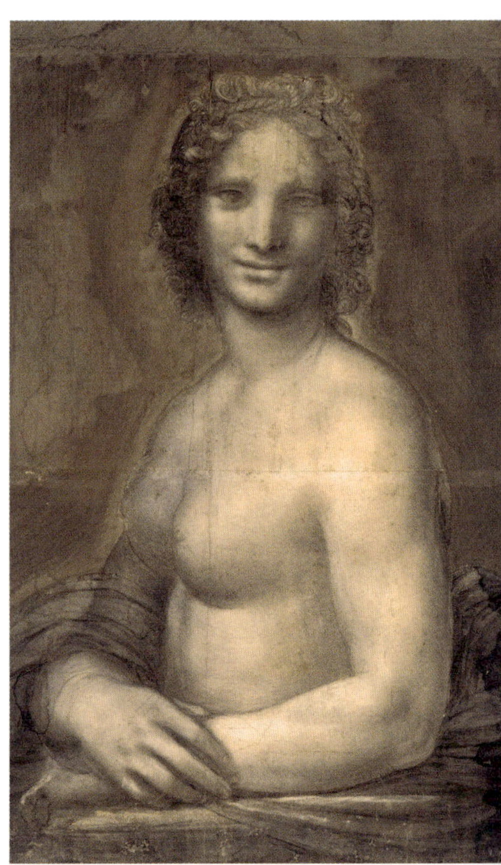

With all its fame, perhaps less well known is the surprising fact that nude versions of Mona Lisa were also made at the time, such as that shown on page 79 by a rebellious apprentice of Leonardo da Vinci. Leonardo took in Gian Giacomo Caprotti da Oreno (1480-1524) to train when the boy was aged ten, swiftly nicknaming him Salaì (The Devil or The Little Unclean One). Leonardo frequently complains about Salaì in his notebooks, describing him as a 'thief, liar, obstinate, glutton' (Salaì stole from Leonardo on at least five separate occasions), but he had a fondness for the beautiful curly-haired youth. At Leonardo's studio Salaì produced the nude Mona Lisa known as the *Mona Vanna* with the same famous smile.[2]

In fact there are around twenty similar existing artworks of the Mona Lisa appearing nude – see Joos van Cleve's *Mona Vanna Nuda* in Prague's National Gallery, or *La Belle Gabrielle* (sixteenth century, author unknown) in the collection of the Earl of Spencer, for example – which has led to the theory that they are all based on a lost original nude version by Leonardo

---

2 It seems Leonardo suffered much in the way of irreverent behaviour by Salaì. There is a purported page of a Leonardo folio discovered in the 1960s that carries drawings added by another hand, showing a bicycle-like device and some crude sketches of an anus labelled 'Salaì's bum', which is being chased around by ambulant penises.

himself. The nearest we might have to this original work is a charcoal sketch known as *La Joconde Nue* (*Naked Mona Lisa*) in the collection of the Condé Museum, Chantilly, which shares identical formal elements. After a month of reappraisal at the Centre for Research and Restoration of the Museums of France in 2017, the experts concluded that the sketch was done at least in part by Leonardo himself, likely as a preparatory drawing of the Louvre masterpiece.

Incidentally, one popular misconception is that there is only one *Mona Lisa*. As well as the famous work hanging in the Louvre, there is also the *Mona Lisa* in the collection of the Prado Museum in Madrid (opposite). It depicts the same figure and scene, but is painted from a slightly different angle of perspective, sharing each *pentimento* (change) to the bust, veil outline and finger position in Leonardo's original. This suggests that it was painted simultaneously by one of Leonardo's students – quite possibly by Salaì – at the neighbouring canvas.

A theory has also been put forward that Salaì himself might even have modelled for the *Mona Lisa* paintings, not Lisa Gherardini, as popularly thought. In 2016 Silvano Vinceti, head of the Italian National Committee for Cultural Heritage, pointed to the nose, forehead and smile as being strikingly similar to the features of Salaì. The idea was rejected by the Louvre but it remains a fringe theory (aided in part, regrettably, by the coincidence that the letters of *Mona Lisa* can be rearranged to form Mon Salaì).

BELOW: *The* Isleworth Mona Lisa, *dated to the early sixteenth century, curious in that it shows Lisa Gherardini in identical pose but noticeably younger in appearance. Since its public debut in 1913, when it was acquired from a private collection by the English collector Hugh Blaker, experts and critics have been divided on whether authorship can be attributed to Leonardo da Vinci himself.*

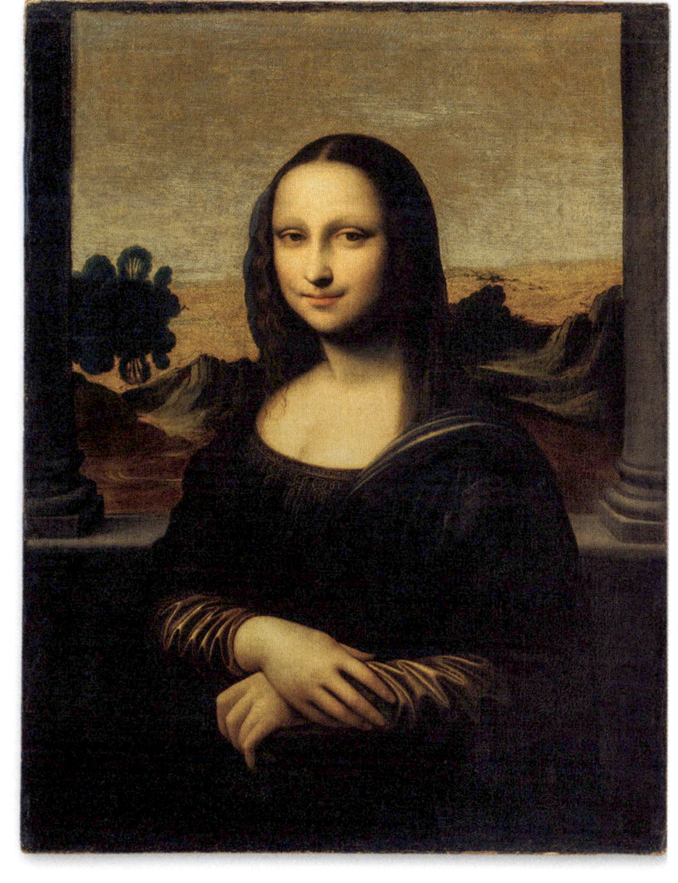

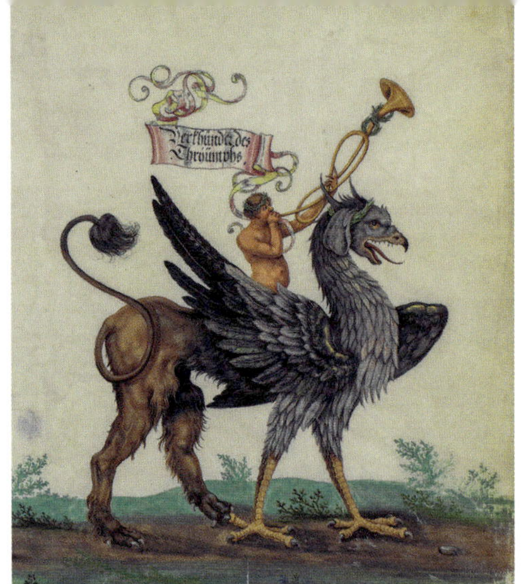
Verkhündt des
Thrŏumphs

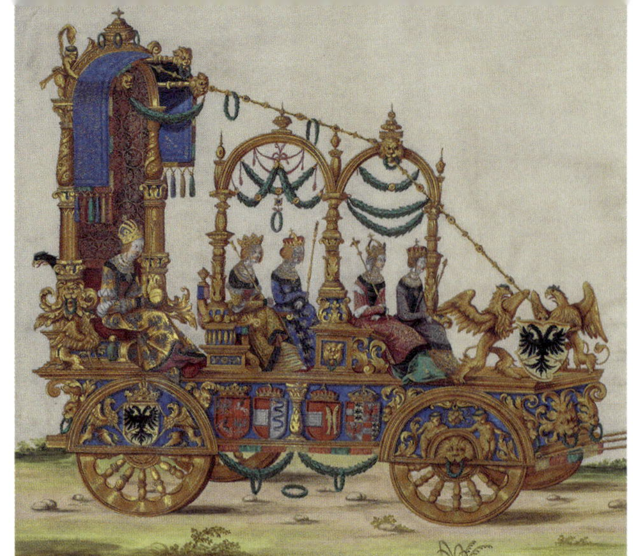

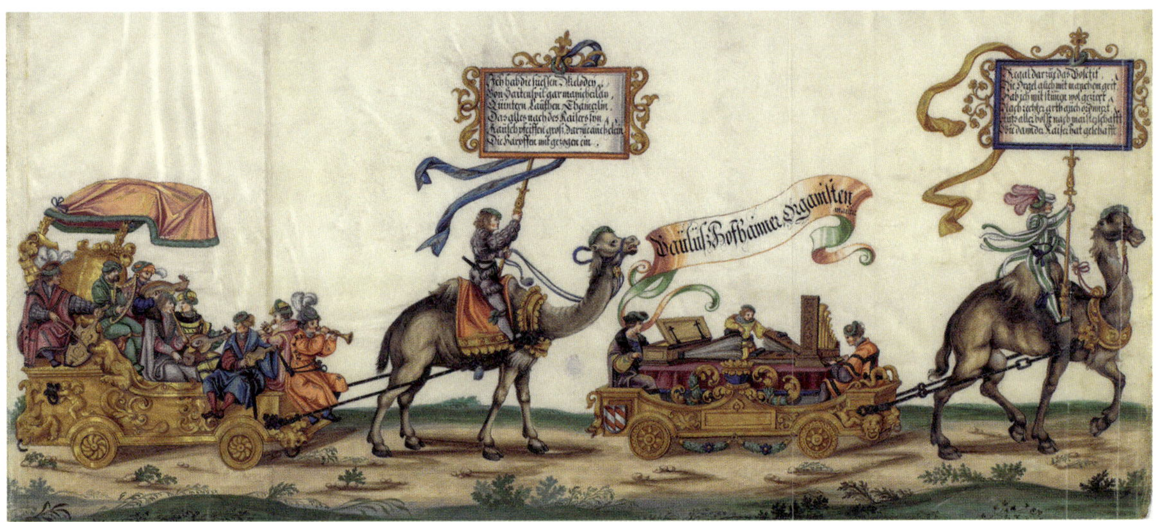
Paulus Hofhaimer Organisten

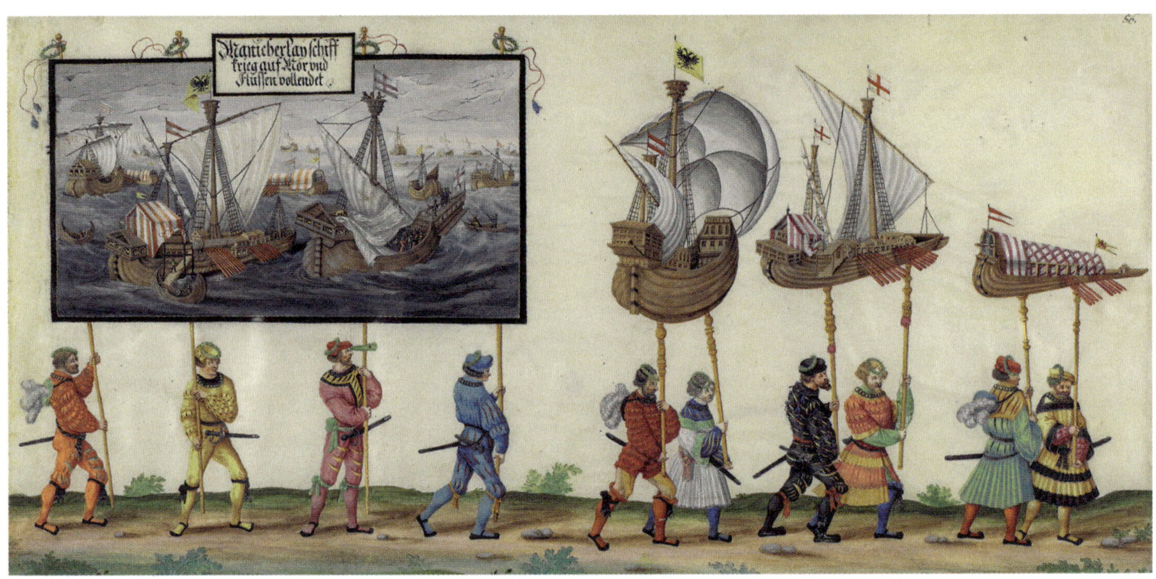
Manicherlay schiff
krieg auf Mör vnd
Flussen vollendet

TRIUMPHAL PROCESSION OF EMPEROR MAXIMILIAN I (1512-26), HANS BURGKMAIR THE ELDER AND OTHERS

To celebrate his own magnificence, in 1512 Maximilian I, Holy Roman Emperor (1459-1519), set about planning the grandest procession the world had ever seen. Epic in proportion and imagination, Maximilian's *Triumphal Procession* comprises a seemingly endless and quite glorious parade of thousands of plumed and festooned soldiers, courtiers, nobles, jesters, crowds of common folk and hunters. They march, ride and dance around huge trundling festival vehicles – there's even a giant treadwheel carriage powered by the courtiers running on it like hamsters. Interspersed among them are rejoicing packs of camels, bears, wild boar, all led by a naked herald astride a giant griffin.

If the appearance of this last celebrant strikes you as a little odd then you've cottoned on to the actual nature of the spectacular event, for the truth is that no such procession ever took place. The perennially impoverished Maximilian couldn't afford it, thanks to the cost of his relentless expansionism and the fact that he'd run up so much debt that it would take his family until the end of the century to pay back the 6 million guilder he owed, equivalent to a decade's worth of tax revenue. But what he lacked in funds he made up for with a flair for publicity and legacy-building. 'He who does not provide for his memory while he lives,' he reasoned, 'will not be remembered after his death, so that this person will be forgotten when the bell tolls. And hence the money I spend for my memory will not be lost.'

The grand procession known as the Triumphal Procession would exist in artistry alone, and quite frankly the imaginary ceremony is all the more wonderful for it. The work forms an

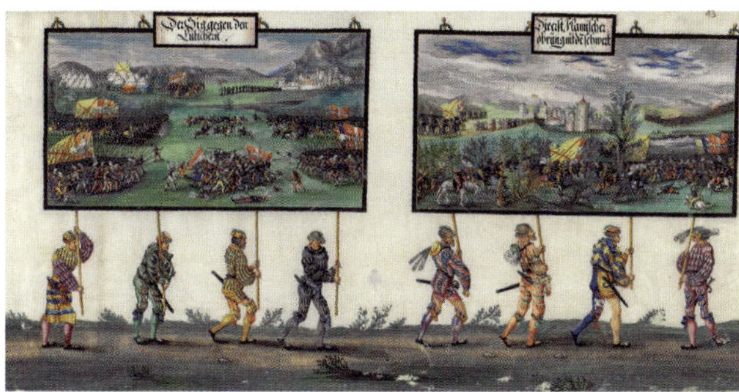

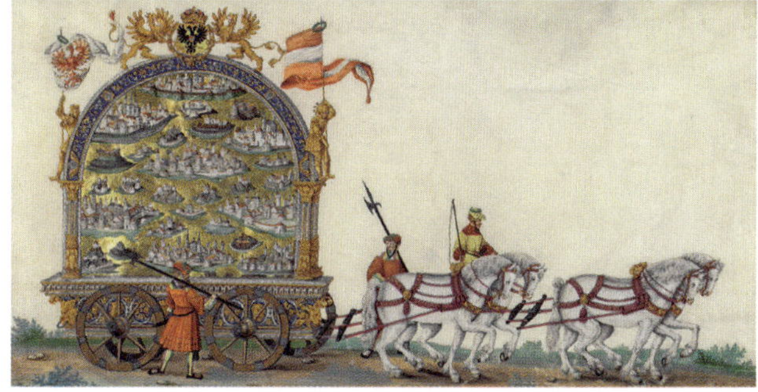

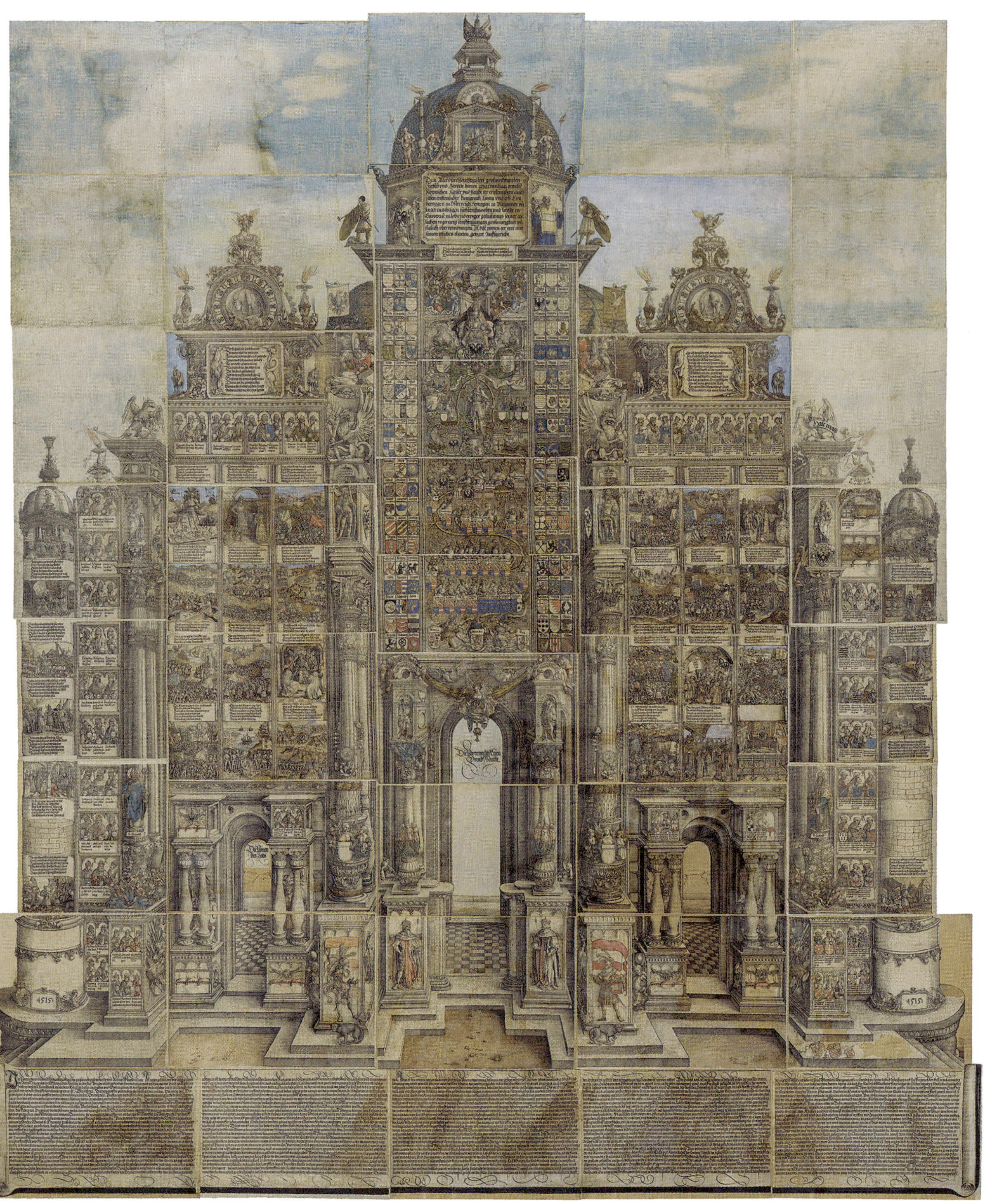

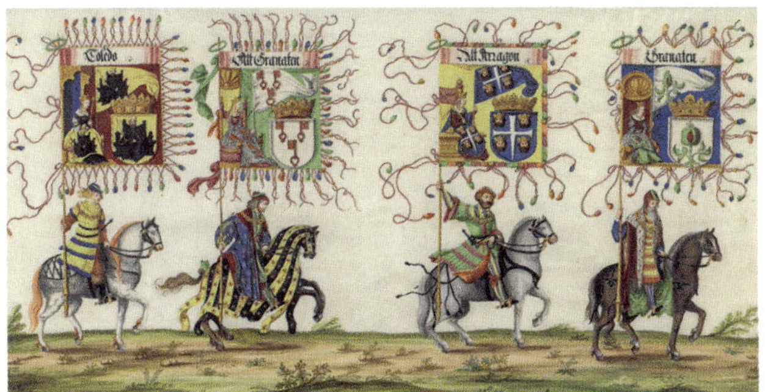

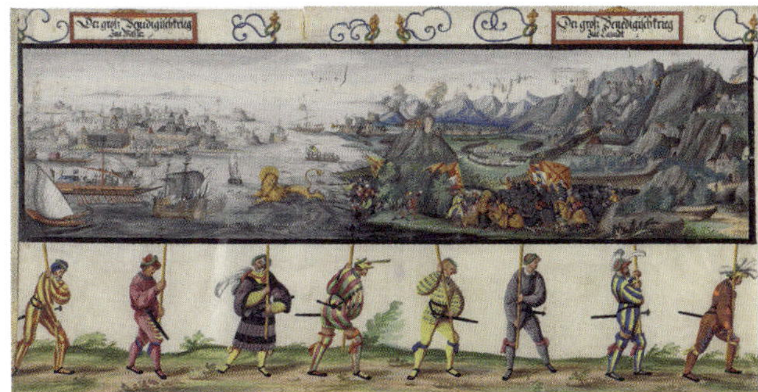

allegorical litany of Maximilian's achievements – see, for example, scenes of the battles he'd fought, symbols of his glorious genealogy (he modestly traced his lineage back to the mythical Trojan prince Hector, Julius Caesar and King Arthur). The noble female passengers on the parade vehicles, meanwhile, represent the glittering cities of his empire.

While the overall programme was planned by Maximilian I and the Austrian cartographer Johannes Stabius (1450-1522), the illustrations were created on the latest graphic technology – the woodcut – by the great artists of the era, including Albrecht Altdorfer, Hans Springinklee, Albrecht Dürer, Leonhard Beck and Hans Schäufelen. The lion's share of the work, though, is attributed to Hans Burgkmair the Elder (1473-1531), though an honourable mention should be made of the large team of block-cutters needed to manifest the artists' vision.

Together with two sister sections created by Dürer, the *Triumphal Arch* and the *Great Triumphal Carriage*, the huge artworks formed a giant frieze that would – according to Maximilian's own recorded dictations – 'Grace the walls of council chambers and great halls of the empire, proclaiming for posterity the noble aims of their erstwhile ruler.' All three sections are truly gargantuan in scale – when pieced together, the *Arch* measures 3.5m (11½ft) high by 3m (10ft) wide,

OPPOSITE: *Albrecht Dürer's* Arch of Honour for Emperor Maximilian I *(1517-18), showing his ancestry, territories, accomplishments, talents and interests.*

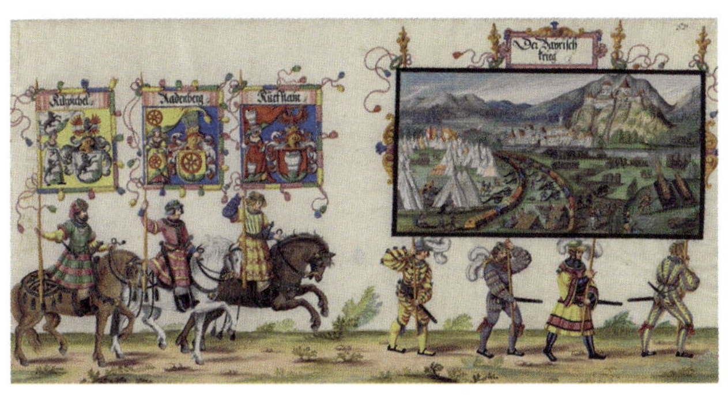

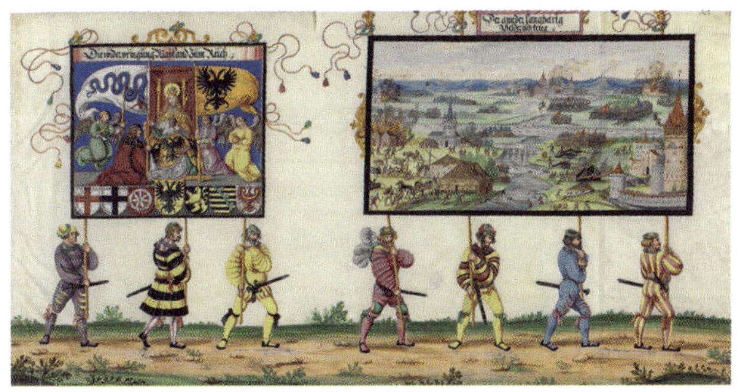

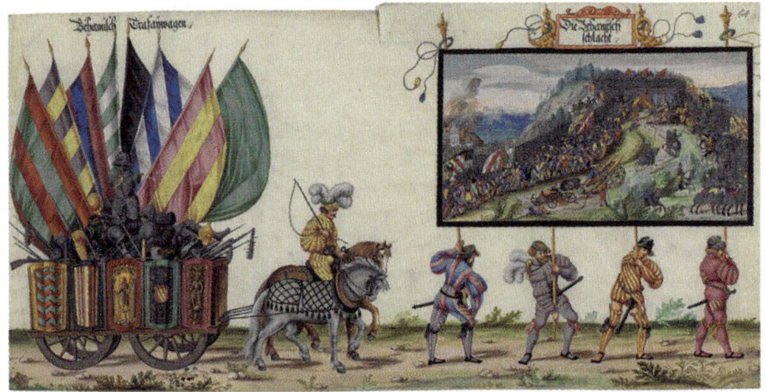

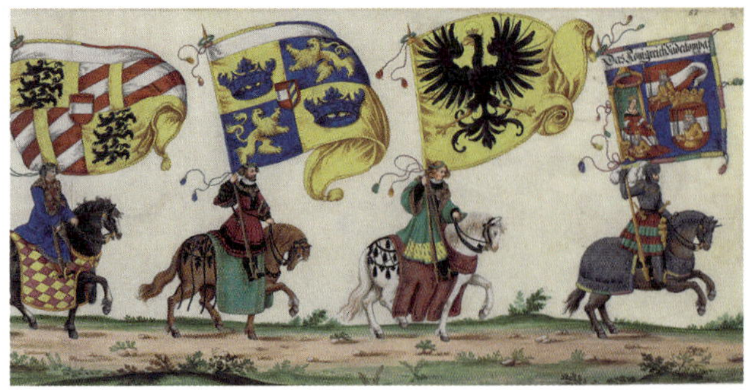

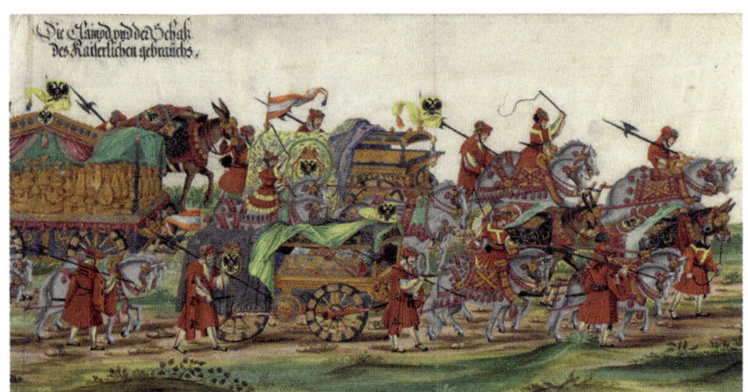

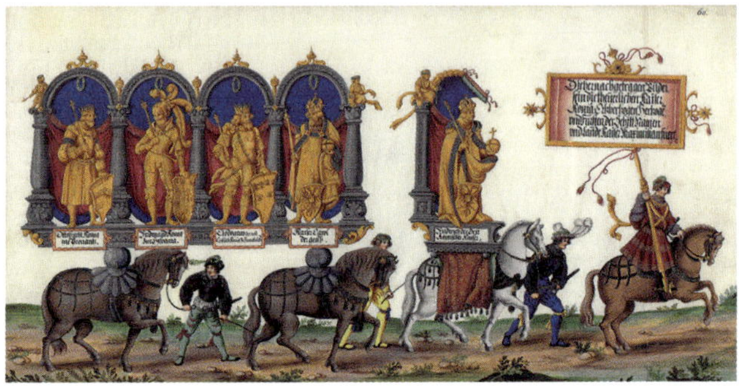

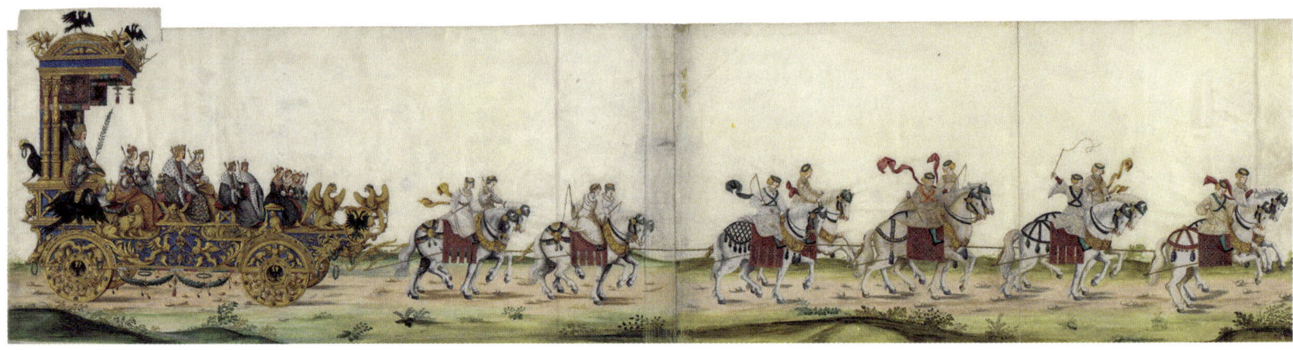

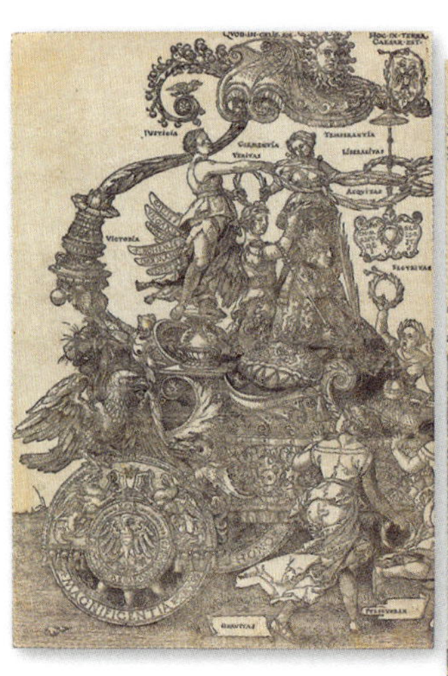

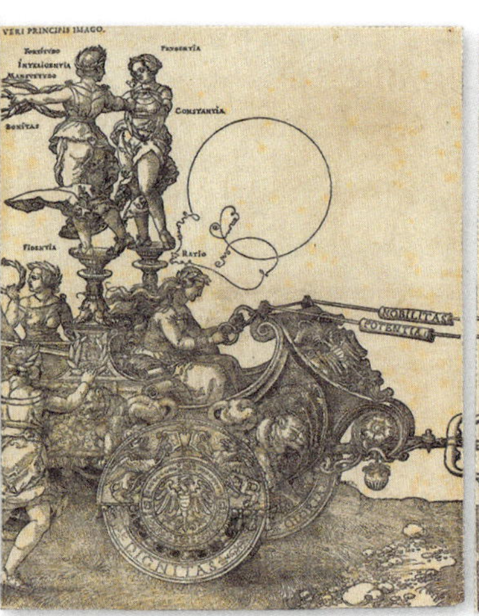

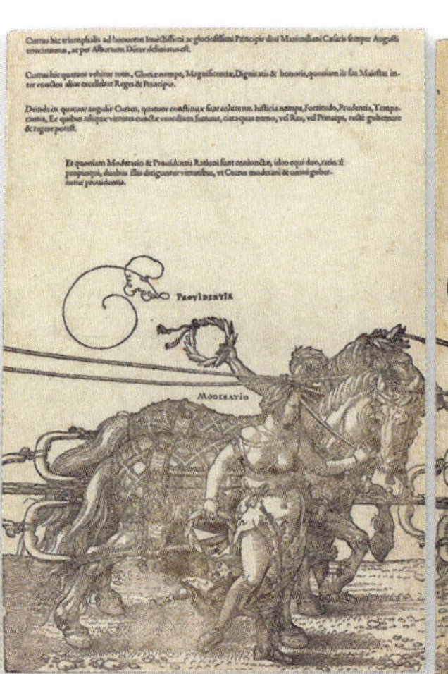

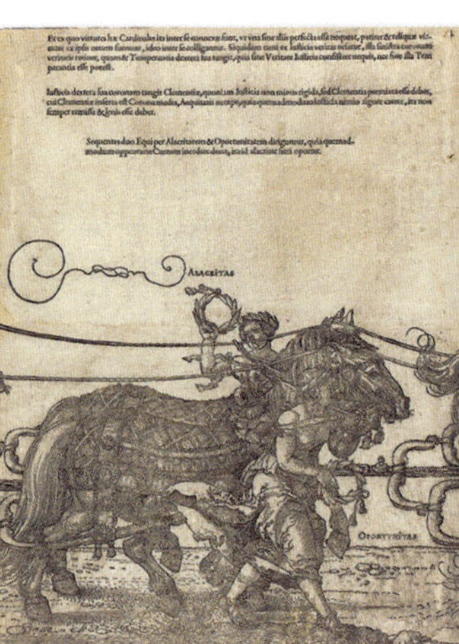

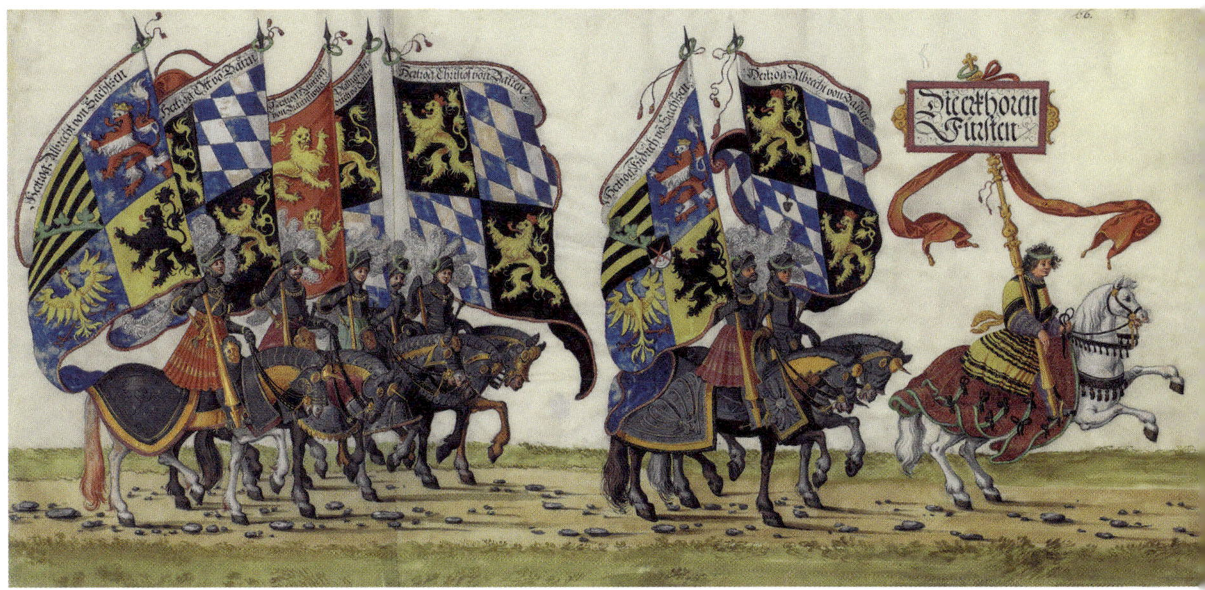

while the *Carriage* is 0.46m (1½ft) high and 2.4m (8ft) long. The cavalcade of woodcut prints, of which 139 are known to have existed, that form the *Procession*, however, runs to a phenomenal 54m (177ft) in length, one of the largest prints ever made.

Maximilian would not live to see the completion of his opulent posterity project. Death took him in 1519, following a morbid depression that had led him to insist on spending his final five years taking a coffin with him everywhere he went. The *Triumphal Procession* was eventually published and distributed in 1526, a vibrant propagandistic victory in its imperial architect's design to secure a lasting legacy.

Below: The Great Triumphal Carriage *(1522) by Albrecht Dürer, composed of eight separate woodblock prints.*

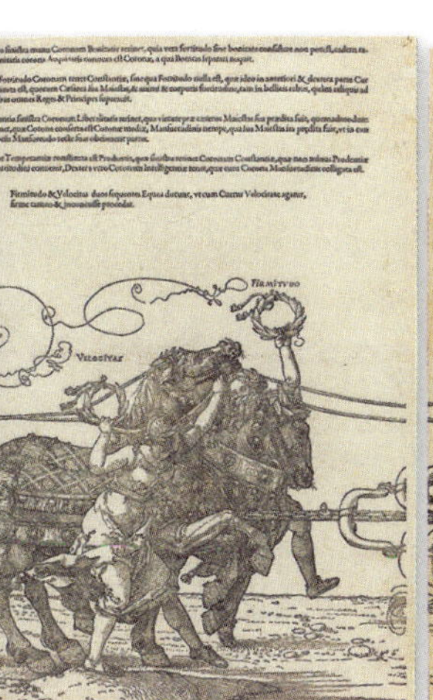

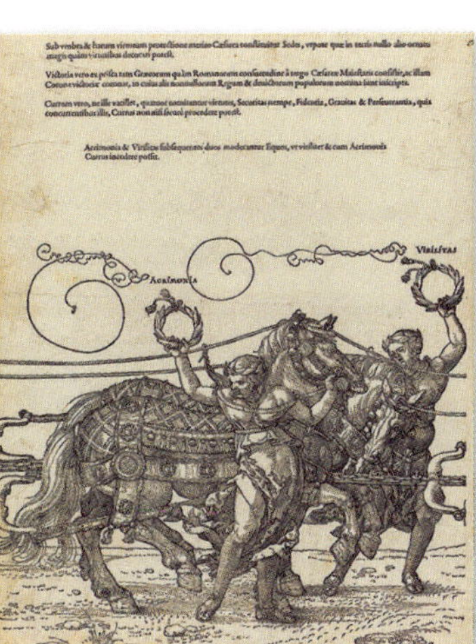

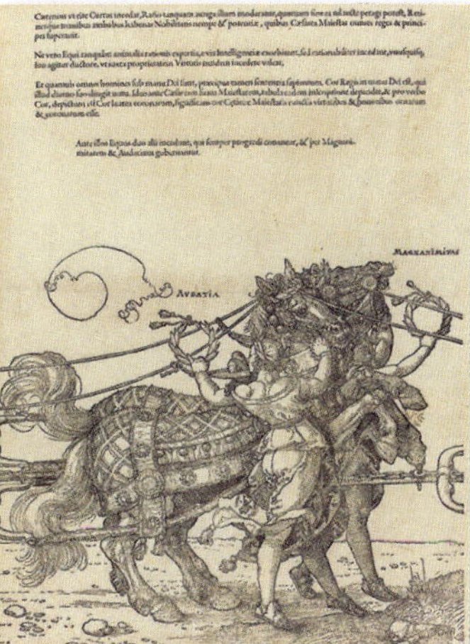

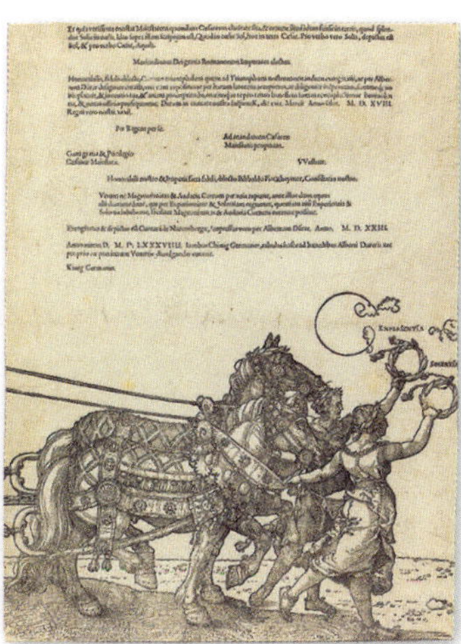

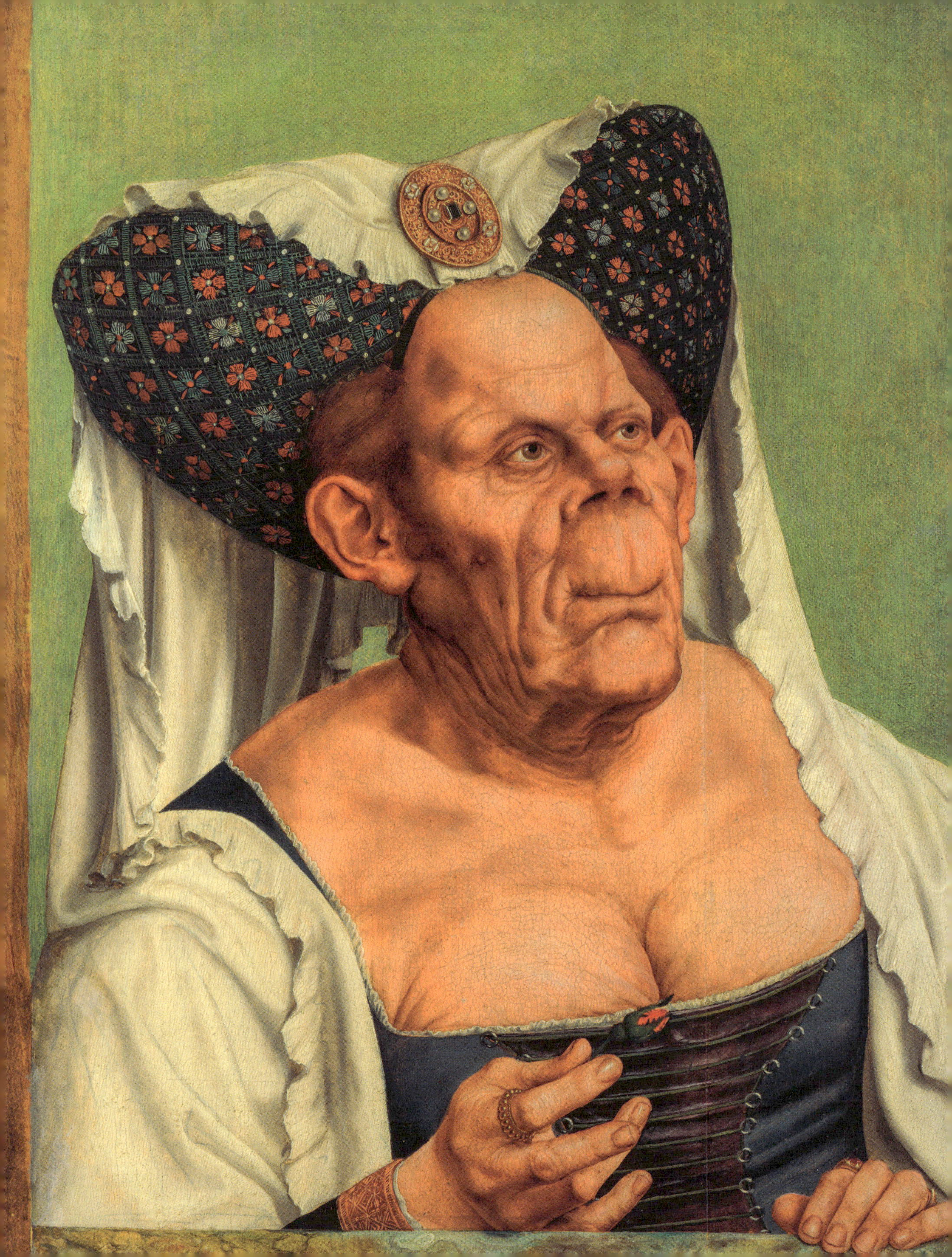

THE UGLY DUCHESS (*c*.1513), QUENTIN MATSYS

'Beauty belongs to the sphere of the simple, the ordinary, whilst ugliness is something extraordinary,' once wrote the Marquis de Sade (1740-1814), who knew a thing or two about peculiarity. 'There is no question but that every ardent imagination prefers in lubricity the extraordinary to the commonplace.' It is difficult to think of a more strangely beautiful study of ugliness in Western art than the painting known as *The Ugly Duchess*, or *An Old Woman* by the Flemish artist Quentin Matsys (1466-1530), which for years has stolen the attention of visitors to London's National Gallery away from many of the more conventionally attractive works hanging on the walls. It is offered as a kind of anti-portrait – who would commission such a painting? At first glance one is both repelled and pulled in by this cartoonish grotesque, and it is only upon surrendering to the latter instinct that one finds there is more exquisite detail and story than than it initially appears.

The first question is: who, or what, are we looking at, exactly? The apparently toothless old woman has striking, animalistic facial features: the large, protruding ears; the beady eyes; the masculine jaw, hairline and brow; the long, ape-like upper lip and shortened nostrils; the hairy warts and emphatic wrinkles. These are contrasted by her rich aristocratic costume, and the equally luxurious artistic effort involved in its depiction: the gold rings on her fingers, the beautifully stitched horned headpiece held in place with a diamond-and-pearl-set gold brooch, rendered using the painstaking *sgraffito* technique in which one scratches into the surface layer of paint to reveal contrasting colours beneath. (The same technique is evident in the minuscule embroidery of her sleeve.) The elegant flowing material falls delicately about her broad, hunched shoulders, and about the corset and neckline, both of a style more commonly worn by younger women.

And this is, of course, the satirical pointedness of both this work and the accompanying piece *Portrait of an Old Man* on page 90 (though, let's be honest, to a much kinder extent in the latter). Matsys mocks the vanity of material culture, and its participants who refuse to acknowledge the fading of the bloom of their rose and continue to dress – to borrow a crude modern phrase – like 'mutton dressed as lamb'. The point is really hammered home with the juxtaposition of a young budding rose held between thumb and forefinger in front of her wrinkled bosom. The moral? Accept yourself as you are, warts and all.

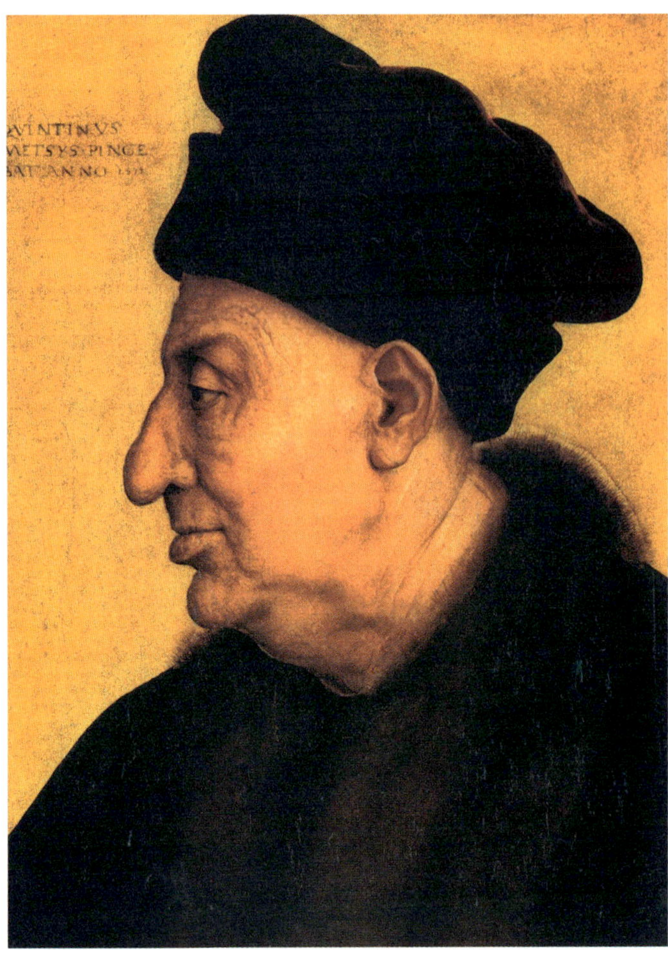

Portrait of an Old Man*, the lesser known 'partner' painting, which bears a striking resemblance to a portrait of Philip the Bold, Duke of Burgundy.*

But perhaps there is more to it. While this is the widely accepted interpretation, the curious nature of the work has inspired readings from other perspectives. Michael Baum, professor emeritus of surgery at University College London, has for years claimed to have found conclusive indications that the woman in the portrait is suffering from Paget's disease, a chronic disease of the skeleton, which causes bones to form abnormally large and irregular shapes. To add to this, a separate modern discovery was made on the originality of the painting. It was assumed that Matsys had copied the design of the work from *The Bust of a Grotesque Old Woman*, a work drawn either by Leonardo da Vinci or one of his apprentices, produced at around the same time. (Da Vinci made a number of grotesque sketches and it's thought that he and Matsys exchanged works.) However, technical analysis with infrared reflectograms revealed a great deal of underdrawing, with several changes made to the face and the hands in different poses, apparently proving the Matsys to be the original.

So was *The Ugly Duchess* based on a real person, and if so were they afflicted with Paget's? One school of thought is that the painting is a historical rumour made manifest, perhaps based on Margaret, Countess of Tyrol (1318-69), who was pejoratively nicknamed 'the She-Wolf of the Tyrol', 'the Ugly Duchess' and *Maultasch* (bag-mouth, meaning whore or vicious woman) in savage ecclesiastical propaganda of the time, critical of her divorce and remarriage. Contemporary chroniclers like

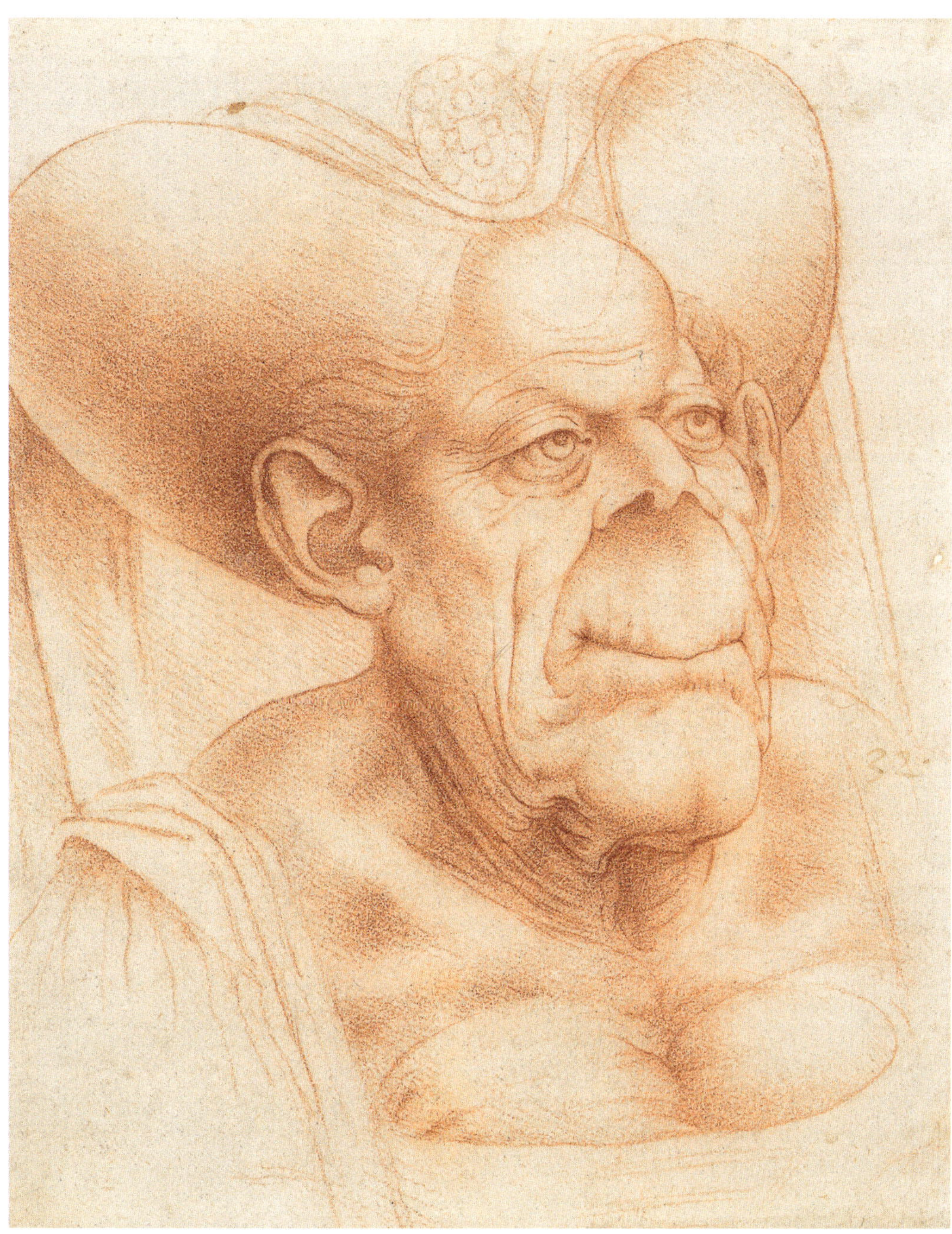

The Bust of a Grotesque Old Woman (c.*1510-20), after Leonardo da Vinci.*

John of Winterthur (*c.*1300-after 1348) actually describe her as exceptionally beautiful, but thanks to a lack of contemporary portraiture the *Maultasch* insult led to the assumption that Margaret was physically deformed. Poor Margaret was slapped with the historical reputation as the ugliest woman who had ever lived, and so perhaps it's this misogyny that is the ugliness we see in the painting.

ST CHRISTOPHER DOG-HEAD
(SIXTEENTH-EIGHTEENTH CENTURIES)

Surely one of the most instantly fascinating images of all Christian religious iconography is the Eastern Orthodox portrayal of St Christopher, patron saint of travellers and, as he is illustrated here, towering military warrior with the head of a dog. Christopher is traditionally venerated by several Christian denominations as a martyr killed sometime during either the reign of the Roman emperor Decius (r. 249-51) or Emperor Maximinus Daia (r. 305-13), and by the seventh century European churches and monasteries dedicated to his name began to appear.

So why the noticeably canine appearance of Christopher Dog-head? At the time it was believed that such men existed. Eastern Orthodox tradition holds that the production of Christian icons dates all the way back to the birth of the universe. The paintings are commonly inscribed with their date of production as being Creation, which in the tradition was believed to have taken place 7000 years ago. While not quite that old, the widely held medieval belief in a foreign race of dog-headed men living somewhere at the edge of the world goes back to antiquity. (Likely it has its roots in sightings of baboons, though it has also been suggested that the dog-headed confusion may have been contributed to by a misreading of the Latin term *Cananeus* (Canaanite) as *caninus* (canine).)

Describing Libya in his *Histories* (4. 191. 3) of 430 BC, Herodotus wrote: 'In that country are… the Dog-headed and the Headless men who have their eyes in their chests, as the Libyans say, and the wild men and women…' Other early accounts locate dog-headed men in India. According to a story by the Greek historian Ctesias, their population numbered around 120,000. Gaius Julius Solinus (*fl.* early third century) also writes of the dog-headed Simeans of Ethiopia, who were ruled by a canine king. This was the accepted knowledge of the time.

With that primer the legends of St Christopher flourished. The medieval *Irish Passion of St Christopher* reports that 'this Christopher was one of the Dog-heads, a race that had the heads of dogs and ate human flesh'. This was confirmed by the German bishop and poet Walter of Speyer (967-1027). There is also a hagiographic narrative of a man named Reprebus (the scoundrel) in the reign of the emperor Diocletian, who was

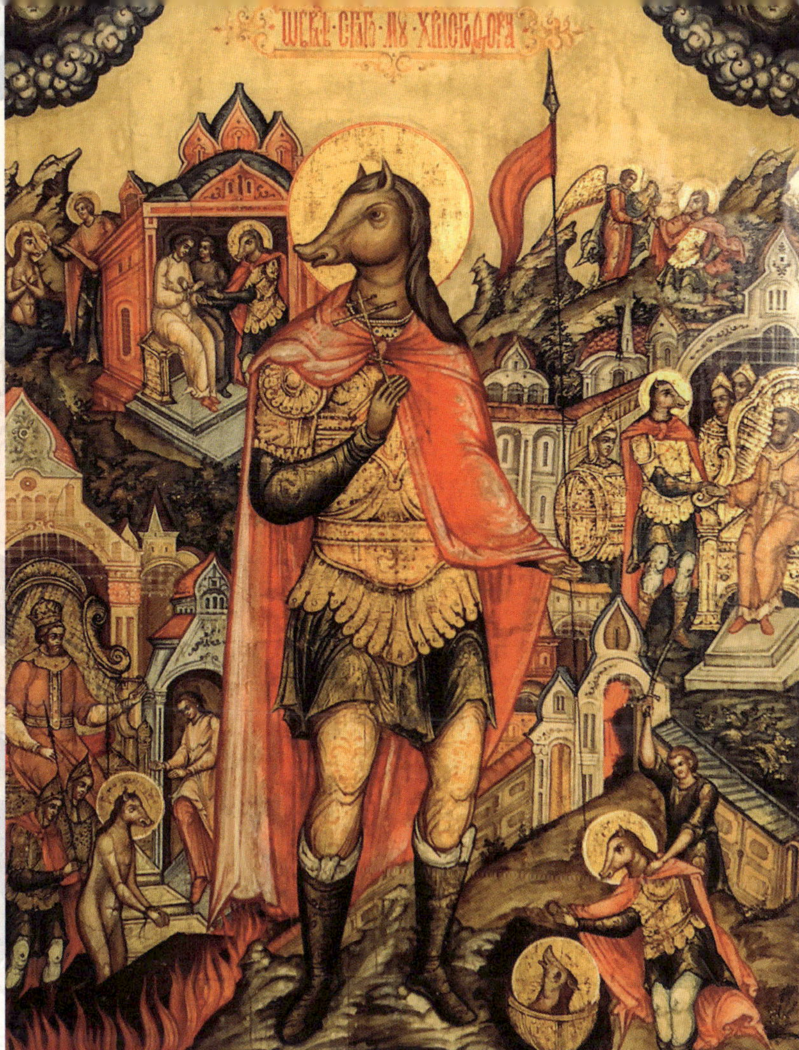

An eighteenth-century Russian icon of the dog-headed St Christopher.

taken prisoner by Roman soldiers battling tribes to the west of Egypt in Cyrenaica. Reprebus, who is described as being of enormous size with the head of a dog, was press-ganged into joining the Roman *numerus Marmaritarum* (Unit of the Marmaritae), a platoon of werewolf-like soldiers. When he and his unit were transferred to Syrian Antioch, Bishop Peter of Attalia baptised him Christopher. He was martyred there in 308.

Since 1722, under the modernist reign of Peter the Great, the 'Holy Synod' banned the depiction of Christopher Dog-head in Russian icons, but this was commonly ignored in everyday practice, particularly by the Old Believers who maintained the tradition. An eighteenth-century Russian painters' manual gives instructions as to how to form his image: 'A dog's head, in armour, in the hand a cross and in the other a sword in sheath; outer robe cinnabar with white, under green…' Today, icons of the dog-headed saint are much sought-after by collectors.

OTHER CHRISTIAN CURIOSITIES

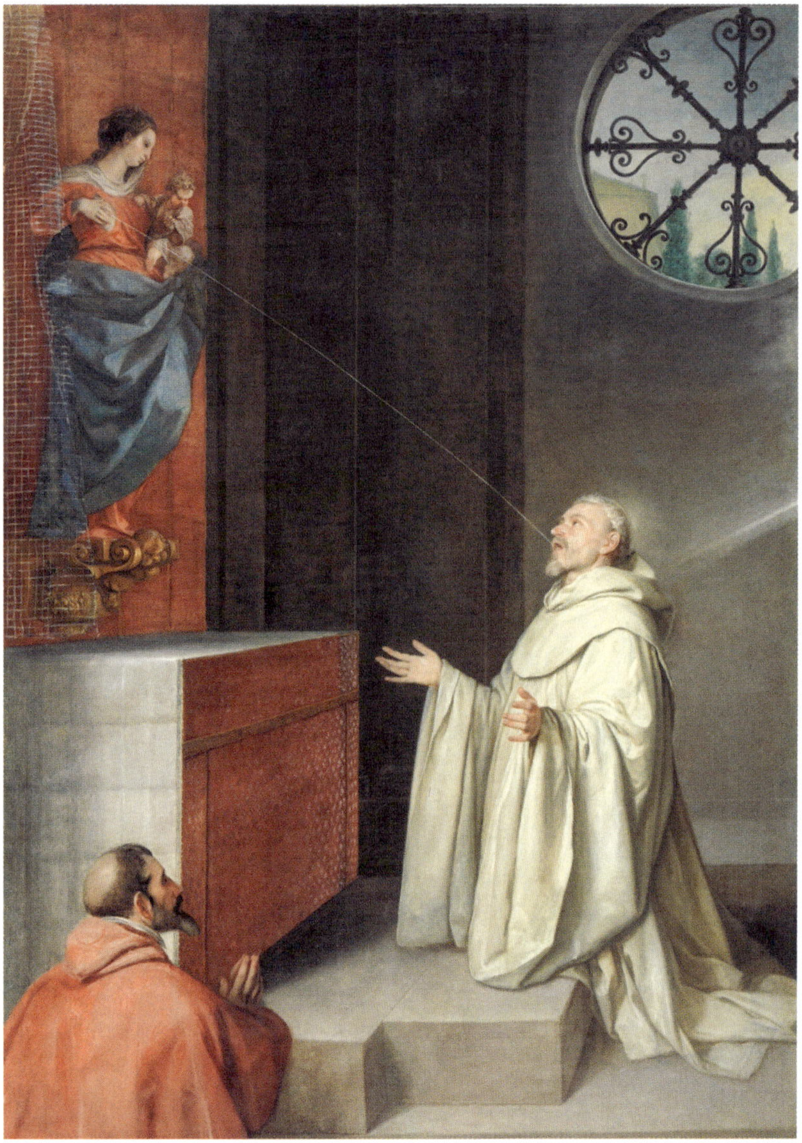

OPPOSITE TOP LEFT: *Jean Bourdichon's illustration from the* Book of Hours for Use of Parisians (c.*1475-1500) of St Denis of Paris. The third-century Christian martyr was beheaded by sword on orders of the Roman governor. St Denis is said to have then picked up his head and walked for several kilometres while preaching a sermon along the way.*

ABOVE: *In* The Miraculous Lactation of St Bernard *(1645-52) Alonso Cano depicts the moment when the twelfth-century St Bernard received a miraculous stream of milk from a statue of the Virgin and Child.*

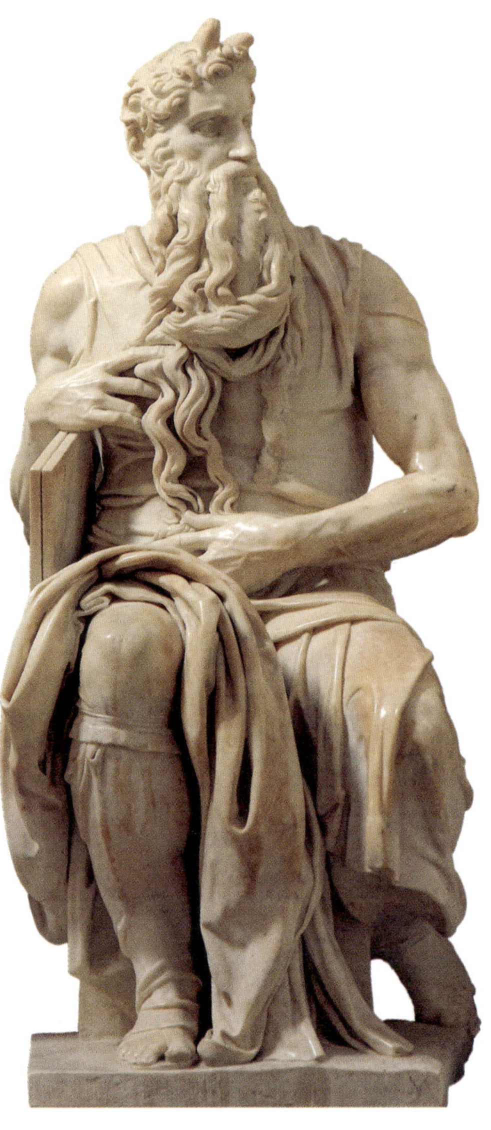

RIGHT: *In Michelangelo's sculpture* Moses, *and in iconographic tradition, the biblical figure Moses is sometimes depicted with horns. This stems from a mistranslation by St Jerome when writing the Vulgate Bible from earlier Hebrew manuscripts, confusing the word for 'shining' or 'emitting rays' with 'horned'.*

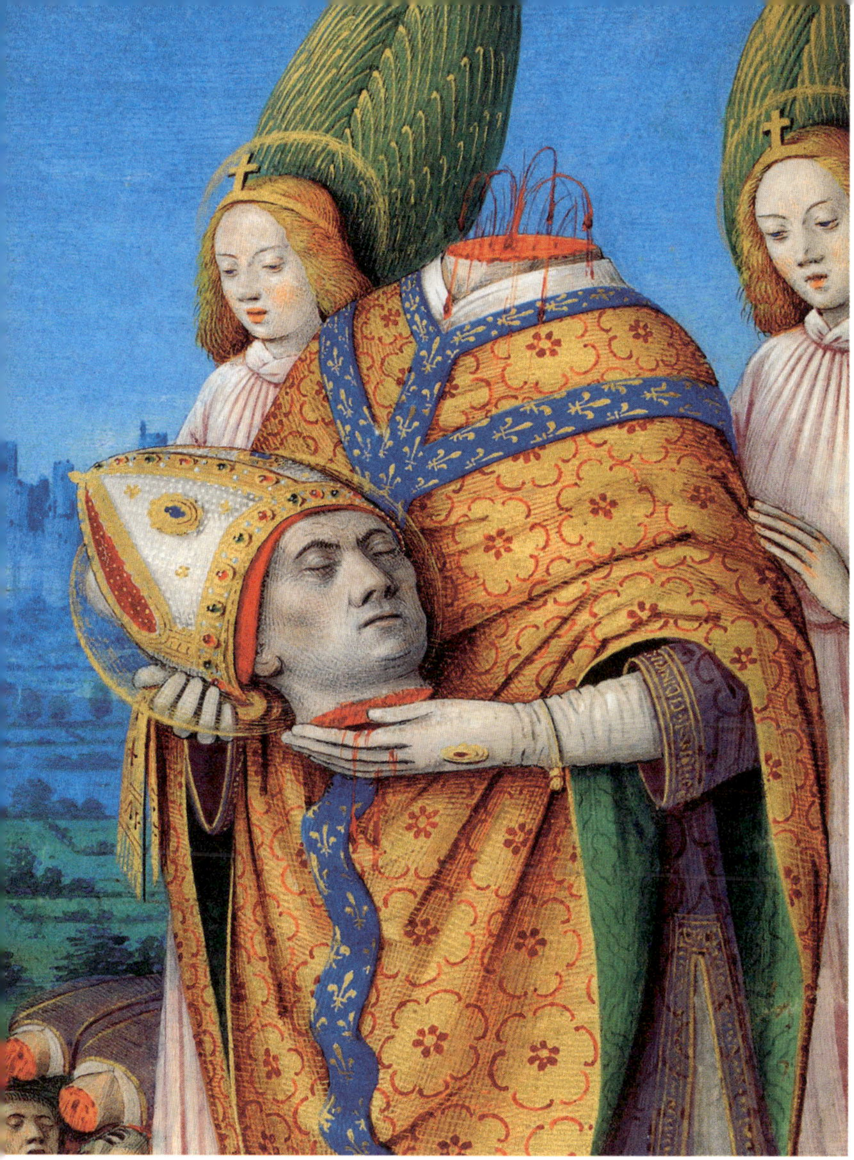

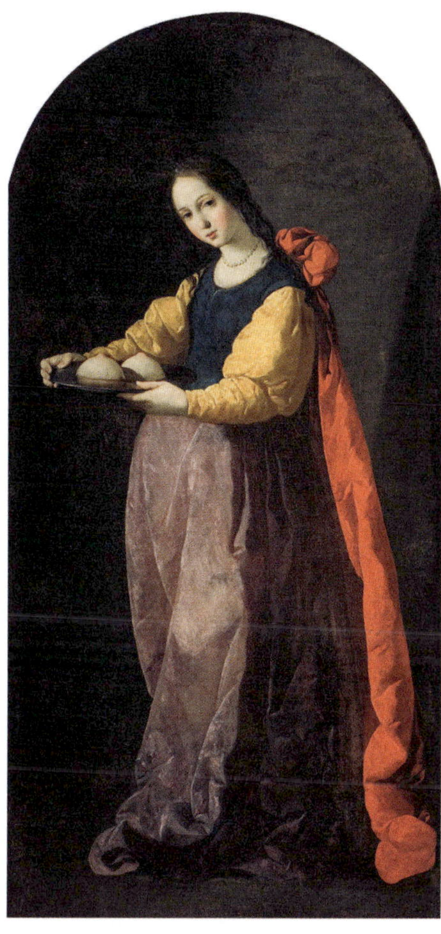

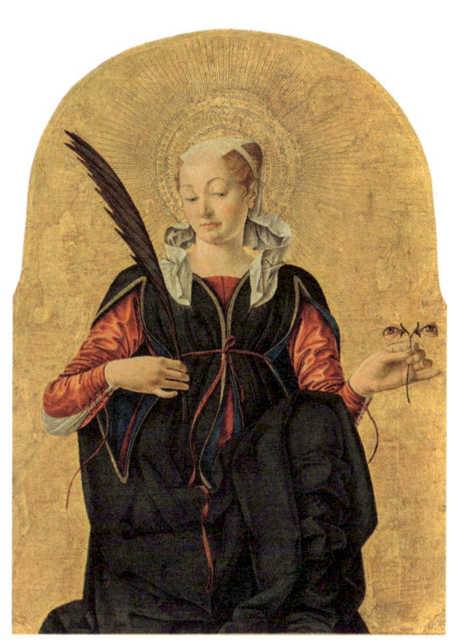

RIGHT TOP: *According to the thirteenth-century collection of hagiographies known as the Golden Legend, St Agatha of Sicily was tortured after spurning the advances of Roman prefect Quintianus, who ordered her to be stretched on the rack, burnt with torches and for her breasts to be excised with pincers. She is often depicted contemplating the breasts on a platter, as shown in this 1630-33 work by Francisco de Zurbarán.*

RIGHT BOTTOM: *Francesco del Cossa's altarpiece panel St Lucy (c.1473-4). In medieval accounts St Lucia of Syracuse (283-304), who was killed during the great Diocletianic Persecution of Christians, was first tortured by having her eyes gouged out. She is therefore often shown holding up the eyes on a stem in Renaissance art.*

FOOL'S CAP MAP OF THE WORLD (*c.*1580-90)

A characteristic common to the historical curiosities collected in this book is a strangeness that lends the work an anachronistic feel – it can appear so unusual that at first one suspects it must be a modern hoax or forgery. The *Fool's Cap Map of The World*, with its startling appearance, certainly qualifies. It is almost as if we are staring into the reflective visor of an astronaut, viewing the Earth from space, or into the face of some sinister inscrutable creature. It is amazing to think that this image was published in or just after the year 1580. The exact date is unknown, as is the artist, the country of origin and the motive, making this map the strangest mystery in the history of cartographic art.

In it, the figure is clothed in the dress of a court jester, complete with bells on his flopping donkey-like ears, and the traditional parodic sceptre. The artist has completely replaced, or covered, the face with a cordiform (heart-shaped) world map, a stretched, spherical projection that lends the image a more threatening, three-dimensional feel. This appears to be in imitation of the cordiform style employed by the great cartographers Oronce Finé, Gerard Mercator and Abraham Ortelius.

There have been different interpretations as to the meaning of the *Fool's Cap Map of The World*, but all are based on the factor suggested by the use of the jester: mockery. The late sixteenth century was the golden era of European exploration, missions of global intelligence-gathering that often tipped into vainglorious obsession. Just as *memento mori* artworks serve to remind us of our mortality, so *vanitas* artworks remind us of the worthlessness of earthly pursuits, pleasures and treasures within this mortality. Perhaps that is the nature of *The Fool's Cap Map of The World* – a *vanitas* map that lampoons modernity (and its heralds, the explorers and mapmakers), satirising the contemporary rapacity for land and gold that defines the period and making the ultimate point that, in the words of Robert Burton in *The Anatomy of Melancholy* (1621), 'all the world is mad'.

This point is hammered home by the scattering of quotes around the image: 'Vanity of vanities, all is vanity' reads the quote from Ecclesiastes on the fool's sceptre. 'O head, worthy of a dose of hellebore' translates the inscription on the fool's cap (hellebore being a poisonous flower historically used in the

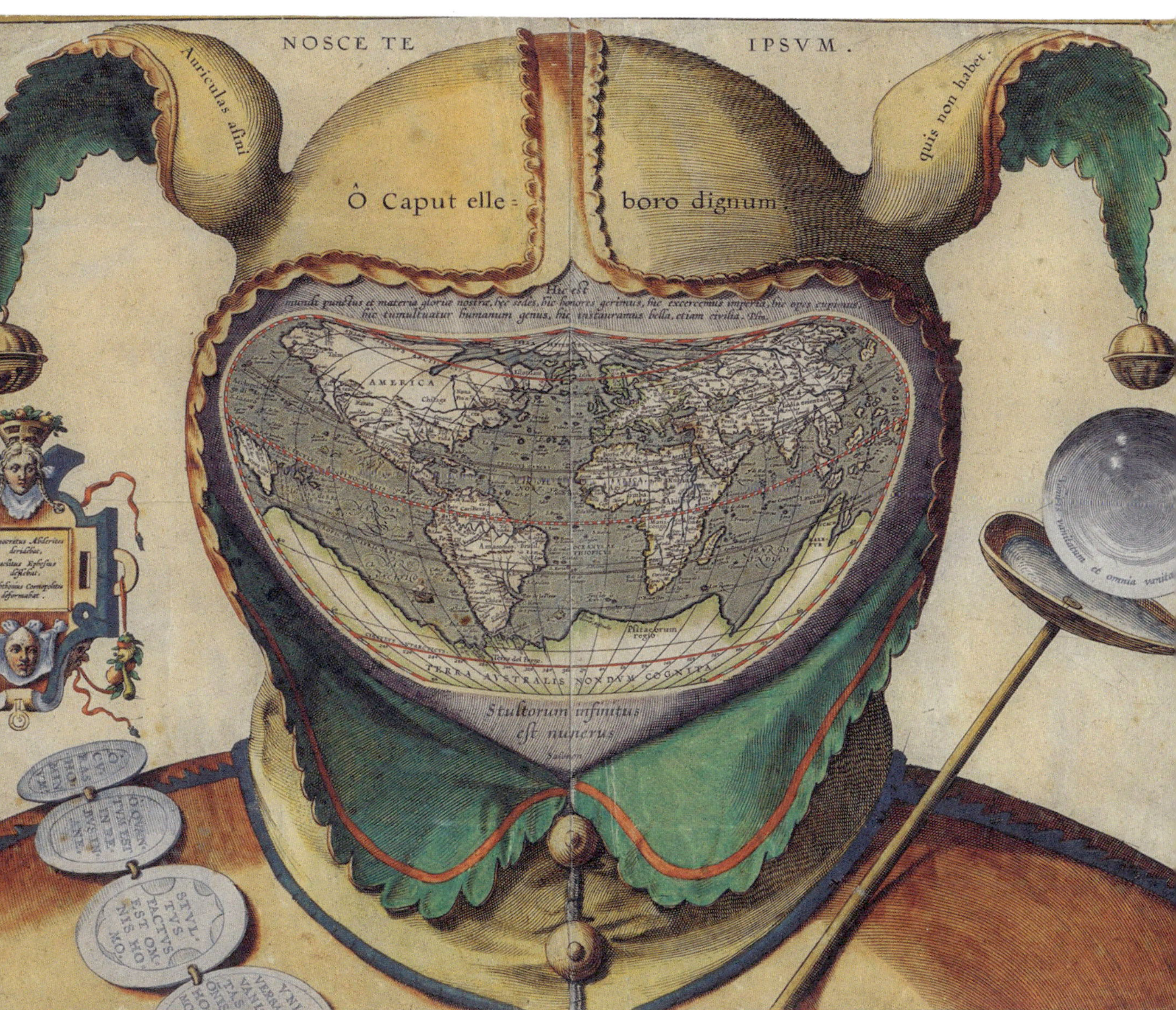

treatment of madness). And, 'Who doesn't have donkey's ears?' reads the quote on the ears, a quip of the first-century Roman philosopher Lucius Annaeus Cornutus. Whatever the shape of this world and wherever its boundaries, the artist declares, we would do well to remember we live in a land of fools.

THE COMPOSITE ART OF ARCIMBOLDO (1563-*c.*1590)

'A triumph of abstract art in the sixteenth century' is how the Austrian art historian and dealer Benno Geiger (1882-1965) once declared the work of the Italian painter Giuseppe Arcimboldo (*c.*1526-93). As portraits go, his *Vertumnus* (*c.*1590), shown opposite, is strange enough even before we take into account the fact that this is an imperial portrait, depicting his patron Rudolf II (1552-1612), Holy Roman Emperor. One might assume that rendering a likeness of the most powerful figure in the land by cobbling it together with foodstuffs was a dangerously unflattering technique, but in this case the composition of fruit and vegetables is a high compliment. Rudolf is here portrayed as the Roman god of the seasons, built from the food of each time of year and so imbued with a godly harmoniousness with nature's power. This symbolised the flourishing artistic and intellectual fecundity under his rule, a public relations broadcast to help remedy Rudolf's unpopularity at the time.

Though it is this style of personification through assemblages of objects – natural and otherwise – by which Arcimboldo is best known, it only emerged after traditional beginnings. Having begun his career designing stained glass and murals for cathedrals, Arcimboldo was appointed court portraitist to Ferdinand I (1503-64) in 1562, and the following year produced the conventional portrait *Maximilian II, His Wife and Three Children*. That same year he had an epiphany that would plunge him headlong into his full Mannerist style (a term that often defies simple definition but was essentially a rebellious movement away from Renaissance classicism through experimentation with tradition and proportion). Arcimboldo revealed his *Four Seasons* series, in which each season is personified as a human figure composed of nature's produce. Spring is a woman with blossom skin, Summer is made of bright fruit, Autumn is a man with a broken barrel for a body, while Winter is a man made of tree stump and bark. Arcimboldo later followed this with a similar portrait series drawing on the *Four Elements*, commissioned in 1566 by Holy Roman Emperor Maximilian II.

Arcimboldo's traditional works have been all but forgotten, but his personifications were, are and always will be fascinating. While critics over the years have wondered if

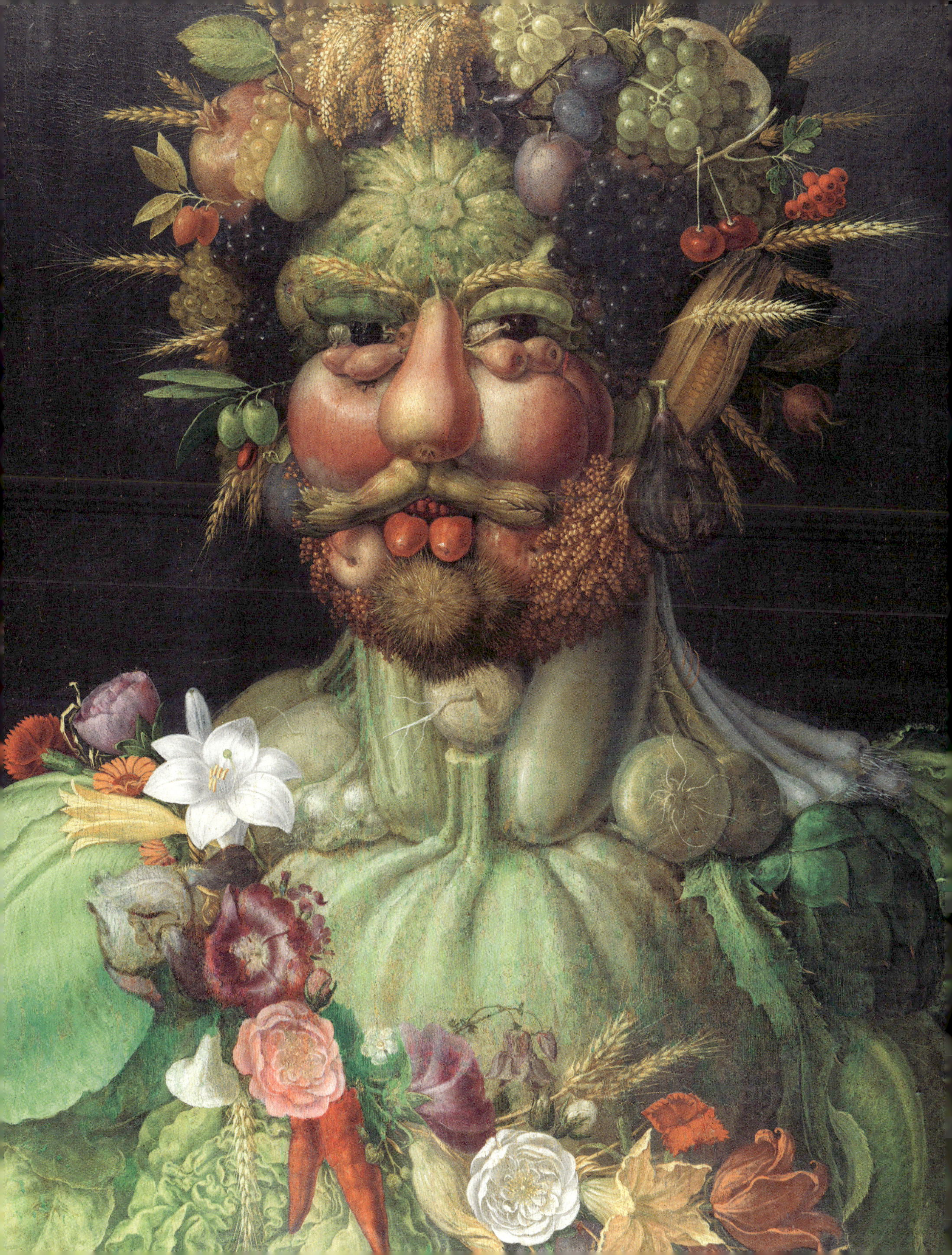

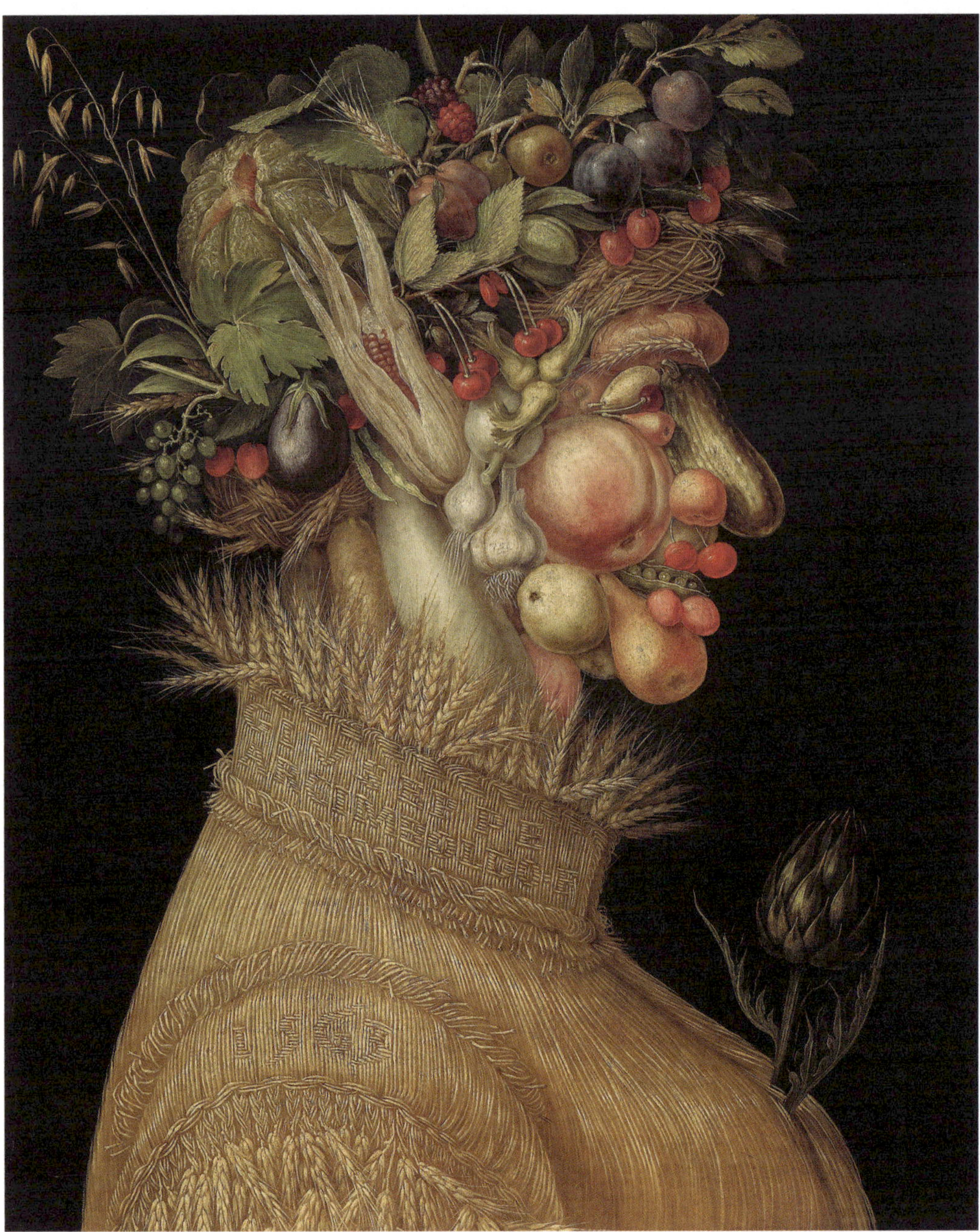

they were perhaps the product of a mentally disturbed mind, it seems clear that they are compositions of wonderful humour and playfulness, woven with flattering symbolism. With wit Arcimboldo captures the Renaissance fascination with riddles and puzzles, and the curiosity-cabinet owner's passion for collecting the bizarre; indeed many of his works were featured prominently in the *Wunderkammer* (wonder room) collection of Rudolf II.

ABOVE: Summer *(1563) by Giuseppe Arcimboldo. His signature and the date are gently woven into the straw.*

OPPOSITE: Fire *(1566) from Arcimboldo's* Four Elements *series.*

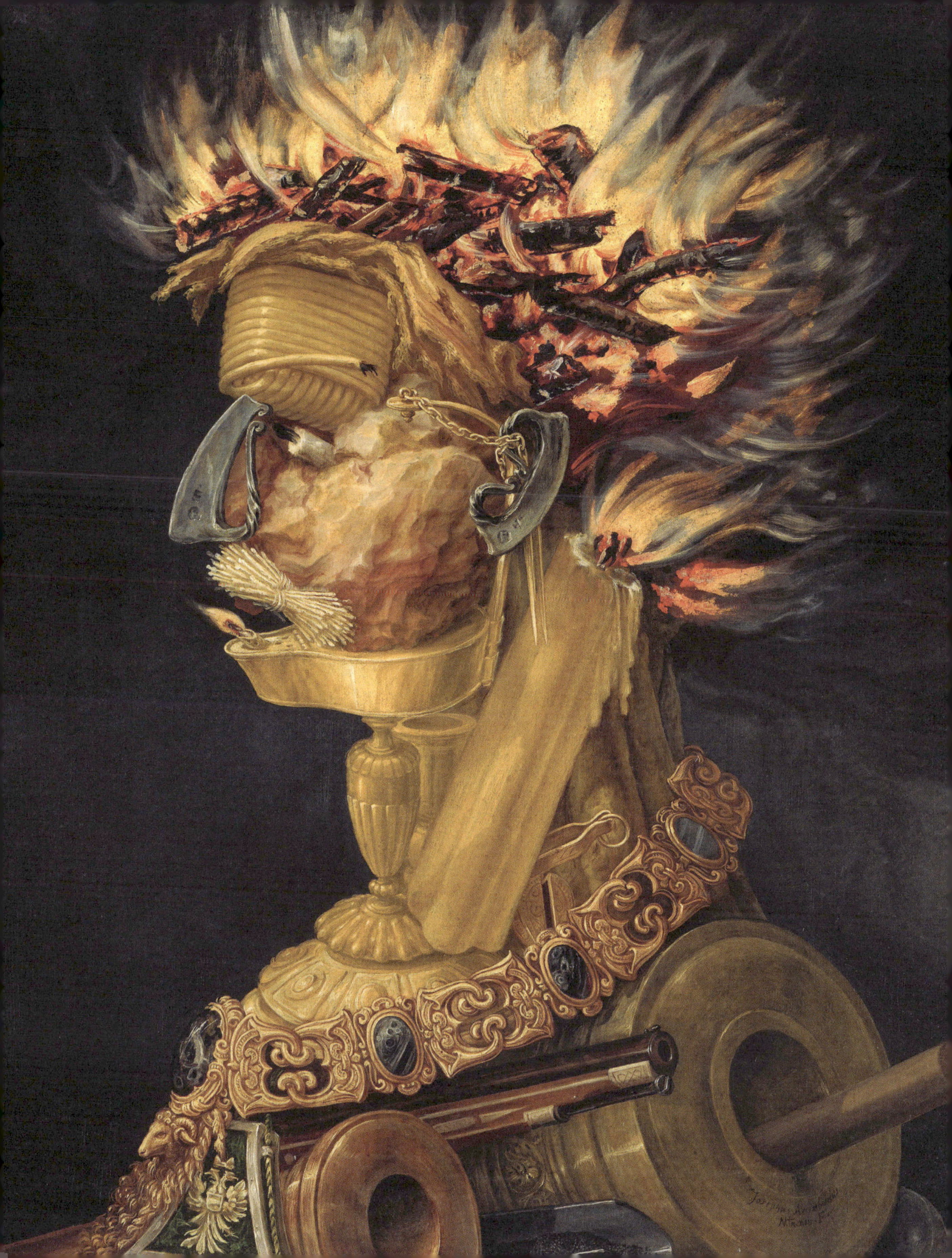

GABRIELLE D'ESTRÉES AND ONE OF HER SISTERS (*c.*1594)

Gabrielle d'Estrées (1573-99), mistress and most trusted adviser to King Henri IV of France and mother of three of his children, sits in a bathtub with her sister the Duchess of Villars delicately squeezing her nipple with fingers in a c-shaped pincer. The two women, painted with achingly pale porcelain flesh by an unknown artist apparently under the influence of the Flemish style, stare directly at the viewer, unabashed, the heavy red curtains pulled aside to reveal the intimacy of the startling scene as if the two are on stage. There are other symbols to take in: the gold ring in the fingers of Gabrielle's left hand; the painting in the background of a woman in a red dress, stitching material; the painting in the background of *that* painting, showing the lower half of a naked male figure, his modesty barely protected by a strip of red fabric.

The unknown artist is thought to be of the second period of the Fontainebleau School, when a group of Flemish and French painters were invited by King Henri IV (1553-1610) on his accession to the throne to help decorate the previously abandoned Palace of Fontainebleau (located 55km/34 miles southeast of the centre of Paris). Many of the works, rich with encoded symbols, are now lost, but were dramatic tableaux of fictional and mythological scenes inspired by Italian and ancient Greek literature, often galvanised with erotic charge. Indeed *Gabrielle d'Estrées and One of Her Sisters*, which hangs in the Louvre, has traditionally been interpreted as a scene of almost overwhelming erotica. More recently, though, has emerged the now-leading interpretation that it is an announcement, made by the pinching sister, of Gabrielle's pregnancy with Henri's illegitimate son. The fingers that grip the nipple point to her fertility; the woman in the background apparently sewing baby's clothes. This does not, of course, preclude the simultaneous sexualised intent of the artist in portraying a mistress stripped in company.

The French historian Pierre de Bourdeille (*c.*1540-1614) reported seeing a group visit the painting, one of whom was so overcome upon viewing it that she seized her companion and hurried away to make love, with the words: 'Let us now straightway take [my] coach and go to my lodging; for… no more can I hold in the ardor that is in me. Needs must away and quench it; too sore do I burn.'

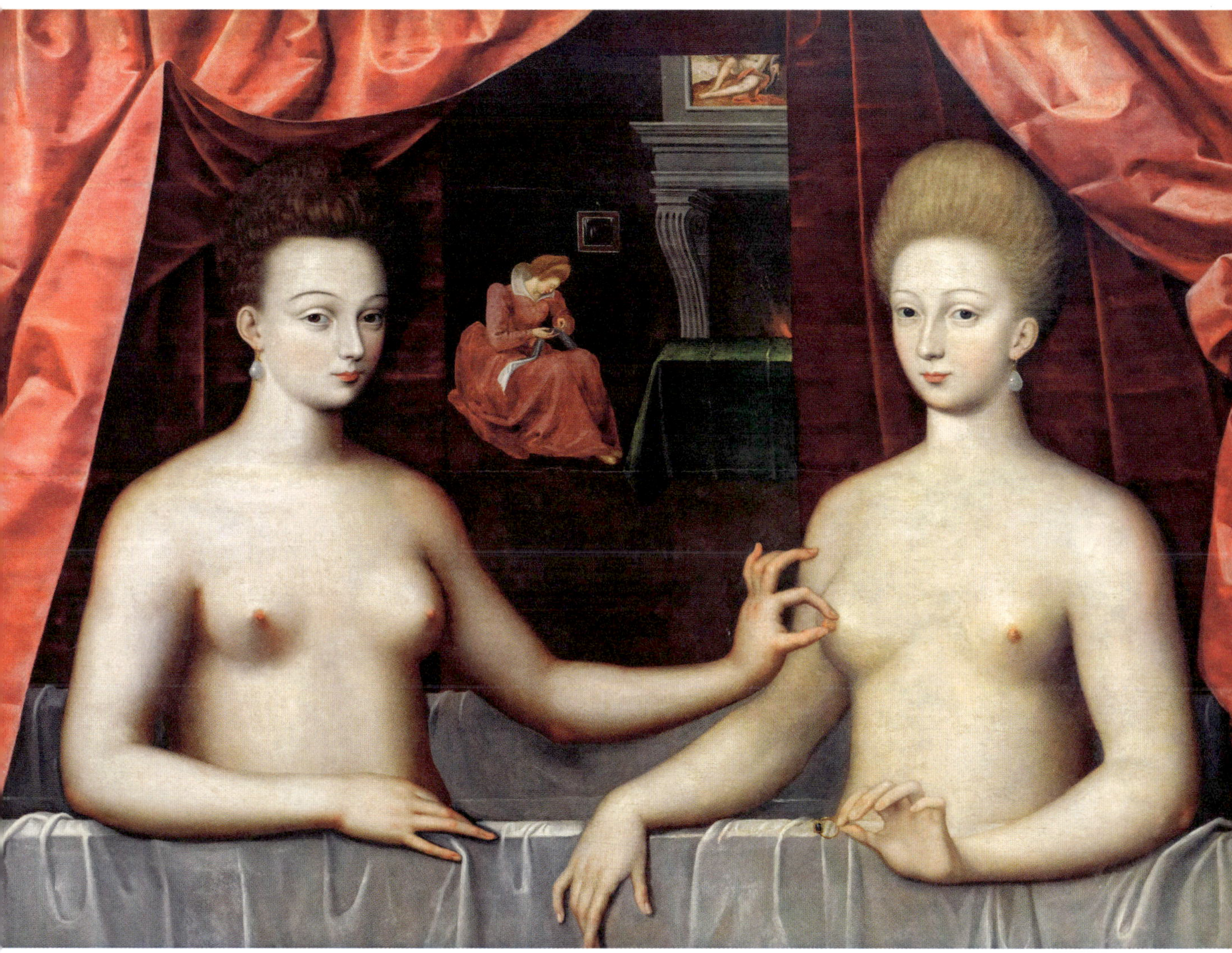

In the early nineteenth century *Gabrielle d'Estrées and One of Her Sisters* was hung in the Prefecture of Police in Paris but was so distracting that it was covered with a green curtain. When preparations were later being made for an upcoming civic function with an artistic crowd, it was thought a good idea to have the painting cleaned to have on display. But when the curtain was drawn back, all that was found was an empty frame – the Sapphic scene had at some point even overwhelmed a police station employee to the point of lustful theft, and it was returned only much later.

Presumed portrait of Gabrielle d'Estrees and her sister the Duchess of Villars.

THE LEGEND OF THE BAKER OF EEKLO (*c.*1550-1650), AFTER CORNELIS VAN DALEM

It's a question we've all asked ourselves at one time or another: if I was to have my head lopped off and baked in an oven, which vegetable should I temporarily replace it with? Little is known about Cornelis van Dalem (*c.*1530 - *c.*1573), a Flemish painter working in Antwerp. The son of a wealthy Tholen nobleman, van Dalem's principal occupation was as a cloth merchant, and despite his many contributions to the landscape art of the Low Countries he remained an amateur, painting purely for enjoyment. The startling work shown here is a whimsical veer away from his usual pastoral and farmhouse scenes, a collaboration with fellow Flemish artist Jan van Wechelen (*c.*1530-70) depicting a scene of a popular legend known as 'the baker of Eeklo'. This example is in the collection of the Rijksmuseum, Amsterdam, a copy of the lost original, produced sometime between *c.*1550 and 1650, but a number of other contemporary examples attributed to the artists' circle are known to exist.

Legends from the Middles Ages of rejuvenation by drinking magical elixirs of eternal life or bathing in the Fountain of Youth are well known but more obscure is this magical cabbage-filled bakery. The story goes that in Eeklo, a Belgian municipality in the Flemish province of East Flanders, townsfolk who wished to improve their looks would seek not the doctor but the village baker. In *The Legend of the Baker of Eeklo*, we can watch the entire process: with the help of his apprentices, the baker would decapitate his customers and stem the bleeding by planting cabbages atop their necks. (Cabbages were traditionally associated with medical use, but also in vernacular colloquialisms were associated with madness and stupidity – their use here is therefore a warning against vanity.)

The unsightly heads would then be reshaped and finished with a beautiful glaze and returned to the body. It was not a process without risk of failure, however – the woman in the background wielding a man's severed head is in discussion with the baker, apparently complaining about the remaining ugliness of her husband's new head. It was crucial, the legend warned, that the head was baked for the exact right amount of time: too long in the oven and the person would suffer a hot temper; too short and they would come out foolish and prone to 'half-baked' ideas.

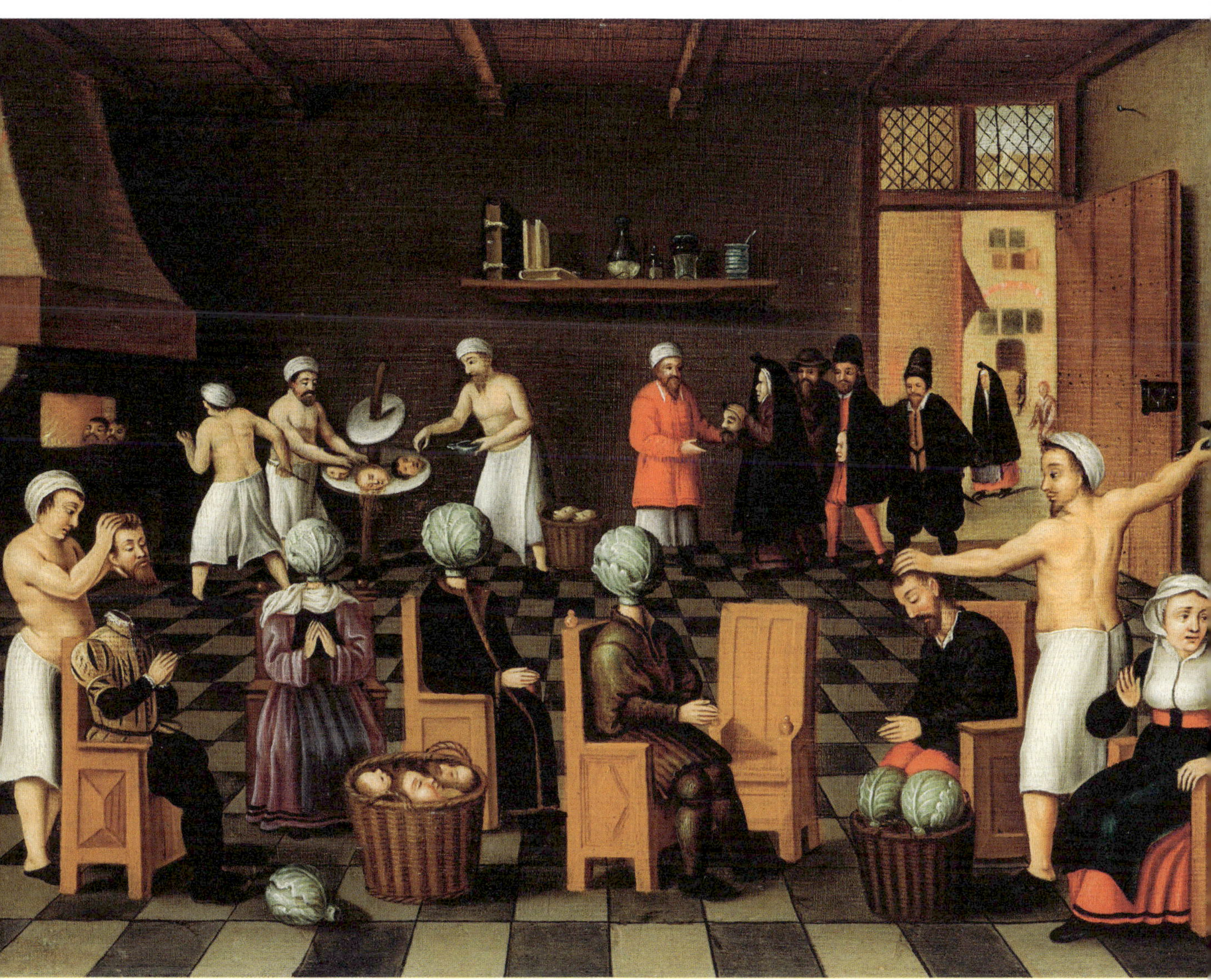

The Legend of the Baker of Eeklo *(c.1550-1650), after Cornelis van Dalem*

MAN CONSUMED BY FLAMES
(1600-10), ISAAC OLIVER

A man is engulfed in fire and yet, like the legendary salamander of antiquity, he is untouched by the flames that dance around him. His cool expression and the absence of a single singed hair suggest him to be wholly unfazed by his situation. Around his head curl the words *Alget, qui non ardet* (He grows cold, who does not burn). But who is this perpetually burning man, and how did he find himself in this predicament?

Isaac Oliver's (*c*.1556-1617) highly detailed miniature portrait, which in its frame measures just 5.2 × 4.4cm (2 × 1¾in), is perhaps the most intriguing example of the English Renaissance art of miniature portraiture. The tradition emerged from the techniques of manuscript illustrators, who would fashion complicated initials and vignettes of just a few centimetres in size. The word 'miniature' comes from the Latin word *miniare* (to colour with red lead) – a practice of manuscript scribes. In the minds of wealthy patrons, these small images would look even better as a luxury accessory worn around their necks or carried in pockets, as mementos, devotional objects and tokens of love and admiration given to family, friends or lovers for private contemplation, in contrast with larger paintings designed to be displayed.

Miniaturists, who from 1460 had been competing with the printed book and in need of business, were only too happy to oblige, despite the demands of the task. Possessing a steady hand was, of course, vital, as the artist had only two or three sittings to capture a likeness on a scrap of vellum about the size of a playing card. In fact, playing cards were often used to support the painting: a miniature portrait of Queen Elizabeth I (1533-1603) in the collection of the National Portrait Gallery, for example, has the Queen of Hearts wryly fixed to its reverse.

In the 1520s portrait miniatures began to appear at the French and English courts, often ceremoniously presented by monarchs as tokens of royal favour. In the circle of Elizabeth I in the 1580s, the wealthy wore her portrait as a display of allegiance. When James I ascended the English throne in 1603 the practice continued with artists like Isaac Oliver and, most

Below: *A self-portrait* c.*1450 by Jean Fouquet (1420-81). The earliest surviving portrait miniature and likely the earliest formal self-portrait.*

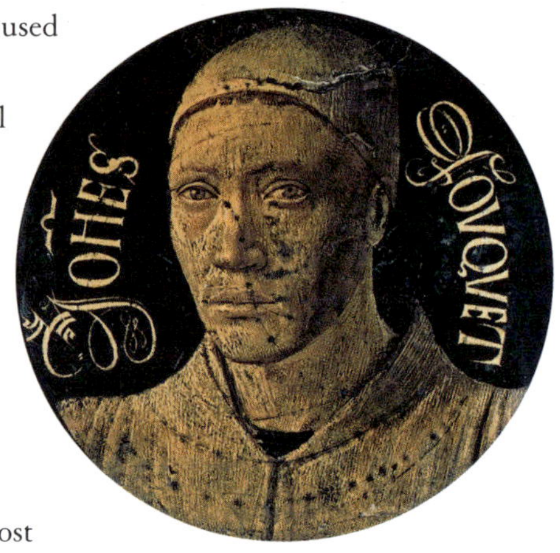

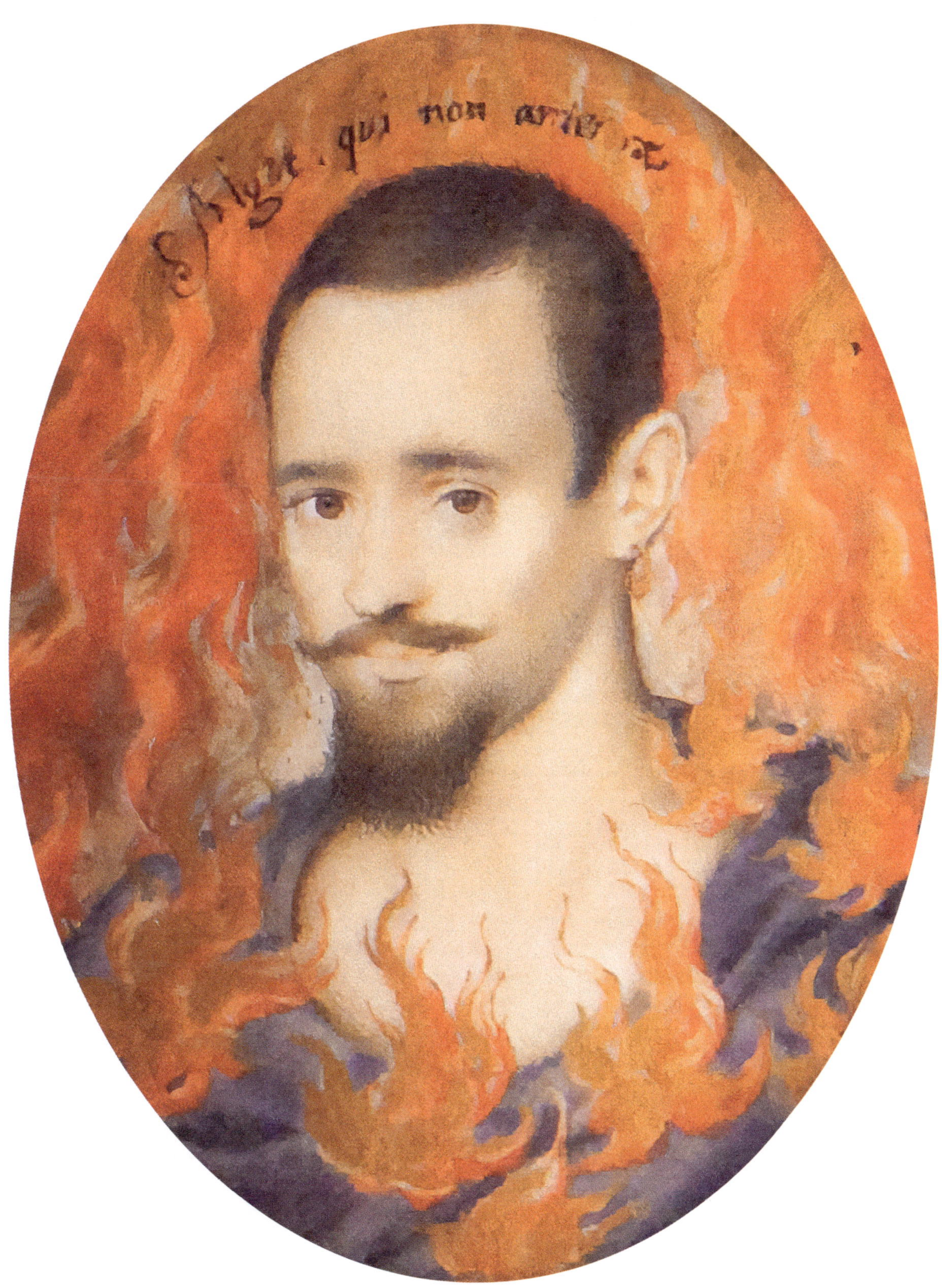

Man Consumed by Flames *(1600-10), Isaac Oliver*

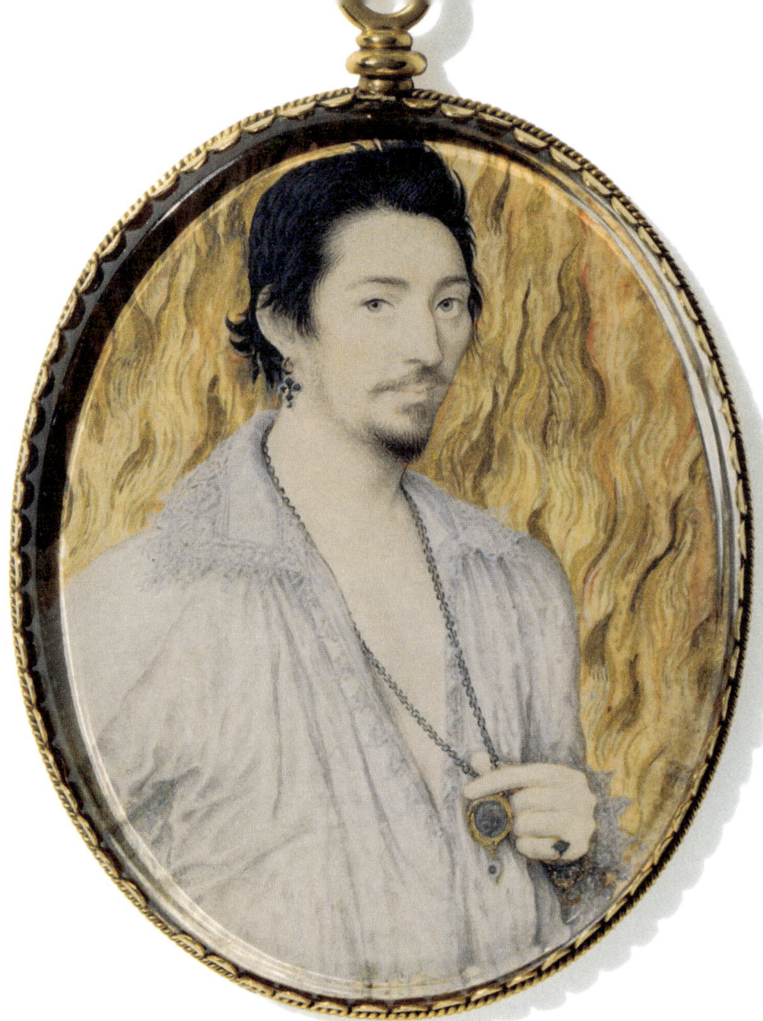

Left: Young Man Against Flames *(c.1600), Nicholas Hilliard. Thought to have been painted a few years earlier than Oliver's work, again the identity of the subject is unknown. The young man chivalrously turns towards his heart the picture box hanging around his neck to hide the image of the object of his devotion. The goal of the miniaturist, wrote Hilliard, was to capture 'those lovely graces, witty smilings and those stolen glances which suddenly like lightning pass'.*

Below: *'Eye miniatures' were a brief trend in miniature painting towards the end of the eighteenth century, presenting the window of the soul as love tokens that were worn as bracelets, brooches, pendants and rings.*

famously, Nicholas Hilliard (1547-1619), under whom Oliver trained. Together they painted numerous miniatures of the royal family, whose portraits are easier to identify than that shown on the previous page.

Although there is no record as to the identity of the subject in Isaac Oliver's *Man Consumed by Flames*, nor original explanation for the flame motif, there are clues to be read. The subject is posed like the bust of a classical hero, the flames bouncing off his cool, statue-like skin (a rigidity broken by the hint of a smile) in his state of (relative) undress. His gaze travels to connect with the intended recipient, an intimacy into which we are intruding across the centuries. The traditional interpretation, given the nature of miniatures serving as love tokens, is that this is a man caught in the flames of passion, perhaps the suffering of unrequited love, with the Latin motto implying a burning love that only death can extinguish. It's a theme popular in Renaissance literature but rare in this art – the only other known example is an earlier work by Hilliard.

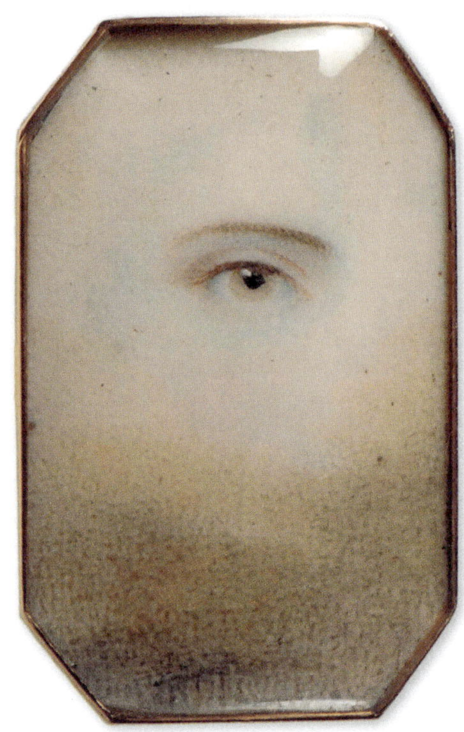

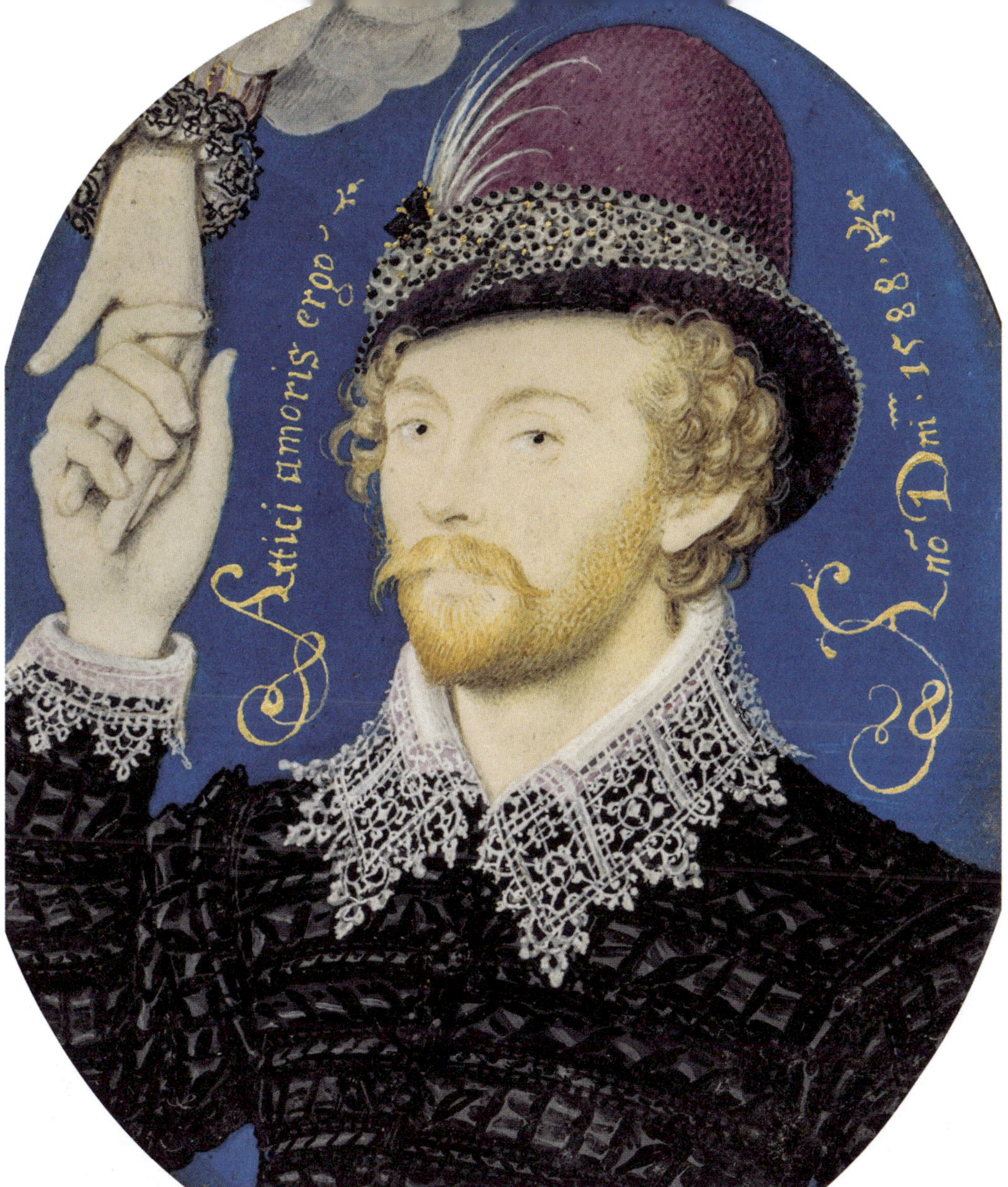

Unknown Man Clasping a Hand from a Cloud *(c.1588), Nicholas Hilliard. An enigmatic miniature showing a man symbolically linking his hand with one descending from the heavens. The identity of the subject has over the years been suggested as Robert Devereux, second Earl of Essex; Edward de Vere, seventeenth Earl of Oxford; and, inevitably, William Shakespeare.*

But is there more to it? Instead of romantic love, could the flames perhaps be an expression of the subject's Protestant devotion in defiance of the Spanish Catholic threat? A more recent reassessment was inspired by the discovery of the same rarely used Latin motto in the title page of a pamphlet by William Strachey (1572-1621), an investor in the English colony at Virginia. Strachey had been aboard the vessel *Sea Venture* on his way to America in 1609 when the ship was wrecked off the coast of Bermuda. News of the disaster was said to have inspired William Shakespeare to write *The Tempest* (*c*.1610-11). Could Strachey be the sitter, surrounded by his fiery devotion to establishing a successful colony at Jamestown and spreading the Protestant word to the natives of a new continent?

ARTEMISIA GENTILESCHI'S *JUDITH SLAYING HOLOFERNES* (1612-13) AND THE ART OF REVENGE

It's hard to imagine there being a more powerful subtext to a painting than this work of the early Baroque Italian artist Artemisia Gentileschi (1593-*c*.1654). It is a biblical scene, albeit of the apocryphal Book of Judith, that has been popular with artists since the Renaissance. Holofernes was an Assyrian general sent by Nebuchadnezzar, the sixth-century-BC king of the Neo-Babylonian Empire, to invade and destroy the Jewish city of Bethulia. A young and beautiful widow named Judith takes it upon herself to deal with the invaders swiftly by seducing and assassinating Holofernes. She prays to God, then dresses in her finest clothing and approaches the general's tent, confident that her attractiveness will gain her access. As Holofernes entertains her, Judith encourages him to drink wine until he is so intoxicated that she seizes his own sword and with the help of her maidservant, Abra, decapitates him. Then she smuggles his head away in a basket.

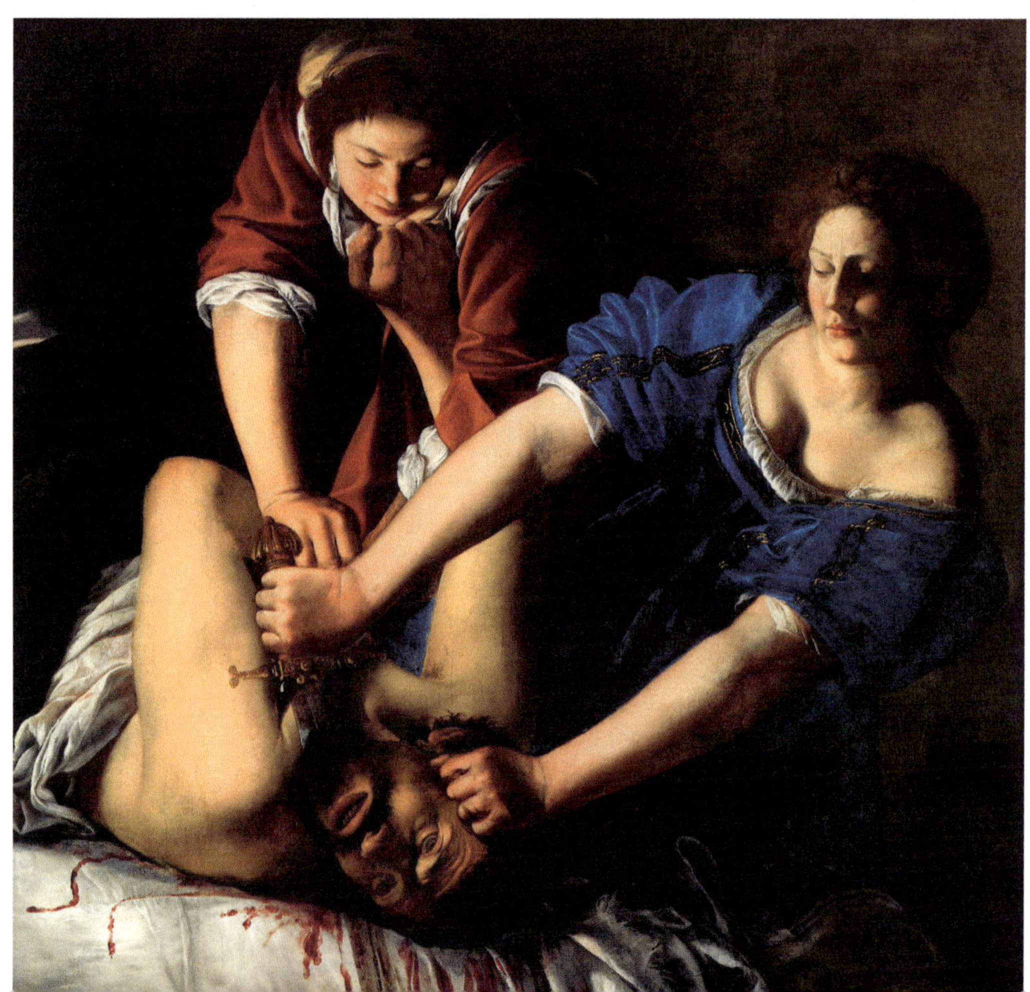

Artemisia Gentileschi completed this painting during 1612-13, and she painted a second version sometime between 1613 and 1621 (which is now in the collection of the Uffizi Gallery, Florence). It is a scene of obvious intensity, magnified many times upon learning of an episode in Artemisia's own biography just a year before she commenced the first version of the work. In 1611 her father, the Tuscan artist Orazio Gentileschi (1563-1639), hired a landscape painter named Agostino Tassi to tutor his daughter. At first he attempted to woo his young student with false promises of marriage, but when these failed he raped Artemisia.

Rather than shrink from her attacker, she sought to prosecute him for the crime and so began a seven-month trial. Tassi denied everything, and Artemisia was asked if she was willing to stand by her statement, even under 'judicial torture' if it came to it. She held firm. The torture came in the form of the *sibille*, in which cords were tied around her fingers and gradually tightened. Artemisia said nothing but the repeated words: '*È vero, è vero, è vero*' (It is true, it is true, it is true).

Tassi was convicted in 1612 of the rape of Artemisia Gentileschi. During the trial it emerged that he had been accused of similar crimes in the past, that he had also planned to steal a number of Orazio's paintings, and that his wife had been missing for some time – murdered, it was suspected, by bandits on his orders. He was sentenced to two years' imprisonment, a sentence that was later annulled, and he walked free in 1613.

When we gaze at *Judith Slaying Holofernes* it is impossible not to feel the pain and anguish of the artist during this terrible experience in this revenge painting, or the fury she must have felt at being powerless to stop her attacker walking free. The two women in the scene are powerful, unwavering avatars of justice – Holofernes's eyes are wide, his body helplessly twisted, as the women hold him down and dispatch him with the same calm determination as the farmer slaughtering an animal. His fist, shown almost as large as the women's heads, wilts at the end of a crooked arm, weaker than the firm, straight forearms of the women.

Not only did Artemisia Gentileschi overcome the traumatic episodes of rape, torture, humiliation and injustice, but in a time when the legacies of female artists were often short-lived, the strength of her talent saw her gain lasting success and admiration across Europe. She was the first woman to gain membership to the artists' academy in Florence, and for forty years she enjoyed a career as one of the most eminent artists of her time.

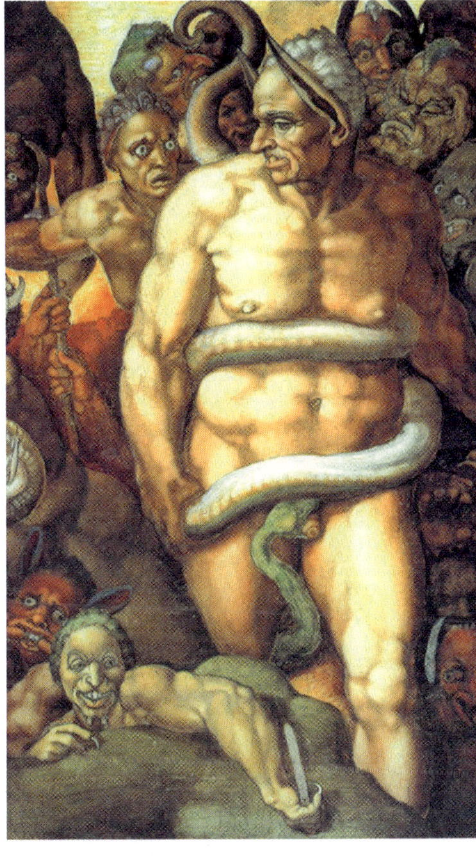

When Michelangelo's (1475-1564) painted ceiling of the Sistine Chapel was revealed in 1512, the Papal Master of Ceremonies, Biagio de Cesena, criticised the nude figures as being 'disgraceful' and better suited to a tavern or public bath. Michelangelo took his revenge by adding this likeness of de Cesena behind the Chapel's altar, showing him as Minos, hated judge of the underworld, with the ears of a jackass and a serpent biting his genitals. When de Cesena complained to Pope Paul III (1468-1549), the pontiff replied: 'Had the painter sent thee to purgatory, I would have used my best efforts to release thee; but since he hath sent thee to hell, it is useless to come to me, as I have no power there.'

CHRIST IN THE STORM ON THE SEA OF GALILEE (1633) AND THE ART OF THEFT

At 1.24 a.m. on 18 March 1990, two moustachioed men dressed as police officers talked their way into Boston's Isabella Stewart Gardner Museum and overpowered the two security guards. 'Gentlemen, this is a robbery,' one of the robbers announced before leaving the guards in a basement tunnel bound with duct tape. Over the following 81 minutes the two thieves stole thirteen artworks, brutally smashing the glass and slashing canvases out of their frames with a razor knife.

The stolen pieces include the beautiful *The Concert* (1658-60) by Johannes Vermeer (1632-75), by whom only 33-35 works exist; Rembrandt's (1606-69) portrait *A Lady and Gentleman in Black* (1633), and a self-portrait etching of 1634 by the same artist; a Chinese bronze beaker dated to 1200-1100 BC in the Shang Dynasty, the oldest piece stolen; five works on paper by Edgar Degas (1834-1917); an Édouard Manet (1832-83) painting called *Chez Tortoni* (1878-80); and, oddly, a finial from a Napoleonic flag that the thieves took the time to unscrew, despite the fact that it's considerably less valuable than the other stolen items.

The lost jewel of the raid, however, was the work shown here, also by Rembrandt. *Christ in the Storm on the Sea of Galilee* (1633) is the Dutch painter's only seascape. Tragically, it's likely that the image printed on the opposing page is now the closest you will ever come to seeing it. Like the rest of the burgled artworks, the masterpiece has not been seen since the theft, nor have the thieves ever been identified, despite a reward offered of $10 million for information leading to their capture. The combined worth of the thieves' haul is today estimated at around $500 million, making it the most significant art theft in history. Bizarrely, due to a quirky clause in the will of the museum's founder, the eccentric Isabella Stewart Gardner, the empty frames of the stolen paintings still hang on the walls of the museum she built. It was stipulated that the displays must be kept as they were originally designed, meaning the curators are prevented from hanging new works in their place, and so the frames remain as poignant reminders of the as-yet-unsolved crime.

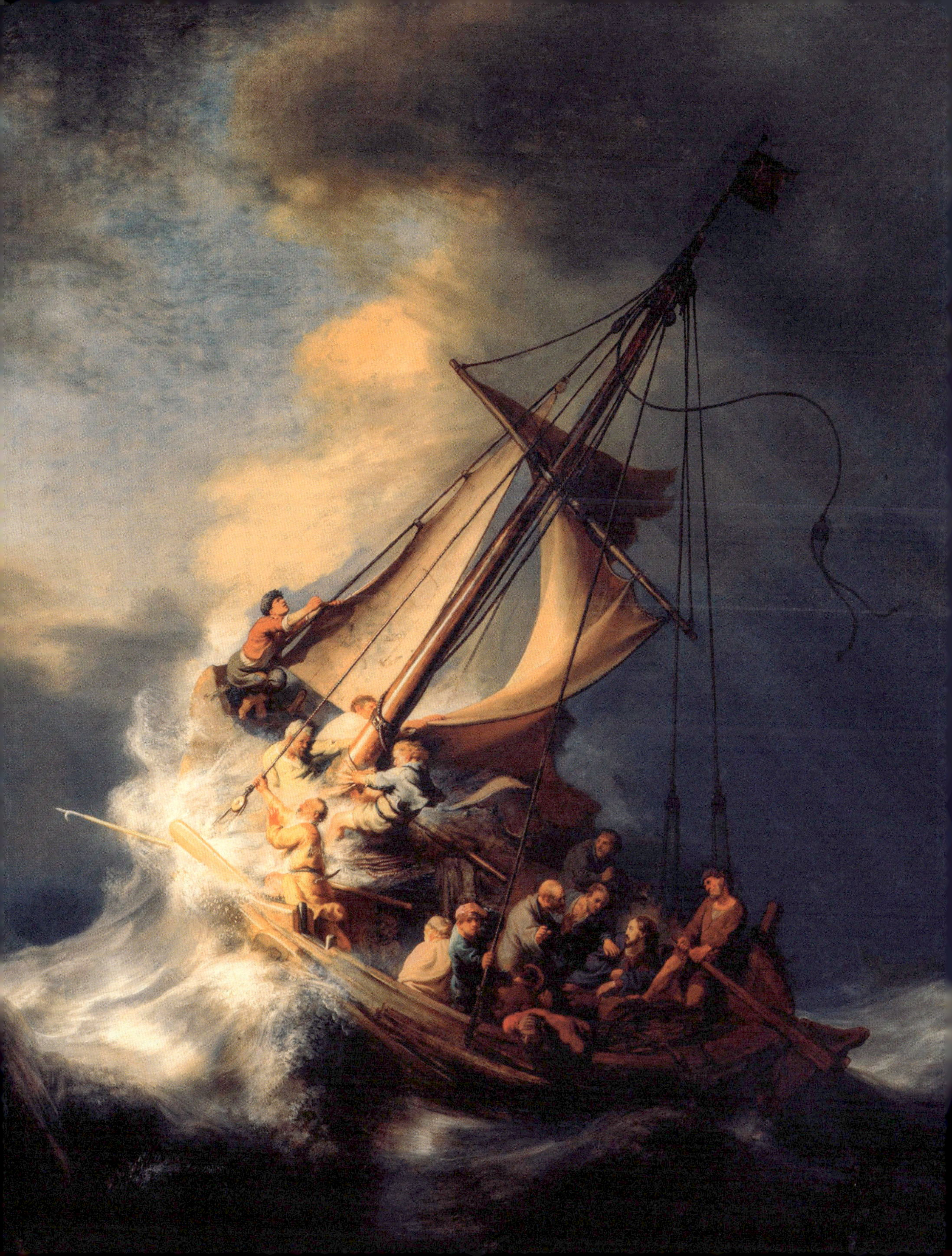

According to the Art Loss Register, only 15 per cent of stolen art is recovered. One reason for this is that valuable stolen artworks, which can't, of course, be displayed or legally resold, can serve as currency in the criminal underworld and so they change hands frequently. They can also be used as leverage. In 2002 thieves used a sledgehammer to break into Amsterdam's Van Gogh Museum and snatched the first two paintings to hand, leaving behind more famous works like *Sunflowers* and *Self-Portrait*. Over a decade later, the Italian mobster Raffaele Imperiale was arrested along with Mario Cerrone, a fellow member of the Camorra organised crime syndicate, for involvement in drug trafficking. Cerrone turned informer and revealed to police that Imperiale had bought the paintings on the black market and stashed them in a luxury villa, leading to the swift recovery of the works.

Despite the precautions and technology in place, it seems that those with the means simply can't resist the idea of taking a world treasure for themselves. At the time of writing, the US hedge-fund billionaire and art collector Michael Steinhardt has received an unprecedented lifetime ban from ever again purchasing antique art, and agreed to surrender 180 looted and illegally smuggled antiquities stolen from eleven countries, the total value of which is said to be $70 million. Among the items were the *Stag's Head Rhyton*, a beautiful ceremonial vessel in the form of a stag's head dating to 400 BC and valued at $3.5 million, and the *Ercolano Fresco* (valued at $1 million), showing an infant Hercules strangling the snake sent to kill him by Hera. The latter was bought from convicted antiquities traffickers for $650,000 in 1995, the same year it was looted from a Roman villa in the ruins of Herculaneum, near modern Naples. Steinhardt was described as 'displaying a rapacious appetite for plundered artefacts' by the Manhattan district attorney Cyrus Vance Jr. In a statement, Steinhardt's lawyers said: 'Mr Steinhardt is pleased that the district attorney's years-long investigation has concluded without any charges, and that items wrongfully taken by others will be returned to their native countries.'

TAPUYA WOMAN (1641)
AND THE ART OF CANNIBALISM

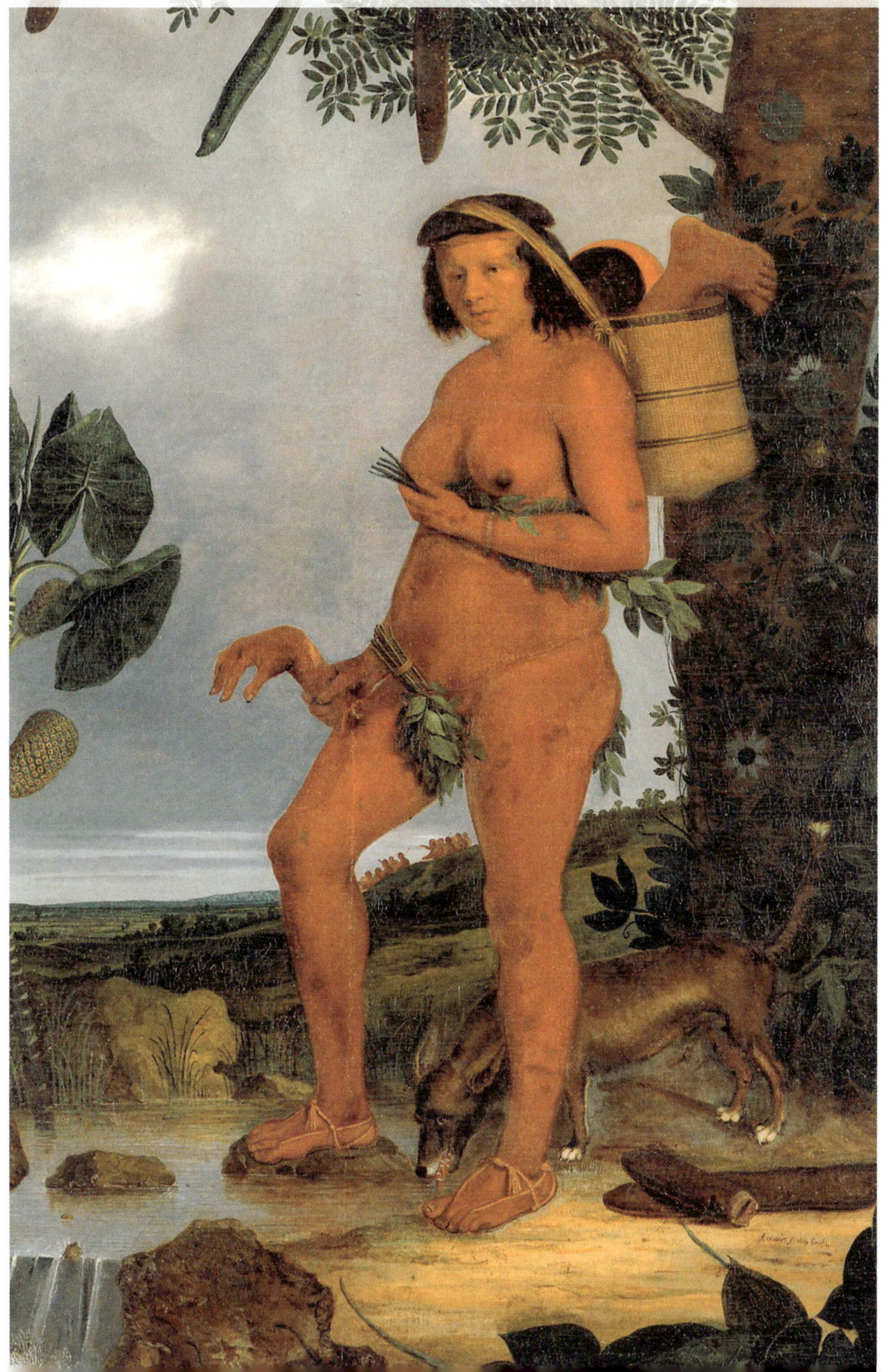

Her face is a vision of serenity and her posture relaxed as she steps across a small waterfall, with the verdant Brazilian country opening up for kilometres behind her. So calm is the scene, and so rich in local flora and fauna, that we almost don't notice the human foot protruding from her sack, nor the severed hand tense with rigor mortis that she holds casually in her own. *Tapuya Woman* (1641) by Albert Eckhout (*c.*1610-66) is the first portrait of a cannibal, painted by one of the first European artists to travel to the New World and graphically record the discoveries of the colonists.

In 1636 the Dutch rule of New Holland, the northern portion of the Portuguese colony of Brazil, had been established for over six years when Count Johan Maurits van Nassau-Siegen took up his new role as Dutch governor-general of Brazil. It was immediately apparent that he had great ambitions beyond simple diplomatic service. Landscapers, architects, scientists and artists were brought over from Europe to the capital city, Mauritsstad, to help with the realisation of the count's dream to build a base for the Dutch West India Company's trade in sugar, which would also be a magnificent beacon of European civilisation among the 'savage wilds' of the New World.

One of those called to this duty, who leapt at the chance to see the wonders with his own eyes, was Albert Eckhout, a Dutch portrait and still life painter. Together with fellow painter Frans Post (1612-80), Eckhout was tasked with documenting the people, plants and animals of the region. The result was a series of life-size (2.66m × 1.65m/8ft 9in × 5ft 4in) portraits of Tupi and Tapuya people from the native population of Brazil, including the cannibalistic Tapuya woman shown on the previous page.

These are ethnographic portraits, which are somewhat paradoxical in that they are an attempt to form a realistic depiction of their subject, even if the specific person depicted never existed. The figure on the canvas of *Tapuya Woman* represents someone from the region, while much care and attention were given to filling the canvas with as many accurate representations as possible of the plant and animal life to be found in the region: the large tree to the right of the scene, for example, appears to be *Cassia grandis* (pink shower tree), native to the neotropics.

Though such paintings are, of course, problematic in that they are often infused with European stereotypical elements of the time, they are rich documents of record when seen as evidence of the informational 'mapping impulse' (a term of the art historian Svetlana Alpers) of Dutch Golden Age

African Man*, another of Albert Eckhout's 1641 life-size ethnographic series.*

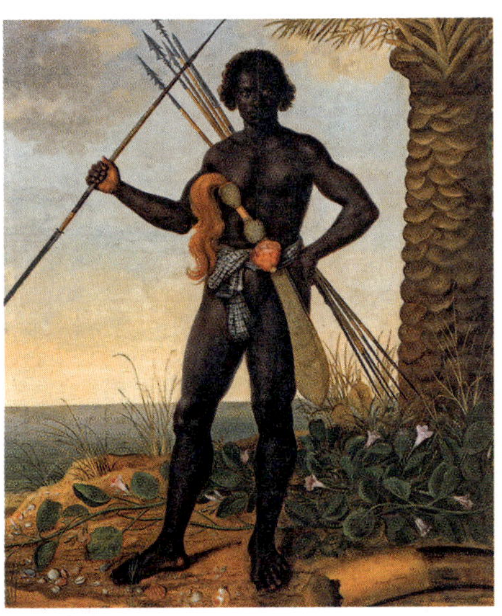

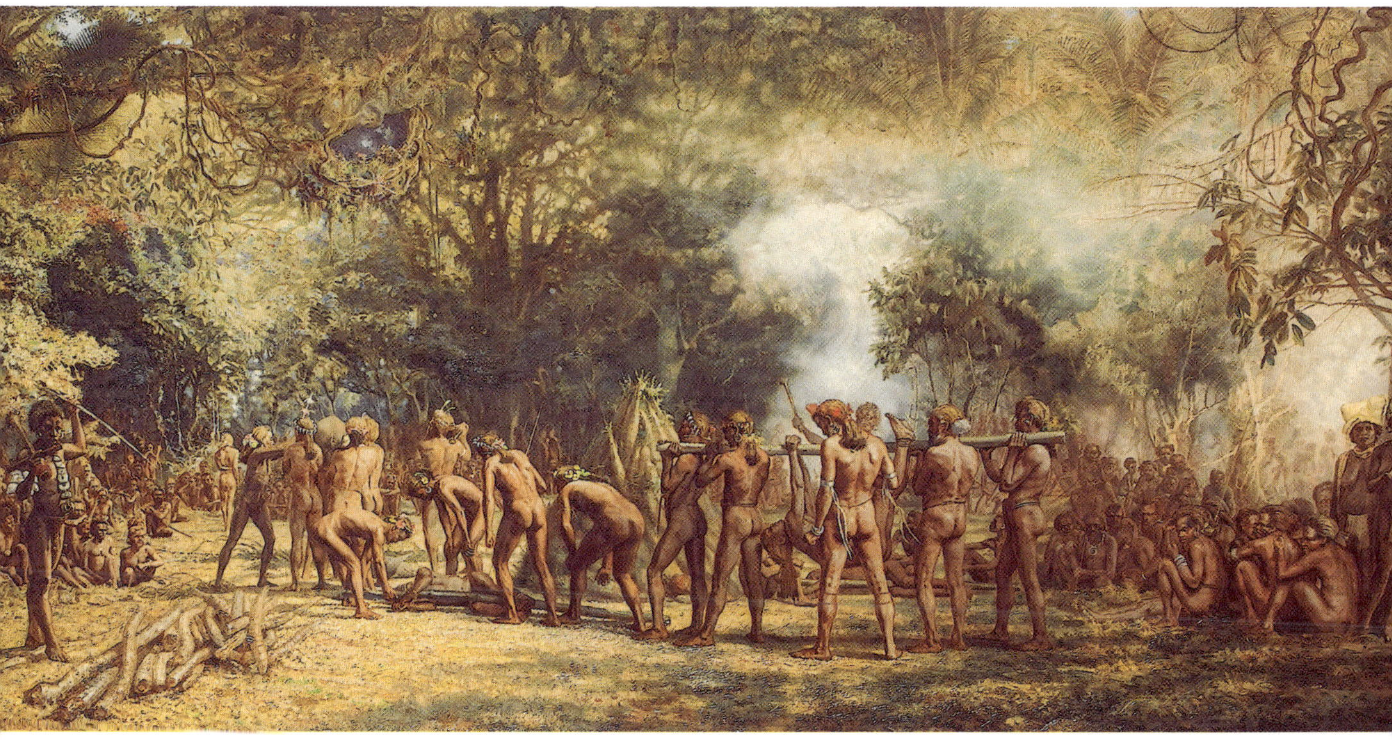

artists. It was with art such as this that the vast flood of new knowledge of alien plants, animals and peoples was organised, processed and telegraphed home.

So where does one hang the image of a cannibal? Eckhout's series of life-size local figures were almost certainly intended to decorate the two-storey grand hall of Vrijburg, the new governor's palace. They were to be in a side-by-side gallery display that progressed from the least 'civilised' people – i.e. the Tapuya woman eating a compatriot – to images of the 'Brazilians' (Tupinambás), who wear clothes, are depicted as more physically attractive and are shown within cultivated countryside. The implied meaning of this order was that the Brazilians are the success story of the transformative civilising presence of the Dutch.

Today Eckhout's Brazilian paintings can be found in the collection of the National Museum of Denmark. The paintings did not remain in Brazil for long – shortly after their completion, Count Maurits gifted the lot to his cousin, King Frederick III of Denmark. One wonders whether there might have been something about the sight of amputated limbs in a cannibal's backpack that led to a loss of appetite with the governor's dinner guests.

Cannibal Feast on the Island of Tanna, New Hebrides *by the British-Australian painter Charles E. Gordon Frazer (1863-99). During his travels in Australasia, the New Hebrides (Vanuatu) and New Guinea, Frazer witnessed this scene of New Hebridean villagers suspending captured enemies on poles 'who afterwards are dragged to the fires to form the nucleus of a prolonged feast'. Frazer was the only white man to witness such a ceremony and survive.*

PORTRAIT OF BARBARA VAN BECK (*c.*1650)

On 15 September 1657 the English diarist John Evelyn (1620-1706) was accompanying friends to see a Turkish rope-dancer when he was delighted to encounter at the show a woman he'd met twenty years earlier as a young boy. Barbara van Beck, born Barbara Ursler near Augsburg in Bavaria in 1629, spoke several languages, played the harpsichord and revealed a sharply educated mind, speaking knowledgeably on a variety of subjects. She also had a face thick with hair. 'Her very Eyebrowes were combed upward, & all her fore-head as thick & even as growes on any womans head, neately dress'd: There come also two locks very long out of Each Eare: she had also a most prolix beard, & mustachios, with long lockes of haire growing on the very middle of her nose, exactly like an Island [Iceland] dog.'

Born with the congenital Ambras syndrome, also known as hypertrichosis, the little girl with the abnormal amount of hair growth had been exhibited by her parents Anne and Balthazar Ursler, and had travelled with shows around Europe ever since, becoming something of a celebrity. 'She was now married,' wrote Evelyn, '& told me [she] had one Child, that was not hairy, as nor were any of her parents or relations: she was borne at Ausburg in Germanie, & for the rest very well shaped, plaied well on the Harpsichord &c.'

This oil portrait of Barbara van Beck is thought to have been painted by an unidentified Italian artist *c.*1650 and was acquired by London's Wellcome Collection in 2017. While her unusual appearance, presented just as Evelyn describes, certainly catches the eye, what is arguably more striking is the tone with which the artist presents her. So familiar are we with the sleazy indignity of the later Victorian 'freak show' that we are caught off guard by the respectful traditional form of this study.

Van Beck is here captured with dignity, composure and femininity; her casual but sure gaze is levelled at the viewer, a gentle challenge to any indecorous staring. Her dress is fashionable – the low-cut grey silk, the soft lace edging, the scarlet bow and ribbons chiming with the red of her lips. 'This is a beautifully executed, high-status painting,' says Dr Angela McShane at the Wellcome Collection, and shows her to be 'a woman with great self-possession and presence, painted at a

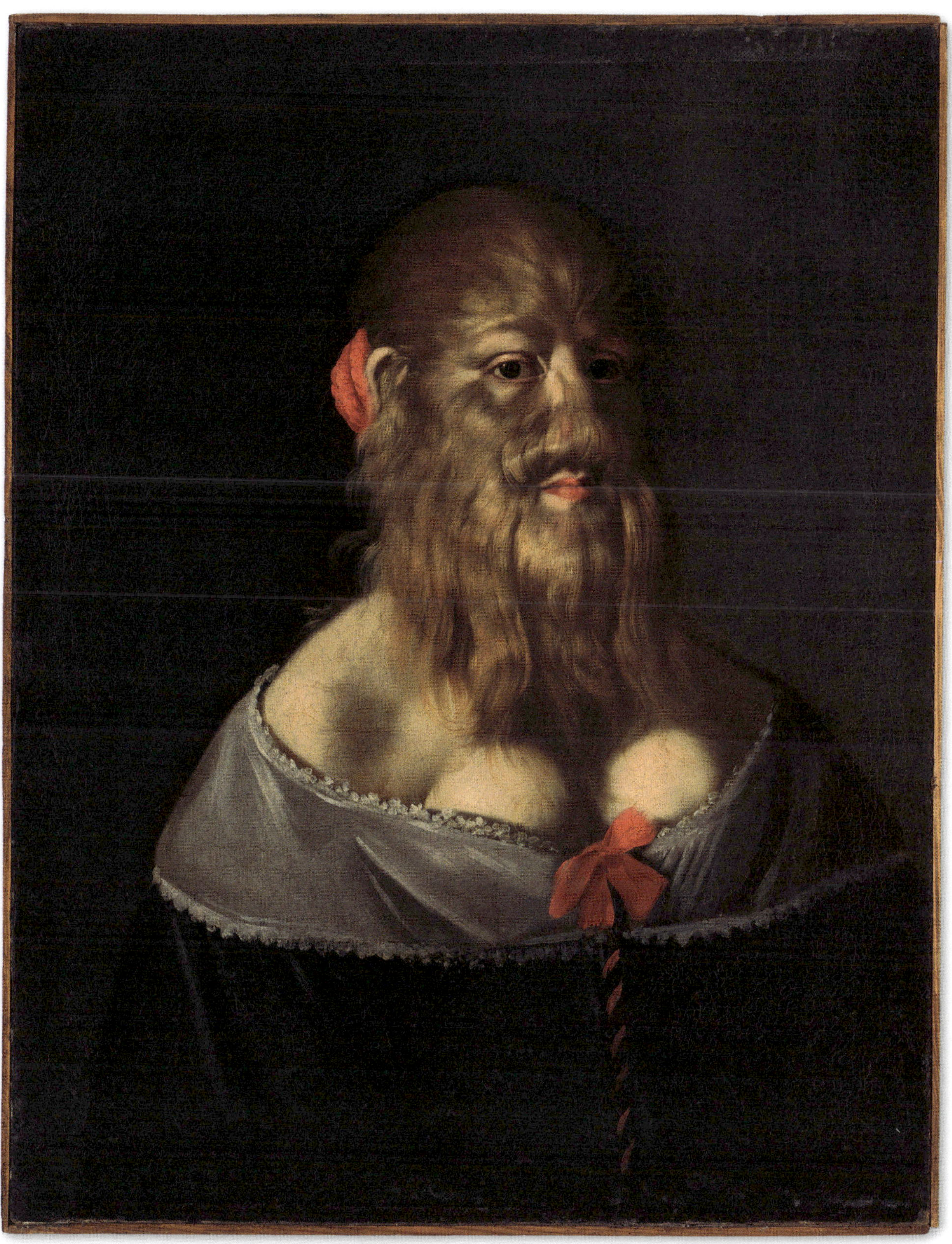

Portrait of Barbara van Beck *(c.1650)*

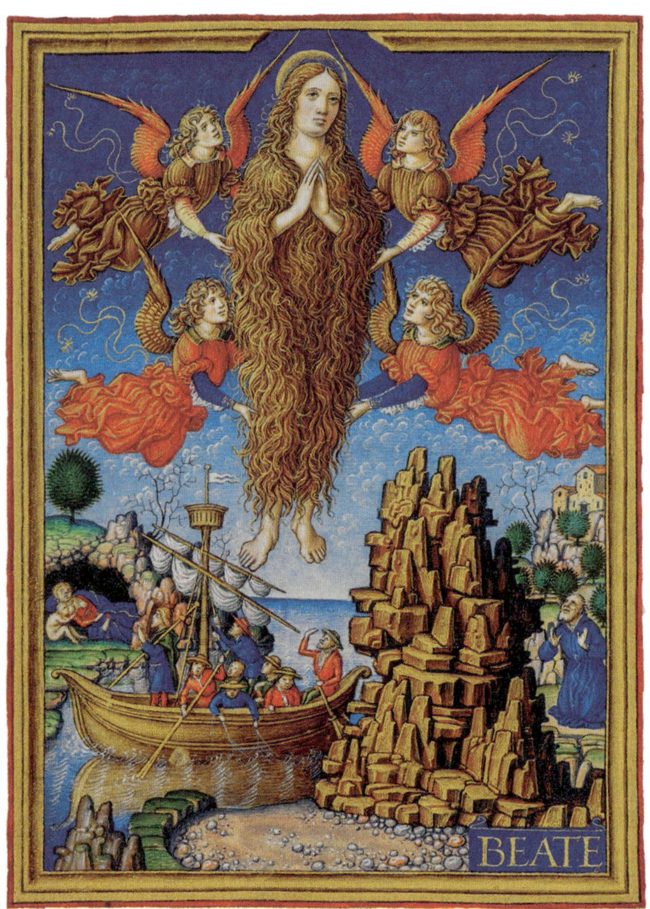

Miniature accompanying prayers relating to Mary Magdalene, from the Italian Book of Hours *manuscript known as the* Sforza Hours *(1490-1521).*

time when she would have been viewed, as Evelyn saw her, as wonderful, a natural wonder.' The painting also forms the last record of van Beck before she is lost to history.

The history of hirsute women in art goes back at least as far as the story of St Mary of Egypt (*c*.344-*c*.421), who according to the theologian Sophronius (*c*.560-638) spent her early life granting sexual favours around Alexandria, only to become a hermit when this behaviour led to her banishment from the Church of the Holy Sepulchre. Out in the wild she grew a thick coat of hair (out of modesty, but also serving as symbolism of the wildness of life outside of God's love), which is how we find her depicted in medieval manuscripts. Her story and artistic tradition then occasionally get muddled with

A statue of the bearded fourteenth-century folk saint Wilgefortis, in the Diocesan Museum Graz-Seckau, Austria. Having taken a vow of perpetual virginity, Wilgefortis sought to avoid an arranged marriage to the king of Sicily by praying to God for help. A full beard sprouted from her face, and the wedding proposal was rescinded. Her furious father had her crucified.

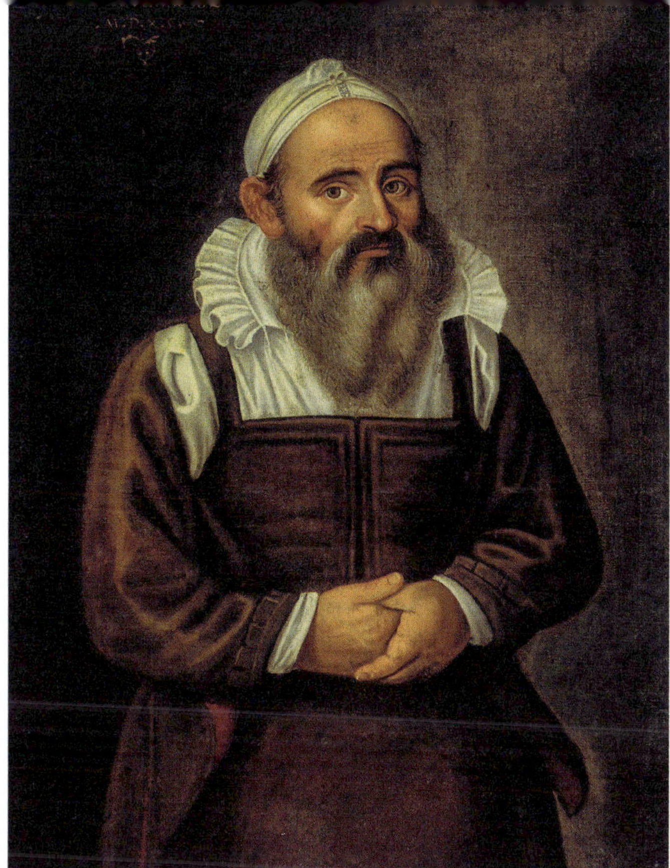

Brígida del Río, the Bearded Lady of Peñaranda *(1590), by Juan Sánchez Cotán.*

another historically licentious female figure, Mary Magdalene (despite the fact that the gospels never actually describe her as a prostitute). In the illuminations of medieval manuscripts, such as that of the *Sforza Hours*, shown on the opposite page, Mary Magdalene occasionally pops up in penitent pose and as hairy as the day is long.

This established tradition of 'hairy Mary' images certainly paved the way, if only subconsciously, for the seventeenth-century Italian author of the van Beck portrait, but there are also more recent works that may have had greater influence. While the van Beck portrait is sometimes held up as the earliest depiction of Ambras syndrome, on this wall of our curiosity gallery we can also hang an earlier painting by Juan Sánchez Cotán (1560-1627) known as *Brígida del Río, the Bearded Lady of Peñaranda*. In Spain, del Río enjoyed a similar level of celebrity to that of van Beck, causing a sensation when she made an appearance at the court of Madrid in 1590. In typically meticulous style Sánchez Cotán creates a fascinating confliction of signifiers, amplifying the masculinity of certain features of del Río such as the size of her hands but countering these with a submissive posture and wide doe-eyes more commonly seen in female portraiture.

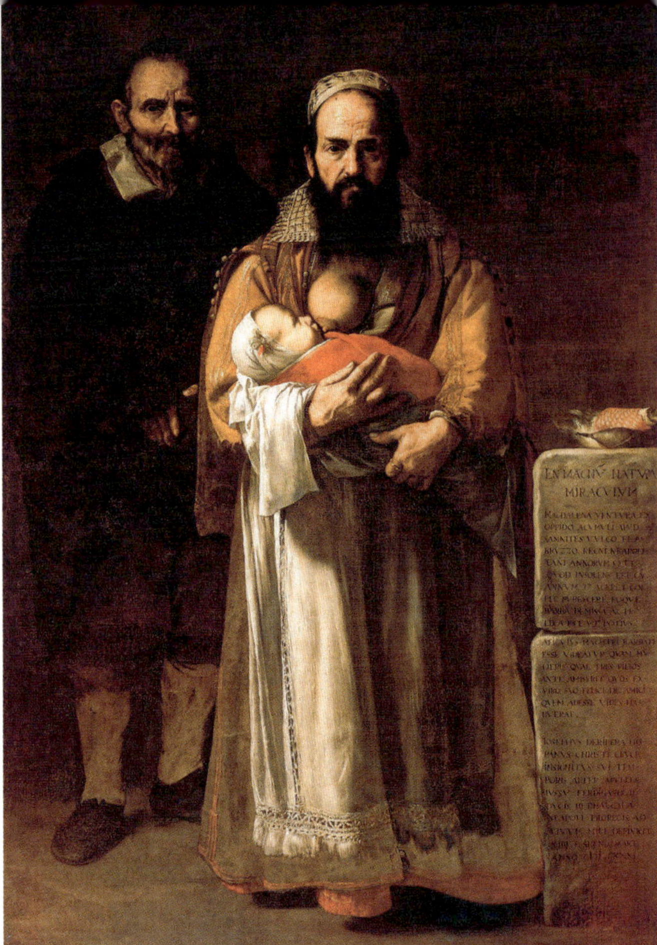

LEFT: *Jusepe de Ribera's* Magdalena Ventura with Her Husband and Son *(1631).*

A similarly bearded female is the subject of the strangest work of Jusepe de Ribera (1591-1652), who in 1629 was asked by the Duke of Alcalá, one of Ribera's major patrons, to produce the work shown here, *Magdalena Ventura with Her Husband and Son*. Again, the motive was to record a natural wonder, as the extensive Latin inscription informs us. Magdalena Ventura of the Abruzzi region of central Italy began to grow a beard at the age of thirty-seven. Fifteen years later she gave birth to the first of three children. It is this unusual family that is portrayed in Ribera's oils, as Ventura nurses her infant with her husband behind in shadow. Her prodigious beard, the inscription notes, 'seems more like that of any bearded master than that of a woman who has borne three sons'.

Most reminiscent of the van Beck portrait, however, is that of Antonietta 'Tognina' Gonzalez (sometimes Gonsalvus), born *c.*1588 to Pedro González, who was more famously known as 'The Wild Man of the Woods' (shown here in the image to the right). She, her father and three of her siblings were all affected by Ambras syndrome and were the subject of a number of paintings of the late sixteenth century. Like her father,

BELOW: Pedro González (Petrus Gonsalvus) and His Wife, Catherine*, a watercolour and gouache painting on vellum of* c.*1575-80.*

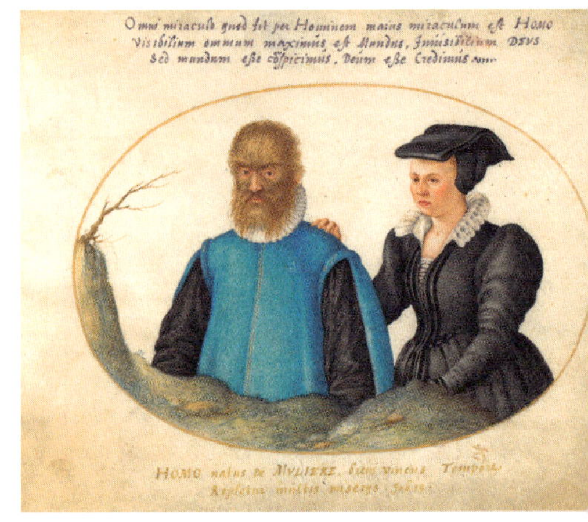

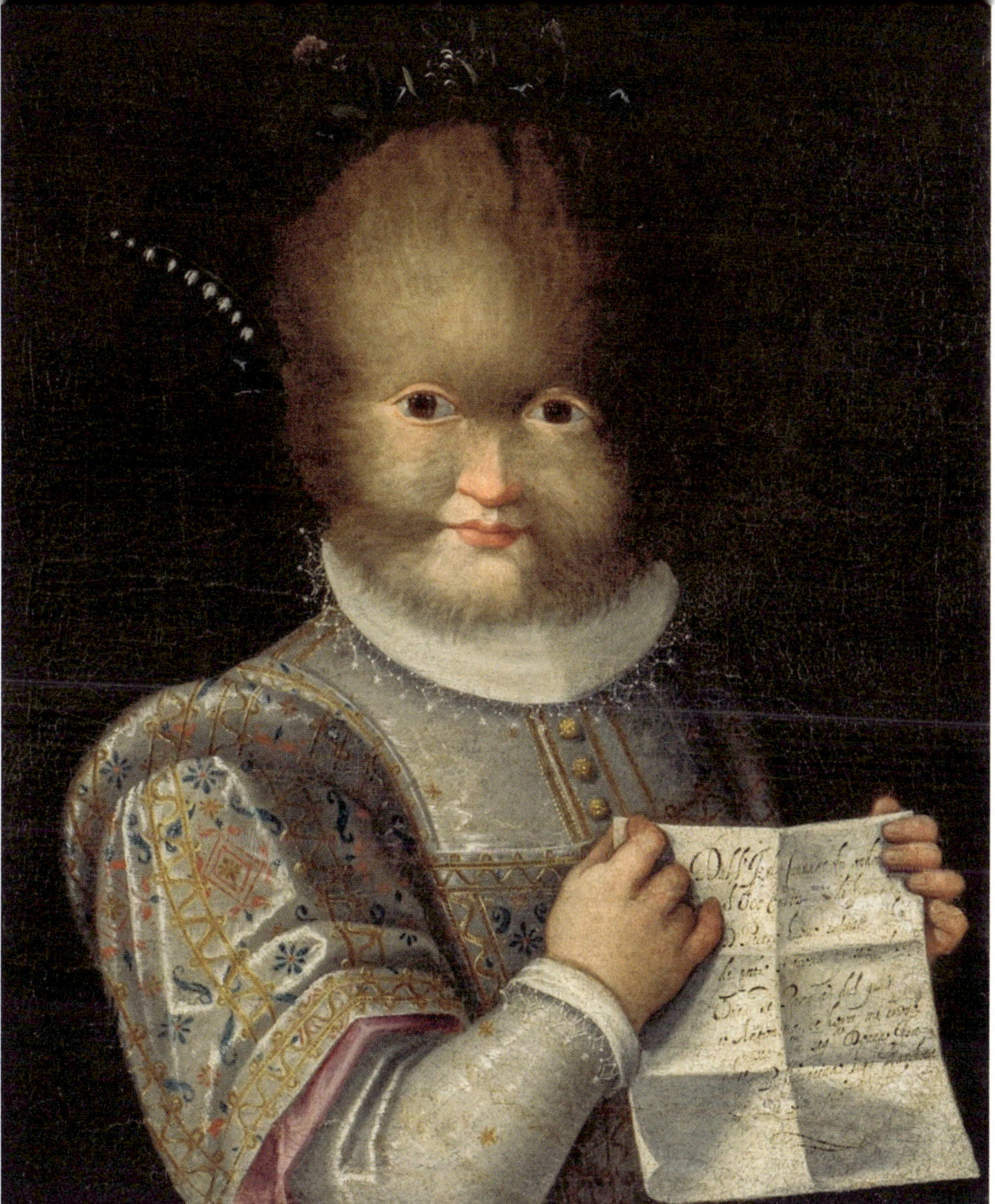

Above: *Portrait of Antonietta Gonzalez.*

Antonietta spent her life at various European courts, having grown up at Fontainebleau, part of the court of King Henri II, where they were dressed in fine clothes and exhibited at social occasions for the entertainment of guests. In this portrait, Antonietta is around ten years old, wearing a court dress and proudly brandishing a handwritten note that tells the story of her family's history: 'Don Pietro, a wild man discovered in the Canary Islands, was conveyed to his most serene highness Henry the king of France, and from there came to his Excellency the Duke of Parma. From whom [came] I, Antonietta, and now I can be found nearby at the court of the Lady Isabella Pallavicina, the honourable Marchesa of Soragna.'

THE TEMPTATION OF ST ANTHONY (*c.*1650), JOOS VAN CRAESBEECK

The Temptation of St Anthony has long been a favourite theme for artists – the competitive opportunity to portray an attack by weird hellish creatures as creatively as possible is irresistible – and it's rare to find a national art museum without its own variation by one of the great masters. In the National Museum of Ancient Art in Lisbon, for example, you can find a triptych of the scene by Hieronymus Bosch (1450-1516), while the enormous *Isenheim Altarpiece* by Matthias Grünewald (*c.*1470-1528) in the Musée Unterlinden in Colmar, France, shows St Anthony standing defiantly with staff in hand as a demon hisses and beats on a window behind him. But the image with arguably the most detail to unpack is the extraordinarily nightmarish *The Temptation of St Anthony* (*c.*1650), by Joos van Craesbeeck (*c.*1605-*c.*1660), in the Staatliche Kunsthalle in Karlsruhe, Germany.

Born in the Hellenised Egyptian village of Coma, Anthony is often referred to as the 'First Monk' or 'Father of All Monks'. Though there had previously been ascetics (those who abstain from sensual pleasures out of piety), Anthony was the first to sell his belongings and venture out into the wilderness to find isolation in which to reflect on his faith. In *c.*360, Athanasius of Alexandria writes that the saint ventured into the Nitrian Desert on the border with the Western Desert (about 95km/60 miles west of Alexandria) and lived as a desert hermit, receiving a number of strange visions so powerful they felt like physical experiences.

The saint did not have to wait long for the first unusual episode. Offended by Anthony's holy mission, the Devil set about tormenting him. Initially this was done seductively, with inflictions of boredom and laziness, false lures of family warmth, scantily clad women offering sexual favours, and mountainous piles of gold pieces. After enduring this without waver, Anthony decided to move to a cave nearer to his native village, but the Devil continued his campaign to sway the saint, dispatching a cavalcade of vicious demons to cause him unbearable physical suffering, inflicting beatings that left him near death.

A particularly severe demonic attack succeeded in killing Anthony, but as a group of hermit followers gathered around

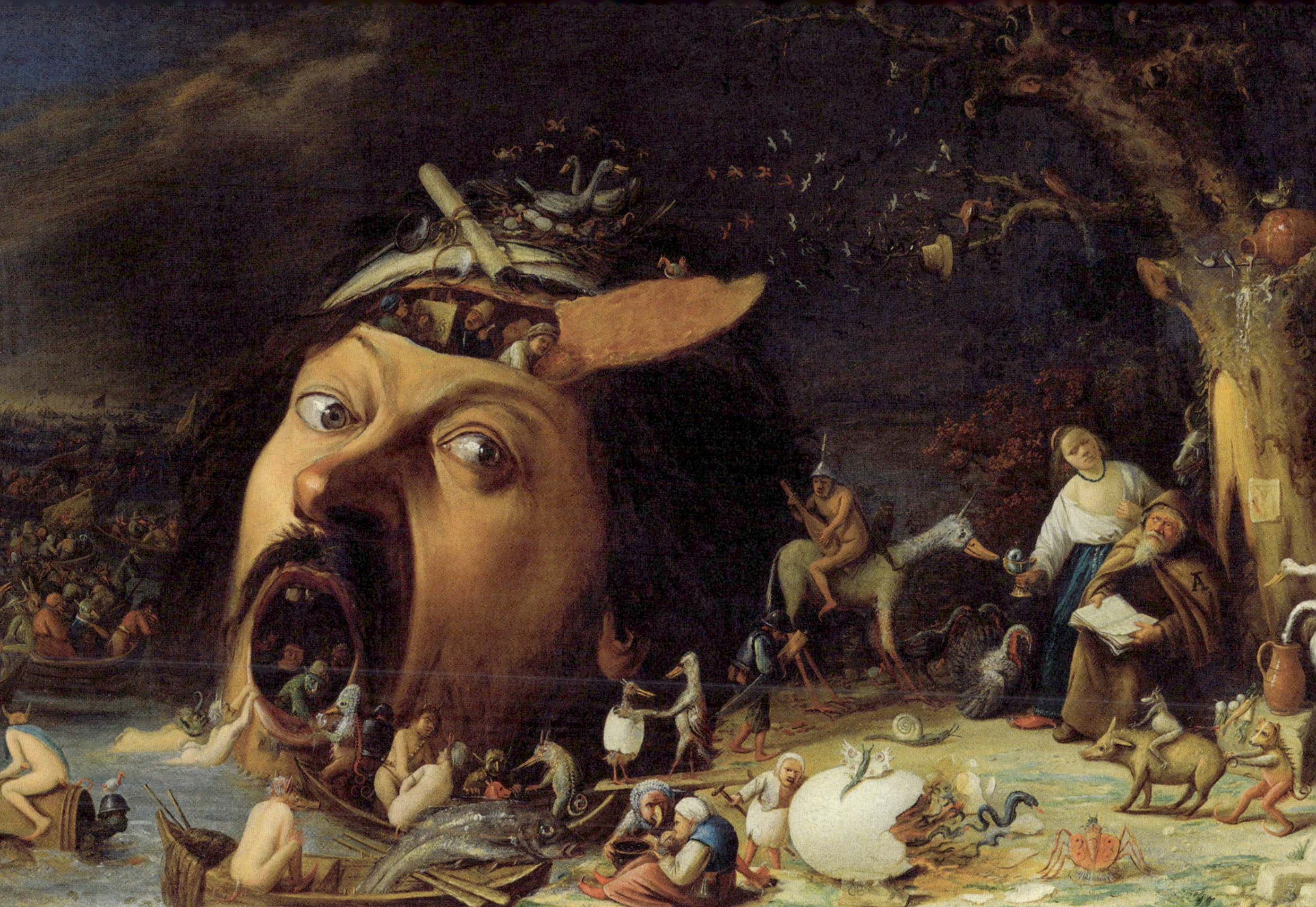

his body he came back to life and immediately demanded to return to the cave where the demons had assaulted him. The devils returned again in the form of wild beasts, but a blinding flash sent by God split the sky, and the animals ran away. For fifteen years Anthony lived this way, until at the age of thirty-five he retreated farther into the desert for absolute solitude. At a mountain by the Nile called Pispir (now Der-el-Memun), he lived within the walls of an abandoned Roman fort, surviving off supplies that were occasionally thrown to him over the wall by visiting pilgrims whom he refused to meet.

The startling painting by Joos van Craesbeeck radiates the terror, bewilderment and panic induced by a demonic vision, and yet on closer inspection there are elements of humour and self-reference that make it even more intriguing. Giant screaming disembodied heads tend to draw the eye, but when our gaze finally moves on from this hypnotically horrifying feature we then find the subject, Anthony (helpfully marked with a small 'A' on his shoulder), sitting under the tree on the right, clutching a Bible.

The Temptation of St Anthony *(c.1650), Joos van Craesbeeck*

He is beset on all sides by a chaotic army of demons in mixed animal form. One creature pours wine on the saint from a high branch, threatening to soak Anthony's woodcut of Christ nailed to the tree. A woman beside him tempts with lust by lowering her shirt and offers a nautilus cup with all the riches of the world. (On closer inspection, the claws of her feet tell us she's one of the many demonic apparitions.) The goat behind his head represents the medieval rumours of goats whispering lewd thoughts to taint the minds of the virtuous. Serpents slide out of a large egg that has shattered on the ground, symbolising original sin, the moment when evil slithered into the world.

And that giant, wild-eyed, wailing head? Interestingly it's very similar to a self-portrait by Craesbeeck of himself smoking. The artist has inserted himself into the nightmare – the strip of skin peeled back from his forehead reveals a miniature version of the artist at work painting a scene of people in a brothel or inn. These naturalistic scenes were a genre popular at the time and were known as 'Low life' painting. Craesbeeck is essentially illustrating his mundane day job, inverting the nightmare with absurdity. Furred and feathered demons pour out of his mouth and head like

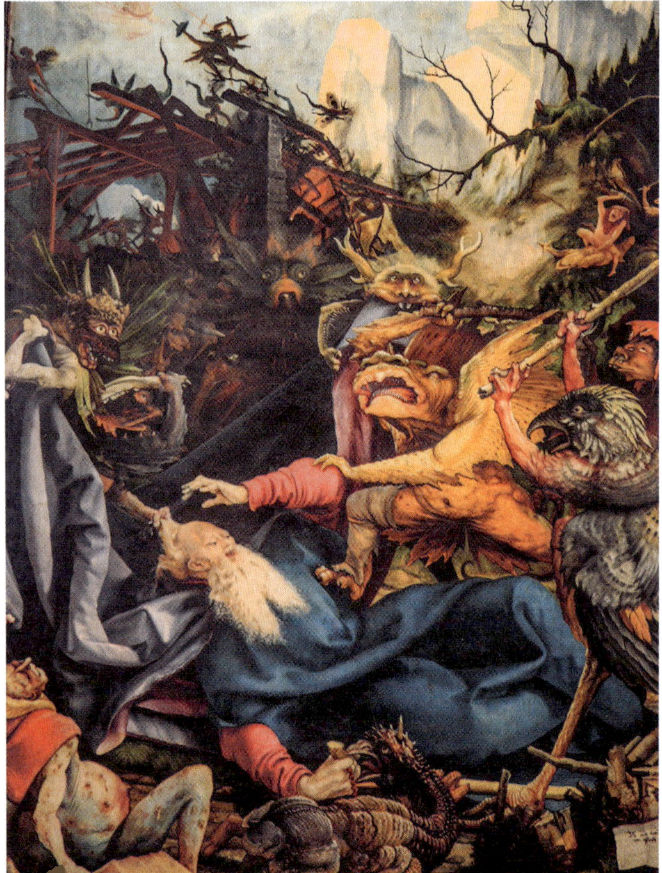

St Anthony is tormented by wonderfully weird demons, from the inner wing of the Isenheim Altarpiece *(1512-16), painted by Matthias Grünewald (c.1470-1528) for the Monastery of St Anthony in Issenheim near Colmar.*

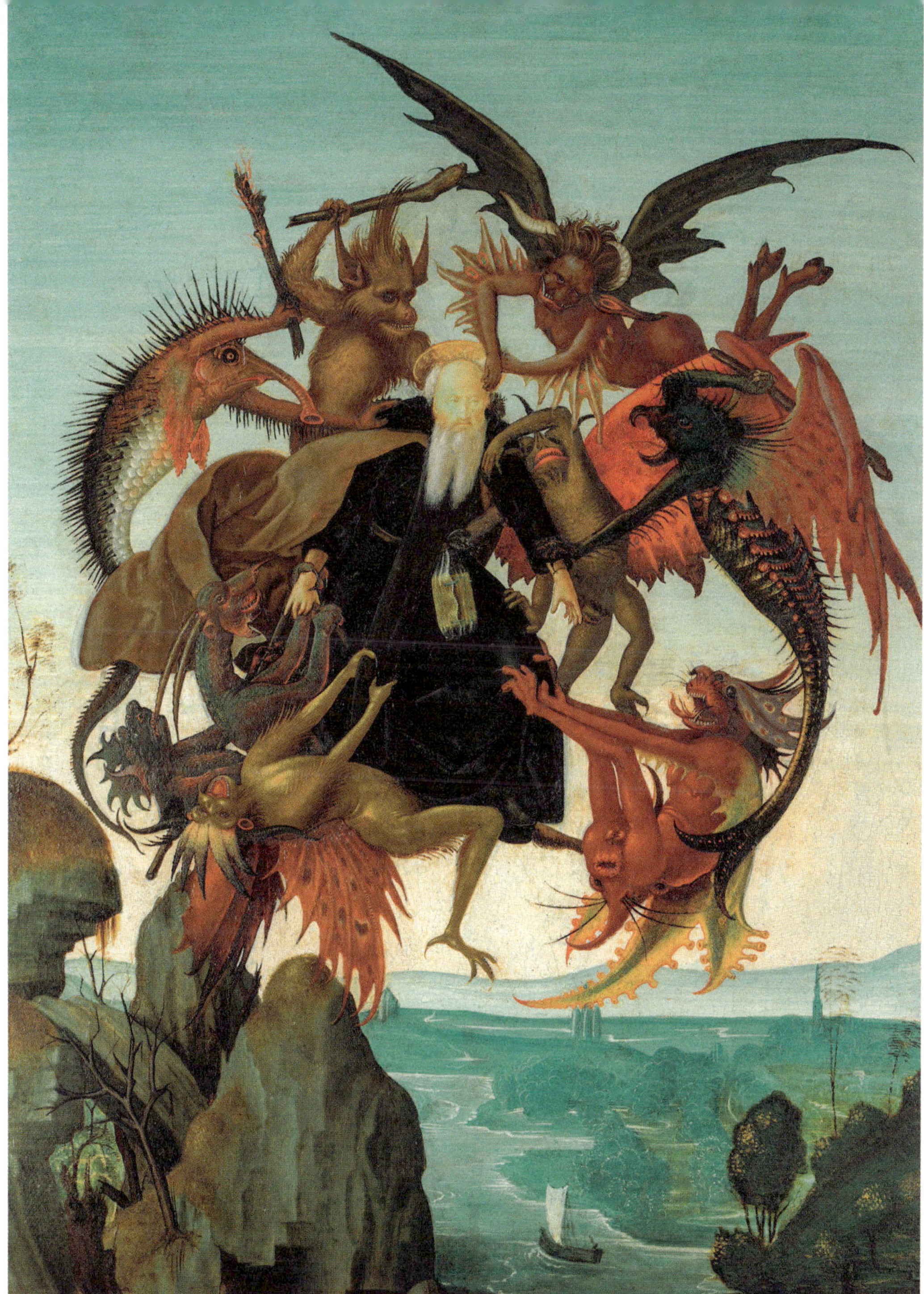

The Torment of St Anthony *(1487-88) by a young Michelangelo (1475-1564).*

evil thoughts, in weird and imaginative forms. With these Craesbeeck is performing a temptation himself, luring the viewer's gaze away from the saint, in favour of the much more enjoyable examination of all the playful creatures of the comical, demonic pantomime – with no qualms about how problematic this seduction might be.

ÁNGELES ARCABUCEROS – THE ART OF THE ANGEL MUSKETEER (SEVENTEENTH CENTURY)

The sacred art of the 'Cusco school' is named after its city of origin, which sits in southeastern Peru near the Urubamba Valley of the Andes (Cusco). There, among the high cities of the Altiplano region, a culture war raged in the seventeenth century, and the soldiers at the forefront of this battle were heavily armed angels.

Behold the *Ángeles Arcabuceros* (harquebusier angels or angel musketeers), gun-slinging soldiers of heaven dressed in luxurious martial outfits of seventeenth-century Spanish-Andean nobility. Examples of this painting tradition simply explode with exotic colour, from the angelic plumage of their hats and their own swooping wings, to the gilt embroidery of their brocaded tailoring. All the while they wield their arquebuses (a type of matchlock rifle commonly used in warfare at the time).

While clearly very beautiful works of art, what we are seeing with these paintings are documentations of cultural synthesis, an assimilative technique of conquerors that is as old as conquest. Here the imperial magnificence of Christianity is introduced and proselytised in a form recognisable and comprehensible to indigenous eyes, incorporating native spirituality, for the pre-Christian deities of the region were believed to have been young and handsome winged warriors, or 'deities of the stars'. The paintings represent a place and period undergoing immense forced cultural integration.

The idea of using art for indoctrination had first been proposed by the Council of Trent (the nineteenth ecumenical council of the Catholic church) between 1545 and 1563. But it was the church's missionaries who effected it, answering local superstitions by introducing the flock of angels in the apocryphal *Book of Enoch*, which reveals that angels control the stars and other natural phenomena. (There is Salamiel the peace of God; Aziel, the fear of God; Aspiel, drawn with gun reversed as if at a prince's funeral; Aspiel, God's lightning; Laeiel, the Forbearance of God; and so on.)

The Cusco artists drew inspiration from local fashions – the decorated feathered hats, the balloon sleeves, the lace,

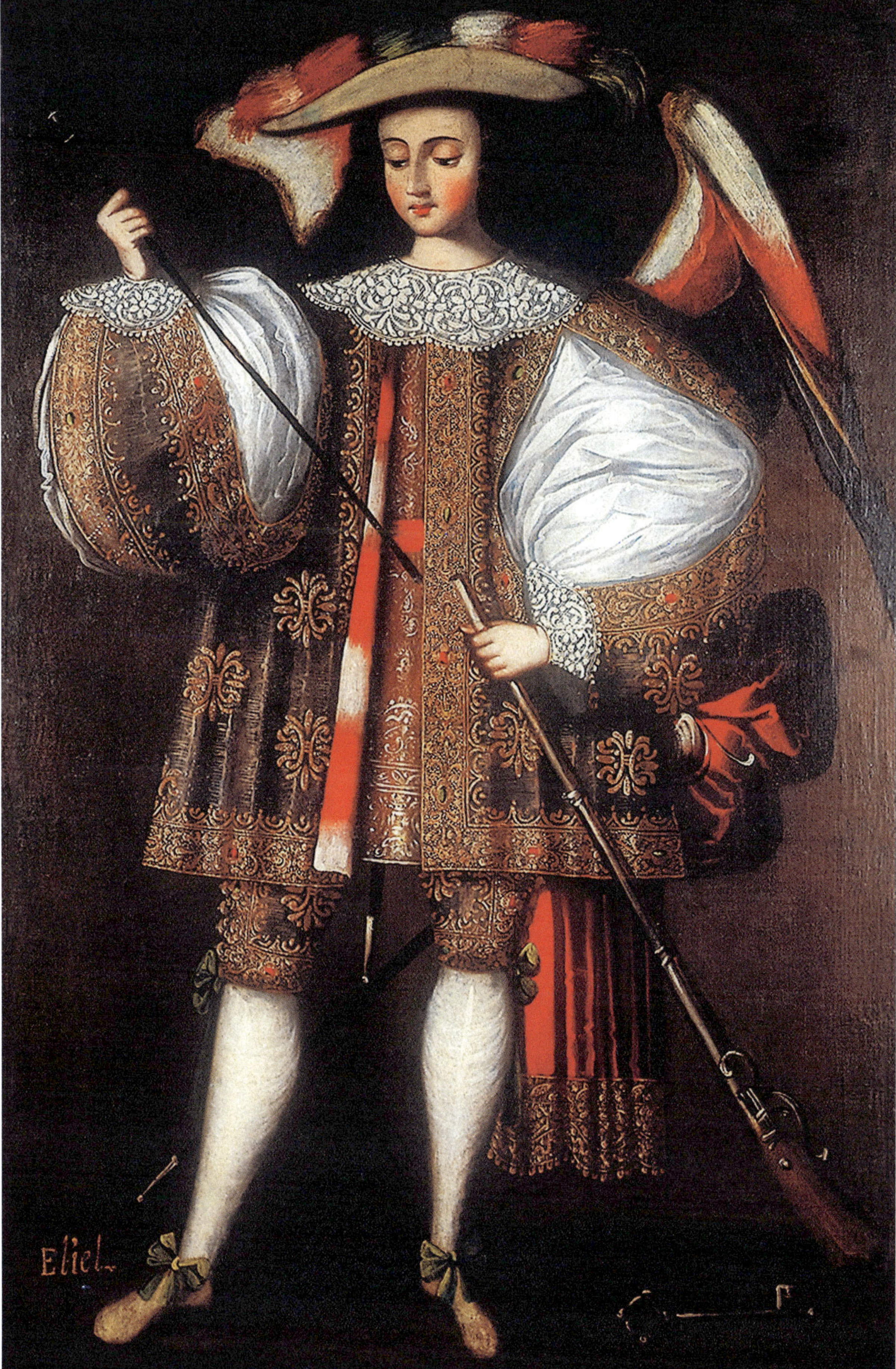
Eliel.

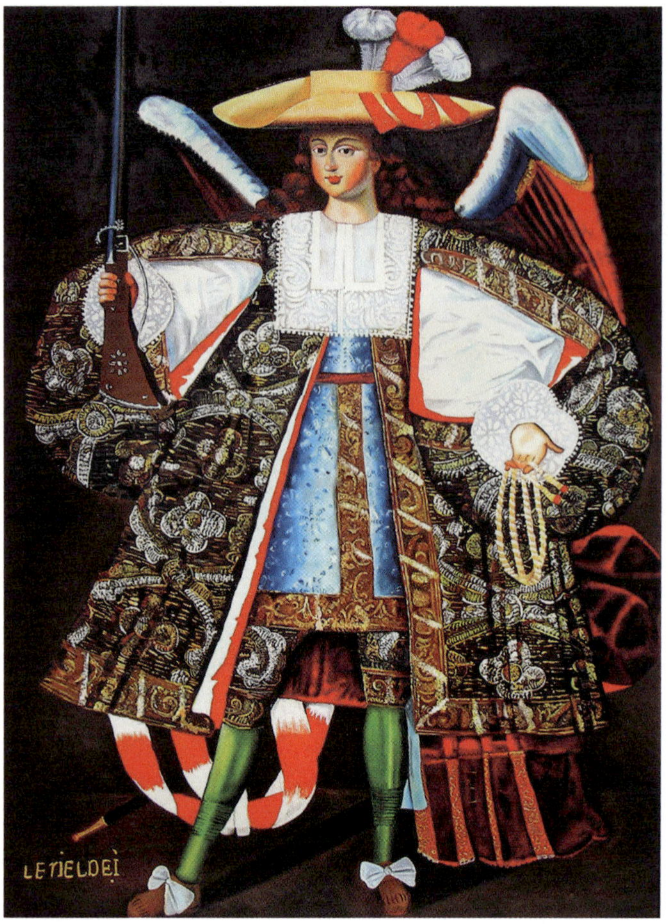

Left: *The angel Letiel as an* ángel arcabucero, *painted by a Bolivian artist known as the Master of Calamarca.*

Opposite: *Another* ángel arcabucero – *the seventeenth-century artist known as the Master of Calamarca.*

Below: *A hand-coloured plate from* The Exercise of Armes… *(1607), a guide to contemporary military exercises by Jacob de Gheyn.*

frilly cuffs, ribbons and stylish shoes, all in iridescent colours of both pre-Columbian and Spanish styles. Inspiration was also drawn from the style of Flemish Baroque art, and the more specific lodestar of Jacob de Gheyn's *Exercise of Armes…* (1607), a book of engravings of contemporary military exercises in which we find figures in identical poses.

Today surviving *Arcabuceros* works can be found widely not just in Peru but also Chile, Argentina and Mexico, and in collections of institutions around the world including Oxford University. But that is not to say it is a tradition that now lies relegated to the dust of basement archives – rather, it is an industry that thrives today. Though initially used as evangelical instrumentation, the paintings were popular into the twentieth century and continue to be produced today, largely for the tourist market, though still created with much the same materials and techniques as their ancestors of the seventeenth century.

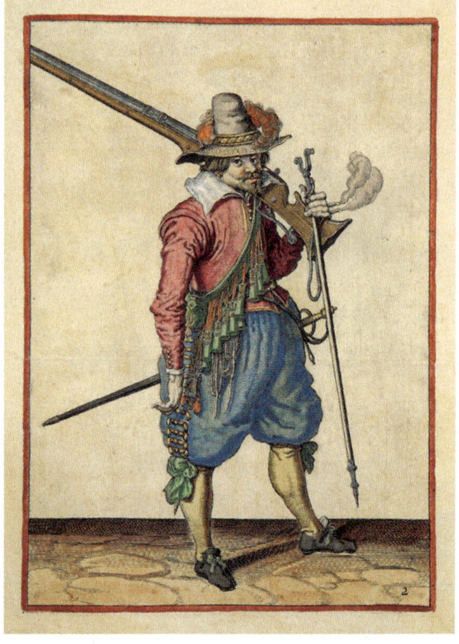

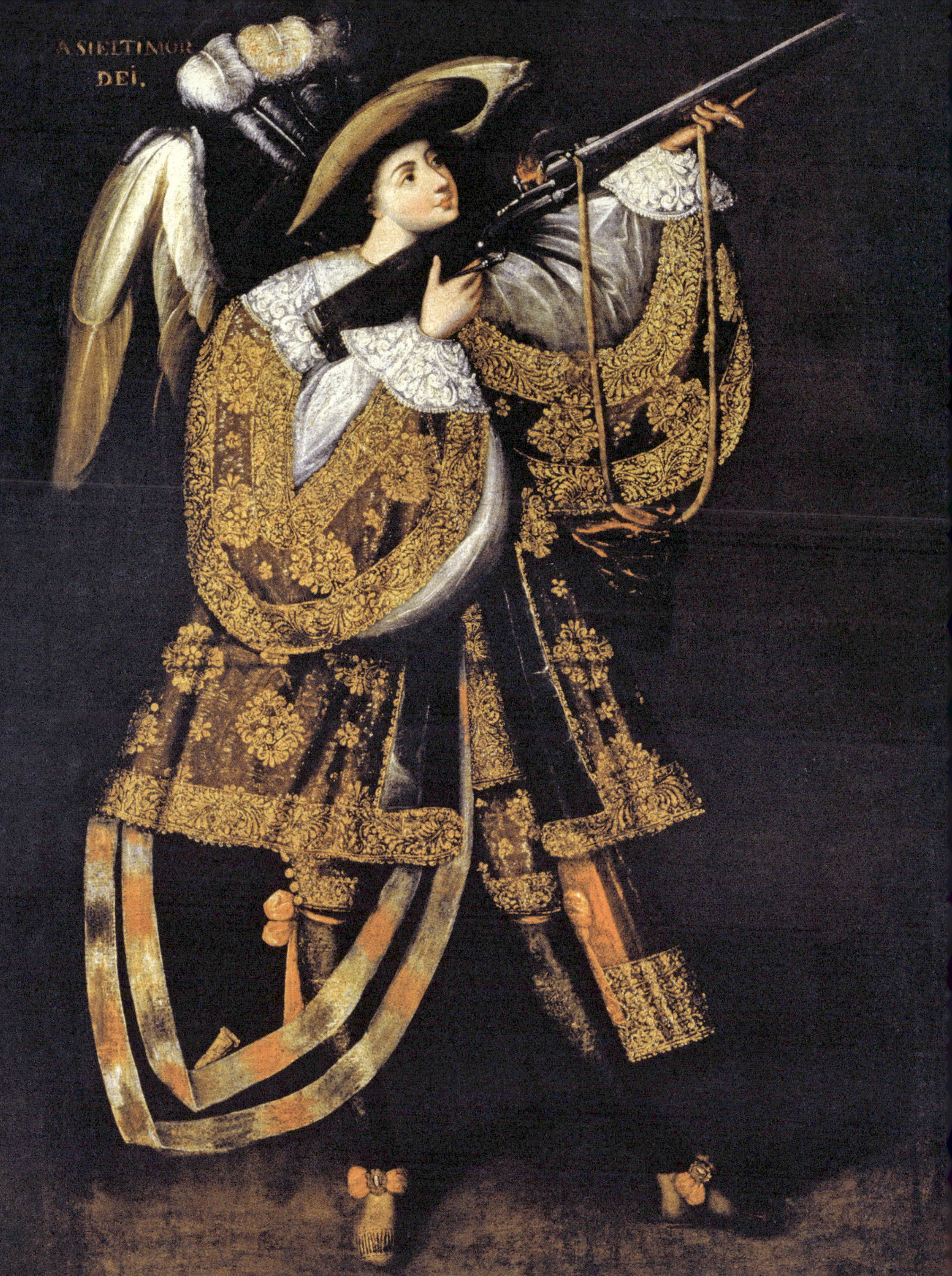
A SIELTIMOR
DEI.

CENTRAL AFRICAN *MINKISI* POWER FIGURES (SEVENTEENTH-TWENTIETH CENTURIES)

At first glance it might appear that these are statues of figures undergoing torture. Open-mouthed, apparently in a grimace of pain, the *nkisi* (power figure) shown here was made by a master working along the coast of Congo and Angola towards the end of the nineteenth century. The figure is embedded with a whirlwind of nails and shards of metal, which have been rammed into his torso, knees and feet and around his jawline. *Minkisi* (the commonly used plural term of *nkisi*) pieces are perhaps the most instantly eye-catching among Central African art, but their meaning is not the horror story that one first assumes.

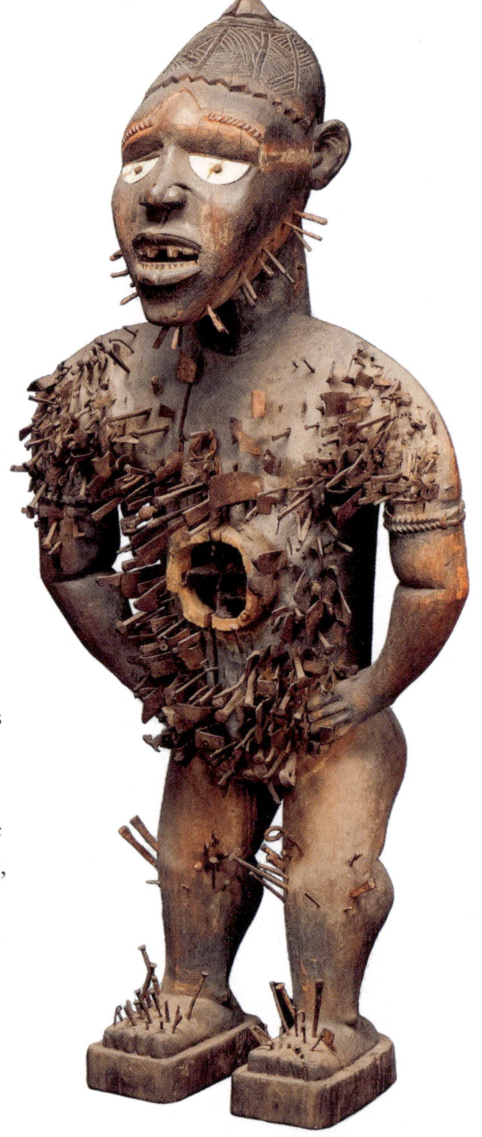

When the first Dutch explorers of the early seventeenth century entered the pre-colonial Kingdom of Loango, in what is now the western part of the Republic of the Congo, southern Gabon and Cabinda, they were introduced to the *mokissie* (as they translated it in Dutch), a term that referred to both the artwork of *minkisi* and the spirit that occupied it. The *minkisi*, which usually take the shape of human or animal figures, are complex instruments of great power that have various functions. As spiritual capacitors, they are at the centre of divination ceremonies, exorcism rituals to destroy the presence of evil or punish evil-doers, and rituals for protection against said evil. Some are used for healing, others for successful hunting and trading.

In order to house mystical power, the *minkisi* are the product of a collaboration between the sculptor and a *nganga* (healer or spiritual mediator). When the hollow wooden form is completed, the *nganga* fills it with *bilongo* (potent medicines) made from both organic and inorganic components of pigments, fibres, stones and other relics. These ingredients transform the object into an instrument of power, and soon it is deployed to help settle arguments and protect the peace. The example shown here, for instance, is identified with Mangaaka, the force of jurisprudence. The statue's authority is reinforced by the presence of its distinguished headdress, usually worn by chiefs and priests, and by its posture, which is an aggressive, challenging stance.

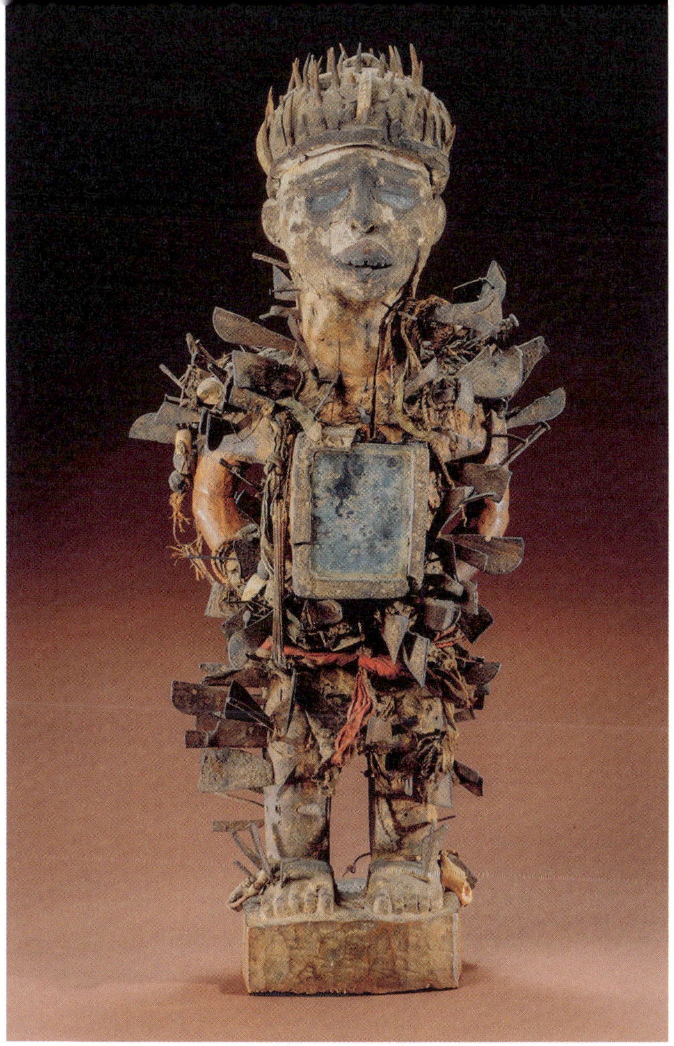

Left: *Another* nkisi *of the Kongo people from the nineteenth century, sheathed in iron. Potent substances would have been placed in the mirror-box of the chest and the upturned bowl on the head. The white clay on the face is a reference to the land of the dead, the source of the object's power.*

Below: *A late nineteenth-century* nkisi *in the form of a two-headed dog – an animal that the Kongo people considered to be a mediator between the worlds of the living and dead. Medicines were places on its back, and then a blade inserted into its body to initialise its power.*

So why the nails and shards of metal? While lending the figures an intimidating presence (and so serving as a warning about transgressing the codes of social conduct), every nail inserted into the body serves a specific documentary purpose. Each time the power of the *nkisi* was called upon, the *nganga* would insert a new piece of metal to activate its power, and so the metal pieces serve as records of disputes resolved, illnesses treated and evil spirits banished. What we see when we look at the *nkisi* is the documented history of a group dynamic – their relationships, worries, maladies, superstitions and desires. Their gruesome impression evaporates when we understand them to be practical objects, regulatory devices essential to maintaining group harmony by calling on the power of the spirits and the dead – artworks fuelled by the power of the past.

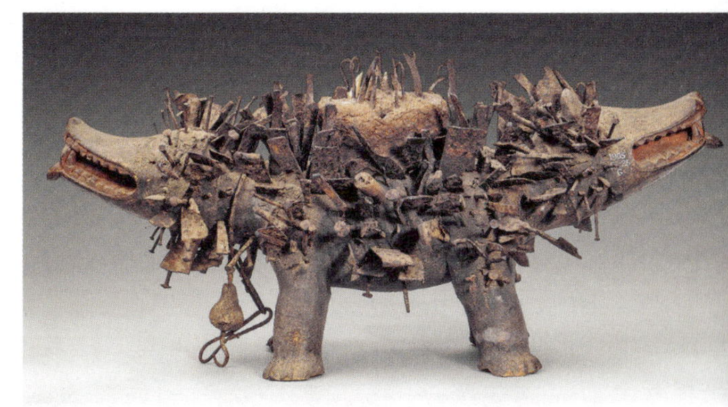

COMPETITION ON THE PONTE DEI PUGNI IN VENICE (1673), JOSEPH HEINTZ THE YOUNGER

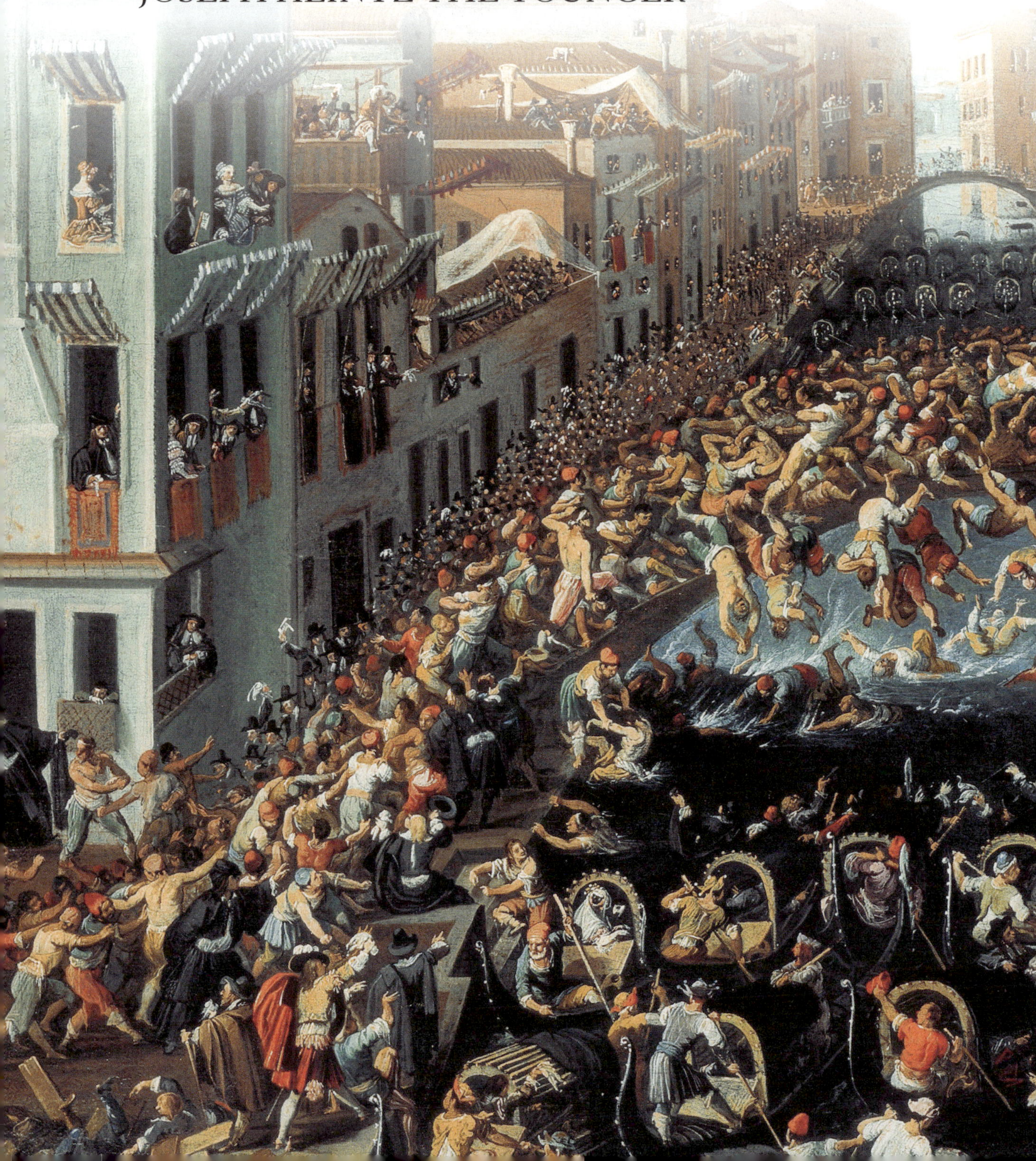

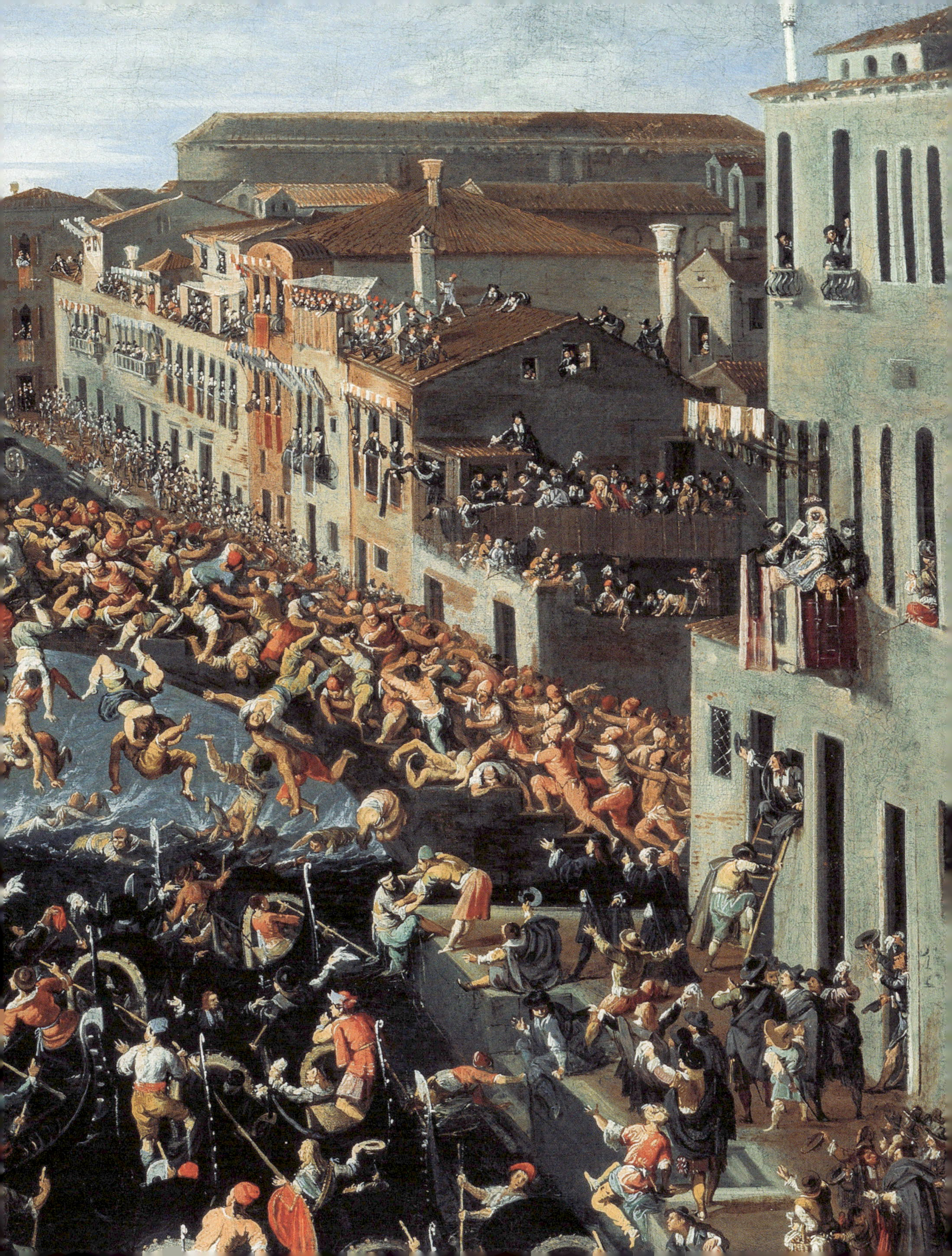

In *Competition on the Ponte dei Pugni in Venice* (1673) by Joseph Heintz the Younger (1600-68), two furious opposing forces charge at each other across a bridge, fists and weapons raised, battle cries filling the air. Men beat men with bare knuckles, knocking each other senseless from the bridge to tumble into the sewage-choked waters below. Heintz, who was German but settled in Venice in 1625, throws us into the midst of a brutal, bloodthirsty martial conflict – at least, this is what we assume. The strange fact is that in Venice, and indeed other cities around Italy, this was for centuries an annual organised event. Even stranger, it was done for fun. Welcome to the 'city battle' tradition: grand mock battles that were – theoretically – nonlethal, held between September and Christmas in which all citizenry could participate. Usually they were divided between north and south parts of the city, combatants represented their various wards and factions, allowing them to vent anger and frustration and enjoy the thrill of 'safe' battle by braining each other with clubs, stones and even snowballs.[1]

The scene on the previous pages is the *Guerra dei pugni* (Wars of the Fist), which began in official form *c.*1600. Venice's ruling Council of Ten reluctantly allowed the event to go ahead, as the bare-knuckle fistfighting was ultimately deemed an improvement on the previous tradition of the citizenry beating the merry hell out of each other with fire-toughened sticks. Plus, it was thought, with the populace directing their anger towards each other, there was less chance of an uprising against their governors.

As early as 1306, the city of Bologna played host to the *ludus graticulorium*, in which crowds of people furiously hurled raw eggs at each other (an early forerunner of the modern Spanish tomato-throwing festival, *La Tomatina*, which continues to take place in the Valencian town of Buñol). Most dangerous of all was the *battaglia dei sassi* (battle of the stones) held in Perugia. Organised by the *Compagnia del Sasso* (Company of Stones), thousands of players took part in a battle that saw the occupants of the northern

---

1 As unlikely as it sounds, mass snowball fights were historically dangerous affairs in which injury was common and death occasional. (An Italian document from 1438 records a Dominican friar who must have been harassed with one too many snowballs by a street youth, because he threw one back so forcefully that the child died of his injuries fifty-two days later.) Fearing the people would render each other unfit for military service, officials were quick to stamp out any unauthorised snowball skirmishes – in Basle, for example, decrees banning snowball fights were repeatedly made between 1378 and 1656 – but it didn't always work. A report from Perugia in 1371 describes one such subduing, and how the snowball throwers chose to completely ignore the guards sent to break up the fight with clubs, in favour of continuing their battle.

part of town clash with those of the southern, hurling rocks at each other. This was only the first part of the game: after the opening salvos, the men set upon each other with clubs and fists, protected in part by helmets, wooden armour and shields.

Identical to this was the *gioco delle pugna* (game of fights) held in Siena. A disapproving author of a record from 1425 describes the carnage: 'Go on, then! Tomorrow you will see charming bloodshot eyes, fine pale faces, many bandaged arms and legs, as many lacking teeth, let alone internal injuries... Two-thirds of the entertainment belongs to the audience, only the rest to the players, and in addition they suffer broken sides, cut foreheads, sprained and broken extremities, ribs, chins...'

The government frequently opposed these battles, but the citizenry doesn't seem to have taken much notice of this. The Sienese diarist Allegro Allegretti referred to the *pugna* as *un belissimo giucco* (a beautiful game) in 1494, and when Charles V visited the city in 1536 a battle was held in his honour, which he is said to have enjoyed tremendously.

One type of these battles was the *mazzascudo* (club and shield), the most famous of which were staged in Florence. The last one to be held, in 1582 at the behest of Grand Duke Francis I of Tuscany, was the most notorious. The Duke paid 88 *scudos* to have it as part of the celebrations for the wedding of his daughter, Eleonor de' Medici, to Vincenzo Gonzaga. Things got a little out of hand, however, and the romantic gift had to be brought to a close early so that the multiple dead and wounded could be carried away.

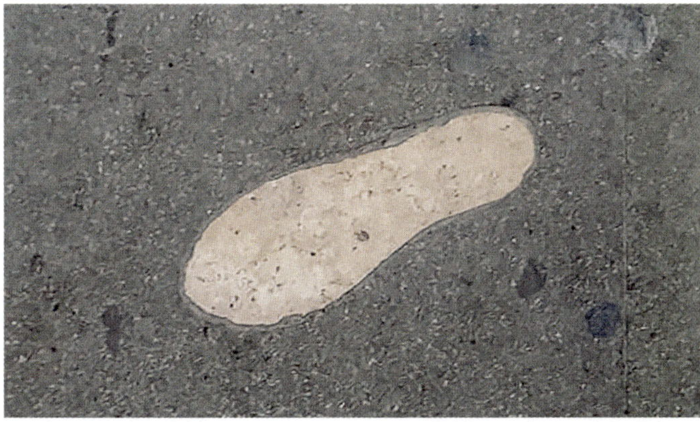

One of four white marble footprints at Venice's Ponte dei Pugni that mark the starting point for combatants.

TYPUS RELIGIONIS (*c.*1700) AND THE ART OF BLASPHEMY

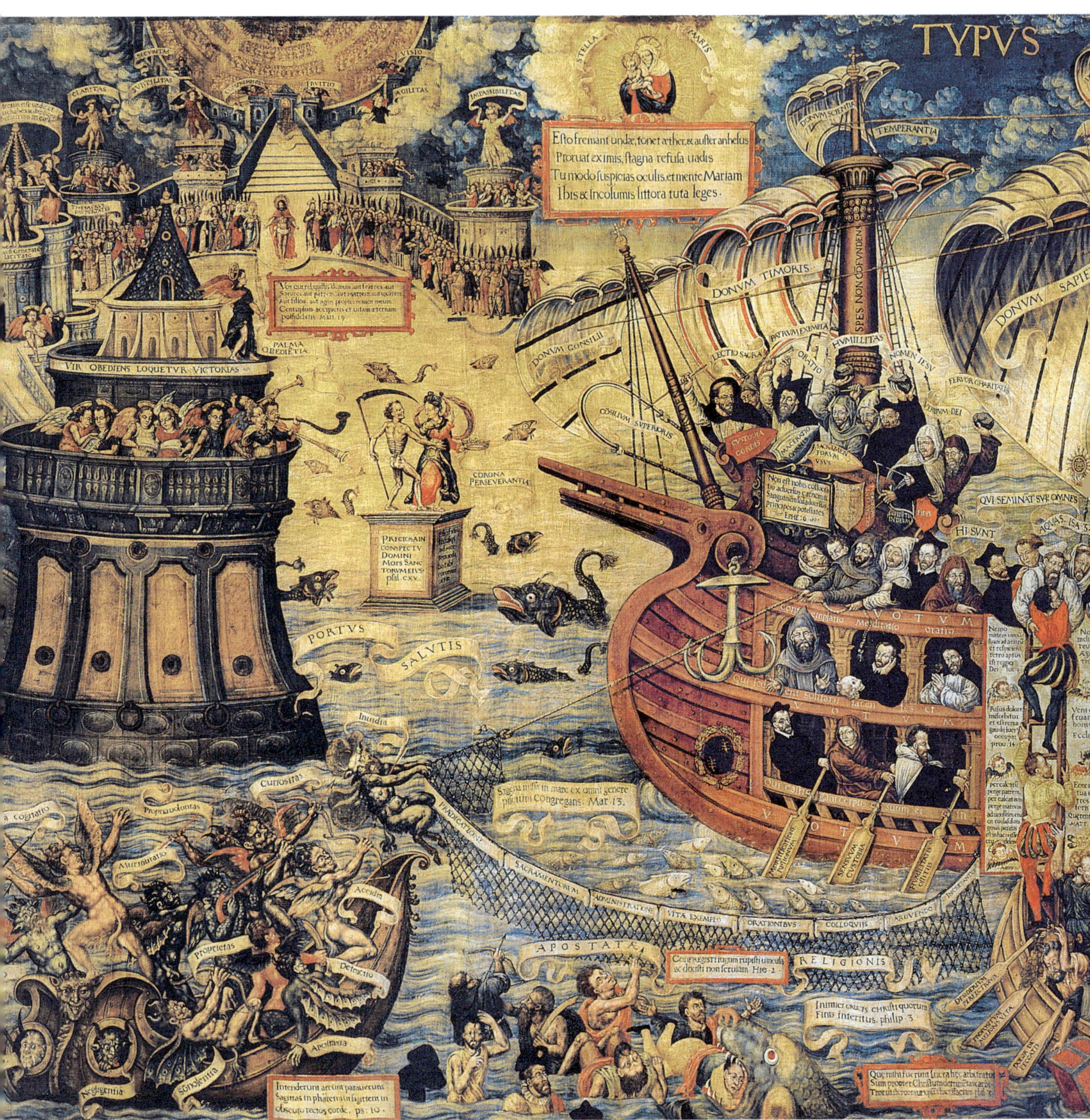

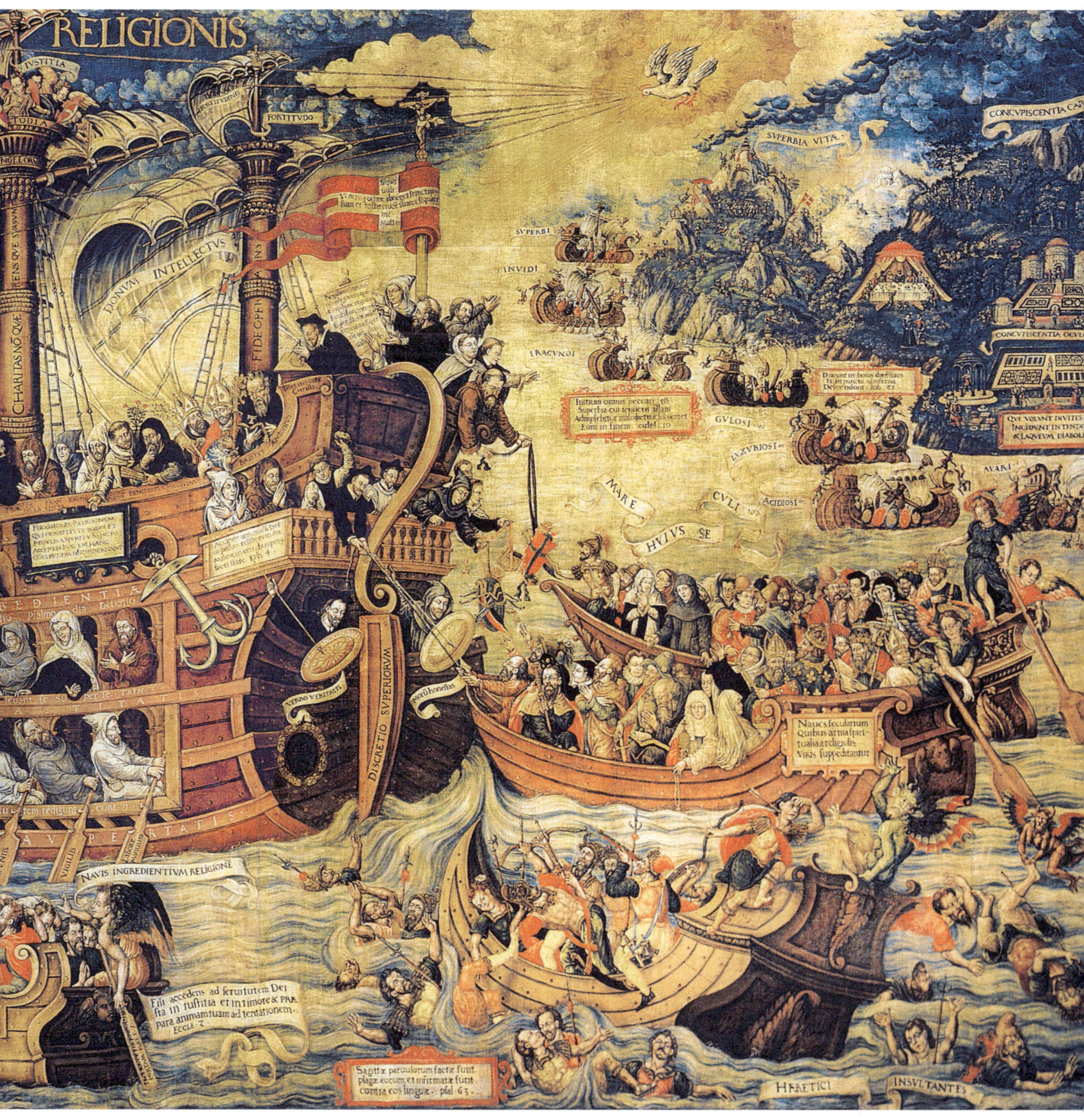
RELIGIONIS
IVSTITIA
FORTITVDO
DONVM INTELLECTVS
SVPERBIA VITÆ.
CONCVPISCENTIA CA
SVPERBI
INVIDI
IRACVNDI
CONCVPISCENTIA OCVL
Initium omnis peccati est
Superbia qui tenuerit illam
Adimplebitur maledictis et subvertet
Eum in finem. eccl: 10
Ducunt in bonis dies suos
Et in puncto ad inferna
Descendunt. Iob. 21
GVLOSI
LVXVRIOSI
QVI VOLVNT DIVITES
INCIDVNT IN TENTA
& LAQVEVM DIABOL
AVARI
MARE
HVIVS
SE
CVLI
ACIDIOSI
VERBO VERITATIS
DISCRETIO SVPERIORVM
Naues fecularium
Quibus arma spiri-
tualia a religiosis
Viris suppeditantur
NAVIS INGREDIENTIVM RELIGIONE
Fili accedens ad seruitutem Dei
sta in iustitia et in timore & PRÆ
para animam tuam ad tentationem.
ECCLE. 2
Sagittæ paruulorum factæ sunt
plagæ eorum et infirmatæ sunt
contra eos linguæ. psal 63.
HÆRETICI
INSVLTANTES

Since antiquity, blasphemy and acts of sacrilege were often considered the worst of crimes. In ancient Greece, for example, the sculptor Pheidias was brought up on criminal charges for carving his own image on the shield of the colossal bronze statue of Athena erected at the Acropolis of Athens *c.*456 BC. In 1987 New York artist Andrés Serrano (b.1950) created his notorious *Immersion (Piss Christ)*, a photograph of a plastic crucifix submerged in his own urine. It was, he said, a critique of the commercialisation and misappropriation of religion. The New York senator Al d'Amato tore up a photo of the work in the US Senate in 1989. When the Netherlands Groninger Museum exhibited Serrano's work in 1997 it was forced to close for the first time since its founding, due to the bomb threats it received. In the same year Serrano exhibited at the National Gallery of Victoria, Australia, to similar outrage, and it was attacked with a hammer. The state premier Jeff Kennett suggested offended parties could just 'go and play tennis instead'.

Much greater impact was made by the relatively obscure, 3 × 1.8m (10 × 6ft), allegorical work *Typus Religionis* (Model of Religion), as it came to be known, by an anonymous artist of the late sixteenth or early seventeenth century. Today it can be found on display at the Hôtel de Soubise, Paris – very different surroundings to its original home of the Jesuit College at Billom. The painting shows a galleon ship embodying Faith, carrying its passengers away from the trappings of the material world and taking on other believers saved from smaller ships sinking in a sea of labelled sins – *superbi* (pride), *invidi* (envy), *iracundi* (anger), etc.

The faithful ship sails for the golden Port of Salvation on the left-hand side, passing Death on a podium engraved with Psalm 116:15 'Precious in the sight of the Lord is the death of his saints', to be greeted by trumpeting angels and Christ with arms wide at the base of the steps of Heaven. The ship's passengers hurl rocks at a boat of demons (lower-left corner) and resist attacks by heretics (lower-right corner). A positive allegory of the benevolent Jesuits and their mission to guide everyone around the world across the satanic sea to salvation, one would initially assume. But an altogether different and damning interpretation was made in the eighteenth century, which we can lead into by examining the painting's details more closely.

In prime position at the centre of the Faith Ship, at the foot of the central mast, we find St Ignatius of Loyola, one of the co-founders of the Society of Jesus. In one hand he holds a Bible and in the other a glowing, floating Christogram of the Society's official seal, which appears to be filling the billowing mainsail with its powerful force. St Ignatius oversees other

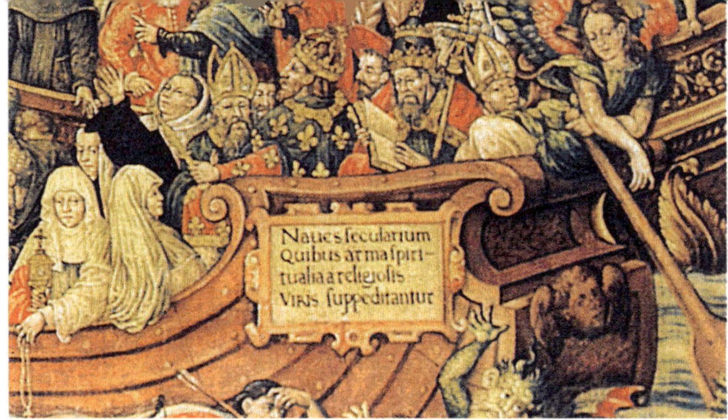

LEFT: *The Pope and the King of France are towed behind the Faith ship.*

shipmates, who include several Jesuit priests as well as – and here's where things start to get a little problematic – other founders of Christian religious orders, like St Francis of Assisi (Order of Friars Minor), St Bruno (Order of Carthusians), St Dominic (Order of Preachers), St Basil (Eastern monasticism); and St Anthony (Western monasticism).

But the most dangerous details can be found in the small *Naves Seculariom* (secular ship), helplessly towed with a rope behind the principal Faith ship. The hapless passengers of this secondary vessel, desperate to keep up, include King Henri IV of France and the Pope, who is absently lost in the pages of a book. (This sacrilegious detail was clearly too much for the colourist of a print of the painting at Chicago's Newberry Library, who covered up the passengers in the rear half of this boat with a large smudge of brown paint.) These helpless passengers are forced to rely on the assistance of the Jesuits to reach the Port of Salvation on the left-hand side.

'This coarse painted image is the work of some tenth-order dauber,' sniffed the French art historian Jules Guiffrey (1840-1918), but a considerably more severe and consequential criticism of *Typus Religionis* had occurred earlier, in 1762, when the canvas was ripped from the walls of the Jesuit College and confiscated as evidence at the trial of the Billom Jesuits. The work was held up as proof of both the arrogance of the order and, more importantly, their denigration of Catholicism and the Crown, with the portrayal of those outside the order as helplessly reliant on the Society to avoid sinking into a sea of sin.

In the notes of the trial it is recorded that the most scandalising aspect was that the Pope was towed cargo, when he should have been in command of the ship of Christianity. In depicting the Jesuit fathers as directing both Church and State, the painting was instrumental in discrediting the Society of Jesus in the trial brought by the French government in 1763, leading to the closure of the college at Billom and ultimately to the dissolution and expulsion of the Jesuits from the realm of France.

BELOW: *This bizarre work by an unknown artist is thought to have been painted in the Netherlands sometime in the seventeenth century. The floating form of a Catholic pope is at first recognisable from his bejewelled headpiece but, as the canvas is rotated 180 degrees, it morphs into a devil's head with pointed bestial ears and horns. The satire is part of a long thematic tradition of the 'inverted world', especially popular towards the end of the Middle Ages – wise men are actually fools, kings are paupers, etc.*

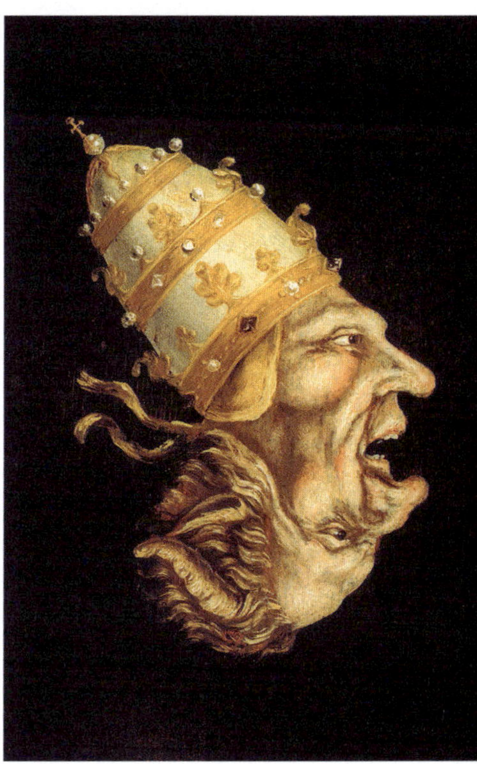

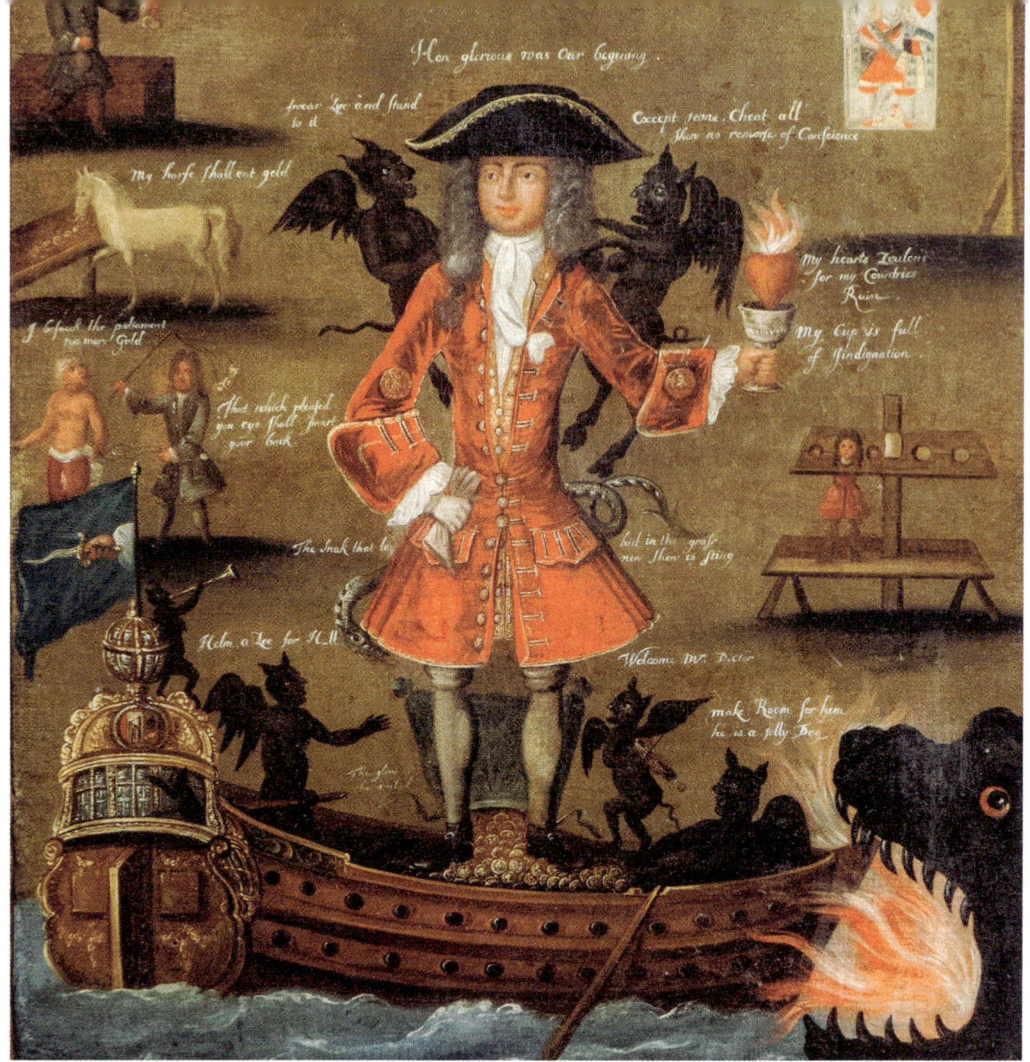

LUCIFER'S NEW ROW-BARGE (*c*.1722)
AND THE ART OF SATIRE

Here for your viewing pleasure is a portrait by an unknown artist of one of the most hated men in eighteenth-century England. Robert Knight (1702-72), financier, co-founder and cashier of the South Sea Company and all-round odious fraudster, is shown riding on a gilded barge heading straight for the fiery jaws of hell.

He stands shameless on a pile of his ill-gotten gains, celebrated by his admiring demonic crew. 'I am the faithful cashier,' says the devil-headed figure in the upper-left corner of the painting. 'Swear Lye and Stand to it,' cries the devil to the left of Knight's shoulder while the other whispers into his ear, 'Except none, Cheat all. Shew no remorse of Conscience.'

The vitriol was well earned. The mercantile South Sea Company had been founded in 1711 to traffic African slaves to the islands in the 'South Seas' and South America. At the time, however, Britain was caught up in the War of the Spanish Succession, and Spain and Portugal controlled the majority of the South American continent, so there was never a chance of the company turning a profit, which indeed it didn't. So the company looked for alternative income.

In 1719 Knight headed the negotiations of a grand deal with the British government, which would see the South Sea Company incorporate the national debt, an agreement that would trigger the largest financial crisis of the century. While it initially seemed like a good deal for all involved – the government received a cash injection and the promise of low interest rates on its future debt – the value of the South Sea Company stock was vastly inflated artificially by its new position as an apparently safe government-backed investment.

Herds of investors clamoured to be a part of it, and Knight and his company cohorts were suddenly making huge amounts of money. By the end of the summer of 1720, share prices of the South Sea Company had exploded from around £100 earlier in the year to almost £1000.

The mother of all speculative financial bubbles burst at the end of September 1720. Thousands of investors from every walk of life were left bankrupt, their lives in tatters. Parliament was recalled in December, and the subsequent investigation found evidence of widespread fraud among the company directors and bribery of Cabinet members including the Chancellor of the Exchequer, the Postmaster General and the Southern Secretary.

The newly appointed First Lord of the Treasury, Robert Walpole (1676-1745), removed thirty-three of the company directors and stripped them of an average of 82 per cent of their wealth, to be distributed among the victims of the scheme. Knight, though, had fled to the France, with his little green book in which he had recorded the details of every bribe paid to members of the government and aristocracy. Perhaps, it was reasoned nervously by those in authority, it was best to leave him to his voluntary exile.

The painting *Lucifer's New Row-Barge*, then, by an unknown artist, is the closest Knight came to any form of justice, his reputation still suffering the tarnish of the furious painter centuries later. 'My Heart is Zealous for my Countries Ruin' and 'Heads I win, tails you lose' read the inscriptions; 'The glory of the wicked'.

Top and Tail *(1777) (artist unknown) is another curious example of eighteenth-century satirical art in a genre known as 'no-body prints'. These figures of just legs and heads (i.e. with no brain in between) mocked fashions of the time – in this case the oversized wigs worn by women in Britain and France before the French Revolution.*

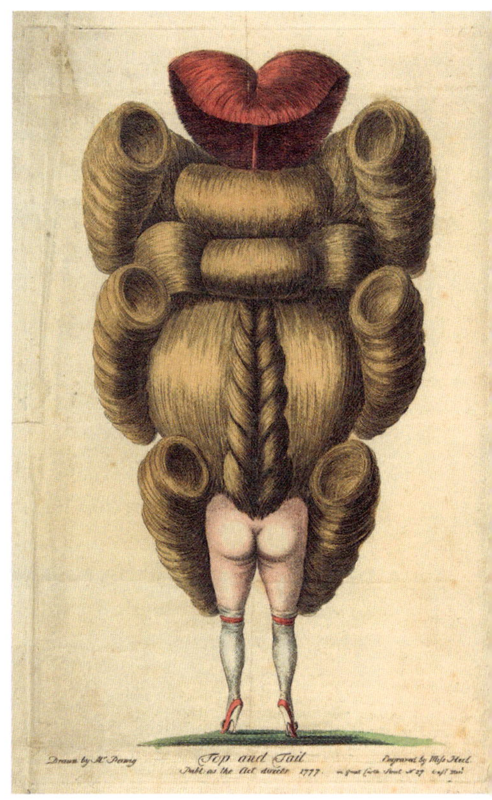

JOSEPH OF CUPERTINO TAKES FLIGHT... (EIGHTEENTH CENTURY), LUDOVICO MAZZANTI

So frequent were the levitations of St Joseph of Cupertino (1603-63), an Italian Franciscan monk who magically flew in moments of religious fervour, that he enjoys recognition as the patron saint of aeroplane passengers. When it comes to tales of airborne holy figures there is, in fact, much in the way of source material. Simon Magus, the Samaritan sorcerer recorded in the Bible in Acts 8:9, is also described in the apocryphal *Acts of Peter* as having the ability to soar into the air. When he demonstrated this power in the Roman Forum, Peter prayed for God to intervene and Simon fell to the ground, shattering his legs, and he was stoned to death by a crowd.[1]

St Teresa of Avila (1515-82) told of receiving a rapturous 'spiritual visitation' that resulted in her levitating 0.5m (1½ft) off the ground for just under an hour. St Francis of Assisi (*c*.1181-1226) was popularly said to have been able to suspend himself above the ground, as was St Alphonsus Liguori (1696-1787), who in 1756 was reported by Canon Casanova of Amalfi Cathedral to have flown with 'his body raised almost two foot [0.6m] above where he stood, as if about to wing his flight for the skies!'

But back to Joseph of Cupertino. One eighteenth-century hagiographer, Fr Angelo Pastrovicchi, wrote that: 'Not only during the sixteen years of the saint's stay at Grottella, but during his whole life, these ecstasies and flights were so frequent, as attested in the acts of the Process of beatification, that for more than thirty-five years his superiors would not permit him to take part in the exercises in the choir and the refectory or in processions, lest he disturb the community.' The power of flight could take hold of him at any moment. One Christmas Eve, for example, Joseph was celebrating with a group of shepherds when the men started playing their bagpipes. Joseph was so inspired that he shot into the air and hung suspended over the altar for fifteen minutes, his robes dangling amid the candles but not catching fire.

---

1 The Italian church of Santa Francesca Romana, located beside the Roman Forum, claims to have been built on the exact spot of this crash landing and to contain a piece of marble dented by the knees of Peter as he prayed for Simon's failure.

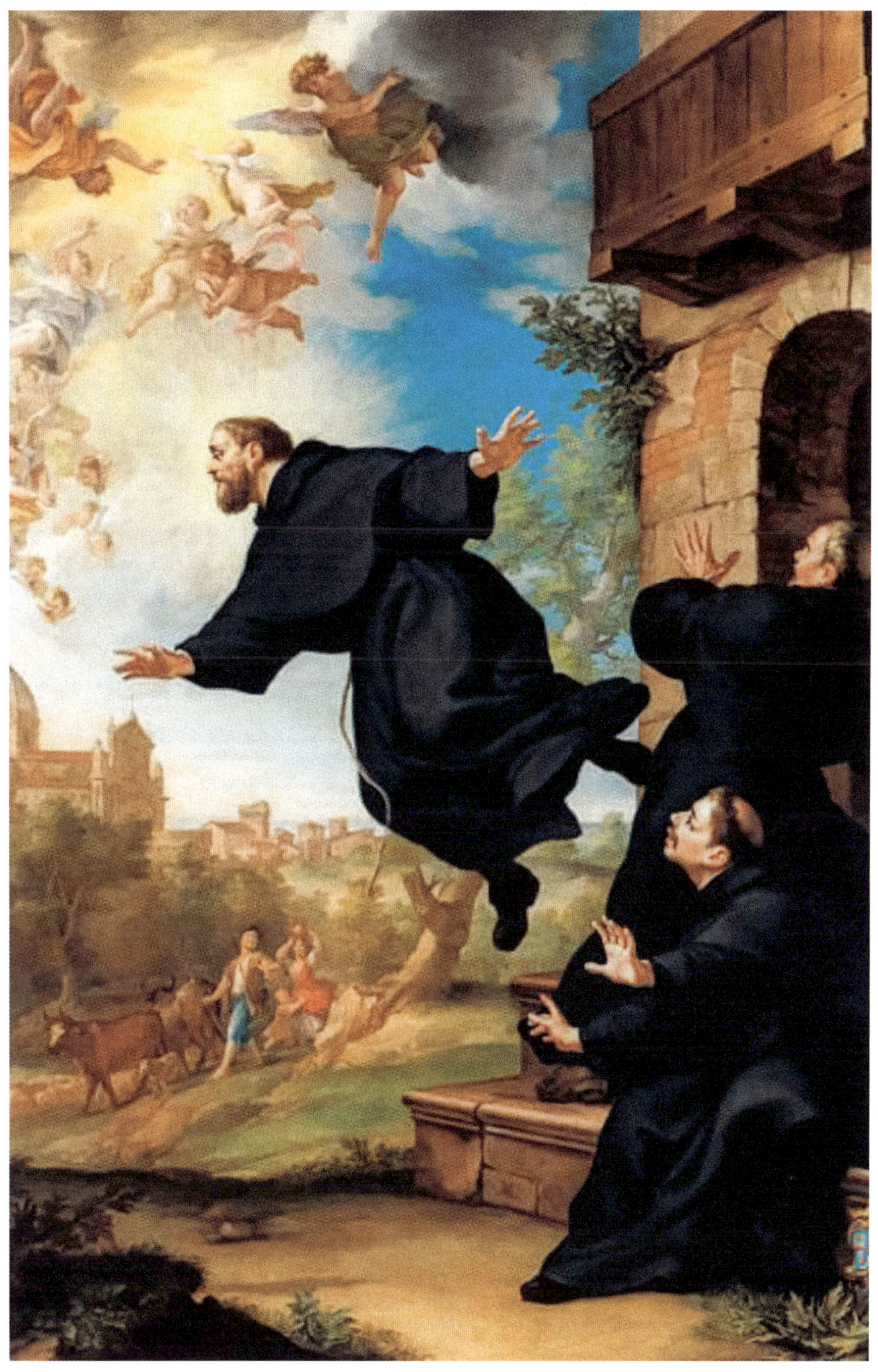

Joseph of Cupertino Takes Flight… *(eighteenth century), Ludovico Mazzanti*

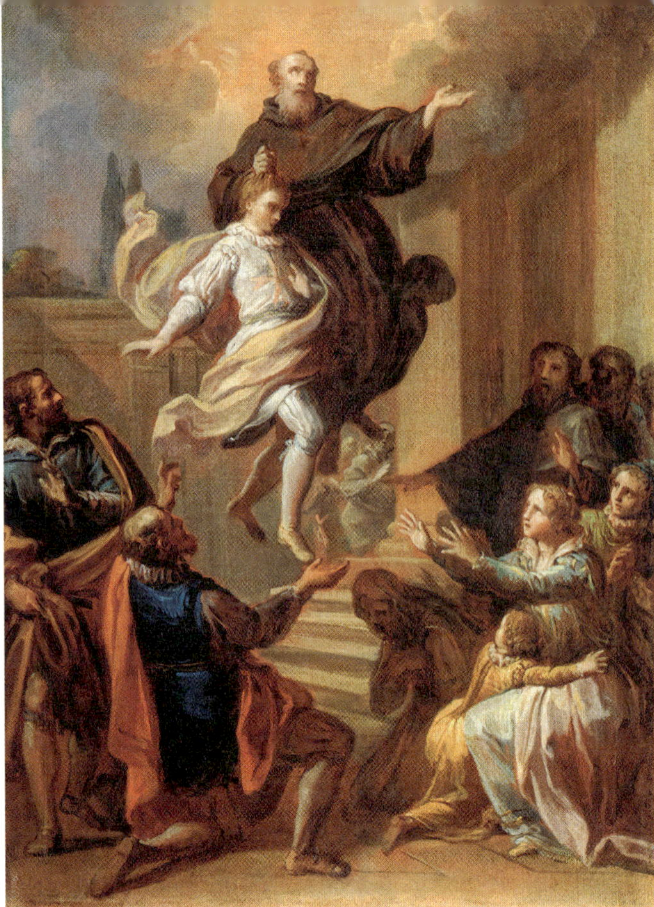

Left: A Miracle of St Joseph of Cupertino (1603-1633) *(1750), by Placido Costanzi. St Joseph of Cupertino exorcises a possessed youth while holding him by the hair in midair.*

Opposite: *A panel from the* Blessed Agostino Novello Triptych *(c.1328) by the Italian painter Simone Martini (c.1284-1344). The Blessed Agostino Novello (1240-1309) is shown miraculously appearing to save a child falling from a balcony.*

During a journey to Naples to visit a new statue of St Anthony of Padua, Joseph caught sight of the monument and flew over the heads of his brethren to inspect it. As the legend goes, word of his miracles reached the Inquisition, who commanded him to say mass in their company at the Church of San Gregorio Armeno. Again he took flight, ending up suspended above the altar to the shrieks of nuns warning that the candles would set him alight.

Another biographer, Domenico Bernini (1657-1723), mentions in 1722 the time that Joseph was walking through a beautiful garden with a priest named Antonio Chiarello, when a comment was made on the magnificence of God's creation. Joseph gave an excited shriek in agreement and shot into the air, finally coming to rest atop an olive tree, where he remained kneeling for half an hour, the branch swaying 'as light as if a small bird had perched on it'. In the *Acta Sanctorum* (the official records of Joseph's beatification process), seventy separate incidents of his levitations and ecstatic flights are officially noted. These inspired several artworks over the years, but none quite so colourful as that of Ludovico Mazzanti (1686-1775) shown on the previous page.

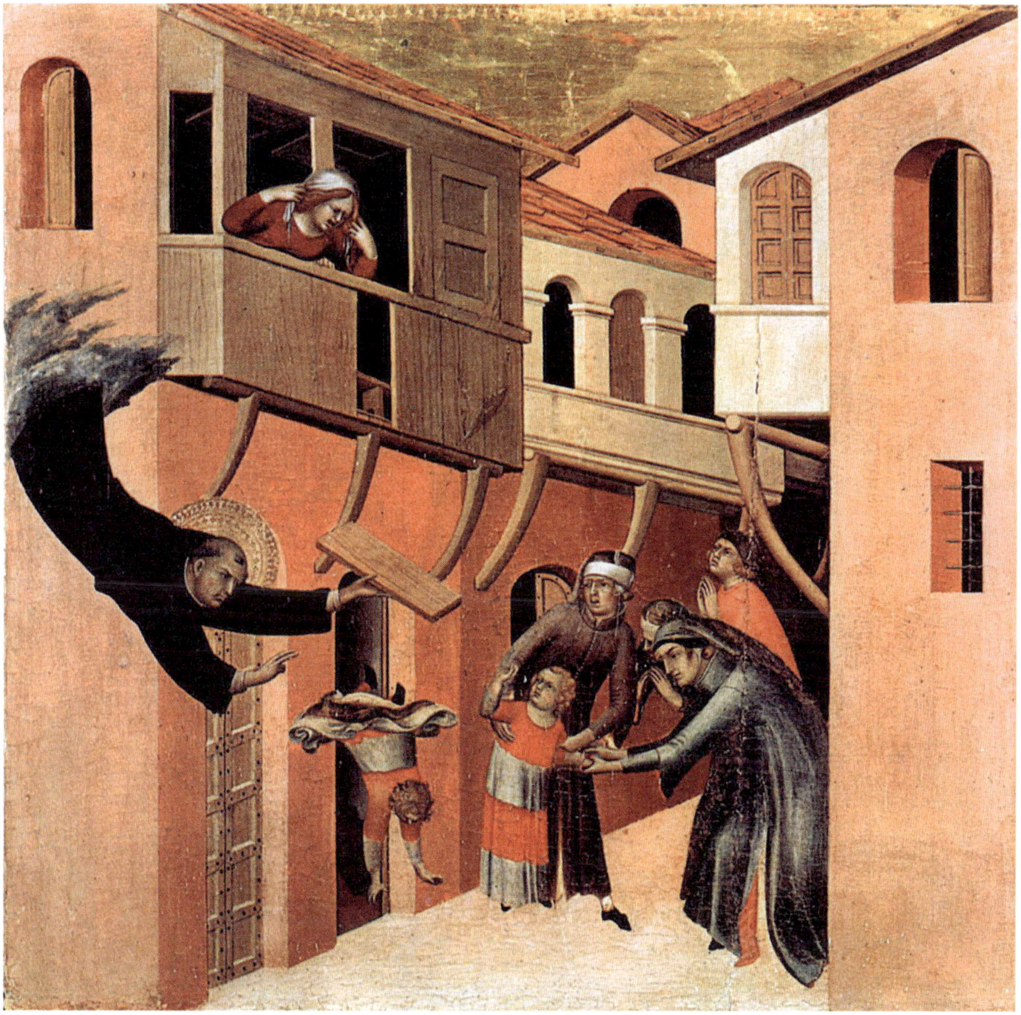

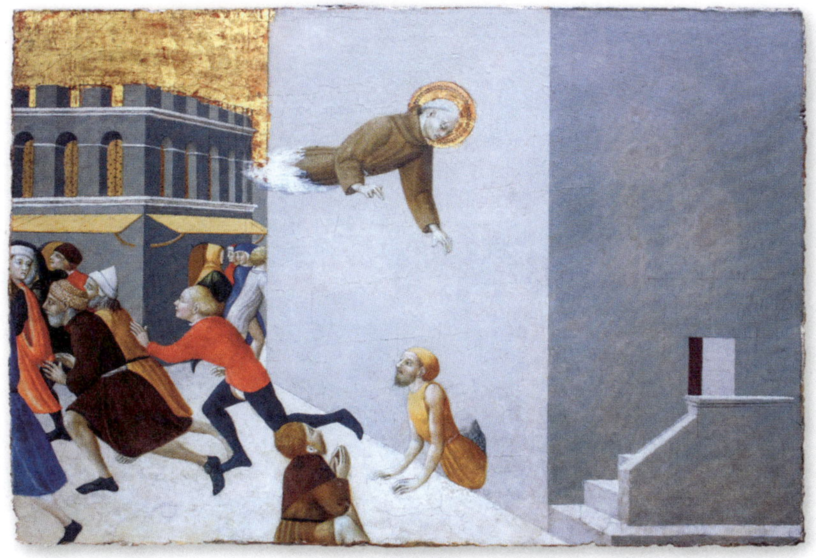

LEFT: The Blessed Ranieri Frees the Poor from a Jail in Florence *(c.1437-44) by the Sienese Renaissance painter Stefano di Giovanni di Consolo (c.1392-1450) is part of an altarpiece commissioned by the authorities at the Church of San Francesco in the town of Sansepolcro. The Blessed Ranieri Rasini (1250-1304) was renowned for helping the poor and performing miracles such as that shown here, in which he responds to a letter from prisoners in Florence by floating outside the prison and miraculously effecting a jailbreak.*

Joseph of Cupertino Takes Flight… *(eighteenth century), Ludovico Mazzanti*

THE IMAGINARY PRISONS OF GIOVANNI BATTISTA PIRANESI (1750)

To explore his etchings of imaginary prisons is to wander through the dark brain of the Venetian artist Giovanni Battista Piranesi (1720-78) himself. Italian prisons were small dungeons, but here they are – paradoxically – boundless. Giant arches support giant arches, seemingly for no structural purpose, with gates and ladders leading nowhere. Chains and ropes swing and dangle into view with the threat of torture, or perhaps part of some great dormant industrial machine, as do the huge wheels that rise up in this underworld, reminiscent of the fiery spoked wheel to which the Greek mythological figure Ixion was bound by Zeus. Bridges twist around pillars like serpents, leading both their pedestrians and the eye of the viewer on endless journeys around the cavernous complexes. And yet with all the space on display we still feel the claustrophobic pressure of the confining walls and the dank chill of the air, and taste the grime and char of the fires that puff here and there.

The *Carceri d'Invezione* (Prisons of the Imagination; or, ambiguously, the imprisonment of imagination) etchings were first published anonymously in 1750, and were republished under Piranesi's name in much darker and in even more nightmarish form in 1761 with a total of sixteen etchings (from which are taken the images shown here). They have fascinated ever since. They are, wrote the French novelist Marguerite Yourcenar (1903-87), 'one of the most secret works bequeathed us by a man of the eighteenth century', the dreamlike quality of the images representing the 'negation of time, incoherence of space, suggested levitation, intoxication of the impossible reconciled or transcended'. The first series gave little away in terms of their creator's intention; the second series, however, makes several allusions to the justice system of the Roman Republic and the notorious cruelty of certain emperors.

Opposite: The Drawbridge *from the darker second edition of the* Carceri *series (1761).*

The 'capricious inventions', as they are described on their title page, are a subterranean world away from the picture-postcard work produced by Piranesi's contemporaries – the *vedutisti* (view makers) like Canaletto (1697-1768) – who were churning out colourful, sunlit, idealised scenes of Venice and its pageantry. Piranesi's imagination took him to deeper, more mysterious and inventive places – 'their intensity, their

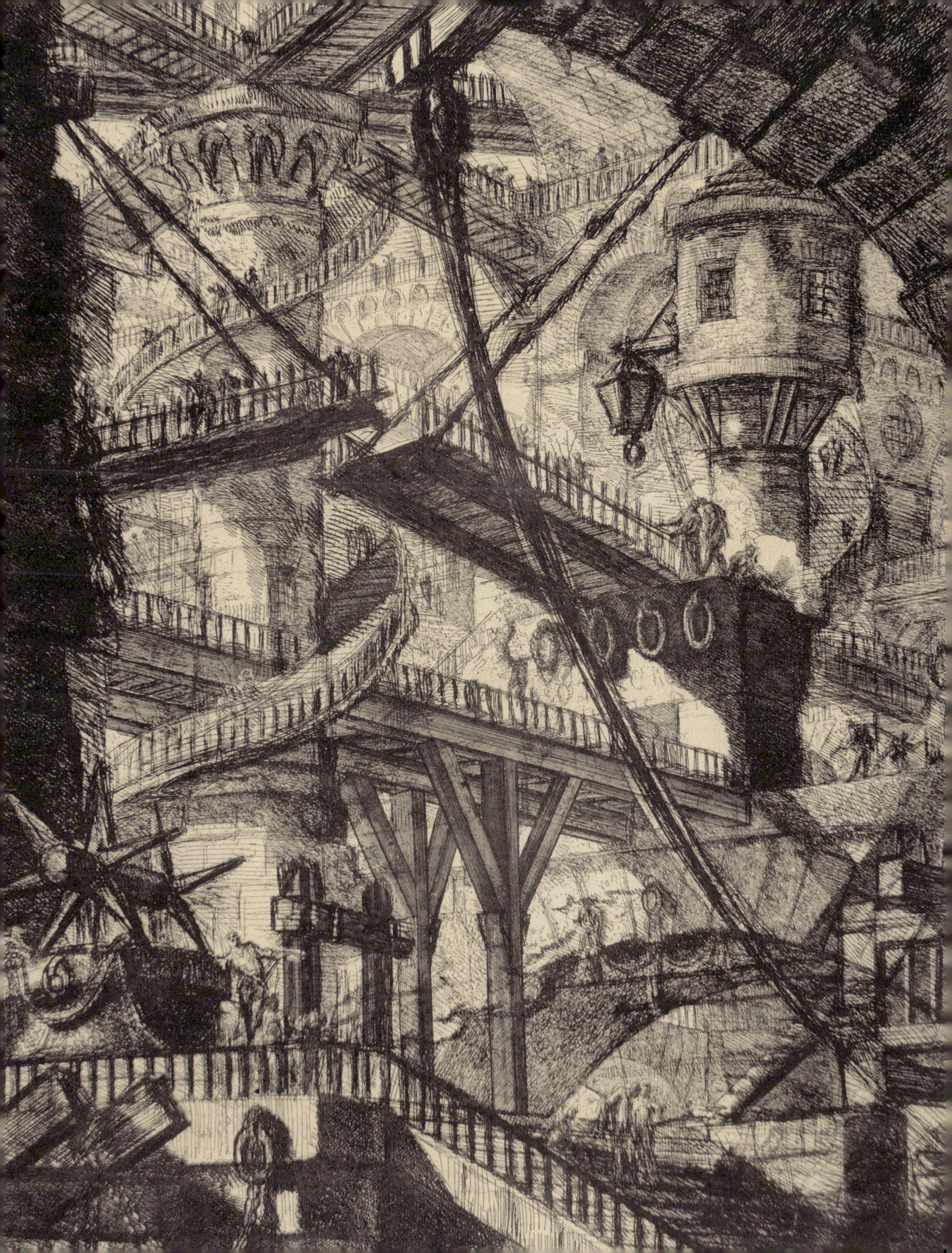

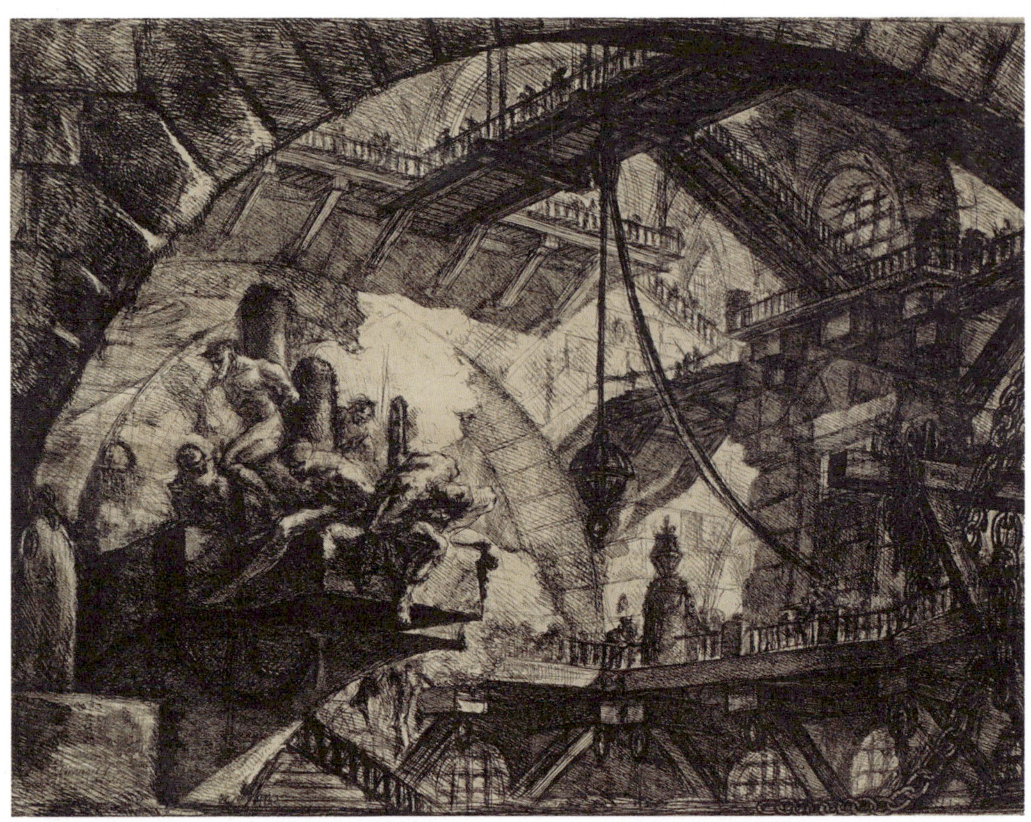

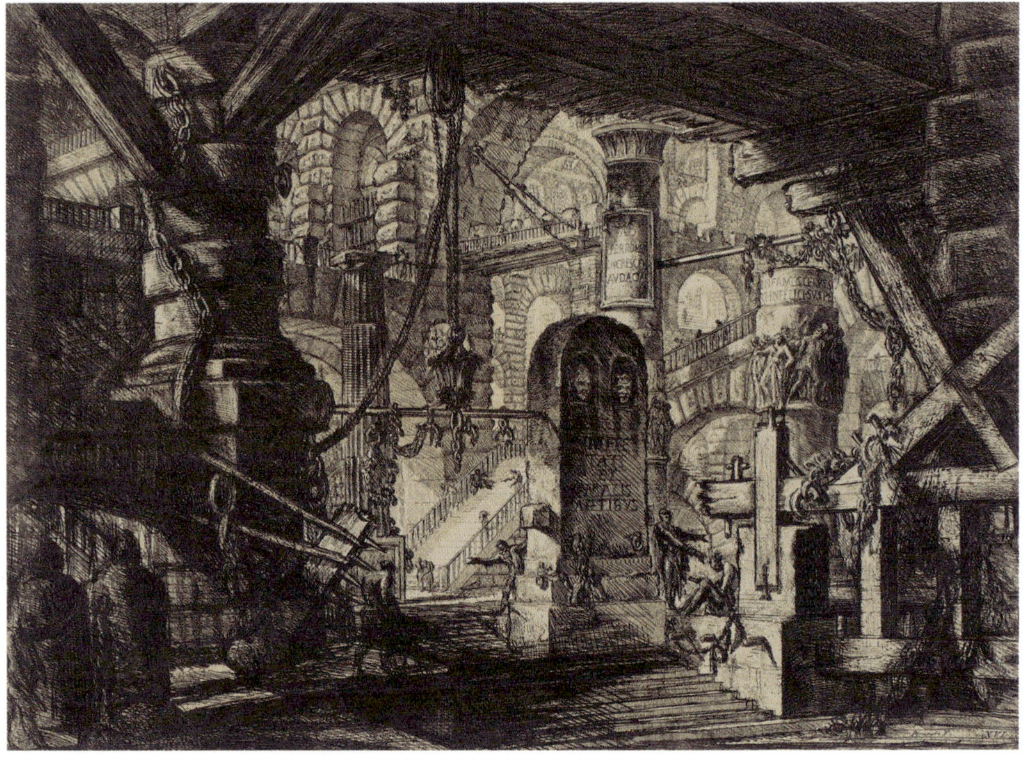

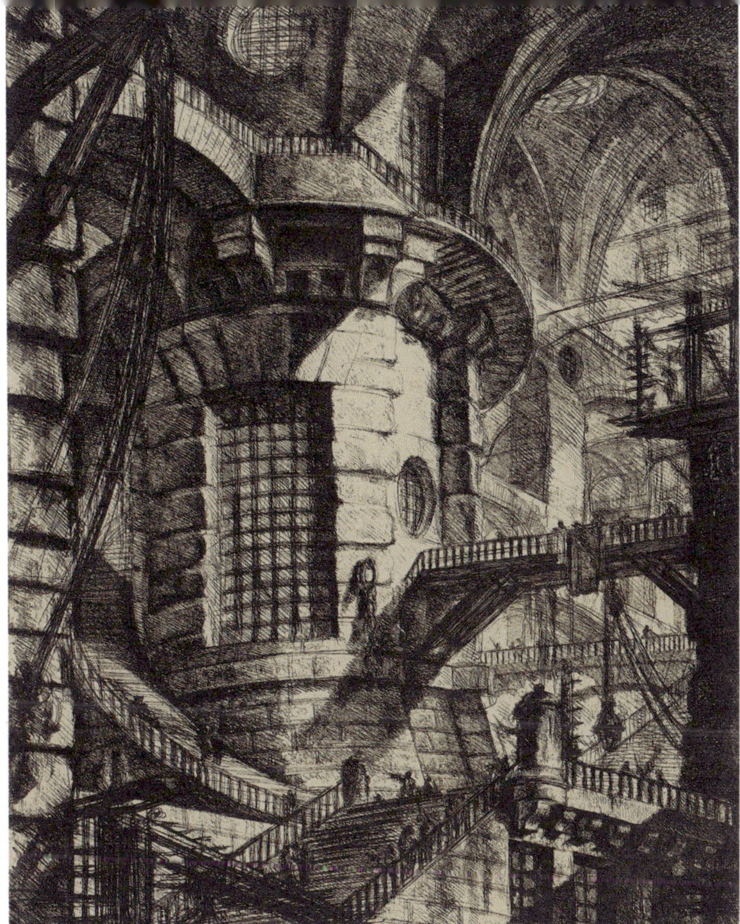

Left: The Round Tower.

Below: The Gothic Arch.

Opposite Top: Prisoners on a Projecting Platform.

Opposite Bottom: The Pier with Chains.

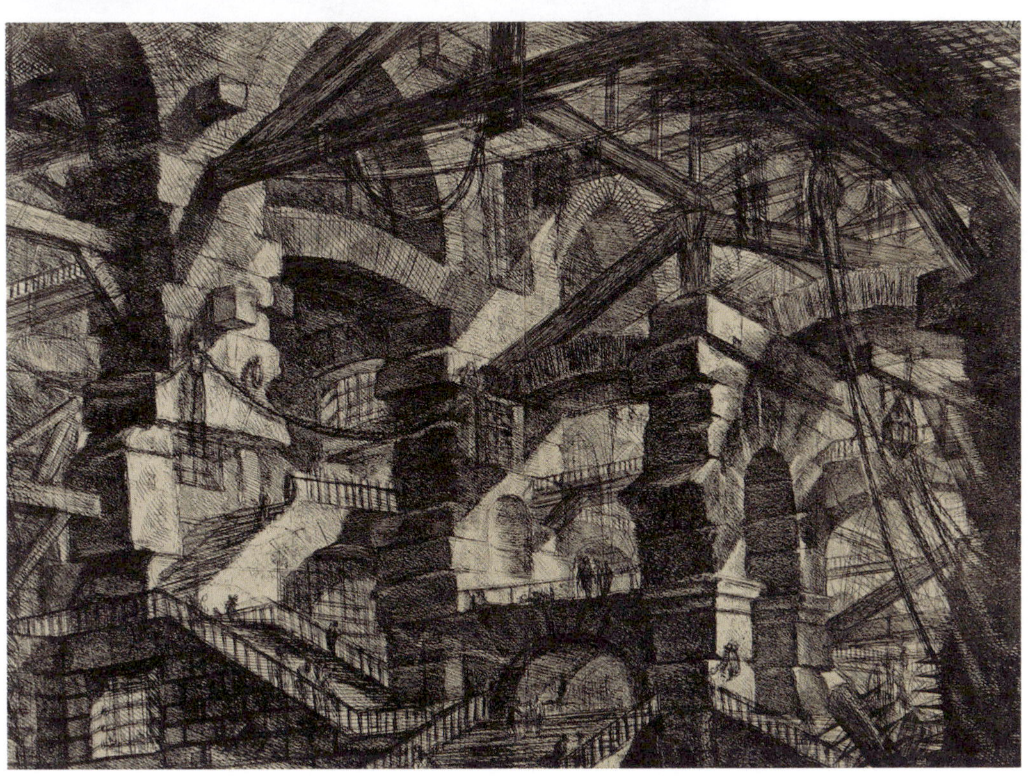

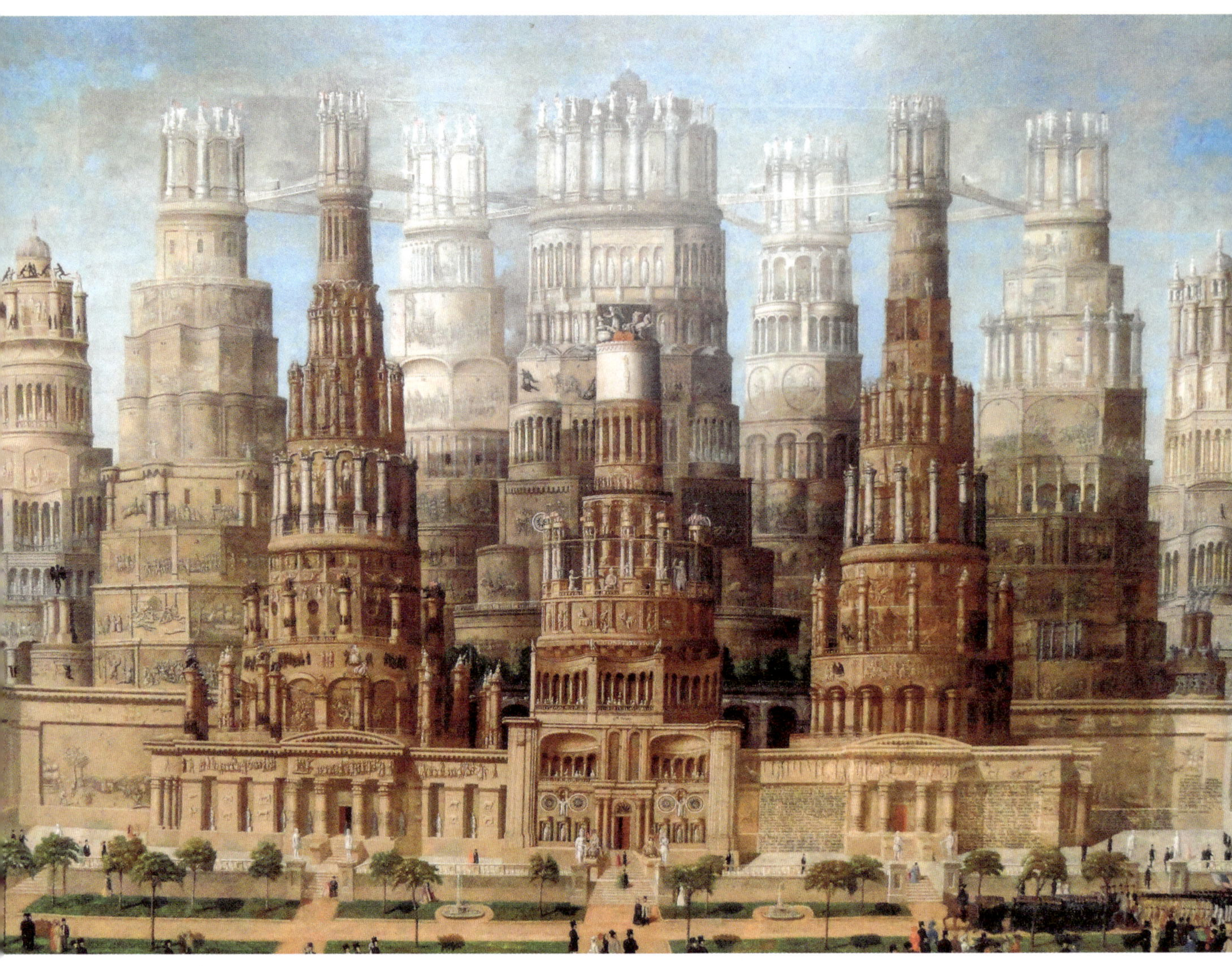

strangeness, their violence – as if struck by the rays of a black sun,' wrote Yourcenar. As a result, Piranesi is an artist who far outlives his colleagues and is animate in his influence over artistic expression through the subsequent centuries. In these prisons we can see the future echoes of the moody drama of romanticism, the playful surrealist engagement with the subconscious, Kafkaesque disorientation and helplessness, the chiaroscuro (sharp contrast of light and dark) of German expressionist cinema, the twisted paradox of the unending stairs of M. C. Escher (1898-1972), and so on.

It wasn't always nightmarish architecture that poured from Piranesi's pen. Having trained as an architect and in theatrical scene-painting, Piranesi's early published work

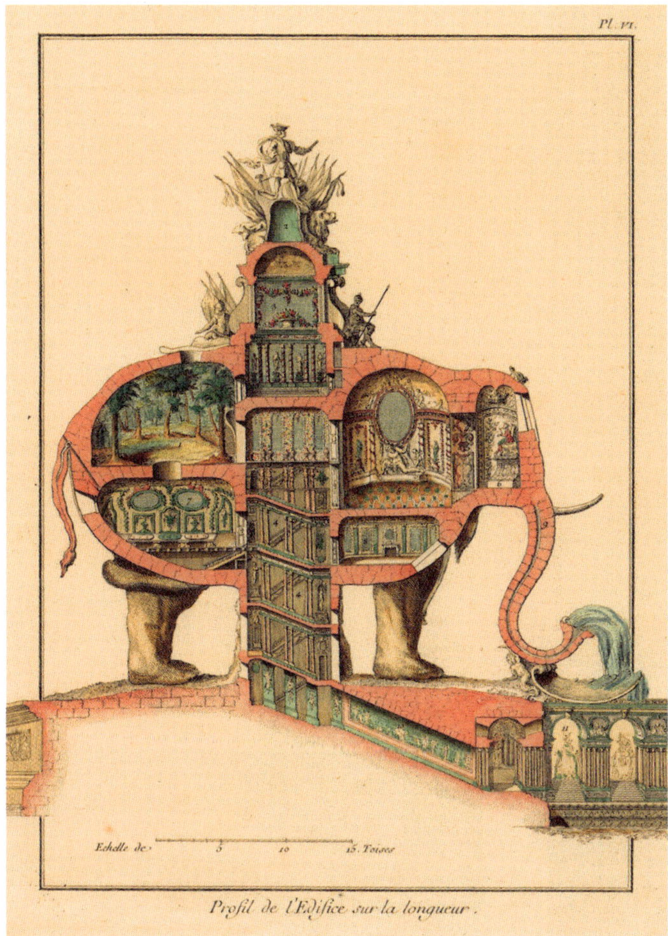

was the product of an obsession with the classical architecture with which he was surrounded. In his sketches of the scattered, crumbled ancient monuments of the Roman Empire, one can feel awe at the scale and the power that must have been involved in their construction, and the sense of being adrift in time in a city and country of such magnificent relics. It's this awe that underpins the prisons, amplified and extrapolated, to create a heightened feeling of existing somewhere just outside regimented time and space, a separate dimension. Unlike the first publication, the 1761 publication was signed 'G Battista Piranesi, Venetian architect': the immensity, and absurdity, of his vision now fully realised.

Opposite: *Erastus Salisbury Field (1805-1900) started work on his* Historical Monument of the American Republic *in 1867, representing 250 years of American history in 130 panels, to complete it in time for the 1876 centenary of American Independence. He was still applying the finishing touches to it in 1888. If built, the towers would have reached some 150m (500ft), connected by a steam railway across the top. 'A professed architect, on looking at this picture, might have the impression that a structure built in this form would not stand,' wrote the artist, admitting, 'I am not a professed architect, and some things about it may be faulty.'*

Left: *A design for a proposed Parisian structure to celebrate a victorious Louis XV after the War of the Austrian Succession had ended in 1748, by an engineer from Béziers named Charles-François Ribart. Louis XV stands atop a colossal elephant, inside which are various decorated rooms. The painted forest at the rear is a dining room, complete with stream and mechanisms for playing birdsong. The table drops down into the room below to allow servants to change courses without intruding on the privacy of guests. Ribart proposed building the monument where the Arc de Triomphe now stands, and having a fountain pour from the elephant's trunk.*

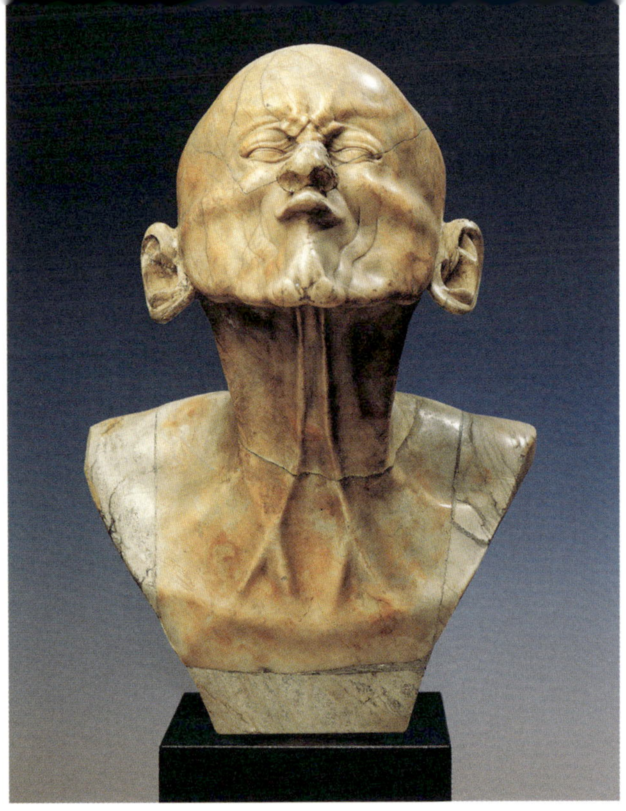

Second Beak Head.

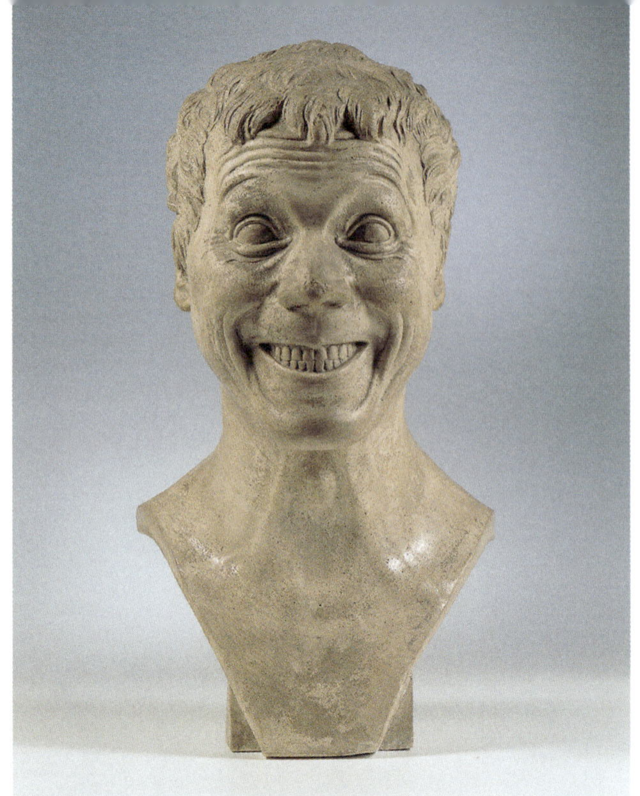

The Enraged and Vindictive Gypsy.

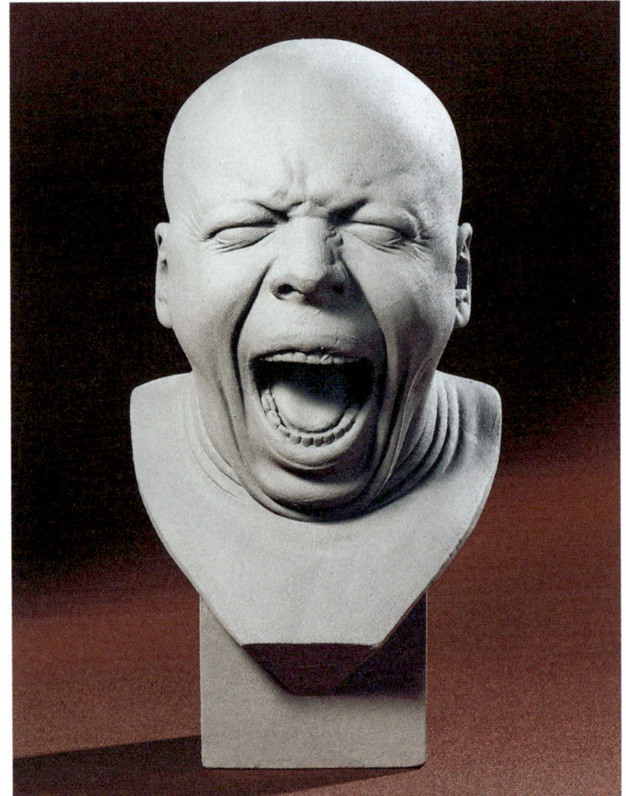

The Yawn.

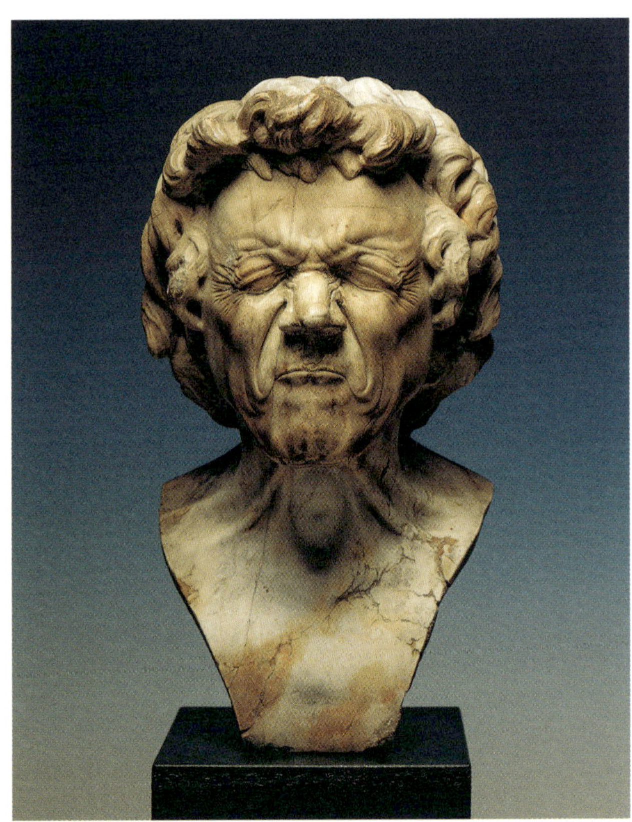

An Emaciated Old Man with Eye Pain.

THE GHOST HEADS OF FRANZ XAVER MESSERSCHMIDT (1770-83)

Franz Xaver Messerschmidt (1736-83) screams, grimaces, yawns and gurns for all eternity in his self-portrait sculptural series of over sixty *Character Heads*, that have fascinated viewers since their first public exhibition, in 1793 in Vienna, a decade after his death. The heads had passed to his brother Johann Adam Messerschmidt, who really didn't know what to make of them, and so they soon found their way to Franz Xaver's nephew by marriage, Johann Pendel. Pendel was even more baffled, but was certain of one thing: the world needed to see them.

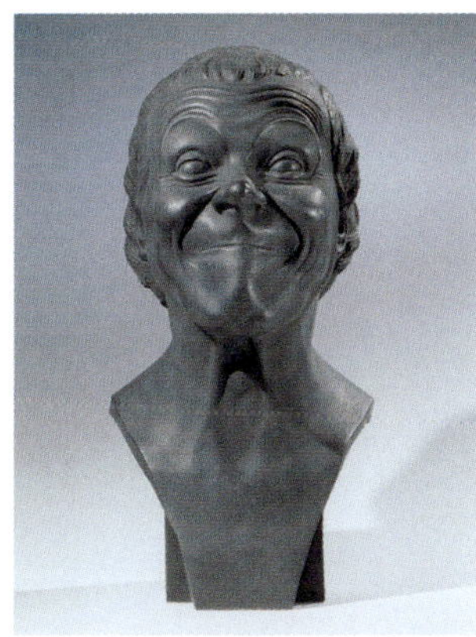

A Nosy, Petty Mocker.

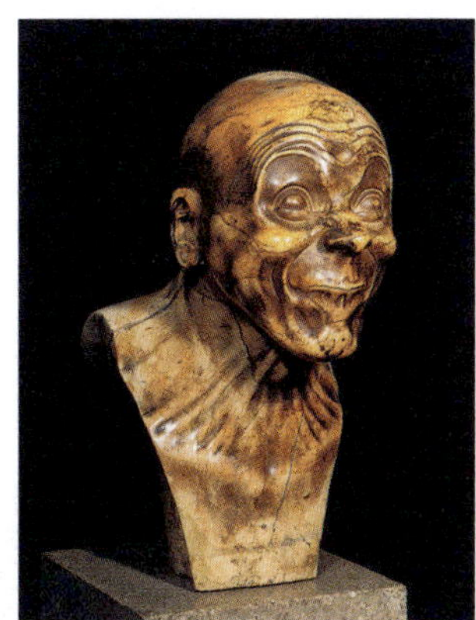

The Sheep Head.

Messerschmidt had never titled the heads himself, leaving their meaning mysterious. But it was decided they needed names for their public viewing, and so someone, likely Pendel, christened them with titles including *The Inept Bassoonist*, *The Strong Odour*, *The Constipated One*, *The Enraged and Vengeful Gypsy*, *A Deliberate Rascal*, *A Nosy, Petty Mocker* and *An Emaciated Old Man with Eye Pain*. While these eccentric names do fit the jolting first impression the sculptures make, it is a shame that they rather obscure the masterful skill and intensity of purpose in their creation. See how, for example, the inherent flaws and cracks of the alabaster are incorporated into the landscape of the facial skin, melding with the creases and wrinkles and lines of tensed muscle.

Born in the southwestern German town of Wiesensteig into a family of craftsmen, Franz Xaver Messerschmidt graduated from the Vienna Academy of Fine Arts in 1755. Almost immediately he was on the fast track to stardom – his works of the early 1760s included commissions for conventional sculptures of the physician Franz Mesmer, and a large tin statue in florid rococo style of Empress Maria Theresa as Queen of Hungary, which currently sits in the entrance to Upper Belvedere palace in Vienna. Emperor Joseph II prized his work and commissioned several pieces. Messerschmidt bought a large house in Vienna, and the Academy of Fine Arts promoted him, promising full professorship.

But then things took a strange turn. By 1770 friends and colleagues noticed Messerschmidt starting to behave erratically. (A later 1774 document written by Wenzel Anton, Prince of Kaunitz-Rietberg, describes the artist as struggling with a 'confusion in his head'.) It was at this point that Messerschmidt began working on his *Character Heads*, with which he would be solely obsessed for thirteen years until his death. Alarmed by his behaviour, the Academy denied Messerschmidt the position of professor. He resigned in outrage, sold his home and went to live with his brother Johann Adam Messerschmidt in Pressburg (modern Bratislava), working on the heads in near-total isolation.

The only insight we have into Messerschmidt's thinking is a strange account written by the German philosopher Friedrich Nicolai in 1788, when he visited Messerschmidt's studio. Nicolai reveals that Messerschmidt believed the invisible spirits responsible for the design of the world resented his art for approaching divine perfection. The shooting pains he suffered in his lower torso and legs during his studio sessions, causing him to grimace, were tortures sent by the Spirit of Proportion out of jealousy.

What's more, Messerschmidt claimed to have discovered a secret correlation between the face and the body through art – when sculpting a particular expression or part of the face, he would feel a sensation in a corresponding part of his body. This secret physiology, he believed, was known to Egyptian sculptors but had since been lost. Though his discovery of this had further angered the spirits and his pain had intensified, he was determined to persevere with the *Character Heads* to preserve for mankind this knowledge of the face-body system.

As Messerschmidt did not leave any text, Nicolai is the sole source of this information and we are left to speculate as to its veracity. The story certainly lends the statues an added hum of vibrancy. When confronting a Messerschmidt head, the viewer is confronted right back – neoclassical busts usually have preoccupied, dreamy stares at an angle, looking off into the distance. Messerschmidt's work stares the viewer down, conveying the full cargo of a troubled psyche with an intense facial expression. (This would have been especially unnerving in restrictive eighteenth-century society, when there were strict rules about who could look at whom.)

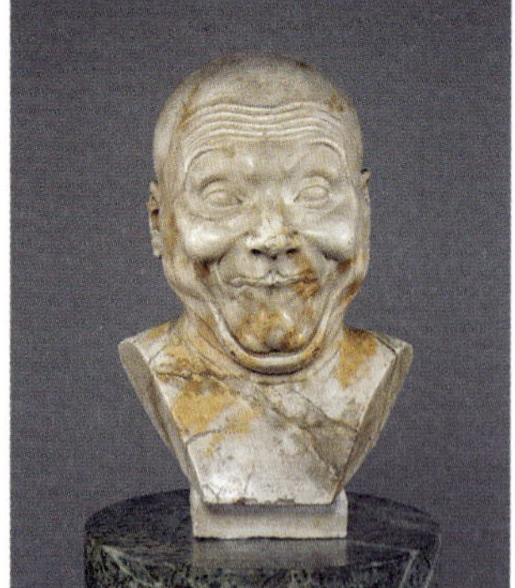

A Deliberate Rascal.

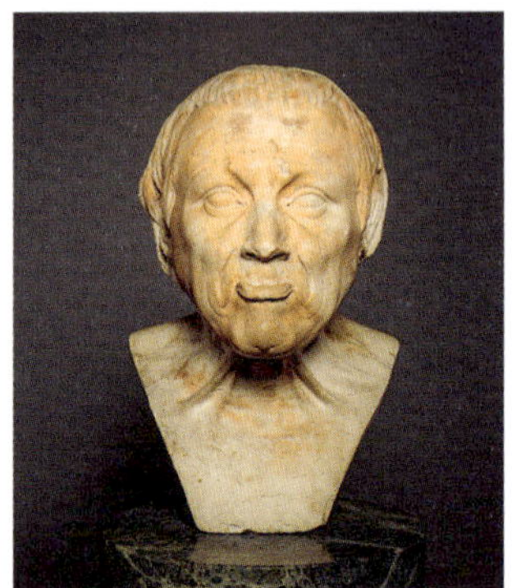

The Old Man.

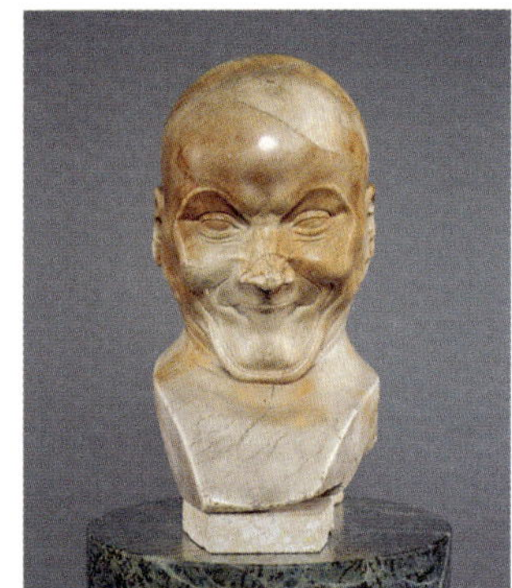

A Scoundrel.

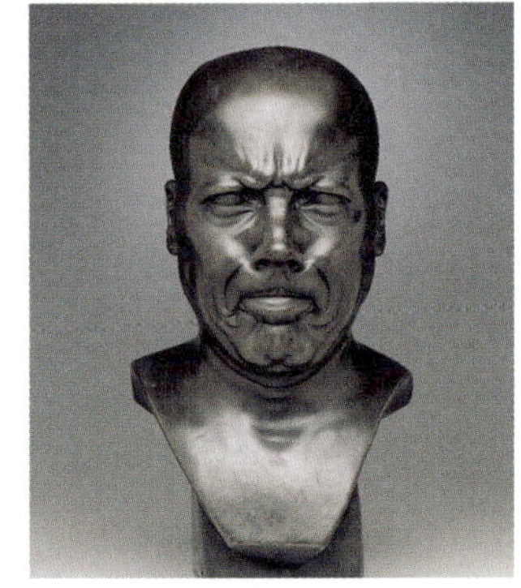

A Hypochondriac.

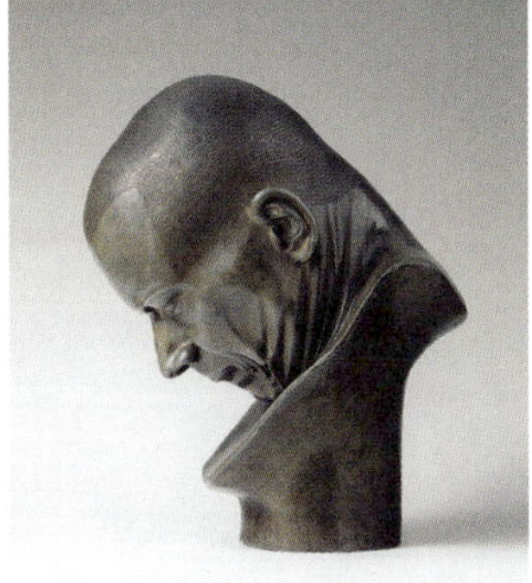

A Hypocrite and a Slanderer.

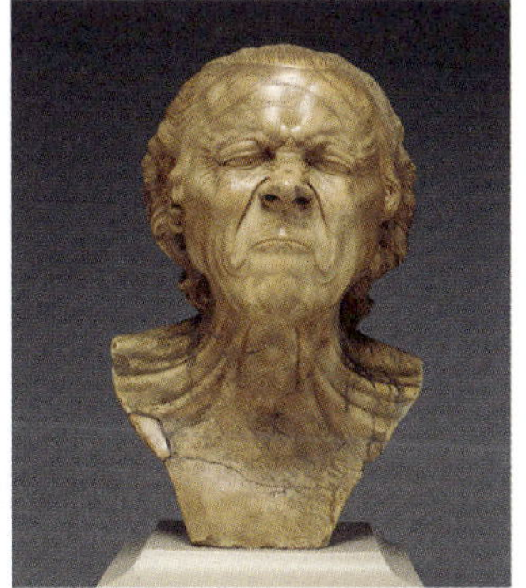

The Vexed Man.

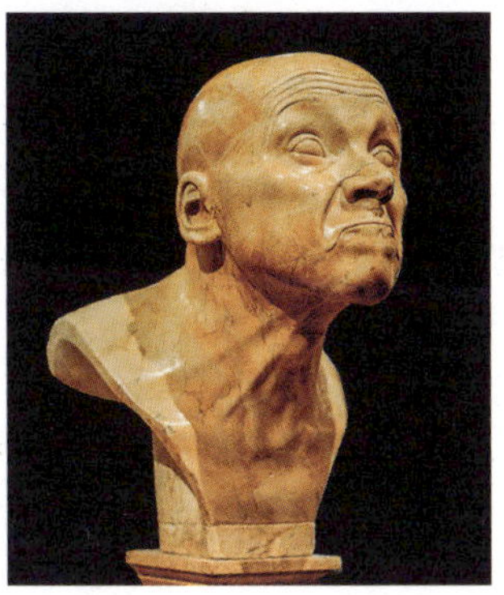

Simplicity of the Highest Degree.

With his fascination with the face, Messerschmidt's work has much in common with the contemporary ideas of the German philosopher and satirist Georg Christoph Lichtenberg (1742-99). Lichtenberg wrote in *Das menschliche Antlitz* (The Human Face): 'We can see nothing of the mind if it is not present in the facial expressions. The faces of a great assembly could be called the history of the human mind written in a kind of Chinese picture writing. The mind arranges the face around itself as a magnet does iron-filings, and the variation in the position of these parts is determined by the variations in that which has created them.'

Maybe this idea informs us as to what it is we see in Messerschmidt's heads, so distinctive in a pre-Freudian world. In recreating the face – in all its expressive range – as an abstraction of the inner workings it represents, Messerschmidt is recording a new, fluctuating language of the self – the closest a sculptor had (or, perhaps, has ever) come to manifesting the human mind in stone.

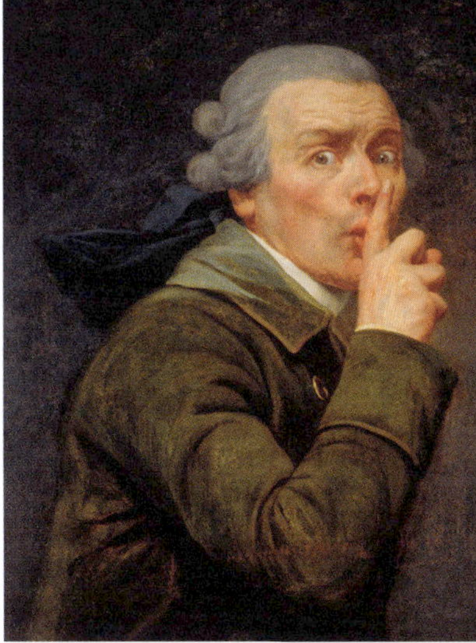

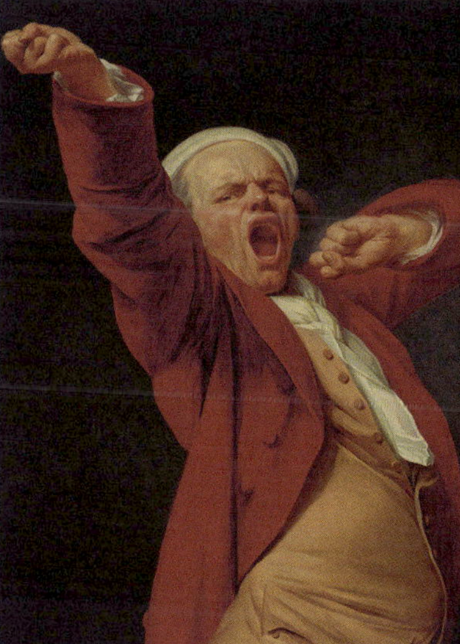

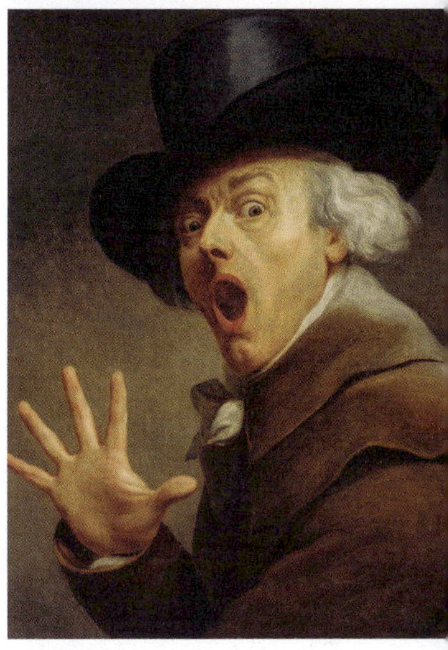

Opposite Bottom Left: Screaming Child, Stung by a Bee *(c.1615), attributed to Hendrick de Keyser (1565-1621). While possible de Keyser was attempting to capture his own horrified experience of a screaming infant, it's likely this sculpture depicts Cupid, god of love, who was said by the Greek poet Theocritus to have been stung by a bee after stealing honey.*

Top, Middle and Bottom: *Joseph Ducreux (1735-1802) played with the traditional limitations of self-portraiture with his broad and humorous self-portraits in unconventional poses of him stretching and yawning. Ducreux shared Messerschmidt's interest in the study of physiognomy, and his paintings burst with life through direct engagement with the viewer.*

HENRY FUSELI'S *THE NIGHTMARE* (1781) AND THE ART OF DREAMING

The Nightmare is a painting that wrenches its viewer in every direction. One's eyes dart repeatedly around the canvas, snapping between the three extraordinary figures of the terrible scene, recognising the themes of folklore and superstition, science, sexual desire and classical art.

The grand icon of Gothic horror caused shockwaves on its exhibition at the Royal Academy in 1782. The Swiss-English painter Henry Fuseli (1741-1825) never recorded what it was he meant to convey with the artwork, but it's likely the initial reaction of both terror and titillation was just as he intended.

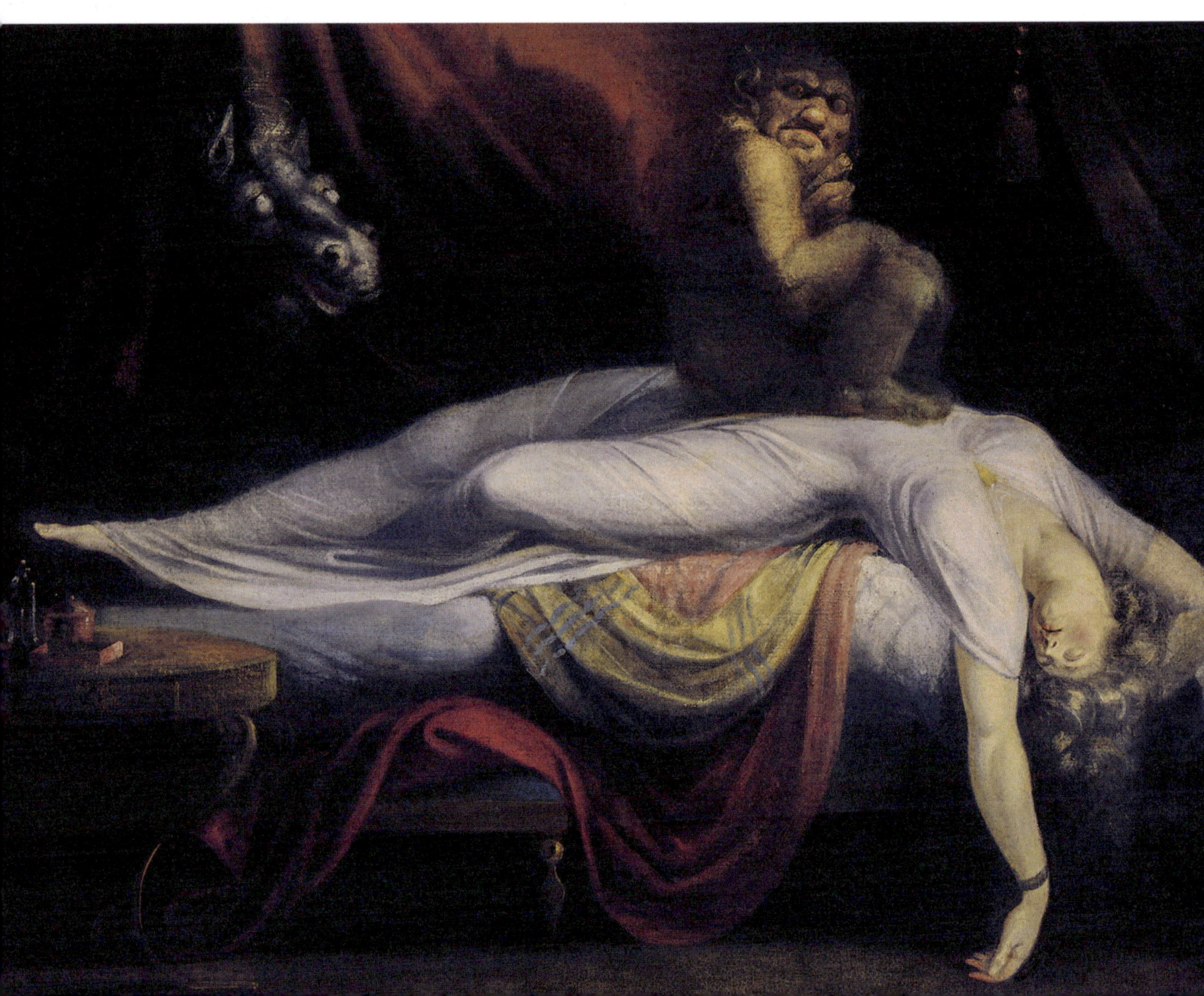

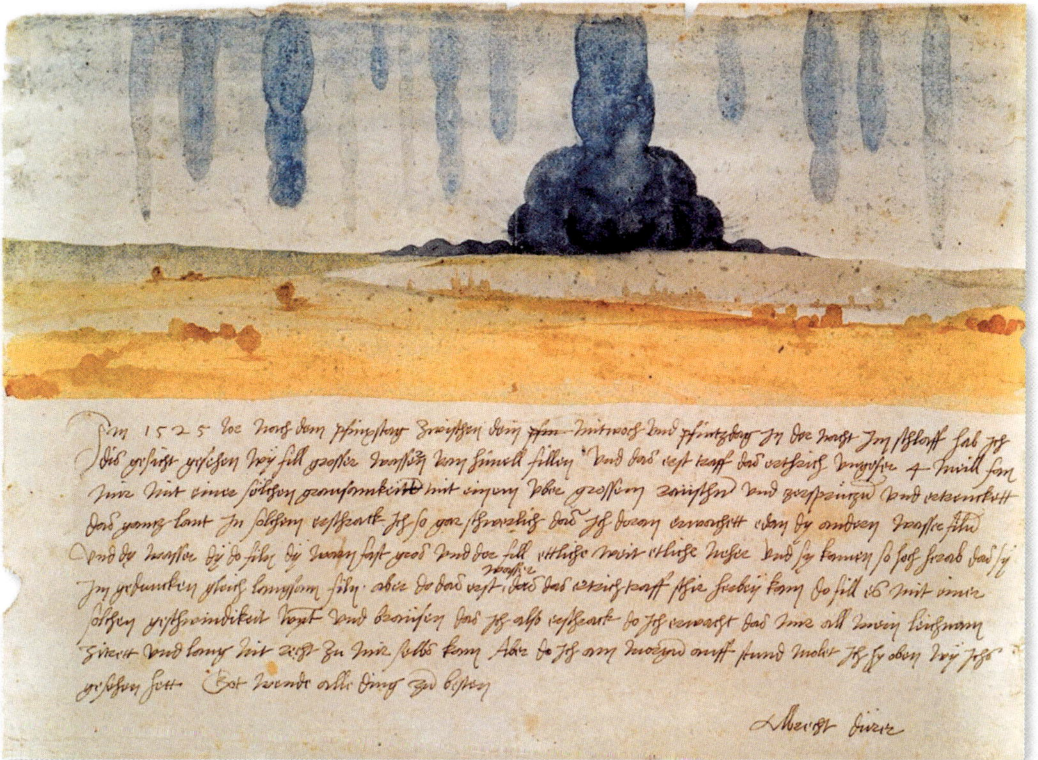

Above: Dream Vision; a Nightmare *(1525) by Albrecht Dürer (1471-1528) of an apocalyptic dream he had on the night of 7-8 June 1525. He describes in the text: 'I had this vision in my sleep, and saw how many great waters fell from heaven. The first struck the ground about 4 miles away from me with such a terrible force, enormous noise and splashing that it drowned the entire countryside... When I arose in the morning, I painted the above as I had seen it. May the Lord turn all things to the best.'*

Unlike the other paintings in the same exhibition, there is no moralising on display, as was popular at the time – no positive message of metaphor, no biblical or traditional literary reference. *The Nightmare* is a dark conjuring from Fuseli's own imagination, showing an apelike creature, an imp or incubus, glaring daggers at the viewer while squatting heavily on the chest of a sleeping woman, while a black horse with glowing eyes, flared nostrils and the hint of a grin watches on from the shadows.

The monstrous characters remain startling, and the theatrical power of the scene is largely undiminished with the masterful use of chiaroscuro to heighten the intensity. The sleeping woman's pale dress and her dramatic swooning erotically exaggerate her vulnerability, helpless under the weight of the incubus – a creature of superstition believed to press on the chest of sleepers and even ravish unconscious women. The horse (or 'mare') too, is a figure from popular contemporary superstition, drawn from Germanic tales of sleeping men visited by horses and hags. But, while its presence here is also a play on the term 'nightmare', the etymology of the latter is derived not from horses but from the Old Norse word *mara* (a spectre that tortured sleepers).

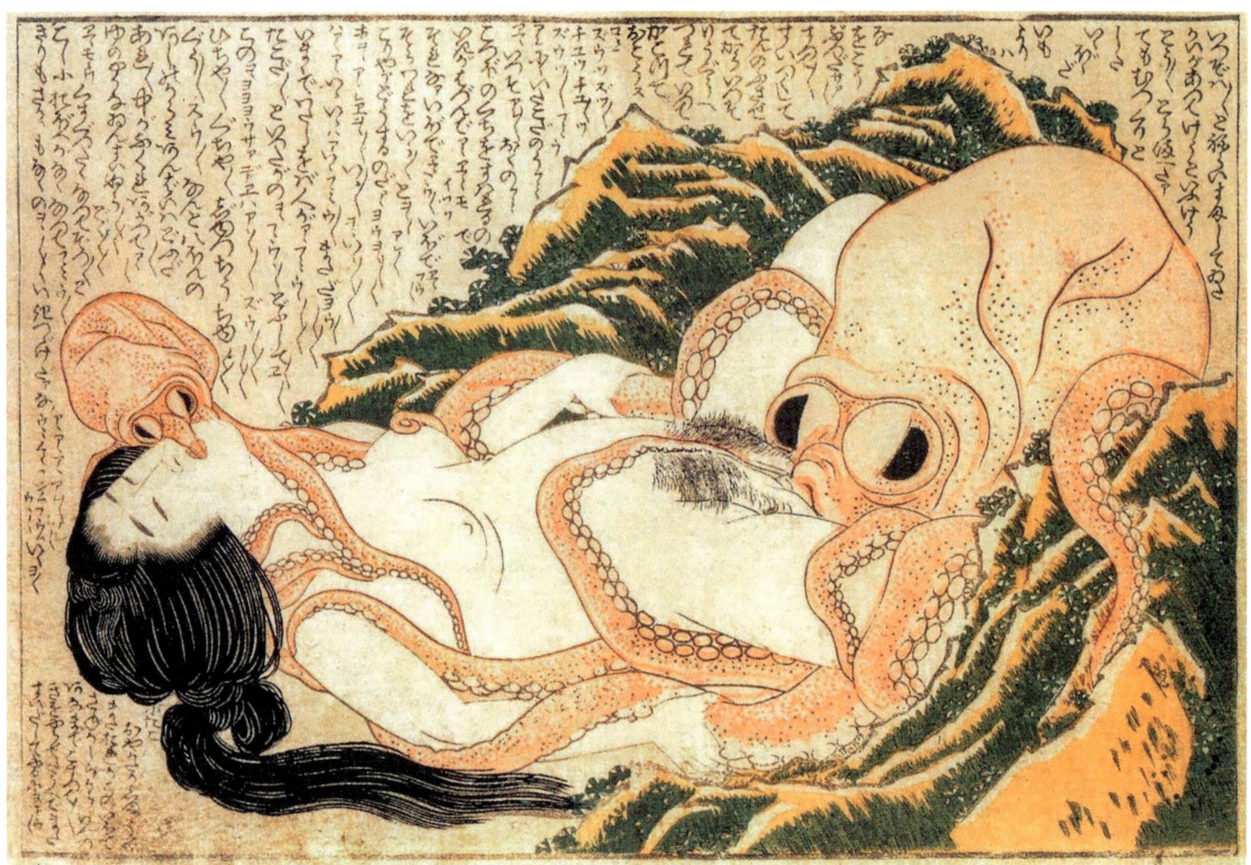

The Nightmare has traditionally been interpreted as a study, and warning, of the powers of the unconscious, anticipating Jungian ideas long before the arrival of psychoanalysis in the late nineteenth century. (Sigmund Freud must have agreed, as he kept a copy of the painting on his wall.) But perhaps the most terrifying aspect of the painting is that the incubus depicted has its roots in reality. The fear of such a creature developed independently in the popular beliefs of cultures around the world, thanks to the common phenomenon of sleep paralysis, in which a waking or dozing person is aware but unable to move, often with fearful hallucinations.

In China, sleep paralysis is known as *guǐ yā shēn* (ghost pressing on body) or *guǐ yā chuáng* (ghost pressing on bed), while in Japan it's referred to as *kanashibari* (bound or fastened in metal). And in Arabic there is the *Ja-thoom* (literally, what sits heavily on something), a kind of *shayṭān* (evil spirit) that sits on and chokes a sleeping person. Visitations by the creature can be warded off, however, if one simply lies on one's right side and reads the *Ayat al-Kursi* (Throne Verse) of the Qur'an each night.

Above: Dream of the Fisherman's Wife, *from the three-volume* Kinoe no Komatsu *(1814), a work of* shunga *(erotic art) within the* ukiyo-e *genre by the Japanese artist Katsushika Hokusai (1760-1849). A young* ama *diver enjoys sexual congress with a pair of octopus. 'Yes, it tingles now;' reads the text, 'soon there will be no sensation at all left in my hips. Ooooooh! Boundaries and borders gone! I've vanished!'*

MR BARKER'S MONSTER PANORAMAS (1789)

In London's Leicester Square in 1794, Queen Charlotte, wife of King George III, was so nauseated by a work of art that it caused her to decorously vomit into a lace handkerchief. Even stranger, in this decidedly landlocked part of central London, it was because she had been made seasick.

The Roman Catholic Church of Notre Dame de France in Leicester Square is defined by its great circular dome, a hint of the building's all-but-forgotten past life as London's most popular entertainment attraction. 'The Rotunda', as it was known, was built by the Scottish architect Robert Mitchell on commission for Robert Barker (1739-1806) to display the latter's artworks – the largest paintings ever made at that time. These were the gargantuan, 360-degree 'panoramas' (a term coined by Barker), hand-painted works that spanned a staggering 250 sq. m (300 sq. yd) and were designed to give the Georgian equivalent of a virtual-reality experience with

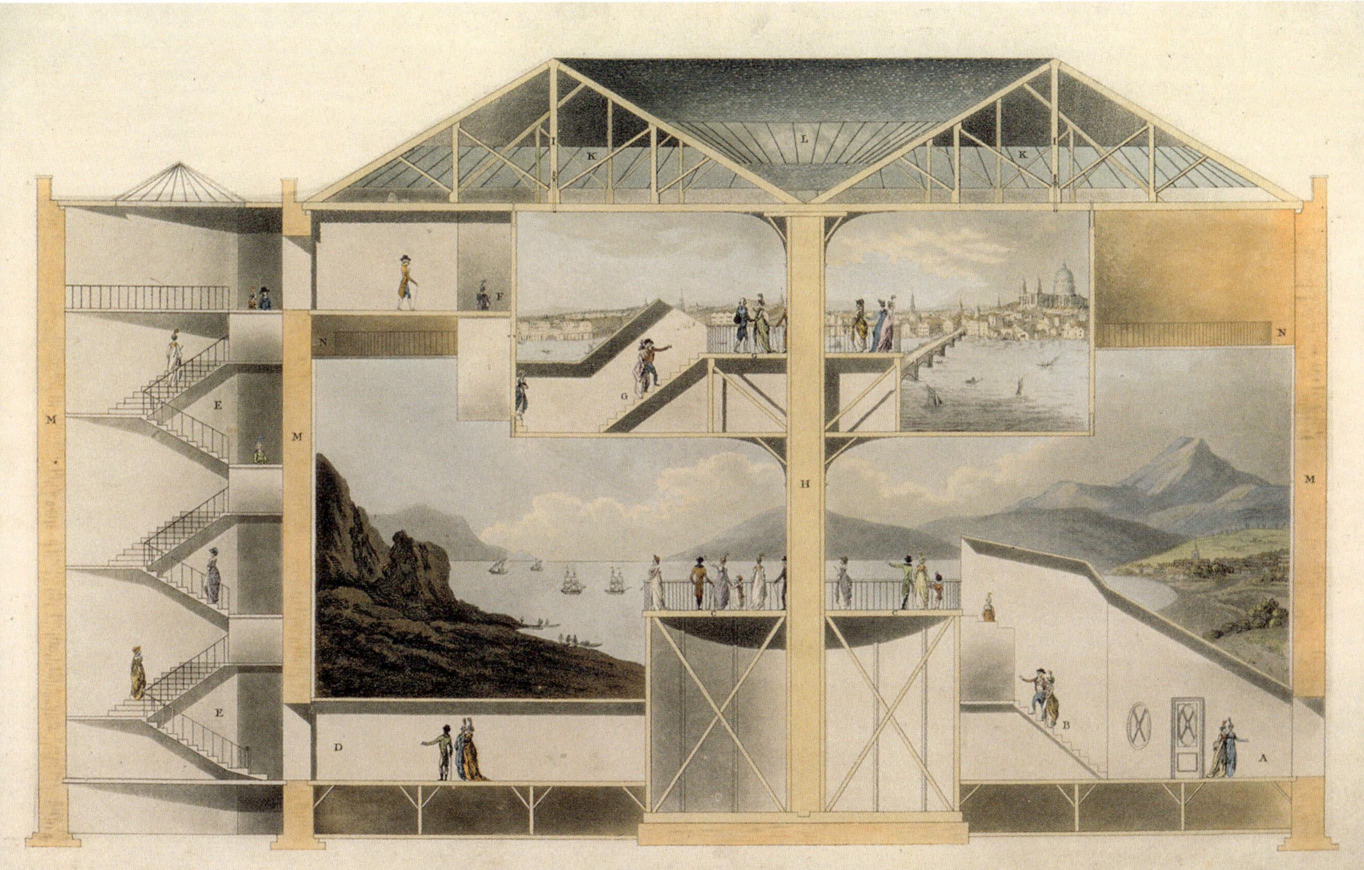

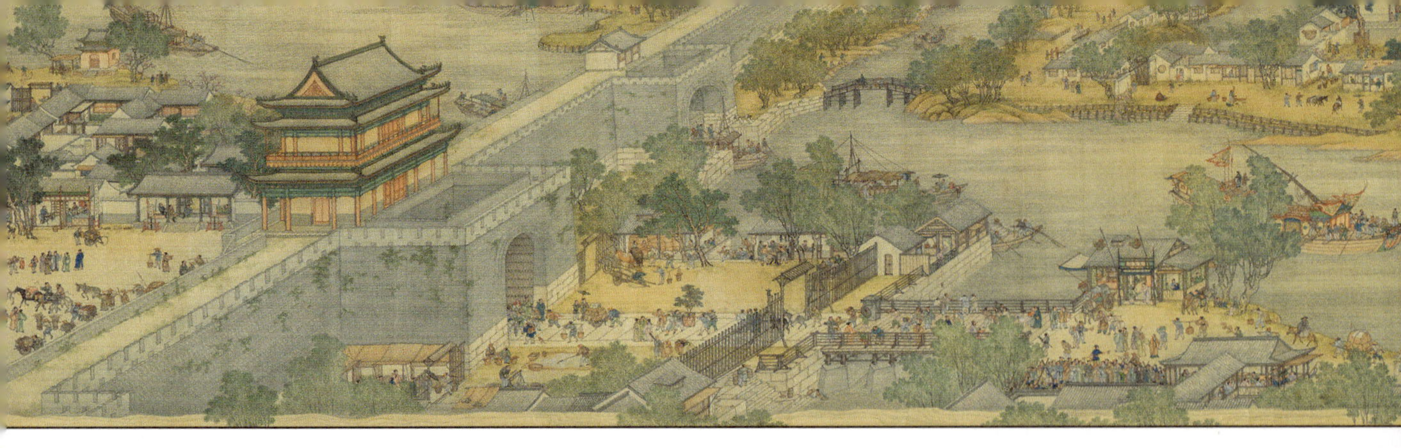

tremendous city views, seascapes, countryside and battle scenes in which the dwarfed spectators could lose themselves.

To aid this effect, the borders of the canvases were hidden, and props were introduced in the foreground. (The example shown on the previous page is one of Barker's earliest from 1789, of the Edinburgh Hills.) The perfectly round building had both a lower and an upper circle, which meant that two panoramas could be exhibited at the same time, one above the other, underneath an enormous conical glass roof, that offered even lighting on the artworks. The dark corridors and staircases that linked the two panoramas were meant to act as a 'palate cleanser' for the viewer between paintings before they experienced the next sensory overload.

The paintings were so large that visitors were given maps to find their way around. In 1794, King George III and Queen Charlotte were given a private viewing. Barker's vast panorama of a naval scene was so realistic and overwhelming that Queen Charlotte, after staring out across the painted ocean, was struck down with seasickness. This story, of course, did wonders for Barker's publicity, and panoramas became the entertainment hit of the time. Londoners paid three shillings for views of London, which were made so effective by Barker's accomplished technique of manipulating perspective better than the 'wide-angle' style used by previous artists.

The artworks were hugely profitable for Barker but also for London's artistic community. Copycat panorama shows sprang up all over town evidence reveals that between 1793 and 1863 at least 126 different panoramas were exhibited in London, and all were in need of skilled painters.

Such monster panoramas sit at the heart of modern cinema – the popularity of the static panorama gradually giving way to the

ABOVE: *Robert Barker may have coined the term panorama, but he did not, of course, invent the artform. In twelfth-century China, for example, the seminal landscape painter Zhang Zeduan (1085-1145) painted the minutely detailed* Along the River during the Qingming Festival *at a width of 5.25m (17.2ft), though later copies were made as wide as 11.5m (38ft). Just a section is shown here.*

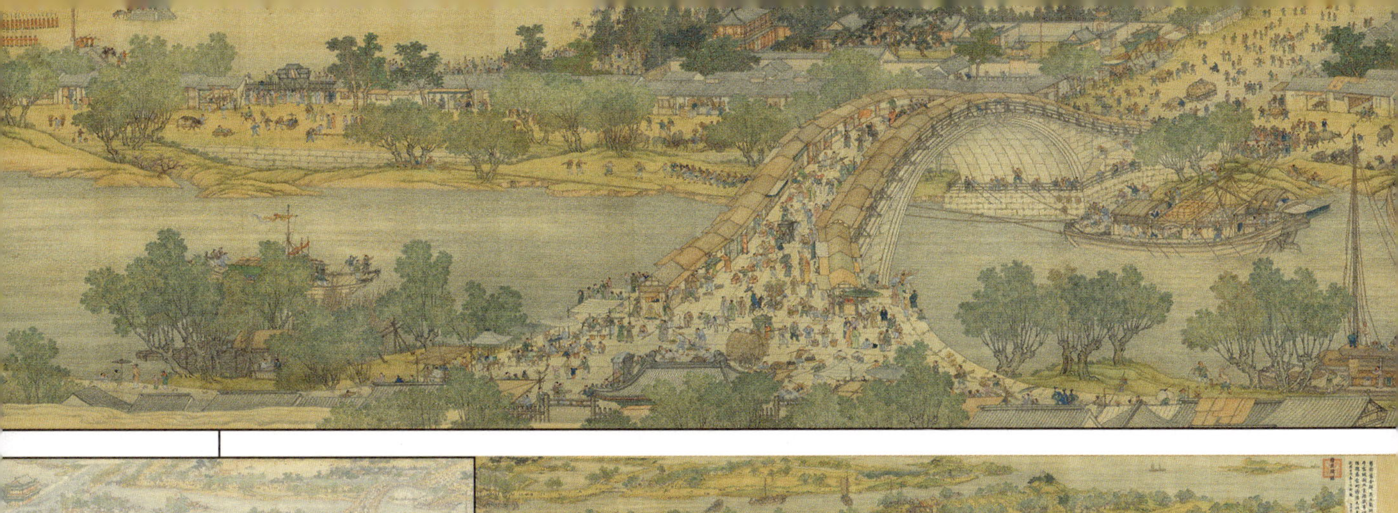

'moving panorama', which were enormously long paintings that an operator slowly rolled before an audience like scenery passing by a train window. In America, for example, the most famous of these were the panoramic scenes of the Mississippi Valley by John Banvard (1815-91), which he toured from 1840. Banvard's largest panorama was his 'three-mile canvas' (as he branded it), which was actually about 0.8km (½ mile) long. With the profits from touring his work he was able to build a giant imitation of Windsor Castle on Long Island, which was nicknamed 'Banvard's Folly'. Gradually, these moving panoramas gave way to the popularity of moving pictures – and cinema was born.

Below: Wyld's Monster Globe *was a similarly gigantic work of art to be explored by the paying public of London's Leicester Square between 1851 and 1862. Visitors to the 18m- (60ft-) diameter globe were led around a perfect recreation of the Earth's surface viewed from the interior, with rivers, mountains and volcanoes, designed by the mapmaker James Wyld (1812-87).*

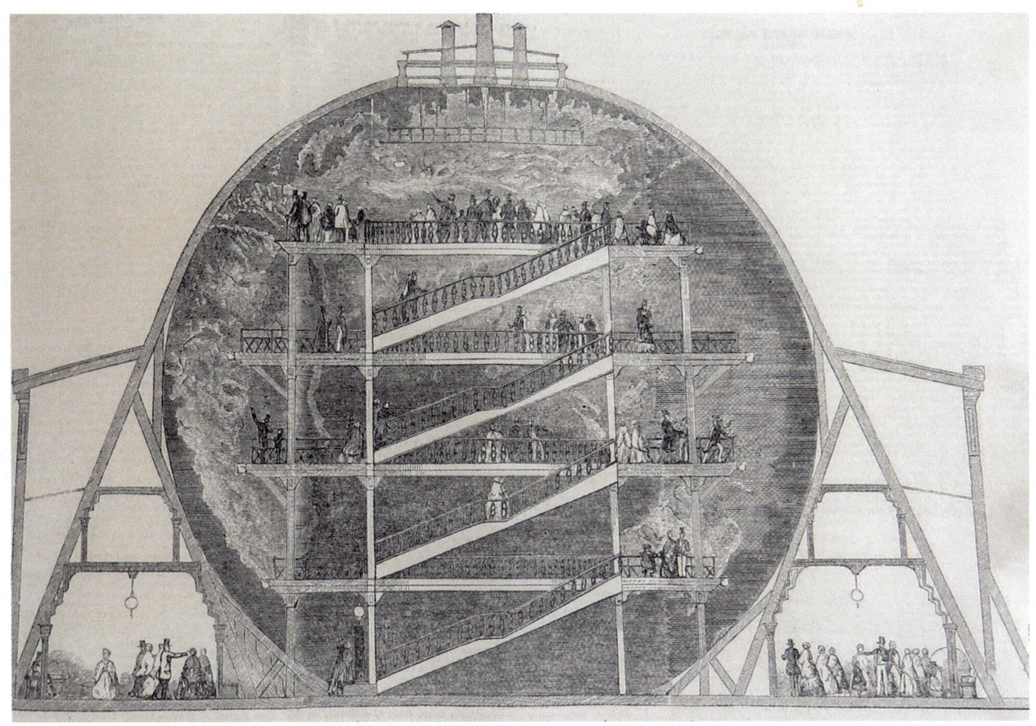

INTERIOR OF A KITCHEN (1815), MARTIN DRÖLLING

The origins of colours are wonderfully varied and far-reaching. The exuberant Tyrian purple, for example, was first used by the Phoenicians as early as 1570 BC and was prized for its resistance to fading – it actually brightens with sun exposure.[1] And where was this chemical found? In the mucus secretion of a predatory sea snail of the eastern Mediterranean Sea. (Royal blue was also extracted from a similar marine snail.) By the nineteenth century purple remained a fashionable colour, but the molluscs were no longer a practical option for sourcing colour on a mass scale. Fortunately, an alternative appeared in the form of the colour mauve, which was accidentally created in 1856 by a nineteen-year-old Londoner named William Perkin while attempting to synthesise quinine from coal tar in the home laboratory he'd set up in his parents' loft. Perkin's method for making purple was instantly preferable to the alternative source at the time. This was a substance called murexide, which was named after the murex snail in honour of Tyrian purple but was, in fact, bird excrement.

But there is arguably no colour in the history of art stranger than the brown paint used in the seemingly innocuous *Interior of a Kitchen* (1815) by Martin Drölling (1752-1817), which

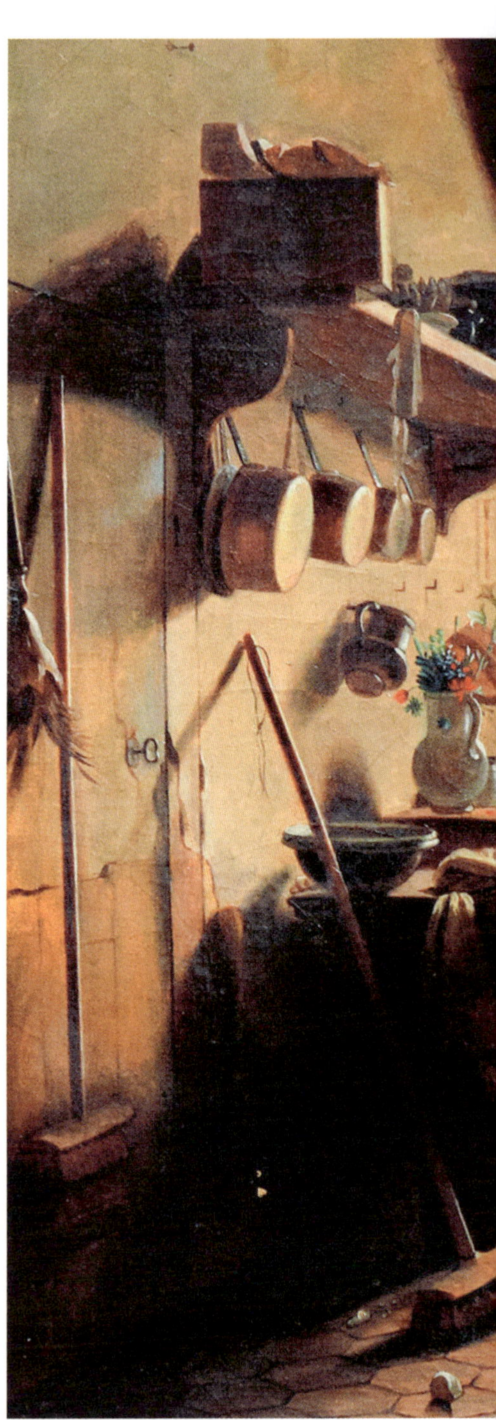

---

1 Such is the impermanence of artists' colours that, for example, it means no one alive today has ever seen a painting by J. M. W. Turner in its original intended state. Many of the bright pigments he used in his works were known at the time to quickly fade – they're referred to as 'fugitive colours'. Carmine-red is particularly elusive – in the Turner work *Waves Breaking against the Wind* (*c.*1840) it was used to paint the last colours of the sun striking the clouds, but today it has faded to a grey, completely changing the tone of the work. Turner was aware of this and had a reputation for treating his work poorly, keeping paintings stacked in damp corners (where mould flourished on the egg-based primer). He even tore a hole in a corner of one masterpiece to form a cat flap for his seven Manx cats.

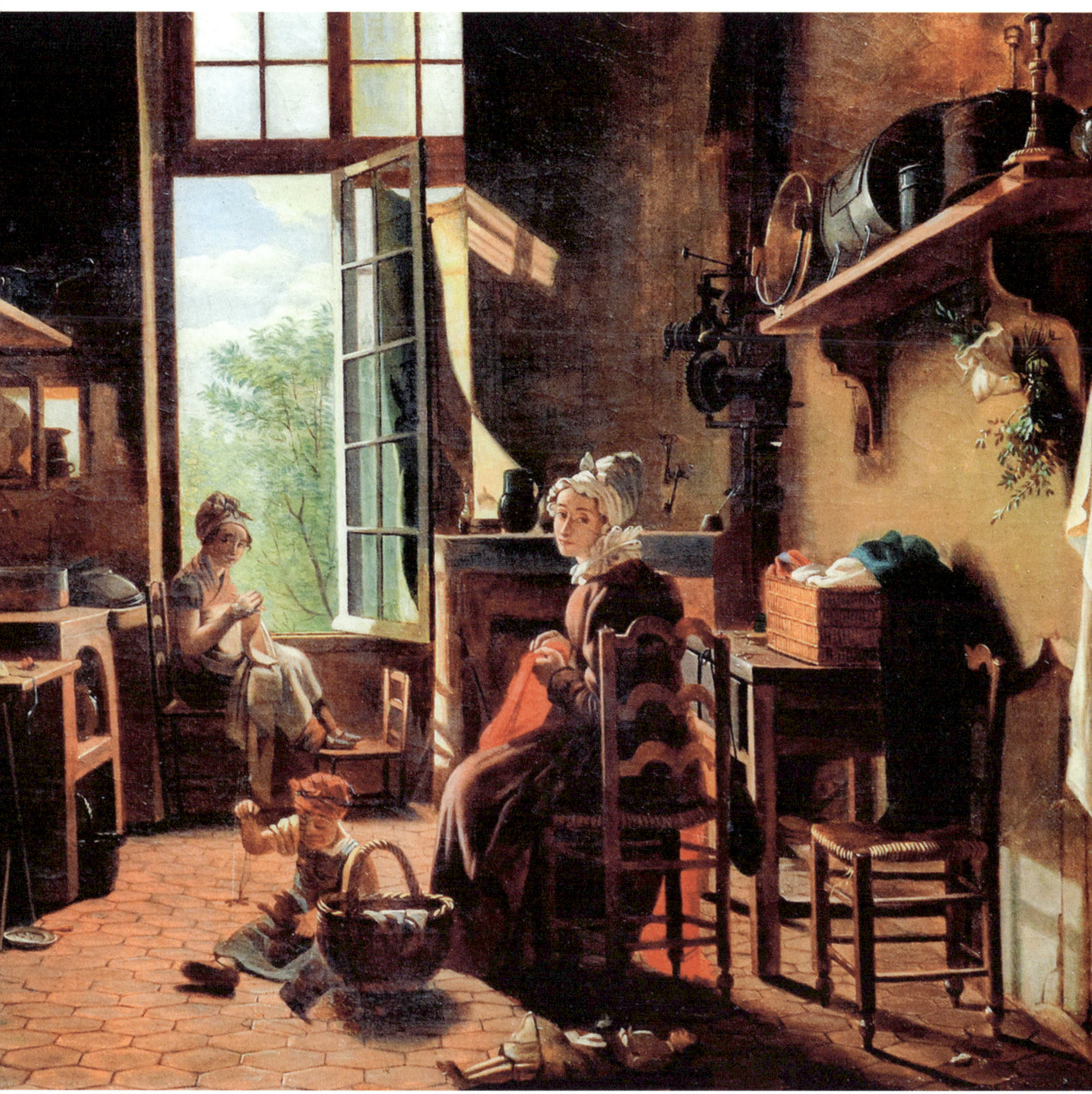

Interior of a Kitchen *(1815), Martin Drölling*

was exhibited at the grand Paris Salon of 1817 and can now be found in the Louvre. Known as 'mommia', 'mummy', 'Egyptian brown' and most revealingly *caput mortuum* (dead man's head), the tarry substance was sourced from the most gruesome of means: by grinding up the desiccated corpses of ancient Egyptians as well as, at one point in its history, mummies of the Guanche people of the Canary Islands, and during shortages the corpses of slaves and executed criminals. Traditionally mixed with white pitch and myrrh, recipes for its concoction vary – some advise pulverising the whole corpse, while others call for using 'only the finest muscle'. Its viscosity meant that it had no use as a watercolour but was excellent for dark shading, and it enjoyed popularity in Europe from the sixteenth to – astonishingly – the early twentieth century, despite its tendency to crack and react with other colours due to its elements of ammonia and fat.

The British chemist George Field recorded receiving a delivery of mummy from Sir William Beechey in 1809, the consignment arriving 'in a mass, containing and permeating rib-bone etc. – of a strong smell resembling Garlic and Ammonia – grinds easily – works rather pasty – unaffected by damp and foul air.' Towards the end of the nineteenth century, though, mummy brown was falling out of popularity with artists when its grisly origin became better known. According to Rudyard Kipling (1865-1936) he was with the Pre-Raphaelite artist Edward Burne-Jones (1833-98) when the artist learnt of the origin of his tube of paint. 'He descended in broad daylight with a tube of "Mummy Brown" in his hand,' recalled Kipling, 'saying that he had discovered it was made of dead Pharaohs and we must bury it accordingly', which he did in his garden.

The paint was still desperately sought by some, however. An advertisement in the *Daily Mail* in 1904 appeals for a mummy 'at a suitable price', reasoning: 'Surely a 2000-year-old mummy of an Egyptian monarch may be used for adorning a noble fresco in Westminster Hall... without giving offence to the ghost of the departed gentlemen or his descendants.'

By 1960 the colour had disappeared completely. 'We might have a few odd limbs lying around somewhere,' said Geoffrey Roberson-Park, managing director of London colour-makers C. Roberson and Co. in a 1964 *Time* Magazine piece, 'but not enough to make any more paint.' Thankfully, those pining for mummy brown following its retirement did not consult

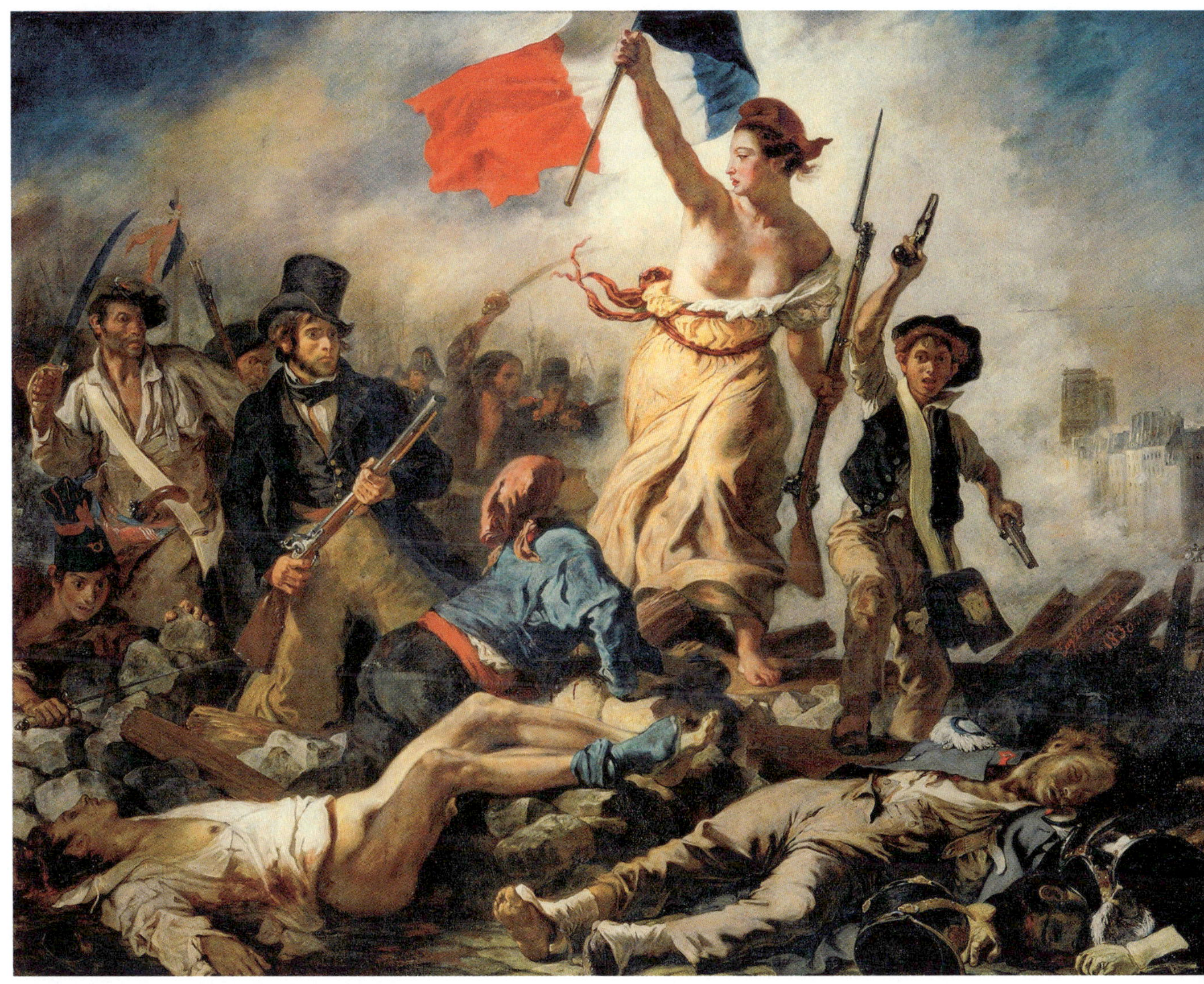

Liberty Leading the People *(1830) is believed to have been painted with mummy brown by Eugène Delacroix (1798-1863), who regularly used the pigment in his work.*

the 1691 journal of William Salmon, a 'Professor of Physick' of High Holborn, who proposed solving the contemporary shortage of Egyptian mummy supplies by using freshly dead Londoners. Salmon also recommended drinking the ground-up corpse mixture as a restorative when feeling gassy. 'Take the carcase of a young man (some say red hair'd) not dying of a Disease but killed,' writes Salmon, 'let it lie in 24 hours in clear water in the Air; cut the flesh in pieces, to which add Powder of Myrrh and a little Aloes, [and] imbibe it 24 hours in the Spirit of Wine and Turpentine.'

One can buy a modern pigment named mummy brown, incidentally, but that is composed of a mixture of kaolin, quartz, goethite and hematite – and no human ingredient.

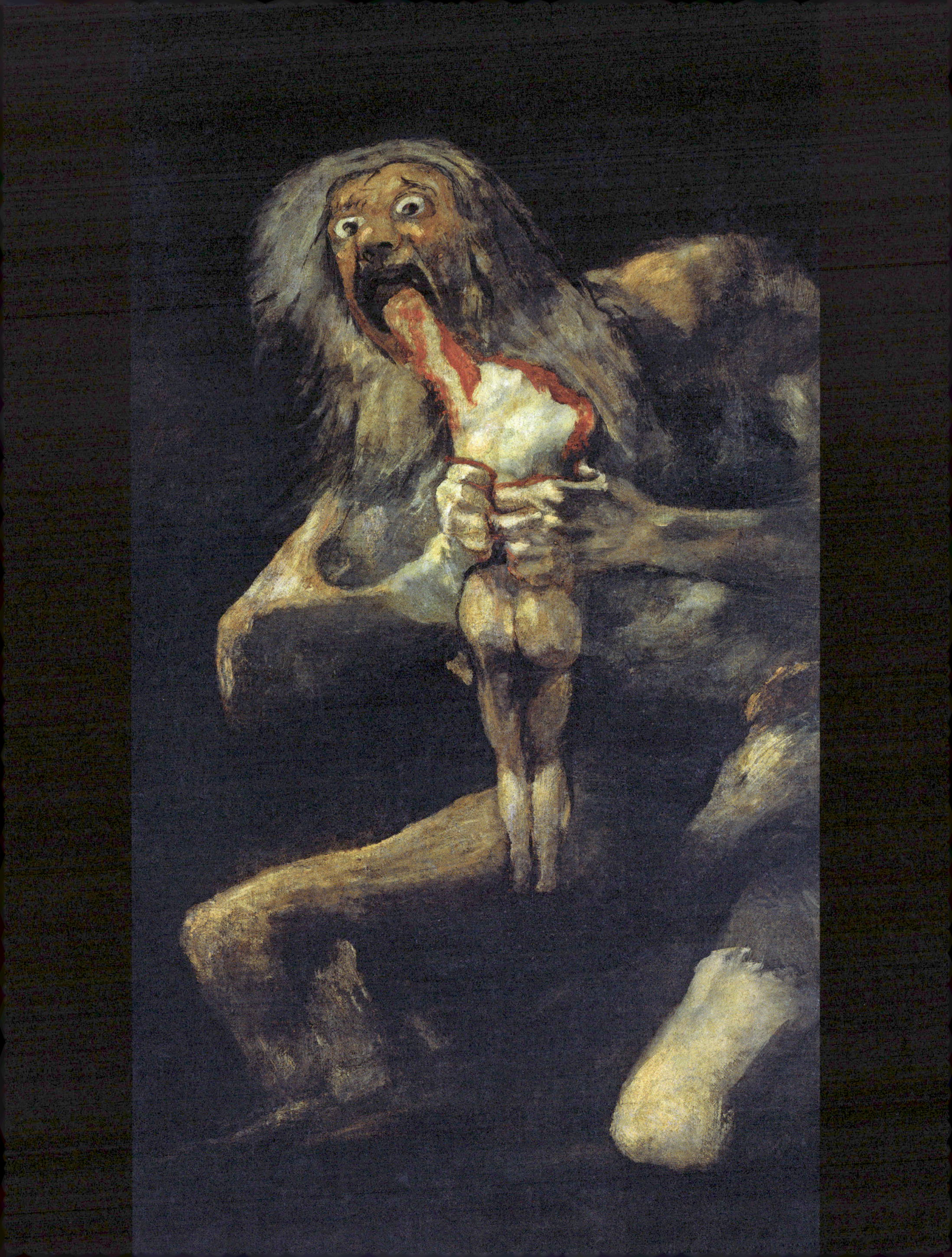

FRANCISCO GOYA'S *BLACK PAINTINGS* (1819-23)

From the darkness of mummy brown we sink further, into the depthless gloom of the phantasmagorical *Black Paintings* of Francisco Goya (1746-1828), last of the Old Masters and first of the modern. This extraordinary group of works was painted in oil in 1819-23 directly onto the walls of Goya's villa, Quinta del Sordo (House of the Deaf Man) outside Madrid, to which the artist had retreated at the age of seventy-two. By that stage Goya had witnessed so much tragedy, both national and personal, that his disillusionment with the politics and social developments of his time had caused him to seek near-total isolation. He and his wife, Josefa Bayeu, had lost several children to miscarriages following their marriage in 1773, and in 1793 he was struck down with a severe illness that ultimately resulted in the total loss of his hearing.

In 1808 Goya watched first-hand as the French occupied Spain, with Napoleon Bonaparte using the pretext of reinforcing his army in Portugal to seize the Spanish throne and appoint his brother Joseph to rule. When attempts were made to remove members of the Spanish royal family from Madrid, a widespread rebellion erupted. From this episode came Goya's *Disasters of War* series and his infamous 1814 painting *The Third of May 1808*, a work that features in every collection of the most significant paintings in history, of a ragged group of Spanish freedom-fighters facing an unflinching French firing squad. In the next few years, until 1819, he toiled on a series of bleak works on the themes of persecution (*The Inquisition Tribunal*), the grim conditions of lunatic asylums (*The Madhouse* or *Asylum*) and the impotency and tyranny of Ferdinand VII's disastrous rule (*The Junta of the Philippines*).

The *Black Paintings*, however, stand out as the deepest tunnels into the psyche of the artist, while also remaining utterly mysterious. For, despite the survival of letters and some of his writings, we know little of his personal thoughts and even less about his ideas behind, and intentions for, the *Black Paintings*. None of the works is formally dated or named, and there is no record of Goya having written or even mentioning them to anyone, nor even intending for the public to ever see them. Fears of mortality and civil strife ripple through the artworks like veins of silver.

OPPOSITE: Saturn Devouring His Son *(1819-23) by Francisco de Goya.*

FOLLOWING PAGE: *Goya's* Black Paintings *series.*

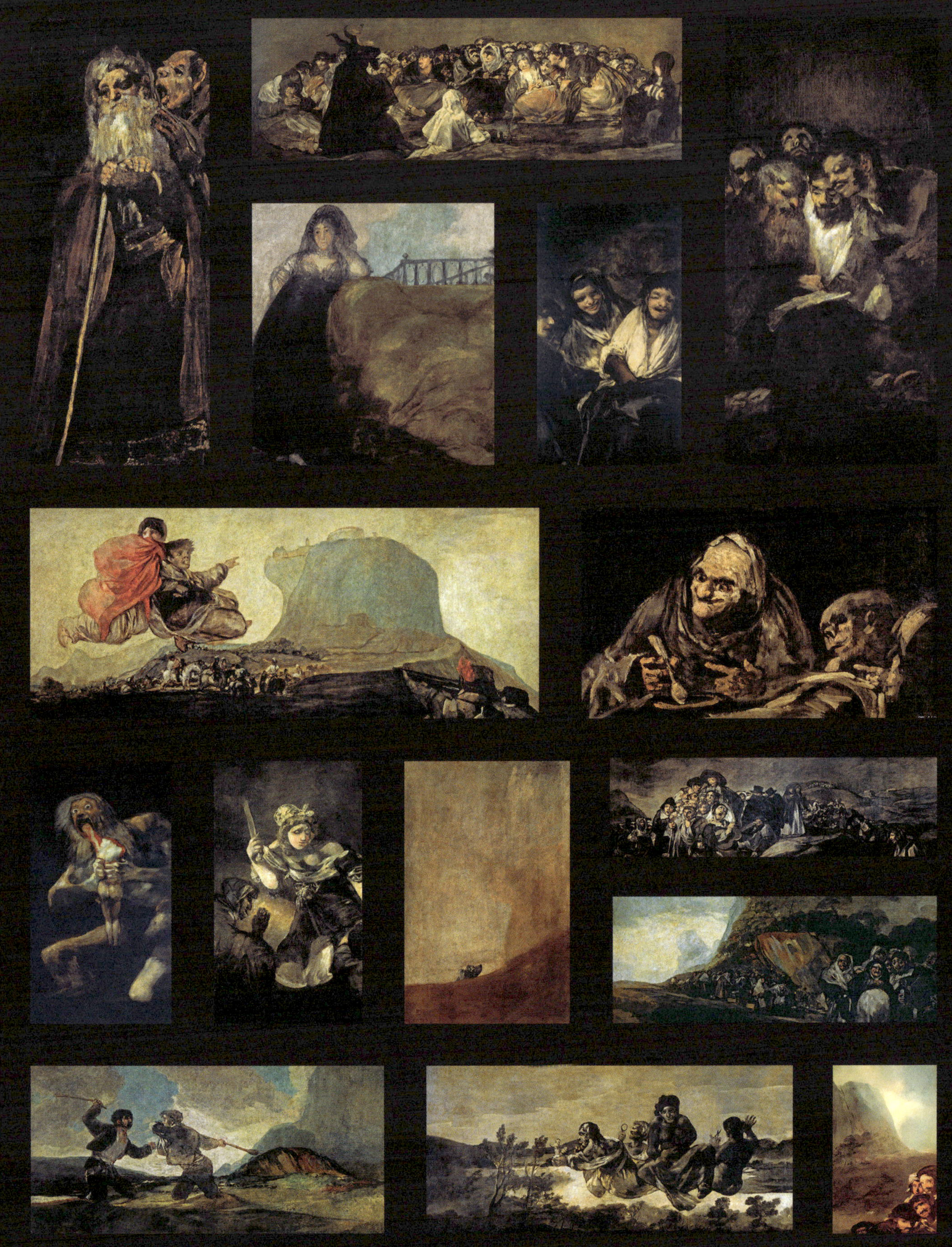

Arguably the most striking is the horrifying *Saturn Devouring His Son*, which according to traditional interpretation depicts the Greek myth of the Titan Cronus (or Saturn when romanised), who was so afraid that one of his children would overthrow him that he would feast on them just after their birth. In this we might find reflection on the conflict between youth and old age, or perhaps Goya's own relationship with his son Xavier, and his guilt that the latter was the only survivor out of six children born. There is also the idea that, as the sex of the body could be either male or female, the image is linked with Goya's live-in housekeeper and possible mistress Leocadia Weiss.

Or perhaps this is too obvious an interpretation. Maybe the disasters he endured forged in Goya not an outlook of despondency and pessimism but of darkly comic wit; perhaps with these paintings he is not blackly bemoaning the state of the society and nature of the people that he left behind, but caustically satirising them.

One of the paintings, today known as *Two Old Ones Eating Soup* or *Witchy Brew*, is a terrible scene: two wizened aged figures in near-skeletal form are slumped at a dinner table in a state of near-death. As sinister as the image is, it could well be a cartoon of greed that Goya painted for his own amusement, the kind of caricature he produced years earlier, in 1799, with a series of eighty prints titled *The Caprices*, which mocked the follies of Spanish society.

Following Goya's death, the new owner of Quinta del Sordo, Baron Frédéric Émile d'Erlanger, stripped out the *Black Paintings*, transferred them to canvas and exhibited them at the Paris Exposition Universelle of 1878, where they horrified their Victorian audience.[1] The British critic P. G. Hamerton decried Goya as a 'hyena', describing his scenes as having erupted from 'a hideous inferno… a disgusting region… shapeless as chaos'. Today, however, together with those of Diego Velázquez (1599-1660) and Peter Paul Rubens (1577-1640), Goya's works are in pride of place at Madrid's Prado Museum.

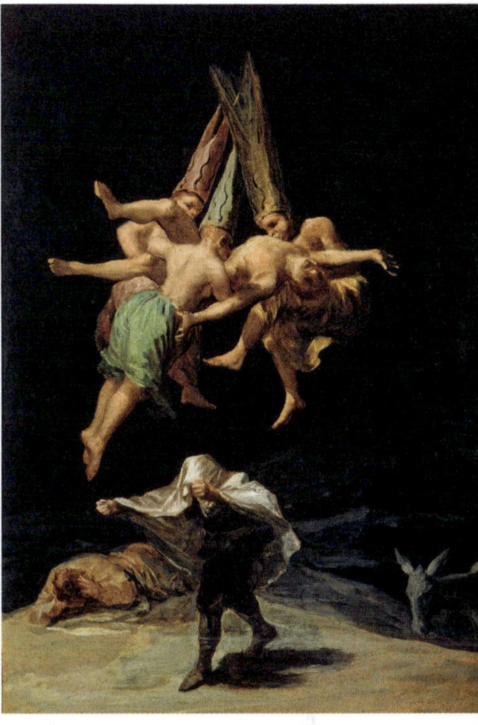

Witches' Flight *(1797)*
by Francisco Goya.

1 Goya himself was also the subject of brutal transfer. Having been buried in Bordeaux, France, on 16 April 1828 at the age of eighty-two, his body was dug up in 1919 by the Spanish and moved to the Real Ermita de San Antonio de la Florida in Madrid. His skull, however, could not be found, reported the Spanish consul to his superiors in Madrid. Soon came the famous response: 'Send Goya, with or without head.'

HIKESHI-BANTEN (NINETEENTH CENTURY) AND THE ART OF FIGHTING FIRE

In March 1657 a priest in a temple of the Hongō district of Edo (the former name of Tokyo) decided to burn a kimono that was said to be cursed. Things got out of hand as the flames leapt to the walls of the wooden temple, then its roof, then engulfed the neighbouring building and then the rest of the neighbourhood. After three days, the Great Fire of Meireki (or the Furisode Fire) had destroyed 60-70 per cent of the Japanese capital city and claimed over 100,000 lives. In the 266 years between 1601 and 1867, the dense city of wood-and-paper buildings suffered approximately forty-nine great fires. In fact, fires were so frequent in Edo that today it is still remembered as the 'City of Fires', with the popular saying: 'Fires and quarrels are the flowers of Edo.'

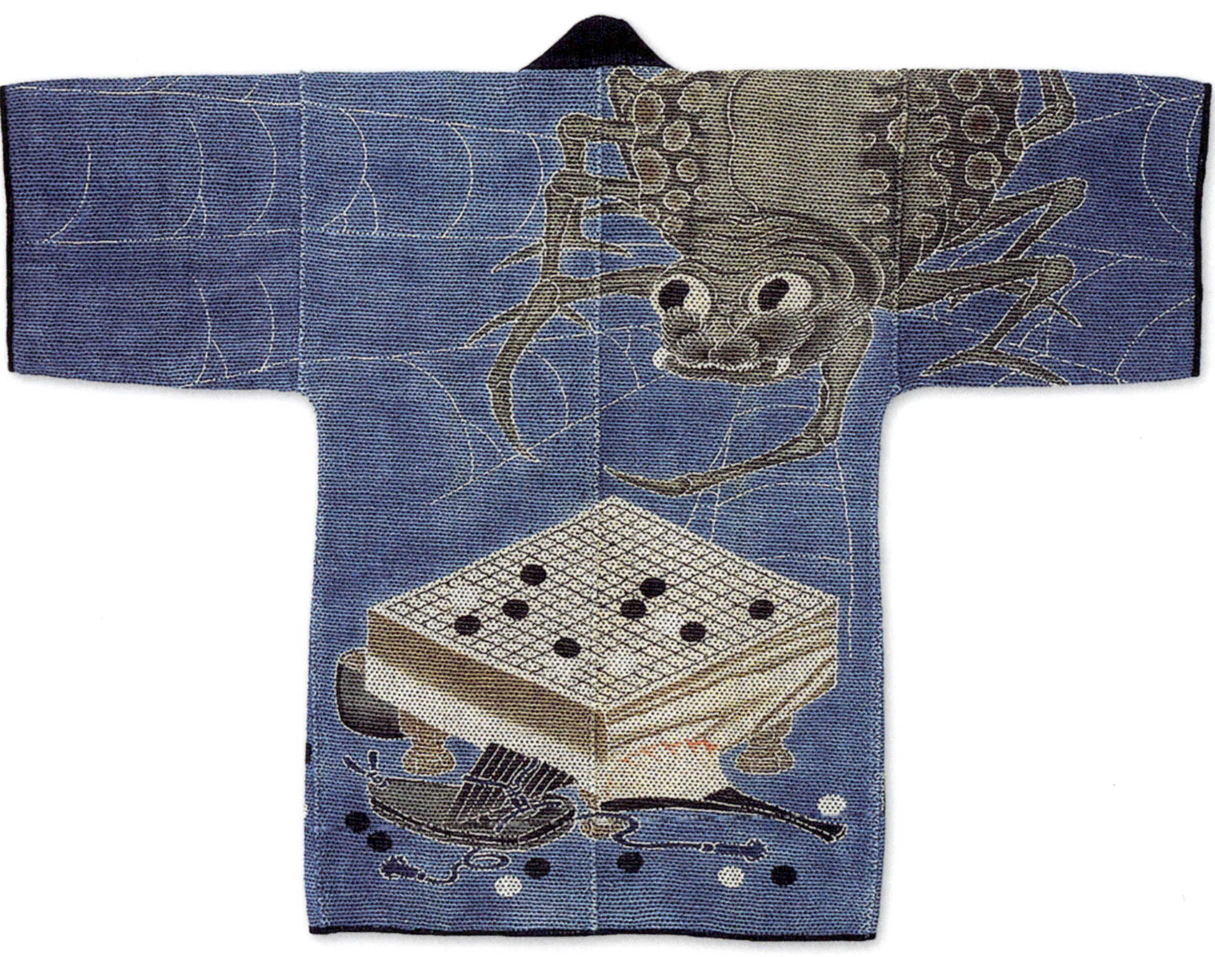

In the early Edo period, firefighting was not officially organised, but after repeated catastrophes the *hikeshi* (firefighting) system was established. The primary technique of the samurai firefighters was to demolish the buildings surrounding the blaze. A wooden pump worked by hand and called *ryūdosui* (dragon spraying water) was employed but the lack of a reliable water supply made it unviable. (In the meantime, in an effort to reduce outbreaks of fire, a law was introduced in 1723 that ordered arsonists be paraded through the streets and burnt at the stake.)

The artworks displayed here are examples of *hikeshi-banten*, the thick multilayered jackets worn by the samurai firefighters. The coats were soaked in water before the men threw them on and entered the boiling fray. The layers of padding retained the water, while also cushioning the wearer from falling objects. Such items are relics of the time following the Meiji Restoration of 1868, when practical imperial rule was restored in Japan under Emperor Meiji. Firefighting techniques were by then more advanced and incorporated pumped water supplies, and building materials were more fire-resistant, but ultimately the saving factor was the extraordinary bravery of the *hikeshi*.

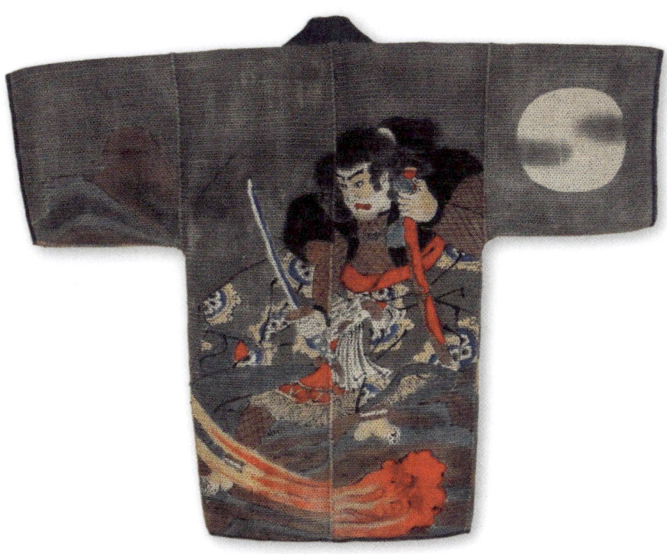

While the exterior layer is made from *sakiori* weaving, the inner liner fabric shows intricate close rows of *sashiko* stitching. To achieve the vibrant colour palette, a method of resist dyeing called *tsutsugaki* was used, over a period of around three weeks. The jacket's artwork was inked onto the jacket cotton with rice paste, and the details were then dyed with their colours individually, using rice paste to stop dye spilling into the other areas. Then the whole object was repeatedly dipped in indigo, dried, and soaked in hot water until finally the rice paste could be scraped off to reveal the multitude of colours.

The *hikeshi-banten* are reversible. The plain side is marked only with the bold pattern of the firefighter's brigade. When the fire was out, the fireman would triumphantly turn his jacket inside-out so that the decorative liner was on display, to the cheers of the crowd celebrating the successful outcome.

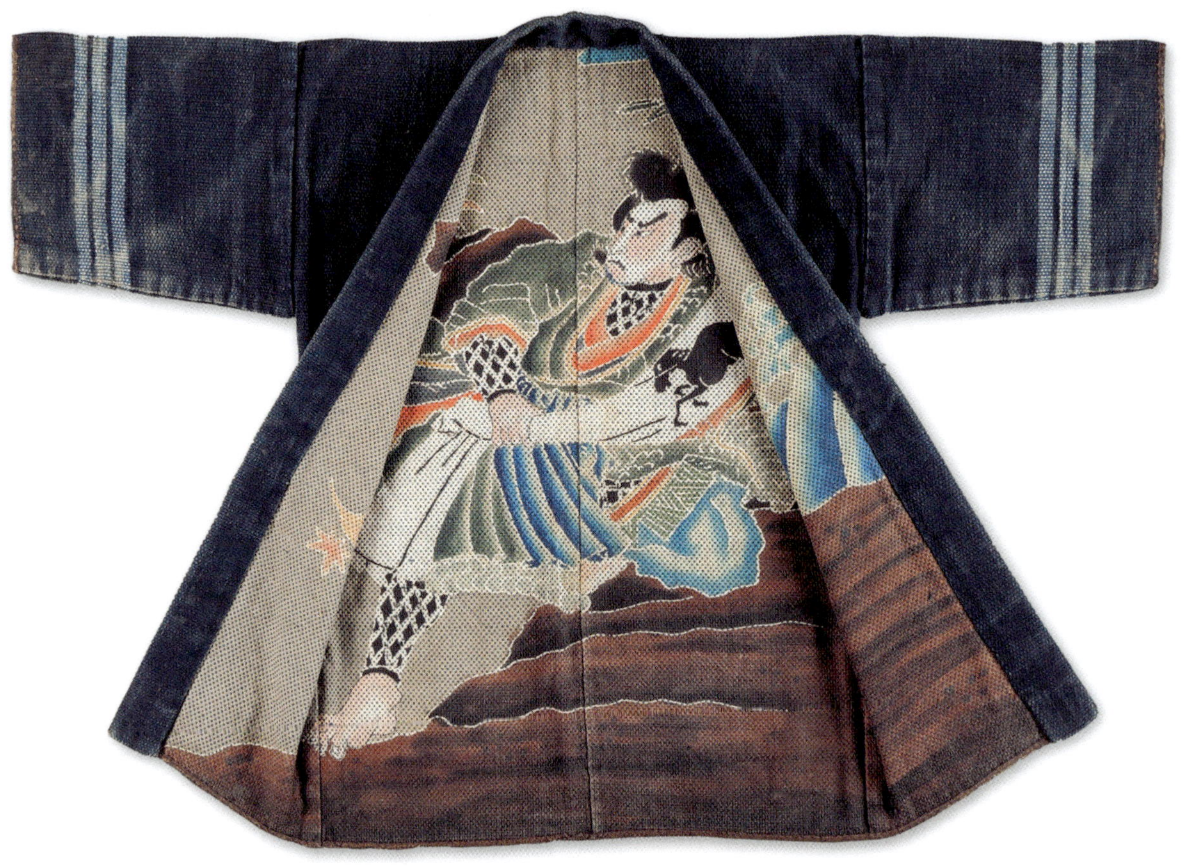

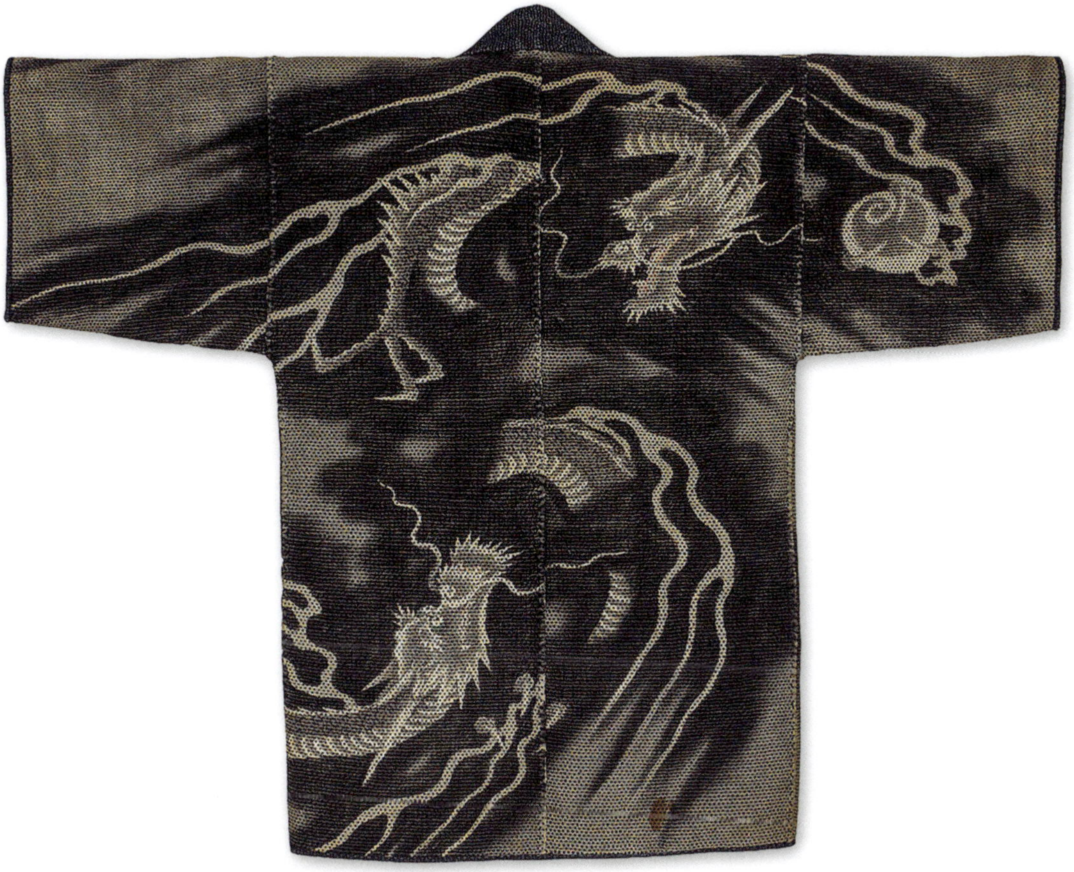

While clearly beautiful, the designs often held special meaning to the firefighter who wore them. The main image on page 172 of *hikeshi-banten* featuring a spider, for example, tells a story from the life of Minamoto no Yorimitsu (948-1021), a hero of numerous legends. One day Yorimitsu was recovering from an illness in bed when he was visited by a kindly priest who was actually a *tsuchigumo* (a giant earth spider in disguise). Yorimitsu saw through the ruse, grabbed his sword and fought off the creature. His four attendants, the Four Heavenly Kings, then leapt up from their game of *weiqi* and hunted the spider back to his den. The image shows the moment the game was interrupted, and the *tsuchigumo* retreating – a symbolic tale of bravery that not only inspired the *hikeshi* but also acted as a talisman of protection as they strode into the hell-mouths of burning buildings.

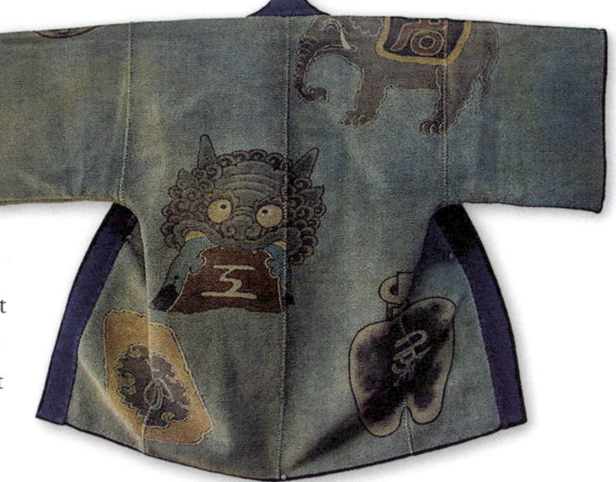

THE CORONATION OF INÊS DE CASTRO IN 1361 (*c*.1849), PIERRE CHARLES COMTE

The French artist Pierre Charles Comte (1823-95) first exhibited this painting at the Paris Salon of 1849. Titled *Le Couronnement d'Inès de Castro en 1361* (The Coronation of Inês de Castro in 1361), the oil on canvas captures one of the strangest episodes in Portuguese history: the crowning of the wife of King Peter I of Portugal (1320-67). Peter stands beside his wife in a packed hall, overseeing the kneeling courtier paying homage to his queen. Nearly all eyes in the room are turned downwards – out of respect, one would assume, unless one knew the story unfolding here, which is hinted at by the new queen's sunken, sallow skin. The averted gazes are more likely to be out of fear and disgust, for the hand that the courtier kisses is that of a corpse. At the time of her coronation in 1361, Inês de Castro had been dead for four years.

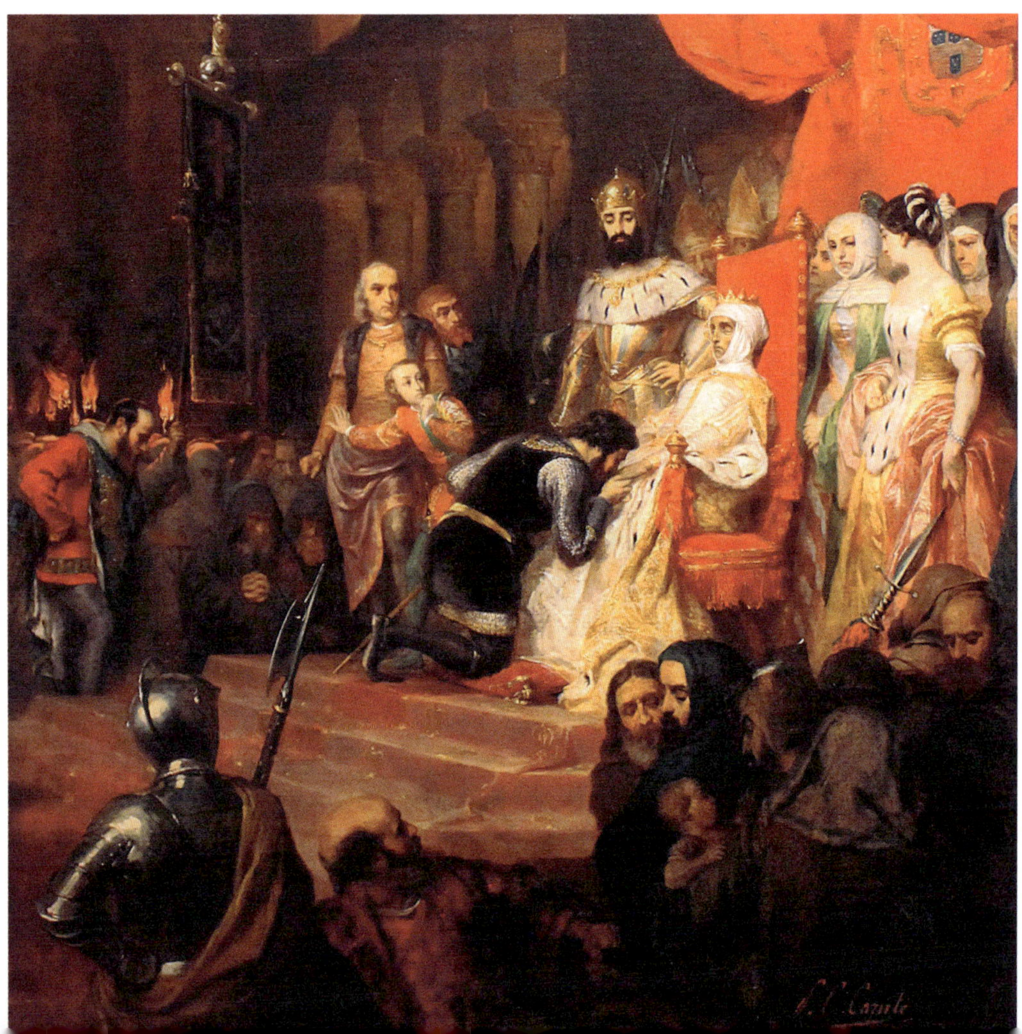

Peter and Inês had met in 1340, when at fifteen years old she was sent by her Castilian family to be lady-in-waiting to Peter's first wife, Constanza of Castile. Peter and Inês began an affair, and five years later, when Constanza died shortly after giving birth to Ferdinand I (future king of Portugal), Peter sought permission from his father King Alfonso IV to marry Inês. Alfonso deemed her unsuitable and banished her from the court, but the couple continued their relationship nevertheless, having four children between 1346 and 1354 at a villa outside Coimbra, a home that would be known as the Villa of Tears. King Alfonso, meanwhile, continued to worry that Inês would exert Castilian influence over his son, and so finally dispatched three assassins to murder her. The killers found her in the villa courtyard beside the fountain and butchered her.

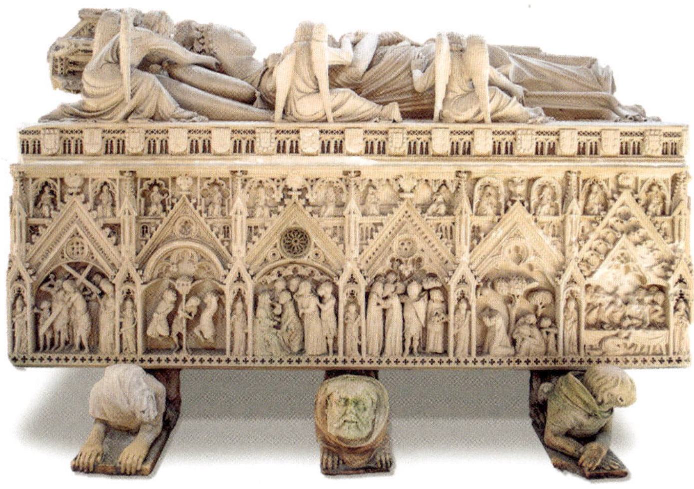

The exquisitely carved tomb of Portugal's posthumous queen, Inês de Castro.

A distraught Peter buried Inês at Coimbra's Monastery of Santa Clara-a-Velha. When he inherited the throne in 1357, following his father's death, Peter immediately sought revenge. Two of his wife's murderers were captured and brought before him, whereupon he ordered that their hearts be ripped out in front of him. He then revealed that he and Inês had, in fact, married in secret, which meant that she was now the rightful queen of Portugal, regardless of her cardiopulmonary status. (While some sources say Peter demanded the coronation of Inês take place during his own ceremony of 1357, this painting is tied to the alternative version of the story that her body was dug up and crowned in 1361.) The body of Inês de Castro was exhumed, dressed in royal robes and placed on the throne for the ceremony. A romantic gesture, in some eyes, but there were also practical reasons behind it, as it legitimised the children that the two had had together. Her body was then buried at the Alcobaça Monastery in a tomb carved with effigies. Peter's tomb was built opposite so that on the day of the Last Judgement, when all the dead will be resurrected for admission to heaven, the two will meet again.

THE FAIRY FELLER'S MASTER-STROKE (1855-64), RICHARD DADD

In *The Fairy Feller's Master-Stroke* (1855-64), in the collection of the Tate Gallery, London, the Victorian English artist Richard Dadd (1819-87) reveals a secret scene of 'Fays, gnomes, elves and suchlike', a playful and charming setting betraying little of the story of its artist. At the time of its painting, Dadd had been incarcerated in a lunatic asylum for almost ten years, having murdered his father on the suspicion that he was the Devil in disguise. He also believed himself to be under the control of the ancient Egyptian god of death, and that the Pope was plotting against him. After the murder of his father, Dadd had attempted to flee to Paris, but when he attacked another man with a razor he was hospitalised at the State Criminal Lunatic Asylum of Bethlem Royal Hospital.

The Fairy Feller's Master-Stroke was a commission for the head steward of the hospital, George Henry Haydon. Before Dadd had fallen ill – with what is today suspected to have been paranoid schizophrenia – he had already begun a career painting Orientalist scenes, inspired by his 1842 tour with Sir Thomas Phillips of Greece, the Levant and Egypt. He then became drawn to fairy painting, a genre popular in the Victorian era that often drew on Shakespearean scenes for inspiration and involved pleasingly precise and minute details. In Dadd's work, the obsessive attention to detail is palpable. He spent nine years working on the 54 × 39.5cm (21 × 15½in) *The Fairy Feller's Master-Stroke*, using a complex multilayered technique to give it an almost three-dimensional effect as we peek through the wisps of grass that conceal the scene behind.

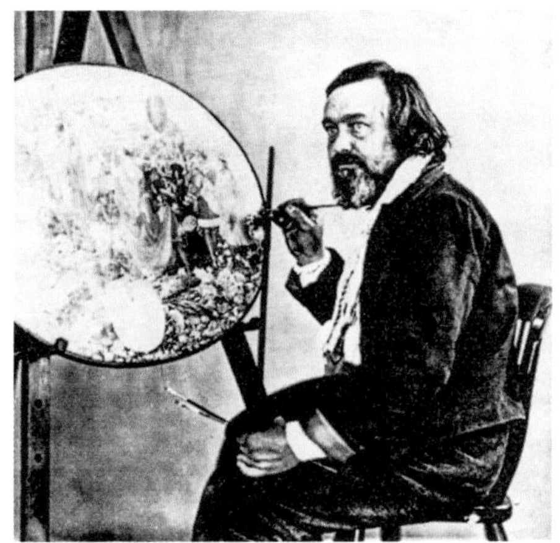

Richard Dadd (c.1875).

Dadd wrote an extensive poem called 'Elimination of a Picture & its Subject – called The Fellers' Master-Stroke' in which each character is named and their purpose explained. Shakespeare's Oberon and Titania appear in the centre of the upper half of the picture, presiding over the rest of the figures invented by Dadd. At the centre is the Fairy Feller, who is about to split a large chestnut from which will be built a fairy carriage for Queen Mabs. Just above him, a white-bearded figure appears to command him to stay his axe until a signal is given, while the other fairies look on eagerly. Much interpretation has been made of this charivari – the bearded figure, though father-like, with his three-tiered crown seems

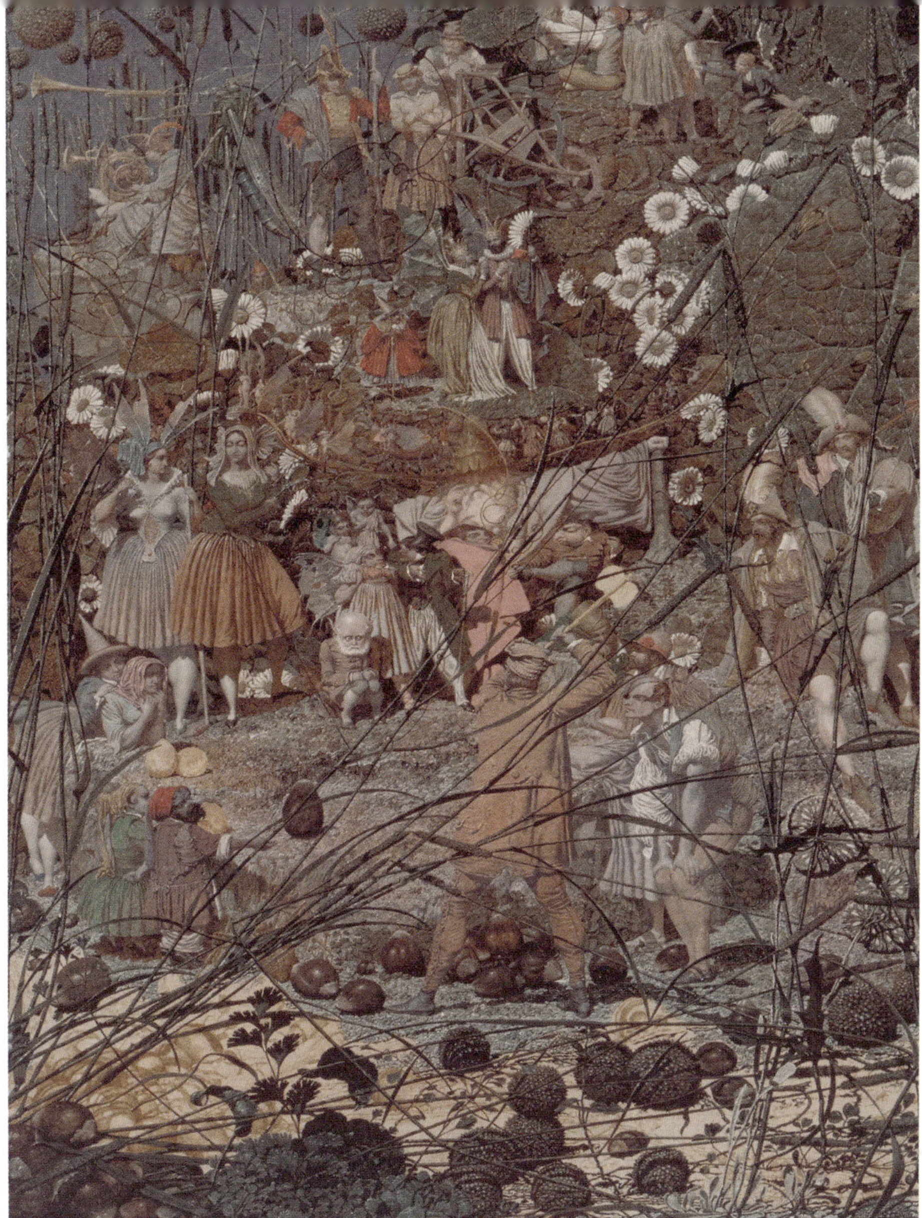

to represent the Pope, while Dadd's father is drawn as the apothecary with pestle and mortar in the upper-right corner. Some symbols are a little harder to decode, like the standing dragonfly playing the trumpet in the upper-left corner.

The Fairy Feller's Master-Stroke is technically an unfinished work – the background of the lower-left corner is only drawn in. Dated 'quasi 1855-64' on the reverse (it's thought that by 'quasi' Dadd meant it took a long time to begin), the end date of 1864 is the year that Dadd was transferred to Broadmoor Hospital in Berkshire, which is why he was never able to finish the work. He would be confined there until his death almost twenty-three years later.

PORTRAIT OF MADAME X (1884), JOHN SINGER SARGENT

When the modern viewer regards the notorious *Portrait of Madame X* by John Singer Sargent (1856-1925), it might seem like an almost conservative image. The black gown flows decorously all the way to the floor, and the subject's face is turned away, with little in the way of legible facial expression to infer any licentiousness. But the fact is that upon its debut at the Paris Salon in 1884, originally titled *Portrait of Madame* ***, the painting was met with such a scandalised reaction that its artist was eventually forced to leave the country, and its subject was never quite able to restore her damaged reputation.

John Singer Sargent was one of the pre-eminent portrait artists of the luxurious Gilded Age of the nineteenth century, born to American parents in Florence, trained in Paris and an inhabitant of London – his travels through Europe being reflected in his prolific output of about 900 oil paintings and 2000 watercolours. While living in Paris in the early 1880s, he sought to solidify his representation as the go-to portraitist of the fabulously wealthy and pursued. The way to accomplish

Below: *A photograph from 1884 of Sargent at work on the painting in his Parisian studio at 41 boulevard Berthier, XVIIe arrondissement.*

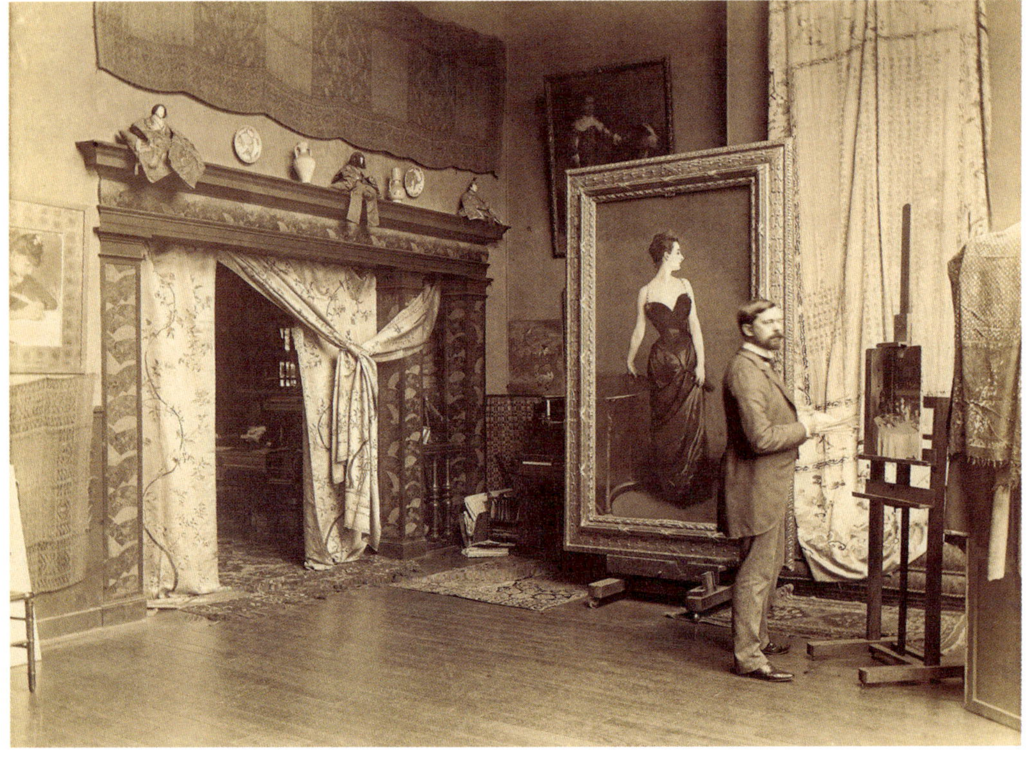

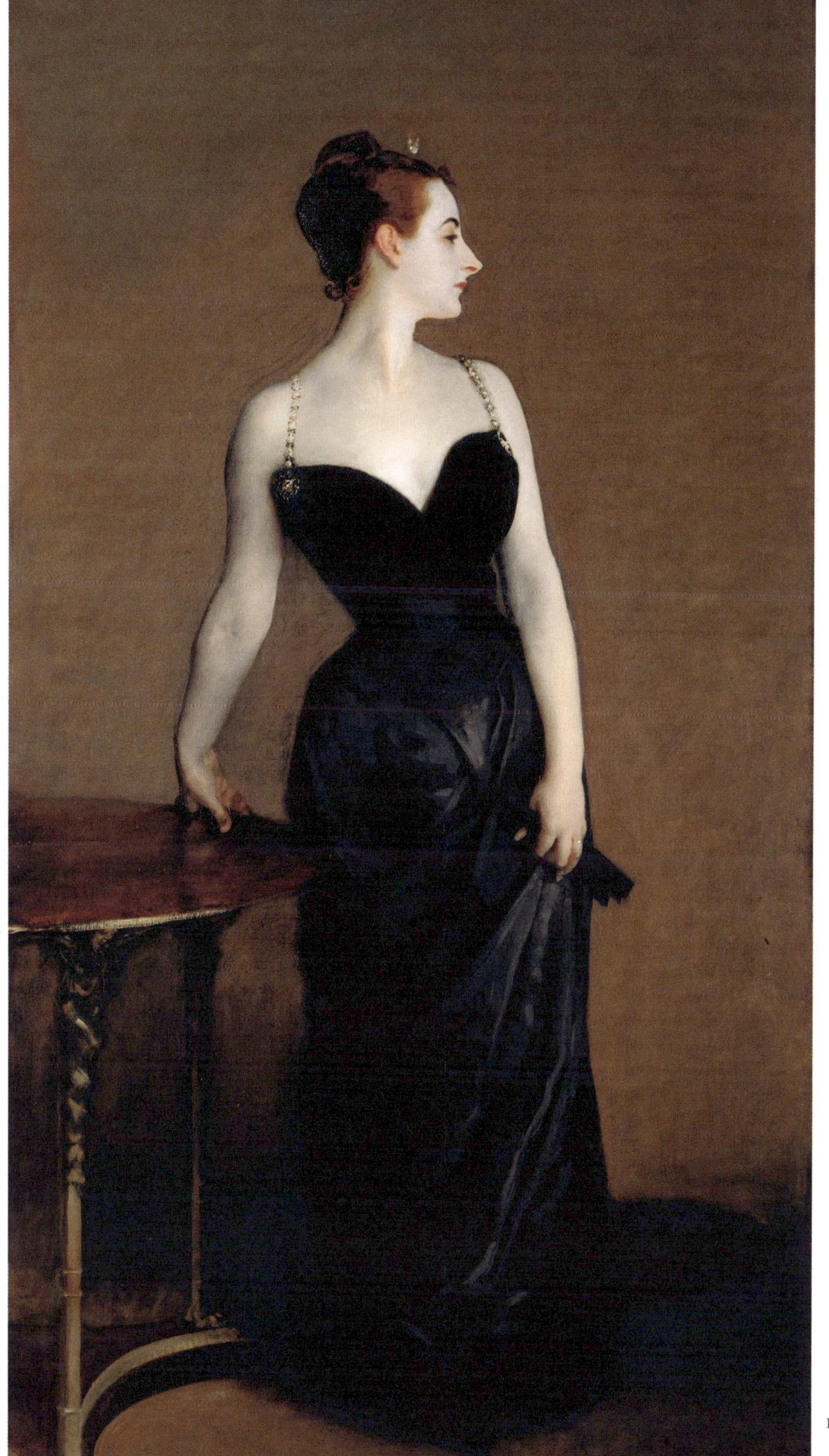

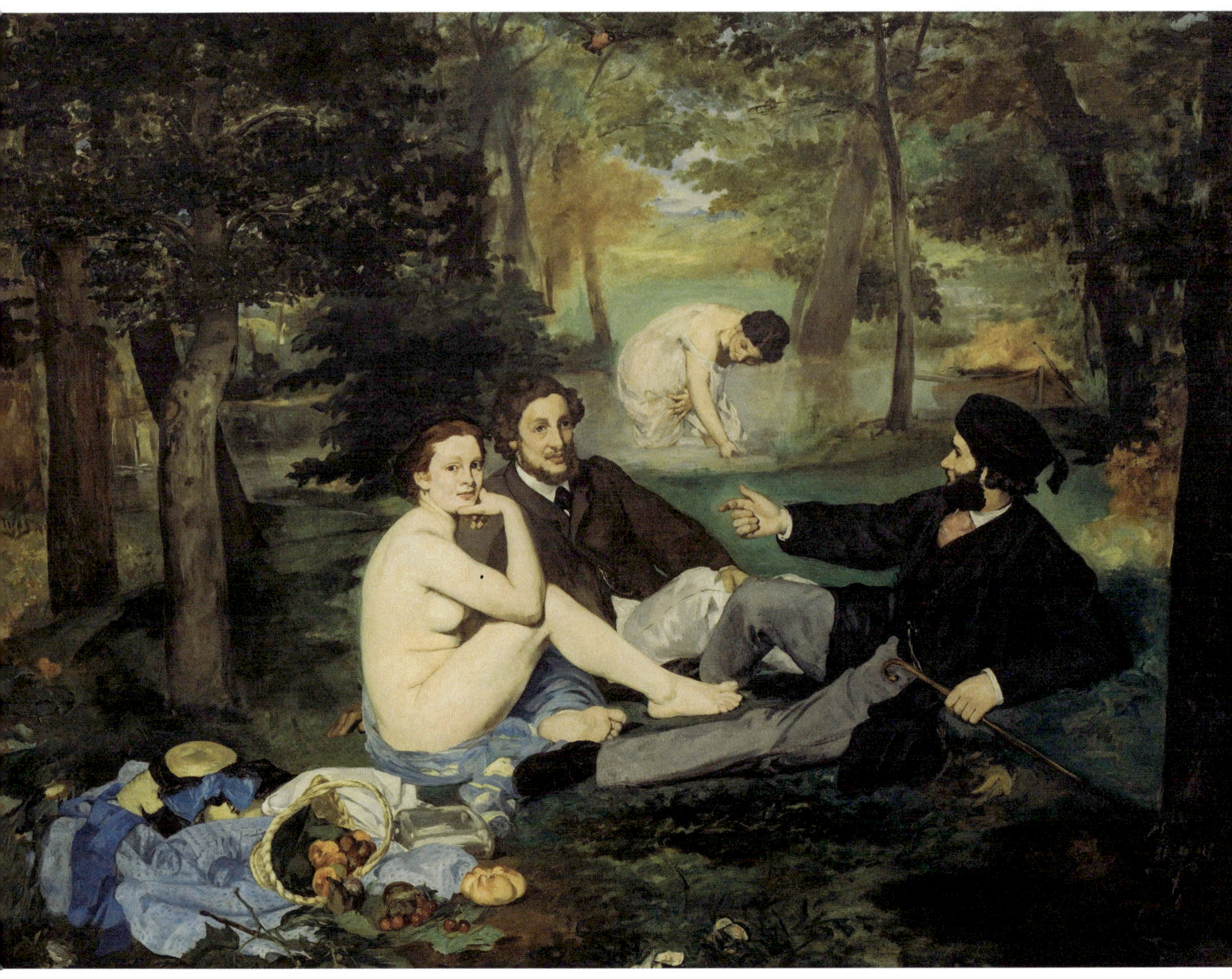

this, he reasoned, was to secure as a model the most admired socialite of the Parisian scene: Virginie Amélie Avegno Gautreau (1859-1915), the young wife of a wealthy and much older banking and shipping magnate. (He was not the only one seeking to paint her – the artist Edward Simmons (1852-1931) wrote that he 'could not stop stalking her as one does a deer.')

Madame Gautreau possessed a strikingly elegant and pale appearance, which she amplified by dying her hair with henna, wearing lavender face and body powder and – it was said – by eating arsenic-laced wafers. (In the painting Sargent contrasts her skin with the dark dress and use of a dark background.) She was a figure who wore the rumours about her as proudly as her mink stole, doing little to mitigate the attention: there

Édouard Manet's (1832-83) Déjeuner sur l'Herbe *(Luncheon on the Grass) (1863), which also scandalised nineteenth-century Paris for breaking the tradition of setting nudes in classical scenes. The work was rejected by the Paris Salon on the grounds that it was obscene. Today it is displayed prominently in the Musée d'Orsay.*

were murmurs of extra-marital affairs, including with a Dr Pozzi, whom Sargent had painted previously. Knowing this biography, suddenly there is a charge to the painting – the impossibly pale flesh with a coolness one can almost feel, the spellbound male gaze of the painting as we regard her while she looks away, the seductiveness of her shoulders on display with her confident indifference to the enamoured attention surrounding her.

Sargent had hoped for comparisons to classical and Renaissance profile portraiture; instead, the painting was met with horror. Though he had attempted to preserve her modesty with anonymity, everyone knew the identity and reputation of the model. (In its original state, Sargent omitted the left shoulder strap – the bare shoulder, coupled with Gautreau's adulterous rumours, rendered the painting shockingly indecent.)

Crowds of visitors came to mock the painting. Louis de Fourcaud, critic for the *Gazette des beaux-arts*, described the visitors' reaction: 'Epithets crisscross in the air – Detestable! Boring! Curious! Monstrous!... One could darken 10 pages with the one-word comments heard in front of this picture.' Gautreau's own mother begged Sargent to remove the painting from exhibition to salvage her daughter's reputation. 'All Paris is making fun of my daughter,' the *Tribune* reported her complaining to Sargent. 'She is ruined. My people will be forced to defend themselves. She'll die of chagrin.' Sargent refused to remove it. Critics hated the painting on a purely technical level, too. A *New York Times* reporter reviewing the Salon wrote: 'Sargent is below his usual standard this year... The pose of the figure is absurd, and the bluish colouring atrocious. The features are so exaggerated that the natural delicacy of outline is entirely lost.'

In the wake of the furore, Sargent moved to London, and the painting hung on the walls of his studio for thirty years before he finally sold it to the Metropolitan Museum of Art in 1916 for £1000 following the death of Gautreau. The sale was agreed on one condition: that the Museum would continue to disguise the identity of the sitter. And so *The Portrait of Madame X* retains its alluring title to this day. 'It is a great success of curiosity,' writes Sargent's contemporary, the Ukrainian artist Marie Bashkirtseff (1858-84). 'People find it atrocious. For me it is perfect painting, masterly, true. But he has done what he saw.'

REPLY OF THE ZAPOROZHIAN COSSACKS TO SULTAN MEHMED IV (1880-91), ILYA REPIN

Historically, artists haven't exactly shied away from hurling insults – most gleefully when it comes to the works of other artists. 'He bores me,' said Pierre-Auguste Renoir on Leonardo da Vinci, 'he ought to have stuck to his flying machines.' Jackson Pollock's style was, to Salvador Dalí, 'the indigestion that goes with fish soup.' Gustave Courbet summed up Édouard Manet's *Olympia* (1865) with: 'It's flat, it isn't modelled. It's like the Queen of Hearts after a bath.' 'What a genius, that Picasso,' mused Marc Chagall, 'it's a pity he doesn't paint.' When asked about his thoughts on Jasper Johns, Andy Warhol replied: 'Oh, I think he's great. He makes such great lunches.' Warhol later got a taste of his own medicine when bumping into Willem de Kooning at a party, who roared at him: 'You're a killer of art, you're a killer of beauty, you're even a killer of laughter. I can't bear your work!' With a more understated cattiness, Frederic Leighton poked James McNeill Whistler with: 'My dear Whistler, you leave your pictures in such a sketchy, unfinished state. Why don't you ever finish them?' Whistler replied: 'My dear Leighton, why do you ever begin yours?'

But the biggest (literally) insult in art history began to take shape in 1880, when the realist painter Ilya Yefimovich Repin (1844-1930), commonly regarded as the greatest Russian artist of the nineteenth century (and so nicknamed 'the Tolstoy of art'), attended a party thrown by the historian Dmytro Yavornytsky (1855-1940). The host performed a reading for his guests from a letter purportedly written in 1676, of which a copy had recently been discovered. Repin was so fascinated by the story that he immediately began the first of his studies for a historical tableau of the episode, which he would spend the next eleven years painting.

In 1676 Mehmed IV, sultan of the Ottoman Empire, dispatched a threatening ultimatum to the Zaporozhian Cossacks, who lived beyond the Dnieper Rapids in today's central Ukraine and who until then had successfully resisted Ottoman expansion. 'No one in the world held so deeply freedom, equality, and fraternity,' said Repin admiringly of them. The Sultan's message reportedly took the following form:

As the Sultan; son of Muhammad; brother of the sun and moon; grandson and viceroy of God; ruler of the kingdoms of Macedonia, Babylon, Jerusalem, Upper and Lower Egypt; emperor of emperors; sovereign of sovereigns; extraordinary knight, never defeated; steadfast guardian of the tomb of Jesus Christ; trustee chosen by God Himself; the hope and comfort of Muslims; confounder and great defender of Christians – I command you, the Zaporozhian Cossacks, to submit to me voluntarily and without any resistance, and to desist from troubling me with your attacks.

Turkish sultan Mehmed IV

The Cossacks were so incensed by this that they decided to take their time in penning the most insulting reply they could come up with, and in doing so created one of the most spectacularly insulting messages in the history of comebacks. Repin's enormous, 4m- (13ft-) wide painting shows this raucous scene, with the Cossacks roaring with laughter as they draft their magnificently profane reply parodying Mehmed's many titles.

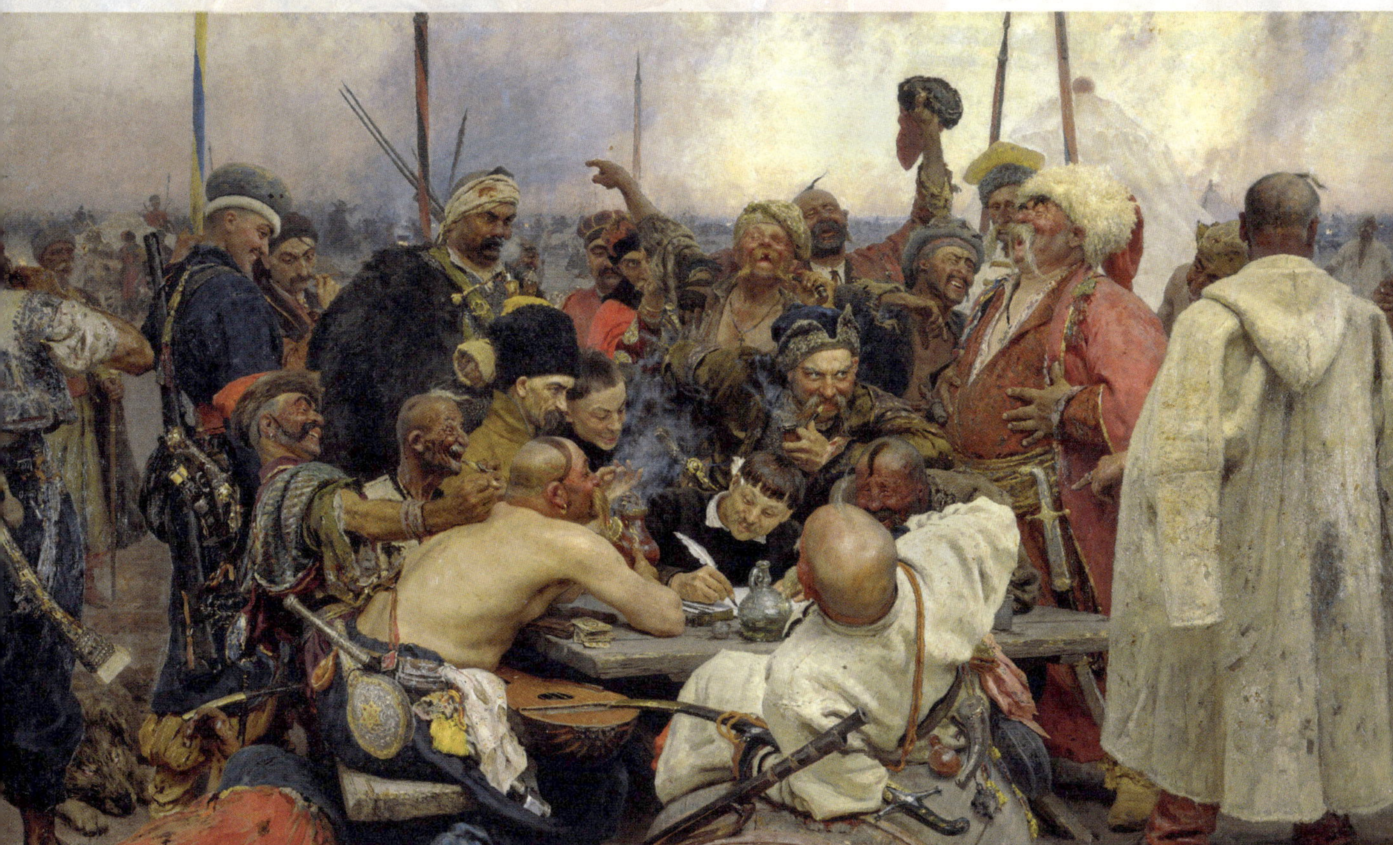

Reply of the Zaporozhian Cossacks to Sultan Mehmed IV *(1880-91), Ilya Repin*

The following is as close a translation as possible of their original dispatch to the Sultan:

> *O sultan, Turkish devil and damned devil's kith and kin, companion to Lucifer himself, Greetings! What the devil kind of knight are you, that can't slay a hedgehog with your naked arse? The devil shits, and your army eats. You will not, you son of a bitch, make subjects of Christian sons; thy army we fear not, and by land and on sea we will do battle against thee, fuck your mother.*
>
> *You Babylonian scullion, Macedonian wheelwright, brewer of Jerusalem, goat-fucker of Alexandria, swineherd of Greater and Lesser Egypt, pig of Armenia, Podolian thief, catamite of Tartary, hangman of Kamyanets, and fool of all the world and underworld, an idiot before God, grandson of the Serpent, and the crick in our dick. Pig's snout, mare's arse, slaughterhouse cur, unchristened brow, fuck your mother!*
>
> *So the Zaporozhians declare, you lowlife. You won't even be herding pigs for the Christians. Now we'll conclude, for we don't know the date and don't own a calendar; the moon's in the sky, the year with the Lord, the day is the same over here as it is over there; for this kiss our arse!*
>
> *Koshovyi Otaman Ivan Sirko, with the whole Zaporozhian Host*

Repin wasn't the only one who loved the story. Shortly after he completed the painting, it was purchased by Alexander III, who happily paid 35,000 rubles, a record-breaking sum at the time. Since then, it has been exhibited in the State Russian Museum in St Petersburg.

The mocking laughter of the Cossacks of Repin's insult painting reminds me of this 1852 painting by William Powell Frith (1819-1909), showing the disastrous moment the poet Alexander Pope (1688-1744) confessed his undying love to Lady Mary Montagu (1689-1762), causing her to howl with laughter.

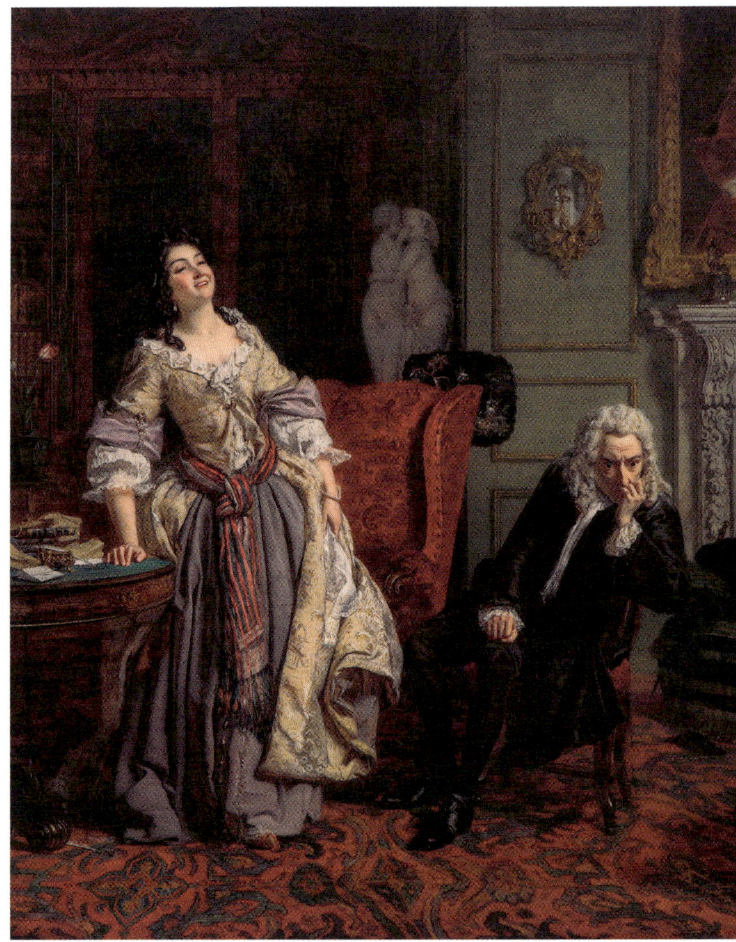

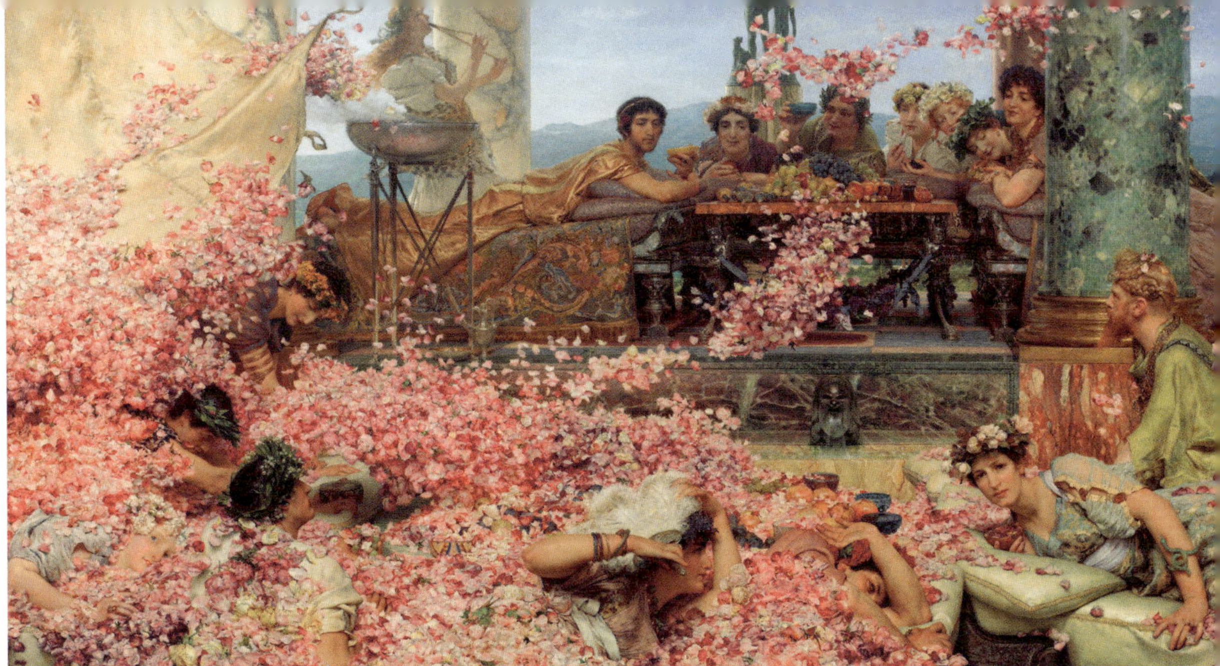

THE ROSES OF HELIOGABALUS (1888), SIR LAWRENCE ALMA-TADEMA

Say what you will about the Roman boy-emperor Elagabalus (*c.*203-222) – and when historians do, it's usually with terms like 'debauched psychopath' – the fellow had a sense of humour. Of a sort. In *The Roses of Heliogabalus* (1888), gentle showers of rose petals tumble from a false ceiling onto the heads of dinner guests at a banquet thrown by the young emperor, who reclines behind them in a gold silk robe and tiara. A peaceful scene, but what we're actually witnessing is a multiple homicide in progress for the entertainment of a whimsical maniac. The people under the flower bombardment are not lazing but are gradually suffocating to death under the sheer weight and density of the petals, to the amusement of the garlanded guests on the higher imperial platform. 'In a banqueting-room with a reversible ceiling,' notes the author of the *Historia Augusta*, likely written towards the end of the fourth century, 'he once buried his guests in violets and other flowers, so that some were actually smothered to death, being unable to crawl out to the top.'

The painting by Sir Lawrence Alma-Tadema (1836-1912), in the classically influenced academic style, takes its inspiration from one of the many darkly eccentric stories in the short but punchy legacy of Elagabalus (or Heliogabalus). Born in *c.*203 and raised to the principate to become emperor at the age of just fourteen years, Elagabalus's rule is marked by just the kind of vigorous sexual scandals and mad practical jokes that one would expect from an unhinged teenage boy given limitless power. In his short reign of just four years Elagabalus managed to terrify and infuriate just about everyone, before he was enthusiastically slaughtered by his own Praetorian Guard and replaced with his cousin Severus Alexander at the instigation of his grandmother, in 222.

From sources such as the *Historia Augusta* we learn various examples of Elagabalus's depravity, and how one's heart must have sunk on receiving an invitation to dine at the imperial palace. One story tells how he enjoyed having broken glass mixed into his guests' food, which he would force them to eat. On another occasion, he waited for his guests to reach a suitably drunken state after finishing their meal of camel heels, nightingale tongues, parrot heads and flamingo brains, before releasing live lions and leopards into their room. At a separate feast, he ordered some of the guests be tied to a slowly rotating water wheel, and ordered everyone to watch as they drowned. Elagabalus's 'shenanigans' weren't confined to the dining hall. He was also said to have harnessed a group of naked women to pull his chariot around the palace while whipping them, and to have caused a deadly panic at a gladiatorial games when he had venomous snakes let loose among the packed crowd.

'Indeed, for him life was nothing except a search after pleasures,' writes the author of the *Historia Augusta*, articulating the philosophy that Alma-Tadema is targeting here with his prim Victorian paintbrush. Academic art was criticised for its clichéd idealism and smooth 'false surface' textures, and unlike other movements has seen little resurgence in popularity since. What is most interesting is how it operated like match paper to ignite the brighter flames of the realists and the impressionists, many key figures of which – Claude Monet, Gustave Courbet, Édouard Manet, Henri Matisse – began their training in academic ateliers before rebelling against the style. Indeed it was the polished academic sheen that inspired the realist Théodule Ribot (1823-91) to experiment with rough, raw textures in his painting.

Alma-Tadema's reputation declined following his death in 1912, and this painting changed hands in the subsequent years for relatively unremarkable figures. Until June 1993, that is, when the Victorian style chimed with the Spanish billionaire art collector, Juan Antonio Pérez Simón, who purchased the work for £1.5 million at Christie's in London.

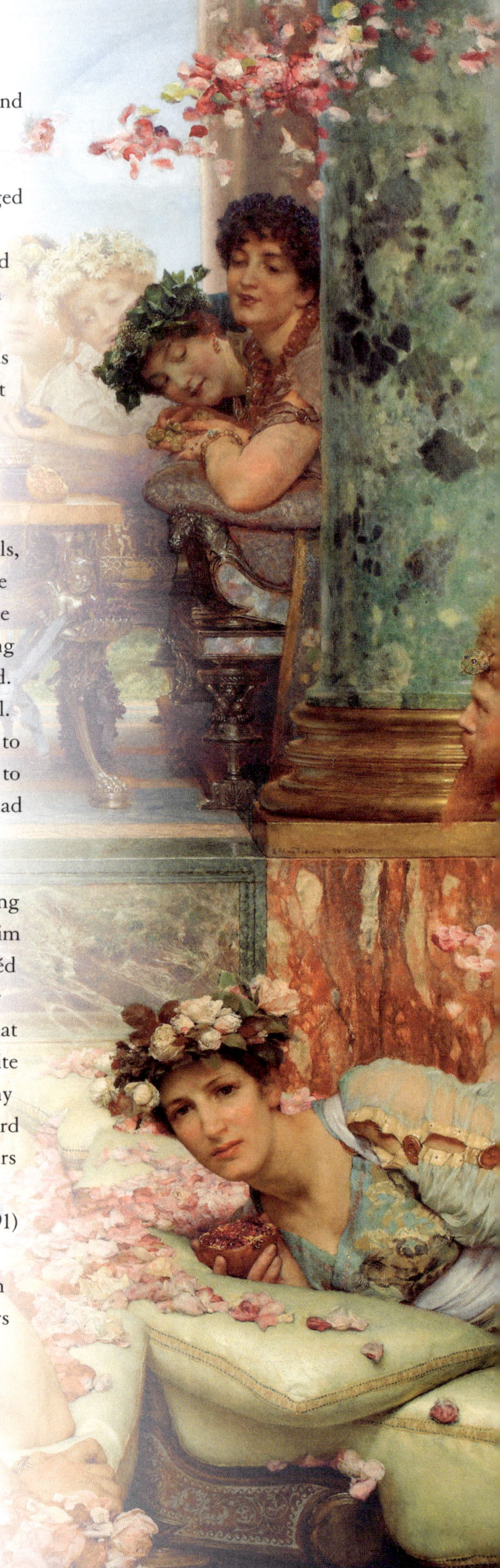

BREAM IN 25 FEET OF WATER OFF THE WEST COAST OF SCOTLAND (1910), ZARH PRITCHARD

He was meant to be an army surgeon – that, at least, was the compromise a young Zarh Pritchard (1866-1956) had reached with his military family. For a year he studied medicine in Edinburgh, until one night, as the students quizzed each other, he was asked the simplest of test questions as a joke and he didn't know the answer. Ten months of study had evaporated from his mind. He fled to New Zealand to paint instead, and returned to England in 1891 to work as a paid artist.

The name Zarh Pritchard (full name Walter Howlison Mackenzie Pritchard) very rarely appears in general histories of art, and for the vast majority of people today it is not a name that rings even the faintest of bells. And yet he was an extraordinary artist with a unique medium: Zarh Pritchard was the first person to paint underwater.

By 1892, following his New Zealand escape, he was building renown for himself in London when he came to the attention of the famed French stage actress Sarah Bernhardt (1844-1923). She commissioned him to design her a fabulous oceanic-themed costume for her Cleopatra and, with it, Pritchard took his first steps into worldwide awareness. In 1902 he arrived in America with eight underwater scenes painted from his memories as a child, which were warmly received in Santa Barbara, California. He decided to produce more accurate submarine seascapes, first with just goggles, standing in the shallows and then using a suit to dive deeper.

His techniques were simple but effective. In the customary diving costume of leaded shoes, air hose and signal ropes, he would descend to depths of 10-20m (30-60ft), which was usually sufficient – any deeper and the lack of light became a problem. After familiarising himself with his surroundings, he'd choose his spot and tug the signal rope, and his easel and box of paints would be lowered to him by assistants on the surface.

Pritchard used brushes with oiled bristles, and his maulstick (a kind of arm support) and easel were both weighted down with lead to prevent them drifting off. Canvas, of course, could not survive the soaking and so he used calfskin and lambskin

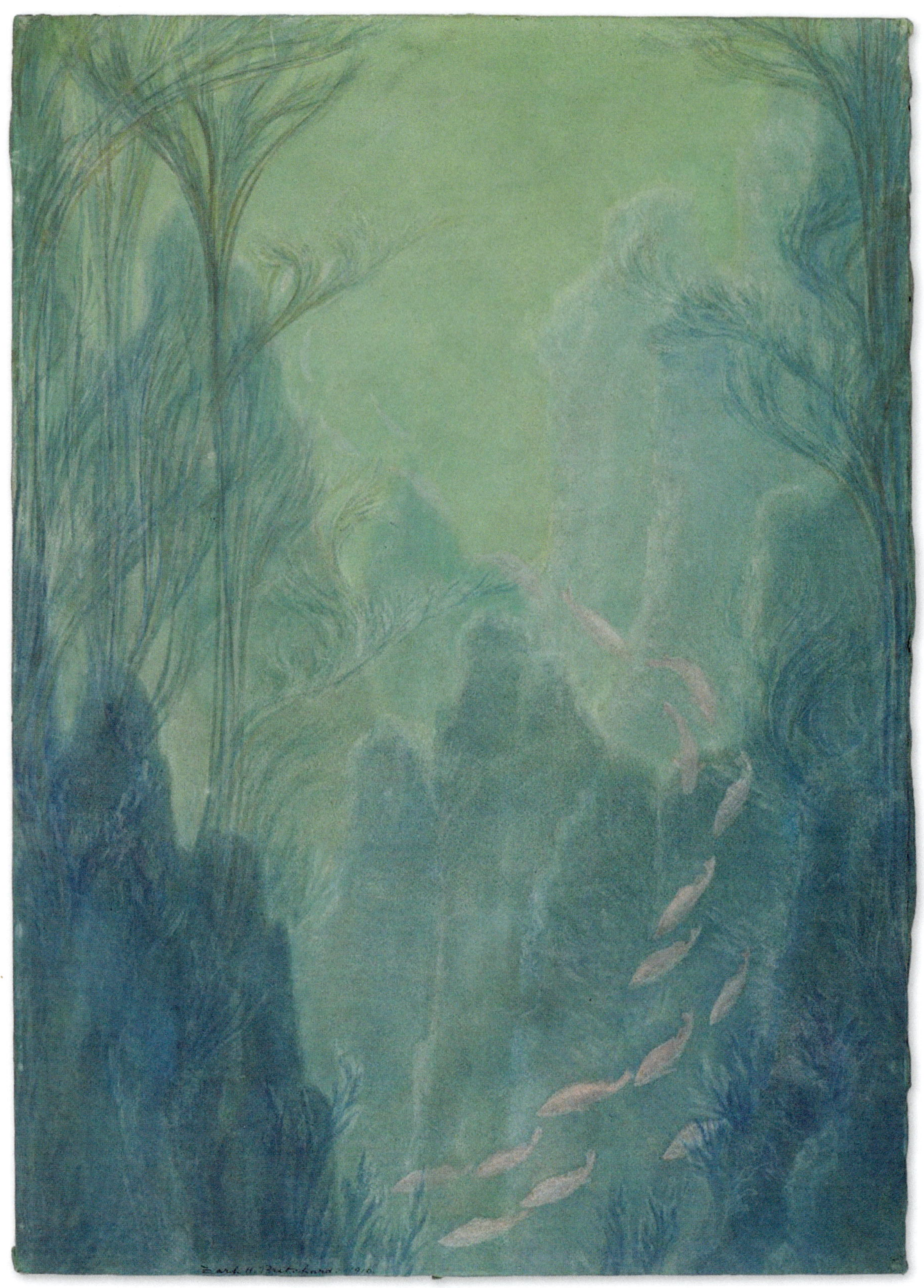

that he'd prepared with oil or a heavy wax. The material worked well but also made it difficult to correct mistakes. 'A wrong colour, or a mistake because a fish comes too near, and the whole thing is spoiled,' he told the *New York Times* in August 1923. (Fish would often come too near, drawn by the smell of gum and to catch the floating flakes of paint that haloed his canvas.) Gloves prevented dexterity, and so Pritchard's suit ended with tight rubber cuffs at the wrists, and he'd rub oil on his hands instead. The labels on the paints would, of course, disintegrate and so part of his preparation was to dab a spot of colour on each tube to help identify it underwater. Hiring the right help was also important – more than once local assistants thought it funny to respond to his two-tugs-on-the-line call for slack by pumping his suit so full of air that he floated away.

In 1905 Pritchard was working in Tahiti, having managed to acquire the only diver's suit in the country. When he returned to California it was with a portfolio of fifty-four large subaquatic landscape paintings and forty-two smaller artworks, every one painted underwater. They were all deliberately signed along the edge of the canvas, where the frame would cover the autograph, so as not to ruin the effect. Ironically, given the hazardous environment in which they were created, it was only after being brought onto dry land that his body of work was put at risk. The entire lot of fifty paintings was destroyed in the 1906 San Francisco earthquake. Pritchard ploughed on, relocating to New York and then to Samoa, where nonstop torrential rain hampered his plans. In 1919 he was exhibiting at a gallery in Tokyo, where he caused panic among the audience of the Nobles' Club by casually yet graphically describing the precariousness of Tokyo's perch on the edge of the Japan Oceanic Trench, which is 8046m (26,398ft) at its deepest point.

Though little-remembered today, Pritchard was a truly inventive pioneer. His work was purchased by prestigious art collectors and naturalists like Sir Joseph Duveen (1869-1939) and Albert I (1848-1922), Prince of Monaco, a keen oceanographer, and they were hung on the walls of the Galérie Georges Petit in Paris, the Cleveland Museum of Natural History and the American Museum of Natural History in New York City. 'It is a dream world in which everything is enveloped in soft sheen,' Pritchard once wrote of his submarine studio. 'On reaching bottom, it is as if one were temporarily resting on a dissolving fragment of some far planet. Nowhere does substance appear beyond the middle distance, and material forms insensibly vanish into the veils of surrounding color.'

FATE OF THE ANIMALS (1913), FRANZ MARC

On 28 June 1914 the powder keg of the First World War was ignited when Archduke Archduke Franz Ferdinand, heir to the throne of Austria-Hungary, was assassinated in Bosnia. Tensions had been rippling through Europe for years previously. Among those living with the grim and gnawing sense of inevitability was the German painter Franz Marc (1880-1916), one of the most significant figures of German expressionism and co-founder – along with a group of other artists including Paul Klee (1879-1940) – of *Der Blaue Reiter* (The Blue Rider), an art journal and movement.

The painting shown here, *Fate of the Animals*, is one of Marc's most famous and shows a dramatic shift in theme. The scene is frantic and disastrous. The blue deer in the centre of the canvas rears in anguish; the two green horses in the upper left are

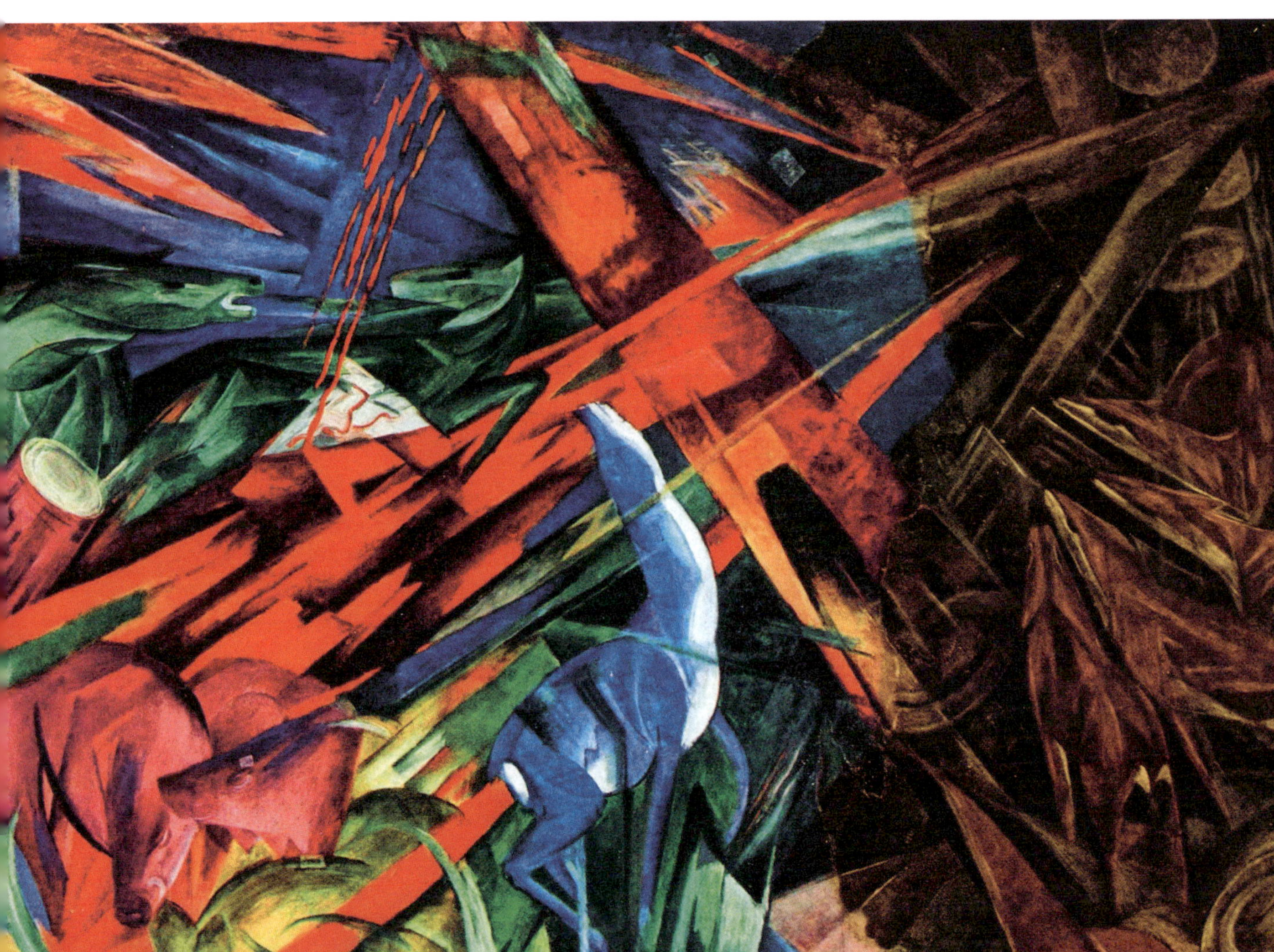

fleeing in terror. Nature has turned on them, their forest setting is being devoured by flames, and burning trees tumble around them. It's an apocalyptic glimpse of the natural world destroyed: whether subconsciously or coincidentally, Marc was predicting the global conflict that was imminent and the helplessness of those caught in the violent collapse.

From a letter he sent to fellow artist Auguste Macke (1887-1914), we learn that Marc originally gave the painting another title: *The Trees Show Their Rings, The Animals Their Veins* (see the tree rings in the far left, and the veins in the belly of the horse to the right of that tree), but he then took the suggestion of Paul Klee to change it to the more doom-laden *Fate of the Animals*. Despite the change to a more fatalistic outlook, Marc still told the story in his customary colour symbolism, which he explains in another letter to Macke in 1910. 'Blue is the male principle, astringent and spiritual,' he writes. 'Yellow is the female principle, gentle, gay and spiritual. Red is matter, brutal and heavy and always the colour to be opposed and overcome by the other two.'

On the back of the *Fate* canvas, Marc reinforced the biblically apocalyptic tone by writing: 'And All Being is Flaming Suffering'. Ironically this too was unwittingly predictive, for the painting was damaged in a warehouse fire in 1916 that scorched the right-hand third of the work. It was Klee who took on the restoration of his friend's work, repainting the damaged area in more muted tones of brown and mustard. Why Klee chose these colours, in contrast to Marc's own bright hues, is unknown. But perhaps it was out of mourning for his friend.

At the outbreak of war, Marc was drafted to serve in the Imperial German Army as a cavalryman, but was then promoted to military camouflage, painting large tarpaulin covers (in styles ranging 'from Manet to Kandinsky', he joked in a letter to his wife) to hide artillery from aerial observation. His name was added to a list by the government of important artists to withdraw from service but, before the reassignment orders could reach him, he was killed by shelling while fighting at the Battle of Verdun in 1916.

Before his death, while fighting on the frontline, Marc was sent a picture postcard of *Fate of the Animals*, which was experiencing success in his absence. He was astonished. 'It is like a premonition of this war, horrible and shattering,' he wrote. 'I can hardly conceive that I painted it!'

RAOUL HAUSMANN'S *THE ART CRITIC* (1919-20) AND THE ART OF DADA

The First World War, which Franz Marc preemptively reflected in his *The Fate of Animals* (1913) and that later claimed his life, would also inspire an entirely new art movement. At the outbreak of that war, many German artists and intellectuals fled to exile. Among them was the writer Hugo Ball (1886-1927), who after witnessing the invasion of Belgium wrote in horror: 'The war is founded on a glaring mistake – men have been confused with machines.' Together with the cabaret performer Emmy Hennings (1885-1948), he swapped Berlin for Zürich and with a group of other artists and performers opened the Cabaret Voltaire nightclub. To this group, and indeed other intellectual circles around Europe, the irrationality and brutality of the war induced a profound collapse in the established culture of rationality with which Europe had proudly defined itself since the Enlightenment. In Ball's words, he wanted to shock any who saw 'all this civilized carnage as a triumph of European intelligence' with absurdist art, Dadaism, which would highlight the absurdity of a senseless war and those who regarded it with complacency.

Dada created through destruction. All traditions and rules had to be thrown out. 'The image of the human form is gradually disappearing from the painting of these times and all objects appear only in fragments,' wrote Ball. 'The next step is for poetry to decide to do away with language.' This he carried out himself, appearing onstage of the Voltaire Club in a bizarre metal outfit to perform a 'new genre' he called 'sound poems'. *Gadji beri bimba*, began the first nonsense poem, *Glandridi lauli lonni cadori…* The Romanian artist Tristan Tzara (1896-1963), part of the Voltaire group, describes their nightly shows as 'explosions of elective imbecility'. Beauty was for them 'a boring sort of perfection, a stagnant idea of a golden swamp.' Ball and the German artist Richard Huelsenbeck (1892-1974) came up with the name Dada for this absurdist outlook by flicking through a German–French dictionary. The word means 'hobby-horse' in French.

The 'virgin microbe' – as Tzara called it – of Dadaism quickly spread around the world in a wild variety of forms, from performance art and poetry like that of Ball, to photography, sculpture, painting and collage. In Berlin the artists Hannah Höch (1889-1978), George Grosz (1893-

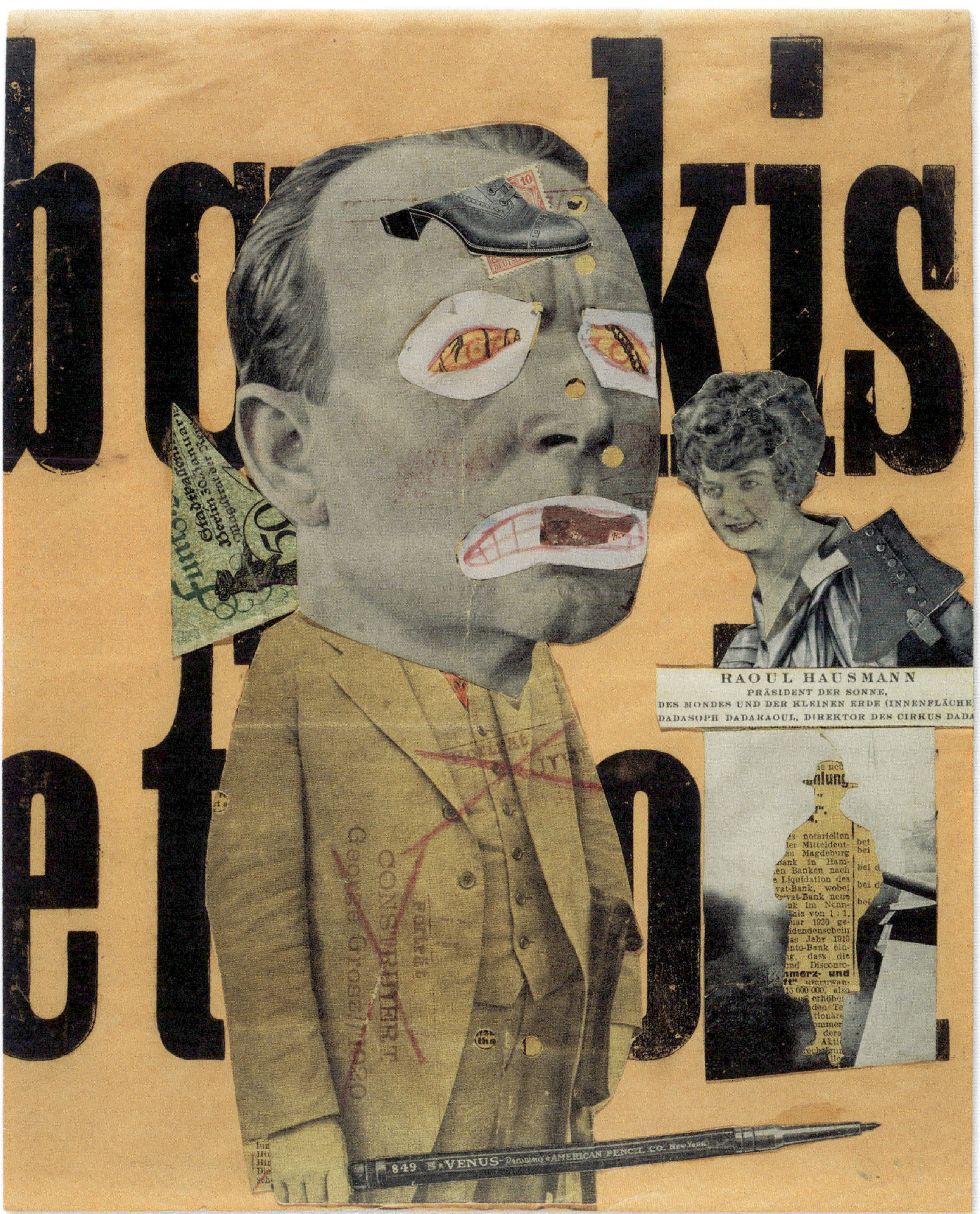
RAOUL HAUSMANN
PRÄSIDENT DER SONNE,
DES MONDES UND DER KLEINEN ERDE (INNENFLÄCHE
DADASOPH DADARAOUL, DIREKTOR DES CIRKUS DADA
849 B VENUS
AMERICAN PENCIL CO. New York
CONSTRUIERT

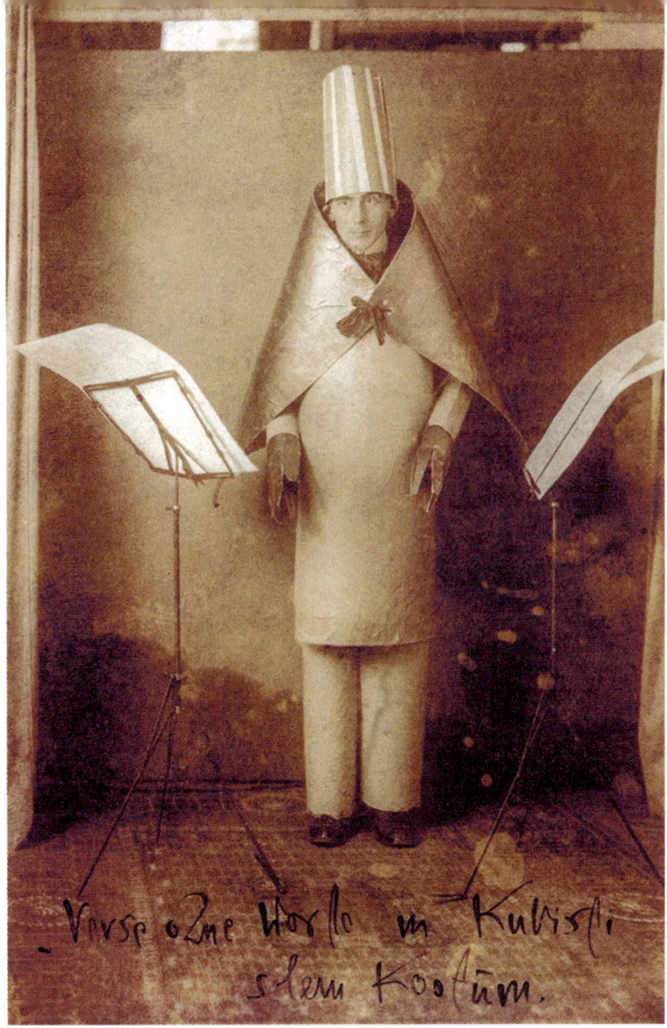

A photograph of Hugo Ball reciting the sound poem Karawane *in a metal costume, taken in Zürich in 1916.*

1959) and Raoul Hausmann (1886-1971) defenestrated every traditional technique to create art that broke natural law – creating photomontages, for example, from newspaper and magazine cuttings, like Höch's *Cut with the Dada Kitchen Knife through the Last Weimar Beer-Belly Cultural Epoch in Germany* (1919) and Hausmann's *The Art Critic* (1919-20), which is shown on the previous page. Hausmann was known as the 'Dadosopher' for his extensive writing on the theory of the movement, and in this image he attacks a true figure of hate, the art critic. The triangular section of a banknote pressed against the critic's neck suggests his opinions are easily swayed or bought by those trading in the reviewed artworks, while the black lines scrawled across his eyes imply blindness, and with his tongue out he pants sycophantically towards the high-society lady on the right.

In New York, Dadaism arrived in 1915 with Marcel Duchamp (1887-1968), who stunned with his series of 'readymades', in which he took prefabricated industrial objects and presented them as art with little to no alteration. Most famously this took the form of his *Fountain* (1917), a white urinal placed on its side and signed 'R. Mutt', a play on the manufacturer's name – J. L. Mott Works – with the addition of 'Richard', French slang for 'money-bags'. The world was introduced to the idea of artwork not actually created by the artist and to Duchamp's Dadaist questions of what constituted art and what were its purposes and values.

In Dadaism we find one of the most influential movements in modern art, underpinning the genres of abstract and conceptual, performance, pop and installation art, but it would burn out after less than a decade, fading away with the arrival of surrealism. This, really, was the only acceptable fate for Dadaists, who would often cry the slogan 'Dada is anti-Dada'. 'Dada Knows everything, Dada spits on everything,' reads a section of one of numerous manifestos.

> *Dada has no fixed ideas. Dada does not catch flies. Dada is bitterness laughing at everything that has been accomplished, sanctified... Dada is never right... No more painters, no more writers, no more religions, no more royalists, no more anarchists, no more socialists, no more politics, no more airplanes, no more urinals... Like everything in life, Dada is useless, everything happens in a completely idiotic way... We are incapable of treating seriously any subject whatsoever, let alone this subject: ourselves.*
>
> *Gardner's Art Through the Ages,* 1926

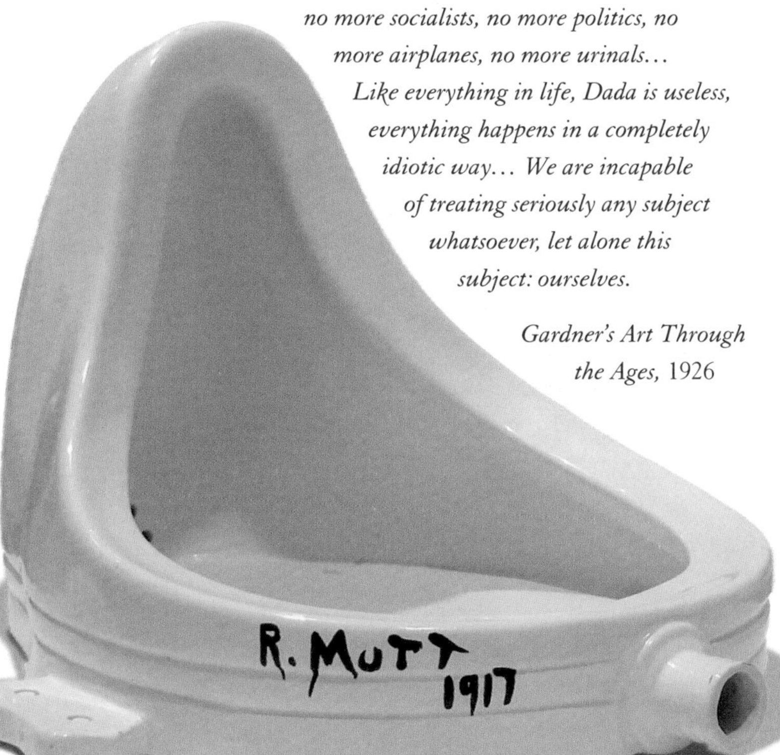

A replica of Marcel Duchamp's infamous Fountain *(the original is long lost).*

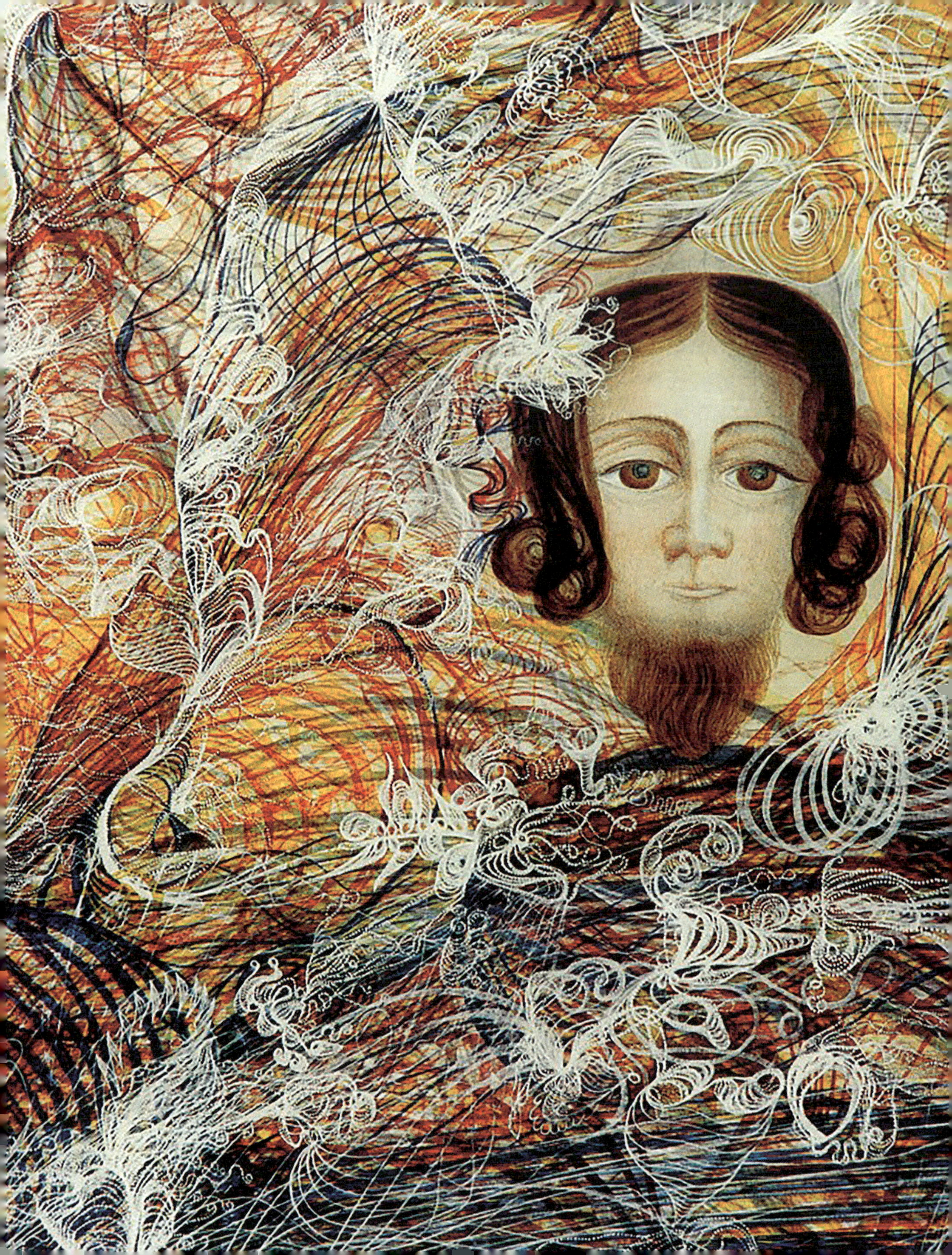

GEORGIANA HOUGHTON AND SPIRITUALIST ART (NINETEENTH-TWENTIETH CENTURIES)

In the same decade as the Dadaist nonsense protest, another art style rose in popularity: spiritualist art, whose proponents sought post-war comfort in the reassuring order of the metaphysical. It was a style that had been around since the mid-nineteenth century, with its Victorian fame largely down to the work of British artist and spiritualist medium Georgiana Houghton (1814-84).

Opposite: *A psychic portrait of Christ in heaven (1860s-1870s) by Georgiana Houghton.*

Houghton had started producing 'automatic' artworks while holding séances in 1859, using a planchette (wheeled pen holder) under her hand to channel the creative talents and messages of souls from the beyond, including those of the Renaissance artists Titian (*c.*1488-1576) and Correggio (1489-1534). In the summer of 1871, Houghton enacted her plan to bring her spiritualist art to the mainstream, and rented the prestigious New British Gallery on Bond Street to exhibit 155 of her spirit drawings. Her looped, indefinable shapes and vague explosions of colour were presented to a public still three years away from witnessing the first major impressionist exhibition, and decades before the arrival of abstract art in the early twentieth century.

A critic from *The Era* newspaper reviewed Houghton's show as 'the most astonishing exhibition in London at the present moment', while the *Daily News* critic decided that the 'tangled threads of coloured wool' should be seen by all 'as the most extraordinary and instructive example of artistic aberration'. Unfortunately, the paying public could not find the same excitement in the puzzling works, and the exhibition was a commercial failure that nearly bankrupted the painter.

Houghton was just one of a number of artists, largely female, who claimed to receive messages and visions of worlds beyond. In France we know of a spiritualist and pencil-sketch artist named Madame Favre operating *c.*1858-60, thanks to the discovery in 1970 of a single exercise book filled with drawings, entitled *The Natural Talent of Mme Favre*. (Like most work of historical spiritualists, her sketches have since become fought-over collectors' items.) Madame Favre's drawings are technical

Below: *A strange drawing (c.1858-60) of the French spiritualist artist known as Madame Favre.*

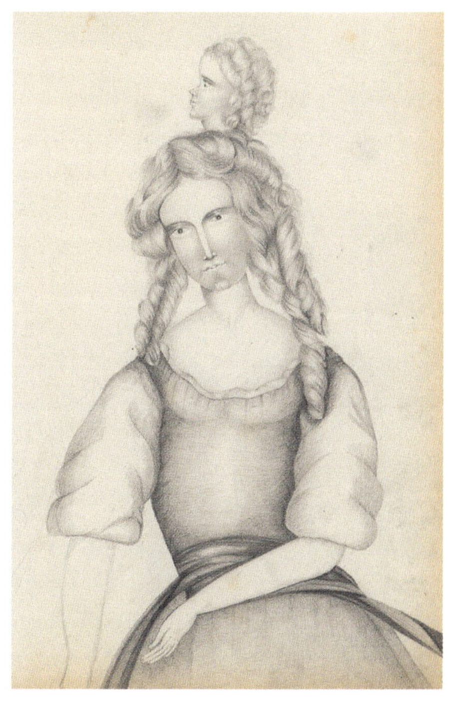

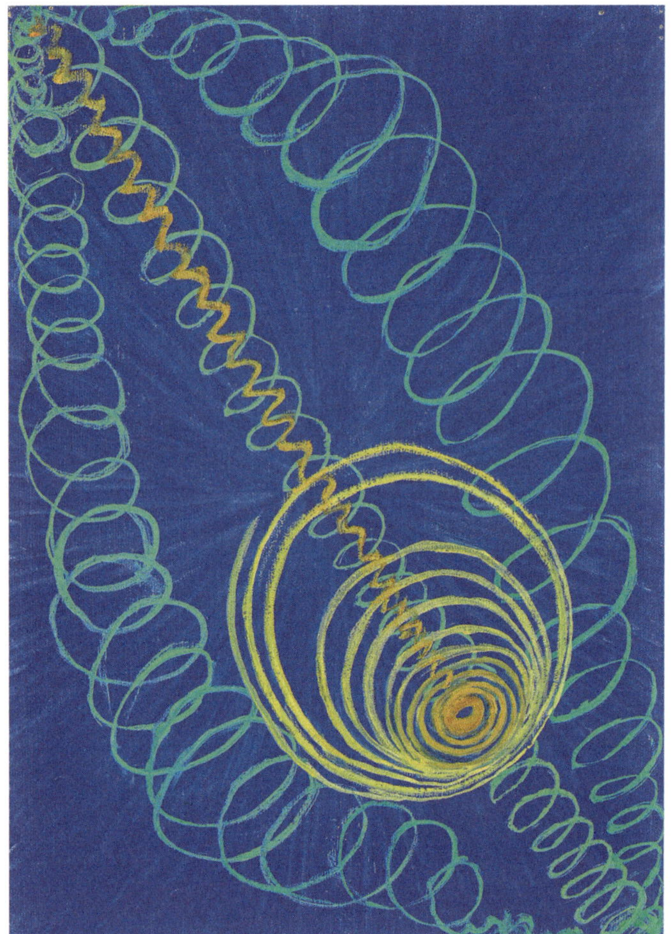

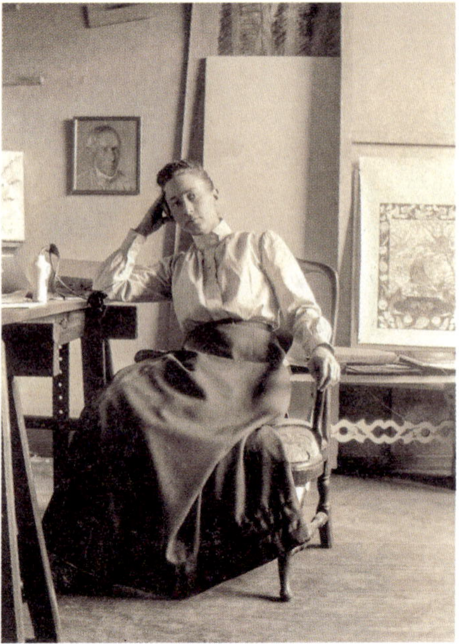

Above: *Swedish artist Hilma af Klint in her studio in Stockholm, c.1885.*

Left: Grupp 1, Urkaos, nr 16 *(Group I, Primordial Chaos, No. 16) (1906-1907) by Hilma af Klint, from The WU/Rose Series (Serie WU/Rosen).*

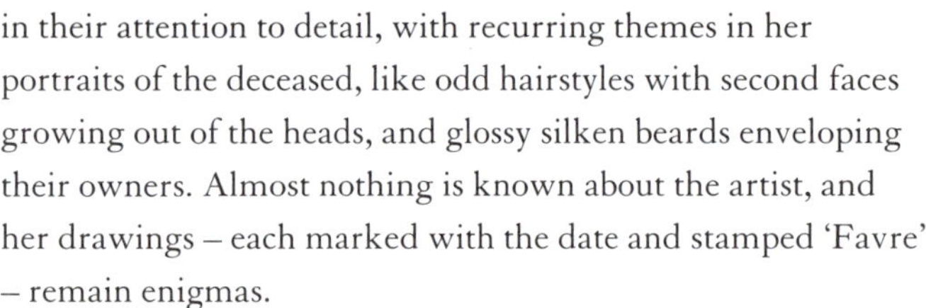

in their attention to detail, with recurring themes in her portraits of the deceased, like odd hairstyles with second faces growing out of the heads, and glossy silken beards enveloping their owners. Almost nothing is known about the artist, and her drawings – each marked with the date and stamped 'Favre' – remain enigmas.

In spiritualist art we can recognise an influence on the later abstract work of artists such as Vasily Kandinsky (1886-1944), Piet Mondrian (1872-1944), Kazimir Malevich (1879-1935) and František Kupka (1871-1957), but only in recent years has the work of the Swedish artist and mystic Hilma af Klint (1862-1944) been credited as the first abstract works in the history of Western art. Following the death of her sister Hermina in 1880, Klint developed an interest in spiritism, and the symbolism in her work is a direct result of this influence. An adherent of theosophy (an occult religion of Western esotericism), she was part of a female group who called themselves The Five, who were determined to contact the Masters of the Ancient Wisdom, the superior enlightened beings identified in the religion. The complex meanings of her paintings are locked behind and hidden within grids and intersecting patterns, vibrant technical floral shapes, painted numbers, loops and curves, pyramids and bursting suns. Af Klint rarely showed her paintings to anyone, conscious of the restrictions against female artists who defied cultural mores. She maintained the secrecy throughout her life and beyond – so concerned was she that her contemporaries would not be able to understand her esoteric pieces that she forbade their exhibition until twenty years after her death.

In this particular wing of our curiosity gallery, one should also mention Marguerite Burnat-Provins (1872-1952), a Franco-Swiss artist and poet who suffered a hallucinatory bout of typhoid while in Egypt, and turned her brush to reproducing the strange sights she saw. She embarked on an extraordinary series of 3000 paintings and drawings titled *Ma ville* (My Town), based on psychic hallucinations of figures glimpsed from beyond the grave who also dictated how they should be drawn, the colours used and their biography, which Burnat-Provins would dutifully record on the reverse of the canvas.

An untitled ink-on-card by Madge Gill, 1950s.

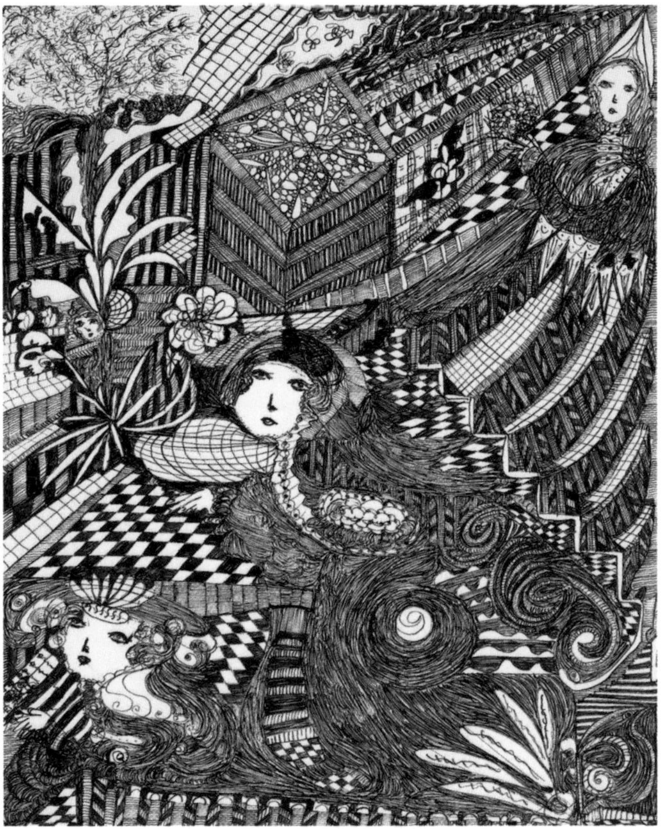

Burnat-Provins's work has traditionally been allocated to the category of *art brut* (raw art), another term for Outsider art, which is where we find also Madge Gill (1882-1961), a British spiritualist born in London's East End. At the age of thirty-eight, having suffered tragedy throughout her life including the loss of two of her four children and the use of an eye, she built up an income from working as a medium. She conducted séances with her spiritual partner Myrninnerest, whom she would summon and channel while playing music, knitting, writing and painting. She produced hundreds of postcard portraits of Myrninnerest and larger works on rolls of calico.

Meanwhile, in America, Marianne Spore Bush (1878-1946) left behind a successful dental practice in Michigan to become a professional painter, moving into a studio in Greenwich Village, New York City. She produced large surrealist works throughout the 1920s that were, she said, inspired by communications from 'beyond the veil'. Her brand of psychic art was prophetic, employing unusually thick paints to create scenes of disaster that she claimed were predictions for the future passed to her from dead artists of history. Many of these scenes appeared to be of a second global conflict on a scale similar to the First World War.

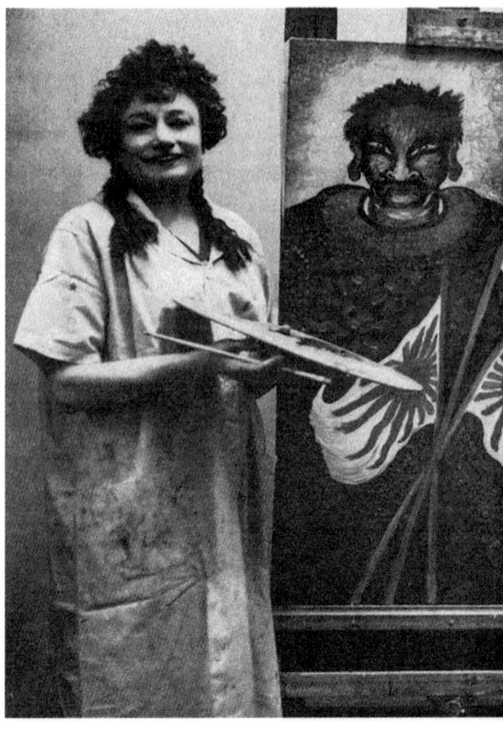

Dentist-turned-psychic-painter Marian Spore Bush at work.

Harry Houdini (1874-1926), who made it his mission to expose fraudulent psychics, found her art fascinating. In 1924 he was quoted in the New York *Sun* as saying: 'I am certain of Miss Spore's honesty. I have never excluded the possibility of supernatural intervention from my belief. I have been engaged in the exposure of criminal fakers... there is no question of that here. Miss Spore has something beautiful and is conveying it to her fellow men.'

'I should be inclined to refer to her work in this field as that of a primitive mystic,' wrote Edward Alden Jewell, the *New York Times* art critic in 1943. 'The large black and white canvases seem at once crude and powerful... All the war paintings are symbolic in nature. Their impact is sharp and disturbing. If accepted as manifestations of psychic phenomena, they are mysterious.'

The outbreak of the Second World War confirmed that Marianne Spore Bush's predictions of a coming war were eerily prescient. The resolution of that conflict may also have had something to do with an artist of the *art brut* category. Fleury-Joseph Crépin (1875-1948) of Calais, France, was a plumber and roofer by trade, but like others was inspired by the working-class spiritualist movement and decided to pack up his tools in favour of spending early retirement as a medium and healer. At the age of sixty-three Crépin picked up the paintbrush as part of his sessions in which he'd enter a trance, and he rapidly built up a prolific portfolio of intricate, symmetrical works that caught the attention of the surrealist artist André Breton (1896-1966), whose own work was directly inspired by the creative spiritualists. Crépin allowed his hand to be guided by spirits, drawing technical, architectural shapes on a pad that he would transfer precisely to canvas and colour and transform into palaces and temples filled with creatures. Crépin held his own work in high esteem – the completion of his three-hundredth painting, he announced, would bring about world peace, as promised to him by angels. As it happens, he finished his three-hundredth painting on 5 May 1945 – three days later, the German Instrument of Surrender was signed and the Second World War was declared over.

My personal favourite, though, ever since purchasing at auction one of only a few copies of her self-published artwork collection *A Goodly Company* (1933), is the work of the London-based artist and spirit medium Constance 'Ethel' Le Rossignol (1873-1970), a former First World War nurse who was awarded the British War Medal and the Victory Medal.

Between 1920 and 1933, she produced a series of forty-four dazzling paintings of the spirit world or, as she calls it, the 'Sphere of Spirit'. In psychedelic colours and kaleidoscopic shapes, the afterlife is revealed to be a realm of dazzling light and golden energy, through which swing beautiful, acrobatic sylphs (spirits of the air) accompanied by bejewelled apes and tigers. 'This sequence of designs is shown to open the eyes of all men to the glorious world of spiritual power which lies about them,' she writes in *A Goodly Company*. The paintings were based on visions she credits to a spirit known only to her as J. P. F., which explained that it was sharing details of the spiritual plane to reassure the living with sights of the worlds to come.

Ethel Le Rossignol's vision of the afterlife from A Goodly Company *(1933), as channelled through a spirit guide.*

Very little is known about Le Rossignol's life other than the fact that she was born in Argentina and the sadness she records in her writing at losing loved ones in the First World War. The loss spurred her interest in channelling communications from the spirit world, and to produce the paintings, which one reviewer describes as comparable to 'William Blake at his mystical maddest'.

THE PERSISTENCE OF MEMORY (1931), SALVADOR DALÍ AND SURREALIST ART

Given the size of its impact, the most famous work of the surrealist movement, Salvador Dalí's *The Persistence of Memory* (below), is surprisingly small at just 24 × 33cm (9½ × 13in). Dalí (1904-89) painted it in 1931, seven years after the poet André Breton (1896-1966) had launched surrealism with a manifesto and the first issue of the radical journal *The Surrealist Revolution*. For Breton and his surrealist writers and painters, there was much to admire of Dadaism in its iconoclasm and inventive techniques like collage, but at the same time the Dadaists were nihilistic, opposed to all art including their own. The surrealists sought to incorporate Dadaist spontaneity but with a reversion to traditional techniques like oil and canvas, and to instead engage with the subconscious, which they held to be the furnace of all creativity.

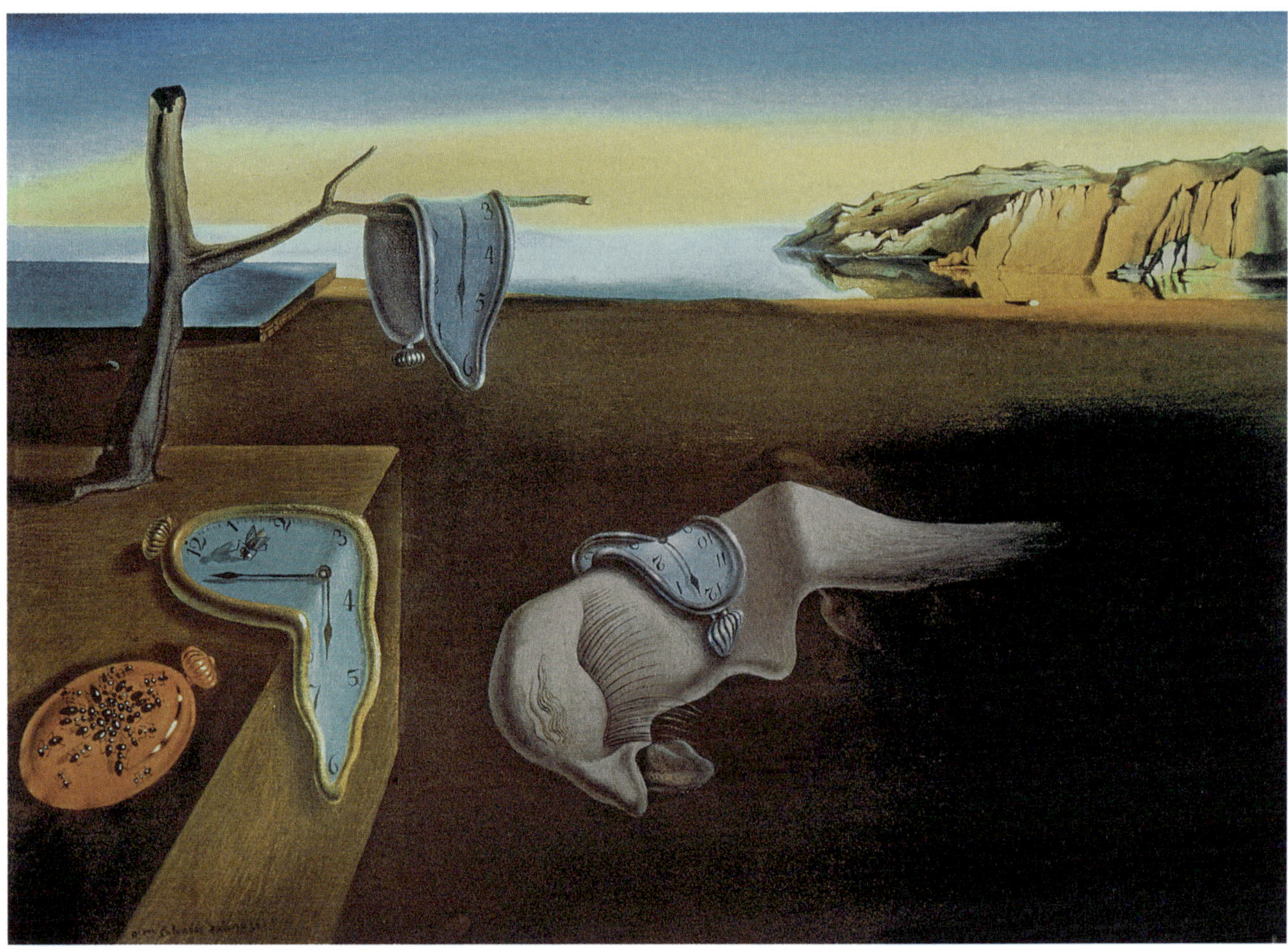

Surrealism is, writes Breton, 'psychic automatism in its pure state'. In this primary stage, surrealist art blossomed out of a variety of new idiosyncratic methods. Max Ernst (1891-1976), for example, produced collages in Dadaist style. He also introduced *frottage*, in which one rubs a pencil across paper laid down on an uneven and/or textured surface, and *grattage*, which involves placing a canvas covered in oil paint on top of a textured object and then scraping the paint off to reveal an unexpected surface. From the lines and features this produced, the artist would develop strange detailed images – the idea being that this image recognition was direct communication with the subconscious. Bulletism works in much the same way, in which one shoots ink at a blank piece of paper and develops the resulting ink blot into an entire painting.[1] Wolfgang Paalen (1905-59) popularised the *fumage* technique, by which one forms impressions on a surface using the smoke of a candle or kerosene lamp. The surrealists were also fond of a game they called 'the Exquisite Corpse': a piece of paper is passed around a group of artists, each one adding their own detail and then folding it to hide it from the next player. At the end, the paper is unfolded to show the Frankenstein combination of each artist's subconscious production.

These 'automatic' methods then gave way to attempts to more directly engage with the subconscious. The impoverished Catalan artist Joan Miró (1893-1983) is said to have taken inspiration at this time from hallucinatory visions brought on by starvation, producing wild landscapes of strange, colourful amoebic figures and sharp technical shapes. Others turned to dreams – Sigmund Freud (1856-1939) had shown that dreams were windows into the unconscious mind in *The Interpretation of Dreams* in 1899, and a new raft of oneiric surrealist painters – most notably Salvador Dalí, René Magritte (1898-1967) and Yves Tanguy (1900-55) – worked by directly tapping into this internal resource. Magritte believed in challenging the viewer to not accept the reality that they were offered, often with visual riddles. This is the philosophy at the heart of his famous work *The Treachery of Images* (1929), the image of a smoker's pipe above the words *Ceci n'est pas une pipe* (This is not a pipe).

---

1 As with so much of modern invention, Leonardo da Vinci seems to have got there first, having once written: 'just as one can hear any desired syllable in the sound of a bell, so one can see any desired figure in the shape formed by throwing a sponge with ink against the wall'.

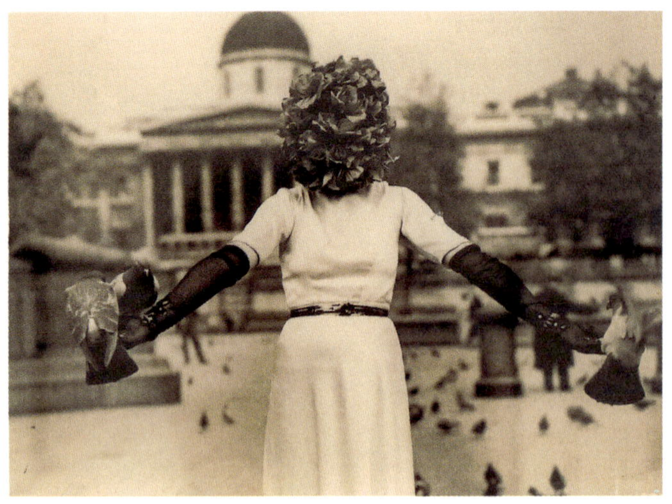

In 1936 Sheila Legge (1911-49), known as the 'Phantom of surrealism', was so inspired by Dalí's Woman with Head of Roses *that she dressed in a bridal gown and, with her head entirely covered in roses, marched round London's Trafalgar Square, startling passersby.*

While surrealism had no designated leader, the arrival of Salvador Dalí in 1929, with a spectacular first show in Paris, was the catalyst in bringing surrealism into mainstream awareness. Like Magritte, Dalí wanted to induce a radical revision in the way that ordinary objects are viewed by the public, and by himself. To this end he developed a working technique he called the paranoiac-critical method, in which he would cause himself to enter a paranoid state, retrieving 'irrational knowledge' based on a 'delirium of interpretation'. 'Paranoiac-critical activity organizes and objectivizes in an exclusivist manner the limitless and unknown possibilities of the systematic association of subjective and objective "significance" in the irrational,' he wrote. Essentially, 'it makes the world of delirium pass onto the plane of reality.' This took the form of inducing in himself states of extreme anxiety and distress, to dissolve the boundaries of what he perceived as real. One of Dalí's techniques was to sit in an armchair to fall asleep, while holding a key in his hand above a plate on the floor. At the moment he fell into unconsciousness, the key would slip from his grip and the sound of impact would jolt him awake. In that split second between waking and sleeping reality, he would pull out the images he glimpsed.

This brings us back to the diminutive yet powerful *The Persistence of Memory*, with its melted liquescent clocks, swarm of black ants, barren landscape and strange, central, eye-lashed shape, produced using his oneiric chair technique. Surreal elements litter a landscape of the real: the coastal cliffs are thought to be that of Portlligat, where Dalí lived with his wife Gala, and which also features in his *The Madonna of Port Lligat* (1949), *Crucifixion (Corpus Hypercubus)* (1954) and *The*

Sacrament of the Last Supper (1955). The shadow that stretches horizontally across the foreground in *The Persistence of Memory* is probably that of nearby Mount Pení. The dead olive tree, upon which one of melted clocks is draped, is a symbol of broken peace, reflecting the turbulence of Spanish society at the time, which would eventually erupt into civil war in 1936. The tree also recalls an etching from Francisco Goya's *Disasters of War* series (as mentioned on page 169), in which a similar tree holds mutilated bodies of executed men. The melted clocks, meanwhile, broadcast the surrealist belief that metamorphosing everyday objects in unusual ways can powerfully subvert reason.

Dalí explained the painting with: 'Be persuaded that Salvador Dalí's famous limp watches are nothing but the tender, extravagant and solitary paranoiac-critical Camembert of time and space.' This statement reveals the painting to contain references not only to Freud but also to Einstein's theories of relativity of 1905 and 1915, in which time and gravity – previously thought to be fields similar to that of electromagnetism – were radically re-envisioned as a kind of malleable fabric: space time. How perfectly this melded with the surrealist sensibility.

In *The Persistence of Memory*, then, we can see both science and art working together in wildly different fashion to achieve the same goal: to radically overturn the notion of an ordered universal reality.

In this detail of the Persistence of Memory *(below left), Dalí pays tribute to his great hero Hieronymus Bosch (c.1450-1516) with the anthropomorphic blob in the centre of his painting, believed to be a self-portrait, resembling a detail (below right) from Bosch's* The Garden of Earthly Delights *(1490-1500).*

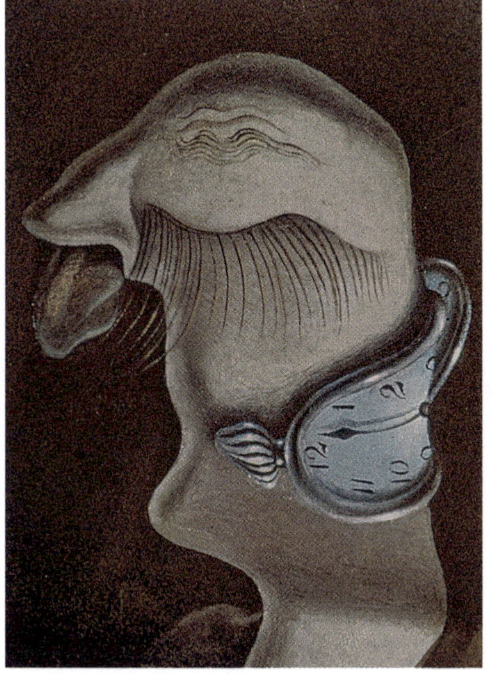

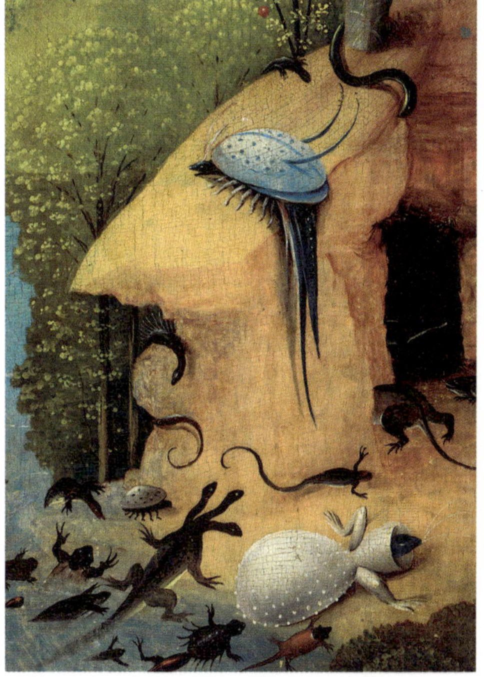

OTHER SURREALIST CURIOSITIES

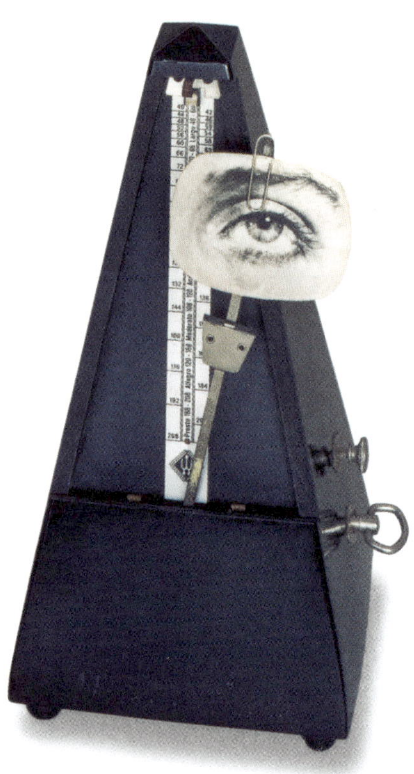

LEFT: *Man Ray's* Indestructible Object. *Ray (1890-1976) first created the combination of a metronome with a photograph of an eye attached by a paperclip to the swinging arm in 1922-3 under the title* Object to Be Destroyed, *smashing it to pieces shortly after. 'The faster it went, the faster I painted; and if the metronome stopped then I knew I had painted too long, I was repeating myself, my painting was no good and I would destroy it.' The photo of the eye created an audience to work before.*

BELOW: *Joan Miró* Harlequin's Carnival *(1924-5), one of the highlights of the first surrealist show at the Galérie Pierre in Paris, where it hung beside work by Picasso (1881-1973). Miró was 'the most surrealist of us all,' says André Breton.*

OPPOSITE TOP: *René Magritte's* Les Amants *(The Lovers, 1928). An alien image of the clichéd close-up kiss, our voyeuristic pleasure hampered by the shroud that covers the faces of the couple, in keeping with the surrealist fascination with what lies hidden beneath the surface.*

OPPOSITE BOTTOM: Eine Kleine Nachtmusik *(A Little Night Music) by the American surrealist Dorothea Tanning (1910-2012). 'It's about confrontation,' Tanning would later explain. 'Everyone believes he/she is his/her drama… there are always stairways, hallways, even very private theatres where the suffocations and the finalities are being played out, the blood red carpet or cruel yellows, the attacker, the delighted victim…'*

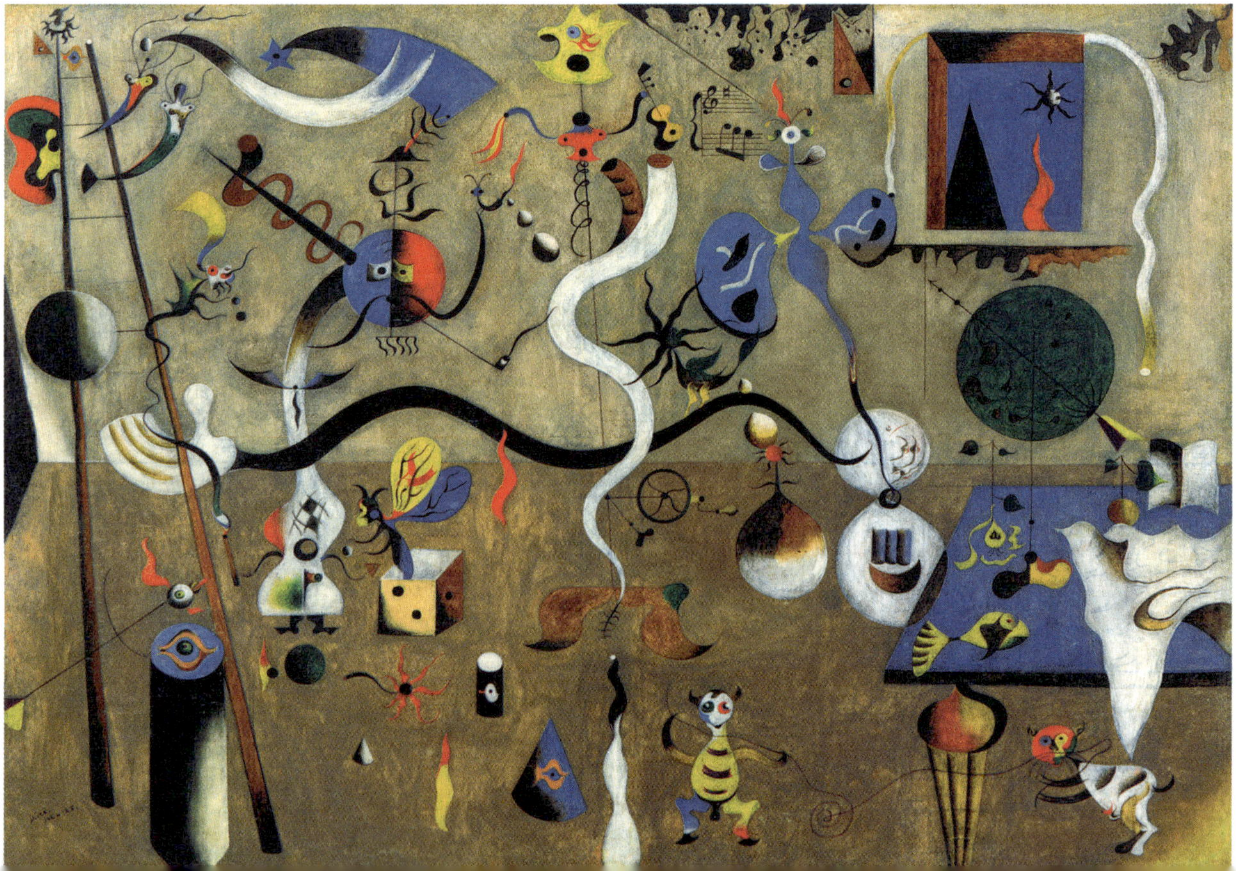

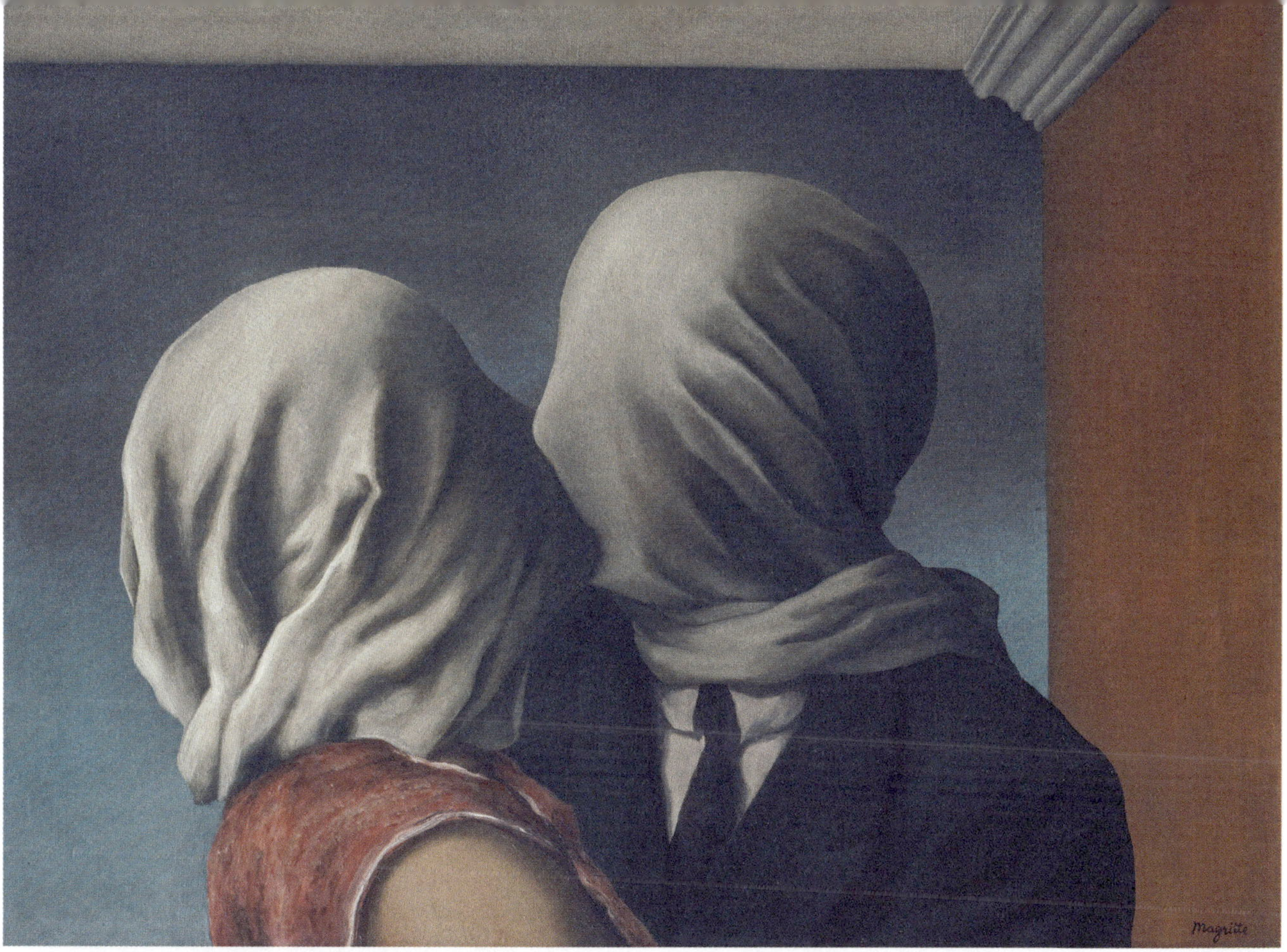

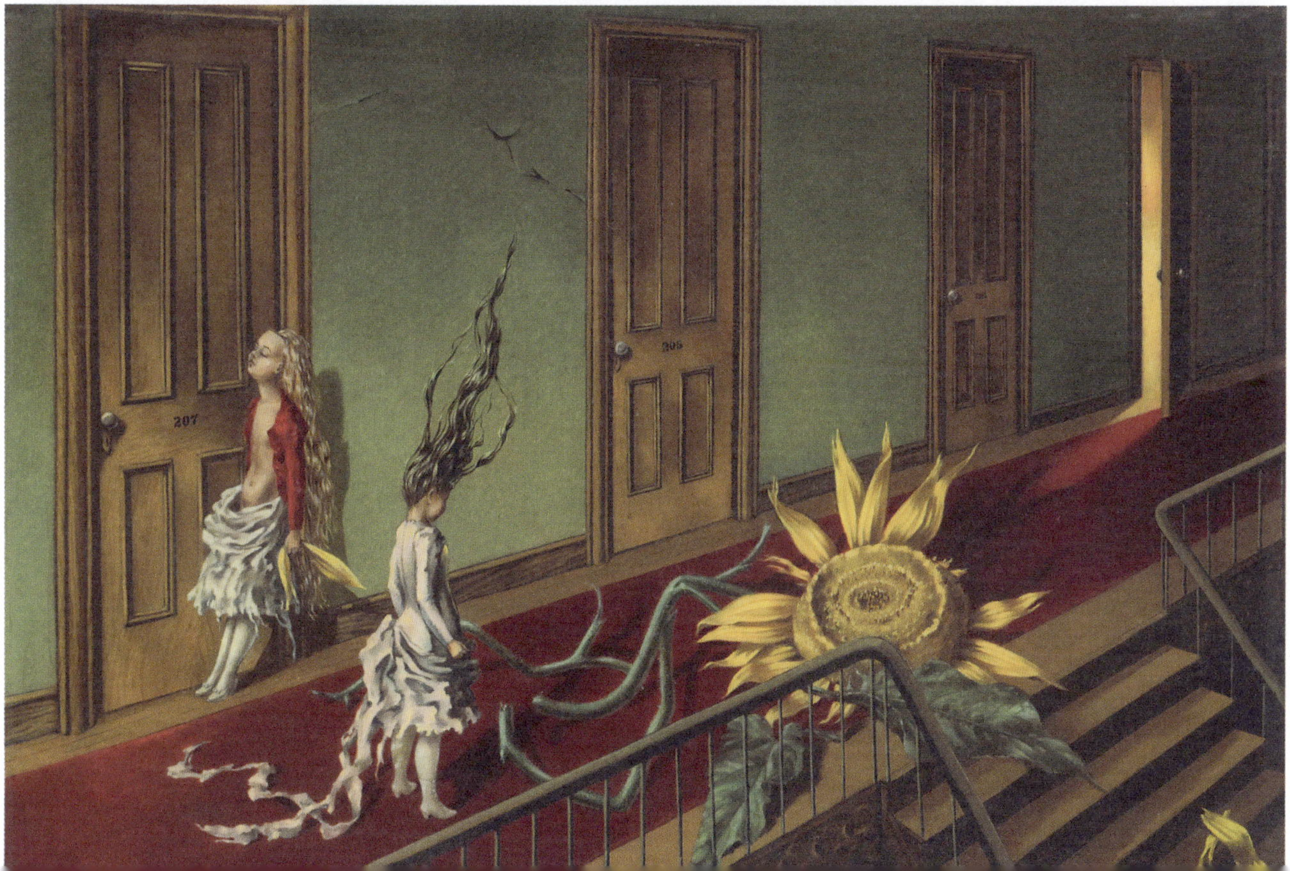

THE WOUNDED DEER (1946), FRIDA KAHLO

For the first major exhibition of Frida Kahlo's work, at the Julien Lévy Gallery in New York in 1938, an accompanying essay was commissioned in which the surrealist founder André Breton hailed her work as 'a ribbon around a bomb' and claimed her as a self-formed surrealist. As much as Kahlo (1907-54) enjoyed the appreciation of her work, she disagreed with the label, and resisted it throughout her career. 'They thought I was a surrealist but I wasn't. I never painted dreams. I painted my own reality.'

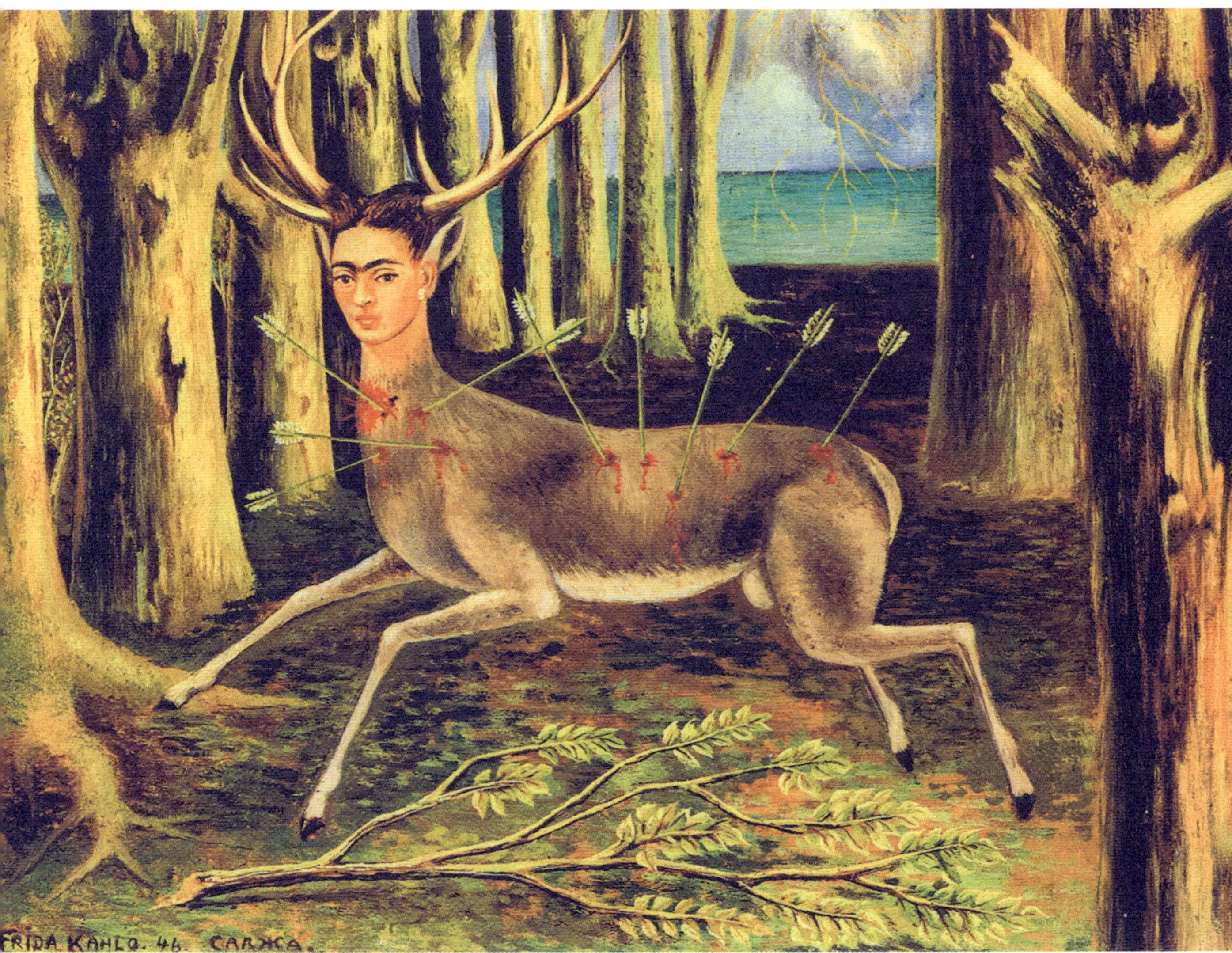

The charmingly strange painting shown on the opposite page was selected for how it best and brutally communicates a significant factor in Kahlo's reality: pain. On 17 September 1925, Kahlo and her boyfriend, Arias, were on a bus when it was struck by an electric tram. An iron handrail punctured her pelvis, abdomen and uterus: 'the way a sword pierces a bull,' she wrote later. The handrail was then wrenched from her body by Arias and some other passengers, to her agony. Her spine was broken in three places, her right leg broken in eleven places (it would eventually be amputated in 1953, a year before her death). Her injuries would worsen and torture her throughout her life – Andrés Henestrosa (1906-2008) once said of his friend that she 'lived dying'. By the mid-1940s, Kahlo's back pain was overwhelming, and so in June 1945 she went to New York for an operation to fuse a bone graft and steel support to her spine in order to straighten it. It was a procedure on which all her hopes were pinned, and it failed. Shortly after, in devastation, she painted *The Wounded Deer.*

The deer/Kahlo hybrid is a muscular, masculine stag, its stoic gaze held by the viewer, but it lies on the ground in a forest of dead trees, defeated by its many bleeding wounds. The broken branch before it is perhaps a nod to the Mexican tradition of laying a branch on the grave of a loved one. In the background the dense forest opens up to a plain beneath swirling blue skies riven with lightning (hope?), but it is not somewhere that the deer will go. At the bottom of the painting besides her signature, Kahlo wrote *Carma* (destiny, or fate), in this setting a word heavy with sorrow and futility. 'I leave you my portrait to remember me all the days and nights that I am away from you,' she wrote in the note that accompanied this painting as a wedding gift to her friends Lina and Arcady Boitler on 3 May 1946. 'The sadness is portrayed throughout all of my paintings, but that's how my condition is, it cannot be fixed.'

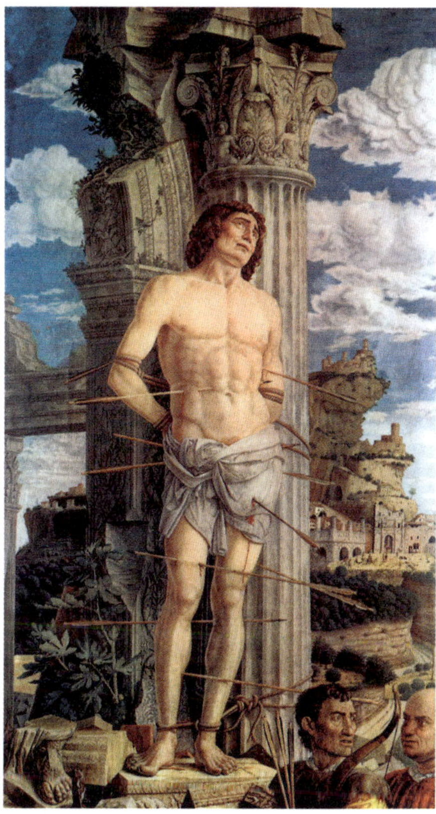

ABOVE: Martyrdom of St Sebastian *(c.1480) by Andrea Mantegna (c.1431-1506), a scene of suffering clearly referenced in Kahlo's* The Wounded Deer.

LEFT: *Between 1940 and 1954, to treat her worsening spinal issues Frida Kahlo wore twenty-eight different supportive corsets, some made from steel, some leather and some plaster, which she would decorate to transform into works of art.*

THE *ETERNITY* OF ARTHUR STACE (1932-67)

One night in November 1932, a word appeared on a pavement in the city of Sydney, Australia: *Eternity*. Written about 30cm (1ft) in length with waterproof chalk in beautiful copperplate handwriting, the graffiti didn't inspire much curiosity and was largely ignored. That is, until it was noticed that the word was also appearing elsewhere – everywhere – on pavements, bridges, roads and walls both interior and exterior across the city. *Eternity*, insisted the unknown author/artist, *Eternity*, *Eternity*, *Eternity*...

This continued into the next year. There were a few public guesses as to the writer's identity, but nobody had been caught in the act – the words mostly appeared late at night – and the mysterious writer became something of an Australian folk hero. This went on for another year, and another and into the next decade. For thirty-five years, between 1932 and 1967, *Eternity* appeared on the streets of Sydney, over 500,000 times, with its simple message written in perfect calligraphy.

Arthur Stace (1885-1967) had grown up in desperate circumstances. Born in inner west Sydney he was a ward of the state by the age of twelve and working in a south-coast coal mine until he was fired for drunkenness. His sisters turned to prostitution while he and his brothers to drink. He enlisted in the Australian Imperial Force to fight overseas in March 1916 but was medically discharged three years later, and by 1932 Stace was an illiterate, alcoholic, petty thief wandering the streets. But in November of that year he overheard the sermon of the preacher John Ridley: 'Eternity, Eternity, I wish that I could sound or shout that word to everyone in the streets of Sydney. You've got to meet it, where will you spend Eternity?' The words caused Stace to have a profound epiphany. 'Eternity went ringing through my brain,' he said in a later interview, 'and suddenly I began crying and felt a powerful call from the Lord to write "Eternity".' Despite his illiteracy (evidenced by the crude signature on his army enlistment form), 'the word "Eternity" came out smoothly, in a beautiful copperplate script. I couldn't understand it, and I still can't.'

Stace's identity was eventually revealed to the *Sunday Telegraph* in early 1956 by Rev. Lisle Thompson, the minister of the Burton Street Tabernacle in Darlinghurst, a Sydney

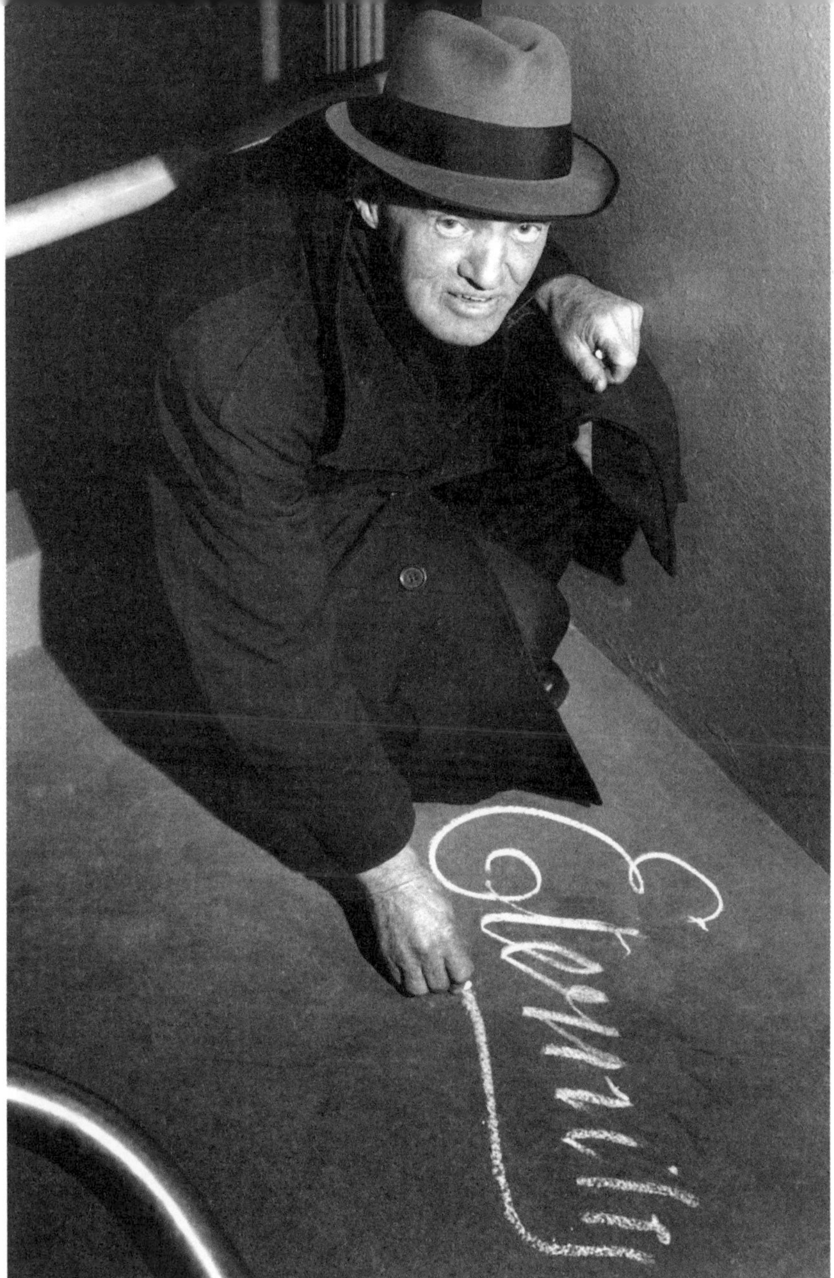

suburb. The photograph shown here was taken when Stace was subsequently interviewed while at work writing in the old Fairfax building in Hunter Street, Sydney. At his peak rate when he was 'running hot', Stace could write *Eternity* fifty times in one day, which would cost him 'six bob a day in chalk'. The graffiti would ironically not last long – about three to six months on average – and only two examples survive today. One is inscribed on a fragment of cardboard given as a gift to a friend. The other is the only one *in situ*, located where few people have been able to interfere with it – inside the bell of the Sydney General Post Office clock tower.

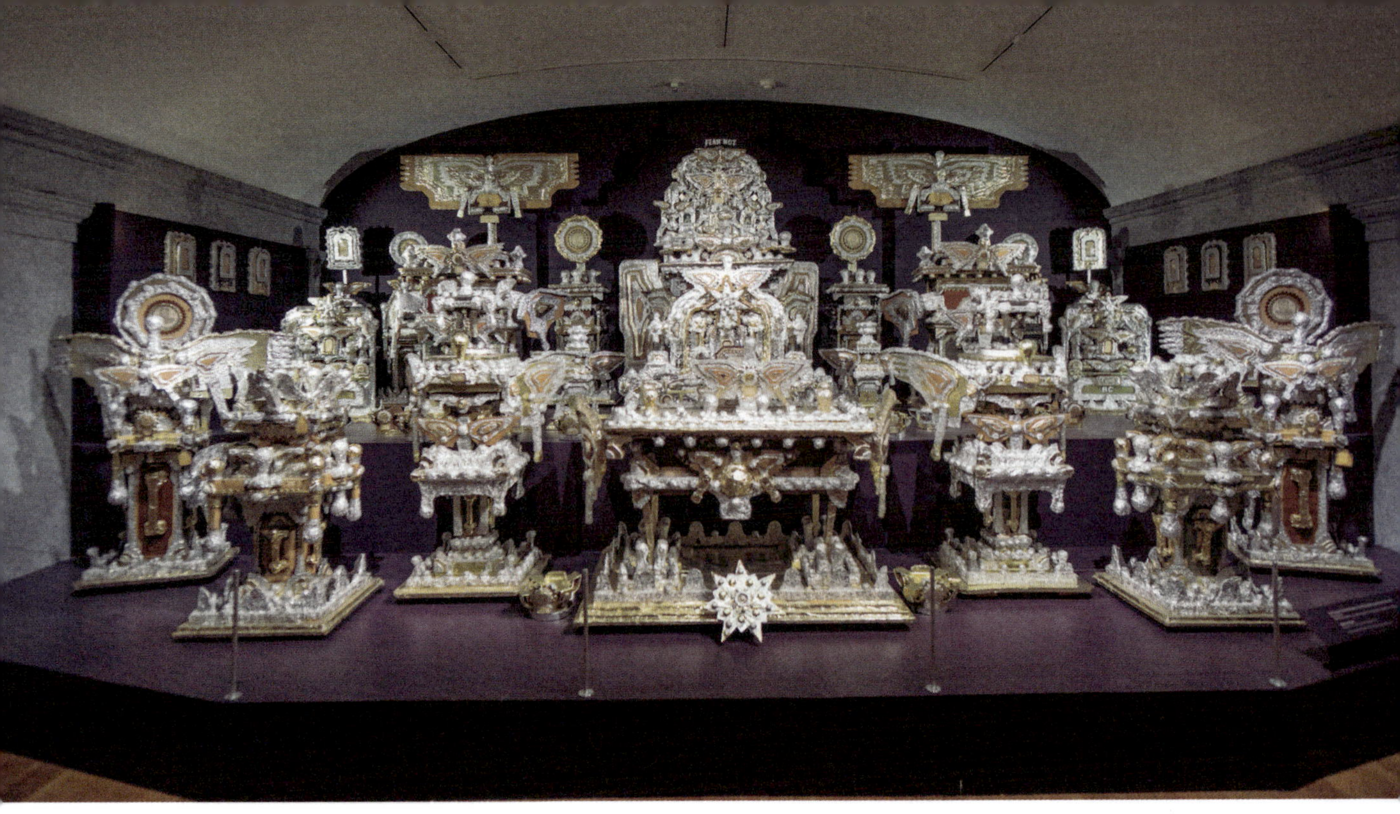

JAMES HAMPTON'S *THE THRONE OF THE THIRD HEAVEN…* (*c.*1950-64) AND OTHER OUTSIDER ART

The term 'Outsider art' was coined in English in 1972 as an equivalent to the French label *art brut* (raw art) to categorise the art of the self-taught, 'naïve' artist – those completely independent of the mainstream art world and stylistic influences. Outsider art is the product of an internal world, often created by those possessed of extreme mental states and unconventional and elaborate, fantastical notions. The Outsider artist is an art movement of one, often using its own invented techniques, and there are few better examples of such creative minds than the African-American Outsider artist James Hampton (1909-64).

Hampton lived two lives. After receiving an honourable discharge from the United States Army Air Forces in 1945, he found work as a janitor for the General Services Administration in Washington, DC and spent his days cleaning the premises of federal agencies. Upon his death in 1964 from stomach cancer, it was discovered he had engaged in a quite different pursuit outside work. In 1950 he had secretly rented a garage in northwest Washington, and spent the next fourteen years crafting a collection of 180 objects of religious devotion essentially made from junk, using materials scavenged from his janitorial job. Aluminium foil, light bulbs, cardboard, gold paint, shards of windows and mirrors, car parts, plumbing and electrical fittings – all were combined to shape pulpits, altars, crowns and lecterns in a dazzling gold and chrome finish.

Hampton writes that the inspiration had come from a series of visits from God he had received throughout his lifetime, as well as an appearance by Moses in 1931, the Virgin Mary in 1946 and a vision of Adam on the day of President Truman's inauguration in 1949. These made him determined to prepare for the Second Coming by creating a 'monument to Jesus' in Washington, in the form of surroundings that Christ would be accustomed to in heaven.

Much of the work is derived from the descriptions of gold and silver thrones in the Book of Revelation and the gold crowns worn by the holy creatures seated on them. The centrepiece of Hampton's iteration is the main throne itself, which is 2.1m (7ft) tall and built upon an antique armchair with a maroon seat cushion. Wall plaques ring the objects, written with the names of the prophets and saints, while the words *The Throne of the Third Heaven of the Nations' Millennium General Assembly* are written across the objects in Hampton's handwriting.

Hampton recorded the details of his visions in a 108-page notebook entitled *St James: The Book of the 7 Dispensation*, which is as intriguing as the monument itself. Most of the book is written in an unknown spiritual language that is yet to be deciphered, but, from the portion of the writing that is in English, we learn that Hampton titled himself 'Director, Special Projects for the State of Eternity' and 'Saint James', and records a new set of ten commandments passed to him by God. His hope was that his work could be used by his local church as a teaching tool, and that perhaps also the world's media would take notice and spread word of it far and wide, but alas no such outcome materialised. Instead, it stayed covered in the small rented garage until his death. Today it finds itself in grander surroundings, fully reassembled in all its glory at the Smithsonian American Art Museum, where it has been on public display since 1970. *Time* magazine's art critic Robert Hughes wrote of the *Throne* that it 'may well be the finest work of visionary religious art produced by an American.'

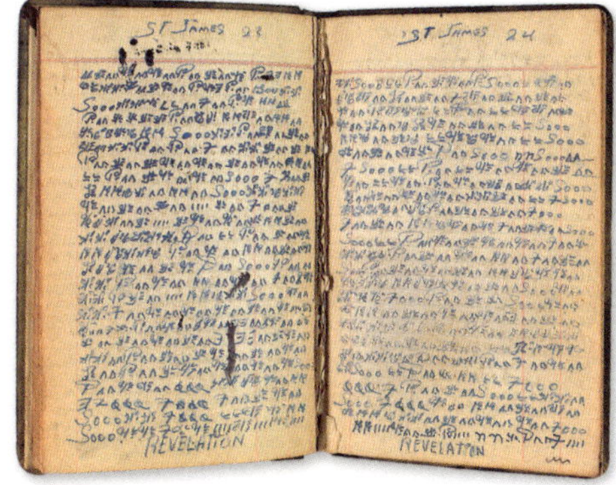

James Hampton's cryptic book.

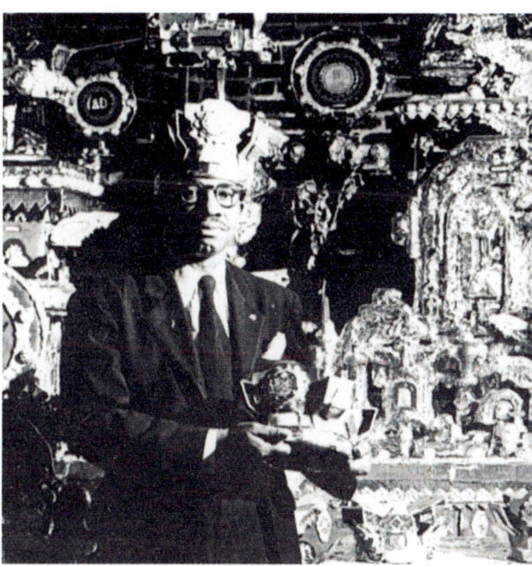

Hampton wearing his crown.

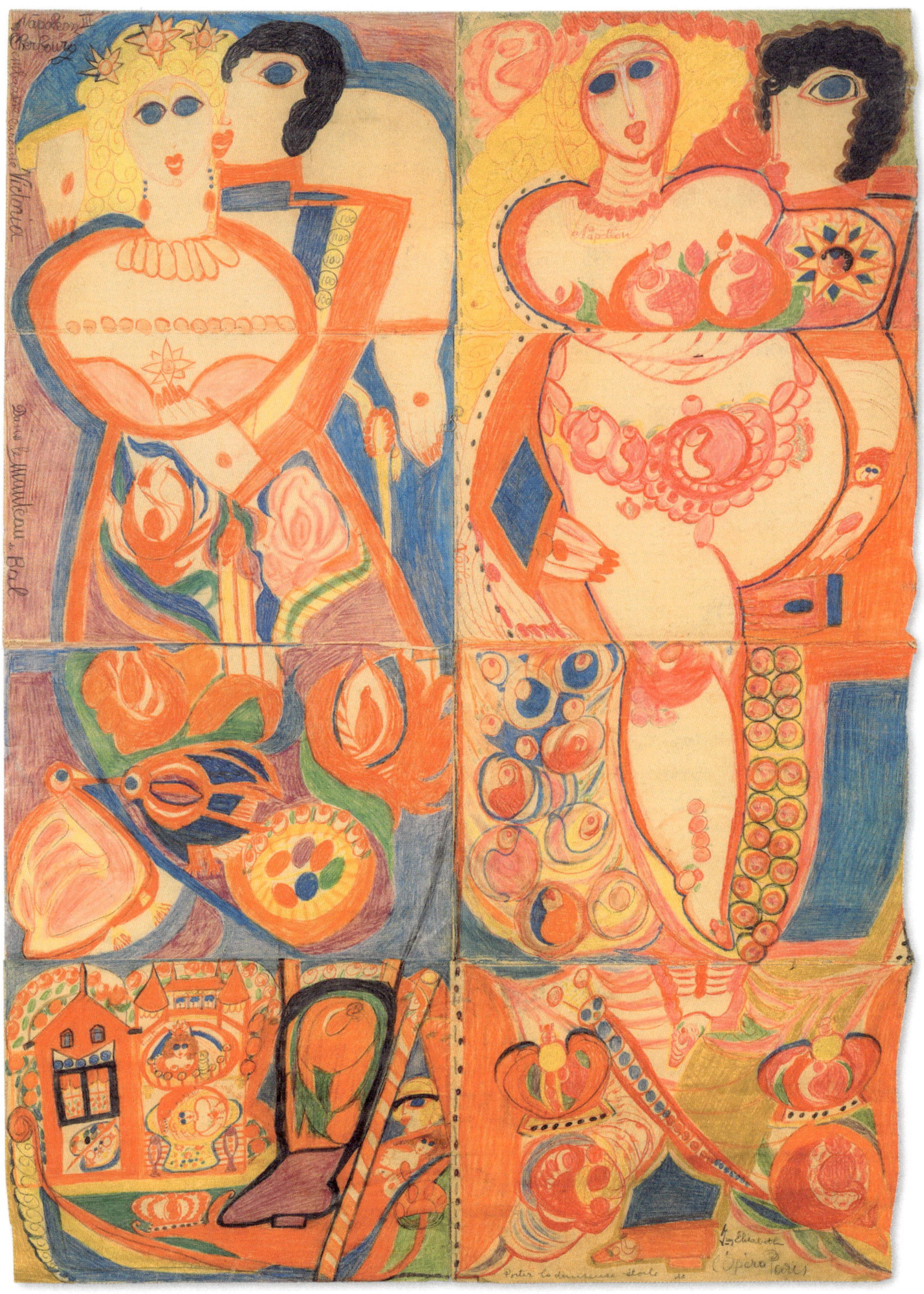

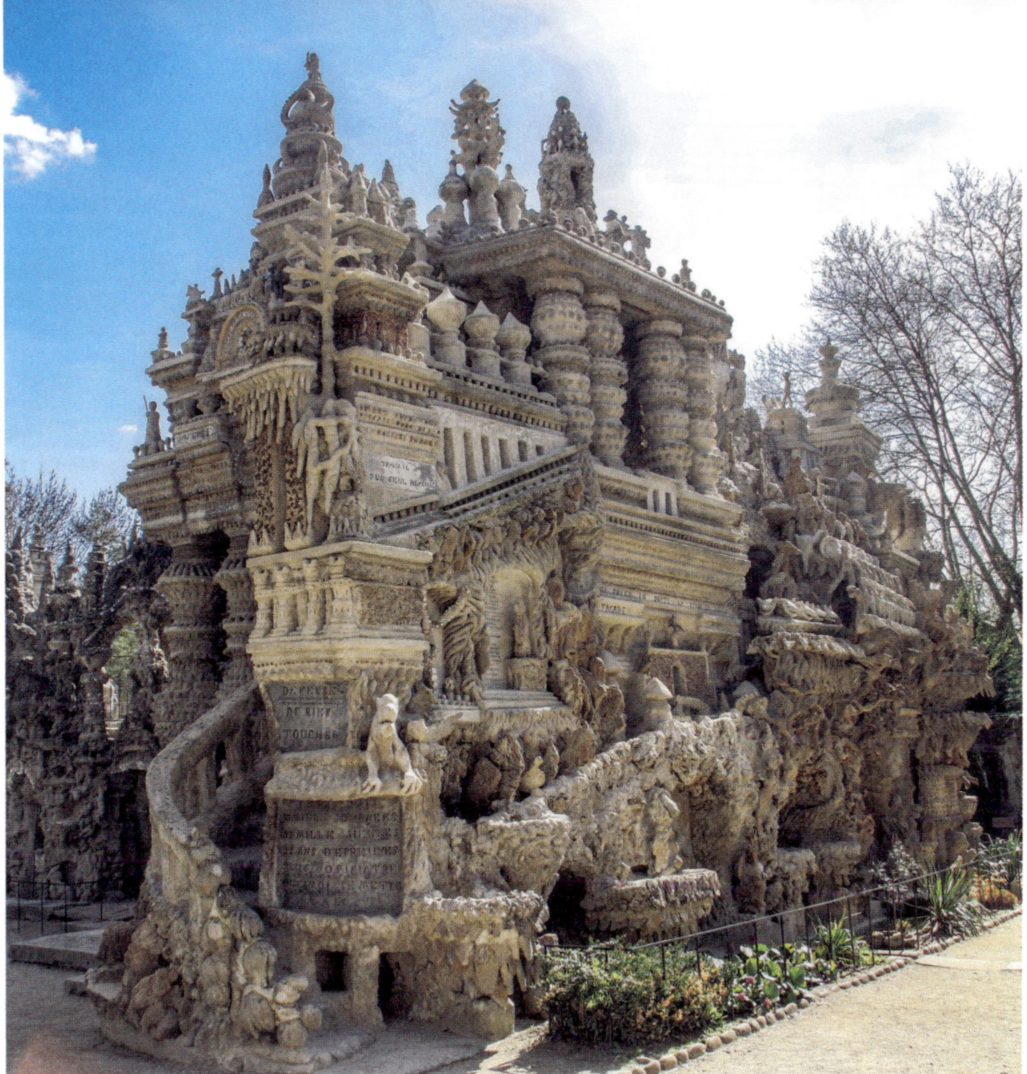

Opposite: *Aloïse Corbaz (1886-1964) was a Swiss artist celebrated in the* Art brut *or Outsider art genre. Wrenched from a new relationship by an older sister who disapproved, she was sent to Germany, where she found work as a governess in the court of Kaiser Wilhelm II. The two developed an intensely passionate romance, which continued when Aloïse was forced to return to Switzerland at the outbreak of the First World War. There it was discovered that the relationship had been entirely in her head – she was diagnosed with schizophrenia and committed to the Hôpital du Cery in 1918, where she continued to fantasise about the relationship and produced many paintings inspired by it.*

Above: *In April 1879, at the age of forty-three, a French postman named Ferdinand Cheval (1836-1924) began building* The Ideal Palace *at Hauterives, France, using pebbles he picked up each day during his delivery rounds. He finished thirty-three years later. The interior is covered with Cheval's original quotes, such as 'The work of one man', 'This is of art, and of energy', 'The ecstasy of a beautiful dream and the prize of effort', 'Dream of a peasant', 'Temple of Life', 'Out of a dream I have brought forth the Queen of the World' and 'Palace of the Imagination'.*

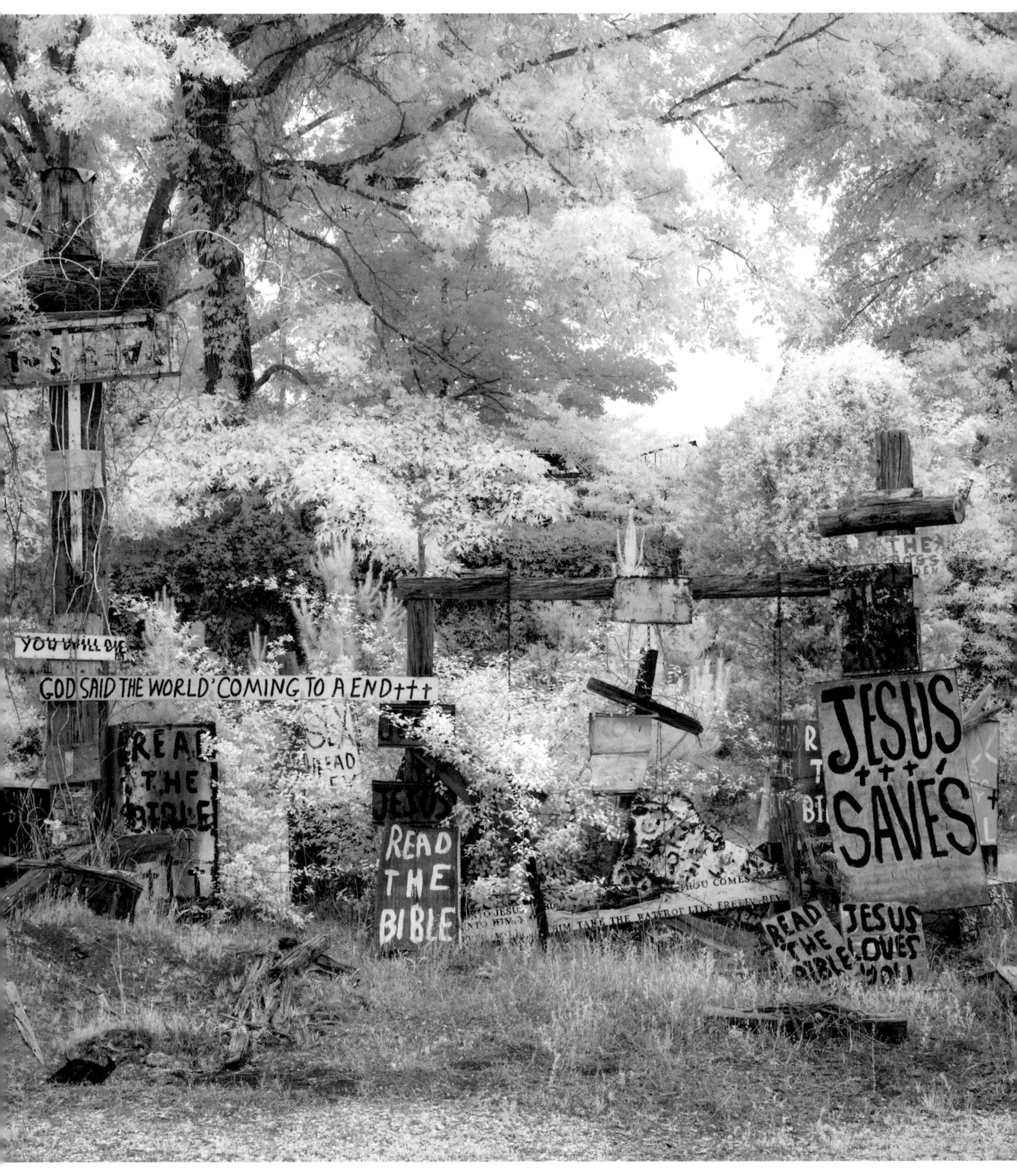
YOU WILL DIE
GOD SAID THE WORLD' COMING TO A END+++
READ THE BIBLE
JESUS
READ THE BIBLE
JESUS +++ SAVES
READ THE BIBLE
JESUS LOVES

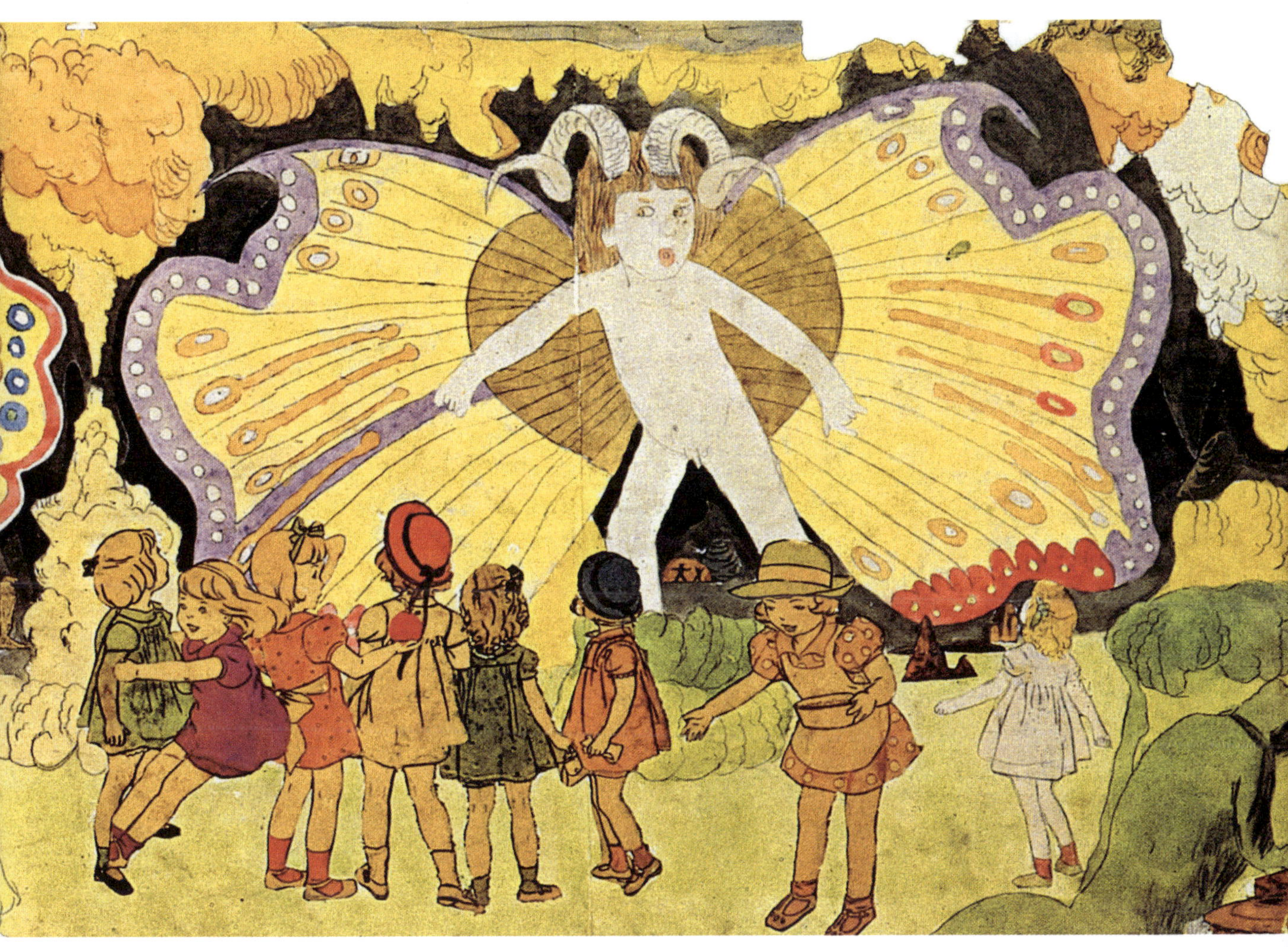

Opposite: *W. C. Rice's* Cross Garden *at Prattville, Alabama, USA. William Carlton Rice (1930-2004) was a soft-spoken house painter who felt God heal him of stomach ulcers on the night of 24 April 1960. In return, Rice spent the next forty years building his* Cross Garden *on his 1.2 hectares (3 acres) of land, which over the years would draw visitors from all over the world. A number of the hundreds of painted white crosses dabbed with red paint and signs with slogans like 'HELL IS HOT HOT HOT' were sold and are sought-after by collectors of Outsider art.*

Above: *Henry Darger (1892-1973) was a reclusive hospital janitor in Chicago, Illinois. Following his death, Darger's landlord discovered over 300 original drawings and watercolour paintings, some painted on sheets 3m (10ft) wide, filling his apartment. These accompanied a 15,145-page manuscript of over 9 million words, titled* The Story of the Vivian Girls, in What Is Known as the Realms of the Unreal, of the Glandeco-Angelinian War Storm, Caused by the Child Slave Rebellion, *which recounts the adventures of seven heroines who led a rebellion against the child-snatching Glandelinians. Today Darger is one of the most famous examples of an Outsider artist, and his art can sell for hundreds of thousands of dollars.*

MERDA D'ARTISTA (1961), PIERO MANZONI

Conceptual art arrived in the 1960s as a rejection of the classifications by galleries, museums and traditionalists of what qualified as art – an intellectual rebellion dating back to the Dadaists of the 1910s-20s. The term conceptual art was officially coined in 1967 by the artist Sol LeWitt (1928-2007) in an article for *Artforum*, but earlier in the decade the road was already being paved in Italy by one of the most radical and wildly inventive artists of the twentieth century – Piero Manzoni (1933-63), full name Count Meroni Manzoni di Chiosca e Poggiolo.

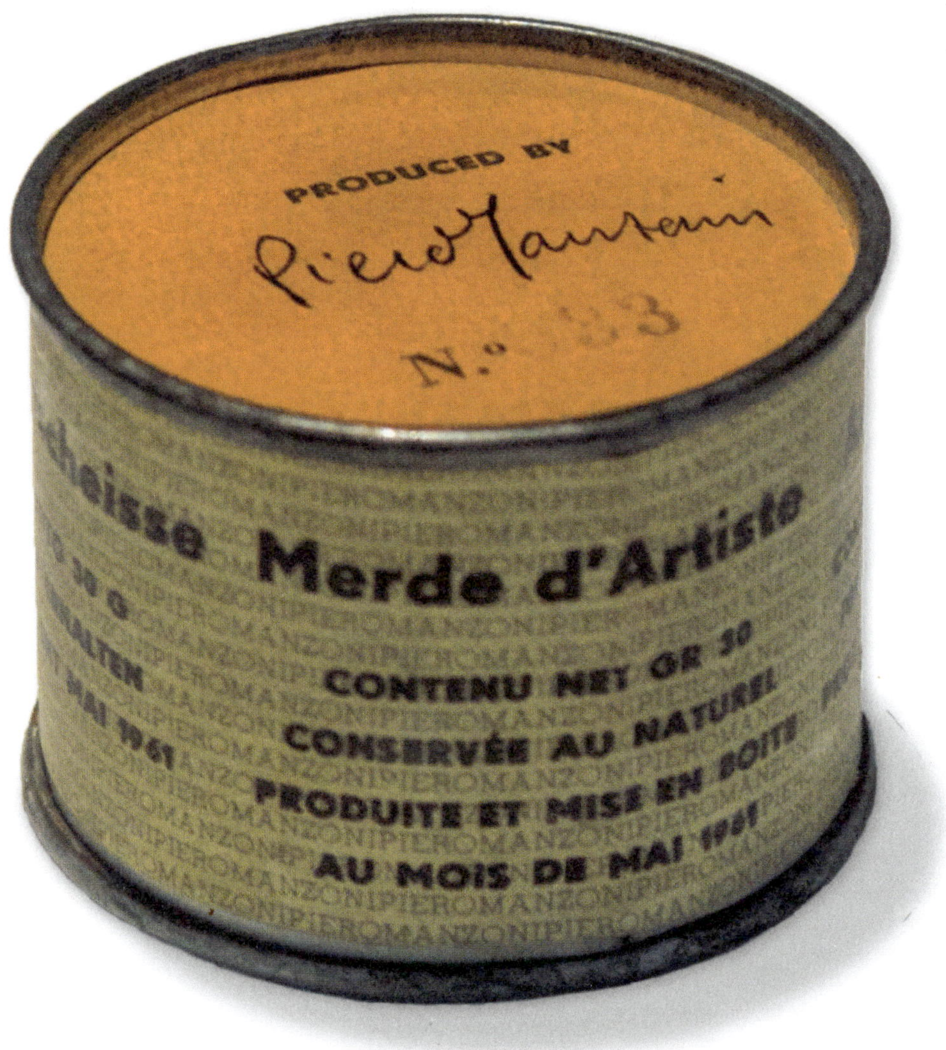

Manzoni started his career as an abstract painter before questioning the traditional techniques. A visit in 1957 to an Yves Klein (1928-62) show at the Galleria Apollinaire, Milan, revolutionised his outlook. Klein's *Proposte Monochrome, Epoca Blu* (Monochrome Propositions, Blue Period, 1957), an exhibition of eleven near-identical monochrome blue paintings (see page 224), prompted Manzoni to work on his *Achrome* series between 1957 and 1963, which all draw on colourless materials, from plain white canvases covered in kaolin and gesso, to framed sections of cotton wool, rabbit fur and even bread.

Manzoni then fell deeper into the investigation of what constitutes an artwork, with some fabulously imaginative and wry proto-conceptual ideas. In 1959 he began producing his pneumatic works *Corpi d'Aria* (Bodies of Air), in which forty-five balloons attached to tripods could be blown up by the visitor/purchaser or, for an extra fee, by the artist himself. Then there is *Magisk Sockkel* (Magic Bases, 1961), a set of wooden plinths that, when stood on by the viewer, transforms their status to 'Living Sculpture'.

Similarly, *Socle du Monde* (Base of the World, 1961) is a large plinth inscribed with 'The Base of The World, Homage to Galileo', which was placed upside down in a field in Herning, Denmark, turning the entire world into a work of art. *Linee dalla lunghezza eccezionale* (Lines of Exceptional Length, 1960-61) comprised lines drawn on rolls of paper using a rotary press and a large dripping bottle of ink – the longest of these lines ran for 7.2km (4½ miles). The plan was for a *Linee* to be produced for each major city in the world, where it would be kept in a steel tube. If all were to be unrolled and joined together, the total length of the *Linee* would equal the length of the equator and circle the world. (Sadly, Manzoni died before this project was finished.)

At the Galleria La Tartaruga, in Rome in 1961, Manzoni began signing his name on models (and visitors) who wandered into the gallery, providing them with a stamped document that they were officially part of his body of work titled *Sculture viventi* (Living Sculptures).

In the same year, Manzoni produced his most notorious work: *Merda d'artista*. A series of sealed, 30g (1oz) cans, limited to a set of ninety. Each can carries a label written in Italian, English, French and German that claims the contents of the can to be Manzoni's own excrement: 'Artist's Shit. Contents 30 gr net. Freshly preserved. Produced and tinned in May 1961.'

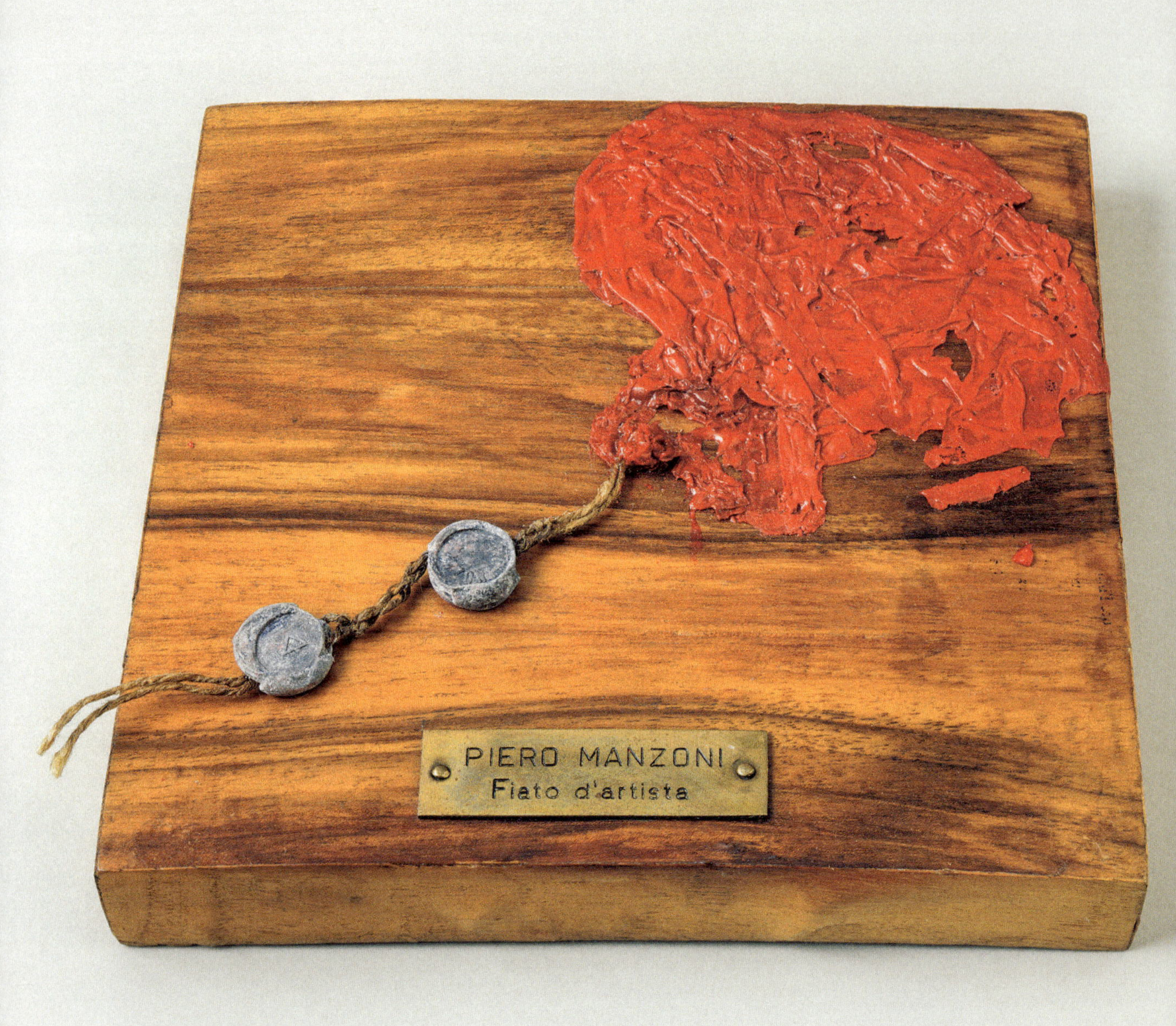

Artist's Breath *(1960), the remains of a balloon inflated by the artist that became stuck to the board as it gradually deflated. 'When I blow up a balloon, I am breathing my soul into an object that becomes eternal', Manzoni said.*

Each can was priced to match the market value of gold ($37 at the time). 'I should like all artists to sell their fingerprints, or else stage competitions to see who can draw the longest line or sell their shit in tins,' he writes to his friend Ben Vautier in December 1961. 'If collectors want something intimate, really personal to the artist, there's the artist's own shit, that is really his.' *Merda d'artista* was, claimed his colleague Enrico Baj, simply 'an act of defiant mockery of the art world, artists and art criticism.' At this time, Manzoni's country was undergoing the Italian Miracle, the post-war economic boom of industrial and commercial development. *Merda d'artista* is seen as a provocative challenge to this consumerism and mass production, in which art was increasingly seen as a commodity, too.

A heart attack claimed his life in 1963 but, had he lived to see the next century, would Manzoni have been disgusted, or perhaps grimly amused, by the amounts that his protest cans are today traded for, as the very commodities he was lampooning? In 2000 the Tate bought one tin for £22,350 from Sotheby's. In May 2007, another original *Merda d'artista* tin was sold for €124,000, and another in October 2008 for £97,250. In October 2015, *Tin 54* sold at Christie's for £182,500, then in August 2016 this record was smashed at an art auction in Milan with another tin selling for €275,000.

Most likely, Manzoni would have found this far from surprising, having once said that with the tins he was exposing 'the gullibility of the art-buying public'. Perhaps this is connected to the contents of the cans themselves, about which the question has, of course, always been: are they *really* filled with the artist's excrement? The cans are steel and therefore can't be X-rayed, and no one has dared open a tin to check, for this would severely reduce its value. Agostino Bonalumi (1935-2013), who worked with Manzoni, wrote in 2007 that Manzoni had actually filled the cans with something else. 'I can assure everyone the contents were only plaster,' he wrote. 'If anyone wants to verify this, let them do so.'

MONDO CANE SHROUD (1961), YVES KLEIN

The story goes that, at the age of nineteen, the man who would be labelled 'the last French artist of major international consequence' by the American art critic Peter Schjeldahl was lying in a field in southern France with two artist friends when the trio decided to divide the world between them. Arman (1928-2005) claimed the earth; Claude Pascal (1921-2017) took words. Yves Klein (1928-62) chose the ether, and with a flourish symbolically signed the sky. This interest in the void, the space between, would fuel him through his life and career.

Klein is best known for the nearly two hundred monochrome paintings that he began in 1949 – most famously his 1957 blue series, for which he used a specially created type of ultramarine that he patented for his sole use and which he labelled IKB – International Klein Blue. None of these paintings was titled or dated by Klein but the early works can be distinguished from the later by their rougher textures, and following his death in 1962 his widow, Rotraut Klein-Moquay (b.1938), gave them numerical identities. The idea behind these plain blue abstractions on canvas was, says Klein, to create an 'open window to freedom, as the possibility of being immersed in the immeasurable existence of color.' He believed his blue to possess a quality near to the purity of space, holding invisible values beyond the tangible. The monochromes would 'make visible the absolute' as part of his mission to 'liberate colour from the prison that is the line'.

The painting chosen for this section, however, while a part of this campaign against the restriction of the lines of the paintbrush, is not part of Klein's monochrome series but of his later *Anthropométries* series. Here, he replaced paintbrushes with naked female models, doused in paint and dragged across the canvas – his 'living brushes'.[1] The process would turn into an early form of performance art. In 1960, Klein conducted one such painting session in front of an audience dressed in formal evening

---

1 The series didn't just involve human brushes – at one point Klein painted 'recordings' of rain by driving around at speeds of 112km/h (70mph) with a canvas strapped to the roof of his car; he also used gas burners to 'paint' canvases in soot.

Mondo Cane Shroud *(1961)*, *Yves Klein*

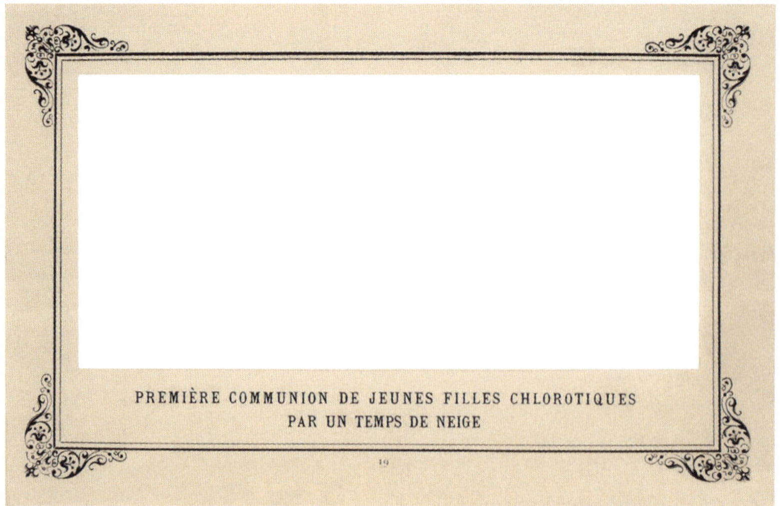

Et sic in infinitum .

wear and nibbling hors d'oeuvres, who looked on as naked women were dragged about the canvas while musicians played Klein's own instrumental composition *The Monotone Symphony* (1949).

An Italian documentary crew making a film called *Mondo Cane* (Doggish World, 1962) recorded one such performance at the offer of Klein, who hoped the resulting film would spread his reputation like Hans Namuth's photographs did of Jackson Pollock, and Henri-Georges Clouzot's filmmaking did for Picasso.

The work shown on page 225, *Mondo Cane Shroud* (1961), was produced for the Italian film, with Klein choreographing his models as the cameras rolled. The 3m- (10ft-) wide, resin-on-gauze is strikingly beautiful, possessing a ghostlike quality characteristic of Klein's ethereal obsession. Though he was delighted with how his painting process was shown in the initial cut of the film, the film was recut for a more trashily provocative and amusing tone, becoming the world's first 'exploitation' film. A humiliated Klein suffered a heart attack while watching the premiere of *Mondo Cane* at the Cannes Film Festival on 11 May 1962; a later coronary episode claimed his life shortly afterwards, on 6 June 1962.

In 2004, the Walker Art Center, Minneapolis, USA, acquired the painting after years of effort, adding it to its collection along with the wooden tub splattered with IKB paint in which the models had bathed, as a key piece in the history of painting and performance art.

OPPOSITE TOP: *In 1882, a Parisian writer named Jules Lévy (1857-1935) founded a satirically irreverent art movement called Salon des Arts Incohérents, with the banner 'An exhibition of drawings made by people who cannot draw'. One contributor was the writer Alphonse Allais (1854-1905), who painted this work of a piece of plain white Bristol paper, and titled it* First Communion of Young Anaemic Girls in a Blizzard *(1883). Also popular was his* Apoplectic Cardinals Harvesting Tomatoes by the Red Sea *(1884), a solid red rectangle, and* Stupefied Naval Cadets Seeing Your Azure for the First Time, O Mediterranean! *(1884), a blue rectangle.*

OPPOSITE BOTTOM: *Klein is known for his blue monochromes, but we can trace the spiritual ancestry of such painting back through the history of avant-garde art to this illustration by the physician and occultist Robert Fludd (1574-1637) in his* Utriusque cosmi… *of 1617-21. The black square is a depiction of the pretemporal nothingness before the light of Creation – an empty universe.*

THE ART OF PIERRE BRASSAU (1964)

'A mysterious painter astonishes the Swedes,' announced the *Paris Match* headline of 7 March 1964, reporting on a unique exhibition of avant-garde art that took place at the Gallerie Christinae in Göteborg, Sweden in February 1964. The show featured new work by English, Danish, Austrian, Italian and Swedish creators, but the star of the show was a previously unknown French painter named Pierre Brassau, of whom little in the way of biographical detail was revealed. His art, however, spoke for itself. 'Brassau paints with powerful strokes,' gushed Rolf Anderberg of the *Göteborgs-Posten*, 'but also with clear determination. His brush strokes twist with furious fastidiousness. Pierre is an artist who performs with the delicacy of a ballet dancer.' Not everyone was a fan, though: 'Only an ape could have done this,' sniffed one critic, unaware of just how accurate the statement was.

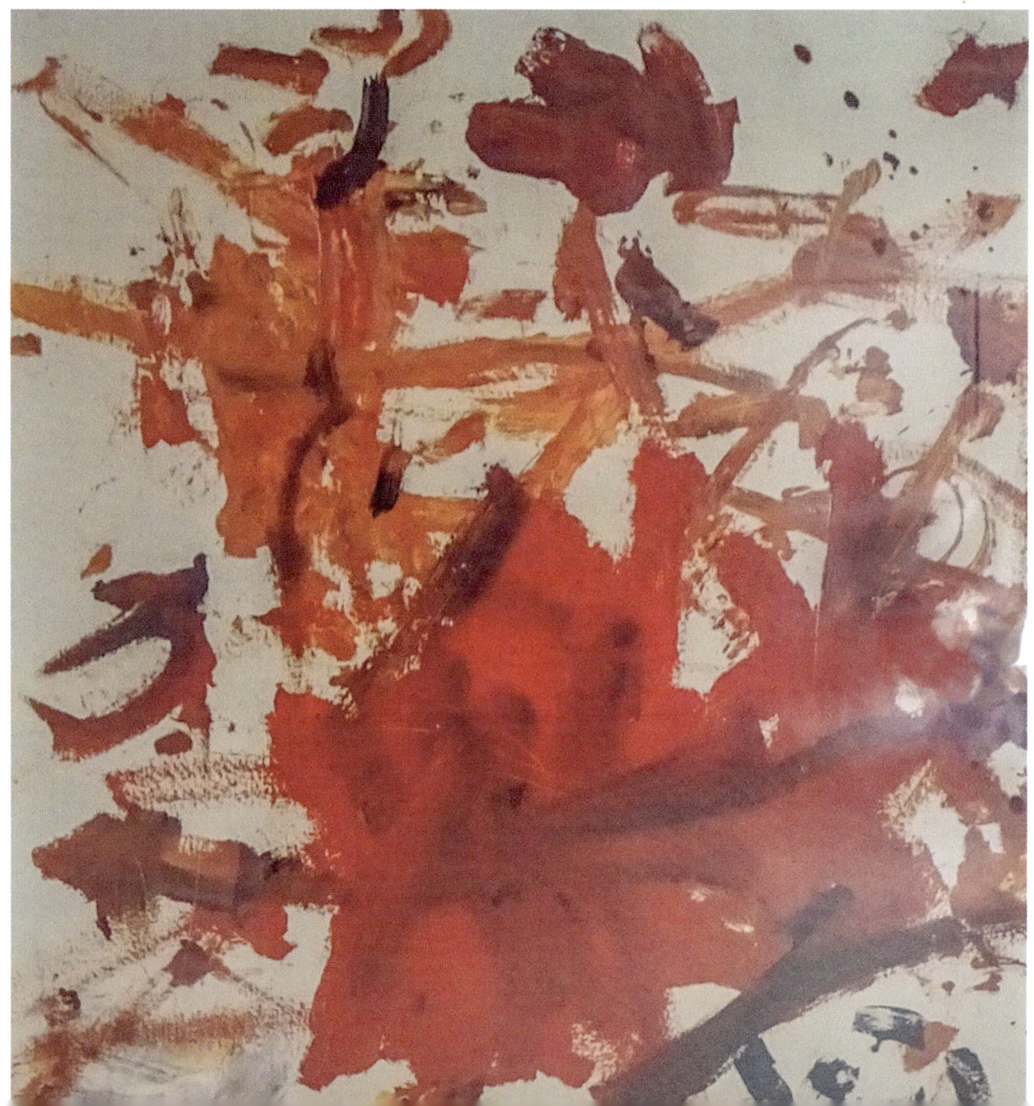

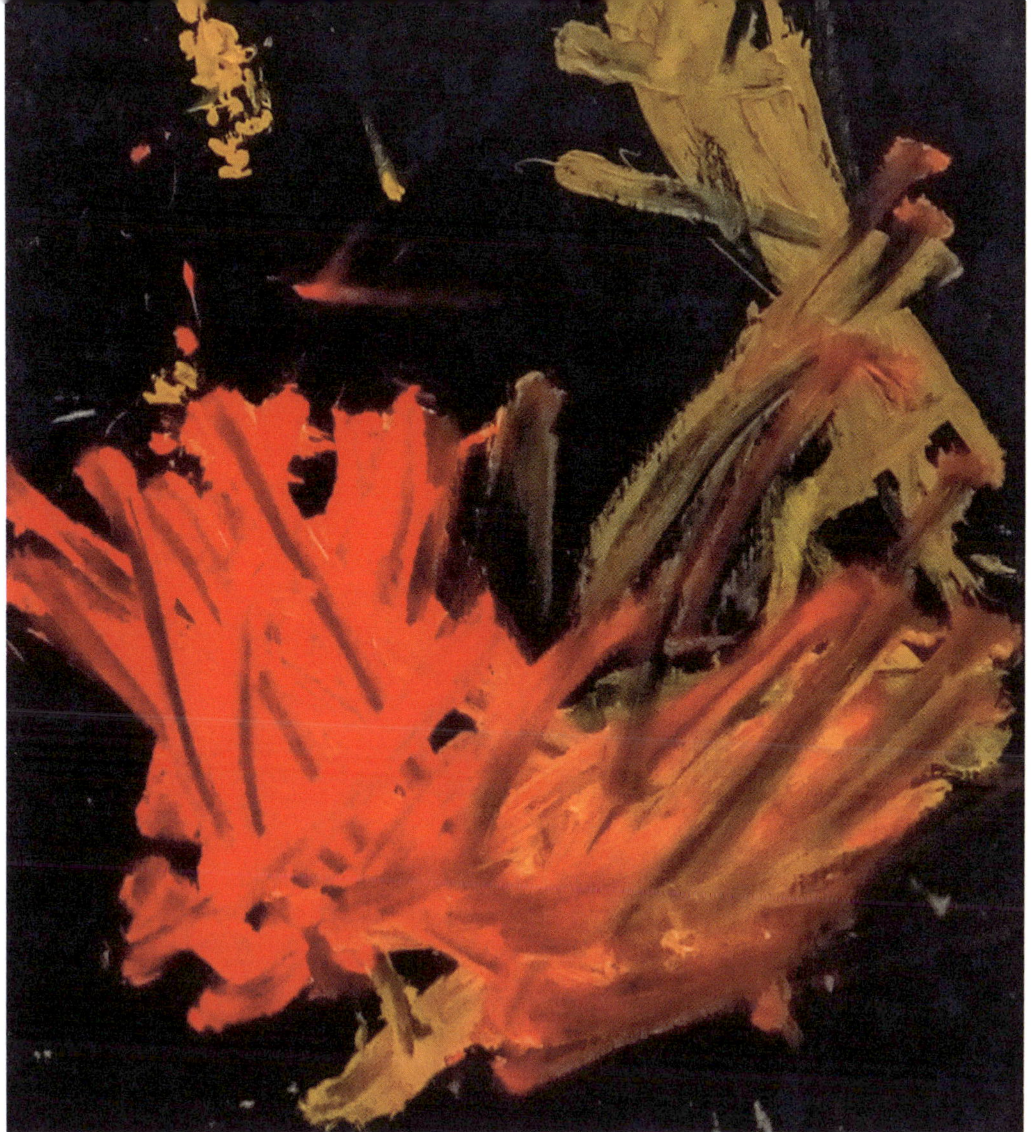

It wasn't abstract art itself that Åke Axelsson, a journalist at the Swedish newspaper *Göteborgs-Posten*, detested; it was the pomposity with which critics claimed to be able to tell the good from the bad. It seemed only logical to put this confidence to the test. And so, in the city of Borås in west Sweden, he visited the Borås Djurpark Zoo and convinced a young zookeeper to give Peter, a four-year-old West African chimpanzee, some canvases and some paint, in the hope that artistic inspiration would strike. Things got off to a rocky start when Peter insisted on eating the paint – the cobalt blue was particularly delicious, which might explain why he favoured it in his work. Peter painted the floor; he painted his keeper; and occasionally he even managed to get some paint on the canvases. Bananas helped aid his concentration. At his peak painting rate, Peter ate almost a banana a minute.

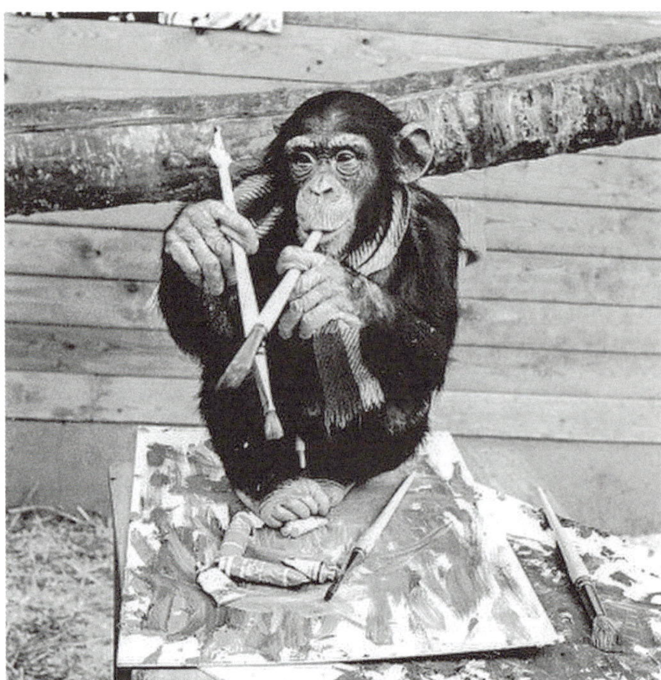

The artist at work in his studio/enclosure.

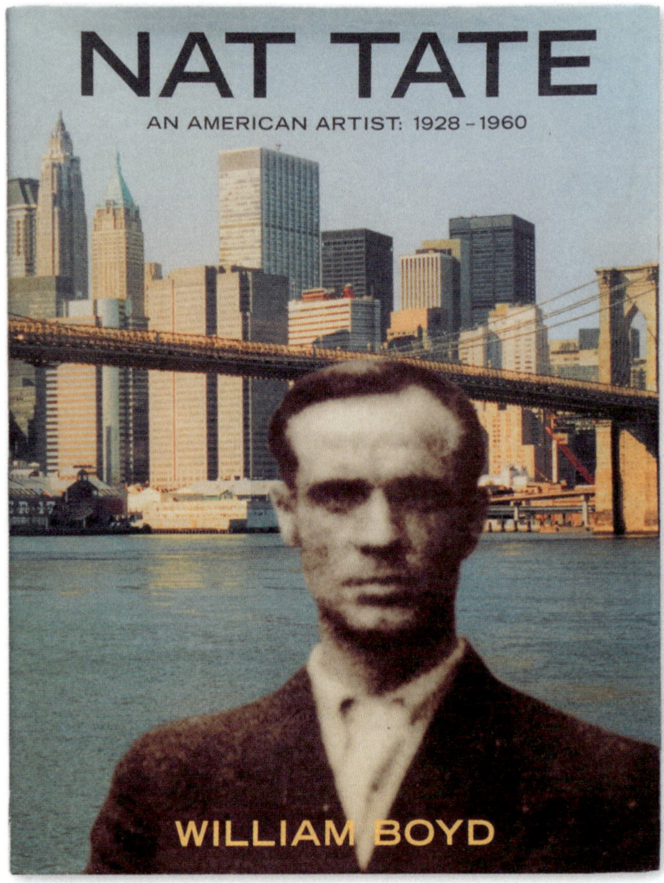

The cover of Nat Tate: An American Artist 1928-1960 *(1998), a hoax biography of a fictional artist, written by the author William Boyd and launched at a party in 1998 organised by his accomplice David Bowie, in which fake artworks by the fake artist were shown. ('Nat Tate' is a combination of National and Tate Gallery.) The art world was, for one wild evening, completely fooled.*

Axelsson scooped up four of the paintings that most resembled deliberate acts, and sidestepping banana skins headed off to organise the Gallerie Christinae show. The exhibition was a hit. 'Pierre Brassau' even made a sale to a private collector for the equivalent of £600 today. Axelsson revealed the hoax soon after. 'Someone is trying to make a monkey out of modern art,' reports *Time*. Rolf Anderberg, the journalist who had so admired M. Brassau's artwork, simply shrugged. Peter's work, he said, was 'still the best painting in the exhibition'.

While Peter is no longer with us, having lived out his retirement in England following a transfer to Chester Zoo in 1969, his reputation lives on, helped by occasional similarly inspired episodes like one in December 2005. A story ran in German newspapers that Dr Kajta Schneider, director of the State Art Museum of Moritzburg in Saxony-Anhalt, had been presented with a modern piece and was challenged to identify the artist responsible. After careful examination she concluded that it seemed to her to be the work of Ernst Wilhelm Nay (1902-68), one of the most important painters of German post-war art. In fact, it was painted by a 31-year-old female chimpanzee named Banghi, artist in residence at Halle Zoo (who apparently loved to paint, though much of her oeuvre was destroyed by her mate Satscho). When the true author was revealed, Dr Schneider replied, 'I did think it looked a bit rushed.'

In 1924 a literary scholar and American universalist minister with no painting ability named Paul Jordan-Smith (1885-1971) invented the pseudonym Pavel Jerdanowitch, and masqueraded as an avant-garde Russian artist, inventing an 'art movement' he called Disumbrationism. His motive? Revenge. The jury of New York's Exhibition of the Independents had snubbed his wife's skilful still life paintings, and so 'Jerdanowitch' entered his crude painting Yes, We Have No Bananas, *showing a Pacific islander woman holding a banana over her head, into the 1925 exhibition. The jury praised it, and 'Jerdanowitch' continued painting to critical acclaim, receiving comparisons to Paul Gauguin, among others. He finally revealed the truth to the* Los Angeles Times *in 1927.*

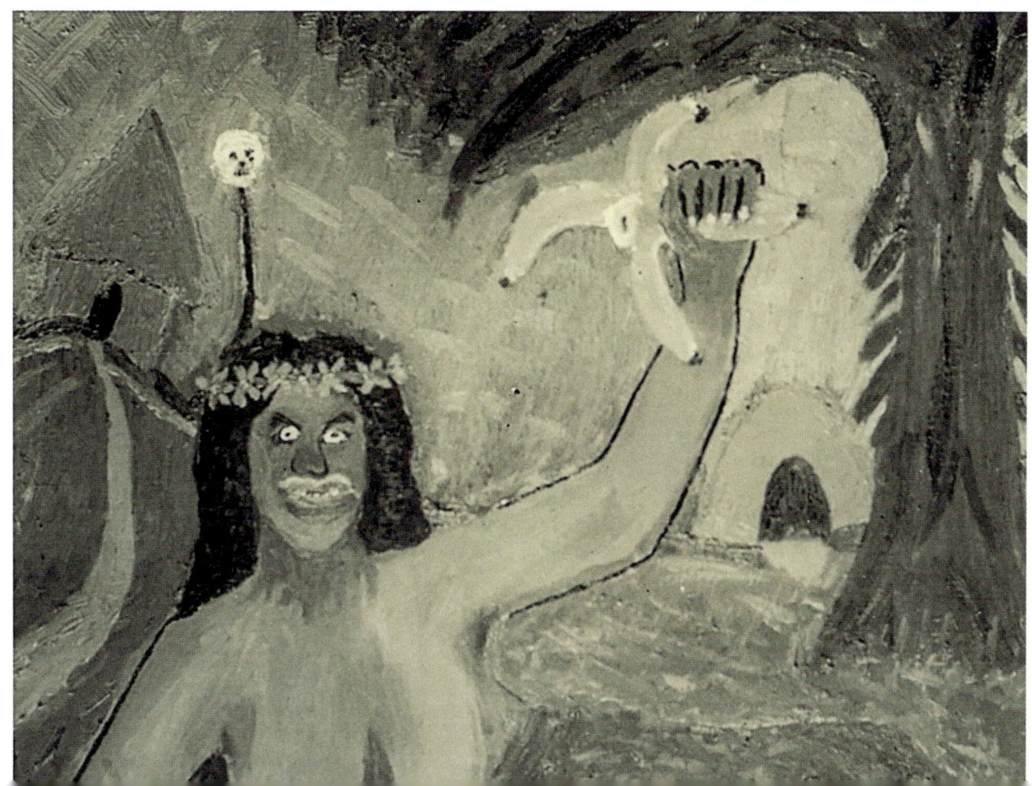

THE *GETTY KOUROS* (TWENTIETH CENTURY) AND OTHER FAKES AND FORGERIES

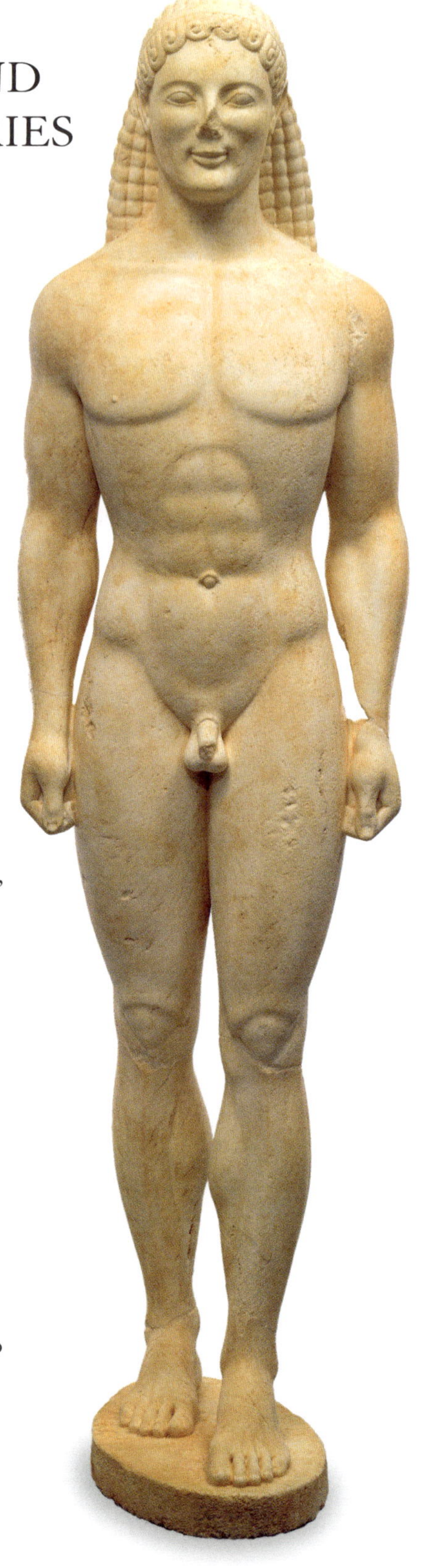

Fake artworks are a real problem. In fact, the odds are good that, at some point during a visit to even the most prestigious art gallery or institution, an artwork you have admired on the wall was not authentic. In 2014, a shocking report by Switzerland's Fine Arts Expert Institute (FAEI) concluded that at least half of the artworks in circulation in the global market are fake. And it seems that the problem is only getting worse.

In Italy in 2017, for example, twenty-one paintings by Amedeo Modigliani (1884-1920) were exhibited at Genoa's Palazzo Ducale, and all but one were announced as fake. The show was closed, and the paintings handed over to the authorities. (The French Modigliani expert Marc Restellini estimates there to be over 1000 fake Modigliani paintings in circulation at the highest levels of the market.) In January 2018, the Museum of Fine Arts in Ghent launched an exhibition of twenty-six works by the twentieth-century Russian artists Kazimir Malevich (1879-1935) and Wassily Kandinsky (1866-1944). Every one of the works was found to be a forgery. In April of that same year, the Étienne Terrus Museum in southern France discovered that eighty-two paintings, or 60 per cent of their collection of the work of Étienne Terrus (1857-1922), was fake. The investigator they hired mentioned that 'on one painting, the ink signature was wiped away when I passed my white glove over it.'

These are European examples, but art forgery is rampant worldwide. In China in 2015, for instance, a former chief librarian of the Guangzhou Academy of Fine Arts named Xiao Yuan admitted to stealing and substituting 143 artworks with fakes that he made himself. Between 2004 and 2011, he is thought to have profited by 34 million yuan (£3.94 million) by selling 125 of the stolen items, while the eighteen original pieces he chose to keep for himself were valued at over

70 million yuan (£8.11 million). His defence? Everyone else was doing it. Even *his fakes* were being stolen and replaced. 'I realized someone else had replaced my paintings with their own,' Xiao told the Guangzhou People's Intermediate Court, 'because I could clearly discern that their works were terribly bad.'

Gary Vikan, former director of the Walters Art Museum in Baltimore, revealed to the *New York Times* in September 2021 that the museum has hundreds of fakes in its collections. 'They're mainly Roman, medieval and Renaissance works acquired by the founder Henry Walters, in 1902,' he said. 'Some of the works had been sold to him as paintings by Michelangelo, Titian and Raphael.' Many gratefully received donations to institutions turn out to be fake yet still serve a purpose. New York University and Harvard University, for example, use high-quality forgeries to educate their art history students on how to tell the fake from the authentic.

It is one thing to suspect forgery; it is quite another to prove it 'beyond all reasonable doubt'. One of the most intriguing works that today continues to be heatedly pulled in all directions by claims of authenticity and forgery is a 2m (6½ft) tall statue of a standing nude youth carved from Dolomitic marble, known as the *Getty Kouros* (opposite). 'Greece? About 530 BC', read its exhibition card, 'or modern forgery'. It certainly has all the hallmarks of a *kouros*, a type of statue representing the notion of youth that was commonly deployed in temples by the ancient Greeks as dedications to the gods.

There were, initially, no doubts as to its authenticity when the Getty completed its purchase in 1985, as shown by the exorbitant price paid: $9 million. It was only when looking into its provenance that things started to get

BELOW: La Bella Principessa *is claimed by some to be a c.1495 portrait of Bianca Maria Sforza (1472-1510) by Leonardo da Vinci, and by others to be the work of an early nineteenth-century German artist imitating the Italian Renaissance style. The debate rages on.*

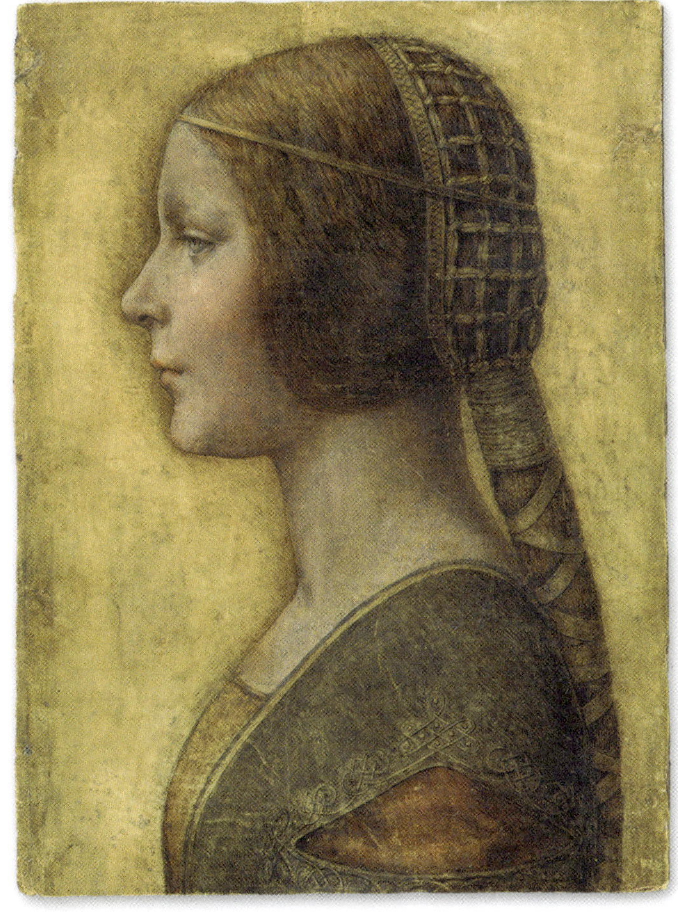

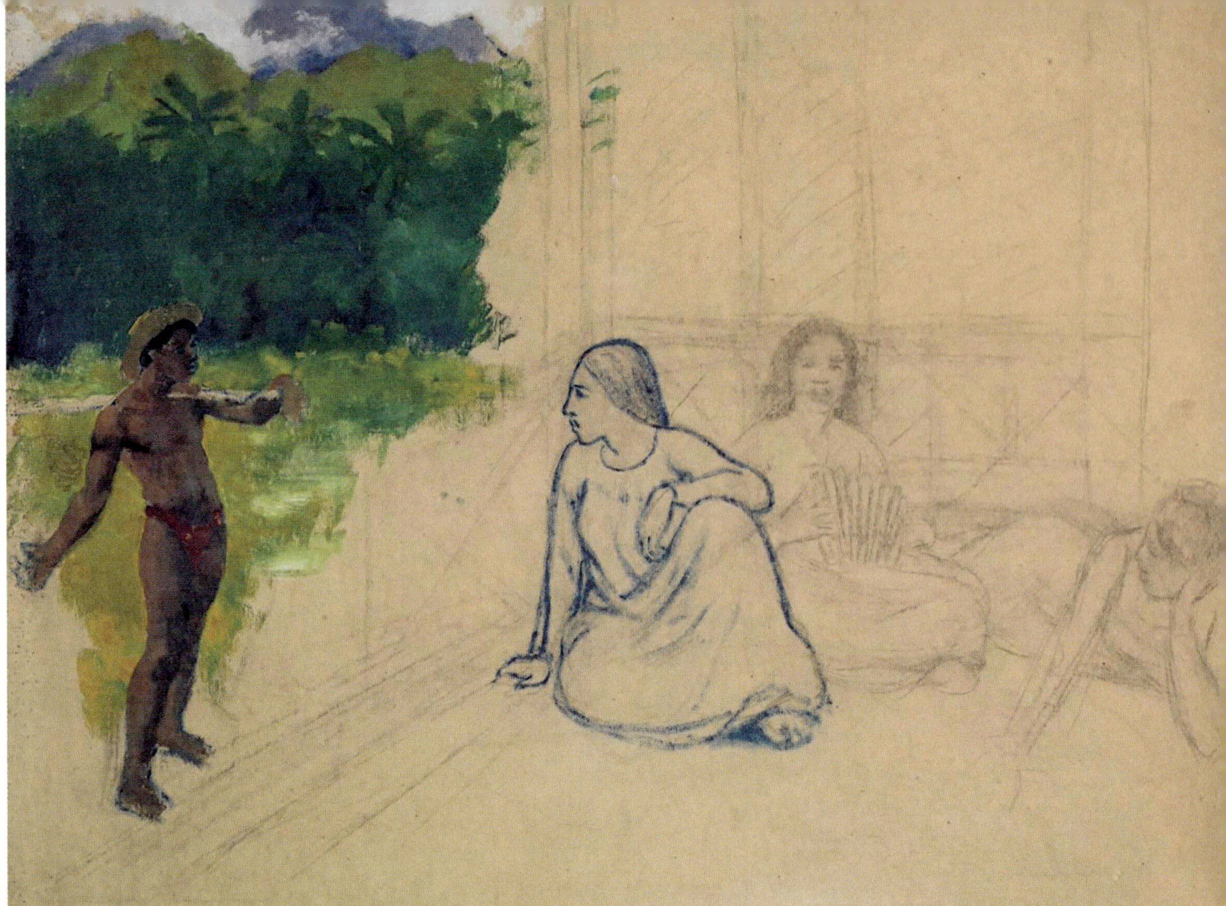

suspiciously hazy. The piece had popped up on the market in 1983, offered by the Basel dealer Gianfranco Becchina. The Getty's curator of antiquities, Jiří Frel, eventually bought it and stored it at the Getty Villa Museum in Malibu together with a packet of documents that traced the provenance to the collection of Dr Jean Lauffenberger of Geneva, who had acquired it in the 1930s from a Greek dealer. There was also a letter dated 1952 from the Greek sculpture expert Ernst Langlotz, discussing the sculpture's similarity to the Anavyssos youth in Athens. Only later was it discovered that the postcode on the 1952 Langlotz letter only came into use in 1972 and that a bank account mentioned in a separate supporting letter of 1955 was not opened until 1963.

Despite suspicions raised by these inconsistencies, as well as the statue's confusing mixture of early and later styles, no one has yet been able to conclusively prove the statue is a fake. Perhaps these questions are simply down to our limited knowledge of Greek sculpture of the Archaic period – only eleven other such *kouroi* are extant. Today, however, the *Getty Kouros* is available to visit by appointment only, having been quietly removed from public exhibition in 2018.

ABOVE: Tahitians, *in the collection of the Tate and acquired in 1917 from the eminent art historian Roger Fry (1866-1934), who coined the term post-impressionism. Attributed to Paul Gauguin (1848-1903), the painting has recently been classed as a fake. A French art historian named Fabrice Fourmanoir began to raise concerns in 2020 about its authenticity, claiming Gauguin's composition to have been more primitive. It has since been omitted by the authoritative* catalogue raisonné *of Gauguin's work published by the New York-based Wildenstein Plattner Institute. The Tate announced that they will 'keep the work under review'.*

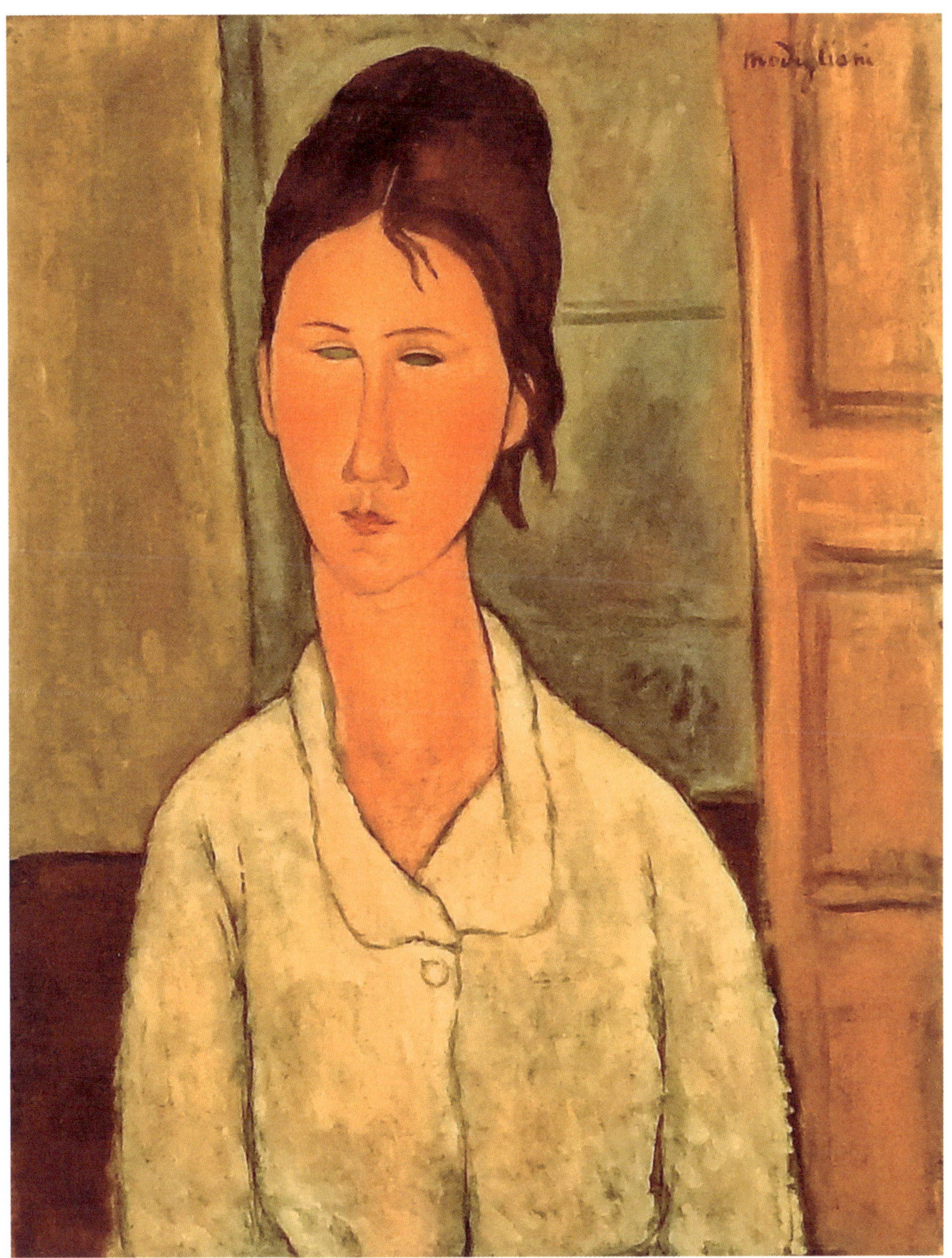

The Hungarian-born painter Elmyr de Hory (1906-76) was one of the most prolific art forgers in history. Having survived a German concentration camp during the Second World War, he travelled to Paris to start a career as an honest painter but discovered a talent for imitating the styles of masters including Modigliani (1884-1920), as demonstrated here. He is believed to have sold over a thousand fake works, including the above painting in the style of Modigliani, to art galleries and museums around the world.

MARINA ABRAMOVIĆ
AND PERFORMANCE ART

It is a curious contradiction at the heart of performance art that is at once the most physical and also the most ephemeral form of conceptual art. Performance in the visual arts traces back to at least as early as the sound poems of the metal-clad Hugo Ball and other Dada cabaret performances of the 1910s (see page 196), but it was only in the 1970s that it became widely used and accepted as its own artistic medium. In keeping with the Dada spirit, performance art was a rejection of artistic convention while simultaneously bringing to physical life concepts long expressed by artists working in two-dimensional mediums.

One early notable performance work is *Following Piece* by the New York-based artist Vito Acconci (1940-2017), which was carried out in 1969. Acconci would follow the first passerby he saw as he stepped out of his Manhattan apartment – sometimes this would last for just a few minutes, sometimes for five and a half hours. The casual pursuit would come to an end when the stranger entered a private location. Acconci performed one *Following* piece each day over one month, each one documented with photographs and written reports. 'I am almost not an "I" anymore,' he said of the activity, 'I put myself in the service of this scheme.'

Joseph Beuys performed extraordinary pieces as part of the Fluxus collective of artists that included John Cage and Yoko Ono. Take his *I Like America and America Likes Me* work of 1974, for example, in which he flew to New York to be ferried by ambulance to spend three days sharing a room with a wild coyote at the René Block Gallery. He slept on a bed of straw, and intermittently threw leather gloves at the animal. (The coyote is an object of worship for Native Americans, and Beuys's intention was to criticise the treatment of the indigenous culture.)

In 1976, Ana Mendieta (1948-85) explored the relationship between the female body and the natural landscape, and the pain of being a Cuban exile. In the performance *Tree of Life*, she caked her naked body in mud and stood for hours at the base of a living tree with her arms raised.

The Belgrade-born artist Marina Abramović (b.1946) and self-described 'grandmother of performance art' has said she

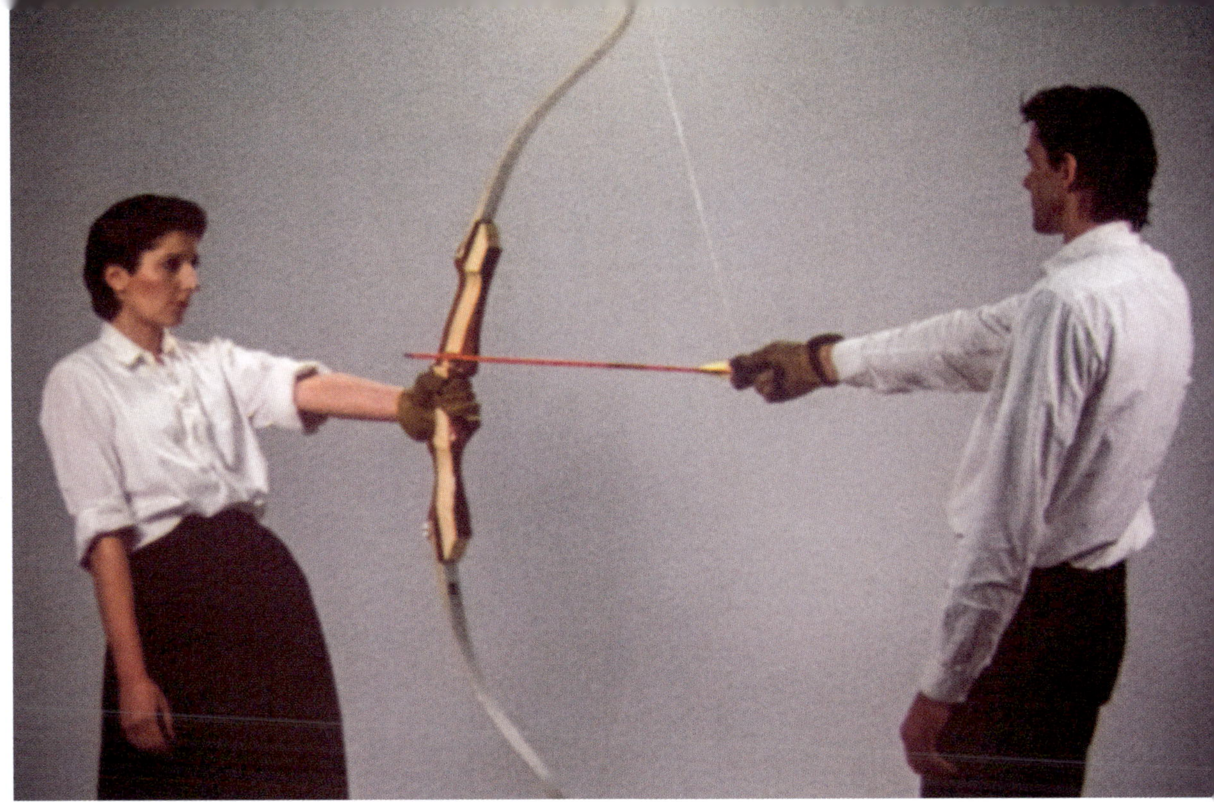

Marina Abramović and Ulay performing Rest Energy *in 1980.*

was entirely unaware of the existence of the medium when she began holding public performances. Her international event – *Rhythm 10*, the first of her *Rhythm…* series – took place in Edinburgh in 1973. In it she played the 'Russian game' or 'the knife game', in which she stabbed a knife back and forth between her fingers. Each time she cut herself she would pick up a new knife, until all twenty were used. She'd then listen back to the performance on a tape recorder and attempt to recreate it as a way of blending past and present. Then came *Rhythm 5* (1974), in which she leapt into the centre of a large, star-shaped wooden frame set on fire, and collapsed to the ground. As the flames grew closer, a doctor intervened when it was realised that she had passed out from lack of oxygen in the blaze. Abramović was irritated at having lost consciousness, and so for her two-part piece *Rhythm 2* (1974) she ingested a medication normally given to catatonia patients, which caused her muscles to violently contract, though she remained aware. After a ten-minute break, she then took a pill that was commonly prescribed to calm violent schizophrenic patients. She became completely mentally removed and later couldn't recall the five hours that elapsed. In *Rhythm 4* (1974) Abramović suffered unconsciousness again from attempting to inhale as much air as possible from the industrial fan she approached while naked and alone in a room.

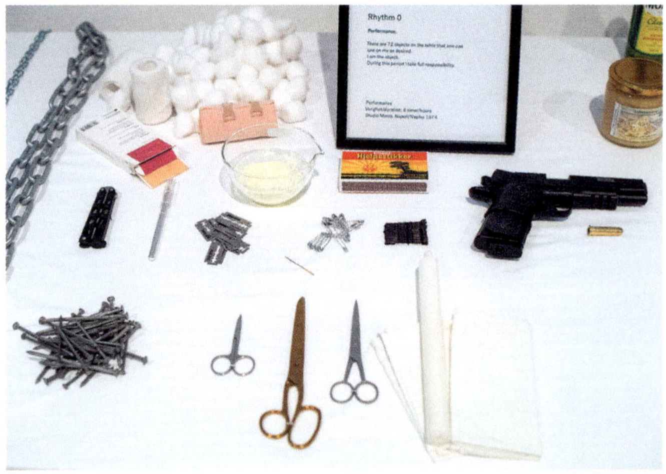

The array of objects used in the performance of Marina Abramović's Rhythm 0 *(1974).*

The image featured on the previous page is of *Rest Energy* (1980), a collaborative performance with her long-time partner, Ulay, in which Abramović again made herself vulnerable through a lack of control. 'In *Rest Energy* we actually hold one arrow on the weight of our body and arrow is pointing at my heart,' Abramović explained. 'We have two small, little microphones on our hearts where we can hear the sounds of the heart beating. As our performance is progressing, heart beats become more and more intense and it's just four minutes and ten seconds, for me it was forever. So, it was really a performance about complete and total trust.'

Abramović's *Rhythm O* is her most notorious work, however, staged at Studio Morra, Naples in 1974. A table was laid with seventy-two objects. Some were for causing pleasure (a rose, a feather, honey, perfume) and some for pain (a scalpel, nails, a gun with a single bullet). The public were invited to interact with the objects and with Abramović, who stood passively beside them. 'There are 72 objects on the table that one can use on me as desired,' read her instructions. 'Performance. I am the object. During this period I take full responsibility. Duration: 6 hours (8 pm – 2 am).'

'It began tamely,' reported the art critic Thomas McEvilley, who was present:

> *Someone turned her around. Someone thrust her arms into the air. Someone touched her somewhat intimately… In the third hour all her clothes were cut from her with razor blades. In the fourth hour the same blades began to explore her skin. Her throat was slashed so someone could suck her blood… Faced with her abdication of will, with its implied collapse of*

human psychology, a protective group began to define itself in the audience. When a loaded gun was thrust to Marina's head and her own finger was being worked around the trigger, a fight broke out between the audience factions.

'What I learned,' said Abramović afterwards, 'was that if you leave it up to the audience, they can kill you.'

In 2010, she revisited public engagement with the remarkable performance piece and act of endurance *The Artist is Present*, at the Museum of Modern Art, New York City. Seated in a chair, she invited members of the public to in turn take the seat across from her. In silence, she would simply hold their gaze. Over nearly three months from March to May, for eight hours a day, she locked eyes with 1000 strangers, a number of whom were moved to tears. Some sat for five minutes; others the entire day. The extreme endurance of such extensive time periods was, Abramović believed, key in altering the shared perception of time and causing a profound engagement in the experience with the audience. Crowds filled the atrium throughout the performance. The chair was never empty. 'Nobody could imagine... that anybody would take time to sit and just engage in mutual gaze with me,' she explained later. 'It was a complete surprise... this enormous need of humans to actually have contact.'

Marina Abramović performing The Artist is Present *in 2010 at the Museum of Modern Art, New York City, where she sat collectively for over 700 hours.*

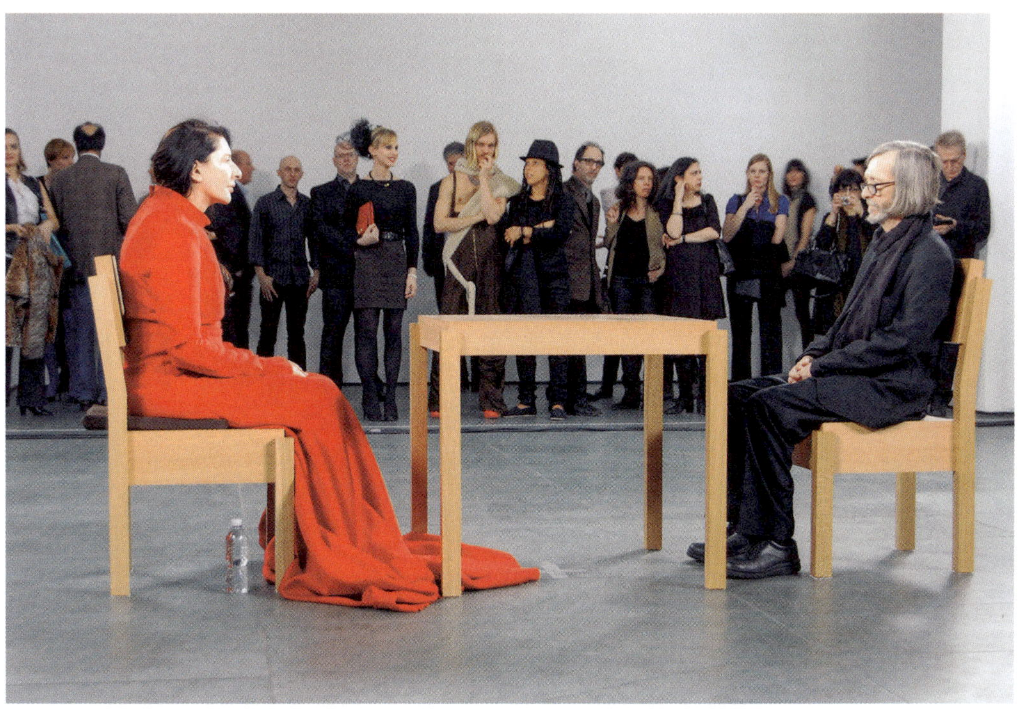

PORTRAIT OF EDMOND DE BELAMY (2018) AND OTHER ART BY ARTIFICIAL INTELLIGENCE

History was made in New York in October 2018 when Christie's became the first auction house to sell a work of art created by artificial intelligence (AI). 'Edmond de Belamy, from *La Famille de Belamy*, generative Adversarial Network print, on canvas, 2018' reads the modest catalogue description. The 70 × 70cm (27½ × 27½in) rendering of an aristocratic gentleman with a slight mouth, no nose and of an indistinguishable era is printed on canvas and 'signed' with the algorithm behind its creation. The estimated value was put at \$7000-\$10,000. The auctioneer's hammer eventually came down at \$432,500. 'Sometimes,' goes the old dealer's saying, 'it's not about being the best, it's about being the first.'

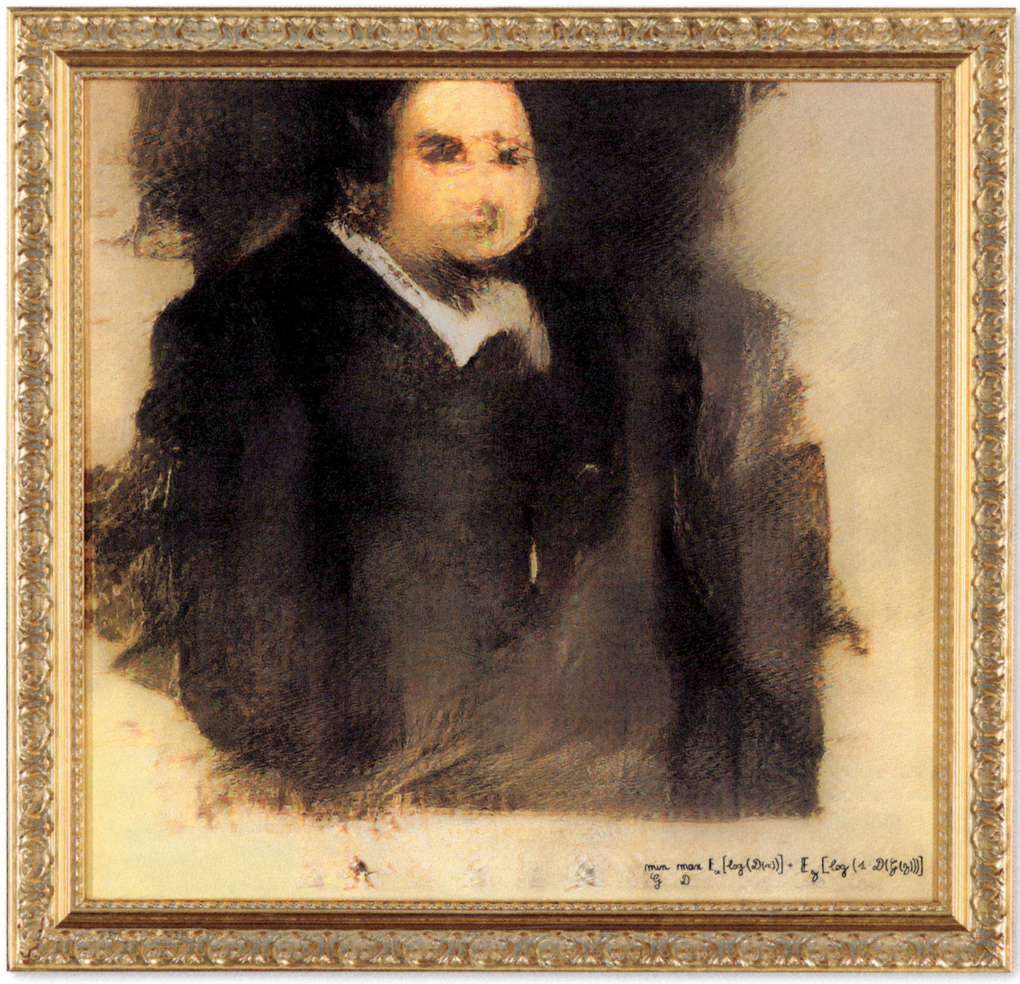

$$\min_G \max_D \mathbb{E}_x[\log(D(x))] + \mathbb{E}_z[\log(1 - D(G(z)))]$$

ABOVE: *The algorithm behind the creation of the* Portrait of Edmond de Belamy *(2018), which also functions as the artist's signature.*

Images generated with AI technology had been in relatively wide use since 2015, when Google revealed art created by their pattern-finding software DeepDream. The software was designed to detect faces and other patterns to automatically classify images. But then it was found it could be operated in reverse, and when run enough times its convolutional neural network generated wild psychedelic and surreal images by seizing on and exaggerating even the faintest hint of a feature or pattern. While magnificent, these results could not technically be classified as a wholly new image, and so the art world took little interest.

Then came Generational Adversarial Networks (GANs), which had been touted as early as 2014 by the researcher Ian Goodfellow as representing the next stage in the evolution of neural networks. GANs are behind numerous recent leaps forward in the development of AI, using interconnected layers of processing nodes, loosely following the model of the human brain. In contrast to Google's DeepDream, GANs can be taught to produce entirely new images by being fed huge amounts of training data sets from which to learn.

In the case of *Portrait of Edmond de Belamy*, the human collaborators of the authorial algorithm, a French art collective called Obvious, influenced the resulting appearance of a classical portrait by feeding their programme over 15,000 portraits painted between the fourteenth and twentieth centuries – an instant crash course in the history of art. From these artistic influences, the algorithm generated new images, which were then put to the test. The pictures were offered to another algorithm, the 'adversary' part of the GAN, which was tasked with spotting the difference between man-made and AI-made images. Like a Turing test but for the AI artist, it must fool its AI colleague into believing its painting is the work of a human mind. *Portrait of Edmond de Belamy*, and another ten portraits of the Belamy 'family', passed the test.

Obvious called the movement 'GAN-ism'. A member named Hugo Caselles-Dupré told Artnet in 2018: 'We really believe that AI can be a new tool for art. In 1850, when the camera showed up, it was only used by highly qualified engineers and so it was not considered for its artistic potential. We think we are in the same situation, because people view us

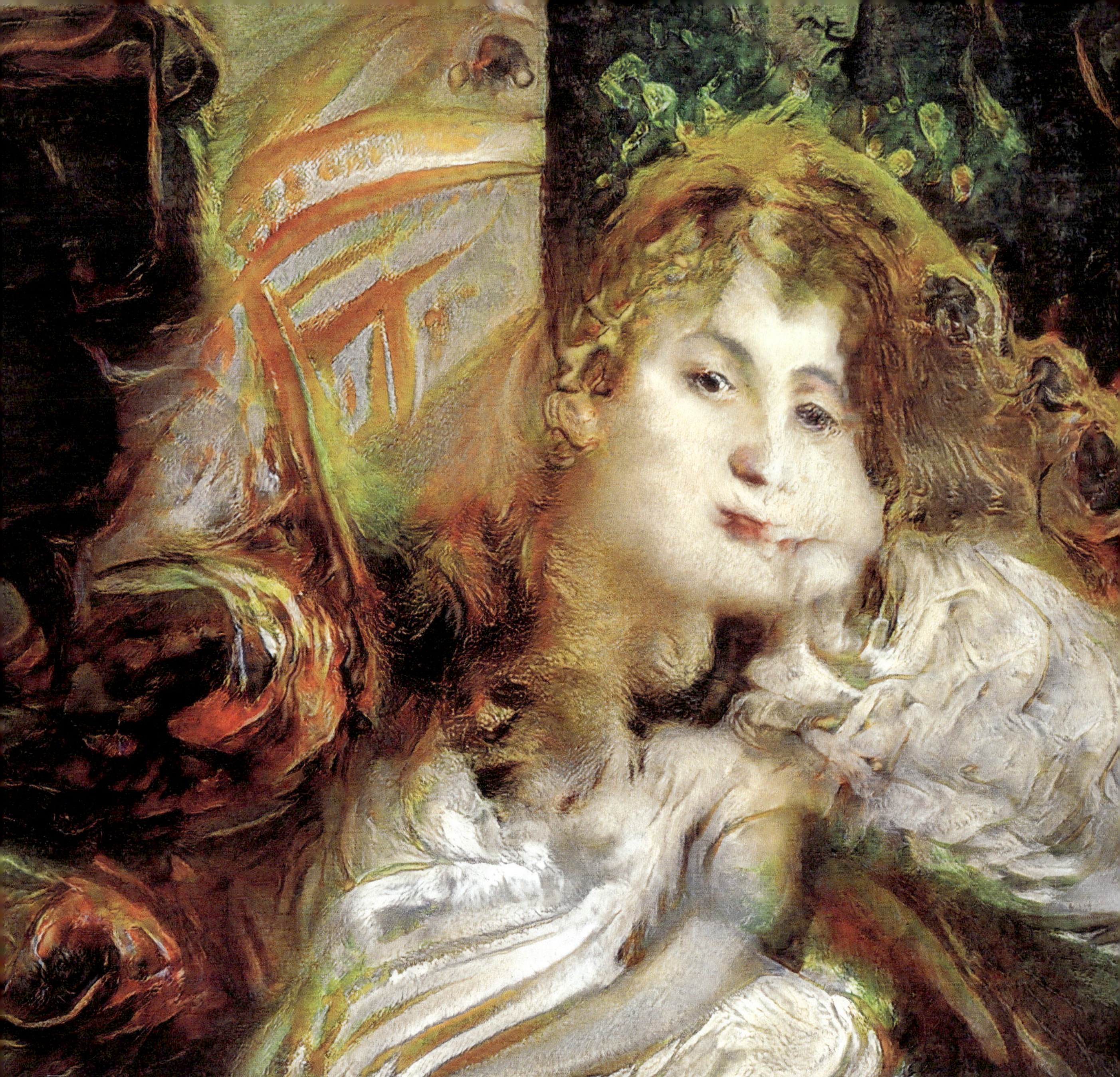

as engineers but we really think this type of technology will be used more and more in art.' The key to the success of the Obvious auction offering is really in the cleverly packaged concept of the artwork. *Edmond de Belamy*, and indeed each of the other members of the fictional aristocratic Belamy family featured in other portraits of the set, came with its own invented identity. The Belamy family name is in tribute to the aforementioned Ian Goodfellow – in French, 'Goodfellow' can be roughly translated to *bel ami*.

ABOVE: Product of Mythology *(2020). Another original AI artwork, in which a scene of landscape and human faces are unnaturally warped together by the programme attempting to produce ordered originality from the chaos of its input material.*

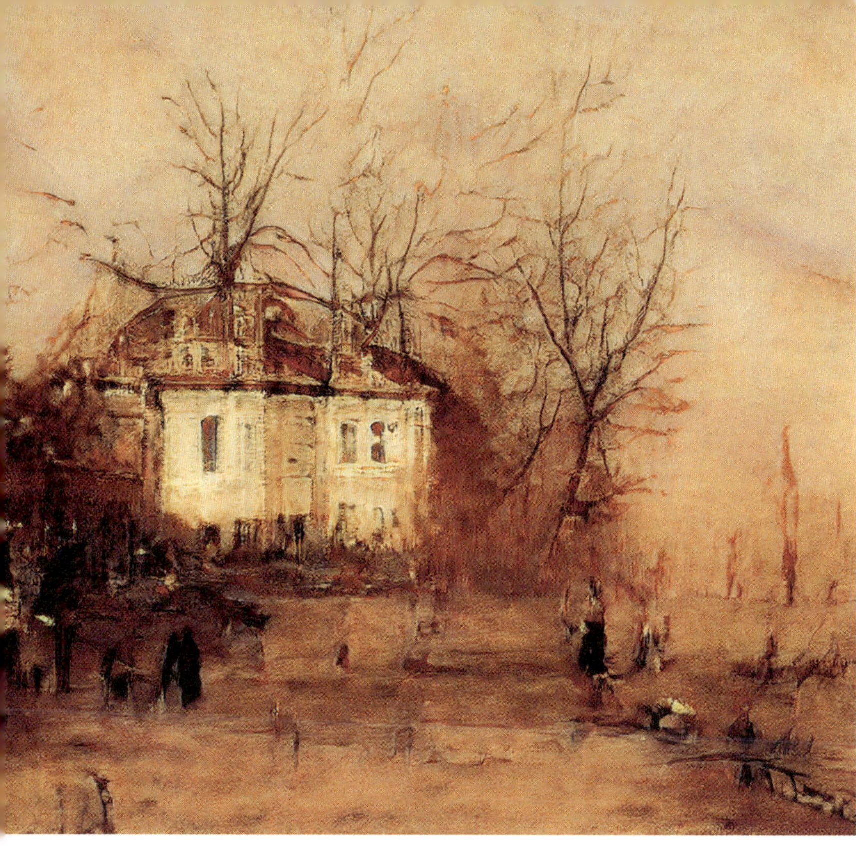

Left: Little House on the Prairie *(2020). A forest bursts from a white mansion, in a bewitching original artwork created by an AI programme operated by the company Art AI.*

Below: DeepDream Mona Lisa *(2021), with DeepDream effect using VGG16 network trained on ImageNet created by P. J. Finlay using code written by Aleksa Gordic.*

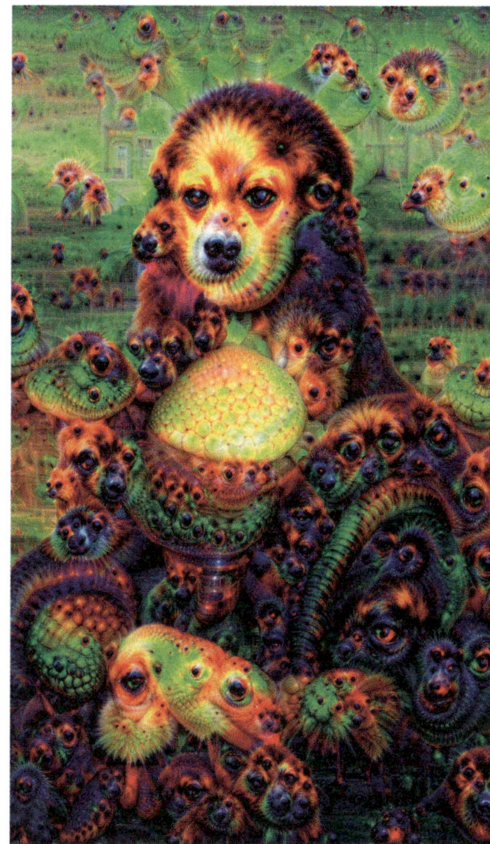

So, with the rise of the machines, will the inevitable human extinction be presaged by the walls of galleries around the world being given over to the creativity of artificial 'imaginations'? Is the future of art the preserve of the algorithm? For now it seems we have little to fear, at least from GANs. The potential of the technology greatly outweighs its current ability, thanks to the fact that teaching a GAN to perform a *new* task requires the complete erasure of everything it has previously learnt, referred to in the science as 'catastrophic forgetting'. So, for example, the GAN that created *Portrait of Edmond de Belamy* cannot also expand its repertoire with landscape or architectural painting.

In this book we've seen how the highway of human development has been, and will always be, illuminated by art. The curiosities collected in this book emphasise the depthless capacity of human imagination, and the chaotic elements of a lived experience that act as creative accelerants. Grief, genius, madness, humour, fury, obsession, passion and shared emotional connection and humour – all are qualities that an efficient, computational system would never tolerate and would never think to adopt. Art is the expression of who we are, the best and the worst. Anything less isn't worth the canvas it's printed on.

SELECT BIBLIOGRAPHY

Armstrong, K. (2005) *A Short History of Myth*, London: Canongate

Arnason, H. H. (2003) *History of Modern Art*, Hoboken: Prentice Hall

Bayley, S. (2012) *Ugly: The Aesthetics of Everything*, London: Welbeck Publishing

Beard, M. & Henderson, J. (2001) *Classical Art from Greece to Rome*, Oxford: Oxford University Press

Benson, M. (2014) *Cosmigraphics*, New York: Abrams

Berrin, K. & Fields, V. M. (eds) (2010) *Olmec: Colossal Masterworks of Ancient Mexico*, New Haven: Yale University Press

Bondeson, J. (1997) *A Cabinet of Medical Curiosities*, London: I. B. Tauris Publishers

Buchholz, E. L. & Kaeppele, S. (2007) *Art: A World History*, New York: Abrams

Charney, N. (2018) *The Museum of Lost Art*, London: Phaidon Press

Cumming, R. (2020) *Art: A Visual History*, London: Dorling Kindersley

Davenport, C. (1929) *Beautiful Books*, London: Methuen & Co. Ltd

Davies, O. (2009) *Grimoires: A History of Magic Books*, Oxford: Oxford University Press

de Rynck, P. (2004) *How to Read a Painting: Decoding, Understanding and Enjoying the Old Masters,* London: Thames & Hudson

Dekker, E. (2013) *Illustrating the Phaenomena: Celestial Cartography in Antiquity and the Middle Ages*, Oxford: Oxford University Press

Dixon, A. G. (2018) *Art: The Definitive Visual Guide*, London: Dorling Kindersley

Ei, N. (2016) *Something Wicked from Japan: Ghosts, Demons & Yokai in Ukiyo-e Masterpieces*, Tokyo: PIE International

Farthing, S. (ed.) (2018) *Art: The Whole Story*, London: Thames & Hudson

Fleming, J. & Honour, H. (eds) (2009) *A World History of Art* (revised 7th edn), London: Laurence King

Ford, B. J. (1992) *Images of Science: A History of Scientific Illustration*, London: British Library

Foster, H. & Krauss, R. (2016) *Art since 1900: Modernism · Antimodernism · Postmodernism*, London: Thames & Hudson

Gerlings, C. (2020) *100 Great Artists: A Visual Journey from Fra Angelico to Andy Warhol*, London: Sirius Entertainment

Goldberg, R. (2018) *Performance Now: Live Art for the 21st Century*, London: Thames & Hudson

Gombrich, E. H. (2007) *The Story of Art*, London: Phaidon Press

Gompertz, W. (2012) *What Are You Looking At?: 150 Years of Modern Art in the Blink of an Eye*, London: Viking

Govier, L. (2010) *One Hundred Great Paintings*, London: National Gallery

Grovier, K. (2018) *A New Way of Seeing: The History of Art in 57 Works*, London: Thames & Hudson

Hartnell, J. (2018) *Medieval Bodies: Life, Death and Art in the Middle Ages*, London: Profile Books

Holzwarth, H. W. (ed.) (2020) *Modern Art. A History from Impressionism to Today*, Cologne: Taschen

Houpt, S. (2006) *Museum of the Missing: A History of Art Theft*, New York: Sterling Publishing
Hughes, R. (1991) *The Shock of the New: Art and the Century of Change*, London: Thames & Hudson
Irving, M. (2018) *1001 Paintings You Must See Before You Die*, London: Cassell
Janson, H. W. (1991) *History of Art* (4th edn), Hoboken: Prentice Hall
Kampen-O'Riley, M. (2001) *Art Beyond the West*, London: Laurence King
Kleiner, F. S. (ed.) (2019) *Gardner's Art through the Ages: A Global History*, Boston: Cengage
Maclagan, D. (2009) *Outsider Art: From the Margins to the Marketplace*, London: Reaktion Books
Marks, A. (2010) *Japanese Woodblock Prints: Artists, Publishers and Masterworks: 1680-1900*, Tokyo: Tuttle
Murray, L. & Murray, P. (eds) (1997) *The Penguin Dictionary of Art and Artists*, London: Penguin
Prinzhorn, H. (2019) *Artistry of the Mentally Ill: A Contribution to the Psychology and Psychopathology of Configuration*, Eastford: Martino Fine Books
Stauble, C. (2015) *The Paintings that Revolutionized Art*, London: Prestel
Stokstad, M. & Cothren, M. (2017) *Art History* (6th edn), London: Pearson
Strong, R. (1983) *The English Renaissance Miniature*, London: Thames & Hudson
Thompson, J. (2006) *How to Read a Modern Painting: Understanding and Enjoying the Modern Masters*, London: Thames & Hudson
Vasari, G. (2008) *The Lives of the Artists*, Oxford: Oxford University Press
Wojcik, D. (2016) *Outsider Art: Visionary Worlds and Trauma*, Jackson: University Press of Mississippi

INDEX

Page numbers in *italics* refer to illustrations. Page numbers followed by an 'n' refer to footnotes.

Abonoteichos 36
Abra 110, *110*
Abramović, Marina 236-9
The Artist is Present 239, *239*
Rest Energy *237*, 238
Rhythm... series 237, *238*
Acconci, Vito, *Following Piece* 236
Acta Sanctorum 146
Adam 50-1, 70, 215
Adickes, David *29*
Agatha of Sicily, St *95*
Agostino Novello *147*
Albero della Fecondità *20*, *21*
Albert I, Prince of Monaco 191
Alcalá, Duke of 122
Alcobaça Monastery 177
Alexander III 186
Alexander of Abonoteichos 36-7
Alfonso IV, King 177
Allais, Alphonse, *First Communion of Young Anaemic Girls in a Blizzard 226*
Allegretti, Allegro 137
Alma-Tadema, Sir Lawrence, *The Roses of Heliogabalus* 187-8
Alpers, Svetlana 117
Altdorfer, Albrecht 85
Anderberg, Rolf 228, 231
Ángeles Arcabuceros 11, 128-31
Anglo-Saxons *41*
Anne of Brittany 76
Anthony, St 124-7, 141
Anthony of Padua, St 146
Anton, Wenzel, Prince of Kaunitz-Rietberg 155
Arcimboldo, Giuseppe 98-101
Fire 101
Four Elements series 98, *101*
Four Seasons series *15*, 98, *100*
Summer 100
Vertumnus 98, *99*
Arman 224
Arnolfini, Giovanni di Arrigio 57
Arnolfini, Giovanni di Nicolao di 57
Art AI *243*
art brut 201, 214, *216*
Art Loss Register 114
artificial intelligence (AI) 240-3
Asclepius 36
astrology, medical 53-5
Athanasius of Alexandria 124
Athena 140
Axelsson, Åke 229, 231
Aztecs 26

Baci, Gregor *14*
Baierland, Ortolf von 53
Baj, Enrico 223
baker of Eeklo legend 104-5, *105*
Ball, Hugo 194, *196*, 236
Banghi (chimpanzee) 231
Banksy, *Dismaland Bemusement Park* 9
Banvard, John 163
Barker, Robert 161-3, *161*
Bashkirtseff, Marie 183
Basil, St 141
battaglia dei sassi 136-7
Baum, Michael 90
Bayeu, Josefa 169
Becchina, Gianfranco 234
Beck, Barbara van 118-23, *119*
Beck, Leonhard 85
Beechey, Sir William 166
Berlin Gold Hat *25*
Bernard, St *94*
Bernhardt, Sarah 189
Bernini, Domenico 146
Bethulia 110
Beuys, Joseph 236
Billom Jesuits 141
bilongo 132
Bird of Hermes 51
Black Death 53
Blake, William 203
Blaker, Hugh *81*
blasphemy 138-41
Boitler, Lina and Arcady 211
Bonalumi, Agostino 223
Book of Enoch 128
Book of Hours *120*, 121
Book of Judith 110
Borås Djurpark Zoo 229
Bosch, Hieronymus, *The Garden of Earthly Delights* 10, 68-71, *68-9*, *207*
Bourdeille, Pierre de 102
Bourdichon, Jean, *Book of Hours for Use of Parisians 95*
Bowie, David *230*
Boyd, William, *Nat Tate: An American Artist 230*
Brassau, Pierre 13, 228-31
Breton, André 9, 202, 204-5, *208*, 210
Browne, John, *Compleat Discourse of Wounds* 53, *55*
Browne, Sir Thomas 73
Bruno, St 141
Buddhism 44-7
bulletism 205
Burgkmair, Hans the Elder, *Triumphal Procession of Emperor Maximilian I* 82-7
Burnat-Provins, Marguerite 201
Burne-Jones, Edward 166
Burton, Robert 96
Bush, Marianne Spore 202, *202*

Cabaret Voltaire 194
Cabinda 132
Cage, John 236
Calamarca, Master of, Letiel *130*, *131*
Campbell, Thomas P. 77
Canaletto 148
cannibalism 115-17
Cano, Alonso, *In The Miraculous Lactation of St Bernard 94*
Carter, Howard 30
Casanova, Canon 144
Casati, Marchesa Luisa *10*
Caselles-Dupré, Hugo 241-2
Central African *minkisi* power figures 132-3

Cerrone, Mario 114
Cesena, Biagio de *111*
Chagall, Marc 184
Chang Yen-yuan 12
Charles V 137
Charlotte, Queen 161, 162
Cheval, Ferdinand, *The Ideal Palace 217*
Chiarello, Antonio 146
China 160, 232
funerary art 30, 30n, *34*
qilin 73, *73*
Christ 39, 74
Arnolfini Portrait 57
Crucifixion Diptych 62
Ecce Homo 61, *61*
The Last Supper 61, 61n
Passion 73, 76
The Throne of the Third Heaven 215
Typus Religionis 140
Wound Man 53
Christianity: Christian curiosities 94-5
Doom paintings 38-41
metal pilgrimage badges 19
St Christopher Dog-head 92-3
using art for indoctrination 128
Christopher, St, Dog-head 92-3
chrysopoeia 48, 50
Church of St Mary and St David, Kilpeck *19*
Church of San Francesco, Sansepolcro *147*
Churchmen's Missionary Association for Seamen *14*
Cleve, Joos van, *Mona Vanna Nuda* 80
Clouzot, Henri-Georges 227
Codex Gigas 42-3
Compagnia del Sasso 136-7
Comte, Pierre Charles, *The Coronation of Inês de Castro in 1361* 176-7, *176*
Conard, Nicholas J. 16
conceptual art 220, 236
Confucius 73
Constantine the Africa 43
Constanza of Castile 177
Corbaz, Aloïse *216*
Correggio 199
Costanzi, Placido, *A Miracle of St Joseph of Cupertino 146*
Council of Trent 128
Courbet, Gustave 184, 188
Craesbeeck, Joos van, *The Temptation of St Anthony* 124-7, *125*
Cranach, Lucas the Elder *11*
Crépin, Fleury-Joseph 202-3
Cronus 171
Crucifixion Diptych 60-3, *60*
Ctesias 73, 92
Cupid *156*
Cusco school 128-30

da Montefeltro, Federico *64*, 64-7, *65*
da Montefeltro, Oddantonio 64
da Oreno, Gian Giacomo Caprotti (Salaì), *Mona Vanna* 11, 78-81, *79*
Dadaism, 194-7, 199, 204, 236
Dadd, Richard, *The Fairy Feller's Master-Stroke* 178-9
Dalem, Cornelis van, *The Legend of the Baker of Eeklo* 104-5, *105*
Dalí, Gala 206
Dalí, Salvador 9, 184
The Persistence of Memory 204-7, 204, 205
d'Amato, Al 140
Darger, Henry *219*
de Kooning, Willem 184
death, Japanese *kusozu* 11, 44-7, *44*, *45*
Decius 92
DeepDream 241
DeepDream Mona Lisa 243
Degas, Edgar 112
del Caso, Pere Borrell, *Escaping Criticism 8*
del Cossa, Francesco, St Lucy altarpiece panel *95*
del Río, Brígida 121
Delacroix, Eugène, *Liberty Leading the People 167*
della Francesca, Piero, *Portrait of Federico da Montefeltro 64*, 64-7, *65*
Denis of Paris, St *95*
Der Blaue Reiter 192
Devereux, Robert, second Earl of Essex *109*
Devil: *Codex Gigas* 42-3
Doom murals 41
St Anthony and 124
di Consolo, Stefano di Giovanni, *The Blessed Ranieri Frees the Poor from a Jail in Florence 147*
Diocletian 92
Disumbrationism *231*
Dominic, St 141
Doom paintings 38-41, *38-9*
Dou Wan, Princess, burial suit of *34*
dreaming 158-9
Drölling, Martin, *Interior of a Kitchen* 164-6, *164-5*
Duchamp, Marcel 196-7
Fountain 197, 197
Ducreux, Joseph *157*
Dürer, Albrecht 26n
Arch of Honour for Emperor Maximilian I 84, 85
Dream Vision, a Nightmare 13, 159
The Great Triumphal Carriage 85, 86-7, 87
Dutch West India Company 116
Duveen, Sir Joseph 191

Ecce Homo 10, 61, *61*
Eckhout, Albert: *African Man 116*
Tapuya Woman 115-17
Edo (Tokyo) 172
Edward de Vere *109*
Egypt, ancient 23, 24, 30, 166-7
Einstein, Albert 207
Elagabalus 187-8
Elizabeth I, Queen 106
Émile, Baron Frédéric 171
The Era 199
Ercolano Fresco 114
Erichsons, Johann 42
Ernst, Max 205
Escalante, Tadeo *40*
Escher, M. C. 152
Estrées, Gabrielle d' 102-3, *103*
Eve 50-1, 70
Evelyn, John 118, 120
Eyck, Jan van, *Arnolfini Portrait* 56-9, *56*, *58*
'eye miniatures' *108*

fake artworks 232-5
Favre, Madame, *The Natural Talent of Mme Favre* 199-200, *199*
Ferdinand I 98, 177
Ferdinand II *14*
Ferdinand VII 169
fertility art 16-21
Field, Erastus Salisbury, *Historical Monument of the American Republic 152*
Field, George 166
Fin, Hernoul le (Arnoult Fin) 57
Finé, Oronce 96
Finlay, P. J. *243*
firefighting 12, 172-5
The Floating Church of the Redeemer of Philadelphia 14
Fludd, Robert, *Utriusque cosmi... 226*
Fontainebleau School 102
Fool's Cap Map of the World 96-7
forgeries 232-5
Fouquet, Jean *106*
Fourcaud, Louis de 183
Fourmanoir, Fabrice *234*
Francis I, Grand Duke of Tuscany 137
Francis of Assisi, St 141, 144
Franz Ferdinand, Archduke 192
Frazer, Charles E. Gordon, *Cannibal Feast on the Island of Tanna, New Hebrides 117*
Frederick III of Denmark 117
Freeman, Margaret 76-7
Frel, Jiří 234
Freud, Sigmund 160, 205, 207
Frith, William Powell *186*
Fry, Roger *234*
funerary art 12-13, 30-5
Furisode Fire (1657) 172
Fuseli, Henry, *The Nightmare* 13, 158-60

Gabon 132
Gabrielle d'Estrées and One of Her Sisters 102-3, *103*
Gaius Julius Solinus 92
GAN-ism 241-2
Gardner, Isabella Stewart 112
Gardner's Art Through the Ages 197
Gascoyne, David 9
Gauguin, Paul *231*
The Little One Is Dreaming 59
Tahitians 234
Gautreau, Virginie Amélie Avegno 182-3
Geiger, Benno 98
Generational Adversarial Networks (GANs) 241-3
Gentileschi, Artemisia, *Judith Slaying Holofernes* 13, 110-11, *110*
Gentileschi, Orazio 111
George III, King 161, 162
German expressionism 192
Getty Kouros 232-5, *232*
Gherardini, Lisa 78, 78n, 81, *81*
Gheyn, Jacob de, *The Exercise of Armes* 130, *130*
Gilded Age 180
Gill, Madge 201-2, *201*
Giménez, Cecilia 10, 61, 61n
gioco delle pugna 137
Glycon, the false snake deity 36-7, *36*
God 70, 125, 215
Golden Legend *95*
Gonzaga, Vincenzo 137
Gonzalez, Antonietta 'Tognina' 122-3, *123*
González, Pedro (The Wild Man of the Woods) 122-3, *122*
Goodfellow, Ian 241, 242
Goodridge, Sarah, *Beauty Revealed 12*
Google 241
Gordic, Aleksa *243*
Göteborgs-Posten 228, 229
Goya, Francisco: *Black Paintings* 168-71
Disasters of War series 169, 207
Saturn Devouring His Son 168, 171
The Third of May 1808 169
Two Old Ones Eating Soup (Witchy Brew) 171
Witches' Flight 171
Goya, Xavier 171
Great Fire of Meireki (1657) 172
Greece, ancient 23, 31, *31*, *32*, 140, 234
Grosz, George 194, 196
Grünewald, Matthias, *Isenheim Altarpiece* 124, *126*
Guanche people 166
Guerra dei pugni (*c.*1600) 136
Guiffrey, Jules 141
gyotaku 13

Hamerton, P. G. 171
Hampton, James *215*
St James: The Book of the 7 Dispensation 215, 215
The Throne of the Third Heaven 214-15, 214
Hausmann, Raoul, *The Art Critic* 194-7
Haydon, George Henry 178
He-Gassen 50
Heintz, Joseph the Younger, *Competition on the Ponte Dei Pugni in Venice* 134-7, *134-5*
Henestrosa, Andrés 211
Hennings, Emmy 194
Henri II, King 123
Henri IV, King 102, 141
Hera 114
Hercules 114
Herman the Recluse 42
Hermes Trismegistus 50
Hermeticism 50
Herodotus 92
Hieronymus Bosch's Butt Song 71
hikeshi-banten 12, 172-5
Hilliard, Nicholas 108
Unknown Man Clasping a Hand from a Cloud 109, *109*
Young Man Against Flames 108
hirsute women in art 118-23
Historia Augusta 187, 188
Höch, Hannah 194, 196
Hohle Fels, *Venus of Hohle Fels* 16-21, *17*
Hokusai, Katsushika, *Kinoe no Komatsu 160*
Holofernes 110-11, *110*
Hopper, Edward 14
Hory, Elmyr de *235*
Houdini, Harry 202
Houghton, Georgiana 198-203
The Hours of Catherine of Cleves 41
Huelsenbeck, Richard 194
Hughes, Robert 215
The Hunt of the Unicorn 72-7

Ignatius of Loyola, St 140-1
IKB (International Klein Blue) 224, 227
Illustrious Brotherhood of Our Blessed Lady 71
Imperiale, Raffaele 114
Inês de Castro 176-7
insults 184-6
Interior of a Kitchen (Drölling) 164-6, *164-5*
International Surrealism Exhibition (1936) 9
Irish Passion of St Christopher 92
Isidore of Seville, *Etymologiae* 42-3
Isleworth Mona Lisa 81
Ixion 148

James I 106
Japan *50*, 160
kusozu 11, 44-7, 44, 45
Jerdanowitch, Pavel, *Yes We Have No Bananas 231*
Jerome, St *94*
Jesuit College, Billom 140, 141
Jesuits 140-1
Jewell, Edward Alden 202
John the Baptist, St, *Crucifixion Diptych* 62
John of Winterthur 91
Johns, Jasper 184
Jordan-Smith, Paul *231*
Joseph 146
Joseph II, Emperor 155
Joseph of Cupertino, St 144
Joseph of Cupertino Takes Flight 144-7, 145
A Miracle of St Joseph of Cupertino 146
Judith 110-11, *110*

Kahlo, Frida, *The Wounded Deer* 210-11, *210*
Kandinsky, Wassily 193, 200, 232
Kennett, Jeff 140
Keyser, Hendrick de, *Screaming Child, Stung by a Bee 156*
Kingdom of Loango 132
Kinoe no Komatsu, *Dream of the Fisherman's Wife 160*
Kipling, Rudyard 166
Klee, Paul 192, 193
Klein, Yves 221
Mondo Cane Shroud 224-7
Klein-Moquay, Rotraut 224
Klint, Hilma af 200-1, *200*
Grupp 1, Urkaos, nr 16 200
Knight, Robert 142, *142*, 143
Komachi, Ono no 47
Kongo people *133*
Kupka, František 200
kusozu 11, 44-7, *44*, *45*

La Rochefoucauld family 76
Langlotz, Ernst 234
Lauffenberger, Dr Jean 234
Le Rossignol, Constance 'Ethel', *A Goodly Company* 203, *203*
The Legend of the Baker of Eeklo 104-5, *105*
Legge, Sheila *206*
Leighton, Frederic 184
Leonardo da Vinci 48, 184, 205n
The Bust of a Grotesque Old Woman (Matsys, after) 90, 91
Isleworth Mona Lisa 81
La Bella Principessa 233
La Joconde nue 80, 81
The Last Supper 61, 61n
Mona Lisa 11, 78, 78n, 80-1, 80
Salaì 80, 80n, 81
Letiel *130*
Lévy, Jules *226*
LeWitt, Sol 220
Lichtenberg, Georg Christoph 157
Life and Death 46
Liguori, St Alphonsus 144
Little House on the Prairie 243
Lomazzo, Gian Paulo 61
Louis XII 76
Louis XV *153*
Louvre 78, 81, 102-3, 166
'Low life' painting 126
Löwenmensch (Lion Man) *18*
Lucas, Arthur 62
Lucia of Syracuse, St *95*
Lucian of Samosata 36, 37
Lucifer: *Codex Gigas* 42-3
Lucifer's New Row-Barge 10, 142-3, 142
Lucius Annaeus Cornutus 97
ludus graticulorium 136
McEvilley, Thomas 238
Macke, Auguste 193
McShane, Dr Angela 118, 120
Magritte, René 9, 205, 206
Les Amants 209
Malevich, Kazimir 200, 232
Manet, Édouard 112, 184, 188, 193
Déjeuner sur l'Herbe 182
Mangaaka 132
Mannerist style 98
Mantegna, Andrea, *Martyrdom of St Sebastian 211*
Manzoni, Piero, *Merda d'Artista 220-3, 220*
Artist's Breath 222
Marc, Franz, *Fate of the Animals* 192-3, *192*, 194
Marcus Aurelius 37
Margaret, Countess of Tyrol 90-1
Maria Theresa, Empress 155
Martínez, Elías García 61
Martini, Simone, *Blessed Agostino Novello Triptych 147*
Mary, *Arnolfini Portrait* 57
Mary of Egypt, St 120-1
Mary Magdalene, *Sforza Hours 120*, 121
Maspero, Luc 78
Matisse, Henri 188
Matsys, Quentin: *The Bust of a Grotesque Old Woman* (after Leonardo da Vinci) 90, *91*
Portrait of an Old Man 89, 90
The Ugly Duchess 88-91, 88
Maximilian I, Holy Roman Emperor 82-7
Maximilian II, Holy Roman Emperor 98
Maximinus Daia, Emperor 92
Maya 26, 31, *32*
Mazzanti, Ludovico, *Joseph of Cupertino Takes Flight* 144-7, *145*
mazzascudo 137
medical astrology 53-5
Medici, Eleonor de' 137
Mehmed IV, Sultan 184-6
Meiji, Emperor 173
Meller, Dr Harald 23
memento mori 11, *46*, 47, *96*
Mendieta, Ana, *Tree of Life* 236

Mercator, Gerard 96
Mersa Matruh 30, *30*
Mesmer, Franz 155
Mesoamerica 26-9, *35*
Messerschmidt, Franz Xaver, *Character Heads* 154-7
Messerschmidt, Johann Adam 155, 156
meteorite dagger 30, *30*
Michelangelo 233
Moses 94
Sistine Chapel 60, 111
The Torment of St Anthony 127
Milan, Duke of 64
miniature portraiture 106-9
minkisi 132-3
Minos *111*
Miró, Joan 205
Harlequin's Carnival 208
Mitchell, Robert 161
Moche funerary art 31, *33*
Modigliani, Amedeo 232, *235*
Monastery of St Anthony, Issenheim *126*
Monastery of Santa Clara-a-Velha, Coimbra 177
Mondrian, Piet 200
Monet, Claude 188
Montagu, Lady Mary *186*
Moore, Alan 37
Moses 215
mummy brown *164-5*, 166-7, *167*
murexide 164
Myrninnerest 201-2

Namuth, Hans 227
Napoleon Bonaparte 61n, 78, 169
Napoli, Mario 31
Nassau-Siegen, Count Johan Maurits 116, 117
Nay, Ernst Wilhelm 231
Nebra Sky Disc 22-5, *22*
Nebuchadnezzar 110
Newton, Isaac 51
nganga 132, 133
Nicolai, Friedrich 156
nkisi 132-3
Notre Dame de France, London 161-2
numerus Marmaritarum 93

Obon (Festival of the Dead) 47
Obvious 241-2
Oliver, Isaac, *Man Consumed by Flames* 106-9, *107*
Olmec, colossal heads of the 26-9, *26*, *27*, *28*
Ono, Yoko 236
Ortelius, Abraham 96
Oteri, Danielle 77
Outsider art 214-19

Paalen, Wolfgang 205
Paget's disease 90
paint 164, 166-7, 224
Pakal, K'inich Janaab' *35*
Palaeolithic age 16-21
Pallavicina, Lady Isabella 123
Panofsky, Erwin 59
panoramas, monster 161-3
paranoiac-critical method 206
Paris Salon 166, 176, 180, *182*, 183
Parma, Duke of 123
Pascal, Claude 224
Pastrovicchi, Fr Angelo 144
Paul III, Pope *111*
Pedro González (Petrus Gonsalvus) and His Wife, Catherine 122, *122-3*
Peeters, Clara, *Still Life with Cheeses, Almonds and Pretzels 59*
Pendel, Johann 155
performance art 236-9
Perkin, William 164
Peru *40*, 128, 130
Peruggia, Vincenzo 78
Perugia 136-7, 136n
Peter (Pierre Brassau) 229-31, *230*
Peter I, King of Portugal 176-7
Peter, St 144, 144n
Peter of Attalia, Bishop 93
Peter the Great 93
Pheidias 140
Philip the Bold, Duke of Burgundy *90*
Phillips, Sir Thomas 178
Philosopher's Stone 50, 51
Phoenicians 164
Picasso, Pablo 78, 184, *208*, 227
Piranesi, Giovanni Battista, *Carceri d'Invezione* series 11, 148-53
Pleiades star cluster 23, *24*
Pliny the Elder 73
Pollock, Jackson 12, 184, 227
Ponte dei Pugni, Venice *137*
Pope, Alexander *186*
Porpora, Paolo, *Flowers* 60
Portrait of Barbara van Beck 118-23, *119*
Portrait of Edmond de Belamy 240-3, *240*, *241*
Poseidonia 31
Post, Frans 116
Pozzi, Dr 183
Pritchard, Zarh H., *Bream in 25 Feet of Water off the West Coast of Scotland* 10-11, 189-91, *190*
Product of Mythology 242
Publius Mummius Sisenna Rutilianus 37
Pussy Goes a Hunting 19

Qin Shi Huang, Emperor 30, 30n
Quinta del Sordo, Madrid 169, 171
Quintianus *95*

Ranieri Rasini *147*
Raphael 233
Ray, Man *10*
Indestructible Object 208
Rembrandt: *Christ in the Storm on the Sea of Galilee* 112-14, *113*
The Night Watch 58, 62-3, 63
Renoir, Pierre-Auguste 184
Repin, Ilya Yefimovich, *Reply of the Zaporozhian Cossacks to Sultan Mehmed IV* 184-6, *185*
Reprebus 92-3
Restellini, Marc 232
restoring art 60-3
revenge 13, 110-11
Ribart, Charles-François *153*
Ribera, Jusepe de, *Magdalena Ventura with Her Husband and Son* 122, *122*
Ribot, Théodule 188
Rice, W. C., *Cross Garden 218*
Ridley, John 212
Ripley, George 50, 51
Ripley Scroll 48-51, *48*, *49*
Roberson-Park, Geoffrey 166
Rockefeller, John D. Jr 76

Rorimer, James 76, 77
Rosen, David 62
Rubens, Peter Paul 171
Rudolf II 98, *99*, 100

Sade, Marquis de 89
St Christopher Dog-head 92-3
Salmon, William 167
San Juan Bautista, Huaro *40*
Sánchez Cotán, Juan, *Brígida del Río, the Bearded Lady of Peñaranda 121*, 121
Sanctuary of Mercy, Borja 61, 61n
Sargent, John Singer *180*
Portrait of Madame X *180-3, 181*
Satan *41*
satire 142-3
Saturn 171
Schäufelen, Hans 85
Schjeldahl, Peter 224
Schneider, Dr Kajta 231
Serpent of Arabia 51
Serrano, Andrés, *Immersion (Piss Christ)* 140
Severus Alexander 188
Sforza, Battista 64, *64*, *66*
Sforza, Bianca Maria *233*
Sforza Hours 120, 121
Shakespeare, William 109, *109*, 178
Sheela na gig *19*
Shepherd, Rev. Henry 38
Simeans 92
Simmons, Edward 182
Simón, Juan Antonio Pérez 188
Simon Magus 144, 144n
sky burials 44
snake deity, Glycon 36-7, *36*
Society of Jesus 140, 141
Soi 36
Sophronius 120
South Newington church 40
South Sea Company 142, 143
Spencer, Earl of 80
spiritualist art 198-203
Springinklee, Hans 85
Stabius, Johannes 85
Stace, Arthur, *Eternity* 212-13, *213*
Stag's Head Rhyton 114
Steinhardt, Michael 114
Stelarc 9, 10
Strachey, William 109
Strebe, Diemut, *Sugababe* 9
Surrealism 9, 204-9, 210

Talhoffer, Hans, *Fechtbuch 67*
Tanguy, Yves 205
Tanning, Dorothea, *Eine Kleine Nachtmusik 209*
Tapuya people 116, 117
Tassi, Agostino 111
Temple of Inscriptions *35*
Teresa of Avila, St 144
Terracotta Army 30, 30n, *34*
Terrus, Étienne 232
theft, art 112-14
Theocritus *156*
Thomas, Dylan 9
Thompson, Rev. Lisle 212-13
Thoth 50
Three Kings, *Wound Man* 53
Titian 62, 199, 233
tomb art 30-5
Tomb of the Diver 12-13, 30-5, *31*, *32*
Top and Tail 143
trompe l'oeil 8
Truman, President 215
Tupi people 116
Tutankhamun 30, *30*
Typus Religionis 138-41, *138-9*
Tyrian purple 164
Tzara, Tristan 194

Ulay, *Rest Energy 237*, 238
Unetice culture 23
Unicorn Tapestries 72-7
Ursler, Anne and Balthazar 118

Van Gogh, Vincent 9, 10, 114
Vance, Cyrus Jr. 114
vanitas artworks 96
Vautier, Ben 223
Velázquez, Diego 171
Ventura, Magdalena 122, *122*
Venus of Dolní Věstonice 20
Venus of Hohle Fels 16-21, *17*
Vermeer, Johannes, *The Concert* 112
Vikan, Gary 233
Villars, Duchess of 102, *103*
Vinceti, Silvano 81
Virgin Mary 53, 62, *94*, 215
Voynich, Wilfrid *51*
Voynich Manuscript 51
Vulgate Bible 42, *94*
Walpole, Robert 143
Walter of Speyer 92
Walters, Henry 233
Wang Shia 12
Warhol, Andy 184
Webster, Daniel *12*
Wechelen, Jan van 104
Weiss, Leocadia 171
Wellcome Collection 118
Weyden, Rogier van der, *Crucifixion Diptych 60*, 62
Whistler, James McNeill *11*, 184
Wilgefortis *120*
Wilhelm II, Kaiser *216*
Wound Man 52-5, *52*
Wyld, James, *Wyld's Monster Globe 163*

Xiao Yuan 232-3

Yavornytsky, Dmytro 184
Yorimitsu, Minamoto no *170*, 175
Yourcenar, Marguerite 148, 152

Zaporozhian Cossacks 184-6
Zapotec 26
Zhang Zeduan, *Along the River during the Qingming Festival 162-3*
Zodiac Man 52, 53-5
Zurbarán, Francisco de *95*

FOLLOWING PAGES: The Experts *(1837) by Alexandre-Gabriel Decamps, in the satirical singerie style that places monkeys in human roles. Here art critics are mocked for their reverence for the art of the past.*

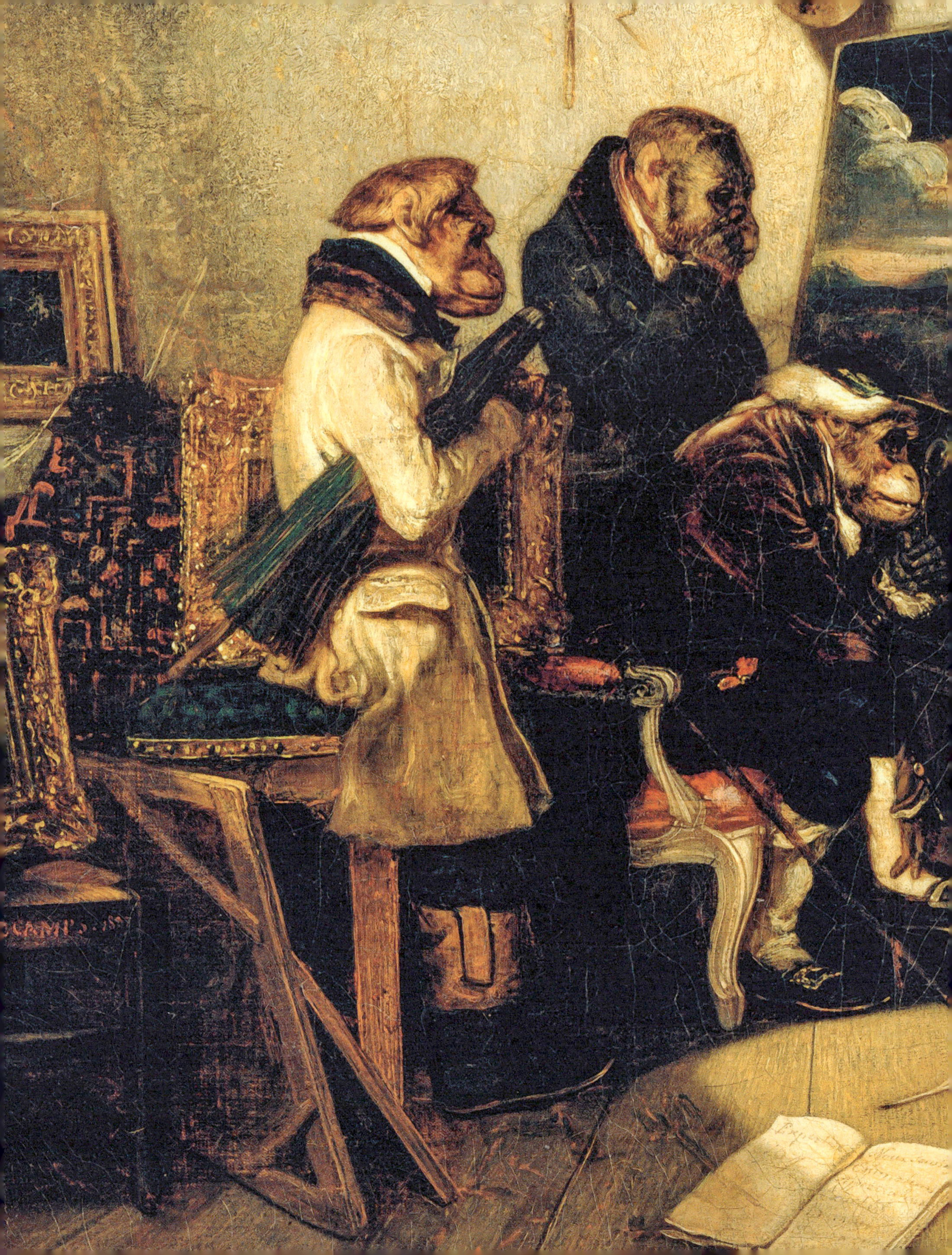

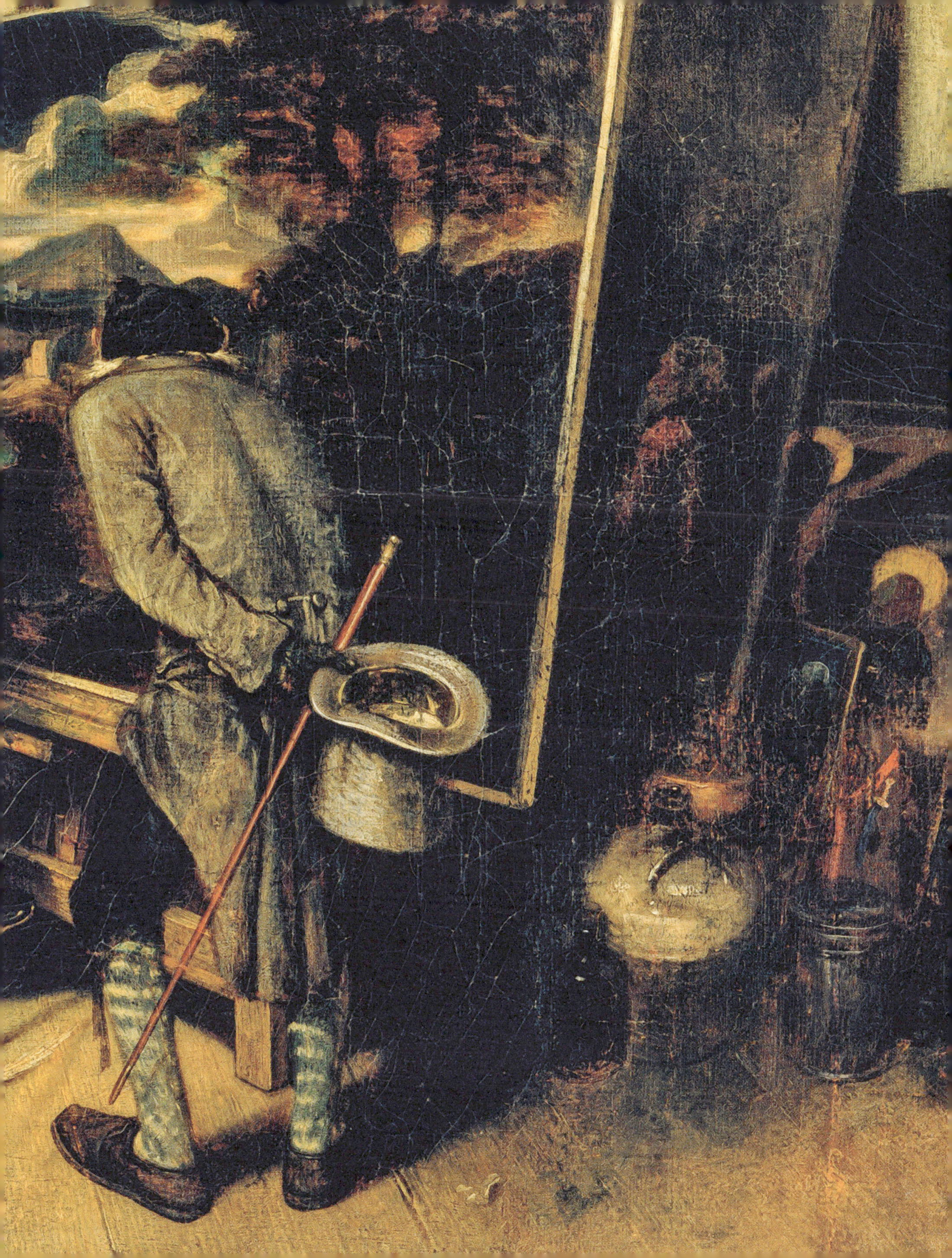

PICTURE CREDITS

pp1, 82-83, 85, 86 top, 87 top Images from the collections of the Biblioteca Nacional de España; **p2, 157 bottom** National Museum, Stockholm in Sweden; **pp4,** René Magritte, *The Lovers,* Paris 1928, © ADAGP, Paris and DACS, London 2022. Location: The Museum of Modern Art, New York Gift of Richard S. Zeisler; **pp7, 52** Wellcome Collection; **p8** Collection of the Bank of Spain; **p10** public domain; **p11 top** public domain; **p11 bottom** Boston Public Library; **p12** Metropolitan Museum of Art; **p13** *A gyotaku fish print*, DigiPub / JG Wang (https://www.flickr.com/photos/pcfannet/66213323/); **p14 top** Ambras Castle; **p14 bottom** Library of Congress; **p15** US National Gallery of Art; **p17** Ramessos, Wikipedia.co.uk; **p18** Dagmar Hollmann; **p19 top** Nessy Pic; **p19 bottom** Edward Brooke-Hitching; **pp20-21** Sailko, Wikipedia.co.uk; **p22** Anagoria; **p24** National Aeronautics and Space Administration (NASA), European Space Agency (ESA) and AURA/Caltech; **p25** Philip Pikart; **p26** Luidger, Wikipedia.co.uk; **p27** Alamy; **p28** Carptrash, Wikipedia. co.uk; **p29** Mobilus In Mobili; **p30** Daniela Cornelli; **p31** Michael Johanning; **p32 top** Alamy; **p32 bottom** Walters Art Museum; **p33** Sculptural ceramic ceremonial vessel that represents a sexually active inhabitant of the Underworld, ML004199. Museo Larco, Lima, Perú; **p34 top** Ann Petersen; **p34 bottom** Greyloch, flickr.com; **p35** Ark in Time, flickr.com; **p36** Cristian Chirita; **p37** Edward Brooke-Hitching; **p39** Edward Brooke-Hitching; **p40** Jeremyboer; **p41** The Morgan Library and Museum; **pp42, 43** Per B. Adolphson, National Library of Sweden, HS A 148; **p44** Wellcome Collection; **p45** British Museum; **p46** Wellcome Collection; **pp48-49** Wellcome Collection; **p50** Waseda University Library (public domain); **p51** Beinecke Library, Yale University; **p54** Wellcome Collection; **p55** Wellcome Collection; **p56** Alamy; **p58 top** National Gallery; **pp58 bottom, 63** Rijksmuseum; **p59 top** The Mauritshuis; **p59 bottom** Ordupgaard, Copenhagen; **p60** Philadelphia Museum of Art; **p61** Alamy; **pp64-66** Livioandronico2013 wikipedia; **p67 top** Yorck Project; **p67 bottom** Royal Library, Copenhagen; **pp68-71** Prado Museum; **p72** Metropolitan Museum of Art; **p73** Hallwyl Museum; **pp74-77** Metropolitan Museum of Art; **p79** Alamy; **p80 top** Alamy; **p80 bottom** unknown; **p81** Wikipedia.co.uk, originaldo.com; **p84** Herzog Anton Ulrich Museum; **pp86-7 bottom** National Gallery of Art, Washington DC, USA; **p88** National Gallery; **p90** CGFA, Wikipedia.co.uk; **p91** Bridgeman Images / © Royal Collection / Royal Collection Trust © Her Majesty Queen Elizabeth II, 2022; **p93** Edward Brooke-Hitching; **p94 left** Alonso Cano (1601-1667), *Saint Bernard and the Virgin.* 1645-1652. Museo del Prado Inv. P003134; **p94 right** Jörg Bittner Unna; **p95 top left** Bibliothèque nationale de France; **p95 top right** Fabre Museum; **p95 bottom right** National Gallery of Art, Washington, DC; **p97** OyZot/HamelCo; **p99** Skokloster Castle, Sweden; **pp100, 101** Kunsthistorisches Museum Vienna; **p103** Oakenchips, wikipedia.co.uk; **p105** Rijksmuseum; **p106** Julia Florenskaya; **p107** © National Trust / Christopher Warleigh-Lack; **p108 top** © Victoria and Albert Museum, London; **p108 bottom** Philadelphia Museum of Art; **p109** Bridgeman Images / Christie's; **p110** National Museum of Capodimonte; **p111** public domain; **p113** Yorck Project; **pp115, 116** National Museum of Denmark; **p117** Bonhams; **p119** Wellcome Collection; **p120 top** British Library; **p120 bottom** Gugganij, Wikipedia.co.uk; **p121** Alamy; **p122 top** Museo Fondacion Duque de Lerma, Toledo; **p122 bottom** National Gallery of Art, USA; **p123** Château Royal de Blois; **p125** State Art Gallery, Karlsruhe; **p126** pxhere.com; **p127** Kimbell Art Museum; **p129** Alamy; **p130 top** Church of Calamarca; **p130 bottom** public domain; **p131** Bridgeman Images / Iberfoto; **p132** Metropolitan Museum of Art; **p133 top** Metropolitan Museum of Art; **p133 bottom** British Museum; **pp134-5** Anagoria, Wikipedia.co.uk; **p137** Grigio60, Wikipedia.co.uk; **pp138-9** Bridgeman Art Library; **p141 top** Edward Brooke-Hitching; **p141 bottom** Museum Catharijneconvent, Utrecht, photo Ruben de Heer; **p142** Woolley & Wallis; **p143** Metropolitan Museum of Art; **p145** Alamy; **p146** Metropolitan Museum of Art; **p147 top** Yorck Project; **p147 bottom** Stéphane Magnenat; **p149** Edward Brooke-Hitching; **p150 top** Daderot; **p150 boap152** Daderot, Wikipedia.co.uk; **p153** public domain; **pp154-5** Photo courtesy of and © Belvedere, Wien. Creative Commons Licence CC BY-SA 4.0; **p156 top three faces** Photo courtesy of and © Belvedere, Wien. Creative Commons Licence CC BY-SA 4.0; **p156 bottom right** Museum of Fine Arts, Boston; **p156 bottom left** Rijksmuseum; **p157 top right** Metropolitan Museum of Art; **p157 middle right** J. Paul Getty Museum; **p157 bottom right** Yelkrokoyade, wikipedia.co.uk; **p157 top right** Spencer Museum of Art; **p157 middle right** J.Paul Getty Museum; **p157 bottom right** National Museum, Stockholm in Sweden; **p158** Detroit Institute of Art; **p159** Kunsthistorisches Museum; **p160** public domain; **p161** British Library; **pp162-3 top** National Palace Museum, Taiwan; **p163 bottom** public domain; **pp164-5** The Art Collection, New York; **p167** Musée du Louvre, Paris; Wikipedia.co,uk public domain; **p168** Prado Museum, Madrid; **p170** Museo del Prado; **p171** Prado Museum; **p172** *Commoner's firefighting jacket (hikeshibanten),* Courtesy Seattle Art Museum, Gift of the Christensen Fund, Acc 2001.414. Medium: Cotton cloth with indigo dye (sashiko and tsutsugaki), 38 1/2 x 50 in (97.79 x 127 cm); **p173 top** Metropolitan Museum of Art; **p173 bottom** public domain; **p174 top** Jim Austin; **p174 bottom** Denver Art Museum; **p175 top and bottom** Jim Austin; **p176** Scailyna; **p177** SaraPCNeves; **p178** public domain; **p179** Sailko, Wikipedia.co.uk; **p180** Wikimedia Commons; **p181** Metropolitan Museum of Art; **p182** GraphicaArtis/Getty Images; **p185** Yorck Project;

p186 Auckland Art Gallery Toi o Tamaki New Zealand; **p187** Wikimedia Commons; **pp189-90** Brooklyn Museum; **p192** Yorck Project; **p195** Raoul Hausmann (1886-1971), *The Art Critic (Der Kunstkritiker)* 1919-1920, Tate London T01918 © ADAGP, Paris and DACS, London 2022; **p196** public domain; **p197** FHKE; **p198** The Courtauld; **p199** Mme Favre, *untitled,* XIXth century, lead pencil on paper, 36 x 23 cm, photo: Claudine Garcia, Atelier de numérisation – Ville de Lausanne, Collection de l'Art Brut, Lausanne; **p200 left** Albin Dahlström, the Moderna Museet, Stockholm; The Hilma af Klint Foundation, Stockholm; **p200 right** public domain; **p201** Madge Gill (1882-1961), *Untitled,* 1950s. Private Collection. Bridgeman Images / Photo © Christie's Images; **p202** public domain; **p203** Edward Brooke-Hitching; **p204** Salvador Dalí (1904-1989), *The Persistence of Memory,* 1931. © Salvador Dalí, Fundació Gala-Salvador Dalí, DACS 2022. Location: Museum of Modern Art, New York, USA. Photo: Bridgeman Images; **p206** Sheila Legge (1911-1949) *Trafalgar Square Performance*, 1936; **p207 left** Salvador Dalí (1904-1989), *The Persistence of Memory,* (detail) 1931. © Salvador Dalí, Fundació Gala-Salvador Dalí, DACS 2022. Location: Museum of Modern Art, New York, USA. Photo: Bridgeman Images; **p208 top** Man Ray, Indestructible Object, 1923, remade 1933, editioned replica 1965. © Man Ray 2015 Trust / DACS, London 2022; **p208 bottom** Jean Miró (1893-1983), *Carnaval d'Arlequin (Carnival of Harlequin),* 1924-1925. © Successió Miró / ADAGP, Paris and DACS London 2022. Location: Albright-Knox Art Gallery, Buffalo, NY, USA, Room of Contemporary Art Fund, 1940. Photo Bridgeman Images; **p209 top** René Magritte, *The Lovers,* Paris 1928, © ADAGP, Paris and DACS, London 2022. Location: The Museum of Modern Art, New York Gift of Richard S. Zeisler; **p209 bottom** Dorothea Tanning (1910-2012), *Eine Kleine Nachtmusik* 1943. © ADAGP, Paris and DACS, London 2022. Tate Purchased with assistance from the Art Fund and the American Fund for the Tate Gallery 1997. T07346; **p210** Alamy; **p211 top** Yorck Project; **p211 bottom** Alamy; **p213** Fairfax Media, Australia: Arthur Stace (1932-1967), AKA Mr Eternity, The Sydney Morning Herald 03/07/1963. Photo by Trevor Dallen; **p214** Wuselig, wikipedia.co.uk; **p215 top** Smithsonian Museum; **p215 bottom** public domain; **p216** Aloïse, "Napoléon III à Cherbourg" from Collection de 'Art Brut, Lausanne. Copyright Association Aloïse Corbaz; **p217** Otourly; **p218** Carol M. Highsmith, Library of Congress; **p219** Alamy; **p220** Jens Cederskjold; **p222** Piero Manzoni (1933-1963), *Artist's Breath,* 1960. © DACS, 2022. Tate T07589, Presented by Attilio Codognato 2000; **p225** Yves Klein, *Suaire de Mondo Cane (Mondo Cane Shroud),* 1961. 274.32 x 300.99 cm overall. Medium: pigment, synthetic, resin on gauze. © Succession Yves Klein c/o ADAGP, Paris and DACS, London 2022. Collection Walker Art Centre, Minneapolis, Gift of Alexander Bing, TB Walker Foundation, Art Center Acquisition Fund, Professional Art Group I and II, Mrs Helen Haseltine Plowden Dr Alfred Pasternak, Dr Maclyn C Wade, by exchange with additional funds from the TB Walker Acquistion Fund, 2004; **p226 top** Bibliothèque nationale de France; **p226 bottom** Wellcome Collection; **pp228-9** Henrik Johansson; **p230 top** Åke Axelsson; **p230 bottom** Edward Brooke-Hitching; **p231** public domain; **p232** The J. Paul Getty Museum, **p233** www.suite101.com; **p234** Vukan Vujović/Facebook; **p235** Elmyr de Hory; **p237** Alamy; **p238** Alamy; **p239** Andrew Russeth https://commons.wikimedia.org/wiki/File:Marina_Abramovi%C4%87,_The_Artist_is_Present,_2010_(2).jpg; **pp240, 241** Obvious Art Collective; **p242** Courtesy of ART AI (https://www.artaigallery.com/); **p243 top** Courtesy of ART AI (https://www.artaigallery.com/); **p243 bottom** P. J. Finlay; **pp252-253**: Metropolitan Museum of Art.

ACKNOWLEDGEMENTS

I would like to express my deep appreciation to all who provided such indispensable help in the creation of this book: to Charlie Campbell at Greyhound Literary; to Ian Marshall at Simon & Schuster; and to Laura Nickoll and Keith Williams for yet another beautiful design, and to Joanna Chisholm, Liz Moore, Henrik Johansson, and Art AI. Thanks to my family for their support, and to Daisy Laramy-Binks, Alex and Alexi Anstey, Matt, Gemma and Charlie Troughton, Kate Awad, Katherine Anstey, Katherine Parker, Georgie Hallett, Thea Lees, Clive Stewart-Lockhart and Ruth Millington; and to my friends at *QI*: John, Sarah and Coco Lloyd, Piers Fletcher, James Harkin, Alex Bell, Alice Campbell Davies, Anne Miller, Andrew Hunter Murray, Anna Ptaszynski, Dan, Fenella and Wilf Schreiber and Sandi Toksvig.

First published in the United States of America in 2023 by Chronicle Books LLC.

Originally published in Great Britain in 2022 by Simon & Schuster UK Ltd.

Library of Congress Cataloging-in-Publication Data is available.

Manufactured in Italy.

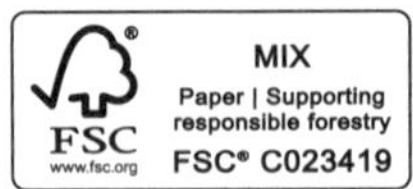

ISBN 978-1-7972-2176-2

Editorial Director: Ian Marshall.
Design: Keith Williams, sprout.uk.com.
Project Editor: Laura Nickoll.

The author and publishers have made all reasonable efforts to contact copyright-holders for permission, and apologise for any omissions or errors in the form of credits given. Corrections may be made to future printings.

10 9 8 7 6 5 4 3 2 1

Chronicle Books LLC
680 Second Street
San Francisco, California 94107
www.chroniclebooks.com

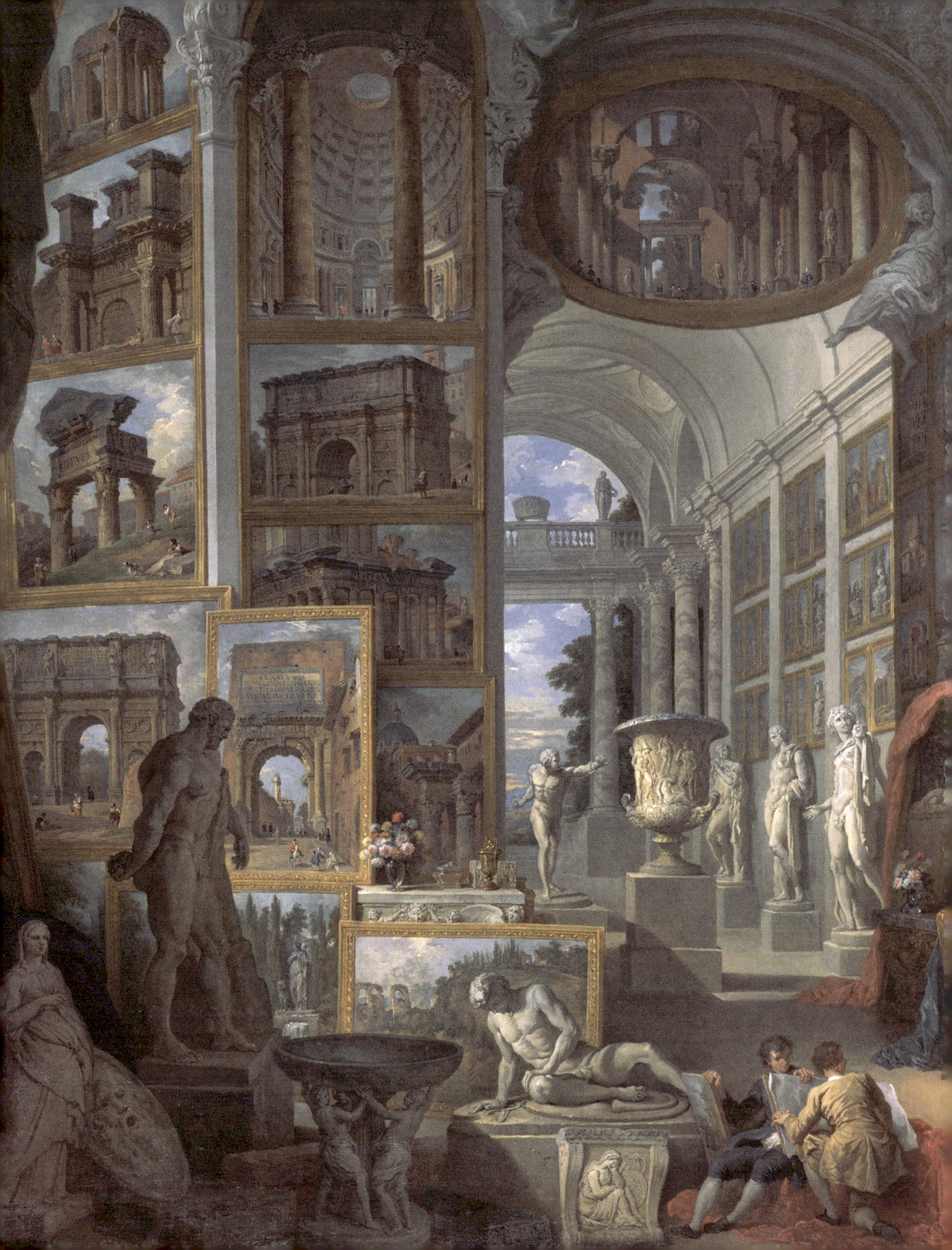